Cook, J. M., + Cl
Multicultural + Soc
Systemic, person-centered, and
approach. Cognella.

MULTICULTURAL & SOCIAL JUSTICE COUNSELING

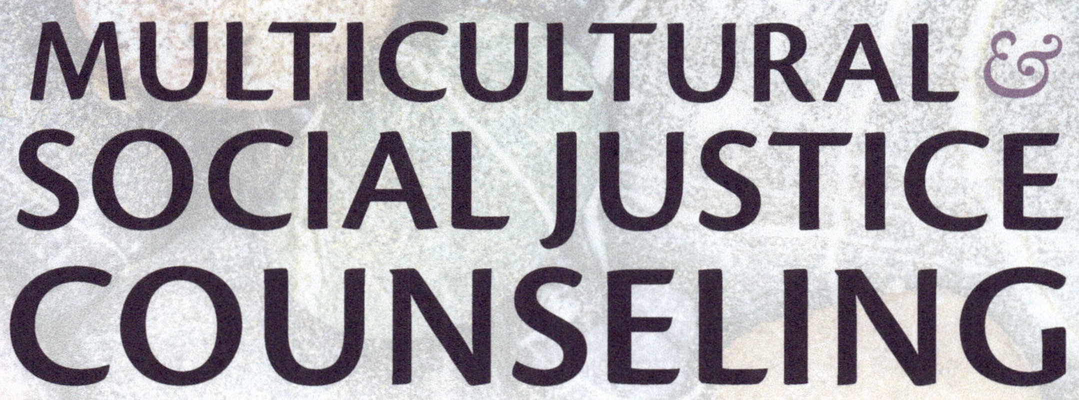

MULTICULTURAL & SOCIAL JUSTICE COUNSELING

A Systemic, Person-Centered, and Ethical Approach

JENNIFER M. COOK & MADELINE CLARK, *Editors*

cognella
SAN DIEGO

Bassim Hamadeh, CEO and Publisher
Amy Smith, Associate Editorial Manager
Susana Christie, Senior Developmental Editor
Jeanine Rees, Production Editor
Jessica Delia, Graphic Design Associate
Kylie Bartolome, Licensing Specialist
Natalie Piccotti, Director of Marketing
Kassie Graves, Senior Vice President, Editorial
Alia Bales, Director, Project Editorial and Production

Printed in the United States of America.

JMC: To all those who fight for justice and those who are discovering the fight they have within them.

MC: For Maxine—I cannot wait to see how far you go in a more equitable world.

ACTIVE LEARNING

This book has interactive activities available to complement your reading.

Your instructor may have customized the selection of activities available for your unique course. Please check with your professor to verify whether your class will access this content through the Cognella Active Learning portal (http://active.cognella.com) or through your home learning management system.

ACTIVE LEARNING

Brief Contents

Introduction xxvii

SECTION I FOUNDATIONS AND CORE COMPETENCIES 1

CHAPTER 1 Overview and Introduction 2
Jennifer M. Cook and Madeline Clark

CHAPTER 2 Cultural Relevance and Counselors' Ethical Responsibility 25
Jennifer M. Cook and Diana Yum Rhyne

CHAPTER 3 Cultural Humility 57
Charmayne R. Adams, Jillian M. Blueford, and Thang S. Tran

CHAPTER 4 Systems and Structural Oppression 77
Madeline Clark, Monica L. Coleman, and Jennifer M. Cook

CHAPTER 5 Social Justice and Advocacy: Skills and Application in Counseling 104
Donghun Lee, ZeVida A. Jones, Derrick Shepard, Tabitha Cude, Jeongwoon Jeong, and Sojeong Nam

CHAPTER 6 Cultural Identity Development Models 131
Alexandria Hepburn, Ryan Wisniewski, Rachel Mattingly, and Madeline Clark

SECTION II CULTURAL GROUPS AND THEIR SOCIOPOLITICAL REALITIES 159

CHAPTER 7 Race, Racism, and Colorism 160
Tanesha Rorie and Janice Byrd

CHAPTER 8 Ethnicity, National Identity, and Ethnocentrism 185
Angelica M. Tello, Alena Pridhidko, and Jennifer M. Cook

CHAPTER 9 Immigrants, Refugees, Diasporas, and Xenomisia 210
John J. S. Harrichand, Krista E. Kirk, Shreya Vaishnav, Joy M. Mwendwa, and Kevin C. Snow

CHAPTER 10 Indigenous, Native, First Nations Groups, and Settler Colonialism 236
Christine Park, Brynn Luger, and Laurie "Lali" McCubbin

CHAPTER 11 **Social Class and Classism 265**
Madeline Clark, Jennifer M. Cook, and Susan M. Long

CHAPTER 12 **Disability and Ableism 292**
Melissa D. Deroche and Elizabeth K. Mautz

CHAPTER 13 **Age and Ageism 323**
Matthew Fullen, Jordan B. Westcott, Mary Chase Mize, Lisa M. Boyd, Julianna Williams, and Nicole Castagna

CHAPTER 14 **Sex, Gender, Patriarchy, and Transmisia 351**
Lena Salpietro, Jacob Perez, and Kassie Terrell

CHAPTER 15 **Romantic and Affectional Identity and Queer Oppression 383**
Clark D. Ausloos, Stacy Pinto, and Chase Morgan-Swaney

CHAPTER 16 **Spirituality, Religion, and Religious Persecution 417**
Erik Braun, Christie Nelson, and Tabitha Fabin

CHAPTER 17 **Emerging Topics in Diversity: Fatmisia, Neurodivergence, Incarcerated Populations, Individuals With Substance Use Disorders, the Individuals Coping With the Climate Crisis 448**
Susan M. Long, Jennifer Rio, and Kaitlyn M. Forristal

SECTION III APPLICATIONS 479

CHAPTER 18 **Applying Culturally Competent Skills Across Counseling Settings: Intake, Assessment, Diagnosis, Case Conceptualization, and Treatment Planning 480**
Madeline Clark, Gwendolyn Hooks, Kathleen Klein, and Renee Stack

Appendix 515
Glossary 527
Bibliography 535
Index 603
About the Editors 615
About the Contributors 617

Detailed Contents

Introduction xxvii

SECTION I FOUNDATIONS AND CORE COMPETENCIES 1

CHAPTER 1 Overview and Introduction 2
Jennifer M. Cook and Madeline Clark

Beginning the Process 4

Considering Diversity, Equity, and Inclusion Within a Multicultural Orientation 5

Building Your Knowledge Base 6

Caucasian Has Racist and Eugenicist Origins 7

White Explains the Relationship to Power and Privilege 8

Dominant and Nondominant Identities 9

Privilege, Power, Marginalization, and Oppression 11

Bias, Stereotypes, Prejudice, Discrimination, and "-isms/misias" 12

Person-Centered Counseling Principles 16

Taking a Strength-Based and Resiliency-Focused Approach 19

Making a Personal Commitment 20

Conclusion 21

Questions for Reflection 22

Applying What You Have Learned 22

Activity #1: Assessing Your Own Unconscious Bias 22

Activity #2: Making Your Personal Commitment Plan 22

Activity #3: Your Cultural Strengths and Weaknesses 23

Activity #4: Your Cultural Resiliencies 24

Activity #5: CRT in the Media 24

CHAPTER 2 Cultural Relevance and Counselors' Ethical Responsibility 25
Jennifer M. Cook and Diana Yum Rhyne

What Is Ethical Practice? 26

Ethical Practice Is Culturally Relevant Practice 27

Professional Responsibility 29

Dispositions and Skills 29

Understanding the Historical Context of Multiculturalism in the Ethical Codes 33
ACA 34
AMHCA 36
Conflicts With "Sincerely Held Principles" 37
ASCA 37
CRCC 38
NBCC 40
Perspectives That Impact Ethical Code Interpretation 41
Perspective 1: How Ethical Codes Are Developed 42
Perspective 2: Ecological Systems Theory 44
Perspective 3: Culture in the Ethical Codes: Direct and Indirect 49
Perspective 4: Social Justice and Advocacy 50
Conclusion 54
Questions for Reflection 55
Applying What You Have Learned 55
Activity #1: Finding the Connections 55
Activity #2: Personal and Professional Values 55

CHAPTER 3 **Cultural Humility 57**
Charmayne R. Adams, Jillian M. Blueford, and Thang S. Tran

Multicultural Orientation Model 58
Model Components 58
Empirical Support 60
Cultural Humility 61
Cultural Opportunities 70
Always a Process: Making and Sustaining Commitment 71
Identifying Areas of Strength and Growing Edges 72
Make a Commitment to Personal Cultural Development 73
Using the Multicultural Orientation Model 74
Conclusion 75
Questions for Reflection 75
Applying What You Have Learned 75
Activity #1: Pop Culture Check—Identifying Beliefs, Values, and Cultural Experiences 75
Activity #2: It's Hard to Be Humble 75

CHAPTER 4 **Systems and Structural Oppression 77**
Madeline Clark, Monica L. Coleman, and Jennifer M. Cook

Systems Theory and Ecological Approaches 78
Systems Theory: General 78

Systems Theory in Counseling 79
Ecological Systems Theory 80
Structural Oppression 82
Understanding the Historical Context of Structural Oppression 83
Structural Oppression Versus Individual Discrimination 84
The Oppressed Versus the Oppressor 89
The Multicultural and Social Justice Counseling Competencies 91
Intersectionality and its Importance in Counseling 92
Black Feminism and its Importance in Understanding Social Justice 93
Systemic Oppression Versus Individual Bias and Discrimination 94
The Outcomes of Structural Oppression and the Social Determinants of Health 96
Counselors' Responsibilities and Interventions as Agents of Change 99
Different Theoretical Orientations That May Foster Systemic Change 100
Conclusion 101
Questions for Reflection 101
Applying What You Have Learned 101
Activity #1: Your Intersectional Identity 102
Activity #2: Dismantling Structural Oppression 103

CHAPTER 5 **Social Justice and Advocacy: Skills and Application in Counseling 104**
Donghun Lee, ZeVida A. Jones, Derrick Shepard, Tabitha Cude, Jeongwoon Jeong, and Sojeong Nam

Social Justice and Advocacy Within Counselor Identity and Practice 106
The Role of Social Justice in Counseling and Advocacy as a Core Component 106
Communicating About Social Justice and Advocacy 107
What Is Advocacy? 108
Understanding the Historical Context of Social Justice and Advocacy in Counseling 109
Ethical Codes Related to Social Justice and Advocacy 110
Social Justice Counseling 114
Historical Knowledge of Social Justice in the Counseling Profession 114
Social Justice Counselors Are Self-Aware 115
Social Justice Skills 116
Advocacy Models in Counseling 117

Advocacy Applications 118
Advocacy in Counseling 118
What Is Your Circle of Influence? 118
The How of Advocating at the Microlevel 119
Building a Circle of Influence 120
Approaches to Social Justice and Advocacy in Counseling Relationships 123
Cultural Humility 123
Cultural Broaching 124
Empowering Clients Through Social Justice
Advocacy and Engagement 126
Conclusion 127
Questions for Reflection 128
Applying What You Have Learned 128
Activity #1: ADDRESSING Model Self-Assessment Worksheet 129
Activity #2: What Is Your Circle of Influence? 129

CHAPTER 6 **Cultural Identity Development Models 131**
Alexandria Hepburn, Ryan Wisniewski, Rachel Mattingly, and Madeline Clark

Defining Identity Development and Introduction to Identity Development Models 132
Brief Overview of Models 133
Race and Ethnicity Identity Development Models 133
Racial/Cultural Identity Development Model 134
Hardiman-Jackson Identity Development Model 135
Minority Identity Development Model 135
American Indian Identity Development Model 136
Asian American Identity Development 137
Black American Identity Development Model 137
Latinx Identity Development 138
White Identity Development 139
Bi/Multiracial Identity Development 140
Ethnic Identity Formation 141
Acculturation Models 142
Extending Existing Racial and Ethnic Identity Development Models 142
Gender Identity Development Models 143
Psychosocial Development Foundations 144
Social Cognitive Theory of Gender Development 144
Feminist Identity Development Model 145

Transgender Identity Development 146
Transgender POC Identity Development 146
Extending Existing Gender Identity Development Models 147
Romantic and Affectual Identity Development 148
Homosexual Identity Formation Model 149
Adolescent Lesbian and Gay Identity Development 149
Lesbian Identity Development 150
Bisexual Identity Development 150
RAI Model Gaps 151
Religious and Spiritual Identity Development Models 152
Fowler's Model 152
Disability Identity Development Model 154
Social Class 155
Areas of Identity Without Developmental Models 156
Conclusion 157
Questions for Reflection 157
Applying What You Have Learned 157
Activity #1: Ethics and Identity Development Models 157
Activity #2: Introducing Identity Development Models to Clients 158

SECTION II CULTURAL GROUPS AND THEIR SOCIOPOLITICAL REALITIES 159

CHAPTER 7 Race, Racism, and Colorism 160
Tanesha Rorie and Janice Byrd
Brief Historical Overview 162
Nondominant Group Identities 162
African American and Black Communities 163
Asian American, Native Hawaiian, and Pacific Islander Communities 169
Latina/o/x and Hispanic Communities 171
Arab and Middle Eastern Americans 173
Ecological and Sociopolitical Contexts 174
Professional Counseling Practice Applications 176
The Counseling Relationship 176
MSJCC Application 177
Counseling Recommendations 178
Resiliencies, Strengths, and Fostering Wellness 180

Ethical Code Application 182
Conclusion 183
Questions for Reflection 183
Applying What You Have Learned 184
Activity #1: Identifying Your Race and Ethnicity 184
Activity #2: It's Still Hard to Be Humble 184

CHAPTER 8 **Ethnicity, National Identity, and Ethnocentrism 185**
Angelica M. Tello, Alena Pridhidko, and Jennifer M. Cook

Understanding the Historical Context 186
Ethnocentrism, Discrimination, and Oppression 188
Counselor Responses to Oppression and Discrimination 189
Nondominant Ethnic Identities 190
Diversity Within Diversity 190
Biculturalism 192
Spectrum of Collectivism and Individualism 192
Ecological and Sociopolitical Contexts 195
Professional Counseling Practice 197
The Counseling Relationship 197
Communicating With Clients Whose First Language Is Not English 199
Attending to Acculturation 199
Spiritual and Religious Informed Support 200
MSJCC Application 201
Resiliencies, Strengths, and Fostering Wellness 203
Ethical Code Applications 206
Conclusion 207
Questions for Reflection 208
Applying What You Have Learned 208
Activity #1: Contextual Ethnicity 208
Activity #2: Expanding Your Professional Knowledge 209

CHAPTER 9 **Immigrants, Refugees, Diasporas, and Xenomisia 210**
John J. S. Harrichand, Krista E. Kirk, Shreya Vaishnav, Joy M. Mwendwa, and Kevin C. Snow

Concepts, Terms, Models, and Definitions 211
Immigrants 212
Refugees and Asylum Seekers 213
Diasporas 214
Xenomisia 214
Acculturation Models 214

Nondominant Group Identities 216
Understanding the Historical Context of Immigration Regulation 218
Ecological and Sociopolitical Perspectives 220
Professional Counseling Practice Application 222
Needs, Challenges, and Barriers Related to Counseling 225
Ethical Considerations: Putting It Into Practice 226
Multicultural and Social Justice Counseling Competencies 227
I-CARE Model 229
Resiliencies, Strengths, and Fostering Wellness: Stories and Counseling Implications 232
Story of Volodymyr 232
Reflection Questions 233
Counseling Implication for Volodymyr: I-CARE Model 233
Conclusion 234
Questions for Reflection 234
Applying What You Have Learned 235
Activity #1: Research and Discuss—Immigration in a Global Context 235
Activity #2: Identifying and Responding to Xenomisia 235

CHAPTER 10 **Indigenous, Native, First Nations Groups, and Settler Colonialism 236**
Christine Park, Brynn Luger, and Laurie "Lali" McCubbin

Understanding the Historical Context of Indigenous and Native People's Experiences 238
Resurgence of Indigenous Peoples 240
Hawaiian Renaissance 240
Columbus Day—Indigenous People's Day 240
Language Preservation 241
Reclaiming Spaces and Land Acknowledgment 243
Cases in Point 243
The Dakota Access Pipeline Conflict 243
Protecting Mauna Kea 245
Essential Models 246
Indigenous Ways of Knowing 246
Native Models of Wellness 246
Symbols and Pathways to Wellness: Balance, Harmony, and Unity 247
Medicine Wheel 250

Multicultural and Social Justice Counseling Competencies 251
Intersectionality 252
Professional Counseling Application 253
Deficit-Based Versus Resilience Focused 253
Rapport, the Therapeutic Relationship, and Ethical Responsibility 255
Culturally Sensitive Approaches 257
The Story of Kau'i 258
Generational Considerations 259
Cultural Connectedness 260
Culturally Appropriate or Cultural Appropriation? 261
Traditional Healing Practices 261
Conclusion 262
Questions for Reflection 263
Applying What You Have Learned 263
Activity #1: Reflection on a Personal and Contemporary Account of Cultural Emergence 263
Activity #2: Cultivating Awareness of Cultural Appropriation 264

CHAPTER 11 **Social Class and Classism 265**
Madeline Clark, Jennifer M. Cook, and Susan M. Long

Unpacking Social Class Terminology 266
Socioeconomic Status and Social Class 267
Classism 268
Nondominant Group Designations: Social Class Stratification 269
Understanding the Historical Context of Social Class 271
Classism in Systemic and Ecological Contexts 272
Poverty 274
The Federal Poverty Level 275
Classism, Microaggressions, and Counseling 276
Counseling Applications 277
Ethical Responsibility 277
Multicultural and Social Justice Counseling Competencies 277
Social Class Counseling Framework 280
Best Practice for Working With Clients Experiencing Poverty 280
Person-Centered and Humanistic Strategies 281
Social Class Assessment 284
Social Class Genogram 284
Wellness and Social Support Strategies 286
Advocacy Interventions 286

Conclusion 288
Questions for Reflection 288
Applying What You Have Learned 288
Activity #1: Best Practices for Counseling Persons Experiencing Poverty 288
Activity #2: Proactive Discussions About Social Class 291

CHAPTER 12 **Disability and Ableism 292**
Melissa D. Deroche and Elizabeth K. Mautz

A Contextual Framework for Understanding People With Disabilities 293
Models of Disability 294
Classification, Onset, Course, and Visibility of Disability 296
Chronic Illness and Spoon Theory 298
Ableism and Ableist Microaggressions 300
Understanding the Historical Context of Treatment of Persons With Disabilities 301
The Disability Rights Movement 303
Section 504 Today 304
Systems and Intersectional Perspectives 307
Professional Counselor Practice Application Considerations 309
Self-Awareness 309
Skills 313
Access and Accessibility 316
Advocacy and Allyship 317
Additional Practice Considerations 317
Conclusion 319
Questions for Reflection 320
Applying What You Have Learned 320
Activity #1: Case Scenarios 320
Activity #2: Identifying Microaggressions 321
Activity #3: Advocacy Activity 322

CHAPTER 13 **Age and Ageism 323**
Matthew Fullen, Jordan B. Westcott, Mary Chase Mize, Lisa M. Boyd, Julianna Williams, and Nicole Castagna

What Is Aging? 325
Cultural Diversity in Aging 326
Understanding Aging Within the Ecological Framework 329
Environment and Aging 332

Understanding Generational Differences: The Age-Period-Cohort Model 332
Applications to Counseling 334
Ageism 334
Ageism Across the Lifespan 335
Intersectionality and Ageism 336
Combating Ageism: Strategies for Counselors 336
Understanding the Historical Context of Aging and Counseling 338
Professional Counseling Related to Aging: Needs, Interest, and Access 339
Multicultural and Social Justice Counseling Competencies 344
Counselor Self-Awareness 344
Client Worldview 345
Counseling Relationship 345
Counseling and Advocacy Interventions 345
Ethical Considerations 346
Conclusion 348
Questions for Reflection 349
Applying What You Have Learned 349
Activity #1: Create Your Own "Age, Period, Cohort" Profile 349
Activity #2: Write Your Obituary 350

CHAPTER 14 **Sex, Gender, Patriarchy, and Transmisia 351**
Lena Salpietro, Jacob Perez, and Kassie Terrell

Terminology and Concepts 353
The Distinct Concepts of Sex and Gender 356
Person-First and Identity-First Language 357
Understanding the Historical Context of Sex and Gender 357
The Time Line of Gender Equality and Visibility in the United States 358
Ecological and Sociopolitical Contexts 361
Microsystem 361
Mesosystem 362
Exosystem 363
Macrosystem 364
Chronosystem 365
Nondominant Group Identities 365
Cisgender Women and Race 367
Transgender People 368

Nonbinary People 369

Professional Counseling Practice Applications 369

Person-Centered Perspectives 369

The Counseling Relationship 371

MSJCC Application 373

Resilience, Strengths, and Wellness 374

Ethical Code Application 377

House Bill (HB) 1557: Parental Rights in Education 377

Conclusion 382

Questions for Reflection 382

Applying What You Have Learned 382

Activity #1: Queer Coding 382

CHAPTER 15 **Romantic and Affectional Identity and Queer Oppression 383**

Clark D. Ausloos, Stacy Pinto, and Chase Morgan-Swaney

Terminology 385

Affectional, Romantic, and Sexual Identity Development 389

Minority Stress, Intersectionality, and Internalized Homophobia/misia 390

Understanding the Historical Context of RAI 392

RAI Across Time, Space, and Culture 392

Dismantling Queer Oppression in Postmodern America (1960–Present) 393

Dismantling Queer Oppression in the Counseling Profession 395

Models of Affirmative and Liberatory Counseling 397

Counseling Standards 397

Nondominant Group Identities 399

Religiosity/Spirituality and RAIs 400

Ecological and Sociopolitical Contexts 401

RAIs, Homelessness, and Youth 401

Micro- and Mesosystems 402

Exosystem and Macrosystem 404

Chronosystem 405

Professional Counseling Practice Application 405

The Counseling Relationship 405

Humanistic and Person-Centered Perspectives 407

The Harm of SOCE 407

MSJCC Application 407

Resiliencies, Strengths, and Fostering Wellness 408

Ethical Code Application 409

Cases in Point: Tremaine and Julianne 410

Advocacy 411

Seeking Consultation 412

Pursuing Continuing Education 412

Conclusion 415

Questions for Reflection 415

Applying What You Have Learned 416

Activity #1: Advocacy and SOCE 416

Activity #2: Accessing Empathy 416

CHAPTER 16 **Spirituality, Religion, and Religious Persecution 417**
Erik Braun, Christie Nelson, and Tabitha Fabin

Distinguishing Religion and Spirituality 419

Spiritual Well-Being 420

Morals and Values 420

Understanding the Historical Context of Religion and Spirituality in Counseling 421

Viktor Frankl 421

Major Religious and Spiritual Belief Systems 423

Christianity 423

Judaism 424

Islam 424

Hinduism 425

Buddhism 425

The Religiously Unaffiliated 426

Religious Trauma 426

Key Features of Cults 426

Nondominant Group Identities Related to Spirituality and Religion 428

Spirituality and Religion Within Ecological and Sociopolitical Contexts and Oppression 430

Ecological Context 430

Oppression Within Sociopolitical Contexts 432

Recommendations for Counselors 436

The Multicultural and Social Justice Counseling Competencies 436

The Counseling Relationship 438

Counseling and Advocacy Interventions 439

Spiritual Genograms and Ecomaps 441

Music Chronology 442
Religion and Spirituality as a Form of Resilience 443
Ethical Code Applications 443
Working With Clients Whose Beliefs Differ From the Counselor 444
Inclusive Language 445
Conclusion 446
Questions for Reflection 446
Applying What You Have Learned 446
Activity #1: A Deeper Dive Into the ASERVIC Competencies 446
Activity #2: Meaning Making isn't Only for the Religious and Spiritual 447

CHAPTER 17 **Emerging Topics in Diversity: Fatmisia, Neurodivergence, Incarcerated Populations, Individuals With Substance Use Disorders, the Individuals Coping With the Climate Crisis 448**
Susan M. Long, Jennifer Rio, and Kaitlyn M. Forristal

Fatmisia 450
Section Overview 450
Learning Objectives 450
Power of Language 450
Lived Experiences of Weight Stigma 451
Microaggressions 451
Fatness in Media 453
Intersecting Identities 453
Professional Counseling Practice Application 454
Ethical Code Applications 455
Neurodivergence 457
Section Overview 457
Learning Objectives 457
Neurodiversity 457
Neurodivergent and Neurotypical 458
Forms of Neurodivergence 458
The Neurodiversity Paradigm and Models of Disability 458
Understanding the Historical Context of the Neurodiversity Movement 459
Professional Counseling Applications 459
Incarcerated Populations 462
Section Overview 462
Learning Objectives 462

The Incarcerated Population 462
Understanding the Historical Context of Incarcerated Populations 463
Counseling Applications 463
MSJCC Application 464
Substance Use Disorders 466
Section Overview 466
Learning Objectives 467
Understanding the Historical Context of SUDs 467
Counseling Applications 469
Climate Crisis and Mental Health 470
Section Overview 470
Learning Objectives 470
Climate 470
Climate Crisis and Well-Being 471
Environmental Justice 472
Counseling in the Climate Crisis 473
Ecological Advocacy and the Climate Crisis 475
Conclusion 476
Questions for Reflection 476
Applying What You Have Learned 476
Activity #1: Advocacy Video 476
Activity #2: See Your Community in a New Way 476

SECTION III APPLICATIONS 479

CHAPTER 18 **Applying Culturally Competent Skills Across Counseling Settings: Intake, Assessment, Diagnosis, Case Conceptualization, and Treatment Planning 480**
Madeline Clark, Gwendolyn Hooks, Kathleen Klein, and Renee Stack
Essential Terms and Models 482
Ethical Considerations by Setting 484
Cross-Cultural Best Practices in Intake 490
Office Spaces and Intake Processes 490
Broaching During Intake 492
Cross-Cultural Best Practices in Assessment 493
Culturally Informed Assessment in School Settings 494
Cross-Cultural Best Practices in Diagnosis 495
Case Conceptualization, Treatment Planning, and Interventions 496

Case Conceptualization 496
Treatment Planning and Interventions 497
Culturally Responsive Interventions 499
Culturally Informed Referrals and Recommendations 500
Referral for Additional Mental Health Assessment 500
Referral for Health-Care Resources 501
Referral for Case Management 502
Referrals and Recommendations for Other Self-Care Resources 503
Referrals for Scope of Practice 503
Referrals for Termination or Full Caseload 504
Considerations for School Counselors and School Settings 505
Culturally Oriented Examples Across Counseling Settings 508
Inpatient Settings 508
Outpatient Settings 510
School-Based Settings 511
Conclusion 512
Questions for Reflection 512
Applying What You Have Learned 513
Activity #1: Creating SMART Goals 513

Appendix 515
Glossary 527
Bibliography 535
Index 603
About the Editors 615
About the Contributors 617

Introduction

Approach and Overview

Welcome in! We're glad you're here! Is this a greeting that's familiar to you—"Welcome in"? It's one that I (Dr. Cook) learned not that long ago when I moved to San Antonio, Texas. It's a common greeting when entering a store, restaurant, bar, etc. Any space you enter, you frequently hear, "Welcome in."

This phrase has become poignant as we cocreated this textbook with so, so many authors. We have welcomed over 60 contributors who bring diverse thought and counseling experiences and settings, and who have diverse, intersecting identities. This book is about welcoming in

- a range of ideas, thoughts, and feelings;
- curiosity and interest;
- the readiness and willingness to learn from others, your life experiences, and your errors;
- openness;
- new experiences; and
- a deeper connection with others.

The "welcome in" philosophy is an important one because it points to relationships and connection, two things we counselors value deeply. Without the relationship and forming of the therapeutic connection, the counseling profession would cease to exist. As such, one of the foundational concepts used throughout this text is *person-centered counseling*, a pioneering contribution of Carl Rogers. The authors address core person-centered skills, and how they can be used and adapted to the wide range of clients they will serve. This is a unique contribution to how counselors learn about diverse identities, as well as how to approach working with clients with diverse identities.

As an extension of the person-centered approach woven through this text, authors focus on *identity intersectionality* or *multiple identities* while simultaneously naming experiences of *oppression* and *privilege*, situating them within *systemic and ecological contexts*. For quite some time, we have struggled with textbooks and teaching methods that attempt to distill who people are into one identity facet only, making few, if any, attempts to account for the identity complexity most individuals experience within the many systems of which they are a part. As a result, the authors in this text rarely, if ever, make sweeping claims about how to stringently work with "this identity" or "that identity." Furthermore, we acknowledge that most people experience privilege and oppression simultaneously. A person's various contexts, particularly the systems in which they are embedded, play a major role in those experiences and determine the extent to which they experience oppression or privilege. Therefore, not only do we include a stand-alone chapter on systems and oppression, but these concepts are integrated into every chapter. Additionally, the authors apply ecological systems theory (Bronfenbrenner, 2005) to the populations they discuss.

Many students struggle with "What do I do?" questions when they dive more deeply or learn for the first time about oppression, what experiences of oppression are like, and how many of the systems of which they are a part support oppression and inequity. As a result, we made social justice and advocacy a priority by including a specific chapter on these topics and addressing the *Multicultural and Social Justice Counseling Competencies* (MSJCCs; Ratts et al., 2016) within each chapter. Finally, in addition to including an independent chapter on the role of ethics in culturally relevant counseling, we have integrated ethical considerations into each chapter. In the spirit of professional inclusion, the authors discuss five major professional ethical codes (i.e., American Counseling Association, American Mental Health Counselors Association, American School Counselor Association, Commission on Rehabilitation Counselor Certification, and National Board for Certified Counselors).

It was a tall order to include so many dimensions within this text, that is true, yet we did so with specific intentionality and purpose. First, life complexity is a given for us as counselors and for the clients we serve. Our clients need us to see that complexity and be able to respond proactively. So, we sought to reveal that complexity, to lay it bear, and to offer students tools to work with it rather than resorting to undue distillation. Second, to handle the demands of complexity, counselors must be able to think critically. Throughout the text, we offer opportunities for reflection and awareness building, as well as ways to take action, all of which are designed to foster critical thinking and a sustained tolerance for ambiguity.

Welcome in. We're glad you're here.

Textbook Composition

This textbook is divided into three sections. Section 1 (*Foundations and Core Competencies*) is intended for you to develop context and lenses through which to understand and work with clients as the diverse cultural beings that they are. A key feature of the chapters in this section is that they are focused on overarching frameworks you will use to inform your practice. No matter your client's identity, you will operate with these core characteristics and competencies in mind.

Section 1: Foundations and Core Competencies

- Chapter 1: Overview and Introduction
- Chapter 2: Cultural Relevance and Counselors' Ethical Responsibility
- Chapter 3: Cultural Humility
- Chapter 4: Systems and Systemic Oppression
- Chapter 5: Social Justice and Advocacy: Skills and Application in Counseling
- Chapter 6: Cultural Identity Development Models

Section 2 is dedicated to helping you learn about different *cultural groups and their sociopolitical realities*. Something you will not encounter in the chapters in Section 2 is prescriptive tropes about how to work with *this group* or *that group*. Instead, we offer information you can apply in a contextual, individualized way for each client you encounter while taking into account the characteristics and competencies you learned in Chapters 1 through 6. Additionally, you will find considerations related to person-centered counseling skills and theory-specific skills you can use with diverse populations embedded in Chapters 7 through 17.

Section 2: Cultural Groups and Their Sociopolitical Realities

- ▹ Chapter 7: Race, Racism, and Colorism
- ▹ Chapter 8: Ethnicity, National Identity, and Ethnocentrism
- ▹ Chapter 9: Immigrants, Refugees, Diasporas, and Xenomisia
- ▹ Chapter 10: Indigenous, Native, First Nations Groups, and Settler Colonialism
- ▹ Chapter 11: Social Class and Classism
- ▹ Chapter 12: Disability and Ableism
- ▹ Chapter 13: Age and Ageism
- ▹ Chapter 14: Sex, Gender, Patriarchy, and Transmisia
- ▹ Chapter 15: Romantic and Affectional Identity and Queer Oppression
- ▹ Chapter 16: Spirituality, Religion, and Persecution
- ▹ Chapter 17: Emerging Topics in Diversity: Fatmisia, Neurodivergence, Incarcerated Populations, Individuals With Substance Use Disorders, the Individuals Coping With the Climate Crisis

Section 3 is the smallest of the sections (*Applications*), yet it should not be overlooked. Chapter 18 offers skills for applying a multicultural orientation to intake, assessment, case conceptualization, and treatment planning across counseling settings.

Ancillaries and Special Features

Earlier in the introduction, we named the foundational components you will find in this textbook that make it quite different from other multicultural counseling textbooks: systems, the ecological context, ethics, person-centered counseling, social justice, and advocacy and applying the MSJCCs, and a strong focus on critical, complex thinking. The structure of this text is a special feature in and of itself!

Additionally, each chapter includes reflection questions and activities, and we have provided robust appendixes with books, blogs, movies, TV shows, and articles to further students' learning. Accompanying this text are podcasts with chapter authors that both students and instructors can access. For instructors, you will find presentation slides, exam questions, and assignment and activity ideas to bolster your work with your students within the instructor resources.

Welcoming You Into Your Journey of Culturally Relevant Counseling

Learning about culture and diversity in a classroom setting is a different experience for each student, and it is certainly different from learning about culture and diversity outside of a formal educational environment. It can take a great deal of effort to welcome yourself and others into the experiences you will have as part of this course, yet we invite you to put forth an effort and begin to imagine what you and your colleagues will gain as a result.

No two students are the same in terms of their identities, experiences, worldviews, beliefs, and values—there is beauty in those differences, yet there can be struggle, too. Group dynamics can be exhilarating, anxiety producing, informative, infuriating, and so much more. Sometimes, the course content can result in high emotions, defensiveness, worry, stress—just to name a few. We get it. The topics the authors discuss in this text are ones many of us have been taught are not *public conversations* or are not to be had *in polite company*. However, the professional counseling relationship is not a public conversation, nor is it one in which counselors maintain unnecessary pretenses. We have real conversations with our clients about what they value most, the hurts that have cut the deepest, the traumas they've endured, and the resiliencies they've developed. All of these conversations are culturally bound because we are cultural beings operating in cultural spaces. So, if we will pursue this depth with our clients, why not with ourselves and each other?

Because no topic is off-limits for clients to discuss, counselors in training practice talking about so-called *taboo* subjects. However, *practice* is not the only purpose. Professional counselors must be knowledgeable about culture and all that it entails: systems and structures, oppression and privilege, values and beliefs, differences and similarities, and so much more. Not only must counselors be knowledgeable, but they must be keenly aware of who they are and who their clients are, and be willing to enter their clients' worldview so they can provide treatment plans and interventions that both align with clients' goals and with who clients are. Awareness and knowledge are translated into a host of skills, and the awareness, knowledge, and skills you develop through this course and beyond will be applicable to every client you serve and be the basis for your future learning as a professional counselor. Finally, you will develop social justice and advocacy skills that will augment the work you do with clients to foster equity and inclusion for individuals, families, communities, and society.

The course you are taking is both an individual and a group process. We invite you into both, welcoming you into both. When the information, emotions, or topics get challenging, we empower you to recall that you are here for a purpose—to become a professional counselor who will be an invaluable resource for the clients and communities you will serve. This truth binds you with your colleagues, no matter your differences. Each of you has an unwavering desire to work with people when they are at their most vulnerable and to see them fully. These commonalities and connections cannot be disregarded because they can be a place to return to when you are struggling to hear, see, or understand one another. We welcome you in and invite you to welcome each other in throughout your learning process.

BOX 0.1 **TIPS FOR ALERT ENGAGEMENT**

Alert engagement is essential for navigating complex topics deeply and thoughtfully. Below, we offer tips you can use while you read this textbook and throughout your educational journey to *engage* with what you are learning so you are better prepared to apply what you have learned with clients.

Take notes about what you read! Simple highlighting is rarely enough. Writing notes in your own voice deepens your learning and ability to think critically about what you read.

Record questions that arise for you. You can take a general approach—that is, questions you would like to ask your instructor—yet you can take the approach of recording questions you would ask the authors if you had the opportunity, questions you would ask professional counselors about how they have applied specific information in practice, or even topics you would like to discuss with your peer colleagues.

Note ideas that strike you as interesting or bizarre, points with which you agree or disagree or find confusing.

Put on your "client hat" just as much as you put on your "counselor hat." When might counselors understand ethical information differently than clients? When might it be the same?

Notice what comes up for you. Are you mostly nodding along as you read, or are you finding yourself having a stronger reaction? Is your stronger reaction, "Yes, yes, yes!" Or is it, "No, no, no!" Or maybe you are constantly saying, "Huh?!" or "What??" Pay attention. Stay alert. Your reactions are important to your learning and your development.

Acknowledgments

This textbook has been a labor of love and an expression of our passion to contribute to building a more equitable society through professional counseling. Neither of us sought the opportunity to write a textbook—it found us by happenstance, as many of the most impactful things in our career journeys seem to do. While we never knew we had a book in us, we are grateful for the opportunity to share our ideas, our care, and, truthfully, our hearts.

There is no way this book could have happened without the over 60 contributors who joined us in our efforts. We are grateful for each word you wrote, each story you told, and each bead of sweat that formed every time you received an email from us asking for something else! We are deeply grateful for the seriousness and care you put into your chapters and for your willingness to share your expertise, knowledge, and spirit with our counseling community.

While the hundreds of students we have served over the years didn't know it, they, too, contributed to the creation of this book. Their stories, their experiences, what we learned from teaching them these concepts—all of this and more went into our approach to this book. Thank you to our students, past, current, and future, for inspiring us and teaching us, sometimes more than we taught you. In addition to our students, we would be remiss if we didn't show gratitude for our clients who not only have immersed us in new cultures but also educated us when needed. Each student and client have opened new opportunities for interpersonal and cultural learning.

A million thank-yous are not enough for what our graduate assistants, future doctors Christine Mayorga (University of Texas at San Antonio) and Karisa Odrunia (University of Nevada, Las Vegas), did for us as we prepared this text. Their organization, keen eye for detail, and patience when we asked for "one more thing" a hundred times over. Thank you for your dedication and spirit!

We are indebted to Kassie Graves for taking a chance on us, new book authors, and our approach to culturally relevant counseling—thank you, Kassie. Kassie gave us a wonderful team of her colleagues at Cognella who made this book what it is in its final form. Thank you for your hard work and dedication!

Maddie Clark: I am grateful for the experiences I've had that led to this specific point in my professional journey. For me, those points, not only my own, are generational. From my grandfather's many challenges and sacrifices as a child growing up in a coal camp in Appalachia to my dad's experience as a first-generation college student, all while being a single father. I can add the love and hope my grandmother poured into me, which has carried past the period of her lifetime. My academic journey led me to counseling and counselor education at Old Dominion University. Every client and student I've had has informed my process. My mentors have informed my process, inspired me to work toward excellence, and often offered validation that I sometimes need! All of that has informed what I have been able to create in this text.

I must acknowledge how instrumental my partner, Viktor, has been in this process. He didn't bat an eye when I started a book proposal in the middle of maternity leave with a 3-month-old baby at home (she's almost 3 now). He supported my desire to create this and understood and provided the time and space I needed to accomplish that creation.

As we shared earlier, we stumbled onto this book opportunity all because Jenn said, "Yes, let's try it." We have been collaborating on various projects for nearly 10 years, and through that time (and distance—we have never worked at the same place and are only in the same room maybe once or twice a year!), we have not only been productive scholars but a great support to each other. This book feels like a culmination of the great relationship we have built. Finally, I am so grateful for all our contributing authors, especially my peers, friends, and former students who answered the call (email) when I asked if they would jump in and write a chapter. My continued relationship with those in this profession is so meaningful and inspiring, and I continue to benefit by being in community with you all.

Jenn Cook: Never in my wildest dreams did I ever think I would be in the position to conceive of a book like this one, let alone be the person to put it together and contribute to it heartily. As a person from a low social class, it is part of my identity to want to name all the people and communities who have contributed to my growth, my personhood—who "raised me" over my 46 years of life. Pragmatically, in conjunction with my dual identity as a person who is also a member of the upper middle class, I will confine my list. Personally, I am grateful for my parents, who instilled in me a love of reading, discovery, cultural curiosity, and, most of all, a love for people and what they have to contribute. Without this start, coupled with being raised in the immense diversity of South Florida with close friends who have supported me, I'm doubtful I would be who I am today. Professionally, I have had the best darn partner in Dr. Maddie Clark in writing this book. I can't imagine having done this with anyone else—we complement each other in all the right ways (most of the time!). I have unending gratitude for the multitudes who trained me as a counselor, educator, supervisor, and scholar, specifically the gifted faculty at the University of Colorado Denver who provided a culturally relevant and justice-focused program and saw something in me to encourage me to become a counselor educator, and the exceptional faculty at Virginia Tech who fostered my abilities, gave me space to learn and grow, and encouraged me when I struck out to study social class when few others were within professional counseling. And finally, the professional-personal combo, my mentor and friend, Dr. Marsha Wiggins, without whom I would not be able to put together a cogent written sentence, nor would I have had the confidence and strength to undertake this book. Thank you to you all.

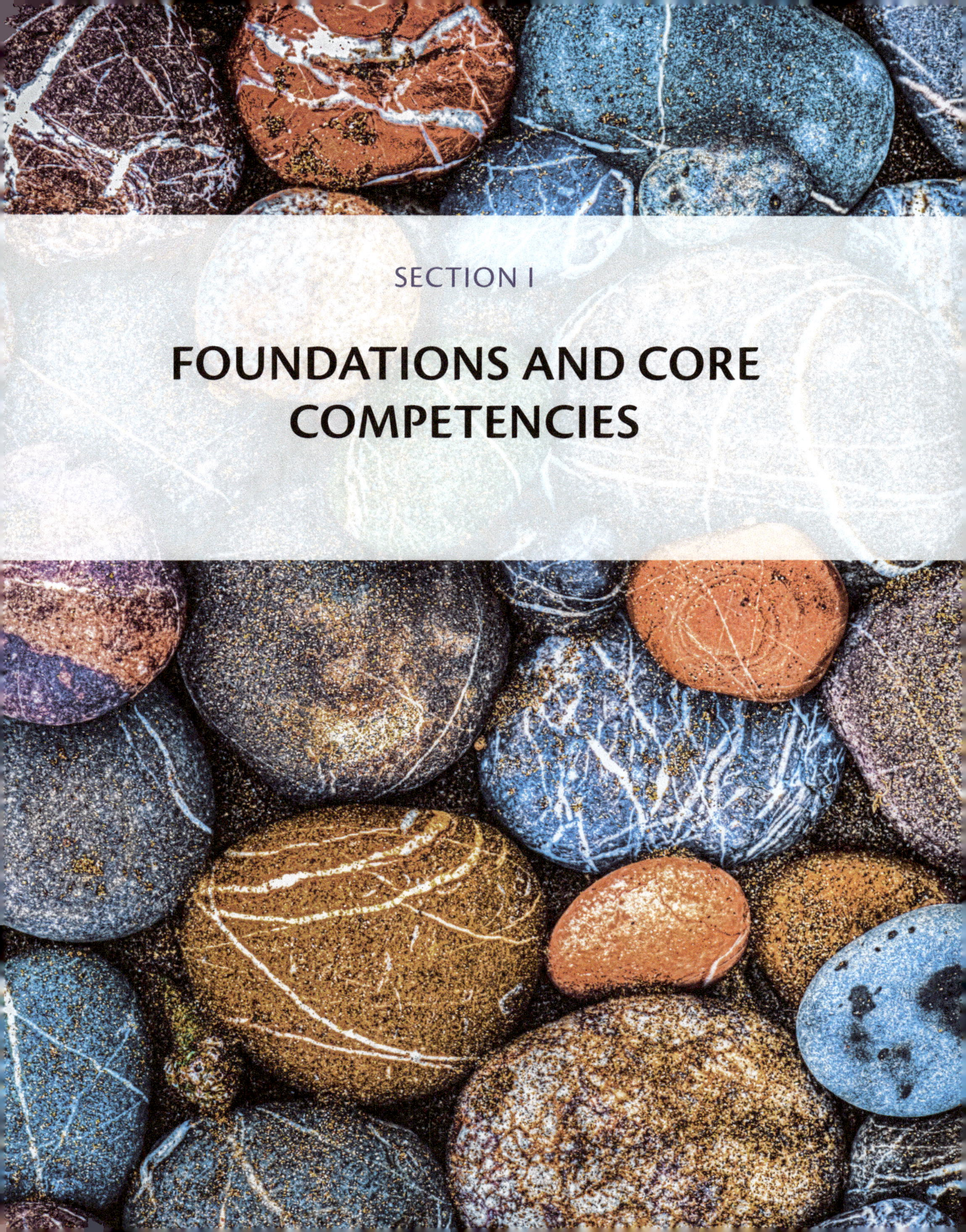

SECTION I

FOUNDATIONS AND CORE COMPETENCIES

CHAPTER 1

Overview and Introduction

Jennifer M. Cook and Madeline Clark

> *Culture makes people understand each other better. And if they understand each other better in their soul, it is easier to overcome the economic and political barriers. But first they have to understand that their neighbor is, in the end, just like them, with the same problems, the same questions.*
>
> —Paolo Coelho

CHAPTER OVERVIEW

Welcome in to the beginning of your journey within your counseling program to becoming a culturally relevant counselor! While the course in which you are enrolled indicates your formal cultural training on your transcript, every person has been having cultural experiences since the day they were born. You were born into a family, you were raised by people and communities with specific cultural identities and ways of being, and you had interactions with cultural similarities and differences in elementary, middle, and high school. In these early instances, you likely began to notice things like who had privilege and eased access to resources, who experienced oppression, and whose path to resources was blocked or filled with barriers to overcome. If you were in the latter group who experienced oppression and barriers, you were keenly aware of inequality, the pain discrimination brings, and the impact of unequal access. If you experienced privilege, your experiences were likely very different. In fact, this could be one of the first times you are taking a deep dive into what cultural identities are, what privilege affords, and the deep impact that oppression has on individuals and communities.

Everyone's experiences, knowledge, and awareness are valid and important. The key to becoming a culturally relevant, ethical counselor begins with the willingness and openness to immerse yourself deeply in your own experiences and the experiences of others. Then, your job is to open yourself to transformation. This is not transformation in the sense of becoming an entirely different person or the person you imagine your professor wants you to be! No, this transformation is about having the ability to think complexly and critically about identities, systems, and experiences so you can fully hear and work with clients from all backgrounds and experiences. Knowledge acquisition and awareness development will go hand in hand—as you acquire knowledge, you will develop deeper awareness, and as you become more aware, you will strive to learn more. Then, you will use your knowledge and awareness to develop your skill set.

In this chapter, you will discover more about the process of becoming a culturally relevant counselor while learning key foundational concepts, such as dominant and nondominant identities, privilege, discrimination, oppression, and microaggressions. Additionally, you will be introduced to the core conditions and how they are applied when building cross-cultural counseling relationships. As you read this chapter, pay close attention to what concepts and applications are familiar to you and which are new. Notice which ones feel comfortable and natural for you and which ones result in discomfort. Remember, everyone's experiences, knowledge, and awareness are valid and important—the key is opening yourself to transformation toward being a counselor who clients trust with their experiences and their healing.

BOX 1.1 **PAUSE AND REFLECT: BEGINNING YOUR JOURNEY**

Graduate school is certainly full of complicated experiences and feelings, and not just a little bit of effort. As you embark on your journey toward becoming a culturally adept counselor, what stands out for you? What identities are you bringing to the table that feel the most relevant at this moment? Do you have strong thoughts or feelings that are coming up related to this course/experience?

LEARNING OBJECTIVES

By the end of this chapter, students will be able to

1. define key terms associated with culturally relevant counseling;
2. identify and describe their own dominant and nondominant identities;
3. discuss how privilege, discrimination, and microaggressions impact counselors and clients; and
4. describe the importance of using the core conditions to build the counseling relationship.

CACREP 2016 STANDARDS

The information in this chapter supports the following standards:

- 2.F.2.d the impact of heritage, attitudes, beliefs, understandings, and acculturative experiences on an individual's views of others
- 2.F.2.e the effects of power and privilege for counselors and clients
- 2.F.2.h strategies for identifying and eliminating barriers, prejudices, and processes of intentional and unintentional oppression and discrimination
- 2.F.5.d ethical and culturally relevant strategies for establishing and maintaining in-person and technology-assisted relationships
- 5.C.2.j cultural factors relevant to clinical mental health counseling
- 5.D.2.s cultural factors relevant to rehabilitation counseling

CACREP 2024 STANDARDS

The information in this chapter supports the following standards:

- 3.B.2. the influence of heritage, cultural identities, attitudes, values, beliefs, understandings, within-group differences, and acculturative experiences on individuals' worldviews

- 3.B.4. the effects of historical events, multigenerational trauma, and current issues on diverse cultural groups in the U.S. and globally
- 3.B.5. the effects of stereotypes, overt and covert discrimination, racism, power, oppression, privilege, marginalization, microaggressions, and violence on counselors and clients
- 3.B.6. the effects of various socio-cultural influences, including public policies, social movements, and cultural values, on mental and physical health and wellness
- 3.B.9. strategies for identifying and eliminating barriers, prejudices, and processes of intentional and unintentional oppression and discrimination
- 3.E.6. ethical and legal issues relevant to establishing and maintaining counseling relationships across service delivery modalities
- 3.E.7. culturally sustaining and responsive strategies for establishing and maintaining counseling relationships across service delivery modalities

Beginning the Process

Counselor training programs are quite distinct from other professional training programs, including many in the allied mental health professions (e.g., social work, psychology). Maybe you know someone who is training to be a physical therapist, an accountant, a lawyer, or a nurse. While all of these professions work with people, they do not work with people in the same ways professional counselors do, so they are trained differently.

Who am I? How did I become who I am? What can I change? Do I *want* to change? What will remain consistent? Why did events unfold as they did? What is my purpose on earth? How can I make a difference? These are root questions that clients ask regularly, even if they do not use these words exactly. Many clients ask these questions in emotional angst, begging for quick, hard-and-fast answers that will free them from the pain, chaos, and consternation they feel. Seasoned counselors know that simple answers rarely exist and that a great deal of clinical time tends to be spent sitting with the emotions that arise from the original questions, in addition to those that arise from unwrapping the complexity of the answers. You've likely spent time learning about that in skills, theories, or other courses you may have taken already. Your friend the physical therapist, the lawyer, or even the nurse, is not prepared to help clients discover answers to these questions, nor are they challenged to refrain from giving answers. In fact, their jobs are built around giving answers, while professional counselors' work is centered on asking questions and sitting with the ambiguity of there not being well-defined answers to offer.

To prepare to sit with clients in the complexity that is their lives (e.g., their thoughts, feelings, experiences, etc.), professional counselors begin by learning about themselves. They dive deep into their values, beliefs, experiences, and worldviews; they identify key experiences that have shaped them; and they become intimately acquainted with their cultural identities and how their cultural identities have shaped their beliefs, values, and experiences. Particularly, professional counselors examine the amount of privilege, marginalization, and oppression they have experienced via their identity intersections. This is not a one-time process. It will not be accomplished during your time in this course. But guess what? You have already begun it! You have been interpreting your experiences through your cultural lenses all your life! Some of you have substantial experience naming these experiences and articulating their impact, while this will be a newer experience for others of you. Neither is wrong, simply different. Yes, this is a very different process than becoming an accountant or a nurse! While we can never know *everything* about ourselves, counselors develop acute awareness about themselves and the world around them so they can be *genuine* and *congruent* when they work with clients. Counselor genuineness and congruence are foundational for building and maintaining the counseling relationship, and they are essential for meeting clients where they are and adapting the counseling process to meet clients' cultural needs.

BOX 1.2 **PAUSE AND REFLECT: YOUR EXPERIENTIAL BACKGROUND**

I (Dr. Clark) love educating counselors (Dr. Cook does, too)! One of the most interesting things about our profession is folks come to it from all backgrounds and walks of life; a counseling graduate degree, unlike many others, doesn't require the same undergraduate experiences. Many of you came right out of your undergraduate program, or maybe you worked for a few years and returned. I also know many students who return after major life changes or even came back to school to change careers or for a second career. This variety of perspectives in my classrooms is valuable and powerful. Everyone can learn from each other, even me.

Take a second to think about your background. What identities, life events, choices, decisions, etc., have led you to become a learner in this course? To your desire to be a professional counselor? What strengths does this experience bring? What growing edges?

Consider how you can build community in your class with your expertise and how you can be a learner from those who have lived experiences that you do not have.

The process of counselors understanding themselves is integral to counselors' ability to practice in culturally relevant and appropriate ways. As you will learn in Chapter 2, culturally relevant practice entails using complex, critical thinking, and recognizing that there is no *one-size-fits-all* approach to working with clients. Further, culturally relevant professional practices affirm clients' cultural identities and experiences in order to promote client-specific wellness, prevention, and intervention efforts. Embracing culturally relevant practice is key to developing a multicultural orientation, which is a shift away from prior models that used the term *multicultural competence.* A multicultural orientation rather than multicultural competence shifts the focus to counselors' *ways of being* during client interactions rather than seeking to meet an evaluative, tiered system of competency standards. In short, a multicultural orientation focuses on the relationship with the client that is relevant to who they are rather than mastering content knowledge about different cultural identities. You will explore multicultural orientation in-depth in Chapter 3.

Considering Diversity, Equity, and Inclusion Within a Multicultural Orientation

Across the United States, there has been substantial debate about diversity, equity, and inclusion (DEI) and the role DEI should play, if any, in our everyday lives, from individual interactions and relationships to broad, systemic applications such as employment, housing, and education. Some see DEI initiatives as ways to include individuals and groups who have been historically unrepresented, underrepresented, or misrepresented, while others posit that DEI advantages individuals and groups with nondominant identities over those with dominant identities and that DEI does not account for individuals' accomplishments and hard work. Is DEI a debate within professional counseling? How does DEI fit within a multicultural orientation?

For the counseling relationship and the work counselors do with clients, DEI is not up for debate because clients' identities and experiences are not debatable. Counselors understand clients both as unique individuals and as part of systems that oppress and privilege individuals and groups based on their sociocultural identities (more on these topics in Chapter 4). Counselors are committed to understanding clients' lived experiences, so culture absolutely plays a role in that because we are cultural beings; however, a multicultural orientation guides counselors to help clients explore *how much* of a role culture plays. A multicultural orientation positions counselors so they are open to hearing clients' vast and varied experiences and *exploring* their impact. Some clients may readily explore sociocultural impacts on their experiences, others may not—counselor are open to both and everything in between, though one thing is certain: Counselors do not force their beliefs, values, or explanations on clients—they guide clients to uncover their own reasons and understandings within the *clients'* worldview and value system.

BOX 1.3 **PAUSE AND REFLECT: THINKING ABOUT DEI**

- What comes to mind for you when hear *DEI*? Does the term have negative connotations? Positive connotations?
- How do you see DEI as separate and as connected to professional counselors' work?
- Despite your personal beliefs about DEI and DEI initiatives, how can you use a multicultural orientation to prioritize clients' needs, values, and goals?

Building Your Knowledge Base

In this section, you will begin to build your knowledge base regarding key terms used throughout this text. You will learn literally dozens of terms throughout this text—some will be new to you, while others will be quite familiar. It's important to know that we are using terms that are considered appropriate and acceptable at this time in history. As societies, cultures, and people grow and change, the words we use change as well. For example, *Caucasian* was once a term used regularly to describe people who are White; however, this term is not appropriate—it has a problematic history, and its continued usage poses problems.

Why White and not Caucasian? It is common to see the term *Caucasian*; you've probably seen it many times on surveys or other forms and maybe have even identified yourself as Caucasian when describing your race! If you had asked me (Dr. Clark) when I went to college (in 2007) how I identified, I might have used that term to describe myself. However, there are more appropriate and precise ways to talk about White folks.

Caucasian Has Racist and Eugenicist Origins

The term Caucasian means to be from the Caucasus—a mountain range in eastern Europe and western Asia spanning multiple countries. This came to be used as a term for White people when an anthropologist discovered a skull from this area, deeming it of good quality due to its large brain. This, through time and racist and eugenicist ideology, was part of the rationale for why White people were superior and people of color deserved to be oppressed. So, this term emerged from a time when it was used as a tool of White supremacy and oppression of any group deemed the "other." The partner words to refer to other racial groups are "Negroid" and "Mongoloid"—incredibly problematic and wrong. We shouldn't use a term that is steeped in this kind of oppressive and harmful ideology.

Beyond these origins, it's also incorrect in terms of ancestry. Most White folks don't have ancestors who come from that area of the world (although some do!), so it doesn't really make sense to describe an entire group in this way.

IMG 1.1.

White *Explains the Relationship to Power and Privilege*

I (Dr. Clark) have found a lot of folks don't like to identify as *White*, even if they are, in fact, White! There is some sensitivity around this term, but we believe it is important to understand that Whiteness is an important identity factor for those in the United States (and across the globe; more on this in later chapters)!

What about European American? Well, in some cases, this term might work, especially for individuals who have recently immigrated to the United States from European countries. For example, I have a close friend who is Italian American; her father was a first-generation American, and her Italian American culture is central to her identity (but she also self-describes herself as White too). For me, however, I'm just White. While I've done a DNA test to figure out what kind of White I am (57% French/German, the rest English/Irish/Scottish, and 2% Portuguese, apparently), I don't have strong cultural or family traditions that are European. My ancestors on one side were poor German farmers who settled in the Midwest in the 1880s. The other side were poor Scot-Irish settlers of Appalachia. If anything, my biggest cultural characteristics are Appalachian family traditions and values (the side of my family that primarily raised me). So, European American doesn't really describe me. I'm White.

As you can see, Caucasian isn't an appropriate term to use (unless someone is literally from those mountains!), and European American might not be the best term either in many cases. White works most of the time, but at the end of the day, when referring to an individual, it is always best to use the identity term that they prefer. Also, we must recognize that using terms like *European American* rather than White conflates ethnicity and race. While this can be appropriate in some instances, most people, especially in the United States, struggle to understand the differences between race and ethnicity, so not confusing the issue further makes sense. More on this topic in Chapter 8! When referring to folks who are of European descent throughout this text, we will refer to that group as White for the reasons we mention above (which is also the term the U.S. Census Bureau uses!).

Another example is the terms we use in the United States to refer to people who are from Mexico, Central and South America, and other Spanish-speaking countries. There is more explanation about this in Chapter 8, though we use several terms simultaneously because they are all acceptable depending on geographic location—Hispanic, Latina/o, Latiné, and Latinx (e.g., in Las Vegas, where Dr. Clark is located, *Latiné* is used most frequently, while in San Antonio where Dr. Cook lives, *Hispanic* wins the day). In Chapter 15, you will learn the many fluctuating terms within the LGBTQI+ community too! While it may seem confusing that multiple terms are acceptable in specific cases and contexts while other terms have fallen out of usage and can even be viewed as offensive, our best advice is to continue to learn and grow and to use the terms each specific client uses to describe themselves.

Given the sociopolitical environment in the United States, it's important to discuss critical race theory (CRT). What does CRT have to do with professional counseling? Just like the terms we use to understand and label groups go through periods of examination and often change with the times, theories and philosophies can go through waves of examination and can change, too. CRT is one such example. Beginning in the 1950s, academic and lawyer

Derrick Bell began to examine critical issues related to race in the United States, beginning with the landmark case of *Brown v. Board of Education*. In the 1970s, Bell joined forces with other legal scholars such as Kimberlé Crenshaw, Richard Delgado, and Cheryl Harris, among others, to develop CRT.

CRT has its roots in law yet has become an interdisciplinary theory used to analyze how power structures are influenced by race, ethnicity, and racism. CRT is not about assigning individual blame but rather about thoroughly critiquing systems to identify if they have privileged dominant groups and subjugated nondominant groups. CRT has been a well-established and used theory for nearly 50 years, yet over that time, it received little public scrutiny or debate until recently. Politicians in several states began to take a stand regarding CRT and whether it should be used and/or taught within K–12 and university-level public education, with governors in some states (e.g., Florida) banning race education in all forms.

What do political debates regarding CRT mean for professional counseling? Actually, they mean quite a bit and have far-reaching implications. Take, for example, the ethical principle of autonomy. Can clients fully embrace their autonomy if they have not been exposed to multiple viewpoints and taught how to develop their own belief system as part of their public education? It's unlikely. What about the ethical principles of beneficence and nonmaleficence? How can professional counselors *do good* and *avoid doing harm* if they are taught to think from only one perspective? It's unlikely they can, and professional counseling would become an act of value imposition.

Sometimes it can be frightening, confusing, or disconcerting to learn about different perspectives and to consider them fully within your own sociocultural identities and experiences. These feelings are often the result of experiencing *cognitive dissonance*, the experience of having thoughts and feelings that are inconsistent with your initial beliefs that cause discomfort as a result of learning new information. Cognitive dissonance is part of the learning process, and we promise no one has ever died from experiencing it! In fact, our clients experience cognitive dissonance all the time when confronted with the need to change to alleviate their symptoms yet being afraid of what change will be like! You have the capacity and are building the skills to *work through* cognitive dissonance rather than avoid it. Learning about different perspectives, perhaps even CRT, is not a threat to you or your personhood but rather than opportunity to learn, grow, and expand your mind beyond its current capacity.

As an extension of the knowledge you are building, we invite you to increase your awareness about your identities, how you perceive others based on their apparent identities, and how others might perceive you. Let's begin with understanding how identities are categorized within the United States.

Dominant and Nondominant Identities

The terms dominant identities and nondominant identities denote how cultural identities are categorized based on power, privilege, and oppression within a specific society. *Dominant identities* refer to identities that hold sociocultural power and privilege, while *nondominant identities* refer to identities that have been marginalized and oppressed because they deviate from the dominant cultural *norm* (Allen, 2023). You may have heard the terms *minority* and *majority* used instead of nondominant and dominant. Intentionally, we have chosen not to use these terms because they do not accurately capture the dynamics of power, privilege, and oppression, and they can create confusion when statistics are applied to them. For example, I (Dr. Cook) am White and reside in San Antonio, Texas. Statistically, I am an ethnic minority in San Antonio because San Antonio is close to 70% Hispanic/Latinx/Latiné. However, these statistics do not change the power and privilege I experience as a member of the dominant culture in the United States based on my race (White). We will discuss this in greater detail in Chapter 4.

Each of us has our own unique, diverse identity makeup. There are scads of identities that make us who we are and impact our experiences. In Table 1.1, we offer a host of identities each of us has. Are you surprised there are so many and that there are dominant cultural identities to accompany each? We humans are fascinating creatures. Our brains love to create order, and with order comes hierarchies—namely, *in-groups* and *out-groups*. In-groups and out-groups can be based solely on dominant and nondominant identity group membership, or they can be used within a dominant or nondominant group to sort preferences further. For example, in Chapter 7, you will learn about *colorism*, a term that denotes *in-groups* and *out-groups* based on the darkness or lightness of skin color in some nondominant racial and ethnic groups.

TABLE 1.1 What Are Your Identities?

Take a few minutes and carefully review this table. As you do so, think about the following questions. What are your identities? Which are nondominant identities, and which are dominant identities? What is your unique identity?

Identity Area	How I Identify	U.S. Dominant Culture Group
Race		White
Ethnicity		Descended from Europe
National Identity		United States
Immigration Status		U.S. born
Language Spoken at Home		English
Sex Assigned at Birth		Male
Gender Identity		Man, specifically cisgender man
Relational/Affectual/Sexual Identity		Heterosexual
Age		35–50 years old
Ability Status		No disabilities
Mental Functioning		"Typical," within normal limits; no mental health conditions

Identity Area	How I Identify	U.S. Dominant Culture Group
Socioeconomic Status (SES) and Social Class		Middle SES and middle social class
Education		High school graduate
Religion		Protestant Christianity
Appearance		Eurocentrically attractive
Family of Origin		Intact, two-parent family
Marital Status		Married (heterosexual)

Another fascinating thing about our brain's desire to create groupings is that very few folks fit squarely into one category or another—that is, have all nondominant identities or all dominant identities. Most of us are a mix of dominant and nondominant identities—this is called *identity intersectionality*. Dominant and nondominant identities can play a role in how people view themselves, others, and situations, yet they do not determine these things necessarily. However, our dominant/nondominant identities can impact how one is perceived and, thus, how one is treated based on whether one's apparent identities are dominant or nondominant. We will dig into this more in Chapter 4 with an in-depth discussion of power, privilege, oppression, and marginalization.

Furthermore, some of our identities remain consistent (e.g., race, ethnicity, sex assigned at birth), some identities can shift (e.g., SES/social class, marital status, gender identity, religion/spirituality), while others change necessarily during the lifespan (e.g., age, ability, mental/physical functioning). These changes can impact the composition of one's intersecting identities and how much privilege/marginalization one experiences. Finally, our perspectives about our identities can both shift and remain stable throughout our lifetimes and development (more about this via identity development models in Chapter 6).

BOX 1.4 **PAUSE AND REFLECT: YOUR STEADY AND SHIFTING IDENTITIES**

Think about some of your identities. Which have stayed consistent over the course of your life? Which are by birth, and which are by choice? Which identities have shifted because of your choices or circumstances? Which identities have changed due to your age/life experiences?

Privilege, Power, Marginalization, and Oppression

In this section, we provide operational definitions for privilege, power, marginalization, and oppression without getting too deep into them because they are covered substantially in subsequent chapters. Consider this an introduction to these important terms and know there is far more to come!

- **Privilege:** Simply stated, privilege is an unearned benefit. In a cultural sense, privilege is what people with dominant identities in all domains experience just for being who they are—the identities with which they were born! As you have learned, some identities can change. For example, someone may be born into a low SES family, and because of education, occupation, and income, they move into middle SES and experience privilege.

  However, privilege that comes from enduring dominant identities (e.g., race, sex, national identity) can sometimes be difficult to manage. For example, some White people experience *White guilt* related to their racial identities. While this is a common occurrence in White racial identity development (see Chapter 6), we offer that White guilt should not last forever. Instead, White guilt must be transformed into anti-racist actions.
- **Power:** In a cultural context, power is how individuals with sociocultural privilege use their privilege within society. Power can be used to *empower*, yet more frequently, sociocultural power is used to oppress and marginalize individuals and groups with nondominant identities.
- **Marginalization:** Sociocultural marginalization is to put a person or a group *at the margins* or the edges of society. *Society* can denote a classroom, club, workplace, etc., as much as it can mean an entire society, like the United States. A key indicator of marginalization is that although a person or group is *permitted* to remain in a specific space (e.g., Black and Latinx students in a school, a Taiwanese American woman in her job), they are viewed as insignificant, unimportant, devalued, and *peripheral* to the dominant culture.
- **Oppression:** Oppression occurs when the dominant culture exercises unjust treatment, power, control, and/or limits or prohibits access to vital resources to people in nondominant cultural groups.

These terms provide an important introduction to the multicultural and social justice counseling competencies (Ratts et al., 2016), an essential professional counseling model, which we will discuss in detail in Chapter 5.

Bias, Stereotypes, Prejudice, Discrimination, and "-isms/misias"

As we shared earlier, our brains love to sort and categorize the world around us. Bias is a form of sorting—it is an inclination or a preference toward one thing over another and can be conscious or unconscious (see Figure 1.1). On the surface, bias isn't wrong or bad necessarily; our brains are wired to scan for similarities and to question differences. In fact, there can be protectiveness associated with some biases based on lack of experience or exposure. For example, a person from Chicago is hiking for the first time in the hills of Colorado. They have lived long enough that they know what a snake is, but they have never encountered one in real life. As they round a curve, they see a long, roundish object slithering on the ground in front of them. Immediately, their brain signals, "Danger!" They stop. They begin to sweat. They might even scream. They have no idea whether the snake is poisonous, but their brain signals "Danger!" based on the instinct to survive and no real-life experience with snakes.

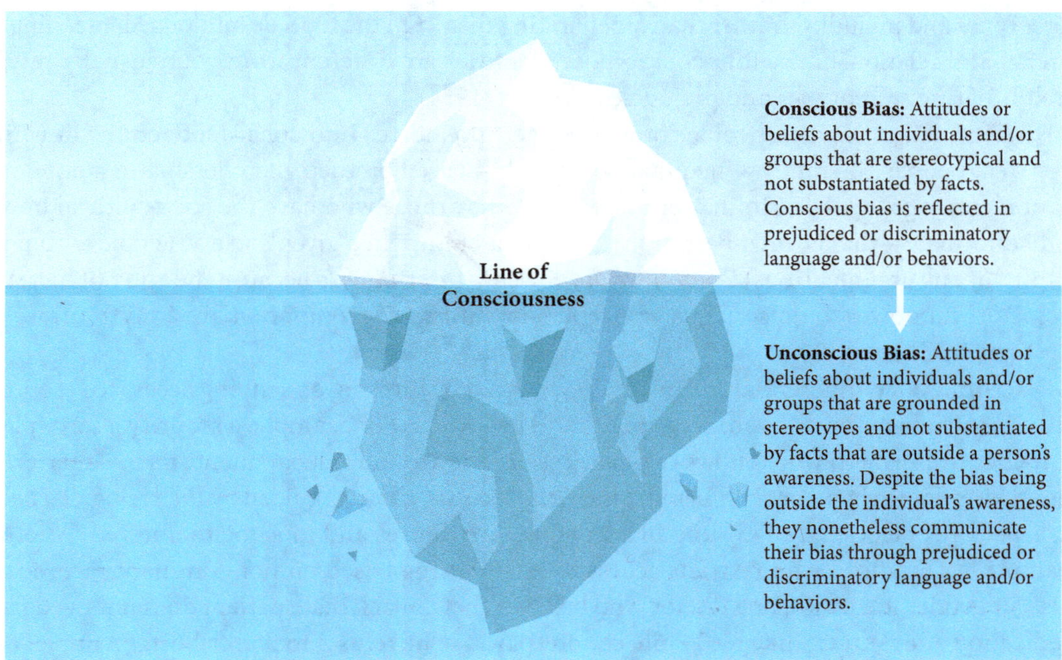

FIGURE 1.1 Conscious and Unconscious Bias

Problems begin to arise when biases are not grounded in personal experience or there is no legitimate need to protect oneself. In this case, an individual might be relying on stereotypes, which are generalizations about groups. To be absolutely clear, *positive stereotypes* do not exist, and this phrase should never be applied to any person from any group. For instance, some have posited that "all Asians are good at math" is a positive stereotype. It's not positive if you're Asian and not good at math! As another example, asking a new gay friend to weigh in about your fashion choice for an upcoming date because you believe all gay men are adept at fashion can be equally problematic and damaging. We will address biases and stereotypes in more depth and detail in Chapter 4.

To return to the above example, what if the hiker from Chicago once read, "All snakes are bad and will kill you if they have the chance," and took this information as fact? They don't look up information about venomous snakes; instead, they join a "People Against Snakes" coalition, joining like-minded people who believe all snakes should be eradicated. This is an example of prejudice, making judgments or assumptions based on stereotypes. Prejudice is "kicking stereotypes up a notch." Prejudices transform stereotypical beliefs into something much more sinister because it is the first step in putting stereotypes into action. Like with stereotypes, prejudices are rarely grounded in facts or real-life experiences; if real-life experiences are part of the equation, they are usually limited experiences. The contact hypothesis states that having brief or limited experiences with nondominant groups different from your own tends to result in strengthening stereotypes and prejudices rather than ameliorating them. On the flip side, prolonged, meaningful contact and relationships with people whose identities are different from yours usually results in eliminating stereotypes and prejudices (Allport, 1954).

Discrimination is when people transform their prejudices into consistent actions in which they treat people differently—inequitably, unjustly—based on their membership in a nondominant identity group. Discrimination is committed by those who have the sociocultural power to discriminate—that is, members of the dominant culture in a given society. People with nondominant cultural identities *do not have the power to discriminate* because they do not have the sociocultural power to do so. Thus, concepts like *reverse discrimination* are a myth (more on this topic in Chapter 8).

Discriminatory, differential treatment is evidenced by limiting or denying access to resources and can include many different areas of life and behaviors. For example, a security guard (plain clothes or uniformed) who follows two Black teenagers around a department store is interfering with their right to shop unencumbered. Likely, the security guard is guided by the prejudicial belief that Black people, especially young Black people, are thieves and must be monitored. Another example is a landlord who restricts access to safe housing based on nondominant race, social class, or gender identities, or a doctor who believes that a Black male patient does not need pain medication after surgery like his White counterparts, so he refuses to prescribe it. Examples can get even more dire: Police brutality against people of color, not believing reports Black people make when criminal activity occurs (check out the Netflix documentary series, *Dahmer-Monster: The Jeffery Dahmer Story* and pay close attention to the role of Glenda Cleveland, played by Niecy Nash), firing or never hiring gender expansive people or people with disabilities, refusing services to queer couples—the list goes on and on.

-isms (e.g., racism, classism, sexism) and **-misias** (e.g., transmisia, homomisia, xenomisia, Islamomisia) are beliefs that one group is better than another and, further, that one has *hatred* for another group based on their nondominant group identity. In fact, the emphasis on *hatred* is what has led to the use of *-misia* over *-phobia* (e.g., transphobia, homophobia, xenophobia, Islamophobia) in recent years (Diversity Pride, n.d.). A phobia is an extreme fear. Those who perpetrate racism, classism, Islamomisia, or transmisia are not expressing fear; they are expressing hate. Furthermore, phobias are a mental illness in the *Diagnostic and Statistical Manual, Fifth Edition, Text Revision* (APA, 2022), and concepts such as homophobia and xenophobia are not listed among the diagnosable mental illnesses (and calling hateful thoughts and behaviors a phobia is ableist and problematic toward folks who do have diagnosed phobias!).

Typically, -isms and -misias result in discrimination, but they can result in microaggressions as well. Microaggressions are everyday, brief interactions in the form of behaviors, verbalizations, or environmental factors that intentionally or unintentionally insult, degrade, and/or diminish the humanity, values, or customs of people with nondominant identities (Sue et al., 2007). While microaggressions may not restrict access to valued resources like discrimination does, they wear down people with nondominant identities so that they do not feel welcome or included in important parts of their lives. Sometimes, microaggressions can sound sort of like compliments, but the receiver is pretty sure they are not. The trouble is that the receiver often feels confused and unmoored, is forced to question the messages they received, and can find themselves using valuable emotional energy trying to decipher them. Sue (2021) likened microaggressions to "death by a thousand cuts."

TABLE 1.2 Some Examples of Microaggressions by Identity

Identity	**Microaggression Examples**
Race	• You're different than any Black person I've ever met. • You're so articulate—did you get a scholarship to a private school? • What does your name mean? It's so unique! • Are you more Black or White? • Wow, your hair looks so professional!
Ethnicity	• You speak English so well! • I wouldn't have known you were Middle Eastern if you didn't tell me—you're so light-skinned. • Will you tell me what this says? It's in Spanish. • You have really pretty eyes for a Chinese girl.
Social Class	• I don't know how you hold everything together with how little money you make. • You know, you just need to budget your money differently—do you really need the new iPhone? • It's a good thing you got away from your family—you're not like them. • You need to move to a different neighborhood. It's not a place where professional people live.
Disability	• You're so lucky that you get to take your dog with you everywhere you go. • Do you *really* need to use a wheelchair? • I don't see anything wrong with that person; why are they parking in a handicapped spot? • I bet she can hear more than she lets on.
Gender	• You should smile more. • Are you a boy or a girl? • I don't see why we can't just use the pronouns we have already. • You should really grow out your hair—you'd look more feminine. • Wow, for a girl, you're really good at math!
Age	• You'll understand this better once you've lived a little more. • Should you really be doing that at your age? • If you want companionship, you should get a dog. • Young people don't have any respect!
Religion/Spirituality	• You're Jewish? But you just paid for dinner! • Everyone has to believe in *something*! • I bet your hair is beautiful under your hijab! • You're so kind and generous. There's no way you're not a Christian. • You're an atheist? You're actually really nice!

(Continued)

TABLE 1.2 *(Continued)*

Identity	Microaggression Examples
Marital Status	• You are so independent! It must feel great to do what you want any time you want. • When are you getting married? • You'll find someone. You just have to stop being so picky. • How many cats do you have? • It must be nice to have a husband who takes care of everything for you.
Affectual/Relational Orientation	• No one is really *bi*. You will pick a side eventually. • Have you ever dated a woman? How do you know you don't like it? • It's so sad that you will never have kids. • What does your husband do?

As you can likely interpret from Table 1.2, microaggressions can have a detrimental impact just as outright discrimination can. In fact, some have posited that we should stop using the term *microaggressions* because their impact is not micro—it is enormous (Tulshyan, 2022). It's essential that counselors understand the phenomena discussed in this section because they affect clients indelibly. Furthermore, it gives counselors the impetus to name what clients are experiencing so they can feel heard, understood, and validated.

BOX 1.5 **PAUSE AND REFLECT: YOUR EXPERIENCES WITH MICROAGGRESSIONS**

What experiences have you had with microaggressions? Take a few minutes to reflect on those experiences and share with a friend or classmate. Where did they occur and what was your emotional response?

Person-Centered Counseling Principles

You are likely beginning to understand how foundational a multicultural orientation and being culturally responsive are as a professional counselor. Person-centered theory (PCT) is another important foundation and one that we use throughout this text. If you've taken a counseling skills class, it is likely you are familiar with PCT. In the 1950s, Carl Rogers established PCT in response to the Freudian and behavioral approaches that dominated at the time. Rogers (1957) identified "several conditions which seem to me to be *necessary* to initiate constructive personality change, and which, taken together, appear to be *sufficient* to inaugurate that process" (p. 95). These conditions are what we now refer to as the *core conditions* and are foundational to all counseling practice, no matter the counselor's theoretical orientation. The core conditions are behaviors counselors demonstrate to build and maintain the counseling relationship throughout the life of the counseling process.

- **Genuineness:** Being fully yourself and not putting on a façade. Never *playing* counselor but rather *being* counselor.
- **Congruence:** The ways in which counselors demonstrate their genuineness—who they know themselves to be and who they present themselves to be are the same thing. Congruence is essential because Rogers believed that clients are in a state of *incongruence* (which is why they seek counseling), so counselors must model congruence.
- **Warmth:** Demonstrating openness, acceptance, and interest in the client. This can be likened to being affable, friendly, and hospitable rather than its opposite, being *cold* toward the client.
- **Empathy:** Accurately communicating the client's affective experiences through perspective taking and slipping into the client's worldview.
- **Unconditional Positive Regard:** Accepting the client for who they are based on their humanity rather than anything they have done or haven't done. Demonstrating nonjudgment, warmth, and care, despite client actions or whether you approve of them.

While PCT, as it was originally devised, used the core conditions as the main mechanism for change, there were no real interventions to accompany PCT. In the decades since PCT's inception, counselors recognized this limitation; however, at the same time, they acknowledged through continued research that the core conditions and the counseling relationship were absolutely necessary, yet not sufficient, for client change. This is how the core conditions became foundational for counseling practice and the counseling relationship. Counselors recognize how essential the counselor-client relationship is and that without it, theory-based interventions fall flat. In fact, Sommers-Flanagan (2015) posited that much of the time, when evidence-based practices (EBP) fail clinically, it is because counselors neglect to integrate the core conditions and to build a strong relationship before delivering EBP interventions. In short, counselors' theoretical orientation and all the fancy interventions that accompany them are not enough, just as the counseling relationship on its own without theoretical backing and appropriate interventions are not enough. Both are necessary for client change.

Now, how do the core conditions partner with counselors' multicultural orientation and cultural responsiveness? They fit together beautifully, yet they require the counselor to engage in sustained, intentional work. As we shared earlier, it is essential for counselors to know themselves and to learn and grow continuously so they are ready to adapt to each specific client and their needs. When taken seriously, the core conditions can stimulate such self-knowledge and growth in a cultural context, though how do you do it? Take a read through the following examples and discern how you might adapt them for your growth.

- **Genuineness.** Have you ever interacted with someone and thought, "Wow, they are trying way too hard!," or "It might just be me, but he seems *fake*!" Clients have this experience with counselors, too, especially when they are *trying to be cool* with a client who has different identities from theirs. To be genuine means counselors don't put on airs, try to demonstrate knowledge they don't have, or act in stereotypical ways they believe a client will connect with. Instead, they are true to who they are, and if there are things they need to learn, they do so on their own time rather than burdening the client with teaching them.

- **Congruence.** Congruence is demonstrating your genuineness. Have you ever heard someone say, "I'm not mad," but heard an edge in their voice and observed their arms crossed tight across their chest? Yeah, right, you're not mad! Something similar can happen during cross-cultural counseling. While the counselor might be using the *right words*, their body language and tone of voice are unlikely to match if they are not genuine. The body doesn't lie and clients notice. For some clients, it might cause confusion, while others feel the incongruence and conclude that the counselor doesn't get them and simply won't return for a second session. Noticing these inconsistencies can be a signal that you have some work to do with your comfort with clients from specific groups or that you would benefit from increased knowledge.
- **Warmth.** Demonstrating warmth is a culturally bound action. In the United States, it's not uncommon to greet someone with direct eye contact, a smile, and a handshake to convey that you are glad they are there and that you're happy to see them. This is not necessarily a warm greeting for people with a host of nondominant racial, ethnic, and gender identities. Counselors who are genuine and congruent pay close attention to how clients react to ways in which they demonstrate warmth. If there is a poor or disconnected reaction, the counselor adjusts. Sometimes that adjustment is natural and needs little to no additional information; other times, counselors consult or even ask the client what would help them to feel the care the counselor wants to show to them.
- **Empathy.** Many people in the United States, not just clients, are unaccustomed to naming their feelings, let alone discussing them. Even more, it is rare outside the counseling relationship for clients to have regular experiences of accurate empathy and to have their feelings normalized and validated. While this is an overarching experience for many clients regardless of cultural identity, it's important to pay close attention to how clients with specific identities respond when you offer empathy because, like warmth, it is culturally bound. For example, men in the United States have been socialized to express a limited range of feelings and have learned that some feelings and feeling expressions are *off-limits* (e.g., sadness, crying). As a result, a client who is a man might feel shame or doubt if you normalize and validate them crying or expressing sorrow. Consider how you can communicate empathy in a variety of ways that clients can relate to so that they accept the empathy you are sharing, and it serves to build the relationship further.
- **Unconditional Positive Regard (UPR).** Many of us have experienced the devastation of someone saying, "I'll always be there for you, no matter what," only to abandon you when you behave in a way they don't like. For some, they cannot point to one person who has supported them and stayed with them consistently for years on end, including family members. For these reasons, you can understand why some clients may struggle to accept and trust the UPR counselors convey. While there can be different words counselors might use to convey UPR to clients with different communication styles, the key across interactions is that counselors have to determine what it means culturally for each client to *trust* the

counselor. For some clients, that trust will be given automatically because they view you as an expert who is worthy of such trust, but for others, especially clients with identities that have been historically marginalized and oppressed, trust is something that must be *earned* over time through behaviors that demonstrate trustworthiness.

With all of the core conditions, consider how you react to them when someone demonstrates them to you. What feels comfortable? What rubs you the wrong way? Even when you share identities with a client, called an *emic perspective,* there can be differences in preferences. Sometimes, it can be easier for your perspective to be *etic,* or outside the experiences of the client, because you are must less likely to make assumptions about what the client prefers. We all have preferences, and the job of the professional counselor is to identify each client's preferences and meet them where they are.

Finally, building the counseling relationship, just like the client's change process, is an ongoing and iterative process. Most simply, iterative means to repeat—to do something over and over again. When working with clients, this can mean returning to a topic, symptom, feeling, thought, or action multiple times within a session or over the course of counseling. It means, too, that we return to the core conditions and relationship building consistently. Within culturally responsive counseling, counselors are prepared to discuss oppression, discrimination, and microaggression experiences as many times as the client needs (more on this in Chapter 3) or return to broaching conversations to learn more about each other's identities as the relationship progresses (more about this topic in Chapter 4). In each session and each step of the counseling process, culturally adept counselors use the core conditions to fully connect with the client and to understand their experiences.

Taking a Strength-Based and Resiliency-Focused Approach

One of the criticisms of counseling, especially cross-cultural counseling provided by counselors from the dominant group, is the focus on client problems and deficits versus their strengths and resiliencies. Strength-based counseling is the alternative to this deficit model and has roots in positive psychology, social work, educational, solution-focused, and narrative perspectives. Strength-based approaches have been found to be effective in various counseling settings and with various cultural groups.

Strengths are an individual's characteristics that help them cope with challenging situations (Smith, 2006). Strengths develop over time and are highly connected to a person's lived experiences, especially those related to their cultural identities. Strengths that are related to culture are called culturally bound strengths (Chang, 2001). Culturally bound strengths vary from culture to culture based on their experiences; what may be viewed as a strength in one culture may be viewed as a weakness or a detriment in others. One example of this is individualism versus collectivism. In many White Western cultures (and very dominantly in the United States), being autonomous, self-sufficient, self-motivated, and some might say even a little bit selfish are viewed as strengths and positive characteristics. However, in Eastern cultures, these facets of individualism are viewed as detrimental; rather, a person should be relational and make decisions with their family and community in mind. You can see the difference between individualism and collectivism being in conflict for those who are from nondominant cultures in the United States. Individualism and collectivism impact counseling, which for many feels like an overly individualistic and maybe even self-indulgent act if the client comes from a collectivist culture. We will discuss this in greater depth and detail throughout the rest of the text. Essentially, culturally bound strengths emerge as individuals and cultural groups deal with adversity and develop resilience. These adversities are sometimes, but not always, related to the oppression experienced by a nondominant group at the hands of a dominant group.

In addition to culture-specific strengths, individuals can develop other strengths that can be identity related. These are called adaptable and functional strengths (Smith, 2006). Adaptable and functional strengths are also known as resiliencies, and are the ability to bounce back and adapt when faced with adversities. These strengths are developed through life experiences—sometimes positive and sometimes negative. Essentially, individuals live to survive and/or thrive in their environment using skills they have learned over the course of their lives. An example is the resilience and knowledge of unhoused people. Many folks view unhoused people as unskilled, unintelligent, or uneducated. These are biases and ignore the strengths of this group. Unhoused individuals have learned and adapted to survive in conditions that most people cannot and have unique strengths and knowledge that cause them to survive and thrive within a community. This applies to all other cultural groups with distinct lived experiences to which they have adapted to survive and thrive.

So, what do we do with this information as counselors? First, we must make a commitment to a wellness and strengths-based paradigm of helping. In this model, we understand that everyone has unique strengths and capabilities that they bring into a session and, obviously, into their day-to-day lives. These strengths are often culturally bound, so we must first seek to understand our own cultural strengths and weakness, and our values related to those concepts. There is an activity at the end of the chapter that gives you the opportunity to explore your cultural strengths and limitations. Then, we must seek to understand what characteristics and values each individual client has and how they may be related to their culture and experiences. One tool is to use the cultural identity models that are outlined in Chapter 6. Once we have a greater understanding of client strengths, we can begin to point them out in session and discern how to use them in treatment plans.

Making a Personal Commitment

As we conclude this chapter, we hope you are feeling excited about the next steps in your journey in your course, with this text, and in your career. There is, without a doubt, some anxiety as well. We outline a few principles we would like you to keep front of mind as you continue along your journey with this text and beyond:

1. Establish/Reaffirm a Growth Mindset. A growth mindset is incredibly important in all areas of your professional preparation, but when considering diversity and cultural development, it becomes even more important. Understand that in this journey you will make some cultural mistakes or missteps. In those cases, once you know better, you do

better, and you appropriately rectify any issues. Humbly accept your error and work hard on not becoming defensive. Listen to individuals who correct you and take their feedback on board. Commit to a growth mindset.

2. Use Person-Centered Skills. A key theme of this book are the core conditions of PCT. When challenged with tricky cultural conversations or content, rely on your person-centered skills and lead with them. Use your listening skills, seek to understand, and show empathy for others' experiences that differ from your own. Commit to person-centered skills.
3. Nontokenization. When discussing cultural groups you or your classmates are a part of, remember, it is not the responsibility of any one person to speak for that cultural group. Everyone has their own unique intersecting experiences and certainly may offer important information in any discussion. However, resist the temptation to pressure a peer to "educate" you about their cultural identity; that kind of emotional labor is a gift from someone of a culture different from yours and should only occur when that person voluntarily shares it. Further, do not make generalizations about cultural groups based on your own experiences (e.g., "My bisexual friend told me ...," or "As a White person, I think that all White people ..."). Speak for yourself and commit to doing your own work.
4. Consider Systems-Level Impacts. As we seek to learn and understand the experiences of different cultural groups, it is important to amplify individual stories and remember the systemic impacts on nondominant groups. While everyone is unique, the experiences of group oppression (e.g., racism, sexism, ableism, etc.) are critically important for you to understand as a professional counselor, especially so you don't replicate that oppression and further harm your client. As you review chapters 7 through 17, keep these systemic issues in mind. You will learn much more about systems in Chapter 4! Commit to understanding systemic impacts.
5. Ethical Behaviors. As you will learn in Chapter 2, professional counselors have an ethical responsibility across settings and specializations to be culturally relevant. Consider professional ethics with every client case and reading across this course. As you engage in challenging course discussions and reflection, practice your ethical responsibilities. Commit to ethical practice.
6. Be an Active Learner. Diversity courses are all about engagement and learning as a part of a community. To do that effectively, you must be an active learner. Complete your readings, engage fully in activities, and come prepared with questions for your instructors. Take the opportunities to reflect on yourself, your own cultural identities, and your future counseling practice seriously. Practice now so you can apply your cultural competence later!

Conclusion

Welcome in; we're glad you're here! In this chapter, we have offered you an overview of the textbook and what you can expect, in part, on your journey to becoming a culturally oriented, informed, and adept counselor. We have introduced you to key terms and concepts essential for your awareness, knowledge, and skill development, as well as offered strategies to help you navigate your developmental process. Again, we're glad you're here—welcome in!

Questions for Reflection

1. What cultural group are you most interested to learn about, and why?
2. What are your thoughts and feelings about learning about diverse identities within your class of unique and diverse learners? What are you excited about? Is there anything that doesn't feel positive?
3. When you think about DEI, what thoughts and feelings come up for you? How might they be congruent or incongruent with professional counseling?
4. What do you believe your culturally relevant counseling strengths are? What areas of identity do you feel well prepared to work with at this time?
5. What about growth areas related to culturally relevant counseling? You can't answer "Everything!" What are the specific cultural groups that you must learn more about to be effective?

Applying What You Have Learned

Complete each of the following activities, considering what you learned from this chapter.

Activity #1: Assessing Your Own Unconscious Bias

Curious about your unconscious biases? Take an Implicit Association Test to learn more about yourself: https://implicit.harvard.edu/implicit/takeatest.html.

Share the results of your test with a trusted friend and make a plan to address your bias that your friend can support you with and hold you accountable for. Remember, we grow with others, not alone!

Activity #2: Making Your Personal Commitment Plan

Using the table below, identify how you can commit to these seven outlined principles in this book and beyond, especially with populations you may have little knowledge about or have some biases toward.

Growth Mindset	
Person-Centered Skills	

Nontokenization	
Systems-Level Impacts	
Ethical Behaviors	
Active Learning	

Activity #3: Your Cultural Strengths and Growing Edges

First, spend some time outlining your cultural strengths/resiliencies and Growing Edges, whether they are culturally bound or adaptive.

Strengths/Resiliencies	**Growing Edges**

Now, consider your lists above. What values are communicated in these strengths and weaknesses? How might these values impact your work with clients? Could they inform any of your biases?

Activity #4: Your Cultural Resiliencies

Return to the cultural identities that you listed when you worked through Table 1.1. Based on your unique identities, what resiliencies did you develop? How will your resiliency development process impact your work with clients? With a partner, discuss your lists, compare the experiences you've had, and discuss your ideas about how your resiliency development can bolster client work.

Activity #5: CRT in the Media

With a partner, identify one media source discussing CRT in the last year. What do you notice? What are your thoughts about how this type of media may or may not affect counselors and clients?

Credits

CHAPTER 2

Cultural Relevance and Counselors' Ethical Responsibility

Jennifer M. Cook and Diana Yum Rhyne

> *The first step in the evolution of ethics is a sense of solidarity with other human beings.*
>
> —Albert Schwitzer

CHAPTER OVERVIEW

From the beginning of counselors' training, terms such as ***ethical practice, cultural relevance***, and ***professional responsibility*** are used regularly. Even if this is your first class in your program, it's likely you have a sense that a great deal goes into these terms, both in theory and in practice. In this chapter, you will learn what ethical practice is and how it functions within the context of being a culturally relevant counselor. You will learn the dispositions and skills you can employ to understand the ethical codes from a culturally relevant perspective, as well as explore history related to the ethical codes. Finally, we offer perspectives to consider that may influence how you interpret ethical codes and the potential impacts on clients.

LEARNING OBJECTIVES

By the end of this chapter, students will be able to

1. define cultural relevance and ethical practice,
2. name perspectives that contribute to a holistic interpretation of the ethical codes,
3. interpret ethical codes using a holistic perspective,
4. list differences and similarities between major counseling ethical codes, and
5. use strategies to engage in ethical, culturally relevant practice.

CACREP 2016 STANDARDS

The information in this chapter supports the following standards:

- 2.F.1.f. professional counseling organizations, including membership benefits, activities, services to members, and current issues
- 2.F.1.i. Ethical standards of professional counseling organizations and credentialing bodies, and applications of ethical and legal considerations in professional counseling
- 2.F.2.c. Multicultural counseling competencies

- 2.F.2.h. Strategies for identifying and eliminating barriers, prejudices, and processes of intentional and unintentional oppression and discrimination

CACREP 2024 STANDARDS

The information in this chapter supports the following standards:

- 3.A.6. professional counseling organizations, including membership benefits, activities, services to members, and current issues
- 3.A.10. ethical standards of professional counseling organizations and credentialing bodies, and applications of ethical and legal considerations in professional counseling across service delivery modalities and specialized practice areas
- 3.B.6. the effects of various socio-cultural influences, including public policies, social movements, and cultural values, on mental and physical health and wellness
- 3.B.9. strategies for identifying and eliminating barriers, prejudices, and processes of intentional and unintentional oppression and discrimination
- 3.B.10. guidelines developed by professional counseling organizations related to social justice, advocacy, and working with individuals with diverse cultural identities

What Is Ethical Practice?

Ethical practice is one of the cornerstones of counseling practice and professional counselor identity. Broadly defined, ethical practice entails applying the ethical codes of one's professional organization(s) to all professional responsibilities and actions. The goals of ethical practice are to provide high-quality, consistent care, to protect the clients and communities counselors serve, *and* to protect counselors themselves. Yes, ethical practice is designed to protect all of us, clients and counselors alike!

The code(s) of ethics to which counselors adhere depend on the state in which the counselor is licensed (or in your case, being trained), as well as counselors' specialized professional identity and the associations to which they belong. These associations include the following:

- American Counseling Association (ACA)
- American Mental Health Counselors Association (AMHCA)
- American School Counselor Association (ASCA)
- Commission on Rehabilitation Counselor Certification (CRCC)
- National Board for Certified Counselors (NBCC)

Each professional organization has its own code of ethics and counselors are responsible for upholding and applying the ethical codes for each organization of which they are members. Counselors may belong to only one organization, while some may belong to more than one because of their professional identities. For instance, rehabilitation counselors may belong to CRCC and ACA simultaneously; school counselors may belong to ASCA and ACA, while clinical mental health counselors may belong to AMHCA and be National Certified Counselors through NBCC. Additionally, each state stipulates which ethical codes counselors must accept as a condition of their license. Some states use more than one ethical code; for instance, ACA and AMHCA, while some only use one. Some states have developed their own ethical codes for which counselors are responsible. Finally, employers may indicate which code of ethics employees must follow, and they will always have policies and procedures to adhere to as well, in addition to local and federal laws.

As you will learn later in this chapter, ethical codes can vary greatly from organization to organization, particularly when it comes to culture, diversity, and social justice advocacy. While some counseling organizations are clear in their commitment to a range of culture-related concepts, others are more ambiguous. Further, you will see differences based on the primary population the organization aims to serve. All counselors must learn how to read, interpret, and apply the ethical codes and, when a counselor belongs to more than one organization, which organization's code they will follow in specific circumstances.

While ethics are foundational for counselors, counselors must pay careful attention and adhere to federal and state regulations too; all ethical codes stipulate that counselors must follow the law. There can be consequences for practicing unethically (e.g., being reviewed by the state licensure board, having one's license revoked), just as there can be consequences for acting unlawfully. For example, practicing ethically includes doing no harm, protecting clients as is feasible, and documenting client interactions accurately. These codes take on specific meaning within the context of laws (e.g., mandated reporting) and can become essential to demonstrating that a counselor acted appropriately in the event that a client dies by suicide or commits homicide. While professional organization's ethical codes and federal laws are applied nationally, counselors must know their state and local laws and any variations in employer ethical codes and regulations to ensure they are acting ethically *and* lawfully.

> BOX 2.1 **ALERT ENGAGEMENT**
>
> As you read through the chapter, stay alert. Recall the tips you read in the Introduction Chapter regarding alert engagement (see Box 0.1) and use them to think critically about what you are learning about ethics and professional responsibility. Pay specific attention to the ethical code aligned with your professional identity, though do not ignore the codes that are outside your specific professional identity. Each organization's code of ethics has something to teach us, whether that's because of what the code includes or what it does *not* include.

Ethical Practice Is Culturally Relevant Practice

Ethical practice and culturally relevant practice have a great deal in common. As you learned in Chapter 1, cultural relevance is defined broadly as engaging in professional practices that affirm clients' cultural identities and experiences in order to promote client-specific wellness, prevention, and intervention efforts. There is no *one-size-fits-all* approach to working with clients in a culturally relevant and appropriate manner. Practicing as an ethical, culturally relevant counselor requires counselors to pay careful attention to:

- Clients' identities, including how their dominant and nondominant identities intersect
- Clients' experiences
- Clients' cultural realities
- Instances of oppression and privilege clients encounter
- How clients' identities may impact the ways in which they navigate the world around them
- How clients make meaning
- How clients share information (e.g., tone of voice, body language, facial expressions)

Culturally relevant and ethical counselors free their minds from preconceived ideas while at the same time, they allow prior information and experiences to inform them. Furthermore, culturally relevant counselors use complex thinking, attend to nuances, and seek feedback from clients and colleagues.

To practice ethically, counselors must think complexly and abandon dichotomous, one-size-fits-all thinking and approaches. Ethical codes must be applied contextually, that is, to the specific event, situation, and client, rather than believing that ethical codes have only one definition or way in which they are applied. However, at the same time, counselors allow their experiences and knowledge to inform their process. It is impossible for your mind to be a *blank slate*—in fact, it would likely do more harm than good if this were possible because counselors would not be able to apply the expertise they have developed! Instead, counselors use their established knowledge and prior experiences to inform them *while avoiding* snap judgments or reinforcing biases/prejudices with their decisions. Concurrently, ethical counselors seek alternate explanations, identify several possible decisions, and engage in discussion with colleagues who can provide additional ideas and perspectives. What we described here is congruent with the ethical decision-making models you will learn in your ethics course.

Are you starting to see the connections between ethical practice and culturally relevant practice? In short, for counselors to practice ethically, they must practice in ways that are culturally relevant. The ethical codes become static and acontextual if counselors do not consider them within the client's specific context, and in fact, the ethical codes can lose their practical relevance if counselors neglect clients' identities, developmental stage, sociopolitical realities, and systems in which they are embedded (more on these concepts in forthcoming chapters!). Counselors must pay attention to these factors about themselves, not just with clients, because clients' and counselors' identities, development, sociopolitical realities, and systemic participation comingle when they come together to form the counseling relationship.

If you're thinking this sounds complicated and challenging, that's because it is! However, don't close the book just yet and think that what we're describing is impossible or beyond your reach because it is attainable. It's normal to feel overwhelmed or perplexed by complex processes, yet you have the capacity to develop the complexity we've described and use it to provide the highest quality counseling services possible.

Professional Responsibility

Although grammatically *professional responsibility* is a noun, it is better understood as a verb because professional responsibility is something counselors *do*—they *take* professional responsibility. There are many ways in which counselors take professional responsibility; ethics and culturally relevant practice are not only part of it, they are foundational! Just like professional responsibility is best understood as a verb, so are ethics. Ethical codes are brought to life and into contextual reality when counselors apply them to specific clients and their day-to-day professional activities. In short, we counselors, in conjunction with our clients, breathe life into the ethical codes because we *take* professional responsibility for keeping our clients safe and ensuring they receive consistent, quality care aimed to result in consistent positive outcomes. Professional responsibility and ethical practice are certainly verbs!

How do counselors take professional responsibility for ethical and culturally relevant practice? In sum, it means that counselors *own and enact* their professional obligation to interpret and apply the ethical codes to all professional activities in culturally appropriate, research-informed, and equitable ways. Pretty straightforward, right? Theoretically, it is, yet there are multiple factors that comprise the *how*. The process is often nonlinear, and each situation and result are unique—remember, there is no one-size-fits-all approach! What remains consistent is that counselors must use their professional dispositions and skills at all times to provide culturally relevant, ethical, and effective client-centered counseling.

Dispositions and Skills

Counselor dispositions are the foundation for taking professional responsibility in ethical, culturally informed ways. Dispositions are counselor qualities that guide and influence their professional behaviors. Dispositions are not fixed traits with which one is born, like hair texture, height, or detached earlobes. Instead, professional dispositions are learned ways of being; admittedly, some are easier to learn and develop than others. Dispositions are developed over time, so they are strengthened and refined as they are nurtured and practiced. Below is a list of core dispositions that are integral to professional responsibility, specifically culturally relevant and ethical practice.

BOX 2.2 **PAUSE AND REFLECT: YOUR DISPOSITIONS**

As you read through the dispositions listed below, consider the following:

- Which dispositions are strengths for you already?
- Which dispositions would you like to develop more?
- Are there dispositions you have questions or uncertainties about?

- **Self-Awareness.** An individual's capacity to examine their thoughts, emotions, values, worldviews, and experiences from a nonjudgmental and curious perspective with the intent to learn and grow from what they learn about themselves. Self-awareness can result in identifying unrecognized strengths and gifts, as well as limitations and areas for growth and change.
- **Nonjudgment.** The ability to suspend critique while taking in information (e.g., listening, reading, experiencing events), making decisions, and interacting with others.
- **Open-Mindedness.** A mental state in which one suspends judgment by bracketing biases, preconceived notions, prior knowledge, and/or prior experiences to fully hear and be present for others.
- **Perspective Taking.** The ability to consider more than one perspective, especially perspectives that are not typical for one to take or those that seem counter to one's worldviews or values.
- **Critical Thinking.** Applying the full information at one's disposal to consider multiple perspectives, processes, causes, and outcomes using depth and nuance. Critical thinkers avoid one-dimensional thinking and do not use limited or one-sided information.
- **Discernment.** The ability to consider multiple perspectives, data sources, and *evidence* to make choices that reflect sound reasoning and thoughtful consideration.
- **Curiosity.** Having interest and demonstrating engagement with ideas, people, concepts, philosophies, experiences, and more, with that which is familiar and unfamiliar. It is the genuine desire to want to learn more.
- **Tolerance for Ambiguity.** The capacity to hold multiple thoughts, ideas, facts, and feelings simultaneously, even if they conflict with one another, without needing to seek resolve.

This disposition list is by no means exhaustive. In fact, you may have been thinking while you were reading them, "What about X?" and wondered if it should be included. Chances are, you may be on to something! Discuss your ideas with your instructor and colleagues because there are many dispositions that can contribute to taking professional responsibility. The list we devised represents the dispositions we discovered we use most often in our practice and have identified as some of the most helpful for students as they learn to interpret and apply the ethical codes from a culturally relevant perspective. Furthermore, these dispositions contribute positively to Rogers's core conditions that you read about in Chapter 1. Now, let's consider some skills that are a natural extension of counselors' dispositions and that are helpful for taking ethical and culturally informed professional responsibility.

- **Active Listening.** Fully hearing others without formulating a response while they are speaking. Active listening involves using all the senses one has at their disposal with the purpose of capturing fully what the person is sharing.
- **Reflections and Summaries.** Accurately capturing content in brief form.
- **Open Questions.** Asking questions that result in detailed responses rather than simple "yes" or "no" or other one-word responses.

- **Empathy.** The ability to tap into and convey the feelings clients express in an accurate and connected way.
- **Immediacy.** Being willing and able to speak to the dynamics that are occurring between the client and the counselor.
- **Attention to Detail and Organization.** Tracking information accurately. This can be what a client says, how they act, the way they say things, what they *don't say*, etc. Additionally, counselors engage in these behaviors when seeking information, documenting sessions and consultations, and creating treatment plans.
- **Supervision.** Seeking feedback and information from a more experienced professional.
- **Consultation.** Seeking information and feedback from others who have specific knowledge and expertise that can assist you with developing additional knowledge, awareness, and skills. Consultants may be other counselors or helping professionals (e.g., psychologists, marriage and family therapists, social workers), just as much as they can be medical professionals, lawyers, activists, employment specialists, clergy, military personnel, and educators.

Note: Counselors practice discernment and use their critical thinking skills when they receive information from supervision and consultation. It's important to consider how culturally relevant the information is and how the other party's knowledge, profession, identities, and experiences may impact their perspective and the direction they offer.

Although we have distinguished dispositions from skills, they are not as separate as one might think. Dispositions are foundational for skills because they give purpose and intention to the skills and behaviors counselors use. For example, let's consider active listening. Anyone can use active listening in their day-to-day lives with friends, family, and coworkers. However, in the counseling context, professional counselors use active listening in specific ways and for specific purposes, like to fully understand what clients are thinking and feeling, to reflect clients' thoughts and feelings accurately, to normalize and validate, and to identify what interventions may be helpful for clients' struggles. When it comes to culturally informed, ethical practice, counselors take active listening further as they listen for key information that guides them to ask focused questions that uncover the client's cultural values and beliefs, to adjust their practice to align with the client's cultural worldviews, and/or to flag potential ethical dilemmas. To use active listening in these ways, counselors must engage their dispositions. Consider this client scenario:

> *Joe is a 28-year-old, gay, cisgender Mexican American man who was born and raised in South Florida. Joe works in IT and was relocated to an Atlanta suburb 6 months ago when he was transferred by his employer. Joe has a close relationship with his family and maintained it after the move by calling and texting daily. Shortly after moving to Atlanta, Joe was sexually assaulted by someone he met in a club. Since that time, he has been drinking throughout the day, including on his lunch break at work, which is something he never did before. His communication with his family has dropped from daily to one to two times a week. Joe was referred to the company's employee assistance program for counseling because of a marked decline in his*

work quality and frequent absences; his manager thought he might be struggling to adjust to his new work environment in a new city. Joe is assigned to work with Mel, a 43-year-old Black, straight, cisgender woman and an Atlanta native who has been a counselor for 3 years.

What are some dispositions Mel might use to actively listen to Joe in a culturally informed and ethical way that demonstrates professional responsibility? Below, we share a few examples to illustrate how dispositions and active listening come together in practice. Pay attention to other skills and dispositions that are present but are not named explicitly and consider how you might approach the situation in similar and different ways from Mel.

- **Nonjudgment.** Mel begins the session by listening to what Joe shares without critiquing or drawing any conclusions about what he shares. She uses nonverbal and verbal encouragers to convey she is listening and that she wants Joe to share more.
- **Self-Awareness.** While Joe is explaining the events that led up to when he was sexually assaulted, Mel notices that she feels uneasy about Joe's decision to leave a club with someone he just met. She would *never* do something like that. She stops using encouragers and is sitting quite still, breaking the eye contact she had been using. Within about a minute, Mel recognizes that her behavior has changed and that her thought process is critical of Joe; she realizes it could stymie the nonjudgment she is trying to display. She wonders if it might be because she does not feel completely comfortable with people who are gay. She resumes her prior eye contact and encouragers.
- **Perspective Taking.** After Mel notices her judgment arise, she quickly considers what it must be like for Joe to live so far away from his family and his home, maybe for the first time ever. She recognizes this would be hard for her and that he probably wanted to have some fun and not feel lonely. Additionally, she thinks about how challenging it must be culturally for Joe, as a Mexican American man, to admit that he was sexually assaulted. These thoughts stimulate Mel to normalize and validate Joe when he states, "I shouldn't have even gone out that night," and to acknowledge how hard it must have been for him to tell her what happened.
- **Critical Thinking.** Mel pays careful attention to any information that might flag an ethical or legal concern. Joe's sexual assault prompts Mel to ask him if he would like to file a police report, knowing that neither of them is required to do so. Joe declines to make a report at this time. Mel validates Joe's decision and offers support whether he files a report or not. Mel makes a note after the session ends to talk with one of her trusted colleagues about what came up for her during the session related to feeling critical about Joe's behavior and her recognition that she feels some discomfort with people who are gay. Ethically, she does not want to convey her discomfort to Joe and knows she has an obligation to work through her discomfort so she can be relationally present for Joe.

Mel did a nice job using her dispositions, though how might this scenario have gone if Mel did not engage her dispositions? For instance, if Mel had not begun the session intentionally

with a nonjudgmental mindset, she may have looked at Joe's intake information and formed opinions about him before ever talking to him based solely on his demographic factors. Despite slipping into some judgment in her thought processes, Mel did not express them because she used self-awareness. If she had not done that, Mel might have spoken the thoughts that entered her mind, that she would *never* leave a club with someone she didn't know rather than bracketing them and potentially conveying that his choice had something to do with his sexual orientation and the reason he was assaulted. If Mel had taken this route, it is unlikely she would have given herself the opportunity to perspective take and to consider even a small portion of what Joe might be feeling and thinking. Finally, without critical thinking, it is likely Mel would have struggled to think critically and discern whether any ethical, legal, or cultural issues were present, and there is a considerable possibility that she would not have made the note to consult with a colleague.

Understanding the Historical Context of Multiculturalism in the Ethical Codes

In this section, we explore the evolution of multicultural integration into professional organizations' codes of ethics. We have chosen the ACA, AMHCA, ASCA, CRCC, and NBCC ethical codes because of their professional influence covering a variety of counseling specialties. While we only provide highlights from the associations' ethical histories, understanding some of the history of the ethical codes gives you a look into how we developed as a profession and can provide insight into where we can or even should go in the future. Use your critical thinking skills and discernment; think through how the codes have developed and the future opportunities you see!

Ethical code development is a group process that involves many constituents over an extended period of time. Typically, it takes years for an organization to revise and finalize its ethical codes using committees, subcommittees, and task forces. These subunits of the organization use feedback from members and organizational leadership, and may also consult with other organizational codes, experts, and professionals outside of the organization for guidance and recommendations. Additionally, some organizations will publish documents between revisions to provide needed updates. This is not a short or quick process; sometimes, it can take up to 10 years to publish revisions!

When analyzing each organization's ethical codes, counselors must approach each document with a critical eye and a curious mind. Consider the following:

- The use of language and any special emphasis on a topic
- The historical context, both within the profession/organization and within the social/political climates at the time of revision)
- How the document is organized (e.g., if there are multicultural considerations, where are they included within the document?)
- The length/the number of pages. Quantity does not always equal quality, yet it's worth paying attention to how much *air time* is given to cultural topics compared to other topics

Also, consider accessibility and transparency. What information is or is not available to the general public? How accessible the information is can say a lot about the organization's values. For example, while preparing to write this chapter, we encountered hurdles in obtaining older versions of the ethical codes from several organizations. We discerned several possible reasons for that, including the most benign—they are not available in an electronic format—and the most troubling—they do not want older versions to be accessed or assessed. Like with most things, it's likely a mix of reasons rather than only one. Finally, it can be easy to jump to conclusions or make assumptions about motives, but we caution you to slow down, use curiosity and discernment, and encourage you to take an informed and proactive approach (e.g., gather more information, reach out to the organizations directly to answer questions, consult with another professional). As is the case in counseling and in life, *assumptions* rarely lead to helpful information.

ACA

The ACA's first *Code of Ethics* was published in 1961 and has gone through multiple revisions over the decades with the most current version published in 2014. While all drafts of the ACA's ethical codes contain foundational concepts such as informed consent, counselor use of consultation, documentation, privacy/confidentiality, and scope of practice, earlier versions' (while under the American Personnel and Guidance Association [APGA] until the 1988 revision) concepts of *diversity* were limited to professional areas of practice, career pathways, and areas of counseling interest. These early versions briefly mentioned the ethical standard of honoring client diversity, mainly as it related to testing and assessment considerations. The 1961 and 1974 *Code of Ethics* used he/him/his pronouns as a default for *members* and *counselees*, which is important to note because those ethical standards were to be applied to *members* of the APGA (now the ACA). The pronoun use may be because the counseling profession was male dominated at the time, but it can also be interpreted to mean the authors' presumed *members* and *counselees* would be predominately male. Alternately, this was the written pronoun convention during that time period. It wasn't until the 1981 revision that pronouns were removed altogether.

The 1995 revision replaced *member* with *counselor*; the term *cross-cultural* was added to the preamble, and respecting diversity and nondiscrimination were mentioned explicitly. It's the only version that includes the *ACA Standards of Practice* within the document to establish "minimal behavioral statements of the Code of Ethics" (ACA Code of Ethics, 1995, p. 23). The *Code of Ethics* was intended to be an extension of the *Standards of Practice* and to be used as a tool to interpret and expand the *Standards*. Additionally, the 1995 version encouraged counselors to examine their own identities and pursue opportunities to learn more about the diverse communities in which they work. Historically, this addition makes sense given that the first multicultural counseling standards were published in 1992 (Sue et al., 1992).

The 2005 version, which was used by all ACA members and nearly two dozen state licensing boards as guidelines for ethical conduct and resolving ethical complaints (Kaplan, 2006), integrated the *Standards of Practice* from the 1995 version to create one document: the ACA *Code of Ethics* (Glosoff & Kocet, 2006). The 2005 *Codes* were clear in that professional counselors were expected to apply cultural context to each section within the document rather than simply applying a blanket consideration of cultural diversity (Glosoff & Kocet, 2006). Notable changes from the 1995 version were that it included the use of language interpreters and translators in counseling communication (A.2.c., 2005) and the prohibition of values imposition (A.4., 2005). These changes are not all that surprising considering the ACA's ethical framework is recognized across 50 countries, including those whose primary language is not English.

BOX 2.3 **TIPS FOR PROFESSIONAL PRACTICE: PROHIBITING VALUES IMPOSITION**

What does it mean for counselors to avoid imposing their values on clients? Since 2005, the ACA *Code of Ethics* has included the code (A.4) that counselors do not impose their values on clients. Counselors are well aware that counseling is not *neutral* or *value-free* because the profession long ago accepted that counselors are not a *blank slate*, as Freud proposed. How do counselors hold in tension that counseling is not value-free while at the same time not *imposing* their values on clients?

Part of the answer to this question lies in the profession's person-centered roots, meaning that counselors focus on the worldviews, values, and beliefs of the *client* rather than their own. Counselors focus on what is important to the client, what they want in life, and how they seek to solve their problems rather than offering what's important to *them*, how they want to live *their* lives, or how they would solve *their* problems. When the focus is squarely on the client, the chance of value imposition is relatively low.

At the same time, it's not uncommon for clients to ask counselors for their opinions, interpretations, suggestions, and advice. This is where many counselors find themselves in tenuous territory. To deal with these situations effectively, first and foremost, counselors need to ensure that clients have *asked* for one of these things or that they have garnered the client's consent to offer them. Next, counselors must continue to focus on and highlight the client's worldviews, values, and beliefs, and bracket their own. While engaging in this process, counselors use appropriate tone, affect, and body language that conveys unconditional positive regard, empathy, and warmth. Finally, counselors give options rather than only one opinion, suggestion, or interpretation. Giving options supports the client's autonomy, decreases the power differential between client and counselor, downplays the expert role, and can instill confidence in the client that they have the capacity to make the best decision for their life and circumstances.

The 2014 version introduced the ACA's ethical principles and was geared toward *all* counselors rather than ACA members only (Meyers, 2014). Also notable was the addition of the terms *diversity, multicultural approach*, and *social and cultural contexts* to the preamble. This version set the standard that counselors "*actively* attempt to understand the diverse cultural backgrounds of the clients they serve" (Section A introduction). Counselors are encouraged to reflect on their own cultural identities and examine how those identities, including principles, attitudes, and beliefs, may influence their counseling approach and process. Under informed consent, "Developmental and Cultural Sensitivity" (A.2.c., 2014) was added to include providing information in "clear and understandable language" (p. 4) with the use of qualified translators and interpreters and the use of accessible, nontechnical language. Finally, and significantly, the 2014 *Code of Ethics* incorporated multicultural components into nearly *every* section of the ethical codes and expanded the definition of diversity to include disability, developmental differences, socioeconomic statuses, race, ethnicity, gender, and sexual orientation. There is no firm date when the next revision of the ACA *Code of Ethics* will be published, but the *Code* is currently under revision and is expected in 2025.

AMHCA

The AMHCA's ethical codes date back to 1978 with its most current version published in 2020. Until 1997, AMHCA was a division of ACA and became an independent association in 1998. The 2010 *Codes* set the standard for mental health counselors' self-awareness of the relationship between their "values, attitudes, beliefs, and behaviors" (AMHCA, 2010, I.A.4.d., p. 4) when working with a diverse clientele; nondiscrimination (I.C.2., 2010); cultural competency as part of the "Counselor Responsibility and Integrity" (I.C.1.g. and l, 2010, p. 9); and implementation/interpretation of testing and assessment tools (I.D., 2010). Additionally, the code spoke to consideration of culture in forensic activities, fee arrangements, bartering, and gifts. Counselors are obligated to include multicultural considerations when developing treatment plans (I.B.1.a., 2010) and to use technology-assisted counseling only when they can "ensure clients are intellectually, emotionally, and physically capable of using technology-assisted counseling services" (I.B.6.c., 2010, p. 6). The 2015 version added that counselors must "*actively attempt*" (I.C.1.m., 2015, p. 16) to learn and understand the cultural backgrounds of their clients, including how their own cultural identities, values, and beliefs impact the counseling relationship and process. This includes counselors reflecting on their own biases about diverse communities as they relate to the counseling process (C.2.c., 2015).

Notable changes in the 2020 AMHCA *Codes* included the addition of the "How Is the AMHCA Code of Ethics Distinctive for the Profession?" prefacing the preamble and changes in language regarding end-of-life care for terminally ill clients. The preface gives a brief explanation of acronyms used throughout the document, the AMHCA's commitment to addressing relevant ethical issues as they arise, and the purpose of their ethical codes. The 2010 and 2015 versions permitted clinical mental health counselors (CMHCs) to refer clients in end-of-life situations if they feel the clients' decisions raised "personal, moral and competency issues" (AMHCA, 2010, I.B.8.b., p. 8 & 2015, I.B.8.b., p. 14) for the CMHC. The 2020 version removed the *personal*, *moral* conditions portion yet permits CMHCs to refer strictly on the basis of *competency*; however, A.4.d is clear that

> CMHCs are aware of their own values, attitudes, beliefs and behaviors, as well as how these apply in a society with clients from diverse ethnic, social, cultural, religious, and economic backgrounds. *CMHCs do not impose their personal values on clients.* (emphasis added; AMHCA, 2020)

Interestingly, 4 years prior to the publication of the 2020 version, the state of Tennessee passed HB 1840, declaring that no mental health counselor would be legally required to provide services to clients whose "goals, outcomes, or behaviors … conflict with the sincerely held principles of the counselor or therapist" (HB 1840, 2016). Rest assured that professional counseling organizations across all specialties were quick to release statements in response to the bill, including the AMHCA. We encourage you to check out these statements on their websites and on other professional sites. Websites are one way that counseling organizations communicate updates and their position on issues critical to the public.

Conflicts With "Sincerely Held Principles"

Tennessee House Bill (HB) 1840 (2016) raised a myriad of questions across the counseling profession and there were innumerable feelings to accompany them. There were counselors who celebrated the bill, while there were far more who were outraged and deeply saddened about what a bill like this could mean for who professional counselors are as a unified profession and whether public trust in professional counselors would waver. In fact, ACA received so much pressure from members that they moved their 2017 annual conference that was scheduled to be held in Tennessee to California.

All counselors must examine critically every bill and law that arises that impacts counselors' work, their professional identity, and *public perception* of the counseling profession. With HB 1840, consider the following:

> Does a client's desired "goals, outcomes, or behaviors" actually impact the counselor?
>
> Is it the counselor's job to assess the client's "goals, outcomes, or behaviors" in terms of their own worldviews?
>
> Does a counselor weighing in on a client's "goals, outcomes, or behaviors" in terms of the counselors' "sincerely held principles" have a functional place in the counseling relationship?

We believe the answer to these questions is "no." Based on the tenants of person-centered counseling that are the grounding principles for professional counseling, we posit that the counselor's role is to join with the client and to demonstrate warmth, empathy, unconditional regard, and congruence. Disagreeing with a client or having a different worldview or belief system does not disrupt congruence. If it did, we counselors would only be able to work with clients who are exactly the same as each one of us, which is impossible! In fact, this is the antithesis of a multicultural orientation (more on this in Chapter 3).

Think critically about bills, laws, and policies, and ask yourself, "Who does this serve?" If the answer does not include clients, it's unlikely to be something we should support, regardless of our principles, sincerely held or otherwise.

ASCA

ASCA first drafted its ethical codes in 1984 and underwent five revisions before publishing the most recent version in 2022. Multicultural considerations can be found in the preamble of their earliest versions, establishing the foundational philosophy of the organization to respect and affirm diversity. The ASCA *Codes* are unique in that they include considerations for the roles of other parties (i.e., parents, guardians, and schools) in the counseling relationship and the lives of students served by professional school counselors.

When examining the ASCA *Codes*, keep in mind that professional school counselors (PSCs) are serving ALL the students in their school AND their families/guardians AND their school/school district (ASCA, 2004). That means they must manage their therapeutic relationships and their multiple roles with each student in relation to other students, adults, and administrators, which is unlike other counseling professionals who serve their clients independent of others. Generally speaking, most early versions of the ASCA ethical codes viewed multiculturalism from the lens of student rights and dignity as human beings and as consumers of counseling services. It isn't until later versions that multiculturalism is expanded to include the context in which the student views themself and interacts with the world, the counseling process, and their relationship with PSC.

ASCA's *Codes* are arguably the most inclusive in their multicultural considerations of all the codes we discuss in this chapter in that they explicitly mention nondiscrimination based on appearance (found in earlier versions), wards of the state, living situations, immigration status, homelessness, and incarceration, all which are not mentioned in other organizations' codes. The 1998 *Codes* even included *marital status* and *character* along with race, ethnicity, disability, and sexual orientation as cultural identities to *respect*. While ASCA's 1998 version used terms like *prejudice* and *respect*, their 2004 version changed the language to *discrimination* and *affirm*. It is in the 2004 version that gender identity/expression was included as part of their multicultural considerations, which made them the first organization to acknowledge gender identity as part of cultural identities. The ACA did the same by including *gender identity* in their 2005 version and other organizations followed in later years. What is remarkable is that the ASCA's 2004 *Codes* were the first to include *gender expression* in their list of diverse identities. Additionally, ASCA directly addressed the current and historical marginalization of students in the education system as part of the introduction of its *Codes*, which is significant given the long history of segregation and desegregation of classrooms and the inequitable distribution of educational resources within the United States.

ASCA's 2004 version was the first to include "guardians" in its "Responsibilities to Parents/Guardians" section (Section B, 2004, p. 2). The term *guardians* was only used once in the 1998 version and only with regard to confidentiality. This is an important expansion because it recognizes that not all students are raised by those whom they consider parents, exalting that there are different family configurations that must be acknowledged. The 2004 *Code* marked the beginning of the collaborative counseling approach between students and PSCs, an important distinction from older versions that emphasized collaboration between PSCs and parents/guardians, school staff/administrators/districts/boards, and other professionals in the *best interests of the students*. From 2004 to 2022, the *Code* increased in length threefold from four pages to 12 pages, which can be attributed to the inclusion of a glossary of terms in 2016 and 2022 and the expansion of sections on technology, as well as the virtual classroom.

CRCC

According to Susan Stark, operations manager for CRCC (personal communication, April 14, 2023),

> Cultural issues were first included in the Code in 2002. Since then, it has expanded dramatically and in the 2023 *Code* there is an entire section now devoted to Multicultural Considerations [and] contains standards related to Bias, Antiracism, Social Justice, Cultural Humility, Avoiding Microaggression, Avoiding Discrimination, Serving Religious Cultures, etc.

Unfortunately, despite publishing "many revisions" (S. Stark, personal communication, April 14, 2023) since its original version of the 1980s, versions of their *Codes* prior to 2002 are "not available in a digital format" (S. Stark, personal communication, April 17, 2023).

The 2002 version of CRCC's *Codes* first mentions cultural considerations as it relates to developing career and employment goals between certified rehabilitation counselors (CRCs) and consumers (i.e., clients), and it is the only one of the four versions that separately addresses *respecting culture* and *interventions* (i.e., culturally relevant interventions), while the later versions condense the concepts. *Code* versions from 2002, 2010, 2017, and 2023 include sections on *respecting diversity* (A.2.), including the expectation that CRCs will not discriminate. *Cultural competence, respecting diversity, culture,* and *nondiscrimination* were introduced in the 2010 CRCC *Codes* and can be seen throughout all subsequent versions. Interestingly, the 2002 and 2010 versions are the only ones that specifically list protected groups (e.g., race, ethnicity, disability, class) under *nondiscrimination* in section A.2. *Respecting Diversity,* whereas the 2017 and 2023 versions mention specific groups in the preamble while using more general references to protected groups in the same section of *nondiscrimination.* Perhaps this was done intentionally to save space (despite the 2023 version being 50 pages long!) and to mitigate redundancy by establishing the reference early on. Either way, the CRCC's *Codes* come in four versions and make up a total of 154 pages—far more than any other organization's codes.

The preamble in the 2017 and 2023 *Commission on Rehabilitation Counselor Certification Code of Professional Ethics* clearly outlines a "commitment to cultural diversity" (p. 1), which establishes the standard that CRCs "are aware of the continuing evolution of the field, changes in society at large, and the different needs of individuals in social, political, historical, environmental, and economic contexts" (CRCC, 2017, p. 5). Also, it sets the standard that CRCs are dedicated to "taking appropriate action when diversity issues occur, and being accountable for the outcomes as they affect people of all races, ethnicities, genders, national origins, religions, sexual orientations, and other cultural group identities" (CRCC, 2023, p. 2). In the *Values and Principles* section of the 2023 version, the language was changed to state "a culturally relevant and responsive approach" (CRCC, 2023, p. 1) rather than a "cultural approach" (CRCC, 2017, p. 4), indicating important nuance and specificity. Additionally, the 2023 version addressed considerations of counselor and consumer values and beliefs when determining an appropriate treatment approach. While the 2017 version used the phrase, *appreciating diversity,* the 2023 version was changed to reflect *respecting* and *understanding* the diversity of consumers. Additionally, the 2023 *Code* changed the language from "fair and adequate" to "equitable and appropriate" (p. 1).

When comparing the 2017 *Codes* to that of the 2023 version, you would almost have to do a word-for-word comparison to notice the subtle changes in language reflecting the evolution of multicultural components integrated into the *Codes*. These subtle differences in language could be the difference between a mere suggestion to establishing an enforceable standard. Remember, all ethical codes are open to interpretation, so what may be considered *fair* may not be *equitable*, and what is *adequate* may not be *appropriate*.

The rehabilitation counseling profession is "primarily dedicated to working with individuals with all types of disabilities" (CRCC, 2023, p. 3). Keeping that in mind, the 2023 *Codes* were the first to require CRCs to ensure access to captioning services in consumer communication, a standard that wasn't specified in previous versions despite a quick Google search showing that captioning services were available well before 2002. Why do you think that is? The 2023 revisions of the *Codes* were the most comprehensive in addressing multicultural considerations under Section D: *Multicultural Considerations*. It is the only set of ethical codes that uses the term *anti-racism* and defines the role of CRCs in actively working to "challenge policies and practices that maintain the oppression of marginalized racial groups" (CRCC, 2023, p. 15). This should not be confused with *advocacy* or simply *challenging* unethical practices within one's organization. *Anti-racism* is defined in the CRCC's glossary of terms as "conscious efforts and actions to counter racism, inequalities, prejudices, and discrimination based on race" (p. 42). This is a much stronger stance than the CRCC has taken in the past and much stronger than the other counseling organizations.

NBCC

The NBCC has three versions of its ethical codes: 2005, 2016, and 2023. The NBCC's website does not indicate how many versions of their ethical codes exist, but the October 2005 version's acknowledgment seems to indicate there may be versions from 1987, 1989, 1997, 2002, and two versions from 2005, one in February and one in October (NBCC, 2005). We were unable to obtain versions from the 1980s to February 2005, so it's unclear how the integration of cultural components has evolved or why there were two revisions in 2005. The October 2005 version does not mention or use the terms *diversity*, *multiculturalism*, or *cultural considerations* anywhere in the document. It isn't until the second page of the *Code* under Section A: General, number 12 that the NBCC mentions "an *awareness* of the impact of stereotyping and *unwarranted* discrimination (e.g., biases based on age, disability, ethnicity, gender, race, religion, or sexual orientation)" (NBCC Code of Ethics, 2005, p. 2) within the context of protecting client rights and dignity. Given the use of the term, *unwarranted*, we question what form of discrimination would be *warranted*. Additonally ,this version sets a standard that certified counselors using electronic and/or computer applications ensure the data and language used in those applications are "nondiscriminatory" (NBCC, 2005, p. 4). However, it does not clarify whether the standard of nondiscrimination applies to clients beyond their intellectual, emotional, and physical limitations, like socioeconomic status, ethnicity, language, and country of origin. While it would be nice to assume that the language would imply nondiscrimination of any kind, it's open to interpretation.

The October 2005 *Codes* preamble makes it clear that the *Code* is a "*minimal* ethical standard for the professional behavior of all NBCC certificants" (NBCC, 2005, p. 1). It's possible that the NBCC may, to an extent, be relying on the ethical codes of the ACA or other counseling organizations despite the fact that the NBCC and ACA have always been independent of one another, unlike the ACA and the AMHCA and ASCA, who were once divisions of the ACA. Between the 2005 version of the *Codes* and the 2023 version, the document doubled from 8 pages to 16 pages. Some updates to the 2023 version include the introduction of multicultural considerations as part of the organization's core values and beliefs, the use of the term *counselors* to indicate that any professional identifying as a *counselor* will be held to these standards, and the inclusion of multicultural considerations in the gatekeeping of the counseling profession. There were additional revisions in the section addressing telemental health, with a heavy emphasis on confidentiality and privacy.

The section on telemental health details standards for providing clients with written procedures but fails to address potential literacy factors and considerations for clients with first languages other than English as potential barriers that could require additional services, qualified translators, or interpreters. The NBCC falls short in its section on professional responsibilities, stating that "counselors shall not engage in unlawful discrimination" (NBCC, 2023, p. 3) but not addressing, for example, the lack of protections for queer and transgender people in certain states under discrimination laws (including North Carolina, the state where NBCC is located). It's clear that the NBCC is making efforts to integrate multicultural considerations into their ethical codes, but when compared to other codes, are they doing enough? With NBCC's affiliation with the Center for Credentialing & Education, the organization that develops and administers the National Counseling Exam and the National Clinical Mental Health Counseling Examination, one of which is the prerequisite for licensure in all states, and one that recognizes the significance of programs accredited by the Council for Accreditation of Counseling and Related Educational Programs (CACREP), we suggest that the NBCC's 2023 *Codes* have room to grow.

Perspectives That Impact Ethical Code Interpretation

For counselors to think critically when interpreting and applying the ethical codes, it is essential that they take a holistic approach. A holistic approach is one that considers multiple factors, components, and perspectives rather than a singular view. Below, we offer several factors specific to understanding the ethical codes from a cultural perspective, though not exclusively so, and the list is by no means exhaustive. There are likely dozens of perspectives one might take; these are some to get you started. Additionally, we invite you to contextualize the perspectives we offer by considering them from different individuals' perspectives, specifically, counselors, clients, the general population, and additional stakeholders (e.g., licensure boards, managed-care systems, educational institutions, the legal system). Each of these individuals and systems has a particular *horse in the race* when it comes to contextualizing counseling ethics, and counselors are wise to put on *different hats*, so to speak, in order to perspective take and understand the potential impact and ramifications of the codes.

BOX 2.4 **TIPS FOR PROFESSIONAL PRACTICE: PUTTING ON DIFFERENT HATS**

As you have learned, perspective taking is an essential skill for professional counselors. Perspective taking is used when interacting with others (i.e., fully hearing a different opinion, thought, feeling, etc., someone else expresses), *and* it is used independently (i.e., considering multiple perspectives within decision-making processes). While perspective taking is a necessary counseling skill, it is not always easy to learn or easy to do, especially when counselors feel passionate about their viewpoint or position. Even when you think you are 100% right, it's essential to perspective take. Here are some tips that might help with your process.

Get Your Mind Right. What this means is to prepare yourself to hear other perspectives and to be open to them. For example, "I am curious about others' perspectives," "I truly want to understand what others believe," and "I know I can't possibly know it all" are ways you can prepare your mindset for perspective taking. Adjust your mindset so you can be as open as possible to what others have to say and apply this openness when perspective taking independently.

Adjust Your Body Language. Perspective taking requires openness, and that openness cannot stop with our minds—our bodies have to match to ensure congruence. Start by opening your hands so your fingers are loose and your hands aren't clenching each other. Then, open your shoulders so you're your arms aren't crossed tightly. Finally, attend to your stance. If you are standing, separate your knees from one another and flex them slightly. When sitting, you can uncross your legs or ensure that your crossed legs are loose rather than tight—you can even choose to cross your legs at your ankles instead of your knees.

Learn Something New! Learning different perspectives means you have the chance to learn something new. In fact, you may even learn that you were *wrong*. It's OK to be wrong (teach your brain this if you haven't already) because it's wonderful to learn something new!

Focus on Professionalism. You've learned that professionalism is a verb and encompasses many skills and dispositions. Use professionalism and all that encompasses when you begin to feel yourself moving away from perspective taking. Draw on the core professional values like respect, autonomy, justice, beneficence, and nonmaleficence. Ask yourself, "Am I respecting that other viewpoints are valid?" "Can I imagine how opinions other than my own support others' autonomy?" "How can I see others' perceptions as good and avoiding harm within their cultural context?"

Perspective 1: How Ethical Codes Are Developed

Let's begin by considering the context in which each ethical code is devised. It's likely obvious that each ethical code was created for a specific type of counselor and, in turn, the specific clients counselors serve. For example, the ASCA *Code of Ethics* was developed specifically for PSCs and the "educational stakeholders" (e.g., students, parents/guardians, teachers/staff, administrators, communities) they serve. The CRCC *Code of Ethics* was established for CRCs and the services they provide to consumers/clients who have disabilities. When reading the ethical codes, it's essential to consider *whom* the code was designed to serve and how cultural relevance may be applied differently based on the client population. For example, clients from low socioeconomic status may face an array of barriers because of financial limitations, yet the ethical considerations addressing barriers to treatment for PSCs may vary from those for CRCs.

In the previous sections, you learned some about the historical development of each ethical code. As you likely noticed, each ethical code was introduced initially at a specific time point and revised at different time points over several decades. It's important to consider what was happening nationally and globally when codes were developed and revised.

- What were the current events?
- What are some influential historical events that may have set the foundation for the development of the nation and profession?
- What was happening politically?
- What movements were occurring?
- What was the economy like?
- What was the cultural milieu related to mental health and help seeking?

Additionally, consider what was happening in the helping professions during the time in which codes were established or revised.

- Did a schism occur within a professional organization (e.g., ASCA or AMHCA becoming independent organizations from ACA)?
- What was happening with counselor training accreditation?
- Did anything change within the allied professions (e.g., American Psychological Association, American Psychiatric Association, National Association of Social Workers)?
- What was happening with state licensure rules and regulations?
- What was occurring at the time the codes were established or revised can have a significant impact on the focus the codes took, how they were worded, and where priorities seemed to lie.

Counseling ethical codes are a reflection of the culture in which they are embedded and cannot be divorced from it because those who wrote the codes are cultural beings who are part of society and the historical present in which they were immersed.

Finally, keep in mind how long it can take for ethical codes to be developed or revised. This is not a short process, and it includes several individuals, groups, and stakeholders. Typically, the process takes a minimum of three years, so, for example, a specific code revision published in 2023 may not reflect contextual variables that occurred in 2022 because the revision process was in its final stages by that time. At the same time, do not hesitate to read the codes with a critical eye toward what the authors may have chosen to ignore in terms of what was happening culturally when the codes were developed/revised. Although the counseling profession continues to make strides with more robust cultural attention, *we ain't there yet.* The counseling profession is in process just like each counselor is continually in process. We learn and grow from our oversights, mistakes, and misjudgments, yet it takes keen awareness and a critical approach to continually do better and serve clients more fully.

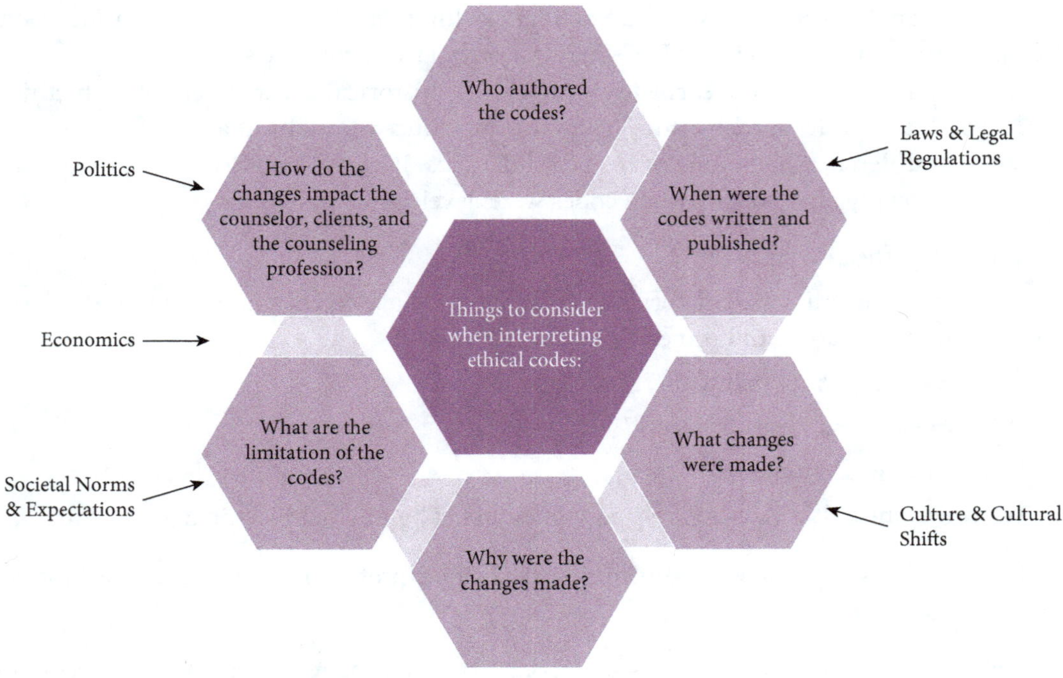

FIGURE 2.1 Considerations for Interpreting Ethical Codes

BOX 2.5 TIPS FOR PROFESSIONAL PRACTICE: KEEPING UP-TO-DATE

Years may go by before an organization publishes another version of its ethical codes (see ACA), but the world does not stop evolving. So, many organizations opt to publish blog posts, statements, or articles on their websites and professional publications in response to events to clarify their stance on issues impacting culturally diverse communities. Check out each organization's website and publications for updated information.

Being informed by current events can provide context to ethical code revisions and context to what your clients/students/consumers may be experiencing in their lives. Being informed will make you a better counselor.

Perspective 2: Ecological Systems Theory

While the United States stands proud in *rugged individualism* and the belief that everyone can *make it on their own* without help from others, it is not literally true that any of us are completely alone. Even in an individualistic society like the United States, every person is rooted within multiple systems, and those systems have individual and group impacts. Bronfenbrenner's (1979) ecological systems theory (EST) posits that the systems in which one is embedded interact and impact their development, beliefs, and behaviors. Although EST was developed to understand child development, it has broader application and is used within this text to understand clients within their multiple contexts. You will learn more about EST in Chapter 4, though in this chapter, you are introduced to it in terms of a way in which to think about the ethical codes.

To understand the ethical codes from a cultural perspective, counselors must consider each system, how they interact with one another, and the impact that may result. As is depicted in Figure 2.2, each system is separate, yet the arrows indicate the interaction between systems. It's important to note that not all impacts can be predetermined. There are plenty of impacts that can't be anticipated; however, the goal is to engage in a thorough process in which counselors do their due diligence to identify potential cultural implications inherent to the ethical codes and their application.

Ecological Systems Definitions

EST is focused on the impact systems have on individuals and their development. Each system denotes factors that can affect an individual's functioning, experiences, and even worldview. Below are the definitions for each system. Keep in mind that each system has the capacity to have both helpful and harmful impacts, particularly as they intermingle with one another.

- **Microsystem:** The individuals and groups with whom the individual has direct contact (e.g., family, friends, intimate relationships, colleagues, clubs, religious involvement). The individuals and groups that impact the individual will likely shift over time depending on where they are in the lifespan (e.g., child, adolescent, adult).

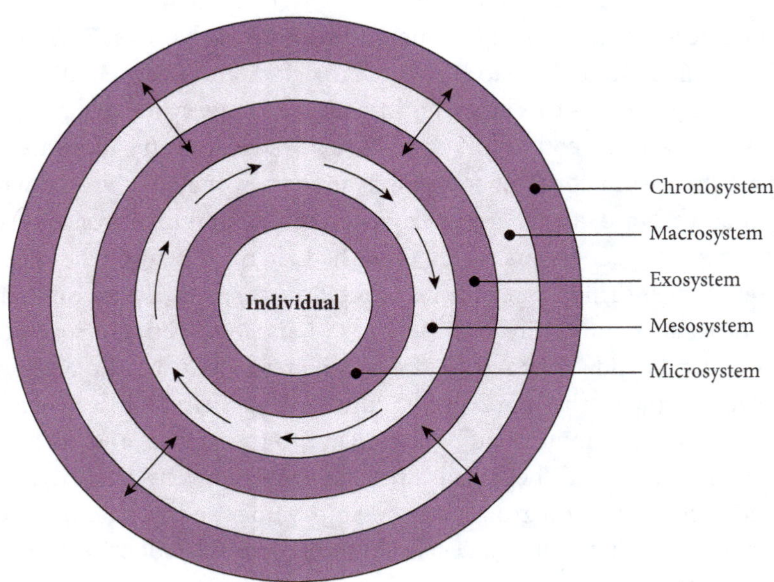

FIGURE 2.2 Ecological Systems Model (Bronfenbrenner, 1979)

- **Mesosystem:** The relationships or interactions between groups within the microsystem that impact the individual (e.g., family's relationship with the individual's school, partner's relationship with the individual's friends).
- **Exosystem:** Systems that affect the individual but with which the individual typically does not have direct contact nor the individual power to influence (e.g., local and nation government, mass media, school boards, company owners, police, social services).
- **Macrosystem:** Cultural identities and the values, beliefs, customs, and ways of being that stem from cultural identities and cultural group membership. Cultural identities can include race, ethnicity, socioeconomic status, social class, ability status, religious/spiritual affiliation, gender, sex, sexual/affectual orientation, immigration status, language, and age. Marginalization, privilege, and power have a central role in individuals' experiences based on their identities.
- **Chronosystem:** This system accounts for how things unfold over time—both what changes and what stays the same. It can include sociocultural and shared historical events (e.g., wars, shared tragedies, social movements, technological advancements), as well as significant individual life events, both normative (e.g., graduating from high school, establishing a career) and non-normative (e.g., death of a sibling in childhood, winning the lottery).

Now that you know the systems that comprise EST and how they are defined, let's talk about what it has to do with ethics and culturally relevant counseling practice.

Counseling ethical codes are situated within the exosystem. Ethical codes are a functional component of each counseling organization and are something that most individuals, clients and counselors alike, did not have a direct hand in developing and are, thus, outside of their control. As you learned earlier in the chapter, although many people are involved in devising each ethical code, ethical codes are established by a governing body. Think about it—AMHCA has over 7,000 members, ASCA over 43,000 members, and ACA has over 56,000 members; there are over 34,000 certified clinical rehabilitation counselors and over 63,000 national certified counselors—with organizations this large, it's impossible for everyone to have decision-making power. That doesn't mean that counselors can't have a voice and can't advocate for changes—it simply means that the vast majority of counselors are not intimately involved with the process.

While counseling ethics are situated in the exosystem, counselors take professional responsibility for how they are applied. We counselors may not have had a hand in creating the ethical codes, yet we are the ones who apply them! This is a weighty responsibility—we must pay careful attention to how we apply them so we do so in a culturally relevant, responsive, and informed way. Specifically, counselors must intentionally attend to how they account for and are responsive to the macrosystem and chronosystem, as well as the impact they have on the individual via their microsystem and mesosystem.

What does it mean to account for and be responsive to the macro- and chronosystems when we apply counseling ethics? Let's begin with the macrosystem. The macrosystem is about the client's cultural identities, cultural group membership, values and beliefs, and the levels of privilege and marginalization they experience based on their cultural identities. When a counselor considers an ethical code in terms of a specific client, they must consider all that is inherent to *the client's* macrosystem and apply the code in a way that is as congruent as possible with the client's macrosystem. Notice the emphasis placed on *the client* in this statement—it is not about the *counselor's* macrosystem. Remember, counselors practice client-centered counseling, not counselor-centered counseling. We suspect this is what you hope for when you attend counseling—that the counselor is focusing on you and your needs rather than their own.

The chronosystem accounts for how things change over time—think big picture and little picture—the world in which one lives and one's individual life. When applying the ethical codes, this means that counselors pay close attention to what the client has experienced over the course of their lifetime, both individually and as a part of groups, as well as what is happening currently—again, both individually and more globally. To gain a sense of the events most important to the client, counselors ask about and explore these events. Remember, these events can be those that have had a positive impact on clients just as much as those that have had a deleterious effect. In both cases, counselors explore the cultural components (macrosystem!) inherent to how the client has made meaning and developed coping mechanisms, and how their values, beliefs, and worldviews have shifted as a result of these events. This is ethical practice because the counselor is attending specifically to the client's worldviews and how they developed, and using that information to inform the counseling process.

Examples of Chronosystem Events

Individual and group events that impact clients are numerous. The list we offer below gives you a starting place in terms of different events that can impact clients and their development.

- Individual Events
    - Family of Origin
        - Parent/Caregiver divorce
        - Death of family members
        - Chronic mental/physical health issues of family member(s) or loved ones (e.g., a sibling with addiction, live-in grandparent with dementia, parent/guardian with bipolar disorder)
        - Moving (e.g., multiple moves, unplanned moves, moves that took the client away from important people or resources)
        - Incarceration of loved ones
        - Historical trauma
        - Abuse and/or neglect
        - Chronic/historical poverty
    - School
        - Bullying
        - Low achievement
        - Difficulty building and maintaining relationships
        - Not reaching developmental milestones

- Personal and Interpersonal Events
  - Addiction
  - Peer group struggles
  - Incarcerations
  - Military service
  - Career failure
  - Workplace struggles (e.g., bullying, low wages)
  - Death of loved ones, particularly *off-time* deaths

- Group Events
  - Weather-related tragedies (e.g., hurricanes, tornados, wild fires)
  - Nonpotable water and *food deserts*
  - War
  - Legislative actions
  - Racism, xenomisia, classism, heterosexism, misogyny, etc.
  - Change movements such as Black Lives Matter, #metoo, feminism, LGBTQ+ rights
  - The 9/11 attacks
  - COVID-19 pandemic
  - Gentrification
  - Neighborhood violence
  - Gerrymandering, restricted voting access

Now that you have some background about what counselors attend to in terms of applying the ethical codes in a way that takes clients' macro- and chronosystems into account, let's apply it to an example by returning to Joe's case from earlier in the chapter. When considering Joe's macrosystem, Mel would explore Joe's cultural identities: race and ethnicity (Mexican American), age (28), geographic region (born and raised in Florida and recently moved to Atlanta), sex (male), gender identity (man), and his affectual orientation (gay). Within that exploration, she would ask questions to understand Joe's values, beliefs, norms, worldviews, and ways of being based on his cultural identities, including the ways in which he believes he has privilege and has experienced marginalization. Remember not to assume which of his identities are most salient to him, especially as it relates to his counseling needs. Mel would note what is most important to Joe, using validation and normalization, and displaying empathy regarding challenges he has faced.

Next, Mel would explore Joe's chronosystem. Starting with group events, if Joe is 28 years old in 2023, that means he experienced the COVID-19 pandemic as an adult, so it would be helpful to understand the impact it had on him. Another major event that occurred in Joe's lifetime was the 9/11 attacks, yet he was only 6 years old when they occurred. Mel might assume that this event had little impact on Joe because of his age and location, yet Joe named this as a critical event in his life because his favorite Tia and Tio were visiting the World Trade Center when the attacks occurred and were killed. Although the 9/11 attacks were a group event, they have individual significance for Joe because of the *off-time death* of his aunt and uncle. Also, Joe is a Florida native, the home of the "Don't Say Gay" bill and tragedies like the *Pulse* nightclub shooting (a 2016 mass shooting in a gay nightclub) and the fatal shooting of Trayvon Martin at the hands of George Zimmerman, not to mention the mass deportation of undocumented immigrants that occurred in 2023. These are all events that may have impacted Joe as a Mexican American gay man as well as his family, extended family, and friend group (microsystem). When Mel asked about other individually significant events and changes, Joe named bullying in middle school, his coming out process in high school, and being the first in his family to graduate from college.

The next natural extension is to investigate the impact of the chronosystem and macrosystem on the microsystem and mesosystem. You have some hints about this already from what you read above! The goal is always to understand the impact on the individual client and in turn, how learning this client-specific information will impact the counseling process. The ethical codes are unanimous that counseling goals and interventions must align with the client and their wants and needs. The contextual information you glean from taking an EST perspective equips you to do this because you have far more information about the client, their history, and effective routes you can take to assist them in achieving their goals.

Perspective 3: Culture in the Ethical Codes: Direct and Indirect

When reading the ethical codes, you will notice that some codes are explicit and direct in their wording regarding culture, cultural implications, and/or social justice advocacy actions. These codes are important because of their explicit nature—they express the counseling profession's overt commitment to diverse populations and justice in terms of rights and access to services. However, it is essential to employ two additional critical perspectives of the ethical codes, that is, what is not stated explicitly in the codes and what the implications could be if the codes are not interpreted from a cultural and/or social justice advocacy perspective. Could clients be harmed or, at the very least, not get their needs met? Could a counselor use a code to impose their worldviews and what they deem to be *best* for the client?

After reviewing the ethical codes, you might have noticed some changes that have occurred over time are more obvious than others. For example, all the organizations we reviewed added sections or codes regarding telemental health, the use of technology, and/or codes related to social media use, and ACA, AMHCA, CRCC, and ASCA explicitly mention the use of interpreters and translators for clients whose preferred language is not English or for those with limited English fluency. These are important updates because they reflect changes in the world in which we live and practice, yet it's important to think critically about the specific language each code uses and how direct or general they are.

We encourage you to look beyond the multicultural and diversity sections of the codes and examine other sections with the same critical eye. How can the code be interpreted, or even manipulated, to justify behavior that may be disproportionately harmful to individuals and communities with diverse identities? Take, for instance, the use of the word *unique* or *uniqueness* found in the preamble of many of the organizations' codes. One could argue that those words, by definition, imply the *uniqueness* of each individual's cultural identities, thereby supposing that they are addressing diversity and multicultural by using it. But is it though? We are all *unique*, yet not all of us have nondominant identities that result in oppression and discrimination; in fact, the opposite is true for those who have sociocultural privilege. We posit that sweeping or broad terms that can point to cultural diversity but not necessarily are not quite enough.

To critically read and interpret the ethical codes, we suggest asking yourself and discussing with others the questions listed below. This list is intended to help you broaden your assessment skills and your abilities to perspective take rather than being a prescriptive list or an ethical decision-making model.

- What are my initial thoughts when reading the codes?
- How am I interpreting the codes based on *my* cultural identities? What are my assumptions?
- How might my interpretations differ from the authors' interpretations? What about clients' interpretations?
- What seems to be *missing* from the codes? Are there things you believe should be there that aren't?
- Are the authors making any assumptions about the identities of their audience?
- Why did the authors choose to make changes to the language they used in the codes?
- How will the codes impact the way I conduct myself as a professional counselor?
- How might my interpretation of the codes be perceived by my clients?

Perspective 4: Social Justice and Advocacy

Social justice and advocacy have been named the *fifth force* in the counseling profession (Ratts et al., 2004). Professional counselors value justice, and as such, advocacy is a natural expressive action of that value. Sometimes it comes as a surprise to counselors in training that counselors are advocates; however, how can professional counselors value *justice* and not take action to promote equity and well-being for their clients? In short, they can't. Counselors are called to advocacy action with and on behalf of their clients to confront injustice when it occurs.

You will have the opportunity to explore social justice and advocacy more deeply in Chapter 5, yet we introduce these concepts within this chapter to get you thinking about how a social justice and advocacy perspective is essential for professional counselors and that it influences how we interpret the ethical codes. Most of the ethical codes speak to justice and advocacy in some form (see Table 2.1), though some do so more than others. For example, ASCA mentions advocacy almost 40 times and the CRCC over 30 times, while ACA mentions it only 9 times. This is where a careful reading and interrogation of the codes can result in insights, ideas, and new perspectives.

TABLE 2.1 Examples of Justice and Advocacy in the Ethical Codes

Organization	Code	Code Text
		Justice
ACA (2014)	Preamble #3	Core professional values of the counseling profession: promoting social justice.
ACA (2014)	G Introduction	Counselors who conduct research are encouraged to contribute to the knowledge base of the profession and promote a clearer understanding of the conditions that lead to a healthy and more just society.
ACA (2014)	Glossary	Social Justice – the promotion of equity for all people and groups for the purpose of ending oppression and injustice affecting clients, students, counselors, families, communities, schools, workplaces, governments, and other social and institutional systems.
AMHCA (2020)	–	*No use of the term *justice* in the ethical codes.
AMHCA (2021)	Standards of Practice; Introduction to Forensic Evaluation Section	In the context of forensic evaluation, ethical principles are more broadly applied to all stakeholders of the legal process, not just the client, and ethical principles of veracity (honesty and the pursuit of truth) and justice (equal treatment of individuals in proportion to relevant differences) often predominate.
ASCA (2022)	A.11.b	Advocate for schoolwide policies, protocols and training for response to bullying, harassment and bias incidents centered in safety, belonging and justice.
ASCA (2022)	B.3.g	Develop knowledge and understanding of historic and systemic oppression, social justice and cultural models (e.g., multicultural counseling, anti-racism, culturally sustaining practices) to further develop skills for systemic change and equitable outcomes for all students.
ASCA (2022)	C.i	Providing staff with opportunities and support to develop knowledge and understanding of historic and systemic oppression, social justice and cultural models (e.g., multicultural counseling, anti-racism, culturally sustaining practices) to further develop skills for systemic change and equitable outcomes for all students.
CRCC (2023)	Principles	Justice: To be fair in the treatment of all clients; to provide appropriate services to all.
CRCC (2023)	D.2.c	Social justice. CRCs/CCRCs are expected to understand the client's personal experience, cultural background, the client's awareness of and personal commitment to social justice, as well as the impact of social justice on rehabilitation services outcomes.

(Continued)

TABLE 2.1 *(Continued)*

Organization	Code	Code Text
CRCC (2023)	J Introduction	CRCs/CCRCs who conduct research are encouraged to contribute to the knowledge base of the profession. They promote the welfare of individuals with disabilities as well as a clearer understanding of the conditions that lead to a healthy and more just society.
NBCC (2023)	Core Values and Beliefs	Certified counselors and candidates demonstrate their commitment to ethical behaviors by demonstrating, and representing to their clients, sensitivity to multicultural issues, avoiding discrimination, oppression, and/or any form of social injustice.
Advocacy		
ACA (2014)	A.7.a	When appropriate, counselors advocate at individual, group, institutional, and societal levels to address potential barriers and obstacles that inhibit access and/or the growth and development of clients.
ACA (2014)	C Introduction	Counselors are expected to advocate to promote changes at the individual, group, institutional, and societal levels that improve the quality of life for individuals and groups and remove potential barriers to the provision or access of appropriate services being offered.
ACA (2014)	Glossary	Advocacy – promotion of the well-being of individuals, groups, and the counseling profession within systems and organizations. Advocacy seeks to remove barriers and obstacles that inhibit access, growth, and development.
AMHCA (2020)	Introduction; F.2.a	(Introduction) CMHCs are encouraged to advocate at the individual, institutional, professional, and societal level to foster sociopolitical change that advances client and community welfare. a. CMHCs are aware of and make every effort to avoid pitfalls of advocacy including conflicts of interest, inappropriate relationships, and other negative consequences. CMHCs remain sensitive to the potential personal and cultural impact on clients of their advocacy efforts.
AMHCA (2020)	F.2.b	CMHCs may encourage clients to challenge familial, institutional, and societal obstacles to their growth and development and they may advocate on the clients' behalf. CMHCs remain aware of the potential dangers of becoming overly involved as an advocate.
ASCA	Preamble	School counselors are leaders, advocates, collaborators and consultants who create systemic change to ensure equitable educational outcomes through the school counseling program.

Organization	Code	Code Text
ASCA	Preamble	All students have the right to: Equitable access to school counselors who support students from all backgrounds and circumstances and who advocate for and affirm all students regardless of but not limited to ethnic/racial identity; nationality; age; social class; economic status; abilities/disabilities; language; immigration status; sexual orientation; gender identity; gender expression; family type; religious/spiritual identity; and living situations, including emancipated minor status, wards of the state, homelessness or incarceration.
ASCA	A.1.j	Advocate for equitable, anti-oppressive and anti-bias policies and procedures, systems and practices, and provide effective, evidence-based and culturally sustaining interventions to address student needs.
CRCC (2023)	Values and Principles Section	The values that serve as a foundation for this Code include a commitment to -promoting empowerment through self-advocacy and self-determination; - advocating for equitable and appropriate provision of services.
CRCC (2023)	C.1.b	Self-advocacy and guardianship. CRCs/CCRCs empower clients, parents, or legal guardians by providing appropriate information to facilitate their self-advocacy actions whenever possible. CRCs/CCRCs work with clients, parents, or legal guardians to support understanding of their rights and responsibilities and encourage them to speak for themselves and make informed decisions. When appropriate and with the consent of a client, parent, or legal guardian, CRCs/CCRCs act as advocates on behalf of that client at the local, regional, and/or national levels. To better support clients, CRCs/CCRCs are familiar with guardianship and the range of alternatives available to clients and their support systems (e.g., supported decision-making).
CRCC (2023)	C.1.d	Organizational and system advocacy. CRCs/CCRCs consider how actions taken by their own organization, as well as cooperating organizations impact clients. To ensure effective service delivery, CRCs/CCRCs act as advocates for clients who cannot self-advocate. CRCs/CCRCs make reasonable efforts to partner with client groups and community members to address environmental and systemic issues and to combat ableism and systems of oppression across policies, procedures, and practices. See M.2.f.

(*Continued*)

TABLE 2.1 *(Continued)*

Organization	Code	Code Text
NBCC (2023)	Core Values and Beliefs	Access and equity are essential to the profession of counseling and fundamentally important for the success of any society. Counseling services should be provided to achieve the best mental health outcomes. Counselors provide services to all of those in need, utilizing available resources, and advocating for the expansion of resources in underserved communities.
NBCC (2023)	89	Counselor educators shall advocate for counseling students to address programmatic barriers and obstacles that hinder student academic growth and development.
NBCC (2023)	112	Counselors who use digital technology for professional purposes shall only post information related to professional services, such as information concerning advocacy, educational purposes, and marketing, that does not create multiple relationships or threaten client confidentially.

Professional counselors must consider, too, how each entry in the codes either promotes or potentially stymies justice for our clients. This means that counselors take a social justice perspective when they read codes that are not explicitly about culture, equity, justice, etc. For example, the AMHCA (2010) *Code* stated that counselors "act in the client's best interest" (I.B.2.c., p. 5). This language was not included in the 2020 *Codes*, likely because AMHCA realized that acting in a "client's best interest" could be interpreted widely and potentially detrimentally. However, this is not only a historic concern. Let's take the term *autonomy* as an example. All of the ethical codes speak to valuing client autonomy. What if counselors interpreted this only as clients making independent decisions for themselves without input from others (simply one way of defining autonomy!)? Likely, counselors would run into trouble when working with clients whose culture values family or community decision-making over independent, singular choices. As you can see, defining autonomy in one narrow way would interfere with justice-focused counseling practices. As counselors *perspective take* and consider multiple ways of defining and interpreting terms and codes, they make space for serving clients fully and within clients' cultural context.

Conclusion

In this chapter, you have learned how ethical practice, cultural relevance, and professional responsibility connect and the key dispositions and skills counselors use to put these concepts into practice. Through the history of the ethical codes sections, you have insight into how professional organizations have changed and adapted over time to prioritize culture and clients' cultural perspectives and, additionally, how we still have room to grow as a profession. Finally, you were introduced to key perspectives to help you invoke critical thinking when reading and applying the ethical codes so you can consistently take professional responsibility. Ethical practice is just that: practice. Counselors practice how to be ethical each day they work with clients and become stronger and stronger as they allow themselves to learn and grow throughout their careers.

Questions for Reflection

1. How will cultural relevance and ethical practice come together for you as a professional counselor? How will you know you are applying both appropriately for each client with whom you work?
2. Which dispositions and skills discussed within the chapter are strengths for you? Which do you want to develop further?
3. How will you stay up-to-date on local and state laws that could affect your clients and your practice? How will you work to discern their potential cultural and ethical impacts?
4. Considering the ethical code(s) you will use in your practice, where do you see gaps or troubling language related to culture?
5. In what ways would you like to engage in advocacy related to ethics?

Applying What You Have Learned

Complete each of the following activities, considering what you learned from this chapter.

Activity #1: Finding the Connections

Professional dispositions are foundational for culturally relevant and ethical practice. How do the skills we listed earlier in the chapter connect to the dispositions we outlined? Name specific ways in which you would use the skills as an extension of your professional dispositions. In what ways do the listed dispositions work together? How do the skills overlap with one another? Finding the connections between skills and dispositions will help strengthen your ability to develop and use an integrated approach to counseling.

Activity #2: Personal and Professional Values

Personal values are tenants, guideposts, and/or beliefs each person has that help guide their decisions and to live their lives in ways that are authentic and meaningful to them. *Professional values* are similar to personal values, yet are focused on core professional obligations designed to protect clients so they are empowered to explore and identify their own values, free from judgment and undue influence. The ethical codes are a product of professional values.

It's essential that counselors have personal values that guide their lives so they can live authentically and demonstrate congruence when working with clients. In turn, it's just as important for the profession to have values so the public knows what they can expect from professional counselors. What happens if a counselor's values do not align with professional values or the ethical codes that are derived from these values? This is an important question to explore because struggles with professional values can result in unethical practice, and no counselor wants to unwittingly engage in unethical behavior.

To explore this question for yourself, make three columns on a sheet of paper or in an electronic document. In the first column, list three to five values essential to how you live your life. In the second column, list why these values are important to you and how they came to hold importance in your life. Finally, use the third column to record how your values align or deviate from professional counseling values. If you encounter deviations, brainstorm how you might resolve these differences. Ideas might include talking with another trusted professional, supervisor, or instructor; seeking more information; engaging in continuing education opportunities, such as workshops, webinars, or conferences; discerning whether the differences are all that great; seeking your own counseling. Then, assess your list of ideas and take action! The only wrong way to complete this activity is not to do it at all. The fact is, all counselors encounter value differences at some point—it's what you do with it, in service to working with clients ethically, that is essential.

CHAPTER 3

Cultural Humility

Charmayne R. Adams, Jillian M. Blueford, and Thang S. Tran

Humility is the solid foundation of all virtues.

—Confucius

CHAPTER OVERVIEW

In this chapter, you will learn about cultural humility and how counselors demonstrate it within their work. We center the chapter around the multicultural orientation model that was developed by Owen and colleagues (2011) to guide professional counselors who work with diverse clients. We offer examples of how you can expand your understanding of your cultural experiences and how those cultural experiences impact the ways you engage with clients. The chapter is full of opportunities to explore external resources and to reflect on the content, so we invite you into the space of deeper exploration of yourself, those around you, and the world in which we live.

LEARNING OBJECTIVES

By the end of this chapter, students will be able to

1. describe the multicultural orientation model,
2. outline how the three components of multicultural orientation work together to create culturally inclusive counseling, and
3. apply the multicultural orientation model to enhance the counseling relationship.

CACREP 2016 STANDARDS

The information in this chapter supports the following standards:

- 2.F.2.b. theories and models of multicultural counseling, cultural identity development, and social justice and advocacy
- 2.F.2.d. the impact of heritage, attitudes, beliefs, understandings, and acculturative experiences on an individual's views of others
- 2.F.2.e. the effects of power and privilege for counselors and clients
- 2.F.2.h. strategies for identifying and eliminating barriers, prejudices, and processes of intentional and unintentional oppression and discrimination
- 5.c.2.j cultural factors relevant to clinical mental health counseling

- 5.c.2.j. cultural factors relevant to clinical mental health counseling
- 5.c.3.e. strategies to advocate for persons with mental health issues
- 5.G.2.a. school counselor roles as leaders, advocates, and systems change agents in P- 12 schools

CACREP 2024 STANDARDS

The information in this chapter supports the following standards:

- 3.B.1. theories and models of multicultural counseling, social justice, and advocacy
- 3.B.2. the influence of heritage, cultural identities, attitudes, values, beliefs, understandings, within-group differences, and acculturative experiences on individuals' worldviews
- 3.B.5. the effects of stereotypes, overt and covert discrimination, racism, power, oppression, privilege, marginalization, microaggressions, and violence on counselors and clients
- 3.B.6. the effects of various socio-cultural influences, including public policies, social movements, and cultural values, on mental and physical health and wellness
- 3.B.8. principles of independence, inclusion, choice and self-empowerment, and access to services within and outside the counseling relationship
- 3.B.9. strategies for identifying and eliminating barriers, prejudices, and processes of intentional and unintentional oppression and discrimination
- 5.H.6. school counselor roles as leaders, advocates, and systems change agents in PK–12 schools

Multicultural Orientation Model

The multicultural orientation model (Owen et al., 2011) was built upon the original research of Tervalon and Murray-Garcia (1998) who posed the question: *In physician training, does cultural humility lead to better outcomes than cultural competence*? The multicultural orientation model is a way of being with clients who hold different identities than their own that is composed of three concepts (i.e., cultural humility, cultural comfort, and cultural opportunities). To apply this perspective to the counseling profession, it is important to understand counselor characteristics, motivation, and physiological experience of comfort when working with clients. Also, this model emphasizes the importance of understanding the complexities of privilege and oppression that are inherent to all cultural identities (Owen et al., 2016). Multicultural orientation can be viewed as an extension of the multicultural and social justice counseling competencies (Ratts et al., 2016) that focus on how cultural dynamics impact the counseling process (Davis et al., 2018). Multicultural orientation is specifically focused on how the counselor's cultural worldview and the client's cultural worldviews create a unique relationship experience within counseling. In sum, the model focuses on the counselors' *ways of being* and the impacts they have on the therapeutic relationship. Ways of being are focused on how we are in session with clients in contrast to the information we know about people who are different from ourselves.

Model Components

There are three pillars of the multicultural orientation model (see Figure 3.1). The first pillar is cultural humility, is defined as counselors being simultaneously aware of their own cultural experiences while remaining curious and open to the cultural experiences of others. Cultural humility has been researched as a standalone component of multicultural competence in various mental health settings (Cook et al., 2020; Mosher et al., 2017), professional counseling, and counselor education (Zhu et al., 2021; Zhu et al., 2022b); nursing (Foronda et al., 2016); social work (Fisher-Borne et al., 2015); and with military populations (Lane, 2019). Additionally, cultural humility has been used in a variety of healthcare models, such as the 5 Rs (i.e., reflection, respect, regard, relevance, resiliency; Masters et al., 2019). Cultural humility is the overarching concept that encompasses the internal and external dynamics of this model. Counselors practice cultural humility by interacting with clients in a nonjudgmental, nonhierarchical manner with respect for their own experiences and the experiences of those whom they are counseling.

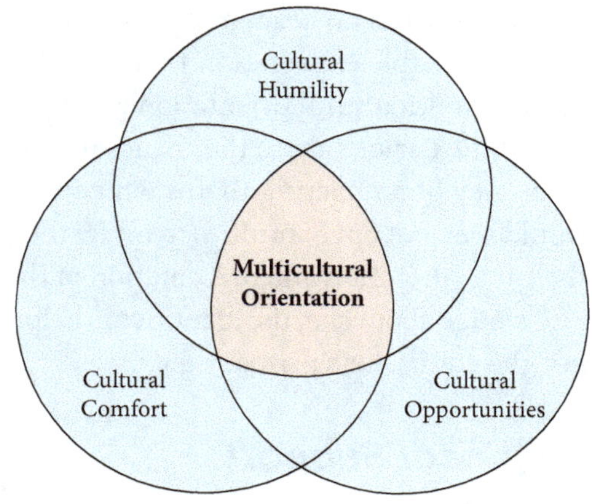

FIGURE 3.1 Diagram of the Three Components of Multicultural Orientation

The second aspect is cultural comfort, which is the physiological sensation of stress or ease experienced by the counselor before, during, and after engaging in conversations about culture. The final component is cultural opportunities, which are the moments in a session that allow for a natural exploration of the client's culture as it pertains to the presenting concern or the content they are discussing.

The multicultural orientation model was created to work in conjunction with any counseling theoretical orientation. Additionally, the creators aimed to shift the conversation away from competencies to focusing on the bigger picture of the quality of the therapeutic relationship and how that relationship is impacted by the client and the counselor's cultural factors (Hook et al., 2017). Moving away from competency language allows counselors to focus on their ways of being or actions in a session instead of evaluation, which is typically associated with the meeting, exceeding, or not meeting tiered assessment of competency standards. This shift is important because it moves the counselor away from trying to master content about specific groups of people toward a more curious stance that encourages the counselor to be open to continuous growth. The aim moves from being *knowledge focused* to being *relationally focused*. As such, the multicultural orientation model does not prioritize mastering the most recent trends and information about singular identities (e.g., women, African Americans, Muslims) but rather approaching clients from a holistic perspective that honors the complexity of their identities and the interaction between them (Davis, DeBlaere, et al., 2020). For example, imagine a counselor working with a 17-year-old Asian American female who identifies as bisexual. Under a competency model of multicultural counseling, to be competent to work with this client a counselor would need to be competent in working with each of those identities independently (adolescent/Asian American/female/bisexual) and competent in understanding how those identities may impact each other from an academic perspective. That feels like a daunting task for any counselor and an unattainable expectation that could leave a counselor feeling anxious and underprepared. From a multicultural orientation perspective, the counselor always views the client holistically, remaining curious about the client's intersectional experiences of their identities, and monitoring what may be impacting their own comfort working with the client. Additionally, a counselor would seek out opportunities to invite the client to explore how their identities may be impacting their interpretation and presentation of the presenting concern. While having some background knowledge about specific identities is helpful, having all-encompassing knowledge is not realistic nor the counselor's primary goal.

Empirical Support

Since 2013, there have been many empirical studies linking the multicultural orientation model and its three components (i.e., cultural humility, cultural comfort, and cultural opportunities) to positive counseling outcomes. In 2013, Hook and colleagues published three studies (Davis et al., 2013; Davis & Hook, 2013; Hook et al., 2013) that correlated cultural humility with the working alliance. Owen et al. (2014) found that cultural humility toward religious and spiritual identity was related to positive client outcomes. Hook et al. (2016) found that cultural humility mitigated the impact of microaggressions in counseling in addition to predicting higher psychological safety.

TABLE 3.1 Multicultural Orientation Research and Outcomes

Research Article and Topic		**Outcomes**
Cultural Humility	Hook et al. (2013) Davis et al. (2013) Davis and Hook (2013)	Stronger working alliance (therapeutic relationship)
Cultural Humility	Hook et al. (2016)	Mitigated impact of microaggressions (including decreased negative emotions) and higher psychological safety
Cultural Opportunities	Hook et al. (2016) Davis et al. (2016)	Missed cultural opportunities negatively impacted the therapeutic relationship
Cultural Comfort	Owen et al. (2017)	Level of cultural comfort predicted therapy termination after the first session with racial/ethnic minorities
Cultural Humility	Zhu et al. (2022a) Zhu et al. (2021)	Ongoing research on cultural humility enactment in counseling and counseling education

One interesting finding was that *missed cultural opportunities* (*cultural opportunities* being one of the three constructs associated with multicultural orientation) in counseling had negative impacts on therapy outcomes, but that impact was less when the counselor had higher cultural humility. This finding was replicated by Davis et al. (2016), who found that cultural humility mediated the relationship between negative emotions caused by counselor microaggressions and the therapeutic relationship. Owen et al. (2017) continued to demonstrate support, finding that lack of *cultural comfort* predicted termination after the first session with racial and ethnic minorities. This prolific group of scholars has produced a robust foundation of knowledge for the multicultural orientation model and its impacts on counseling, specifically as it relates to the therapeutic relationship, which we know is one of the largest predictors of positive outcomes in counseling (Norcross & Wampold, 2011). Specifically focused on professional counseling, Zhu and his colleagues have published multiple scholarly articles focused on measuring cultural humility within counselor education and in the counseling relationship (e.g., Zhu et al., 2021; Zhu et al., 2022a). This team has been hard at work creating and validating a scale to measure cultural humility and how it is enacted in the counseling relationship (Zhu et al., 2022a).

There is also a burgeoning interest in how the concepts of the multicultural orientation model could be used in a group counseling context with its heavy reliance on here-and-now experience (Kivlighan & Chapman, 2018), as well as in clinical supervision (Walkins et al., 2019). At the time of writing this chapter, the articles on the use of this model in group counseling and supervision are conceptual. The authors respectfully made excellent cases for the application of this model in both domains, noting, "[G]roups are inherently cultural reflections of the world and unfortunately not immune to the systems of power, privilege, and inequity that operate within society" (Kivloghan & Chapman, 2018, p. 40) and "supervision often provides multicultural oversight for individual and group psychotherapy services" (Watkins et al., 2019, p. 38). Both articles provide excellent recommendations for further research, which we have no doubt we will see in the coming years. Now, let's shift our focus more deeply into the components that comprise the multicultural orientation model.

Cultural Humility

According to the American Counseling Association (ACA) *Code of Ethics* (2014), a core professional value of all counselors is "honoring diversity and embracing a multicultural approach in support of the worth, dignity, potential, and uniqueness of people within their social and cultural contexts" (p. 3). Both the American Mental Health Counselors Association (AMHCA, 2020) and the Commission on Rehabilitation Counselor Certification (CRCC, 2023) code of ethics assert that counselors have the responsibility to "actively attempt to understand the diverse cultural backgrounds" of their clients (AMHCA, 2020, p. 8; CRCC, 2023, p. 1). School counselors have a similar calling in which they have a "primary obligation" to each of their students, "who are to be treated with dignity and respect as unique individuals" (ASCA, 2023, p. 1). As the U.S. population becomes increasingly older and more ethnically and racially diverse, counselors must rise to help and support human functioning, connection, and well-being on multiple levels (Vespa et al., 2022). Age/generational and ethnic/racial influences are just two among many cultural influences that counselors must consider in their dynamic and evolving relationship with their clients. Though not exhaustive, other influences may include the following:

- Disability (physical, invisible, developmental, or other; see Chapter 12)
- Religion and/or spirituality (see Chapter 16)
- Socioeconomic status and social class (see Chapter 11)
- Sexual, affectual, and romantic orientation (see Chapter 15)
- Indigenous heritage (see Chapter 10)
- National origin (see Chapters 8 and 9)
- Language (see Chapter 8 and 10)
- Gender (see Chapter 14)

Counselors and counselors in training may find themselves asking, "How can I honor the many aspects of my client or student's cultural beliefs, values, background, and experiences while being real about my own?" This is a fair and thoughtful question that you will continue to answer throughout your development—not only now while you are in your training program but also in the years to come as you practice as a professional counselor throughout your career. The world and environments in which you and your clients live will change, so you will adapt, grow, and change too.

Clients, by nature, are a vulnerable population. They are coming to receive mental health support during a time when their well-being is compromised. In working with these unique individuals, culturally adept counselors consider and understand the distinct perspectives and often complex histories of those they serve. An important, intrinsic responsibility that all counselors must maintain is the safety and dignity of every client/student/consumer. This is an ongoing process that requires strong commitment, empathy, genuine care, active engagement, adaptability, and humility. Though current counselor training on cultural sensitivity, responsiveness, and competence is improving, many counselors may still feel frustrated, unprepared, and unsupported to face pressing issues such as racism, classism, ableism, and homomisia, just to name a few. The need for increased culturally relevant counseling remains great. Cultural humility may help to bridge this gap.

Attributes of Cultural Humility

Cultural humility is often described as a "way of being" (Davis et al., 2020, p. 11) or "stance" (Dixon et al., 2021, p. 1) having two main parts or attributes. The first part is intrapersonal: An *inward-focused*, accurate view of self, primarily around one's perceived cultural values, beliefs, experiences, and limitations. The intrapersonal centers around an authentic and accurate understanding of oneself and one's level of cultural awareness. Ongoing self-reflection and self-critique as a lifelong learner are integral to one's intrapersonal development.

The second part is *interpersonal*, honoring others and displaying humble curiosity. Interpersonal dispositions include humble openness, cultural sensitivity, respect, and a high level of acceptance toward others (Hook et al., 2013; Mosher et al., 2017).

TABLE 3.2 Cultural Humility Attributes and Outcomes

	Intrapersonal	Interpersonal	Outcomes
Attributes	Authentic, accurate perception of one's level of cultural awareness (values, beliefs, biases, limitations, experiences)	Humble curiosity, honoring consideration, other-centeredness (their cultural values, beliefs, experiences, history)	Stronger relationships (working alliance) – trust and safety, better care, higher retention rates, easier recovery from cultural mistakes
	Self-reflection and self-critique as a lifelong learner	Non-superiority/ egolessness	Low cultural humility linked to more cultural mistakes/ microaggressions and longer recovery

Specific to counseling, cultural humility has been defined as counselors' ability to hold "an accurate perception of their cultural values as well as maintain an other-oriented perspective that involves respect, lack of superiority and attunement regarding their own cultural beliefs and values" (Hook et al., 2017, p. 29). Important to these dispositions is a bidirectional stance of self-awareness, ongoing self-reflection, client-centered openness, and humble curiosity as counselors work to relate to and counsel diverse clients more effectively.

Understanding the Historical Context

Cultural humility originated during the late 1990s in the medical field and public health as a response to the need to better train medical students and hospital staff to "skillfully and respectfully negotiate the implications of … diversity" (Tervalon & Murray-Garcia, 1998, p. 117). At the time, many medical and health-care students were trained under the banner of *cultural competence*, which some have argued can connote a certain level of mastery of a finite body of cultural knowledge. As a supplement to and, in some ways, a redefinition of cultural competence, Tervalon and Murray-Garcia (1998) introduced cultural humility to redirect the focus from gaining "expertise" (p. 119) in navigating patients' cultural influences toward an ongoing dispositional commitment to self-reflection, self-critique, patient-focused care, and mutually respectful and dynamic partnerships. The goal is that such partnerships could help mitigate the ever-present power imbalance that exists between patient and physician. As the U.S. population continued to diversify, this was especially important for patients of color and those who hold a variety of marginalized identities. It is important to note that cultural humility and cultural competence do not have to be in conflict. Indeed, developing cultural humility necessitates a simultaneous movement away from cultural ineptitude and stereotypical interactions toward skillfully and properly addressing and contextualizing expansive issues of culture within the physician/patient relationship, as well as any other potentially diverse cultural exchange.

BOX 3.1 **PAUSE AND REFLECT: CULTURAL HUMILITY VERSUS CULTURAL COMPETENCE**

How is cultural humility different from cultural competence? When you think of the term competence, what comes to mind? When you think of humility, what comes to mind? How can both contribute positively to your counseling practice?

Over the last 25 years there has been a growing body of research on cultural humility in several professions, including psychology, social work, education, veterinary sciences, religion/spirituality, library sciences, and clinical mental health and school counseling (Dickinson et al., 2021, Dixon et al., 2021; Haynes-Mendez & Engelsmeier, 2020; Hook et al., 2013; Hurley et al., 2022; Mosher et al., 2017; Rovito, 2020; Tran & Rubel, 2022; Winkeljohn Black et al., 2019). A common theme in incorporating cultural humility into the ethos of these professions has been the need for better, more culturally impactful, honoring, and other-centered (i.e., focusing on the interests of others ahead of one's own) training.

Empirical Support

Cultural humility is a protective factor in client-counselor relationships (Dixon et al., 2021; Zhang et al., 2022). Counselors who are more culturally humble exhibit characteristics that reduce negative outcomes and have attributes that positively counter the impact of risk factors. Positive outcomes include healthy working alliances, increased retention rates, and helping to mitigate power imbalances.

Cultural humility helps to form stronger working alliances (Hook et al., 2013; Mosher et al., 2017). Developing a sense of trust and safety is the foundation of a strong counselor-client (i.e., bond). Low cultural humility has been linked with cultural mistakes and microaggressions, while high cultural humility has been shown to help counselors recover more easily from cultural mistakes (Davis et al., 2016). Mosher (2017) described counselors who are higher in cultural humility as engaging in the following actions:

- intentionally self-reflect and make a consistent effort to reduce their limitations and biases;
- focus on learning from their clients' cultural backgrounds and experiences;
- search for opportunities to build respectful, mutual partnerships with their clients; and
- motivated throughout their lives to learn more about various cultural beliefs (p. 224).

BOX 3.2 **PAUSE AND REFLECT: CULTIVATING YOUR OWN CULTURAL HUMILITY**

In what ways are you engaging in the above actions aligned with cultural humility? In which areas can you engage in intentional action more frequently? Jot them down and swap lists with a colleague. Discuss the strengths you see in your lists and how you can use your strengths to increase your actions in areas that need attention.

Cultural humility has been linked to higher retention rates in counseling (Rovito, 2020). Depending on the counseling setting and context, the counselor may have little say with whom they work. For example, a counselor who sees court-mandated clients or school counselors with a caseload determined by students' last names. Many times, the students who may need the most assistance will work with their school counselor on a recurring and possibly frequent basis. If a school counselor lacks an honest and correct assessment of their cultural values or is not open, curious, or considerate of their student's experiences, students may be unlikely to work with them again.

Cultural humility can provide a framework to help counselors and clients address power imbalances within the therapeutic relationship, which was the original intent of the multicultural orientation model (Masters et al., 2019; Tervalon & Murray-Garcia, 1998). Those who are more culturally humble are more open and honoring of new cultural information, interactions, and experiences. A major part of the *other orientation* of cultural humility includes allowing others to inform us of their salient (i.e., immediately relevant) cultural identities. Identity salience will be especially important when we discuss cultural opportunities later in the chapter.

As communities are rapidly becoming more diversified, counselors must professionally and ethically rise to meet the needs of clients and students who look, learn, and live differently from them. Moon and Sandage (2019) stated that one of the major consequences of racism and oppression in the United States for Black, Indigenous, and People of Color is the "self-doubt, self-criticism, and [the] shame one experiences" (p. 79). Cultural humility may be the key to forming stronger working alliances, quicker recovery from cultural mistakes, higher return rates (i.e., lower attrition rates), and addressing power imbalances on multiple levels with students, consumers, and clients of color.

Counselors and counselors in training will inevitably work with clients and students from diverse backgrounds. Professional counselors, regardless of their setting, work in places where individuals with a variety of diverging cultural contexts and backgrounds converge. Counselors must navigate these diverse relationships and the complexity of the intersectionality of their own identities and their clients'. Negotiating relationships within the counselor-client/student working alliance can be complicated. Counselors are often seen as mediators, advocates, leaders, and role models within these mutual relationships and have multiple considerations, making these experiences unique and complex. Cultural influences are often at the top of this list. As cultural diversification increases in schools and communities, all counselors, no matter their specialization, must be "more globally responsive and culturally sustaining in the educational and social environment than ever before" (ASCA, 2021, p. 28), because "all individuals have the right to be accepted for their unique and authentic self" (ACA, 2017a, p. 3).

Cultural Comfort

To sustain cultural humility and enhance counselors' ability to support clients who hold a variety of intersectional identities, counselors must take time to evaluate and increase their *cultural comfort*, the second component of the multicultural orientation framework (Hook et al., 2017). Hook and colleagues (2017) defined cultural comfort as "the feelings that arise before, during, and after culturally relevant conversations in session ..." (p. 37). Cultural broaching is an approach counselors use to discuss racial, ethnic, and cultural identities as they relate to the client's presenting concerns (Day-Vines, Wood, et al., 2007; Day-Vines, Booker, et al., 2018). Research supports cultural broaching related to race and ethnicity (Day-Vines Booker, et al., 2018), gender identity (Toomey & Carlson, 2022), age (Mejia et al., 2018), neurodiversity (Mitran, 2022), and countless other identities. Counselors' comfort levels when broaching and discussing culture impact the counseling process and the overall client-counselor relationship. For counselors to create and sustain a safe therapeutic environment, they must be able to remain at ease and comfortable while discussing their clients' identities.

Counselors who are more comfortable engaging in reflection and dialogue surrounding culture and its impact on clients and their system are more likely to have challenging and meaningful conversations with their clients (Choi et al., 2015). Not addressing one's comfort level can lead to avoiding culturally relevant conversations in the counseling session and potentially harm clients. When counselors remain at ease while discussing culture, it allows clients to be present and authentically engage with their thoughts and feelings. This authenticity can lead to a robust client-counselor relationship in which all topics can be discussed adroitly, thus increasing the quality of the therapeutic alliance and treatment outcomes (Owen, 2013; Sue, 2003).

Increasing cultural comfort can be a daunting task because often, we must first allow ourselves to feel the discomfort and pinpoint its origin. Identifying one's cultural comfort and discomfort with specific cultural demographics can require intensive work and honesty. While counselors would like to possess a strong comfort level engaging with clients of all diverse backgrounds, we must first acknowledge that this can only be achieved through honesty with ourselves and a true reflection of our starting point.

Comfort is cultivated through exposure because anxiety serves as an emotional alarm that something is unknown, new, or potentially dangerous. Anxiety is always going to tell us the worst-case scenario, which is one of the key functions of that emotion. It is our responsibility to manage that emotional experience and counter it with the *most likely scenario* by developing skills on which we can rely. We are not aiming to eliminate all anxiety when we engage in conversations that are new to us because another key function of anxiety is motivation. Rather, you want to manage that anxiety in such a way that it fuels your curiosity, eagerness to learn, and attunement with your client.

For example, imagine you are working with a client who is part of a motorcycle club (called a "biker gang" by your client), and you have no frame of reference for that cultural experience, but you know that it has a large impact on your client's worldview. You may feel some anxiety asking them about their experience, yet a counselor with higher cultural comfort would use that anxiety to lean into the conversation instead of leaning out or avoiding it for fear of looking uneducated or ignorant, offending the client, being perceived as incompetent, or admitting that it is a cultural experience with which they are unfamiliar. This concept aligns with collaborative and constructivist approaches to counseling. Returning to the example, a counselor could invite their client to share how belonging to a motorcycle club impacts their values and relationships, disclose that they don't know much about motorcycle clubs and will do some reading outside of session so they know more by the next time they meet, and ask the client what's important about that part of their identity.

Developing Cultural Comfort

Developing cultural comfort requires effort and reflection in one's intrapersonal, interpersonal, and professional domains. This section provides ideas for enhancing each domain related to cultural comfort. The examples are not an exhaustive list but rather a foundational structure to build on throughout your career.

Intrapersonal. As with most critical concepts in counselor development, it is important to start with inward reflection. Counselors have ethical responsibilities to maintain competency to provide effective services (ACA, 2014; AMHCA, 2020; ASCA, 2022; CRCC, 2023). Researchers have shown that when a counselor's discomfort is high, they are less likely to engage in opportunities to increase their competency (Hook et al., 2017), contributing to higher chances of causing client harm and early termination of services. This research finding needs to be balanced with what was stated earlier in this section: The aim is not to completely remove our anxiety but to channel it into motivation to change and grow. We encourage counselors across their careers to identify their areas of cultural discomfort, with the understanding that comfort levels may change with time, experiences, and intentionality.

A way to pinpoint discomfort is by using formal assessments, such as the *Cultural Comfort Scale* (Pérez-Rojas et al., 2019; see Table 3.3). This assessment is taken by clients to assess the cultural comfort of their counselor. Further, this assessment can be used in the classroom and supervisory settings to create and implement goals based on the scoring, especially while viewing client recordings. For example, a practicum student could have their client take this assessment and share the results with their supervisor while showing a session recording with that client. We very rarely have the client's perceptions available during supervision, so this assessment can create wonderful dialogue between supervisors and supervisees. Also, it can be used in counseling practice sessions, where one student is the client and the other is the counselor. After the practice session, the student playing the client could fill out the assessment and discuss it with the student who was the counselor.

TABLE 3.3 Cultural Comfort Scale

When important parts of my culture come up or are discussed, my therapist ...	**Strongly Disagree**	**Disagree**	**Unsure**	**Agree**	**Strongly Agree**
1. stumbles with words.	1	2	3	4	5
2. becomes defensive.	1	2	3	4	5
3. appears anxious.	1	2	3	4	5
4. seems comfortable talking with me.	1	2	3	4	5
5. changes the focus to another topic.	1	2	3	4	5
6. seems angry.	1	2	3	4	5
7. seems unsure about how to behave.	1	2	3	4	5
8. has a relaxed demeanor.	1	2	3	4	5

(Continued)

TABLE 3.3 *(Continued)*

When important parts of my culture come up or are discussed, my therapist ...	Strongly Disagree	Disagree	Unsure	Agree	Strongly Agree
9. seems comfortable in our interaction.	1	2	3	4	5
10. seems at ease with me.	1	2	3	4	5
11. seems genuine.	1	2	3	4	5
12. appears guarded.	1	2	3	4	5
13. seems annoyed.	1	2	3	4	5

Note. Negative subscale = 1, 2, 3, 5, 6, 7, 12, 13 (reverse code); positive subscale = 4, 8, 9, 10, 11.

Source: Pérez-Rojas et al. (2019).

In addition to educational and clinical conversations, counselors must acknowledge how much or little exposure they have had to cultural identities different than their own. While exposure to diverse individuals and people across one's lifespan can be ideal for increasing cultural comfort, that is not always realistic for every counselor based on geographic location. However, that does not justify limited exposure as counselors enter the field. Instead, using the time during your training program to expose yourself to diverse cultures, perspectives, and worldviews can broaden your understanding and empathy toward others (Day-Vines et al., 2018) and increase your cultural comfort. Counselors need to increase their exposure before seeing clients to build their comfort and humility without relying solely on their clients to teach them.

BOX 3.3 **PAUSE AND REFLECT: THINKING ABOUT MY EXPERIENCES**

1. Are there cultural groups or identities that I have had little personal experience with or that may be new to me?
2. In my day-to-day life, do I engage with people who hold different identities than my own? How comfortable am I in those interactions?
3. When I engage with media (e.g., television, social media, reading), do I seek out stories that help me understand people and places that may be unfamiliar to me?
4. In my community (e.g., neighborhood, religious community, sports community, hobbies), do I interact with people who hold different identities than my own? How comfortable am I engaging in conversations with them that may involve the topic of culture?
5. Growing up, was my school/neighborhood/community diverse?
6. In my household, how did my primary caregivers model engagement with people or topics that were unfamiliar? Was it something they were excited about? Afraid of? Avoided?

Interpersonal. As counselors work to increase their personal comfort, their interpersonal skills can be enhanced. Cultural comfort can foster deep interpersonal relationships and dialogue between the counselor and the client and foster greater rapport and trust, the conditions needed for therapeutic success, especially with clients who have historically excluded identities (Day-Vines et al., 2018; Mejia et al., 2018; Owen et al., 2017; Toomey & Carlson, 2022). An increase in cultural comfort does not mean sessions will be easier. Possessing a solid cultural comfort level means having more challenging conversations, which can evoke emotional reactions and content from the client. Clients' reactions can be challenging for the counselor and warrant further personal reflection on their comfort level. Counselors are encouraged to reflect on these conversations post-session and consider what ruptures, if any, may have developed and ways they can continue the conversation during the next session. Additionally, reflection may include considering your theoretical framework and any interventions you used during the session. In addition to personal reflection, it may be helpful to consult with other counselors about their experiences with broaching culture to glean aspects you may want to implement or to learn from *pain points* other clinicians have experienced.

Professional. Counseling programs are a starting point for growing your skills to work with a variety of clients, but it cannot stop there. Adhering to ethical guidelines, counselors are responsible for maintaining a robust understanding of the most recent empirical data for the various reasons clients may seek counseling. A way to adhere to this ethical practice is by seeking continuing education from reputable sources. Within the counseling profession, many practitioners and scholars have substantial knowledge and experience in increasing cultural comfort and understanding critical components for engaging with diverse individuals. Seeking professional development opportunities through conferences, webinars, books, peer-reviewed articles, and organizational memberships is necessary. Some professional counseling associations and divisions that may be helpful include the following:

- Association for Adult Development and Aging
- Association for Child and Adolescent Counseling
- American College Counseling Association
- Association for Multicultural Counseling and Development
- American Rehabilitation Counseling Association
- Association for Spiritual, Ethical, and Religious Values in Counseling
- Counselors for Social Justice
- International Association for Additions and Offender Counselors
- Military and Government Counseling Association
- Society for Sexual, Affectional, Intersex, and Gender Expansive Identities
- Association for Counseling Sexuality and Sexual Wellness

Ongoing learning, reflection, and collaboration can provide exposure to different thoughts and ideas while validating that every counselor is on a unique developmental journey. In addition, growing and maintaining a diverse network of professional counselors can lead to more supportive supervision and consultation. Counselors should not wait until they need support before developing a professional network but instead, begin building their network as a counselor in training.

Cultural Opportunities

As you have learned, the multicultural orientation model is focused on *ways of being* with clients. The three core concepts of this model deepen the therapeutic relationship by creating a felt sense that the counselor is open to exploring the client's culture at any point in the therapeutic process. You have already learned about the first two components of this model, cultural humility and cultural comfort; in this section, we explore the third component, *cultural opportunities*.

One way to deepen the therapeutic alliance, which we know from research is a major contributor to positive counseling outcomes (Norcross & Wampold, 2011), is by capitalizing on cultural opportunities. *Cultural opportunities* are *guideposts* or *flags* in counseling that indicate a space where the client's "cultural beliefs, values, or other aspects of the client's identity could be explored" (Hook et al., 2017, p. 32). Think of them like exit ramps on the highway that we can choose either to explore or to speed past in a rush to get to our destination. Sometimes we may take the ramp and shortly find out that we need to hop back on the highway to head toward our original destination, and that's okay. Counselors and clients both report that explicitly addressing cultural concerns is not always needed (Huey et al., 2014). But sometimes, we take the ramp and find ourselves in a new place that offers a wealth of opportunities for growth and exploration. Either way, the intention is to clearly communicate to our clients that we are willing and motivated to explore all aspects of their identities because we know that culture impacts help-seeking behaviors, our client's description of their presenting concerns, and their worldview (Arnault, 2009). Factors outside of counseling that are impacted by culture play a significant role in client motivation to access resources, so counselors must explore culture consistently and appropriately.

Cultural opportunities can be client or counselor initiated. Client-initiated cultural opportunities occur when clients explicitly state values and beliefs or share cultural antidotes (Owen et al., 2016). The counselor's role in those instances is to remain curious, nonjudgmental, and respectful of the connection the client makes to their cultural experiences by prompting them to continue to explore that connection. For example, "I noticed that you mentioned religion may be a factor in your feelings of guilt concerning boundaries. Say more." Also, we can see how cultural humility and cultural comfort play a key role in a counselor's awareness of these opportunities and willingness to engage with them. The counselor must have genuine curiosity about the client's lived experience and be comfortable enough to explore an area that they may not be familiar with.

Counselor-initiated cultural opportunities are gentle invitations from the counselor that allow the client space to explore if the presenting concern or if the information that they provided has a connection to their cultural experiences (Owen et al., 2016). For example, a counselor might say, "Monica, I heard you mention that work is a primary area where you are experiencing distress, and I'm curious if your experience as a Black woman in a predominately White work environment might be contributing to some of that stress?" In this example, the counselor's invitation is grounded in previous knowledge of workplace dynamics for Black women, and the counselor leverages that information into an opportunity for the client to determine if it matches their experience.

The key ingredient to successfully engaging cultural opportunities is ensuring that they aren't abrupt interjections in the counseling process or forced; they need to be natural components of the conversation. There aren't set rules for when these conversations need to be had or how often they need to happen (Hook et al., 2016). Ideally, culturally humble counselors with a sense of ease engaging in cultural conversations will view cultural opportunities as a naturally evolving process between the client and the counselor that ultimately leads the client to feel that the counselor is willing and motivated to explore their cultural identities (Owen et al., 2016).

Clients who reported that their counselor took opportunities to have cultural discussions had better treatment outcomes (Owen et al., 2016). This highlights the importance of the counselor's responsibility for not only noticing when clients bring up topics about identity and culture but also engaging clients in further exploration. Hook et al. (2017) hypothesized that counselors may hesitate to engage in cultural conversations for a variety of reasons, including their anxieties, conscious and unconscious bias, and counselor burnout. Although these hesitations may be reasonable initially, they do not let counselors off the hook. Counselors must work through their reluctance so they are culturally present and attentive to clients during sessions.

Capitalizing on cultural opportunities is not only about being attentive to them during sessions but also about how counselors engage in the conversations when they have them. As such, cultural opportunities are influenced by cultural humility and cultural comfort. Cultural humility functions as a buffer in counseling relationships, especially in instances when counselors miss opportunities to discuss culture (Davis et al., 2016). Counselors who either intentionally or unintentionally avoid conversations about a client's culture may be engaging in cultural microaggressions (Sue, 2007) or, at the very least, are communicating to their clients that the complexities of their cultural identities are not a welcome topic of discussion. Clients who rated their counselors as culturally humble tended to provide more flexibility for their counselor in instances when they missed a cultural opportunity, in contrast with clients who rated their counselor as low in cultural humility (Davis et al., 2016). We must remember that all social norms and pleasantries outside of the counseling office are the default inside the counseling office unless counselors intentionally create a space that is more open, nonjudgmental, flexible, and cultivates conversations that some may consider *taboo* or *off-limits*. Being a counselor who truly engages in the core tenets of the multicultural orientation doesn't involve deviating from your treatment plan or adapting any theoretical orientation. It simply involves remaining truly curious about the intersectional factors that impact client wellness and being willing to *exit the highway* for a moment to explore.

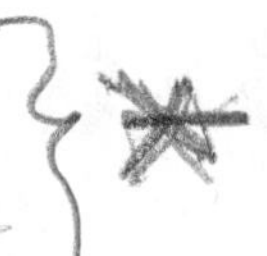

Always a Process: Making and Sustaining Commitment

In this section, we discuss several ways counselors can continue to develop their multicultural orientation. As you will recall, there are both intrapersonal and interpersonal components to this model. The intrapersonal components align well with the reflective nature of many assignments embedded in counseling programs. The interpersonal components stem from cultivating a curiosity about your clients and their worldviews while managing your experiences of stress/anxiety as they pertain to engaging in cultural conversations.

Identifying Areas of Strength and Growing Edges

In the above sections, we provide examples of how to identify your strengths and growing edges as it pertains to cultural humility, cultural comfort, and cultural opportunities. The first step in this process is knowing yourself. Are there specific topics, identities, or life situations that a client might bring into counseling that you aren't familiar with or may feel uncomfortable processing? What are these topics? What knowledge do you believe will help you? Who are people you can discuss your hesitations with? How can you use your comfort with other topics to increase your comfort in these areas?

Another approach to learning more about yourself is to use assessments. There are scales to measure cultural humility (Hook et al., 2013; Zhu et al., 2022a; see Table 3.4), cultural comfort (Pérez-Rojas et al., 2019), and cultural opportunities (Owen et al., 2016). Depending on the scale, some are counselor self-reports, and others survey clients to rate their counselor. We know that counselors often rate themselves higher in cultural engagement than clients do, so it is important to have multiple data points while assessing strengths and areas of growth.

TABLE 3.4 Cultural Humility and Enactment Scale

In general, my counselor ...						
1. is open to exploring cultural topics.	1	2	3	4	5	6
2. is open to changing their views on cultural issues.	1	2	3	4	5	6
3. is curious about what my culture means to me.	1	2	3	4	5	6
4. is interested in my cultural views.	1	2	3	4	5	6
5. is open to cultural views that are different from their own.	1	2	3	4	5	6
6. enjoys discussing ideas of different cultures.	1	2	3	4	5	6
7. asks clarifying questions about cultural issues when they are uncertain.	1	2	3	4	5	6
8. is willing to examine their own biases.	1	2	3	4	5	6
9. recognizes the limitation of their cultural views.	1	2	3	4	5	6
10. seeks corrective feedback for their cultural views.	1	2	3	4	5	6
11. is open to corrective feedback for their cultural views.	1	2	3	4	5	6
12. is willing expand their cultural view(s).	1	2	3	4	5	6
13. recognizes their biases.	1	2	3	4	5	6
14. has a stereotypical view of my culture. [R]	1	2	3	4	5	6
15. pretends to know something when they have no idea. [R]	1	2	3	4	5	6

16. prioritizes their cultural views over mine. [R]	1	2	3	4	5	6
17. is arrogant about their cultural views. [R]	1	2	3	4	5	6
18. imposes their cultural views on me. [R]	1	2	3	4	5	6
19. makes me feel like my cultural views are inferior. [R]	1	2	3	4	5	6
20. patronizes me in discussing cultural views. [R]	1	2	3	4	5	6
21. is defensive when their cultural view(s) are challenged. [R]	1	2	3	4	5	6
22. minimizes my cultural view(s). [R]	1	2	3	4	5	6

1 = Strongly disagree; 2 = Disagree; 3 = Somewhat disagree; 4 = Somewhat agree; 5 = Agree; 6 = Strongly agree

Note. This scale is intended to be completed by a client. The client is instructed to please think about their interactions with their counselor in general. Using the scale below, please indicate the extent to which you agree or disagree with the following statements about your counselor. [R] indicates reverse scoring.

Source: Zhu, et al. (2022a).

Make a Commitment to Personal Cultural Development

Making a firm commitment to anything can be a challenge for many people, including counselors! As you assess your readiness to commit to your personal cultural development, we offer the following ideas to assist you in your process.

- Have a clear understanding of your own cultural identity and the parts of that identity that feel more salient in the counseling relationship (this may fluctuate based on the client, the setting, and what is happening in your personal life).
- Continue to reevaluate your comfort level by engaging with a variety of topics and identities.
- Intentionally sustain engagement in activities that expose you to cultures that are different from your own. You need to go beyond attending a short cultural festival or eating at a restaurant that is different from where you'd typically eat. The key to real cultural development is *sustained* engagement and reciprocal relationships. We don't want to go into other people's cultural spaces and "take" cultural experiences. We want to go into spaces different from our own and authentically engage in cultural experiences.
- Place yourself in situations that make you feel a little uncomfortable, and practice channeling that discomfort into curiosity and attunement.
- Notice when your ego kicks in, and practice leading from your heart.
- Foster curiosity, especially while admitting your limitations.
- Practice noticing cultural opportunities with your friends and family members, and inviting them to expand on how their culture shapes their worldview.
- Seek out and learn directly from people who belong to communities you are not familiar with; so many experts are willing to share their knowledge.

Using the Multicultural Orientation Model

The overarching goal of the multicultural orientation model is to have authentic relationships with clients that allow them to bring their whole selves into the counseling process. Additionally, counselors know themselves well enough to understand their limitations and be *egoless* when admitting they have reached them. It's okay to say to a client, "This seems important to you, but I have limited knowledge of it. I'm wondering if you'd be okay explaining the basics, and I'll do research of my own before our next session." Responses like this allow the client to provide a foundation but do not shift the burden on them to do all the teaching. It can be scary to admit when we don't know or understand something. As graduate students, you are constantly trying to show your peers, faculty, and site supervisors that you understand and know what you are doing. This model is asking you to do something slightly different and embrace the limitations of your humanity. When our minds don't have the information, lead with your heart, not with your ego.

Advocacy

The key to advocacy is to listen to communities who are being marginalized and not make assumptions about what they want or need. One of the most challenging aspects of advocacy is realizing that the process is collaborative and even with the best intentions, professional counselors can be perceived as dominating an initiative sometimes. By default, professional counselors hold privilege and power. We have access to higher education, systems that our clients may struggle to connect with and are perceived as experts in various psychological issues. It can be challenging for us to understand how to use our privilege and power in ways that do not take autonomy away from our clients who are marginalized.

Multicultural orientation and advocacy naturally fit together because some of the strongest advocacy initiatives come from a servant-leadership model (Greenleaf, 2002), which parallels many of the tenets of multicultural orientation. The process of ongoing, in-depth self-reflection and lifelong commitment to self-evaluation and self-critique strengthens advocacy while allowing the focus to be on connection rather than being an expert on clients' cultural experiences (Masters et al., 2019). Servant leaders are viewed as servants first and leaders second (Greenleaf, 1977). They engage in advocacy and leadership when it aligns with their strengths, and they support those around them when the leadership/advocacy position makes more sense for someone else to spearhead. Servant leadership is a hallmark in counseling (Cashwell & Sweeney, 2016). To embody servant leadership and use it as a framework to empower marginalized groups, counselors must know their strengths and limitations, and genuinely take pleasure in watching others step into the spotlight. At its core, that's what the multicultural orientation model is asking us to do. It's asking us to make space in the counseling relationship for our clients' intersectional identities even if we are unfamiliar with them, uncomfortable with them, or have no prior experience with them. These opportunities can and should be faced with curiosity and a commitment to empowering our clients to show up as authentically as they would like to in session. We will discuss advocacy in greater depth and detail in Chapter 5.

Conclusion

In this chapter, you were introduced to the multicultural orientation model, which is a model that encompasses three concepts: cultural humility, cultural comfort, and cultural opportunities. We began by providing a foundation on what this model is and how it can be used alongside the concept of multicultural competence and any theoretical orientation. Then we moved into the specifics of what each of the three concepts entails and how they work together to create multicultural orientation. We finished by discussing ways to continue to develop your multicultural orientation and how it parallels many of the advocacy/leadership tenets embedded in servant leadership. We hope this chapter left you feeling empowered and energized as you think about engaging with clients and students who may hold a variety of intersectional identities.

Questions for Reflection

1. What are areas in which you feel culturally competent? What about areas where you feel culturally humble? Make a list and reflect on these areas and your levels of cultural humility.
2. What are some ways you have seen cultural humility modeled in your personal, professional, or academic life?
3. What are some examples in which you have not seen cultural humility practiced? What was the outcome?
4. When considering the multicultural orientation model, what are your areas of cultural comfort?
5. When considering the multicultural orientation model, what are your areas of cultural opportunities?

Applying What You Have Learned

Activity #1: Pop Culture Check—Identifying Beliefs, Values, and Cultural Experiences

Choose one of your favorite television shows, and pick an episode at random. While you are watching, keep a tally of instances where a character references a belief, value, or cultural experience. Additionally, you can note times when you are curious if culture played a role in the character's reaction. Are you surprised by how often cultural opportunities come up when you are looking for them?

Activity #2: It's Hard to Be Humble

We have all experienced being wrong. Being wrong, depending on the context, can bring about all kinds of feelings—embarrassment, anger, anxiety, incompetence—just to name a few. As professional counselors, there are many times in which we are "right," but there are instances in which we are "wrong," too. It's important to understand what your reactions are when you miss the mark so you're prepared to handle it professionally *when* (not if!) it happens with clients.

Jot down how you react and the feelings you experience when you are wrong within the following contexts: with your parents/caregivers, siblings, close friends, acquaintances, in the classroom, at work with a colleague, and at work with your boss. You can add to this list if you'd like! What is the common reaction you have? With whom are you most likely to have a humble response when you make an error? In which relationship are you more likely to have an adverse response or one that is not so humble? Now, think through how you would like to respond and feel when you slip up with a client—it can be similar, different, or a combination of the examples you listed. How will you work to ensure this is your consistent approach with clients?

Credit

Fig. 3.1: Joshua N. Hook, et al., *Cultural Humility: Engaging Diverse Identities in Therapy*, American Psychological Association, 2017.

CHAPTER 4

Systems and Structural Oppression

Madeline Clark, Monica L. Coleman, and Jennifer M. Cook

> *To have privilege in one or more areas does not mean you are wholly privileged. Surrendering to the acceptance of privilege is difficult, but it is really all that is expected. What I remind myself, regularly, is this: the acknowledgment of my privilege is not a denial of the ways I have been and am marginalized, the ways I have suffered.*
>
> —Roxane Gay

CHAPTER OVERVIEW

Understanding systems and systemic oppression is a complex endeavor because systems, while singular forces, are rarely siloed entities—they are intertwined with one another and have both apparent and hidden impacts on other systems and the individuals who comprise them. Systems, and their subsequent complexity and impact, are discussed throughout this text because counselors cannot ignore the external forces that affect clients' functioning, and in some cases, they cause clients' distress! So, while there is much to learn and discover about systems and their impacts now and throughout your career, we hope you will embrace the intricacies and dive deep into how understanding and applying a systems approach to clinical work can benefit your clients. In the first section, we start with the basics by naming and defining key concepts and terms to start you on your systems journey. Then, we share a brief historical overview and explain structural oppression and how it differs from individual discrimination. Finally, we explore ways counselors can contribute to systemic change both inside and outside the counseling environment.

LEARNING OBJECTIVES

By the end of this chapter, students will be able to:

1. explain the myriad of ways systems impact individuals and groups,
2. list the differences between systemic oppression and individual biases and biased behaviors, and
3. identify their own privileged and marginalized identities and how to address those identities with diverse clients in counseling settings.

CACREP 2016 STANDARDS

The information in this chapter supports the following standards:

- 2.F.2.a. Multicultural and pluralistic characteristics within and among diverse groups nationally and internationally
- 2.F.2.b. Theories and models of multicultural counseling, cultural identity development, and social justice and advocacy
- 2.F.2.c. Multicultural counseling competencies
- 2.F.2.d. The impact of heritage, attitudes, beliefs, understandings, and acculturative experiences on an individual's views of others
- 2.F.2.e. The effects of power and privilege for counselors and clients
- 2.F.2.h. Strategies for identifying and eliminating barriers, prejudices, and processes of intentional and unintentional oppression and discrimination
- 2.F.3.f systemic and environmental factors that affect human development, functioning, and behavior

CACREP 2024 STANDARDS

The information in this chapter supports the following standards:

- 3.B.1. theories and models of multicultural counseling, social justice, and advocacy
- 3.B.2. the influence of heritage, cultural identities, attitudes, values, beliefs, understandings, within-group differences, and acculturative experiences on individuals' worldviews
- 3.B.4. the effects of historical events, multigenerational trauma, and current issues on diverse cultural groups in the U.S. and globally
- 3.B.5. the effects of stereotypes, overt and covert discrimination, racism, power, oppression, privilege, marginalization, microaggressions, and violence on counselors and clients
- 3.B.6. the effects of various socio-cultural influences, including public policies, social movements, and cultural values, on mental and physical health and wellness
- 3.B.7. disproportional effects of poverty, income disparities, and health disparities toward people with marginalized identities
- 3.B.9. strategies for identifying and eliminating barriers, prejudices, and processes of intentional and unintentional oppression and discrimination
- 3.B.10. guidelines developed by professional counseling organizations related to social justice, advocacy, and working with individuals with diverse cultural identities
- 3.C.11. systemic, cultural, and environmental factors that affect lifespan development, functioning, behavior, resilience, and overall wellness

Systems Theory and Ecological Approaches

Systems Theory: General

Systems theory is a broad term that posits that the parts of any whole are best understood by the relationships and connections between them. For example, think about your workplace. Each workplace has a name and an expressed purpose for existing (e.g., a restaurant to feed people, a school to educate, a hospital to heal). However, no business can fulfill its purpose without people.

In every workplace there is a management structure–the folks who are owners, those who make high-level decisions, those who run day-to-day operations, etc. Of course, then, there are the individuals whose jobs are to do the day-to-day work; they provide the services, whatever that is. As you know, there are no workplaces in which people simply complete their tasks and *never* interact with others. They have bosses to please, constituents who rely on them, etc., even those who work independently (e.g., a work-from-home code writer, a janitor who works third shift). These interactions and relationships are connections. There are connections between employees who work together regularly and collaborate, those who just happen to be in the same department and interact infrequently, and connections between those who manage the employees below them, even if they have never met one another. Each person's contributions, or lack thereof, impact the system. This connectional, relational fact cannot be ignored, even if the players involved, the connections between them, and the subsequent impacts are unknown or not readily apparent. *System* denotes connection and when there is connection of any kind, there is the possibility for impact. Notably, while there are individuals who create the whole that is the system, the focus within a systems perspective is the overall *unit* rather than the individuals who comprise it. This is a key point, particularly because U.S. culture tends to be ensconced in an *individual perspective* rather than a systemic perspective.

Systems Theory in Counseling

In professional counseling, *systems theory* is a specific approach to understanding and working with clients. Systems theory underlies approaches to family (e.g., Bowenian, structural family therapy, strategic therapy) and couple/marriage counseling (e.g., emotionally focused therapy, Gottman method). Systems theory within counseling recognizes that individuals are connected through the familial relationships they are born into, brought into, and choose to join. These relationships result in strengths and resiliencies as much as they can inflict pain and teach maladaptive functioning. While couple, marriage, and family therapists/counselors usually work with *the system* (i.e., the couple, the family) and see the relationship as *the client* rather than an individual, counselors who work with individual clients understand and recognize that the individual client with whom they are working does not exist in isolation: They are a family member, a friend, and they can be a worker, a lover, a volunteer, a student, and many, many other roles that involve human relationships and connection.

Counseling systems theories help counselors to understand that even when they are counseling an individual client, that client brings with them all of their connections and relationships and that it can be helpful to conceptualize the client as having all of the people who are part of these important relationships sitting right there in the room with them because of their impact on the client. Moreover, clients bring the external systems of which they are a part with them into session too. These systems can include their school, workplace, religious organization, and clubs, as well as larger systems, such as their neighborhood, community, the town/city/state in which they live, and the overall society and culture, inclusive of values and norms. Ecological systems theory (EST) accounts for these systems and how they interact with and impact the client.

Ecological Systems Theory

Through general systems theory and counseling systems theory we discussed above, we have established that no one exists in isolation because they have relationships and connections, for better and for worse. Now, we discuss an approach that accounts for how systems interact and the impact they have on individuals: *EST*.

Ecological approaches to understanding human connections are not new. There is historical knowledge that the people who lived before the common era (BCE) in what we know as Mesopotamia, Indigenous populations in North America, etc., lived their lives through the shared understanding of multiple connections—connections to one another, the earth, the seasons, spiritual entities, just to name a few—and that these connections were essential for their survival.

While there are many ways in which people conceptualize the interconnectedness of systems and their impact on individuals, we use Bronfenbrenner's (1979, 1994) EST throughout this text. EST was developed originally to explain children's development by understanding their cultural, societal, biological, and interpersonal contexts. While this theory was originally created to understand children's development, it has been adapted to understand the impacts systems have on the lives of all individuals.

EST is comprised of five levels, each of which interacts with one another, with the individual placed in the middle (see Figure 4.1). The circular shape of the figure represents the connected and layered nature of systems and their impact on the individual who resides in the middle of the circle. The arrows indicate movement within a level (i.e., mesosystem) and between levels.

The individual is situated in the middle of the model and the first proximal system is the microsystem. The microsystem reflects the relationships (e.g., family, peer group, colleagues)

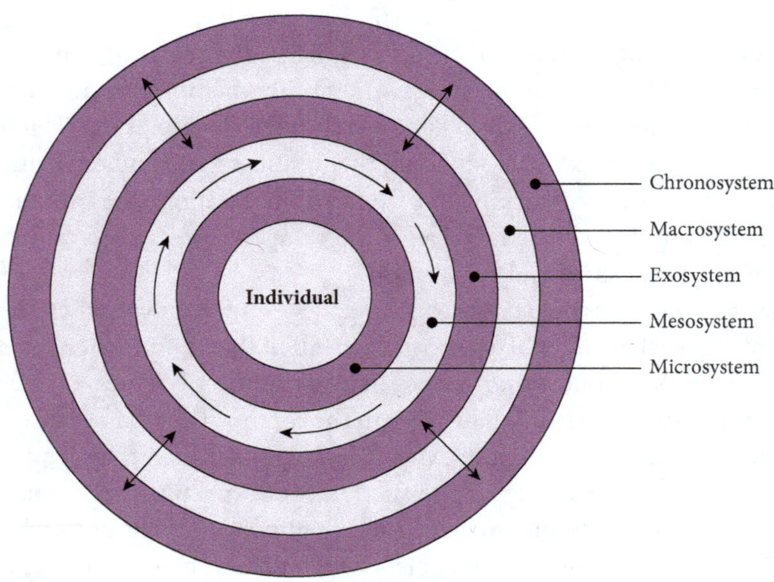

FIGURE 4.1 Bronfenbrenner's EST

and systems (e.g., school, workplace, clubs, religious organizations) of which the individual is a part, while the mesosystem accounts for the interactions between relationships within the microsystem. Such relationships can include parents' relationships with a child's teacher, coach, or peers or a husband's relationship with his partner's friends.

The exosystem accounts for systems that are reasonably close to the individual but with which the individual does not have direct contact. Take, for example, a parent or partner's workplace. What occurs in their workplace can have an indirect impact on the individual depending on if their loved one has predominantly positive or negative experiences there. For example, a parent whose boss demands 30 hours of overtime per week may not be all that pleasant when they come home or may not be readily available for their child physically or emotionally, causing strain on the child and the household. On the flip side, a partner who works balanced hours and experiences fulfillment in their work may have more emotional and time resources to share with their partner, creating the conditions for a healthier relationship.

The macrosystem can be conceptualized as the cultural-societal system. While the person who is situated in the middle of the model has their own intersecting dominant and nondominant cultural identities, the macrosystem denotes the overarching forces of the dominant culture. Facets of the dominant culture include values, beliefs, and ways of being that have been established societally as the *norm*. Inherent to this are power structures, privilege, and oppression that have been institutionalized as *appropriate* and *normal*, yet clear discrepancies are present. Discrimination occurs and manifests as policies and laws because of how individuals and groups function based on these overarching *norms* and structures. Importantly, macrosystem *norms* are communicated and instilled now more than ever through the internet and social media, yet it's important to remember that media communication occurred prior to these modern conventions (e.g., broadcast TV, advertisements, print media). The macrosystem gives insight into why societal change is slow. There are individuals and groups within systems who endeavor to keep these systems in place–overtly and covertly, consciously and unconsciously—because they benefit from the power and privilege they receive from how the system functions currently. Furthermore, we must acknowledge that the United States is an incredibly large country with vast regional differences; this, too, impacts societal change and why it seems unduly slow or even impossible.

The final outer system is the chronosystem. As the term suggests, the chronosystem is concerned with time, specifically, the events that occur over time. These events are both individual and group based. Individual events include expected milestones like starting school, partnership or marriage, and death of a loved one, as well as unexpected events like acquiring a disability, moving to another country, or earning an advanced degree. Group events can occur at the local, state, national, or international levels yet have far-reaching impacts. Examples of impactful community-level events include the water crises in Flint, Michigan, and Jackson, Mississippi, the New York City trash strike, or the Columbine, Virginia Tech, and Sandy Hook school shooting massacres. State-level crises include a variety of events like the wildfires in California, a typhoon in Hawai'i, or even restrictive state laws like limiting abortion rights or educational restrictions that have occurred in states such as Florida. Importantly, local and state events can have national implications. For example, school shooting massacres have led to protests, population outcries, and national policy conversations about gun control, while hurricanes in Florida and wildfires in California have impacted food availability and the cost of food nationally. However, national events occur as well. For instance, national elections and federal law changes impact people in the United States regularly. When thinking about international events, instances of war often come to mind, yet there was no bigger worldwide disruption than the COVID-19 pandemic.

The key to understanding and utilizing EST is to identify the *impact* and then ascertain interventions to mitigate the negative impact. For counselors, the impact we work with most directly and regularly is on individuals, couples, and families, though using EST means we acknowledge and work for change in further reaching ways than these three human points. In sum, EST highlights impact, while also focusing on our attention to areas in which social justice and advocacy are necessary on a larger scale. Now, with a clearer understanding of systems and EST, you are better prepared to understand how these systems work to oppress or empower the clients we serve.

Structural Oppression

Laws, policies, practices, and norms can sometimes become so interwoven into our society that they impact us all without any focused effort to enforce them. In such cases, these matters are considered *structural or systemic*, because they are deeply embedded and self-perpetuating in society. Because power is innate to laws, policies, practices, and norms, they can be empowering or oppressive depending on whether they produce equitable outcomes. When laws, policies, practices, and norms intentionally or unintentionally lead to disparate outcomes for certain groups, we must investigate if *structural oppression* is present.

Structural oppression is the unfair and/or unjust distribution, administration, and application of laws, policies, societal practices, and societal norms in ways that disempower and harm specific groups in society. The cycle of socialization often perpetuates historic structural oppression (Harro, 2000). Structural oppression is difficult to pinpoint because it is often uncritically and passively supported through societal practices and norms, becoming almost invisible to those who navigate life without a critical eye. Though not all, many laws and policies are designed to uphold whatever practices and norms a society considers moral (Greenberg, 2014). Yet, morality itself can be skewed by varying societal practices and norms depending on from where one's morality is derived (e.g., religion, economics). Thus, morality undergirding laws and policies sometimes leads to unfair and unjust outcomes for certain groups. Using a critical perspective, laws and policies that may be intended to promote good can impact groups in ways that deteriorate their health and well-being. When left uninspected and unchallenged, these laws and policies may permeate society and lead to inequities that impact entire populations for generations. For example, consider the wide acceptance and codification of school segregation prior to integration in the 1960s and the negative, enduring impact school segregation has had on the education of children of color in the US for generations. While at one time, segregation was considered to be a *common good*, we learned that it was not good for anyone and, more so, it resulted in numerous deleterious effects for students of color.

The very laws, policies, practices, and norms that create structural oppression are the root causes of social determinants of mental health risk factors, including housing inadequacy, food insecurity, and exposure to community violence, which ultimately lead to poorer health and mental health outcomes. Because social determinants of mental health are conditions in the social environments where individuals live, work, and play that impact their ability to thrive in life, structural oppression is a public health threat that must be addressed to promote well-being for all (Compton & Shim, 2014).

Understanding the Historical Context of Structural Oppression

The history of structural oppression is rooted in power struggles and can be seen throughout the world. In some cases, human-led catastrophic events have left large groups of people marginalized for decades, even centuries (e.g., the trade of enslaved people from the African continent across countries in the Western hemisphere). Common among these tragedies are hierarchical ideologies that promote the attainment and retention of power by individuals and groups with specific social identities over others, whether by force, manipulation, codification, or normalization. In fact, one of the hallmarks of civilization is the development of social and economic classes, which normalized hierarchies that assigned value to individuals and groups based on their attained social and economic statuses. However, a glance into the history of landownership, one of the earliest and most enduring vehicles for building wealth, reveals how frequently land has been obtained through implicit and explicit violence (Blomley, 2019). As such, some of the wealthiest heirs in the world continue to benefit today from historic violence that left others oppressed.

As an example, in the documentary film *Descendant* by Margaret Brown (2022), Black descendants of captured and enslaved Africans from the ship, *Clotida*, share their personal and generational experiences. In this film, a wealthy landowner and enslaver, Timothy Meaher, captures Africans and brings them, illegally, to Mobile, Alabama. The descendants discuss their ancestors' and their personal experiences with historic violence, including how it impacts them and their community today.

The use of violence in creating structural oppression based on race is well-documented in the United States when White colonizers, who largely disregarded the humanity of Indigenous people and communities, violently stole land, goods, people—whatever they decided they wanted. The colonizers thought themselves superior to the Indigenous peoples and forced them to leave their land or risk being murdered. Later, White colonizers would force Black people from Africa into chattel slavery. Chattel slavery secured generational wealth for many White slave owners while creating a pathway to generational poverty for many Black people. At times, both religious texts and academic scholarship have justified racism (Duriez & Hutsebaut, 2000), making it one of the most difficult forms of structural oppression to dismantle. While structural oppression was partially addressed by the Civil War in terms of making it illegal to own slaves, the impact continues today for the descendants of those who were enslaved because structural inequality was not fully resolved.

Often, health and mental health knowledge systems and practices have instigated structural oppression and structural racism, evidenced by early research that promoted ideas that there are biological differences among people based on race, ethnicity, and other identity factors. For example, for centuries medical students were erroneously taught that Black patients could endure more pain than White patients. Despite this information being scientifically debunked, the idea that Black people do not need as much pain management treatment as White people endures (Hoffman et al., 2016), creating a cascading effect of negative health outcomes. Similarly, the mental health field previously classified *homosexuality*, or sexual attraction to the same sex/gender, as a disorder (see Chapter 15 for more information). While evidence has proven otherwise, conversion therapy, the practice that was once used to *treat* homosexuality, persists in some states despite the allied mental health professions opposing it.

Every organization in the allied mental health professions has issued statements that oppose conversion, reparative, and aversion therapies for individuals who identify within the LGB spectrum. Many do not realize that health organizations have issued statements too. Visit https://www.hrc.org/resources/policy-and-position-statements-on-conversion-therapy to investigate the different statements and to compare and contrast how each organization has addressed this harmful practice.

The counseling field is uniquely positioned to address structural oppression in many ways with micro-, meso-, and macrolevel interventions. Birthed out of the vocational guidance movement, counseling has always embraced elements of social justice. A range of frameworks including feminist theory, relational-cultural theory (RCT), and social justice counseling, all illustrate the profession's desire to dismantle structural oppression. However, in practice, this is not clearly discernable but rather obscured by superficial attempts to be a values-free profession. An intentional effort to work against structural oppression in the counseling profession is necessary because our clients and their lived experiences of oppression demand it.

Structural Oppression Versus Individual Discrimination

One of the challenges to understanding structural oppression is that persons who have dominant identities (e.g., White, upper social class, heterosexual, cisgender male) benefit from structural oppression, *whether they want to or not.* In the absence of experiencing oppression, an individual experiences privilege. For example, a person who is Christian or celebrates traditional Christian holidays typically receives days off from work or school that align with their belief system (e.g., winter breaks in the university system tend to align squarely with Christmas, spring break tends to fall at Easter for many primary and secondary schools). White supremacy protects people who are White (and in some cases White passing—see more on this in Chapter 7) from discrimination in the financial system and housing, from police violence, and much, much more. Essentially, these are the policies and societal structures that make life easier in terms of access and safety when you are a privileged person. In many cases, you could likely be benefiting from structural privileges without even knowing it. We (Drs. Clark and Cook) benefit from White supremacy, even though we definitely do not identify as White supremacists. While we are not White supremacists and work very hard to be anti-racist, being White has made our lives (and that of our family's, regarding generational mobility) much easier. You do not sign up to be an oppressor at birth; unfortunately, the system bestows that upon you. As you learned in Chapter 1, privilege is not something to feel guilty about but rather something to use to institute change.

What is challenging about addressing structural oppressions is that there is no one perpetrator because the system(s) itself maintains oppressions to uphold and reinforce the status quo and extant power structures (i.e., homeostasis). These oppressive forces have different names (see Table 4.1). Because these oppressions are systemic, all individuals in society are responsible for their existence, *especially* those of us who are privileged by these structures. There is no one White person to blame for White supremacy; we all must ameliorate it. There is no one man responsible for patriarchy; we all must work against it daily. All of us must actively work to revolutionize the structures and policies that oppress and marginalize others (see Chapter 5 for more information regarding advocacy!). While there are countless examples of structural oppression, we summarize some in the table below, and you will learn far more as you progress through the chapters in this text.

TABLE 4.1 Examples of Structural Oppressions

Cultural Group(s)	Example of Structural Oppression	The Oppressive Force
People of Color (POC)	Because of historical policies surrounding mortgages, housing values/appraisals, POC, especially Black Americans, have been excluded from buying homes (which limits one's ability to build equity), or when they can buy homes, they are frequently under-valued and/or they receive higher interest rates. For more on this housing inequity (redlining), see "What Is Redlining?" from the *New York Times*: https://www.nytimes.com/2021/08/17/realestate/what-is-redlining.html.	White Supremacy, Structural Racism (see Chapter 7)
Nondominant Ethnic Groups	 IMG 4.1. The United States has a long history of ethnocentrism and xenomisia. From early settlers (e.g., Irish) to later stages of settling (Italians, Jews, Chinese, Eastern Europeans), U.S. culture has excluded various groups to maintain power and authority over these ethnic groups. This includes job discrimination, housing discrimination, and violence, among others. Much of anti-ethnic sentiment is driven by White supremacy. For further reading, see the book *Working Toward Whiteness* (2006) by David Roediger.	Ethnocentrism, xenomisia, Racism (see Chapters 8 and 7)

(*Continued*)

TABLE 4.1 *(Continued)*

Cultural Group(s)	Example of Structural Oppression	The Oppressive Force
Immigrants and Refugees	Immigration policy in the United States is often race and class based. Who is offered immigration/citizenship in the United States creates a structural force that limits the composition of who is and can be a U.S. citizen (often driven by White supremacy and classist values). The Trump administration illustrated this oppression by targeting Latine immigrants (specifically Mexicans) as *dangerous* and Asian immigrants and people as *the cause* of COVID-19. Violence toward these groups drastically increased with hate crimes against Asians increasing by over 300% in 2021.	Xenomisia, Racism (see Chapters 7 and 9)
Indigenous Peoples	 IMG 4.2. Indigenous persons in the United States (and all settler colonial countries) experienced oppression at the hands of empires and colonizers. This included the loss of homeland, experiences of racism, and experiences of poverty. As a specific example, Indigenous children were taken from their families to "Indian Schools," where they were forced to speak English, cut their hair, and no longer engage in their cultural practices. These schools were funded by the federal government and were created to force Indigenous children to assimilate into a colonized United States. See more on Indian Schools here: https://www.nytimes.com/interactive/2023/08/30/us/native-american-boarding-schools.html	Settler Colonialism, Racism, Classism (see Chapters 7, 10, and 11)

Cultural Group(s)	Example of Structural Oppression	The Oppressive Force
People Experiencing Poverty	Poverty itself is caused by many structural barriers; poverty experiences themselves have reinforcing structural barriers that make changing those experiences incredibly difficult for individuals. For example, children living in poverty may not only have individual barriers to learning, such as hunger or housing instability, but they are also likely to attend poorer funded schools that have fewer resources and even more burnt-out or less-equipped teachers. Without equitable educational resources, children experiencing poverty will have a more difficult time with educational attainment (Ferguson et al., 2007) and raising their income above that of their family of origin as adults.	Classism (see Chapter 11)
Persons with Disabilities	Persons with apparent and concealed disabilities experience macro and microaggressions. An example of structural oppression toward this group is that individuals who receive Social Security Disability Income (SSDI) cannot have any savings, any additional income, or increase their household income (e.g., get married) without losing access to their benefits. Essentially, it forces them to live in poverty (because SSDI benefits themselves are inadequate). To read more, see *Dismantling the Poverty Trap: Disability Policy for the Twenty-First Century* (Stapleton et al., 2006).	Ableism (see Chapter 12)
Older Adults	A way structural ageism can be identified is through the policies and procedures set forth by governments and even the language used to describe the population who is 65 years and older. For example, the "dependency ratio" is used to describe the population of adults over age 65—seemingly referring to their status as only dependent and not productive for economic success (Backer & Chang, 2023). There is evidence that supports increased ageism leads to an increased risk of violence toward older persons (Chang et al., 2021).	Ageism (see Chapter 13)

(Continued)

TABLE 4.1 *(Continued)*

Cultural Group(s)	Example of Structural Oppression	The Oppressive Force
Women and Femme-Presenting People	There are countless examples of structural oppression against women and femme-presenting people; however, an enduring example is the gender pay gap. For nearly 20 years, this pay gap has remained the same, with women making only 82 cents to a man's $1.00 for the same work. This pay gap is even more extreme for women of color (Pew Research Center, 2023).	Patriarchy (see Chapter 14)
Gender-Expansive People	Imagine being out in public and not being able to use the restroom. This has become a reality for transgender and gender-expansive people in many states across the United States. This structural issue has made simple day-to-day experiences of trans and gender-expansive people more stressful and more dangerous. To learn more about states where these laws are in place, see the following map provided by the Movement Advancement Project: https://www.lgbtmap.org/equality-maps/nondiscrimination/bathroom_bans.	Transmisia, transmisogyny (see Chapter 14)
Queer Persons	The structural oppression of queer people has a long history in the United States and is grounded in the basic safety and human rights of this group. In many states, queer people do not have employment nondiscrimination protections, housing protections, and in some cases, states even allow for conversion therapy. For more, see the Human Rights Campaign Equality Index: https://www.hrc.org/resources/state-equality-index.	Homomisia (see Chapter 15)
People with Nondominant Religious Beliefs (i.e., belief systems and identities outside of Protestant Christianity)	Many schools and businesses allow for holidays that center on the Christian calendar. Employees and students who celebrate other faith traditions are forced to choose between missing school or work (and using their paid time off) or missing holiday celebrations (Haynes & Thomas, 2007).	Religious persecution (see Chapter 16)

BOX 4.1 **PAUSE AND REFLECT: SYSTEMS, STRUCTURES, AND YOU**

What structures and systems benefit you? What systems and structures oppress you? Think critically about the specific structures and the subsequent outcomes in your life.

As you can infer from Table 4.1, many structures work together to oppress individuals, even within identity factors (e.g., immigrants are likely to experience xenomisia and possibly racism depending on the color of their skin). The intersections of oppressive forces are exactly what makes systemic oppression so insidious-it almost exists as multiple ropes binding our society, making it difficult for people who are oppressed to experience equity, inclusion, and justice. Importantly, it is possible and common for individuals to experience privilege and oppression at the same time, so it's important to understand individuals' intersecting identities and which are *leading* in terms of how much privilege and oppression they are experiencing because this helps counselors to identify strengths, risks, and resiliencies. While systemic oppression is not an individual act, the societal and political reality is that individuals operate within systems to maintain the status quo that benefits groups with the most privilege. As counselors, we must acknowledge these realities, their impacts on clients, and ways we can intervene.

The Oppressed Versus the Oppressor

Considering the complexity of structural oppression, it is important to recognize and critically evaluate our own relationship via our identities with oppression. In some cases, we may be the *oppressor* or a member of a privileged group. In other cases, we may be *oppressed* as a member of a marginalized group. In fact, it is absolutely common that you as an individual (and your clients, as well) are going to occupy privileged and oppressed identities simultaneously. However, when we consider the identities of oppressor and oppressed, we have to deeply consider the context in which we exist.

BOX 4.2 **PAUSE AND REFLECT: WHOA, WAIT, I'M NOT AN OPPRESSOR**

What was your reaction when you read that people can be the *oppressor* and *oppressed*? For some, this language can be alarming, and you might feel immediately defensive. For example, you might've thought, "I'm not oppressed!" even though you have nondominant identities. That could be a fair statement for you, yet we encourage you to dive a little deeper. What work has been done in the generations before you that has afforded you the privilege of not feeling oppressed? Do your other identities afford you privilege so that you do not experience oppression based on your nondominant identities? Is there a chance that you have internalized oppression and accepted it as the *norm*?

On the flip side, you may have reacted with, "I am NOT an oppressor! My family never owned slaves!" This is a common reaction. While it may be true that your family never owned slaves (this is true for me, Dr. Cook, as far as I know of my family history), being an *oppressor*, so to speak, is about what our identities represent to other people. While we may not like that our skin color signals oppression to others, it is a reality we must acknowledge. As we accept this reality, we cannot overcome it with words (e.g., "My family never owned slaves.") because such words can convey that we are dismissing another's reality and their generational experiences of oppression. We cannot mitigate our historical lineage of privilege by attempting to dismiss or erase the generational oppression of others.

Instead, we encourage you to learn about your identities, the privilege and power you hold, and the ways your words and behaviors can convey that you are using your privilege to *empower* rather than to oppress. As you have learned, none of us chose the identities we were born with, yet we can choose how we *use* our identities to eradicate marginalization and oppression. As one of my master's professors and clinical supervisors used to say, "How are you going to use your privilege to lift up others today?"

For example, I (Dr. Clark) am a White, queer, femme, neurodivergent person. I am a tenured associate professor, which holds social class privilege. When I am in a room full of diverse women, my Whiteness will give me privilege in that space that other women and femmes may not have because of White supremacy and White privilege. However, when I, just like many other women and femme-presenting people, am in public, I have experienced catcalling, feeling nervous walking or running in the dark alone, and the other things that patriarchy does to oppress women and gender-expansive people (more on how patriarchy also oppresses men in Chapter 14). When I am working with clients who are unhoused, I have a drastic amount of class privilege. When I operate in the workplace (or any space, really), I feel the oppression related to my neurodivergence (more in Chapter 17) and often my gender. My experiences as an oppressor and the oppressed absolutely exist at the same time, but the context varies as to which is most dominant at any time or the one I feel most acutely. In spaces where I have more privilege, I work to ameliorate it and cede it (e.g., at work, monitoring how often I speak first rather than colleagues of color, how much I share, and listening more). In the spaces where I am oppressed (e.g., gender), I work to find allies and accomplices who can support me and my success.

It may be uncomfortable to begin to recognize the identities that you hold are shared with systemic oppression, the ones that make you an oppressor. This work, however, is the pivotally important work toward becoming culturally aware advocate for clients. Without first recognizing your own privilege, it can make advocating for those with oppressed identities more complicated and at times, harmful or even impossible. As you begin or continue your own cultural development journey as a counselor in training, remember to consider how your identities are situated in the place and space you are in at each moment in time. This doesn't invalidate any experiences of oppression, but it can allow you to recognize your own privileges and then use those privileges more effectively as an advocate for systemic change (see Chapter 5 for more). This recognition begins the process to ensure you are able to readily work with clients with different identities than you, those who are privileged and those who are oppressed.

BOX 4.3 **PAUSE AND REFLECT: CONSIDER YOUR PRIVILEGE**

"To have privilege in one or more areas does not mean you are wholly privileged. Surrendering to the acceptance of privilege is difficult, but it is really all that is expected. What I remind myself, regularly, is this: the acknowledgment of my privilege is not a denial of the ways I have been and am marginalized, the ways I have suffered" (Gay, 2014).

Roxane Gay is a writer, professor, and social justice advocate. This quote is from her book *Bad Feminist*.

How does this quote change how you identify your privileges within yourself? The ways in which you have been oppressed? How might you use what you've learned in this chapter to help a friend, colleague, or client identify their own privileges and oppressions?

The Multicultural and Social Justice Counseling Competencies

The multicultural and social justice counseling competencies (MSJCC; Ratts et al., 2015) are discussed throughout this text and, without a doubt, throughout your counseling program. The MSJCC is a model (see Figure 4.2) that highlights the relationship between the privileged and oppressed (i.e., marginalized) identities of counselors and the clients we serve. It is important to understand one's own identity as privileged (oppressor) or marginalized (oppressed) in

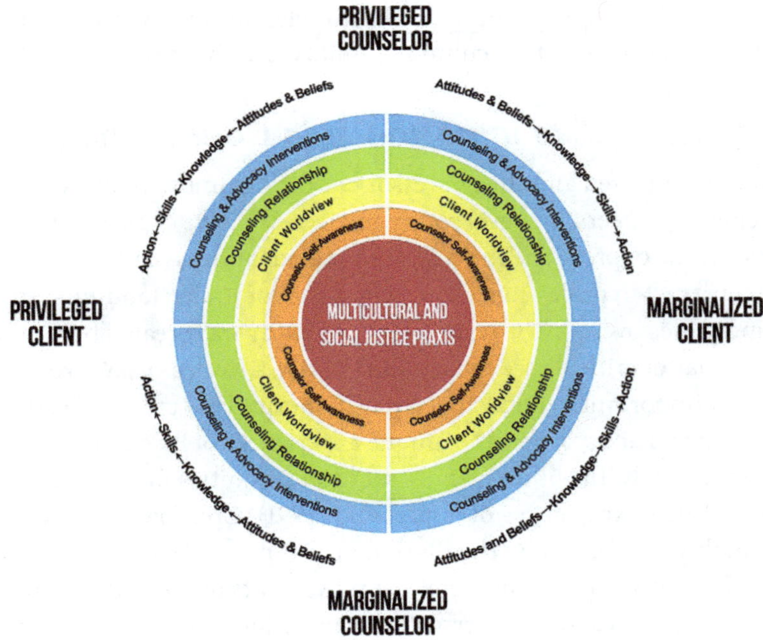

FIGURE 4.2 The Multicultural and Social Justice Counseling Competencies (Ratts et al., 2015)

order to fully engage with the MSJCC. There are four quadrants of the model reflecting this relationship in the counseling setting: (a) marginalized counselor, (b) marginalized client, (c) privileged counselor, and (d) privileged client. It is critical to remember that in one session you may be the privileged counselor and in the next the marginalized counselor. It is identity and context dependent; therefore, you must clearly understand the relationships your identities have to systemic oppression and those of your client! There is a definite reason the phrase "Counselor, know thyself" is a popular mantra!

The quadrants that surround the MSJCC are the dynamics that will impact the counselor's relationship to power, privilege, and oppression that exists in that unique interaction: (a) attitudes and beliefs, (b) knowledge, (c) skills, and (d) action. You will find that the chapters throughout this text are focused on all four of those dynamics to help you improve your attitudes, beliefs, and knowledge about yourself and different groups. Additionally, each chapter spends time supporting your skill development and actions when working with diverse groups.

Within the quadrants are layers that include (a) counseling and advocacy interventions, (b) the counseling relationship, (c) client worldview, and (d) counselor self-awareness. Counseling and advocacy interventions are just that, what you will do with and on behalf of the clients you serve. You'll see those interventions throughout the upcoming chapters of the text. The counseling relationship is the rapport you establish with clients through person-centered counseling skills (see Chapter 1); there are specifics on this in future chapters too. The client worldview is the client's unique way of making sense of their experiences in society; as you can imagine, this will be greatly impacted by their experiences of privilege and/or marginalization. Finally, counselor self-awareness is your understanding of your own identities and their relationships with systemic oppression and privilege—the intrapersonal aspects of cultural humility that the authors describe in Chapter 3.

Intersectionality and its Importance in Counseling

The identities of the oppressed and the oppressor coexist in almost all of us: yourself, your professors, your clients, your peers, and everyone you meet. We have explored this in the context of the MSJCC and systemic oppression. The coalescence of identities is called *intersectionality* and it is an important construct in professional counseling and for understanding systemic oppression and structural inequities overall. The term *intersectionality* was created by Kimberlé Crenshaw (1991), who is a scholar of critical race theory and the law, as well as a law professor at Columbia University. It is very important to know that Crenshaw originally created the theory of intersectionality to highlight and advocate for the unique experiences of Black women—namely, racism and sexism and specifically, the burden and structural inequities Black women experience due to their dual, concurrent experiences of oppression (1991). Crenshaw's work and intersectionality theory are highly influenced by the Black feminist movement; Black feminism was born out of the civil rights, racial justice, and feminist movements of the 20th century. Black women found themselves excluded via these intersecting oppressions—from the civil rights movement by Black men (patriarchy) and the feminist movement by White women (racism). Crenshaw's scholarship has greatly influenced the thinking and writing of social justice advocates across fields, including counseling.

Black Feminism and its Importance in Understanding Social Justice

Black feminism has existed for hundreds if not thousands of years, and activism by Black feminists in the United States has been documented since the anti-slavery movement to today. Black feminists have made incredible contributions to the advancement of social justice movements and inclusion for all marginalized groups. Black feminists are writers, scholars, advocates, and even counselors. We hope you are interested in learning more about Black feminism and reading the works of some of these amazing minds. Here are some for you to look up and learn more about:

- Sojourner Truth
- Ida B. Wells
- Zora Neale Hurston
- Shirley Chisholm
- Audre Lorde
- Angela Davis
- Brittany Packnett Cunningham
- Raquel Willis
- Tressie McMillan Cottom

While intersectionality was originally devised to connect the experiences of racial and gender oppression (Crenshaw, 1991), it has evolved to include a multitude of identity factors and associated oppressions. Each individual has a unique, culminating intersectional identity that is composed of their experiences as the oppressor and the oppressed. We are all intersectional beings with identity factors that have likely made our lives easier (privileges) and those that may have made our lives more difficult (oppressions)—the magnitude of how *much* easier or harder is determined by each person. As you can see, this folds into the MSJCC (Ratts et al., 2015) quite clearly. Because every person has a unique, diverse identity it is important for counselors not to make snap judgments or assumptions, even when they share identities with clients. For instance, not all Black individuals share the same exact intersectional identity, but they all have been oppressed by White supremacy and racism. Not all women have the same intersectional identity,

IMG 4.3. Ida B. Wells

IMG 4.4. Audre Lorde

IMG 4.5. Angela Davis

but again, they have commonly experienced gender-based oppression (patriarchy). There are countless apparent identities (e.g., assumed race, gender) and nonapparent identities (e.g., ability status, social class), so it is paramount that counselors learn from their clients what their intersecting identities are and what they mean to them. Subsequent chapters in this text will discuss these various identities (apparent and nonapparent), the structural oppressions people occupying those identities experience, and what counselors can do to work with and on behalf of people who are members of those groups. So, while we introduce intersectionality here, we encourage you to maintain an intersectional perspective throughout subsequent chapters. No one experience of privilege or oppression is a monolith, and there is incredible diversity of experience within diverse groups.

BOX 4.4 **TIPS FOR PROFESSIONAL PRACTICE: YOUR INTERSECTIONAL IDENTITY BACKPACK**

When I (Dr. Clark) teach about intersectionality, I like to share that an individual's intersecting identities are something we carry with us all the time, like a backpack, a metaphor Peggy McIntosh popularized in the 1990s. As we journey through life, we accumulate experiences that either make that backpack lighter to carry or, in some cases, heavier and more difficult. In the cases where individuals are experiencing multiple intersecting oppressions, the backpack would begin to get very heavy. It can make the journey through life slower and more difficult. The lighter the backpack, the more quickly you can move through the journey with less effort and stress. It doesn't mean the journey isn't difficult, but it means what you are carrying isn't as heavy.

The *multiple minority stress model* (MMSM; Meyer, 2003) expands on this anecdote in a scholarly fashion. The MMSM outlines how individuals experiencing these intersecting oppressions and hostilities experience higher levels of physical, mental, and emotional effects with negative mental health outcomes. Intersectionality and intersectional oppression isn't just a theoretical idea, it will be a lived reality for many clients you will serve.

Systemic Oppression Versus Individual Bias and Discrimination

At this point, you understand that systemic oppression and privilege are not things that any of us had a personal hand in creating; however, they have a significant impact on each person's lived experiences and the challenges they face across the lifespan. Systemic oppressions and subsequent societal values have a substantial influence on the ways individuals and groups within society think, feel, and act. This is often called the overculture (versus the subculture). Overculture influences the morals and values of the individuals who are participants in that culture and aligns with the macrosystem in EST. As we have discussed, the overculture in the United States is based on White supremacy, patriarchy, and classism, among other oppressions, that reinforce the status quo. These turn into cultural values that are learned by individuals who live in that culture, whether they want to learn them or not. As we have discussed previously (see Chapter 3), a multicultural orientation comes from learning but also unlearning. When you are socialized in a culture steeped in oppression, there is much work to do for people with all identities. Some things you may have learned are problematic, racist, sexist, classist—in sum, oppressive. First, you must take stock of what you have learned so you can begin the unlearning process.

BOX 4.5 **PAUSE AND REFLECT: LEARNED STORIES**

What are the stories about other cultural groups or identities that you learned throughout your childhood and adolescence? Where did you learn these values? Your family, the media, religious organizations, other places? Make a brief list and connect them to their origin.

Now, reflect on that list and what you have come to know about privilege and oppression. How much was factual? Incorrect? How much did you have to unlearn or still need to unlearn? Do you think that these things have influenced how you have engaged with (or not engaged with) people from those cultural groups? What has changed about what you have come to know when you take an intersectional perspective?

While we aren't responsible for the identities with which we are born, we are responsible for how we think and act, and how we engage with privilege when we have it! When individuals are unaware of negative and oppressive ideas, they have learned via the overculture to be unaware of their biases.

Uncheck biases are dangerous. Biases, conscious or unconscious, are the foundation of oppressive and violent behaviors by individuals and groups. *Allport's Scale of Prejudice* (Allport, 1954; see Figure 4.3) outlines how these conscious and unconscious biases are required for further actions of discrimination and even violence. Individual biases can lead to biased behaviors (e.g., bullying, slurs, belittling jokes). Without intervention, these biased behaviors can escalate to discrimination (e.g., structural oppression, educational disparities, political marginalization, etc.). When discrimination is present in society it can escalate to bias-motivated violence (e.g., hate crimes, rape, vandalism). When bias-motivated violence is present, it is possible for this violence to progress to genocide or the systematic process to annihilate an entire group of people (e.g., the Holocaust, current anti-transgender legislation and policies).

Allport's Scale of Prejudice provides a stark look at what is possible when human biases are unchecked and allowed to intensify. It can be discouraging to review this scale and compare it to the current state of discrimination and violence against marginalized people in the United States. It is clear that our culture is, and has always operated, closer to the top of Allport's pyramid (e.g., settler colonization and Indigenous genocide, chattel enslavement of Africans and centuries of subsequent structural racism, lynching, violence against women and children, hate crimes against queer people, among countless other examples). These historical and present-day examples of hatred and violence only add to the stress experienced by marginalized groups (e.g., generational trauma—more on this in later chapters). This scale is not meant to scare you, but it should awaken you to the need to take systematic oppression, bias, and acts of bias seriously. No act of bias is too small for intervention; there is no such thing as "it was just a joke." These "small" behaviors provide the foundation for escalating harm and violence toward marginalized groups.

FIGURE 4.3 Allport's Scale of Prejudice

The Outcomes of Structural Oppression and the Social Determinants of Health

Structural oppression has numerous outcomes that impact the lived experiences of clients across multiple domains: housing, health and health care, mental health, education, occupation, and others. The outcomes of structural oppression impact daily living and also increase mortality rates for marginalized populations; this means that individuals from marginalized groups, especially those with intersecting marginalized identities, have shorter lifespans (Centers for Disease Control [CDC], 2022). Increased mortality comes from increased exposure to violence (e.g., biased motivated violence, as Allport described) but also because of the structural barriers that limit access to resources (e.g., financial, education, health care). How structural oppressions (or privileges) impact an individual's health and wellness are called the *social determinants of health* (SDOH). Essentially, SDOH are a client's access to resources (privilege) or lack of access/barriers to resources (oppressions) in five areas: economic stability, education access and quality, health-care access and quality, neighborhood and environment, and social and community context (CDC, 2022). Experiences of oppression may influence client access to resources in all five of these areas, outlined in Table 4.2.

TABLE 4.2 SDOH

SDOH Area	Areas of Oppressions	Some Areas of Intervention to Improve SDOH Outcomes
Economic Stability	Individuals experiencing poverty (about 1 in 10 people in the United States, more in Chapter 11) are significantly more likely to have shorter lifespans. Lack of economic security limits access to quality health care in the United States (including mental health care). Individuals who have physical illnesses or disabilities may also have employment challenges, limiting economic stability. People with higher levels of economic stability have lower mortality rates.	Reduce poverty Help children and adolescents stay in school and complete school Increase employment in working-aged people (CDC, 2022)
Education Access and Quality	The higher a person's education, the more likely they are to be healthy and live longer (which is also related to their economic stability). Children experiencing poverty may experience cognitive changes that make learning more difficult. Children who go to under-resourced schools may have less educational support to attend and complete college.	Increase 4-year high school graduation rates Increase enrollment in college by high school graduates Increase reading proficiency skills in eighth graders Increase the proportion of mental health care in schools (CDC, 2022)

(Continued)

TABLE 4.2 *(Continued)*

SDOH Area	Areas of Oppressions	Some Areas of Intervention to Improve SDOH Outcomes
Health-Care Access and Quality	Access to health care is, of course, related to mortality. About 10% of people in the United States do not have health insurance (again, often related to economic resources in many cases). Individuals without access to health care are more likely to miss preventive care screenings that can prevent or catch chronic diseases and cancer. In other cases, individuals may live too far from health-care resources, making getting to appointments very difficult. Increased health-care access increases lifespan and improves health.	Increase preventive health-care screenings (e.g., pap smears, colonoscopies) Increase the number of insured individuals Increase the proportion of people with substance use disorders who receive treatment in the past year (CDC, 2022)
Neighborhood and Built Environment	Where people live significantly impacts their wellness and lifespan. Neighborhoods that are more violent or are exposed to greater levels of pollution increase an individual's health risk. Safer neighborhoods and communities increase lifespan and improve health.	Reduce pollutants Reduce smoking rates Increase adult access to broadband internet Reduce rates of minors committing violent crimes (CDC, 2022)
Social and Community Context	An individual's access to a safe and healthy relationship is also a protective factor against mortality and health concerns. Increased social support from family, friends, peers, and professionals can improve health. Individuals who don't have access to supportive relationships may have worse outcomes.	Reduce mental health issues in caregivers of persons with disabilities Increase the number of adolescents who endorse having an adult to talk to about serious problems Increase the proportion of children and adolescents who show resilience to stress Reduce bullying of transgender students (CDC, 2022)

As you can see, counselors across settings have an important role in reducing these health inequities and can be a part of the interventions proposed in these five domains. Regarding economic stability (see Chapter 11), counselors who work with children, especially professional school counselors (PSCs), are pivotal in helping children and adolescents complete their K–12 education. Clinical, career, and rehabilitation counselors are critical in assisting individuals with finding meaningful employment and staying employed. The role of the PSC is wholly related to the second domain, educational access and quality. Substance use counselors' work is directly related to SDOH and health-care access (more on substance use in Chapter 17) too. Again, while the neighborhood and built environment may not seem directly related to counselors, the reduction of crime rates in minors is incredibly relevant to counselors who work in juvenile justice and correctional settings (see Chapter 17).

Counselors of all specializations will find their roles are critical in building social and community contexts. Not only can we address specific goals, like ensuring adolescents have an adult they can trust, but counselors can be that supportive relationship that can be preventive and increase health outcomes, too! SDOH are increasingly discussed in professional counseling literature (e.g., Johnson & Brookover, 2021; Sheperis et al., 2023), and the additional research articles in the appendix can provide greater insight into these applications in our field.

Counselors' Responsibilities and Interventions as Agents of Change

Counseling ethical codes call for counselors to promote social justice (ACA, 2014; AMHCA, 2020; ASCA, 2022; CRCC, 2023; NBCC, 2023). When counselors are aware that structural oppression is part of the etiology of their clients' concerns, they are expected to advocate. "When appropriate, counselors advocate at individual, group, institutional, and societal levels to address potential barriers and obstacles that inhibit access and/or the growth and development of clients" (ACA, 2014, p. 5). Not addressing barriers through advocacy when appropriate may have the unintended consequence of perpetuating harm. Counselors are called to avoid harming their clients, trainees, and research participants and to minimize or to remedy harm that cannot be avoided (ACA, 2014, p. 4). However, in practice, this ethos is sometimes not clearly ascertained but rather obscured by superficial attempts to be a values-free profession rather than relying on the fact that professional counselors know how to bracket values to prevent biases from negatively impacting client outcomes. Professional counselors must not confuse *imposing values* with being *value-free*. Counseling is not a value-free endeavor, as evidenced by our ethical codes, which are inherently value-laden. The key is that counselors do not impose their *personal values* on clients and attempt to sway clients toward their worldviews. Instead, counselors work from an ethics-driven perspective that supports client autonomy, veracity, nonmaleficence, beneficence, fidelity, and justice.

Different Theoretical Orientations That May Foster Systemic Change

Theories in the field of counseling address structural oppression in many ways that span micro-, meso-, and macrolevels. Multicultural counseling, the forerunner that paved the way for other theories that illuminate the need to address structural oppression, promotes diversity in the field. For example, feminist theory and RCT suggest that patriarchy is a root cause of poor mental health outcomes and calls for action against systems of patriarchal oppression. Social justice counseling, which has been considered a *fifth force* of the profession, embraces the idea of counseling that addresses systemic oppression with and for clients who identify structural and systemic oppression as a part of the root cause of their symptoms.

The multicultural counseling competencies and standards laid a critical foundation that counselors must be prepared to appropriately serve an increasingly diverse population (Sue et al., 1992). While the framework did not explicitly say how to address structural oppression, the concept is threaded throughout as it relates to counselors' cultural competence mitigating symptoms clients experience as a result of cultural oppression. One major critique has been that counselors have been trained to understand different cultural groups from a stereotypical perspective. Traditional training has focused on teaching techniques about how to work with this group or that group rather than emphasizing intersectionality, structural oppression, and adapting to clients' unique needs rooted in their identities and experiences. This lack of holism has been troubling for many counselors and has fallen short in serving clients fully, an error we hope we begin to rectify with the holistic perspective we have taken in this text.

While there is not a single individual we can identify as the founder of feminist theory, the cumulative contribution of situating the etiology of client concerns in relation to sexism is monumental (Pitts & Kawahara, 2017). Looking at sexism as a root cause of distress has created a demand for advocacy, often going a step beyond individualized interventions. Techniques such as power analysis and social action are common in feminist therapy, as clients are often encouraged to use their power to resist oppression brought about by sexism. One critique of feminist theory is whether it adequately addressed the needs of Black women; this ultimately led to the creation of Black feminist theory (hooks, 2000).

Counselors who practice social justice counseling consider how oppression can interfere with well-being and mental health and use biopsychosocial assessments to determine the root of a client's problem before engaging in counseling or advocacy interventions. If the root is determined to be biological in nature, referrals are made to an appropriate provider if biological (e.g., medical, psychopharmacology) interventions are warranted. Additionally, social justice counselors explore psychological and social factors. If assessment reveals that a client's problem is rooted in psychological factors, individual and/or group counseling are the primary interventions. When assessment indicates social factors as the roots of a client's problem, social justice counselors immediately invoke interventions to alter systemic variables, whether at the individual, social, cultural, or institutional levels. Thus, social justice counselors do not use one method of intervention but rely on data from clients to determine the best constellation of interventions and engage in as many as are necessary (Ratts & Pedersen, 2014). In sum, many, if not all, clients you will serve will experience oppression. It is your responsibility as a counselor not only to address their experiences in session but also via various forms of advocacy, which you will learn more about in the next chapter.

Conclusion

After reading this chapter, hopefully you have a better understanding of what systems are and how systems work to maintain themselves. Many systems maintain themselves through various structures of oppression, which have a very real impact on all of us and the clients we serve. The way individual identities interact with these systems creates privilege and oppression, and can coexist within one individual at the same time (i.e., intersectionality). Using an intersectional approach can help us identify how various systems have impacted our lived experiences and those of our clients in concrete ways.

Structural oppressions result in societal values that include conscious and unconscious biases. These biases can lead to discrimination and even violence toward marginalized groups. Not only physically harmful, but they can also lead to poorer physical health, mental health, and educational and occupational outcomes. Counselors have a significant role to play in helping clients name, address, and navigate structural barriers with and on behalf of those we serve. Counselors also have a personal and ethical responsibility to be social justice advocates against these structural oppressions, which will be discussed in greater detail in Chapter 5!

Questions for Reflection

Consider what you learned in this chapter as you respond to the questions and prompts below.

1. Identify some systems that operate in your life and how you have experienced oppression and benefits.
2. In what ways do you see systemic oppression play out in your school, community, or other systems in which you engage?
3. How might you help a client who is different from you identify how their privilege and oppression have impacted their lived experiences? What interventions are most appropriate in the counseling setting?
4. If you heard a person in your life using biased or prejudiced language toward another group, how might you react? What would you say to intervene?
5. How has learning about your privileges and biases changed your perspective on your lived experience? How will this knowledge impact your work as a future counselor?

Applying What You Have Learned

Complete each of the following activities, considering what you learned from this chapter.

Activity #1: Your Intersectional Identity

*Adapted from Clark, M. (2019). Experiences of intersections of privilege and oppression. In M. Pope, M. Gonzalez, E. Cameron, & J. S. Pangelinan (Eds.) *Experiential activities for teaching social justice and advocacy competence in counseling.* London: Routledge.

A common mnemonic device in counseling for understanding and identifying diverse identities is the RESPECTFUL model (D'Andrea & Daniels, 1997):

R: Religion/Spirituality
E: Economic Class Background
S: Sexual Identity
P: Psychological Development
E: Ethnic/Racial Identity
C: Chronological/Lifespan Challenges
T: Trauma
F: Family Background
U: Unique Physical Characteristics
L: Location/Language

You may notice that this original model is missing gender, a significant identity factor! This activity has been adapted to include gender, RESPECTFUL-G. Using the table below, consider how your intersectional identities represent a privilege or marginalization. First, consider your identity/ies in these domains. Then, compare your identities with those that are privileged in the United States. In the final column, identify if you are privileged or marginalized. Consider how your identities of privilege or marginalization add to the weight of your "backpack."

Once you have completed the table, share your experiences with a classmate or small group. What was it like completing this activity? What did you learn about yourself? Your classmate(s)? How do these results influence your work as a future counselor?

Domain	Privileged Identity in U.S. Society	My Identity	Privileged or Marginalized?
R	Christian		
E	Upper Class		
S	Heterosexual		
P	Not Psychologically or Developmentally Disabled		
E	White		
C	Without Developmental Challenges		
T	Without Trauma		
F	Intact, Nuclear Family		

Domain	Privileged Identity in U.S. Society	My Identity	Privileged or Marginalized?
U	Not Physically Disabled or Different		
L	U.S.-Born Citizens, English Speakers		
G	Cisgender Men		

Activity #2: Dismantling Structural Oppression

As you have learned, structural oppression is mammoth—it has seeped into every corner of society, including education, health care, transportation, economics, employment, religious institutions, clubs—the list goes on and on. While structural oppression is insidious and ever present, that doesn't mean change cannot occur. If each one of us makes small contributions, it can add up to a lot.

What is a form of structural oppression you see in your day-to-day life and with which you interact? By *interact*, we do not necessarily mean that you are a direct contributor—more so, that you are part of that system—it could be your school, workplace, or house of worship, just to give a few examples. What is something you could do that would highlight the oppression you see? Something small—it doesn't have to be anything big—simply something that could get people thinking and maybe even join you in your efforts. For example, maybe you decide not to shop at a particular corporate store because their business practices contribute to structural oppression. You could share this decision with those who suggest you shop there or even go a bit further and post your decision and your reasons on social media.

The goal of this activity is to take a small, reasoned action that could have a positive influence on dismantling structural oppression. Small actions can result in something big—what will you do?

Credits

IMG 4.1: Copyright © by Adam Jones, Ph.D. (CC BY 3.0) at https://commons.wikimedia.org/wiki/File:No_Dogs-Negroes-Mexicans_-_Racist_Sign_from_Deep_South_-_National_Civil_Rights_Museum_-_Downtown_Memphis_-_Tennessee_-_USA.jpg.

IMG 4.2: https://commons.wikimedia.org/wiki/File:Mount_Pleasant_Indian_Industrial_Boarding_School.jpg, 1910.

Fig. 4.2: M.J. Ratts, A.A. Singh, S. Nassar-McMillan, S.K. Butler, and J.R. McCullough, "Multicultural and Social Justice Counseling Competencies". Copyright © 2015 by M.J. Ratts, A.A. Singh, S. Nassar-McMillan, S.K. Butler, and J.R. McCullough.

IMG 4.3: Mary Garrity, https://commons.wikimedia.org/wiki/File:Mary_Garrity_-_Ida_B._Wells-Barnett_-_Google_Art_Project_crop.jpg, 1893.

IMG 4.4: Copyright © by K. Kendall (CC BY 2.0) at https://commons.wikimedia.org/wiki/File:Audre_Lorde.jpg.

IMG 4.5: Bernard Gotfryd, https://commons.wikimedia.org/wiki/File:Angela_Davis_in_a_half-length_portrait_by_Bernard_Gotfryd_-_crop.jpg, 1974.

Fig. 4.3: Anti-Defamation League, "Pyramid of Hate," https://www.adl.org/sites/default/files/documents/pyramid-of-hate.pdf. Copyright © 2018 by Anti-Defamation League.

CHAPTER 5

Social Justice and Advocacy

Skills and Application in Counseling

Donghun Lee, ZeVida A. Jones, Derrick Shepard, Tabitha Cude,
Jeongwoon Jeong, and Sojeong Nam

> *When we identify where our privilege intersects with somebody else's oppression, we'll find our opportunities to make real change.*
>
> —Ijeoma Oluo

CHAPTER OVERVIEW

Today, the role of professional counselors is not merely about addressing individual mental health concerns in counseling sessions. Instead, it embodies a broader mission of social responsibility. It is within this broader context the concepts of social justice and advocacy find a natural home within the identity and practice of professional counselors. Given the evolving landscape of societal challenges, the counseling profession has actively adopted a profound commitment to addressing systemic injustices and advocating for equitable mental health services. In this chapter, we explore a variety of concepts, models, and practical applications, and offer real-world examples pertinent to social justice and advocacy within the counseling context. The journey of this exploration will be guided by the objectives listed below.

LEARNING OBJECTIVES

By the end of this chapter, students will be able to:

1. describe the roles and responsibilities of professional counselors in social justice counseling and advocacy,
2. explain how the counseling profession has evolved toward social justice and advocacy,
3. describe basic concepts and ethical standards related to social justice and advocacy,
4. apply theories and models related to social justice and advocacy in counseling,
5. demonstrate how social justice counseling and advocacy affect the counseling relationships and the overall process, and
6. use culturally relevant counseling approaches/skills and implement humanistic perspectives into counseling.

CACREP 2016 STANDARDS

The information in this chapter supports the following standards:

- 2.F.1.d. the role and process of the professional counselor advocating on behalf of the profession
- 2.F.1.e. advocacy processes needed to address institutional and social barriers that impede access, equity, and success for clients
- 2.F.1.k. strategies for personal and professional self-evaluation and implications for practice
- 2.F.2.a. multicultural and pluralistic characteristics within and among diverse groups nationally and internationally
- 2.F.2.b. theories and models of multicultural counseling, cultural identity development, and social justice and advocacy
- 2.F.2.c. multicultural counseling competencies
- 2.F.2.d. the impact of heritage, attitudes, beliefs, understandings, and acculturative experiences on an individual's views of others
- 2.F.2.h. strategies for identifying and eliminating barriers, prejudices, and processes of intentional and unintentional oppression and discrimination
- 2.F.3.f. systemic and environmental factors that affect human development, functioning, and behavior
- 2.F.3.i. ethical and culturally relevant strategies for promoting resilience and optimum development and wellness across the lifespan
- 2.F.4.g. strategies for advocating for diverse clients' career and educational development and employment opportunities in a global economy
- 5.C.3.e. strategies to advocate for persons with mental health issues
- 5.G.2.a. school counselor roles as leaders, advocates, and systems change agents in PK–12 schools
- 6.B.5.i. role of counselors and counselor educators advocating on behalf of the profession and professional identity
- 6.B.5.j. models and competencies for advocating for clients at the individual, system, and policy levels

CACREP 2024 STANDARDS

The information in this chapter supports the following standards:

- 3.A.5. the role and process of the professional counselor advocating on behalf of the profession
- 3.A.4. the role and process of the professional counselor advocating on behalf of and with individuals receiving counseling services to address systemic, institutional, architectural, attitudinal, disability, and social barriers that impede access, equity, and success
- 3.A.11. self-care, self-awareness, and self-evaluation strategies for ethical and effective practice
- 3.B.1. theories and models of multicultural counseling, social justice, and advocacy
- 3.B.2. the influence of heritage, cultural identities, attitudes, values, beliefs, understandings, within-group differences, and acculturative experiences on individuals' worldviews
- 3.B.9. strategies for identifying and eliminating barriers, prejudices, and processes of intentional and unintentional oppression and discrimination
- 3.B.10. guidelines developed by professional counseling organizations related to social justice, advocacy, and working with individuals with diverse cultural identities

- 3.C.7. models of resilience, optimal development, and wellness in individuals and families across the lifespan
- 3.C.11. systemic, cultural, and environmental factors that affect lifespan development, functioning, behavior, resilience, and overall wellness
- 3.D.11. strategies for improving access to educational and occupational opportunities for people from marginalized groups
- 5.C.8. strategies to advocate for people with mental, behavioral, and neurodevelopmental conditions
- 5.H.6. school counselor roles as leaders, advocates, and systems change agents in PK–12 schools
- 6.B.5.i. models and competencies for counselors and counselor educators advocating on behalf of the profession and professional counselor identity
- 6.B.5.j. models and competencies for advocating for clients at the individual, system, and policy levels

BOX 5.1 **PAUSE AND REFLECT: YOUR JOURNEY TO THE PROFESSION**

Each student is on their own journey to becoming a counselor. In this chapter, two current professional counselors were asked to share their journeys, and now, you are going to be asked to reflect on and share your journey.

Prior to reading the chapter, reflect on the following questions:

- Why did you choose to go into the field of counseling?
- How does your cultural identity shape your counseling journey?
- Which of your cultural identities were most impactful in your decision to become a counselor?
- What is your definition of social justice?
- What is your definition of advocacy?
- How do you view advocacy as a counselor?
- If you are already a counselor, reflect on a time you implemented social justice advocacy as a professional counselor. If you are on a journey to become a counselor, reflect on a way you hope to implement social justice advocacy as a professional counselor.

After reading the chapter, reflect on these questions again. What did you learn? Did anything in the chapter change one or more of your responses? Did your responses become more robust and knowledgeable after reading the chapter?

Social Justice and Advocacy Within Counselor Identity and Practice

The Role of Social Justice in Counseling and Advocacy as a Core Component

Social justice permeates every facet of counseling, demanding that counselors recognize and address disparities, inequities, and systemic barriers impacting individuals' mental health. Counselors are trained to be culturally sensitive and to confront societal issues that contribute to mental health disparities. They are advocates by nature, ensuring culturally competent care and engaging in the dismantling of oppressive systems that perpetuate inequality. Advocacy is the lynchpin of counseling practice, manifesting in various forms. From advocating for individual client rights to engaging in systemic and community-level advocacy, counselors actively ensure their clients' voices are heard and their needs met, both within and beyond counseling. Yet, this endeavor is not without complexities and ethical considerations, necessitating a delicate balance between advocacy and maintaining ethical standards, particularly professional boundaries and client confidentiality.

The integration of social justice and advocacy into counseling practice yields a multitude of benefits. Clients experience improved access to care, enhanced well-being, and increased empowerment as counselors address systemic barriers and advocate for equitable mental health services. Counselors, in turn, find fulfillment as change agents, contributing to broader societal well-being, both with and on behalf of clients. However, to engage effectively in this transformative work, counselors must acquire training and skills, including developing a multicultural orientation, understanding social determinants of mental health, and mastering the intricacies of systemic oppression. Continuous education and training equip counselors with the knowledge and skills required to effectively advocate for their clients and communities, reinforcing their role as essential agents of positive change.

Communicating About Social Justice and Advocacy

In order to embark on the exploration of the concepts, models, and practical applications of social justice counseling and advocacy, it is necessary to first establish clear definitions of the fundamental concepts central in this chapter.

Multiculturalism is a paradigm that acknowledges and values the diverse cultural backgrounds, identities, and life experiences of individuals. Multiculturalism is frequently used interchangeably with terms such as cultural pluralism, cultural diversity, and diversity and inclusion. In the context of counseling, multiculturalism is tied to essential competencies required to work effectively with clients from various cultural backgrounds. Finally, it involves understanding the pervasive impact oppression, prejudice, and inequality have on individuals from diverse backgrounds across multiple dimensions (Sue et al., 1992; Vera & Speight, 2003).

Social justice counseling is an approach that employs a diverse range of strategies and interventions aimed at addressing oppressive systems of power and privilege that impact clients. It includes confronting and rectifying inequitable social, political, and economic conditions that hinder the academic, career, and personal/social development of individuals, families, and communities (Ratts et al., 2016).

Advocacy is, in general, defined as proactively supporting and promoting clients' overall well-being at the individual, community, and national levels by minimizing systemic barriers that prevent them from achieving their optimal potential. In the context of counseling, advocacy represents counselors' strong commitment to addressing injustices and societal challenges, which extends to promoting systemic changes in an optimistic and constructive manner. Advocacy actions encompass activities such as raising awareness about particular issues, working directly with clients who are impacted by these issues, participating in public campaigns and community events, engaging in peaceful protests and demonstrations, and representing the interests of clients within the legal system (Lewis et al., 2002; Ratts, 2009).

What Is Advocacy?

The roots of advocacy in counseling can be traced back to Frank Parson's work in the 1900s with underserved populations in vocational counseling (Bemak et al., 2011). However, it took the American Counseling Association (ACA) over 100 years to develop a core skillset of advocacy competencies (Lewis et al., 2002). Advocacy is such a part of our identity that the profession took the step to address the need for advocacy within the 2020 Vision for the profession (Kaplan et al., 2014). With the updated advocacy competencies in 2018, the authors stimulated counselors to consider current and everchanging sociopolitical challenges and to increase advocacy across ACA and accrediting bodies (Toporek & Daniel, 2018).

The ACA Advocacy Competencies give counselors a framework to address systemic barriers facing students, clients, and consumers (Toporek & Daniel, 2018). Two dimensions, extent of client involvement in advocacy and level of advocacy, organize the framework and guide counselors in determining the appropriate level of advocacy on their part and how much client involvement is needed to accomplish the advocacy goal. Counselors can navigate between supporting clients and client groups or direct system intervention.

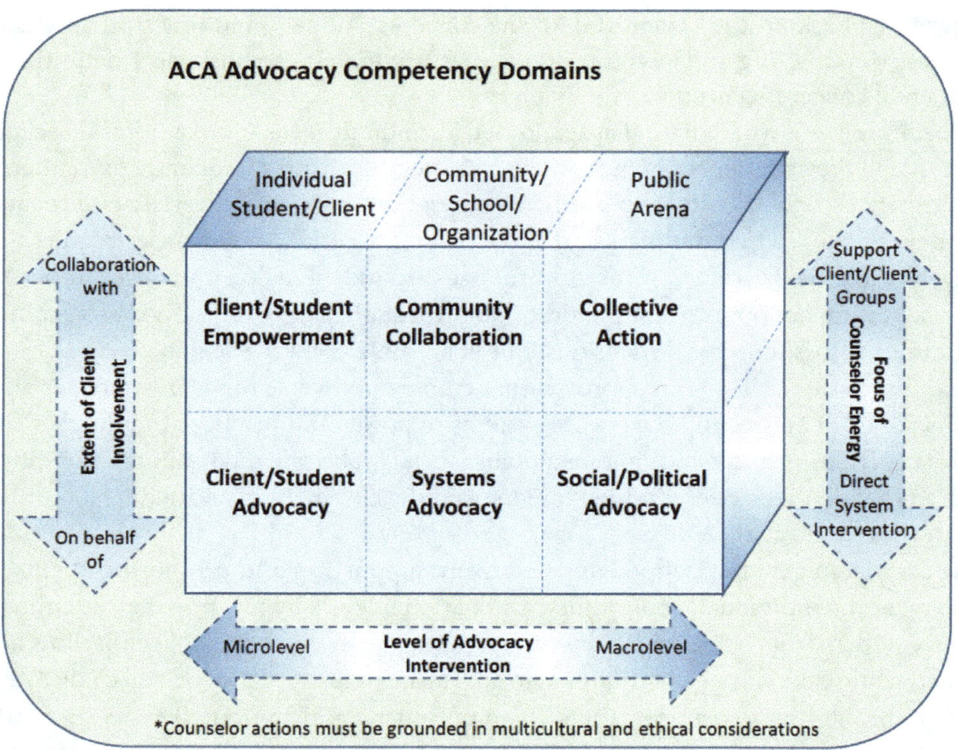

FIGURE 5.1 ACA Advocacy Competencies

Understanding the Historical Context of Social Justice and Advocacy in Counseling

In the field of counseling, social justice and advocacy have taken a central role in addressing a wide range of multicultural and diversity-related issues (Di Giovanni, 2009; Ratts, 2009). Social justice counseling has emerged as a paradigm that employs social advocacy and activism to confront inequitable social, political, and economic conditions that hinder the academic, career, and personal/social development of individuals, families, and communities (Ratts, 2009). The counseling profession has come to acknowledge systemic oppression and inequity exacerbate the marginalization of those lacking power, resources, information, and access to community services. This represents a significant shift from traditional counseling paradigms that primarily focused on the individual, often neglecting environmental and contextual factors (Prileltensky, 1994).

In response to these systemic concerns, scholars and practitioners have collectively worked to develop social justice and advocacy paradigms, effectively establishing a *fifth force* in the field of counseling (Ratts et al., 2004). This approach integrates cultural and sociopolitical factors into the process of understanding clients' presenting issues. Notably, the social justice counseling movement is not entirely new but rather a culmination of long-term efforts by numerous scholars, counselors, and advocates (Smith et al., 2009).

Bronfenbrenner (1979) introduced Ecological System Theory, offering a multilevel framework for comprehending human nature and behavior within their environments. This theory encourages counselors to consider how individuals are reciprocally shaped by their interactions with others and their surroundings. Building on this foundation, McLeroy et al. (1988) developed the Socioecological Model, offering a framework to explore how individuals and their social environments mutually influence each other. This model allows counselors to investigate the extent to which oppressive environmental factors impact individuals' overall well-being (Conyne & Cook, 2004; Cook, 2012; McMahon et al., 2014).

In 1992, multicultural counseling competencies (MCCs) were introduced by Sue and colleagues to raise awareness of the impact of oppression, prejudice, and inequality on diverse clients at multiple levels. The MCCs laid the groundwork for developing competencies tailored to specific populations, deepening the understanding of historically marginalized groups, and incorporating multicultural perspectives into counseling practice (Ratts et al., 2016). Paralleling ongoing efforts to address systemic issues in a broader context, there was a significant push to recognize the importance of advocacy within the counseling profession. This led to the development of the ACA Advocacy Competencies (Lewis et al., 2002). These competencies highlight the vital role of counselors as advocates, both within and outside of counseling sessions, assisting clients in navigating systemic barriers.

Expanding on these initiatives, the multicultural and social justice counseling competencies (MSJCC) was established in 2016 as an update to the original MCCs published in 1992 (Ratts et al., 2016). The MSJCC were pivotal because they underscored the need for a more contextual approach to working with clients and communities within a larger ecosystem. This recognition acknowledged that clients *and* counselors possess intersecting identities and experience both privileged and marginalized statuses. As a result, the MSJCC enhances the role of social justice advocacy as an integral aspect of counselors' professional identity. Consequently, professional counselors are expected to view clients' issues through a culturally contextual framework and implement interventions that address challenges at both the individual and systemic levels.

Following the establishment of the MSJCC (Ratts et al., 2016), the counseling profession has made significant strides in integrating social justice advocacy into its core identity. However, the journey toward equitable and inclusive counseling practice is ongoing. To continue advancing, professional counselors must remain dedicated to learning, self-reflection, and active engagement in addressing the multifaceted challenges faced by individuals and communities. By embracing these principles and taking action, counselors contribute to a more just and equitable society while supporting the well-being of their clients.

Ethical Codes Related to Social Justice and Advocacy

Professional counseling associations have embraced social justice and advocacy as core values and codified them in their ethical standards. These ethical codes bestow upon counselors professional and ethical obligations to practice social justice and advocacy in their various roles and responsibilities, providing principles and minimum guidelines counselors are expected to adhere to in their practice. When it comes to social justice and advocacy, the codes emphasize the importance of promoting fairness and equality, and advocating for the rights and well-being of clients, especially those who are marginalized or disadvantaged. It is crucial for counselors to familiarize themselves with the specific ethical codes and guidelines provided by their respective counseling associations (i.e., ACA, National Board for Certified Counselors, American School Counselors Association, Commission on Rehabilitation Counselor Certification, American Mental Health Counselors Association) as these codes vary. Additionally, counselors should engage in ongoing ethical decision-making and seek consultation when faced with complex ethical dilemmas related to social justice and advocacy in their practice. Below are some examples of key ethical codes related to social justice and advocacy in counseling associations.

TABLE 5.1 Advocacy Codes Across Professions

ACA	
ACA Code of Ethics (2014)	*A.7.a. Advocacy.* When appropriate, counselors advocate at individual, group, institutional, and societal levels to address potential barriers and obstacles that inhibit access and/or the growth and development of clients.
	A.7.b. Confidentiality and Advocacy. Counselors obtain client consent prior to engaging in advocacy efforts on behalf of an identifiable client to improve the provision of services and to work toward removal of systemic barriers or obstacles that inhibit client access, growth, and development.
	E.5.c. Historical and Social Prejudices in the Diagnosis of Pathology. Counselors recognize historical and social prejudices in the misdiagnosis and pathologizing of certain individuals and groups and strive to become aware of and address such biases in themselves or others.

American Mental Health Counselors Association (AMHCA)	
AMHCA Code of Ethics (2020)	*F.2 Advocate*. CMHCs are encouraged to advocate at the individual, institutional, professional, and societal level to foster sociopolitical change that advances client and community welfare.
	F.2.b. CMHCs may encourage clients to challenge familial, institutional, and societal obstacles to their growth and development and they may advocate on the clients' behalf. CMHCs remain aware of the potential dangers of becoming overly involved as an advocate.
	C.2.c. CMHCs have a responsibility to educate themselves about their own biases toward those of different races, creeds, identities, orientations, cultures, and physical and mental abilities, and then to seek consultation, supervision, and/or counseling in order to prevent those biases from interfering with the counseling process.
American School Counselor Association (ASCA)	
ASCA Ethical Standards for School Counselors (2022)	*A.1.j*. Advocate for equitable, anti-oppressive and anti-bias policies and procedures, systems and practices, and provide effective, evidence-based and culturally sustaining interventions to address student needs.
	A.10.f. Advocate for the equitable right and access to free, appropriate public education for all youth in which students are not stigmatized or isolated based on race, gender identity, gender expression, sexual orientation, language, immigration status, juvenile justice/court involvement, housing, socioeconomic status, ability, foster care, transportation, special education, mental health and/or any other exceptionality or special need.
	A.10.h. Actively advocate for systemic and other changes needed for equitable participation and outcomes in educational programs when disproportionality exists regarding enrollment in such programs by race, gender identity, gender expression, sexual orientation, language, immigration status, juvenile justice/court involvement, housing, socioeconomic status, ability, foster care, transportation, special education, mental health and/or any other exceptionality or special need.
Commission on Rehabilitation Counselor Certification (CRCC)	
CRCC Code of Professional Ethics for Certified Rehabilitation Counselors (2023)	*C.1.a. ATTITUDINAL BARRIERS*. CRCs/CCRCs recognize and address attitudinal barriers in applicable settings (e.g., employment, educational, health care, community inclusion) that inhibit the growth and development of their clients, including stigma, stereotyping, and discrimination.
	C.1.c. EMPOWERING THE CLIENT. CRCs/CCRCs work to ensure the voice of the client is heard, valued, and given full consideration by supporting informed choice and client engagement in decision-making and treatment planning. CRCs/CCRCs foster self-advocacy skills of clients to achieve maximum independence.

(*Continued*)

TABLE 5.1 *(Continued)*

	C.1.d. ORGANIZATIONAL AND SYSTEM ADVOCACY. CRCs/CCRCs consider how actions taken by their own organization, as well as cooperating organizations impact clients. To ensure effective service delivery, CRCs/CCRCs act as advocates for clients who cannot self-advocate. CRCs/CCRCs make reasonable efforts to partner with client groups and community members to address environmental and systemic issues and to combat ableism and systems of oppression across policies, procedures, and practices.
National Board for Certified Counselors (NBCC)	
NBCC Code of Ethics (2023)	*Advocacy, 89.* Counselor educators shall advocate for counseling students to address programmatic barriers and obstacles that hinder student academic growth and development.
	Professional Responsibilities, 7. Counselors shall demonstrate multicultural counseling competence in practice. Counselors will not use counseling techniques or engage in any professional activities that discriminate against or show hostility toward individuals or groups based on gender, ethnicity, race, national origin, sex, sexual orientation, disability, religion, or any other legally prohibited basis.
	Research, 71. Counselors conducting research with underrepresented groups must take into consideration their historical, diverse, and multicultural experiences, and only use techniques and approaches based on established, clinically sound theory applicable to underrepresented populations.

These ethical standards of various counseling-related associations share similar fundamental principles. The standards emphasize *advocacy* as one of the key commonalities. Regardless of their focus or specialty, counseling associations recognize the important role of counselors as advocates. We are expected to engage in client advocacy at the individual, group, institutional, and societal levels. This collective acknowledgment highlights the importance of counselors working to address barriers and obstacles that impede the well-being of our clients. Furthermore, the ethical standards commonly stress counselors' ongoing commitment to cultural competence and awareness in order to recognize and address biases, prejudices, and oppression that might affect their clients. This recognition extends to understanding one's own biases, promoting self-reflection, and participating in continuous education to mitigate these biases. The shared focus on cultural competence further specifies counselors' responsibilities of ensuring that the voices of their clients are heard and valued by enhancing both the autonomy and the self-advocacy skills of their clients.

BOX 5.2 PROFILE OF A PRACTITIONER: JUSTIN DODSON, PHD, LICENSED PROFESSIONAL COUNSELOR

Two experienced professional counselors were invited to interviews to gain insights into their paths toward achieving cultural competence in counseling. The interviews, structured around guided questions, aimed to explore their individual journeys and shed light on practical ways to implement social justice and advocacy within the counseling profession. The questions delved into their personal definitions of social justice and advocacy, their perspectives on advocacy within the counseling field, and their firsthand experiences in implementing social justice and advocacy as professional counselors. The first interview is with Justin Dodson, PhD, LPC.

IMG 5.1. Justin Dodson, PhD, Licensed Professional Counselor

Journey to Becoming a Counselor

I identify as a middle-class, African American male with pronouns he/him. I am a counselor educator, licensed counselor, behavioral health consultant, and author. I value education because I was taught knowledge is knowing you can learn more, and education can't be taken away from you. I attended the University of Tennessee, Chattanooga, where I earned my undergraduate degree in psychology. I graduated as the first African American male to earn a master's degree in counseling from Lipscomb University. I am also the first African American male to earn a PhD in counselor education and supervision from the University of Memphis. I am a published author of *The Courage of A Single Freckle*, *Navigating Your Black*, which is meant to create space for race relations, recognizing bias, and identity development.

Living as a minority male in spaces that don't always feel safe is challenging. Many people will tell you to "play the game" or "keep your head down" as a "how-to" in navigating academia or corporate workspaces. I quickly learned that the game I was playing was one that required parts of me that I wouldn't compromise. Writing became how I vented because my words wouldn't judge me or challenge my experiences as a distorted or irrational. My book was my journal throughout both graduate programs, navigating workplace issues, and poses thought-provoking questions at the end of each chapter to allow the reader to write their own story. We can buy textbooks anywhere. However, they are typically from a limited worldview. My book allows readers to reflect on their own experiences. After all, authentic storytelling is how we make sense of the world.

I opened Navigating Courage, Counseling, and Consultation to give men a safe space to feel safe, seen, and challenged. Many times, men don't have the same opportunities as others to experience emotions without being judged—get to acknowledge sadness versus anger, hurt or rejection. Men are expected to only be masculine, providers, aggressive, and handy. The world places its expected definition onto us that we often subscribe to without truly identifying how we define manhood. Unfortunately, that narrative doesn't allow a complete story to be told of the male experience, and definitely not the black male experience. My practice aims at allowing men to exist safely. I believe strongly in this, so I positioned myself to fulfill my purpose and execute my vision. I hope that my practice continues to grow so that more people can be served through purpose-driven work.

My journey as a therapist came about by learning that every challenge we have is not a mental illness, and sometimes our lack of coping is due to limited skills and poor decision-making. Everyone has a role to play in this world; I am glad that I found my purpose through business ownership and formal training as a mental health professional.

What is your personal definition of social justice and advocacy?

Social Justice is the world distributing equal human rights, and rectifying wrongs for future peace. Advocacy is practicing assertiveness for self and others in search of social justice, especially when representing on behalf of someone who can benefit from assistance.

How do you view advocacy as a counselor?

Counselors play several roles on any given day as it pertains to client care. When a counselor is able to advocate for a client, we are teaching and modeling behavior we want the client to exhibit. We are teaching a skill the client will use one day to fill in the gap for themselves. Advocacy as a therapist is being a voice that can be heard for someone others aren't paying attention to.

Discuss a time you implemented social justice advocacy as a professional counselor.

At the start of my career, I worked with minors who had sexually offended another minor. My role included providing individual, family, and group therapy for each client while in my care. The role that was equally as important was to educate members of their interdisciplinary teams on the minors' needs and history of trauma, and ask for what the client didn't have a voice to ask for. Many times, that included fighting with legal teams, the Department of Children Services, staff, families, and a system that appears to work on behalf of minors but is set up to save face and earn money.

Social Justice Counseling

The greatest threat of harm doesn't come from any bomb
The moment you refuse the human rights of just a few
What happens when that few includes you?

Immortal Technique, *Civil War*

Historical Knowledge of Social Justice in the Counseling Profession

The above lyrics ask an essential question of counselors committed to social justice. What happens when you have power and privilege but do not speak up for the oppressed? Paulo Freire (2011) argued that it is incumbent upon those in power to lift the downtrodden and fight to dismantle systems of injustice. This sentiment is embraced by professional counselors: Promoting social justice is an ethical responsibility (e.g., ACA, 2014; AMHCA, 2020; ASCA, 2022) and is woven into the fabric of the profession (Ratts, 2009). Born out of growth from multicultural counseling, the fifth force of counseling, social justice counseling, allows the counselor to take a balanced perspective in the counseling room, and to integrate individually based treatment that accounts for environmental conditions that impact human development (Ratts et al., 2004).

There are several working definitions of social justice counseling in the profession. C. C. Fouad et al. (2006) emphasized the equal redistribution of resources and opportunities by alternating the societal structures. Hipolito-Delgado and Lee (2007) defined social justice counseling as the full participation of individuals in society regardless of race, ethnicity, gender, age, ability status, sexual affliction, or social class. Counselors for Social Justice, a division of ACA, defined social justice counseling as confronting oppressive systems of power and privilege impacting the clients and professional counselors while working for positive change in society (Counselors for Social Justice, n.d.). Finally, Ratts and Pedersen (2014) defined social justice counseling as the role counselors take in a mutually collaborative process with clients that counselors strive to achieve. A critical consciousness, advocacy competency, and a past, present, and future orientation worldview of society and our clients are naturally embedded in social justice counseling.

Social Justice Counselors Are Self-Aware

BOX 5.3 **FOCUS ON CLIENT CARE**

Jesus is a 10-year-old Latinx boy from Guatemala who arrived illegally in the United States 6 months ago. Jesus' family settled in a small, rural town in the southeastern United States. Jesus has extended family in the area, which drew his parents to migrate to the area.

Upon arriving in the area, Jesus and his family received comments and ridicule from community members. Jesus constantly receives messages that he and his family needs to "return back to the country they came from." Jesus even receives threats and bullying at school, which should be a safe space for him. However, he receives little support from his school counselor and teachers. More than once, Jesus has cried and begged his parents to take him back "home."

Jesus' parents do not know where to turn to help him. Although well-intentioned, Jesus's parents do not seek help from a trained Clinical Mental Health Counselor because they are unfamiliar with counseling. In addition, they view the school as a hostile environment because many of Jesus' troubles stem from his treatment in the school environment. At a loss on how to help, Jesus's parents feel their only recourse is to return to Guatemala for the sake of their son.

Pause and Reflect

What emotions does this story elicit? What thoughts on how you could help Jesus and his family as a counselor in training? Did plans and interventions on how you, as a counselor, could help?

Xenomisia is on the rise in the United States (Adnan et al., 2023). Jesus and his family's struggle to migrate to the United States is typical. The dominant culture, which sits in the seats of power and privilege, constructs barriers and systems of oppression to maintain control over nondominant cultures (Johnson, 2018). Most times, however, those in power do not realize the privileges they hold.

BOX 5.4 **PAUSE AND REFLECT: PREPARING TO ADVOCATE AGAINST XENOMISIA**

The term *xenomisia* is defined as hatred of people with actual or perceived nondominant ethnic identities or based on their country of origin. As a future counselor who will be working with a community of people, have you ever experienced xenomisia in your community? Thinking of xenomisia specific to your community, how do you think you can advocate for your clients as it relates specifically to helping others overcome xenomisia? Hint: Use the information you learned about advocacy to help yourself develop a plan to be an advocate.

Counseling ethical codes (ACA, 2014; AMCHA, 2020; & ASCA, 2022) are clear that counselors-in-training should develop self-awareness to be effective practitioners. Moreover, Ratts et al. (2016) stated that counselors should navigate their privileged and marginalized identities while integrating the privileged and marginalized identities into the therapeutic relationship.

The ADDRESSING model is a useful framework counselors can use to explore their identities and biases (Hays, 2008), as well as the identities of their clients. ADDRESSING provides counselors with ten distinct cultural identities to self-reflect on in the therapeutic relationship (Hays, 2008; see activities section at the end of the chapter).

Social Justice Skills

Chan (2021) called for counselors to create deep and intentional partnerships to collaborate with marginalized communities for the betterment of society. The skills needed to be an effective social justice counselor are much like the skills required to be an effective counselor. Counselors use evidence-based treatments and interventions in a collaborative process to help guide their personal growth. At its core, social justice skills mirror the collaborative therapeutic process inasmuch as the skills require self-awareness and the knowledge of the historical, current, and possible future sociopolitical landscape that may impact marginalized communities.

School counselors have similar tools for implementing and promoting social justice. Ratts and Greenleaf (2018) created a model for school counselors to address systems of oppression impacting students in the school environment. The authors posited that school counselors are in a unique position to impact the academic, career, and personal position of students through the MSJCC framework by addressing issues of power and privilege (Ratts & Greenleaf, 2018). The framework requires school counselors to respect the intersectional identities of students while acknowledging the blatant or hidden issues of inequalities in the school environment.

Similarly, the 3-C model (Marbley et al., 2017) provides counselors with a framework to view social justice while challenging one's bias. This relational, collaborative, reciprocal model is centered on developing healthy, egalitarian relationships that are respectful in nature. In addition, the relationships should be collaborative and creative. Finally, reciprocity is essential in the relationship. In essence, social justice is a giving endeavor in which we give ourselves for the greater good and model such a behavior. More to come about skills later in the chapter.

Advocacy Models in Counseling

The profession has several advocacy models. One of the more prominent models is the counselor-advocate-scholar model (CAS; Ratts & Greenleaf, 2018). Counselors can use CAS as a framework to merge their counselor, advocate, and scholar roles in the pursuit of advocating for marginalized communities (Ratts & Greenleaf, 2018). Counselors have different roles in empowering clients and communities. Depending on the situation, professional counselors may need to assume the role of counselor, advocate, or scholar, or we may need to integrate two or more roles to accomplish a goal (see Figure 5.2).

Ratts and Greenleaf (2018) distinguished each role and its responsibilities. In the role of a counselor, different therapeutic modalities can be used to externalize the oppression and privilege clients may have internalized due to socialization and environmental factors. In the advocate role, counselors are viewed as influencers. In this role, counselors should use their power and

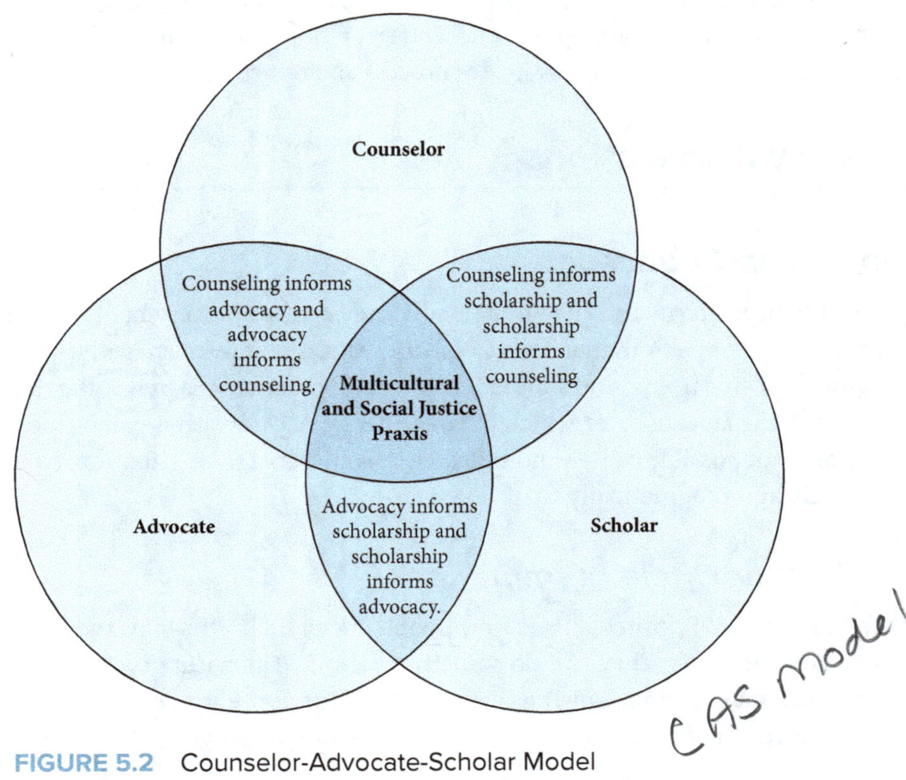

FIGURE 5.2 Counselor-Advocate-Scholar Model

CAS model
– Ratts + Greenleaf

privilege to work within their community to effect change to oppressive barriers that impede the growth of the marginalized community. In the final role, scholar, the counselor understands that research and practice are intimately woven together to inform best practices for giving voice to marginalized communities.

The CAS model is best operationalized through a biopsychosocial perspective (Ratts & Greenleaf, 2018). Biology, psychology, and the environment all affect how humans develop throughout their lifespan (Sigelman & Rider, 2022). Applying that understanding to the CAS model means that the counselor cannot have a narrow worldview of the client; instead, the counselor should factor in and explore the three variables as a cohesive unit. Figure 5.2 gives an operationalization overview of the CAS model.

The need for advocacy extends beyond direct or indirect advocacy for clients. The counseling profession also needs advocacy! Moorhead et al. (2023) called counselors to promote the uniqueness of the profession with legislative bodies. As such, Farrell and Barrio-Minton (2019) developed the three-tiered legislative professional advocacy model to advocate with respective legislative bodies. They break down the model into three phases: advocacy catalyst, advocacy action, and advocacy training.

The advocacy catalyst phase symbolizes what caused the counselor to take action and is internal (Farrell & Barrio-Minton, 2019). The next phase the authors described in the process is the advocacy action. In the advocacy action phase, the counselor moves from internal to external and takes action on the legislative issue. Picking your battles and making the legislative advocacy process their own is vital. The final phase is advocacy training. This phase is marked by collaboration and mentorship with other counselors, self-training, and trial and error. Importantly, the model is iterative and cyclical, reminding advocates the importance of process and returning to critical phases when needed.

Advocacy Applications

Advocacy in Counseling

Advocacy is a broad term and engaging in advocacy can seem overwhelming and daunting. As such, advocacy must be individualized to specific causes that resonate with the counselor, is targeted toward specific needs, and should be direct and practical (Farrell & Barrio-Minton, 2019). In determining what causes for which to advocate, novice advocates can become overwhelmed by the number of possible causes and injustices that deserve their attention, so it's important to choose wisely and pragmatically.

What Is Your Circle of Influence?

Stephen Covey (1989) posited, "Proactive people focus their efforts in the Circle of Influence. They work on the things they can do something about. The nature of their energy is positive, enlarging, and magnifying, causing their Circle of Influence to increase" (p. 83). Mr. Covey's statement conveys a powerful yet largely misunderstood message in the advocacy realm.

We all belong to sociopolitical, ecological systems (Bronfenbrenner, 1979). Moreover, advocating for the marginalized is part of a counselor's professional identity (Gibson et al., 2010). Using Bronfenbrenner's (1979) five-level ecological systems model, Chan et al. (2019) posited an approach for counselor educators to implement student-focused advocacy training within the profession. This is a prime example of the *how* within counselor educators' circle of influence. Figure 5.3 provides an overview of the ecological system in terms of advocacy within counselor education.

The How of Advocating at the Microlevel

The number of causes to advocate for as a counselor in training and even as a professional counselor can feel daunting. To this end, we suggest a microsystem-based approach (Bronfenbrenner, 1979). As mentioned, we exist in a sociopolitical ecological system that starts with your local city and county governments. All too often, the national landscape dictates the charge on an imposing level, but as a novice advocate, entering into that system can feel overwhelming and intimidating. In addition, national issues are often born out of local ones that have caught the eye of the national media and politicians, so we suggest you start by becoming aware of issues at your local level of government. Many local municipalities offer residents the ability to subscribe to meeting agendas and minutes or recordings from previous council meetings in addition to attending live.

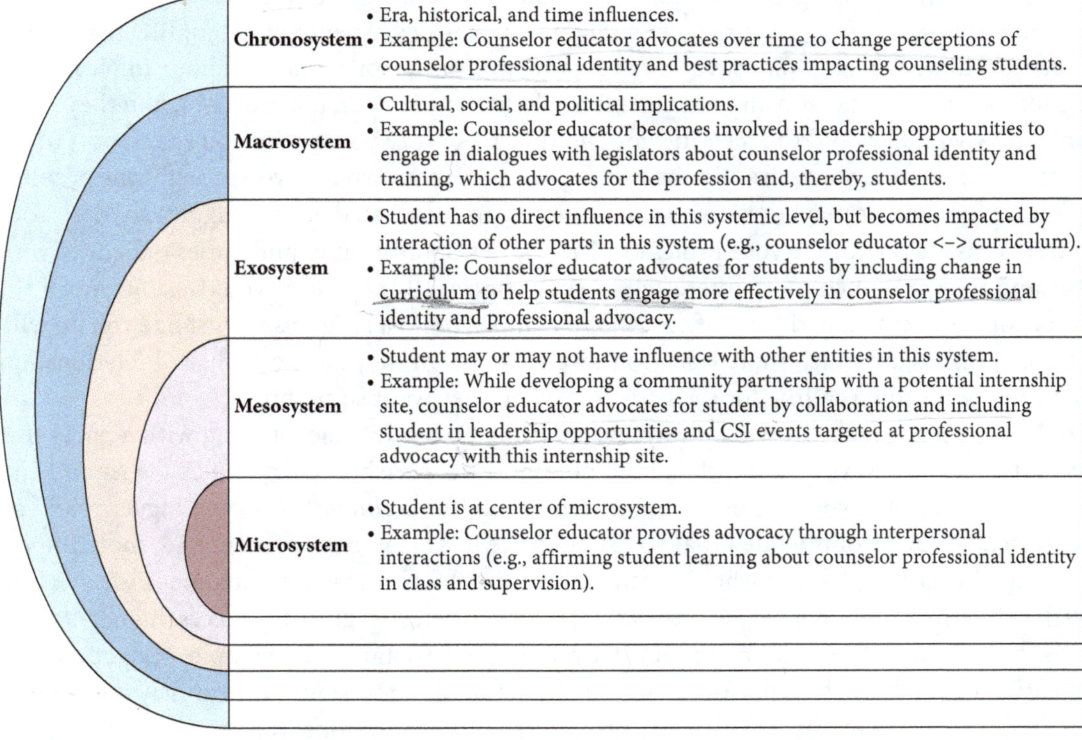

FIGURE 5.3 The Ecological System and Advocacy

Social media is a powerful tool for knowing what is going on at the local level. With the ongoing demise of local newspapers (Bosman, 2019), individuals are turning to social media platforms such as Facebook, X, and news apps to know what is going on locally. Plus, social media allows individuals to take control and distribute news to others in their local networks. Although social media is a valuable tool, it is important and ethical to ensure that the information is accurate and reliable (ACA, 2014; CRCC, 2023). Before circulating information, you should consider the following: (1) Is this an original article or piece of content? (2) Who shared or created the information? (3) When was the information created? (4) Why was the information shared (Calabrese, 2020)?

An example of a possible advocacy action at the local level that impacts LGBTQ+ and African American communities is the widespread initiative of several municipalities to ban books that are considered *inappropriate*. Taking a stand at the local level against censorship by organizing like-minded individuals and having your voices heard can be a positive step. Starting at the local level is akin to putting out a small brush fire rather than a large wildfire.

Building a Circle of Influence

Another advocacy approach is to build relationships with your state representative (Farrell & Barrio-Minton, 2019). State representatives are citizens' voice in Congress and building relationships with them gives you the ability to share your concerns on an ongoing basis, rather than contacting them cold when a pressing issue arises. It might sound daunting to build such a relationship but as a counselor in training, we suspect you might have some experience with building these types of relationships. For example, have you ever gone to a professor at the 11th hour to plead your case for, say, an extension on an assignment? You've never met with the professor, and they really don't know you. How did the meeting go? Did they recognize you, or did you spend part of the meeting introducing yourself? Did the professor express concern that you brought the problem up a little too late, or maybe that you should have communicated your struggles sooner? Your representative is not unlike your professor. They have responsibilities and duties outside of your issue and they are much more interested in your concern if they know you. In short, open the line of communication early and often. And remember, build a *relationship* just like you do with clients. Humans are much more open to those with whom they have established relationships than those who come calling for the first time when they want something.

In the advocacy realm you are always negotiating. To be clear, negotiating with a party that has more power than you do is difficult but not impossible (Fisher & Ury, 1991). Fisher and Ury (1991) suggested that you do not turn the negotiation into a *slugfest*. They are bigger than you are. Instead, they recommended that you stick to the merits of the argument and, more importantly, the key principles and what is needed most to achieve a positive outcome (Fisher & Ury, 1991). While you might not get everything you hoped to get, engaging in a successful negotiation tends to result in getting at least part of what you sought to obtain. For example, a negotiation to increase state Medicaid benefits for mental health to unlimited sessions per year may not happen, but if you are able to increase the limit from 12 sessions to 18 sessions, you are making progress.

Counselors are trained in skills they can apply to advocacy. As a counselor in training, you are learning how to carefully listen and intentionally respond to clients in a therapeutic manner that does not rupture the relationship you are working to build. In short, as advocates, we seek to understand and to be understood as empathic communicators (Covey, 1989). Alexandra Campion (2021) discussed pointers on how best to use social justice language in your TEDx Talk. The speaker discussed agreeing on terms and sticking to the merits of your case while not getting stuck on the labels (Campion, 2021; TED, 2021). They argued that the language you use matters in this divisive world we live in. For example, Campion (2021) addressed how the call to *defund the police* can elicit strong reactions from both sides of the argument, provoking images of the *Purge* movie franchise. Instead of an all-or-nothing approach, Campion (2021) argued that social justice advocates should be mindful of their language and consider a more reformist mindset rather than focusing on abolishing the justice system in its entirety.

An awareness and understanding of the difference between an "-ism," a system of oppression (e.g., racism, classism), and an "-ist" (e.g., racist, classist), individuals who choose to operate within that system to maintain the status quo (e.g., racist, classist), is an important distinction for social justice advocates to know and convey when speaking through a social justice lens (Campion, 2021). Ratts et al. (2016) argued that counselors need to understand the worldview of privileged clients in order to be culturally relevant, effective counselors. In turn, understanding the worldview of those in power and using that understanding to effect change is an essential attribute social justice advocates possess. Therefore, labeling issues as supporting racism or classism and giving evidence for why that's the case tends to be far more effective than labeling a person racist or classist.

Finally, we need to keep the end in mind. Social justice is the fifth force in counseling and is still in its relative infancy (Ratts, 2009). The road is long and fraught with landmines. Furthermore, those in power are not willing to just give away the privileges they have accumulated over the years with a "sure, here you go." As social justice warriors, we need to understand that the small progress and achievements we make on behalf of and with marginalized groups will feed into a greater ethos—a greater aspirational society that benefits all and not just the few. In short, keep fighting the good fight and causing good trouble.

BOX 5.5 **PROFILE OF A PRACTITIONER: TENNILLE A. BROWNRIGG, PHD, CERTIFIED SCHOOL COUNSELOR**

IMG 5.2. Tennille A. Brownrigg, PhD, Certified School Counselor

Journey to Becoming a Counselor

I am walking in my purpose. I am adhering to my calling. My journey to become a school counselor started with my decision to major in language arts education at Tuskegee University in Tuskegee, Alabama. Becoming an educator was always a dream of mine. So, when I became a teacher at Annapolis Senior High School after graduating with my BA, I realized that I was talking to students regularly about their future plans, goal setting, making good decisions, etc. I went to speak with one of the school counselors about all the needs of my students, and she looked at me, smiled and encouraged me to go back to school and get a master's degree in school counseling. As a middle-class, Black American female from a rural town called Leighton, Alabama, I remember the impact that my school counselor had on me and my decision to further my education. I wanted to pour into students in the same way. Nevertheless, I felt I needed to go the extra mile to ensure that future school counselors would have a mentor and support system that would spark their desire to do the same. So, after getting my MS in counseling, I returned to Texas A&M University–Commerce for my PhD in counseling with a focus on children and adolescents and student affairs. Since that time, I have worked with numerous populations. I am a certified teacher and school counselor in Alabama, Georgia, and Texas. I have worked in Xiamen, Fujian, China, at an IB World School, learning the intricacies of school counseling across cultures.

What is your personal definition of social justice and advocacy?

I would define social justice as being the means through which all humans can have access to equal rights and opportunities so that they may live healthy and productive lives. This can only happen through the advocacy and implementation of laws and policies that will ensure equity across the board for every human being. We have a moral obligation to fight for those who cannot fight for themselves. Advocacy means that if I have access to entities that act as gatekeepers, I use my voice to help level the playing field and create change for all people, using my voice to speak for those who have little or no voice. Having the ability to stand in the gaps for others, regardless of race, ethnicity, religious or spiritual affiliation, sexual identification or orientation, or socioeconomic status, means that I must serve as an advocate when their cry is not being heeded.

How do you view advocacy as a counselor?

Our job as advocates should not be taken lightly. We have the power to create change within the field of mental health, and we must help shift the narrative of how it is viewed across cultures. This is the first step to garnering the support necessary to make sure that future generations see wellness in mental health as the standard and not something that only other demographics take seriously or have access to. By advocating for the profession, client well-being, better policies to protect and support vulnerable populations, etc., we will set the stage for change throughout mental health entities.

Discuss a time you implemented social justice advocacy as a professional counselor.

When I moved to China, it was evident that there were cultural differences that often made it difficult to ensure that students' mental health needs were being met. To ensure that we were respectful of culture while supporting a shift in ideology regarding the necessity of mental health support within schools, I worked with my principal to develop and implement cooperation between several local and international schools with mental health agencies that would provide testing and support for their students. Because nothing of this kind was in place, we were able to see more parents attending parent seminars and asking for resources to support the needs of the children at our schools.

Approaches to Social Justice and Advocacy in Counseling Relationships

Every counseling relationship is embedded in society and is susceptible to societal influences but also has the potential to effect changes. While counselors and clients are individuals, they are connected as integral members of history, culture, and society. Their experiences, values, perceptions, beliefs, and even the resources available to them are deeply rooted in the tapestry of sociocultural factors that surround them. Accordingly, mental health, as a fundamental aspect of an individual's well-being, is profoundly influenced by the sociocultural context.

To gain a comprehensive understanding of mental health, it is essential to examine symptoms within the larger framework of societal inequities and oppression. Mental health disparities often mirror broader societal disparities. Discrimination, marginalization, and systemic inequalities can contribute to the development and exacerbation of mental health symptoms. Historical factors, such as a legacy of colonialism, slavery, and other forms of oppression leave lasting imprints on the mental health of individuals and communities. Therefore, counselors must adopt an integrated approach that considers not only the individual but also the society they come from. They must recognize the societal factors that shape their clients' experiences and the barriers that may impede their mental health journeys. By doing so, counselors can play a pivotal role in not only alleviating individual symptoms but also contributing to larger societal shifts toward greater equity, inclusion, and well-being. In this way, counseling becomes a potent tool for social justice and advocacy.

Integrating social justice and advocacy into counseling relationships may range from counselors fostering their own awareness of historical and sociocultural factors and their contributions, whether intentional or unintentional, to motivating clients to participate in social initiatives to promote changes at broader levels. This section will explore diverse approaches, skills, and considerations essential for effectively practicing social justice and advocacy within the context of counseling relationships.

Cultural Humility

Cultural humility, a concept introduced by Tervalon and Murray-García (1998), represents a profound commitment to a lifelong journey of self-examination. As you learned in Chapter 3, cultural humility revolves around the idea that individuals, particularly counselors and other helping professionals in culturally diverse contexts, must engage in continuous critical self-reflection and cultivate deep self-awareness while maintaining a humble and open attitude. This ongoing process unfolds at both the intrapersonal and interpersonal levels. The practice of cultural humility is central to social justice and advocacy within counseling relationships. Interpersonally, counselors embracing cultural humility engage in self-reflection concerning their own cultural identities, which encompass aspects of privilege, oppression, values, and personal experiences. In doing so, counselors acknowledge their position within a larger systemic framework, thereby enhancing their comprehension of systemic power dynamics. This plays a pivotal role in their practice of social justice advocacy as counselors begin to recognize the intersections between their own identities and their environmental context, while also understanding the systematic roles of oppression (Ratts, 2009). With this awareness and understanding, counselors become better equipped to conceptualize their clients and the challenges they face within the broader societal context. This allows counselors to adopt an open perspective that incorporates the impact of power and oppression into all aspects of understanding their clients' experiences.

At the interpersonal level, counselors create a supportive, safe, and encouraging environment for clients to explore their experiences and the influence of sociocultural factors. Through practicing cultural humility, counselors encourage clients to identify themselves as cultural beings and share their lived experiences, strengths, and challenges. Consequently, clients gain a better understanding of their experiences within the sociocultural context and can identify systemic determinants and barriers that affect their mental health. In the pursuit of social justice, counselors may, for instance, invite clients to discuss potential changes needed to address these issues. Such interactions and discussions between counselors and clients provide opportunities for engagement in actions aimed at effecting social change (Singh et al., 2020).

Cultural Broaching

An integral facet of the counseling process that closely aligns with the principles of social justice and advocacy is cultural broaching. In the context of professional counseling, cultural broaching represents a counselor's deliberate and receptive approach to integrating sociocultural elements and individual cultural identities into the counseling relationship. It involves the counselor's readiness and competence in facilitating discussions on diversity, grounded in genuine and open attitudes, and sustained through consistent and ongoing actions (Day-Vines et al., 2007).

While cultural humility serves as the overarching attitude and foundational framework guiding counselors in their approach to the counseling relationship, broaching represents a proactive strategy. The interconnectedness between cultural humility and broaching is profound. In essence, broaching can be viewed as cultural humility in action (Jones & Branco, 2020). While cultural humility lays the foundation by cultivating the counselor's introspection, self-awareness, and receptivity to cultural diversity, broaching translates these attitudes into concrete, real-time practices within the counseling sessions. It is a dynamic, hands-on approach where counselors take deliberate steps to engage clients in conversations about their cultural backgrounds, experiences, and identities. Broaching is characterized by counselors actively initiating and fostering these discussions within the counseling sessions.

The significance of broaching in counseling is multifaceted. First, it empowers clients by acknowledging and validating their cultural identities, thereby fostering a sense of belonging and trust within the therapeutic relationship. Also, it enables clients to explore the impact of their cultural backgrounds on their psychological well-being and personal growth. Moreover, broaching facilitates the identification of potential disparities and injustices that clients may face due to their cultural identities, which is essential for advocating on their behalf and promoting social justice within the counseling context.

In order to effectively implement broaching in counseling, counselors need to be aware of clients' readiness and willingness to engage in cultural discussions. Otherwise, resistance from the client may negatively influence the counseling relationship and counseling process. For example, some clients who are not ready or willing to engage in broaching may become defensive by refusing to accept or discuss social injustice in the current society or its impact on them (King, 2021). Sometimes, they defend themselves by saying that they are not the ones who sustain the status quo or by saying that they don't experience microaggressions, oppression, or discrimination. Therefore, counselors need to be strategic with how they address such resistance by using client-tailored interventions (e.g., reflecting, assessing identity development stages) and not forcing a broaching conversation a client does not want to have.

Through cultural broaching, small changes can begin to take root within individuals, eventually culminating in an impact on society despite their seemingly trivial effect initially. Hence, cultural broaching assumes paramount importance, prompting counselors to implement it in order to create social justice–driven transformations within clients, as well as to better our society.

Frameworks for Broaching in Counseling

To effectively incorporate broaching behaviors into counseling, many counselors employ and adapt relevant frameworks that provide structured guidance and strategies. These frameworks serve as invaluable tools for initiating and navigating discussions concerning sociocultural factors. One such comprehensive framework is the multidimensional model of broaching behavior (MMBB), which equips counselors with specific broaching skills and techniques for racial, ethnic, and cultural (REC) topics within the counseling context (Day-Vines et al., 2020). The MMBB encompasses four critical broaching dimensions (i.e., intracounseling, intraindividual, intra-REC, and inter-REC). According to the authors, broaching the intracounseling dimension may involve discussions of their understanding of REC topics, differences and similarities, or related concerns aimed to create a space in which such discussions are permitted and encouraged and to reduce the power difference between client and counselor. When broaching the intraindividual dimension, counselors acknowledge and address the confluence and intersectionality of identities, which will also facilitate the exploration of oppressions that clients experience.

Broaching the intra-REC dimension includes the discussions of cultural struggles that may arise between clients and others who share the same REC identities. With these discussions, clients gain a better understanding of within-group and between-group differences and similarities. For broaching the inter-REC dimension, counselors and clients acknowledge different forms of oppression (e.g., microaggressions, discrimination) clients experience and discuss how these experiences impact the client's well-being. Broaching in this dimension also involves identifying skills and strategies to disrupt systematic barriers, including implementing social justice and advocacy interventions to bring social changes to the lives of marginalized populations.

In addition to the MMBB, counselors can use frameworks such as the ADDRESSING and RESPECTFUL models to enhance their broaching behaviors. These models offer comprehensive approaches to understanding the multifaceted aspects of cultural identity and the sociocultural factors that influence human development and well-being. The ADDRESSING model introduced by Hays (2001) highlights critical dimensions of cultural identity, including age, developmental disabilities, acquired disabilities, religion, ethnicity, sexual orientation, socioeconomic status, indigenous group membership, nationality, and gender. By comprehensively recognizing these identity facets, counselors gain a deeper understanding of a client's cultural identity and can use this knowledge to initiate meaningful conversations about their lived experiences and potential sources of oppression. The RESPECTFUL Model, introduced by D'Andrea & Daniels, 1997, expands the scope of cultural factors that impact individuals. This expansive framework encourages counselors to consider the broader spectrum of factors that shape a client's identity, thus enabling them to engage in comprehensive broaching conversations that address the client's unique needs and experiences.

BOX 5.6 **THE RESPECTFUL MODEL (D'ANDREA & DANIELS, 1997)**

R: Religious and Spiritual Identity
E: Economic Status and Social Class Background
S: Sexual (Affectual/Relational) Identity
P: Psychological Maturity
E: Ethnic/Racial Identity
C: Chronological/Developmental Challenges
T: Trauma (Big "T" and Little "t" trauma)
F: Family Background/History
U: Unique Physical Characteristics
L: Location and Language

By employing these models, counselors are better equipped to navigate the intricacies of cultural identities and initiate dialogues regarding the impact of these identities and the associated dynamics of power and oppression. Ultimately, these frameworks serve as tools for promoting social justice and advocacy within the counseling relationship by fostering understanding, empathy, and equitable support for diverse clients.

Empowering Clients Through Social Justice Advocacy and Engagement

Empowerment is "a process of increasing personal, interpersonal, or political power so that individuals, families, and communities can take action to improve their situation" (Holcomb-McCoy & Bryan, 2010, p. 262). It is a pivotal concept within the counseling field, with implications for individuals and society. When counselors embark on the journey of empowering clients, they embark on a transformative process that not only enhances clients' physical, mental, emotional, and spiritual well-being but also fosters their ability to practice greater autonomy and control over their health-related decisions and actions (Faridi et al., 2023). However, the significance of empowerment transcends personal health; it serves as a potent catalyst for addressing pervasive power imbalances within society, thereby catalyzing social justice and advocacy efforts

(Goodman et al., 2004). The essence of empowerment, from a counseling perspective, is centered on the client's realization that they possess the inherent power to shape the trajectory of their own life. This profound revelation is a cornerstone of therapeutic empowerment and underscores its importance in counseling relationships.

Empowerment begins with the recognition that clients have the capacity to exercise control over their lives. This autonomy is supported by all counseling *Code of Ethics* (ACA, 2014; AMHCA, 2020; ASCA, 2022; CRCC, 2023; NBCC, 2023). Counselors facilitate this awakening by helping clients identify their strengths, values, and aspirations. By acknowledging their own agency, clients are better equipped to address challenges and navigate life's complexities. Empowering clients also involves a deep exploration of the systems and sociocultural factors that influence their lives, families, and communities. Counselors guide clients in recognizing how these systems impact their well-being and opportunities. This heightened awareness forms the foundation for informed and purposeful action.

Moreover, empowerment is a mechanism through which clients become agents of change within societal systems marked by power imbalances. This proactive stance is crucial in the pursuit of social justice and advocacy. Clients are encouraged to channel their awareness and agency into initiatives aimed at dismantling oppressive structures and promoting equity. Consequently, empowered clients actively engage in initiatives and actions that seek to rectify societal injustices. Clients who become actively involved in social justice work often experience a heightened sense of control over their circumstances. They see themselves as agents of change, capable of influencing and reshaping their environments. Also, empowerment strategies equip clients with the skills and confidence to advocate for themselves and others. Counselors play a vital role in supporting clients as they identify challenges and disparities, confront systemic obstacles, and initiate actions within their communities and society (Savage et al., 2005). In fact, many counselors engage in advocacy actions with their clients!

Empowerment is a collaborative endeavor grounded in the mutual trust and alliance between counselors and clients. This alliance is instrumental in guiding clients toward transformative self-discovery and facilitating their active participation in advocating for themselves and social change. Indeed, empowerment serves as a dynamic force for social justice and advocacy by supporting clients to recognize and harness their innate power and agency. By fostering awareness, imparting skills, and supporting clients' proactive engagement in systemic change, counselors contribute to the dismantling of diverse forms of oppression and the cultivation of more equitable and just realities for their clients and society at large.

Conclusion

Social justice and advocacy are essential components of the counseling profession, embodying the core principles of equity, inclusivity, and ethical responsibility. As the counseling landscape continues to evolve, the acquisition of robust skills in social justice and advocacy have become indispensable for professional counselors. This journey commences with understanding the systemic disparities and barriers faced by diverse populations. It extends to challenging discriminatory policies, promoting inclusivity within institutions, and actively striving to dismantle obstacles hindering marginalized communities. The application of social justice and advocacy skills requires counselors to possess a keen awareness of social justice issues, recognizing and deconstructing subtle biases and microaggressions. Counselors should further foster inclusive environments for clients with diverse cultural backgrounds and amplify the voices of those who have been historically marginalized individuals. We discussed an integrated approach that recognizes the societal factors shaping clients' lives. There are several strategies that will enable us to offer more empathetic and culturally sensitive care:

- By embracing cultural humility, counselors engage in continuous self-reflection, understanding their own cultural biases, and acknowledging systemic power dynamics. This introspection allows them to create a safe space where clients can explore their experiences within the sociocultural context.
- Cultural broaching, a proactive strategy, involves counselors initiating discussions about clients' cultural backgrounds and identities. This approach validates clients' experiences, fosters trust, and enables exploration of how cultural factors affect their well-being.
- To facilitate these discussions effectively, counselors can employ frameworks like the MMBB, ADDRESSING, and RESPECTFUL models, which provide structured guidance for addressing cultural identities and sociocultural factors.
- Empowerment is a central concept in counseling, involving clients recognizing their own agency and ability to shape their lives. Empowered clients, guided by counselors, become advocates for social change, actively engaging in initiatives to dismantle oppressive structures and promote equity.

Questions for Reflection

1. How do you connect the concepts of cultural humility, systemic oppression, and social justice advocacy?
2. What are some areas in your life that you can identify in which you have been an advocate?
3. Are there some causes or social justice issues that you would like to advocate for? Why?
4. Why are social justice and advocacy important in the counseling profession?
5. How would you describe advocacy to a person who has never heard the term before?

Applying What You Have Learned

Complete each of the following activities, considering what you learned from this chapter.

Activity #1: ADDRESSING Model Self-Assessment Worksheet

Use the table below to self-assess biases you may hold in each area. Once you are finished, write down the potential professional implications if you were to *not* work through your biases. Use this knowledge to help you create a plan to work through the biases you currently hold.

ADDRESSING FRAMEWORK

Cultural Influences	Self-Assessment of Biases
Age and generational influence	
Developmental disability	
Disability acquired later in life	
Religion and spiritual orientation	
Ethnic and racial identity	
Socioeconomic status	
Sexual orientation	
Indigenous heritage	
National origin	
Gender	

Activity #2: What Is Your Circle of Influence?

Where do you start to determine your circle of influence? One way is to identify the spaces and places you go regularly. Are you part of a club? Do you have a job? What about school? Do you volunteer? These are all spaces and places in which you have influence or could *choose to have influence* if the circumstances warrant it.

The *circumstances* are an important piece of the puzzle. Are there circumstances you have encountered that are unjust, inequitable, or discriminatory? Do you see a solution, or are you motivated to find a solution? Are you unsure how to answer either of these questions? Cook (2020) suggested that pre-advocacy action planning requires intentional thoughtfulness and that counselors can use the following questions to make advocacy choices.

1. What population do you feel most passionate about?
2. What do you perceive to be a "social problem" in your community?
3. What types of inequality do you see frequently?
4. What systemic inequalities/issues do you notice your clients encounter most frequently?
5. Have you noticed something that "makes your blood boil" when you hear about it? What is it?
6. What are your strengths? List professional and personal strengths.

After you have your answers, read through them and note the following:

- What themes do you notice in your answers?
- Which questions did you write the most about?
- What group/issue do you feel as if you gravitate toward most?
- How will your strengths influence the advocacy choices you make?

Do you have a better idea now of what circumstances might motivate you to advocate? What will you choose?

Credits

Fig. 5.1: R. L. Toporek & J. Daniels, "ACA Advocacy Competencies," https://www.counseling.org/docs/default-source/competencies/aca-advocacy-competencies-updated-may-2020.pdf, p. 3. Copyright © 2018 by American Counseling Association.

Fig. 5.2: Manivong J. Ratts & Arie T. Greenleaf, "Counselor–Advocate–Scholar Model: Changing the Dominant Discourse in Counseling," *Journal of Multicultural Counseling and Development*, vol. 46, no. 2. Copyright © 2018 by American Counseling Association.

CHAPTER 6

Cultural Identity Development Models

Alexandria Hepburn, Ryan Wisniewski, Rachel Mattingly, and Madeline Clark

An identity would seem to be arrived at by the way in which the person faces and uses [their] experience.

—James Baldwin

CHAPTER OVERVIEW

In this chapter, you will learn about several identity development models (IDMs) and their clinical applications. These models encourage clients and clinicians to engage in introspection, reflect on societal positioning, and conceptualize therapeutic processes from an identity development perspective. It is worth noting that a multitude of identities are represented by development models, while some identities have no specific model. These models provide a basis for understanding the cultural development of some clients; however, they do not represent the developmental experiences of *all* clients. It is important that counselors use culturally informed assessment processes (see Chapter 18) to identify cultural identities important to clients and how those identities impact their unique lived experiences.

LEARNING OBJECTIVES

By the end of this chapter, students will be able to

1. identify characteristics highlighted in cultural IDMs across various cultural groups,
2. apply appropriate counseling techniques and theories related to clients' cultural identity development,
3. discuss how counselor and client worldviews impact identification with cultural groups,
4. promote an understanding of the impacts of change across the lifespan based on cultural developmental models, and
5. apply ethical and culturally relevant research strategies to ensure updated and culturally competent care is provided to clients from various cultural groups.

CACREP 2016 STANDARDS

The information in this chapter supports the following standards:

- 2.F.2.b theories and models of multicultural counseling, cultural identity development, and social justice
- 2.F.2.a multicultural and pluralistic characteristics within and among diverse groups nationally and internationally and advocacy

- 2.F.2.d the impact of heritage, attitudes, beliefs, understandings, and acculturative experiences on an individual's views of others
- 2.F.3.f systemic and environmental factors that affect human development, functioning, and behavior
- 2.F.3.i ethical and culturally relevant strategies for promoting resilience and optimum development and wellness across the lifespan
- 2.F.5.a theories and models of counseling

CACREP 2024 STANDARDS

The information in this chapter supports the following standards:

- 3.B.1. theories and models of multicultural counseling, social justice, and advocacy
- 3.B.2. the influence of heritage, cultural identities, attitudes, values, beliefs, understandings, within-group differences, and acculturative experiences on individuals' worldviews
- 3.C.7. models of resilience, optimal development, and wellness in individuals and families across the lifespan
- 3.C.11. systemic, cultural, and environmental factors that affect lifespan development, functioning, behavior, resilience, and overall wellness
- 3.E.1 theories and models of counseling, including relevance to clients from diverse cultural backgrounds

Defining Identity Development and Introduction to Identity Development Models

Identity development is an ongoing, interactive, relationship-based process in which individuals develop a sense of understanding of themselves within a wider context of social and cultural norms (Huffaker & Calvert, 2005). Identity development can be formulated through cultural factors such as race, ethnicity, gender, spirituality, ability status, and social class. Importantly, many clients will develop in more than one identity domain, sometimes concurrently. For example, clients may examine their racial and social class identities at the same time, singularly, or sequentially (i.e., explore their racial identity and then their social class identity). The models presented in this chapter support clinicians' ability to understand clients' subjective viewpoints and experiences while strengthening the working alliance and treatment outcomes. While these models can be helpful tools, it is important to avoid overgeneralizations, confirmation bias, and stereotyping.

IDMs are not only for understanding clients' development—they are useful for counselors to understand their identities as well! As you learned in Chapter 5, the multicultural and social justice counseling competencies call counselors to understand their marginalized and privileged identities and how they may impact the counseling relationship with clients who have marginalized and privileged identities. As you read the models in this chapter, consider where you fit within each one, how you might like to develop further, and how your development may impact the counseling relationship.

TABLE 6.1 Identity Development Model Categories Overview

Model	Description
Racial/Ethnic Models	Provides an understanding of marginalized identities and experiences within the White-dominant culture. Useful in exploring individuals' current racial/ethnic identity experiences across identities. Can be general or specific.
LGBTGEQIAP+Models	Proposes an understanding of LGBTGEQIAP+ individuals' identity formation experiences. Useful in working with clients sharing similar experiences and for counselors to practice effectively with these individuals.
Disability Identity Development Models	Provides an understanding of the experiences of individuals living with disabilities.
Gender Models	Used to identify the general development of one's gender, including experiences outside of the heteronormative narrative.
Spirituality Models	Useful in exploring the development of clients' faith and spiritual experiences.
Social Class Models	Used to identify clients' social class and how classism affects mental health symptoms and diagnosis.

Brief Overview of Models

Before we move into exploring individual IDMs by cultural category, we provide an overview of the IDM categories (see Table 6.1). It is important to note that the *racial/cultural identity development models*, *majority and minority identity models*, *acculturation models*, and *ethnic identity formation* are considered general racial and ethnic development models, while the *American Indian identity development model*, *Asian American identity development model*, *Black American identity development model*, *Latinx identity development model*, *White identity development model*, and *Poston and bi/multiracial identity development models* are specific racial and ethnic IDMs.

Race and Ethnicity Identity Development Models

It is vital to acknowledge clients' racial identities. Racial identity development refers to one's individual and group value systems and ideologies rooted in racial identity and the awareness of how they relate to perceptions of other races, including racism (Helms, 1990; 2020). Racism plays a role in the development of racial and ethnic identity development; therefore, it is imperative to acknowledge its existence and understand the three racism types, as defined by Jones (1982):

1. **Individual Racism:** An individual's attitude, beliefs, and behaviors that enable the superiority of Whites, resulting in the inferiority of other racial groups.
2. **Institutional Racism:** Laws, social policies, and regulations that enable social and economic advantage of people who are White over Black, Indigenous, and People of Color (BIPOC).

3. **Cultural Racism:** Societal beliefs and customs that endorse the assumption that White culture, language, and traditions are superior to those of other races.
4. These three types of racism are represented at the micro- (individual), meso- (institutional), and macrolevels (institutional and cultural). While an individual may not personally identify with or hold overt, individual racist beliefs, they still benefit from and contribute to institutional and cultural racism, and counselors must understand these impacts for themselves and their clients.

BOX 6.1 **PAUSE AND REFLECT: YOUR EXPERIENCES WITH RACISM**

Racism is pervasive in U.S. culture and impacts everyone. BIPOC clients experience oppression and discrimination and their devastating impact, while White clients can participate in racism directly and/or indirectly by benefiting from institutional and cultural racism. While counselors explore clients' experiences and the impact racism has on their lives, they must understand their experiences with racism as well. As you read this section and progress in your counselor development, reflect on these questions:

1. In what ways has racism impacted your lived experience and the experiences of your friends, family, and loved ones?
2. How have you participated and/or benefited from racism, both knowingly and unknowingly?
3. How can your experiences with racism positively impact the counseling relationship or be detrimental to the counseling relationship?

Racial/Cultural Identity Development Model

Cultural oppression is a common, unifying experience for BIPOC in the United States. These experiences impact individual and group cultural identities. Atkinson and colleagues (1998) introduced a five-stage *racial/cultural identity development model* to explain common cultural experiences of BIPOC in the United States. This model illustrates the complexity of understanding one's own culture, the dominant culture, and how oppression has impacted individuals with nondominant racial identities. The five stages explore a person's cultural attitudes toward themselves, others in the same minority group, those of different minority groups, and the dominant group (Atkinson et al. 1998; 2013).

1. **Conformity:** Individuals hold beliefs that the White majority culture and standards are superior to their own culture. They might hold negative views of their own race and view themselves as the *exception* to racial and ethnic stereotypes. They may experience self-deprecating beliefs because of cultural distance from the dominant group.
2. **Dissonance:** A person realizes individual and systemic racism exist and acknowledges their personal interest in minority culture. The person no longer views the dominant White culture as flawless and gains perspective on systemic flaws.

3. **Resistance and Immersion:** The individual begins to reject dominant culture societal views and embrace their own culture and racial identity. Distrust in the dominant culture, because of harm inflicted on racial minorities, begins after gaining awareness and appreciation for diversity.
4. **Introspection:** Individuals begin to feel exhausted by feelings of anger and frustration toward the dominant cultural group and begin to shift emotional energy to strengthening personal cultural identity while respecting other groups. They develop more balanced perspectives about dominant and nondominant cultures.
5. **Integrative awareness:** Individuals develop a secure racial and cultural identity, and this is used to advocate for oppressed groups.

Hardiman-Jackson Identity Development Model

The *Hardiman-Jackson identity development model* examines the racial consciousness and attitudes of White individuals toward people of other racial and ethnic backgrounds (Hardiman & Jackson, 1992). This model contains five stages that involve White individuals' experiences as they work to develop a positive White identity that includes challenging racism, White privilege, and injustices.

1. **Naïve:** There is little awareness of cultural differences, yet they do not fear other racial groups or think much about their own racial identity, as they are the dominant culture.
2. **Acceptance:** There are two phases to this stage: *passive* and *active* acceptance. In passive acceptance, individuals typically avoid contact with racial minorities or adopt a supportive attitude from afar. In active acceptance, individuals are conscious of racial privilege and may express feelings of collective superiority.
3. **Resistance:** A shift occurs from blaming members of minority groups for their conditions to acknowledging the realities of unjust and biased systems. Guilt and shame may occur during this stage because of the historical actions of White people, while others may want to be *adopted* by people of color.
4. **Redefinition:** Individuals attempt to redefine Whiteness and move past guilt, identifying that one culture is not better than another.
5. **Internalization:** Individuals come to positively accept their White identity via challenging racism, understanding the effects of White privilege, and working toward systemic change.

Minority Identity Development Model

The *minority identity model* (Cross, 1971) is based on the premise that racial and ethnic minorities are brought up and live within the context of discrimination and oppression. Racial and ethnic minorities are seen as *different* in relation to the dominant White culture. The change in identity is continual and nonlinear, involving re-socialization through different development levels. Given the nonlinear process, there is no standard time frame or age in which a person matures through the stages (Yakushko et al., 2010). The five stages of the minority identity model are:

1. **Pre-encounter:** The individual may hold color-blind attitudes toward race as well as exhibit the viewpoints of the dominant culture. May hold low self-concept and feel discomfort or shame about their nondominant identity.
2. **Encounter:** Awareness is developed surrounding oppression and discrimination, and they consider what being a minority means to them. Often, experiences of discrimination facilitate reflection.
3. **Immersion-Emersion:** Individuals begin to experience a shift in their alignment with the dominant culture's views and move toward aligning with their minority identity. This necessitates critical thinking and self-reflection in order to discard previous beliefs regarding the dominant culture in favor of their own. Also includes examinations of beliefs from different cultural perspectives.
4. **Internalization:** Individuals begin to feel stable and develop a strong sense of their own identity as well as their identity as part of their racial/ethnic group.
5. **Internalization-Commitment:** Their newly gained knowledge is used to deal with oppression in a way that is socially active and beneficial for their identity group, as well as others.

American Indian Identity Development Model

American Indians, interchangeably called *Indigenous people* throughout this chapter and text, experience struggles with maintaining their identity amid acculturation pressures, historical genocide, colonization, and the theft of land and culture. It is important to understand client empowerment in their own self-identification. The *American Indian identity development model* (Horse, 2001) outlines five influences on American Indian consciousness, defined as "principles or moral values that guide an individual's actions" (Horse, 2005, p. 65). This model differs from the previous models because it is nonlinear. Individuals do not aspire to reach a higher level of American Indian consciousness but rather use this model to explore how they relate to the five influences and the importance each influence has in their lives.

1. The extent to which one is grounded in one's Native American language and culture, one's cultural identity. One's cultural identity can encompass language, clothing, and religious beliefs that one derives from their tribe and their Native American identity.
2. The validity of one's American Indian genealogy.
3. The extent to which one holds to a traditional American Indian philosophy or worldview that emphasizes balance and harmony and draws on Indian spirituality.
4. One's self-concept as an American Indian.
5. One's enrollment (or lack thereof) in a tribe.

The pressures of acculturation have led some Indigenous communities to respond with a deliberate return to practices, language, and knowledge of tribal traditions. Some colleges and universities have been established with these tribal traditions in mind (e.g., Fond du Lac Tribal and Community College, Diné College). A comparative example is the concept of time in mainstream

Westernized American culture to value "every second counts," whereas Indigenous values might reflect "time is relative" (Limb et al., 2008, p. 390).

Asian American Identity Development

While there are numerous Asian American IDMs (e.g., Kitano, 1982; Sue & Sue, 1971) that have made important contributions, many models lack supporting information about the complexities of this identity development process. For this reason, we have chosen to highlight the *Asian American identity development model* (Kim, 1981) because of the emphasis on progressive, sequential stages. Kim (1981) used the term *ethnicity* to describe Asian American identity and the term *race* to express White identity.

1. **Ethnic Awareness:** From ages 3 to 4, family members are the primary representatives of the ethnic group, and the child forms neutral or positive attitudes toward their ethnicity.
2. **White Identification:** School-age children interact with peers and institutions that convey ethnic prejudice that negatively impacts their self-esteem and views of their ethnic identity. The child recognizes differences from the majority White racial group, has feelings of cultural shame, and may seek escape from *otherness* by identifying with White society.
3. **Awakening and Social-Political Consciousness:** With an increase in social and political awareness, individuals develop new perspectives of their racial identity. Typically, there is a decrease in identification with White culture and society and an increased understanding of oppressed racial and ethnic groups.
4. **Redirection:** Individuals reconnect with their culture and heritage and acknowledge tenets of oppression from White society that contributed to negative experiences in their past. Increased sense of pride in Asian American identity.
5. **Incorporation:** Individuals feel positive and comfortable in their Asian American cultural identity, respecting all other races, ethnicities, and cultures equally.

This model highlights the impact of one's social and environmental reference groups that typically change with age, noting the influence of acculturation, exposure to cultural and racial differences, methods of handling race-related conflicts, and the effects of social movements on Asian Americans' identity development (Kim, 1981). Because Kim's (1981) study of Japanese Americans and their identity development is foundational to this model, its use may be limited for Asian Americans from other countries and Pacific Islanders (AAPI). As there is not a comprehensive AAPI identity development model, counselors using the *Asian American identity development model* (Kim, 1981) with AAPI clients should be mindful of this critique.

Black American Identity Development Model

Cross (1971) devised the *Black American identity development model* to address the stages that Black Americans journey through to embrace their Black identity. Cross was one of the first researchers to create a model to examine human behavior in the context of Black America, independent of White culture (DeCuir-Gunby, 2009). Cross identified five stages that promote positive shifts in Black identity development.

1. **Pre-encounter:** Idealism surrounding the dominant White worldview and the condemnation of the Black worldview (Moreland & Leach, 2001). Often associates the world as being non-Black, anti-Black, or the opposite of Black.
2. **Encounter:** A social or personal event shifts the person's frame of reference and allows for new interpretations of their identity. There is increased receptivity to information that challenges negative assumptions that surround being Black.
3. **Immersion/Emersion:** Involves a sense of pride in being Black while engaging in the belittlement of the traditional, dominant White culture. Increased engagement with information and participation in events that expand awareness regarding Blackness and distancing themself from traditional White culture.
4. **Internalization:** Marked by an increase in active participation in one's own culture and acceptance of diversity, individuals develop an idealistic view of being Black. Lengthy or traumatic frustration with unmet expectations can lead to a "Why does it matter?" attitude more than previously experienced. There are three nonproductive things that can happen while in the internalization stage: *disappointment and rejection* (succumbing to a pessimistic worldview), *continuation and fixation* (holding hurtful perceptions and increased aversion toward White people) and *internalization* (not yet dedicated to a plan of action).
5. **Internalization/Commitment:** There is a commitment to an individual's understanding of their identity as a Black American. The individual shifts from having outward concerns about others' perceptions of them to having confidence in their personal standards of being a Black American. Individuals transition from anger toward White people to anger toward racist and oppressive institutions. Individuals experience a transition from anxiety and insecurity toward feeling Black pride, self-love, and a deep sense of Black communalism (Cross, 1971).

Latinx Identity Development

Latinx or Latine is the gender-neutral, pan-ethnic label for people who are Latino/s, Latina/s, and Hispanic. People who are Latinx do not fit into firm ethnic and racial categories in the United States because they have many countries of origin that span multiple continents (see Chapter 8 for more information). Ferdman and Gallegos (1996; 2001) sought to provide this heterogeneous, complex group with a racial identity model that highlights the diversity in national origins, values, experiences, traditions, and relationships to non-Latinx Whites in the United States. Ferdman and Gallegos's (2001) *Latinx identity development model* is an ongoing, complex process comprised of *orientations* rather than linear stages.

1. **Latinx-Integrated:** An individual understands the complexities of other cultural subgroups and their own. Their Latinx American identity is consolidated with their other social identities, and they identify with many different parts of themselves. There is a

balanced awareness, positive and negative, of Latinx American cultural aspects, and they choose to be inclusive of all Latinx subgroups.

2. **Latinx-Identified:** One holds flexible views of other Latinx and non-Latinx groups that increase alliances between individuals and places a high value on Latinx culture and history. Often, individuals who hold this orientation view Latinx people as a distinct race and identify with this group in its entirety, viewing White Americans as a different, rigid racial group. Individuals acknowledge institutional and systemic racism and find value in fighting against racial injustices.
3. **Subgroup-Identified:** An individual views their identity in terms of their own ethnicity or nation of origin subgroup. Identification is distinct from White Americans; they may not identify with other Latinx people or other BIPOC. This group has a narrower, more exclusive view of group identity and prefers to identify mostly with their ethnic subgroup, such as Mexican, Cuban, Colombian, or Guatemalan. They view their subgroup positively and sometimes view other Latinx subgroups as inferior. These Latinx Americans view their nationality, ethnicity, and culture as their primary identity rather than their race.
4. **Latinx as "Other":** Individuals in this orientation identify as Persons of Color (POC) or as a *minority* and are not aware of their specific Latinx history or cultural background. Increased focus on ethnic and racial groups is viewed by those outside the group rather than internally. There is little knowledge of their ethnic group, and they do not participate in Latinx norms or in White cultural norms. Rather than specifically connecting to Latinx subgroups, they feel connected to all POC, unified against the dominant White culture of the United States.
5. **Undifferentiated:** The individual identifies as *just people* and often claims color-blindness, denouncing systemic oppression and avoiding awareness of the unique privileges and barriers of different racial and ethnic groups.
6. **White-Identified:** Individuals embrace the values of White culture and view themselves as racially White and superior to other races. This group is often disconnected from their Latinx subculture and Latinx people in general while also subconsciously understanding that they are separate from White culture. This group accepts the U.S. racial superiority order without question and generally views Whites as superior to Latinx Americans.

White Identity Development

"To be White in America is not to have to think about it. Except for hard-core racial supremacists, the meaning of being White is having the choice to attending to or ignoring one's own Whiteness" (Terry, 1981, p. 120). Helms (1990) advised that to develop a healthy, nonracist White identity, White people in the United States must acknowledge and develop an anti-racist identity, accept their own Whiteness, and define their racial identity without depending on any perceived superiority of one racial group over another. Helms (1990; 2020) created the *White identity development model*, composed of two phases and six schemas, that a White person can experience simultaneously, one at a time, or not at all:

Phase 1: Abandonment of Racism

1. **Contact Schema:** There is a lack of awareness of their Whiteness, and although they acknowledge others' pigmentation differences, they assume others are *raceless* like they are. This stage is characterized by innocence, ignorance, and denial about race and race-based issues.
2. **Disintegration Schema:** When denial no longer works, confusion occurs. The White person accepts that they receive certain societal benefits from being White and possibly fears losing kinship with their socially powerful racial group if they were to cease treating other nondominant racial groups as inferior. They hold the belief that the nondominant racial groups/individuals deserve mistreatment and justify their racist beliefs.
3. **Reintegration Schema:** Racist beliefs result in feelings of superiority to other races, appropriating other races' cultures and customs, and ignoring the societal contributions BIPOC have made.

Phase 2: Defining a Nonracist White Identity

1. **Pseudo-Independent Schema:** Individuals scale down their positive view of Whiteness to be more realistic and balanced, and they no longer need to believe that the White race is superior. They may adopt the view that BIPOC can become equal to Whites with the assistance of programs such as special education and affirmative action. The White person, intellectually, understands that BIPOC are impacted by political and systemic racism; however, they do not take responsibility for enabling racism.
2. **Immersion/Emersion Schema:** Individuals seek to understand the undiluted White history of the United States that highlights racism, assimilation, and acculturation of BIPOC people. There is a well-rounded understanding of the privileges and deficiencies of being White, and they take personal responsibility for racism. To grow beyond this, they must morally reeducate fellow White people, take inventory of personal racist beliefs, and actively confront oppression and racism in their environments while increasing participation in cross-racial experiences.
3. **Autonomy Schema:** The individual prioritizes inclusion and collectivism and feels secure within themselves as they nurture their White racial identity without the need for racial superiority.

Bi/Multiracial Identity Development

Root (1990) aimed to develop a non-oppressive approach to navigating bi/multiracial identity development. The model attends to harmful narratives surrounding biracial identity with consideration to identity intersectionality and how dominant and nondominant cultures impact a person's proximity to aspects of privilege and adversity. Root's (1990) model has four stages:

1. **Acceptance of the Identity Society Assigns:** There is an intentional and empowered approach to accepting one's racial identity as not entirely fitting into one preexisting grouping (e.g., only Black, only White). There is acknowledgment that the systems in

which they operate are often oppressive and non-accepting. Successfully navigating this stage includes receiving support and acceptance from others.

2. **Identification With Both Racial Groups:** Individuals in this stage internally and externally hold space for all their racial identities without favoring one. This is achieved through a more self-accepting view of the power and oppression of their racial identities. They establish tools and constructive strategies for coping with social resistance and oppression.
3. **Identification With a Single Racial Group:** Individuals highlight, display, and more outwardly identify with one racial identity without entirely denying their other identity(ies). Their mono-group affiliation is related to a degree of assimilation and/or their acquired coping strategies. The difficulty at this stage involves processing incongruence they may feel as they differentiate how the world perceives them from how they perceive themselves.
4. **Identification as a New Racial Group:** Individuals achieve the ability to move between their racial identities with confidence in their uniqueness. They no longer hide aspects of their heritage, or they accept that they are not able to change others' minds. The difficulty experienced in this last stage is the lack of accurate representation in their society's classification system. In a literal sense, this includes selection options on documentation regarding racial identity, and socially, this can include a lack of portrayals of bi/multiracial models in entertainment/media.

Ethnic Identity Formation

Inspired by Cross's Black identity model and Erickson's psychosocial development stages, Phinney (1989) developed a three-stage model focused on discerning one's ethnic identity.

1. **Unexamined Ethnic Identity:** Individuals have not explored their ethnicity and tend to absorb the values and attitudes of the dominant culture.
2. **Ethnic Identity Search/Moratorium:** Individuals explore their ethnic identities when provided with the opportunity or forced to do so. Participants of Phinney's (1989) study on ethnic identity formation described this process as "going to festivals and cultural events to help me learn more about my culture and myself" (p. 44).
3. **Ethnic Identity Achievement:** Increased assuredness of ethnicity and clearer understanding of their social positioning as related to their ethnicity and the dominant culture.

BOX 6.2 **PAUSE AND REFLECT: CONSIDERING THE MODELS**

Now that you have learned about several racial/ethnic IDMs:

Which of the models resonated with you most in terms of your racial/ethnic identity development?

How did the model that resonated with you most affirm your development? In what ways did it miss the mark?

How will these models be relevant to your work with clients? How can they positively impact the work you do together?

Acculturation Models

Acculturation is the process people experience when they encounter different cultural groups with different values and beliefs by living among cultural groups that differ from their own (Berry, 2015; Schwartz et al., 2010). This has become a more salient phenomenon because of globalization and the increasing number of people moving to new countries (Song, 2021). For more information on the acculturation experiences of immigrants and refugees, see Chapter 9.

Berry (1992) proposed one of the most widely used acculturation models, aptly named the *Acculturation Model.* This model conceptualizes an individual's adaptation from the nondominant culture into the dominant culture. This model is based on two principles (Fox et al., 2013): (a) retention or rejection of their individual identity within their own culture and (b) the acceptance or refusal of the host culture. Four acculturation strategies/outcomes arise from these two principles:

1. **Assimilation:** Adopt the cultural norms and practices of the dominant culture and reject their own culture.
2. **Separation:** Reject the dominant culture in favor of preserving their culture and identity of origin.
3. **Integration:** Simultaneously adopt the cultural norms of the dominant culture while maintaining their initial cultural identity. This is also known as biculturalism.
4. **Marginalization:** Reject their culture of origin as well as the dominant host culture. Individuals in this category can feel they do not belong to either culture and may develop a de-identified identity.

Extending Existing Racial and Ethnic Identity Development Models

While navigating clinical relationships with clients, it's imperative to avoid pathologizing, stereotyping, and overgeneralizing, especially when using IDMs to understand clients' experiences. When working with clients for whom there are no identity models available, counselors must determine how to understand clients' identity development without a preestablished model. For example, a counselor might inquire about a client's' views on adherence to patriarchal structures, norms regarding expressivity of emotions, collectivist versus individualist cultural norms, citizenship, proximity to religion and spirituality, poverty, colorism, and/or or internalized -isms and -misias (e.g., racism, xenomisia, Islamomisia, transmisia). With or without using a preestablished IDM, counselors can do the following:

- Use genograms to help clients identify and understand immigration history and family structure, and assess levels of acculturation.
- Employ narrative therapy techniques (empowerment through re-storying).
- Use psychoeducation to demystify therapeutic processes.
- Suggest group counseling as an intervention that supports modeling, building cohesion, and networking.

BOX 6.3 **FOCUS ON CLIENT CARE**

Kris, a 26-year-old Black man, recently started therapy with Jeff, a 30-year-old White man related to self-exploration and workplace adjustment. In their third session, Kris shares an incident in which two coworkers at his job made comments regarding Kris's hair, which he wears in dreadlocks. This experience frustrated Kris and made him feel alienated from his coworkers. Jeff begins to conceptualize Kris's experiences using the Black identity development model (Cross, 1971).

As Jeff listens to Kris's experiences, he notices that Kris feels uncomfortable expressing his Black identity (*pre-encounter*). Jeff encourages Kris to explore his beliefs and values around his Black identity and offers support without judgment. Through their sessions, Kris starts recognizing how the dominant culture has shaped his beliefs and starts challenging those assumptions as they relate to his identity.

As Kris and Jeff explore the *encounter* stage, Kris reflects on his experiences of being ridiculed at work, causing him to reflect on the racist nature of that exchange. Kris becomes more open to exploring information that challenges his own assumptions regarding his Black identity. Jeff supports Kris as he navigates this new perspective, and Kris starts developing a sense of pride in his Black identity while distancing himself from the traditional dominant White culture.

In the *immersion/emersion* stage, Jeff encourages Kris to seek out more information and participate in events that expand his awareness of his own Black identity, and he starts to feel more connected to his culture. Jeff helps Kris to explore his sense of pride and to understand his emotions of anger and frustration toward the dominant White culture. Jeff also supports Kris as he works through the *internalization* stage, where he actively participates in his own culture, accepts diversity, and talks through any negative emotions that come up for him during this stage. Kris develops an idealistic view of being Black and gains confidence in his personal standards of being a Black American. Through therapy, Kris can accept his identity as a Black man with pride, reducing his anxiety and insecurities and replacing them with a deep sense of fulfillment in his own identity.

Gender Identity Development Models

Identity models are not just limited to race and ethnicity. In this section, we explore the various models related to individuals' gender identity development (see Table 6.3). Table 6.2 explains the acronym LGBTGEQIAP+ that is used throughout the gender identity and romantic and affectual identity development model sections.

TABLE 6.2 Defining LGBTGEQIAP+

L	Lesbian	Q	Queer/Questioning
G	Gay	I	Intersex
B	Bisexual	A	Agender, Asexual, and Aromantic
T	Trans, Transgender, and Two-Spirit (Indigenous Identity)	P	Pansexual, Pan/Polygender, and Poly-relationship Systems
GE	Gender Expansive	+	Developing Identities Not Included Specifically in the Acronym

TABLE 6.3 Overview of Gender Identity Development Models

Model	Author(s)	Description
Psychosocial Developmental	Erikson	An early chronologically organized model on social-emotional development
Social Cognitive Model	Bandura	An incorporation of internal and external influences on gender roles, expectations, and development
Feminist Model	Downing and Rush	A model of awareness, decision-making, and challenging tenets of gender
Transgender Models	Bockting and Coleman Simons	These models explore the process of navigating gender affirmation, as well as infuse domains of privilege and oppression with the intersection of race and gender

Psychosocial Development Foundations

Erikson (1958; 1963) created one of the first models of human development using psychosocial stages. Erikson's model depicts the complex psychosocial developmental processes people experience throughout the lifespan, including how relationships with self, others, and society influence development. Social and emotional theories are foundational for other models that seek to explain the relationship between identity development and experiences, particularly gender identity.

Social Cognitive Theory of Gender Development

Social cognitive theory (SCT) of gender development places emphasis on the environment (e.g., family, neighborhood) and social norms (e.g., patriarchy, gender roles) in creating and preserving binary gender categories through observation and modeling (Bussey & Bandura, 1999). Conceptions of gender and role behavior are seen as products of a broad network of social influences operating both within the family and societal systems (Bandura, 1986; 1997). Individuals who subscribe to SCT regard gender as emerging through shared and multidirectional influences between personal, behavioral, and environmental factors.

1. *Personal factors* account for gender-related cognitions, judgmental standards, and self-regulatory influences (e.g., thoughts, appraisals, and decision-making).
2. *Behavioral factors* are explicit actions related to gender (e.g., acting out engendered behaviors in specific social groups).
3. *Environmental factors* denote the social influences experienced in day-to-day interactions (e.g., observing gendered behaviors, gender-specific spaces, organizations).

These three factors can influence one another in reciprocal and bidirectional ways. For example, individuals' thoughts can be influenced by the social group they engage with and the type of clothes they choose to wear to conform. As such, a person's thoughts may mirror that of their social group, and clothing choice can be influenced by the individual's social group. In this example, personal factors are shaped by behavior and environmental factors, while at the same time, environmental factors are shaped by behavior factors. Bussey and Bandura (1999) argued that the stability of gender is not a result of copying same-sex models, but rather is a consequence of it. The authors of this model only looked at two dichotomous gender expressions (girl/woman and boy/man). They did not consider any other gender expressions, limiting the model's use with gender-expansive clients (more information in Chapter 14). This model can be used with clients to identify how personal, behavioral, and environmental domains have shaped their gender views and expression, exploring what works for them and what doesn't. Further, notice how clients tend to pursue courses of action they believe will bring valued outcomes and refrain from those they believe will give rise to aversive outcomes—this can be particularly helpful with clients who are exploring gender-expansive identities.

Feminist Identity Development Model

Downing and Roush's (1985) *Feminist identity development* is a five-stage model that describes the process of self-identification toward a feminist identity in persons with oppressed gender identities. Equity, morality, role expectations, and social positioning are underlying tenets of this theory that developed from a series of research studies on moral development, with an emphasis on gender biases, conducted by Carol Gilligan in the 1970s. Although originally created for cisgender women, this model is applicable to all gender identities and expressions, including cisgender men.

1. **Passive Acceptance:** There is a lack of awareness of prejudices and forms of discrimination regarding gender at the micro-, meso-, and macrolevels. Also called *stagnancy* in terms of accepting the dominant culture's gender-based expectations (social positioning, role expectations, etc.)
2. **Revelation:** This stage is initiated by an unavoidable event or circumstance that ignites reflection and a change of reference. One's perceptions are challenged and result in a move away from dualistic thinking. Events may include a direct or indirect experience of gender-based injustice.
3. **Embeddedness–Emanation:** Individuals explore concepts of connectedness with others, proximity to the dominant culture, and increased receptivity to holding a multidimensional perspective of inner group perspectives. Shifts in thinking begin to occur regarding topics of inferiority and oppressive systems, such as pay inequality or freedoms and restrictions regarding bodily autonomy.
4. **Synthesis:** There is increased acceptance, celebration of uniqueness, and autonomy. Also described as "transcending traditional gendered expectations" (Downing & Rush, 1985, p. 702), like challenging gender-oppressive language or finding empowerment outside of the normed rules of dress, behavior, or thinking.
5. **Active Commitment:** Individuals in this stage experience a solidification of value-based goals and implementation of meaningful action. Includes an acceptance of new perspectives about gender and integration of skills to commit to socially just change.

Transgender Identity Development

Transgender identities encompass an array of gender identities in which one's sex assigned at birth is not congruent with their gender identification, and more broadly includes gender-expansive identities. Bockting and Coleman's (2007) model of *transgender identity development* explores living authentically in one's gender identity across five stages.

1. **Pre-coming Out:** An individual may experience feelings of misalignment with their assigned sex/gender and may express themselves as gender nonconforming (i.e., they do not subscribe to norms traditional of their gender like adherences to masculinity, femininity, or socioemotional role expectations). These feelings are not shared with others and are known as a private persona.
2. **Coming Out:** Individuals acknowledge their sex/gender incongruence and their feelings of not identifying as cisgender, and they start to identify those they can trust to discuss their feelings. Trust and safety concerns in this stage can be due to a lack of social support or hostile narratives surrounding transgender identities.
3. **Exploration:** Individuals begin expressing the gender identity that accurately reflects their felt sense of gender via clothing and personal style, integrating into affirming communities (e.g., more time spent in safe and inclusive spaces), and establishing coping tools for experiences of internal dissonance and/or external discrimination (e.g., establishing boundaries). The processes of disclosure and expression are considered a public persona.
4. **Intimacy:** Continued exploration of relationships while expressing their genuine gender identity. This may include vocalizing pronouns and furthering their appearance to reflect their true self more accurately.
5. **Identity Integration:** Individuals begin integrating their private and public personas, resulting in a greater acceptance of the self that comes from no longer existing in shame or concealment. It can include more publicization of hobbies or interests in social groups that empower and advocate for transgender people.

Transgender POC Identity Development

Relevant to transgender identity and transgender people of color (TPOC), the Simons et al. (2021) intersectional approach considers the comprehensive nature of individuals' experiences of their gender and racial identity. Intersectionality is critical to consider with clients of color who identify as transgender, gender non-expansive, and/or as two spirit (diverse spectrum of gender identity and sexuality derived from Indigenous communities; Brown, 1997) because of the overlap of experiences one might have regarding proximities to privilege and oppression related to race and gender.

Understanding the developmental process of identity formation experiences of TPOC clients through an intersectionality framework is relatively new to counseling-based literature. Simons et al. (2021) examined school-aged children who identify as transgender POC as related to resiliency factors and coping in their identity development. The following table depicts nonlinear

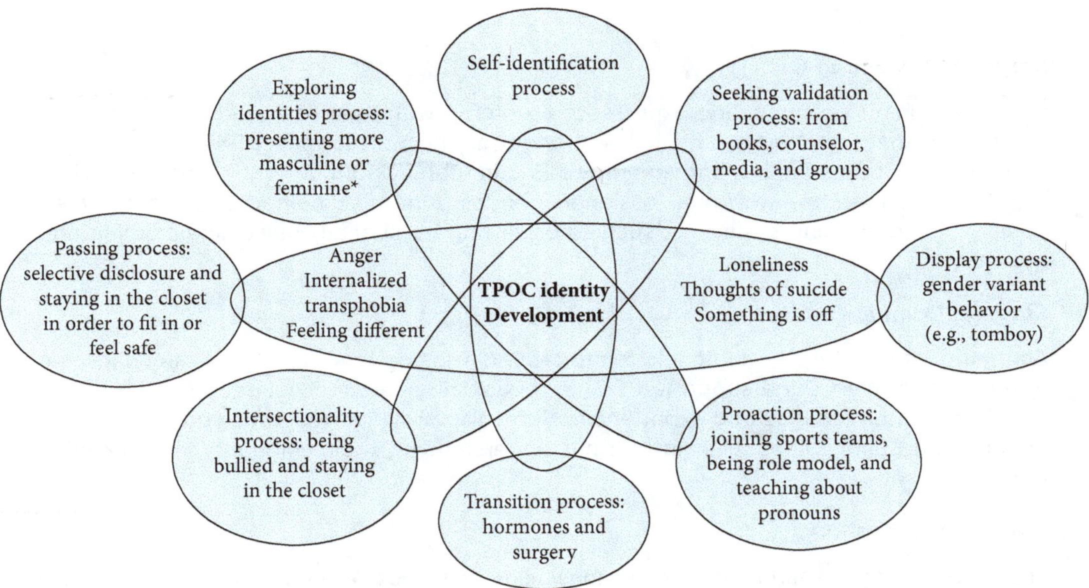

*Cross dressing, in particular, is a critical step and it may or may not affect feelings of difference (levels of dysphoria).

FIGURE 6.1 Transgender Identity Development Among TPOC (Simons et al., 2021)

factors that characterize unique challenges and checkpoints TPOC clients experience and often revisit throughout their lives. The intention of this model is to highlight the duality of resiliencies and adversities TPOC experience that clinicians can incorporate into the clinical relationship.

Extending Existing Gender Identity Development Models

Gender IDMs are designed to be general and not all-encompassing. Counselors must assess how other intersecting identities are considered or not in each model and whether they are well-suited for the client with whom they are working. It is typical that additional identity components are often overlooked in earlier models such as Erikson's and the feminist IDM. Influences such as age, ability status, and social class must be considered when applying these models because clients' experiences are unique based on their identity makeup and often, they do not fit models perfectly.

BOX 6.4 **FOCUS ON CLIENT CARE**

Eric, a 23-year-old college student, sought out a gender-affirming counselor (June) for guidance on their feelings of misalignment with their assigned gender at birth. June employed a person-centered approach, offering a safe, nonjudgmental space for Eric to explore their identity and feelings.

Stage 1: Pre-coming Out

In the beginning sessions, Eric expressed discomfort with their assigned female gender, mentioning that they had always felt a stronger connection to masculinity. June provided empathic understanding and supported Eric in identifying moments in their life when they felt incongruence with their assigned gender. June also helped Eric identify their gender-nonconforming behaviors, such as preferring traditionally masculine clothing and hobbies.

Stage 2: Coming Out

As their trust in June grew, Eric felt comfortable disclosing their belief that they might be a transgender man. June supported Eric in recognizing safe individuals with whom they could share their feelings and experiences. June also provided resources on transgender identity and communities, allowing further understanding their emotions and validating their identity.

Stage 3: Exploration

Eric began experimenting with a more masculine wardrobe and personal style. June encouraged Eric to seek out affirming communities, such as local LGBTGEQIAP+ groups and online forums. Eric also started learning about coping strategies for dealing with internal dissonance and external discrimination. June guided Eric in establishing boundaries and accessing support from friends and family.

Stage 4: Intimacy

As Eric grew more comfortable with their gender identity, they began exploring relationships with others while openly expressing their true self. He shared his pronouns (he/him) with friends and family and changed his appearance to better reflect his identity. June continued to provide support and encouragement in navigating relationships and maintaining open communication with loved ones.

Stage 5: Identity Integration

Eventually, Eric reached a point where he felt more secure in his identity as a transgender man, and his private and public personas began to integrate. He became more involved in social groups and activities that empowered and advocated for transgender people. June affirmed Eric's growth and helped him celebrate his accomplishments, fostering a greater sense of self-acceptance.

Romantic and Affectual Identity Development

This section explores romantic and affectional identity (RAI) development models (see Chapter 15 for more information on this topic). To reflect a more inclusive and current approach, the models will be labeled with their original names, yet we will use updated, more inclusive language as part of the descriptions and discussion. Because the dominant, heteronormative culture is embedded in role expectations surrounding relationships, these models arose from the need to normalize relationships outside of heteronormativity (Fassinger et al., 1995).

Homosexual Identity Formation Model

Originally, this model used *homosexual* to describe same-sex RAI, yet current literature reflects more expansive terminology that specifies an individual's romantic and affectional relationships (e.g., lesbian, bisexual, pansexual). Cass (1979) established this model to explore a person's internal processes and corresponding behaviors in exploring their RAI development outside of heterosexual norms:

1. **Identity Confusion:** Individuals question current assumptions about their affectional identity and attractions to others. This can be followed by feelings of shame.
2. **Identity Comparison:** Individuals often have feelings of isolation and alienation as they stray from their previously held assumptions of their RAI (e.g., heterosexual) and their attraction to others of the same or multiple genders.
3. **Identity Tolerance:** Individuals seek out other queer individuals and are in the early stages of exploration of shifts in identity. They vacillate between feelings of acceptance and incongruence in this stage.
4. **Identity Acceptance:** Individuals begin engaging in selective disclosure (i.e., coming out) to others as they gain assuredness and self-acceptance of their RAI and attraction to others.
5. **Identity Pride:** Individuals immerse themselves in a culture that de-centers heterosexual values, rejecting heteronormativity.
6. **Identity Synthesis:** Individuals transition to a more congruent identity that accurately reflects their RAI.

Adolescent Lesbian and Gay Identity Development

Individual *coming out* processes vary, and this model attempts to synthesize what one might experience while navigating this process as an adolescent. Inspired by the Cass (1979) *model of homosexual identity formation*, Coleman (1982) created the *adolescent lesbian and gay identity development model*, a five-stage process for coming out in adolescence.

1. **Pre-coming Out:** Characterized by secrecy, sense of dissonance, confusion, fear, and denial of romantic and affectional feelings for people of the same or multiple genders. This often results from concerns of punishment (e.g., rejection, ostracization) if they disclose their feelings.
2. **Coming Out:** Demonstrated by reconciliation, the individual in this stage admits to themselves that their romantic or affectional feelings are outside of those represented in the dominant heterosexual culture. This is followed by disclosing their RAI to others, which can result in acceptance or rejection. Acceptance or rejection by others deeply impacts the trajectory of further navigating RAI. This stage is characterized by a spectrum of willing vulnerability, assessing trust, and honesty with self and others.
3. **Exploration:** This stage includes sexual and social-based experimentation. Characterized by intrigue and peer-to-peer consultation in search of validation, expertise, and support.

4. **First Relationships:** Individuals in this stage begin to consider themselves eligible partners in a relationship and seek intimacy and/or connection. Through trial and error in first relationships, the individual gains insight and experience that can either be used to positively inform the next relationships or solidify maladaptive and destructive relationship patterns.
5. **Integration:** The individual gains confidence and skills that promote healthier, self-accepting attitudes toward their identity that is reflected in their relationships.

Lesbian Identity Development

McCarn and Fassinger (1996) developed the *lesbian identity development model* to better support, articulate, and normalize experiences for lesbians. The following describes the four-step process of lesbian identity development:

1. **Awareness:** The individual experiences awareness of feelings or desires outside of heteronormativity, though not to the extent of self-identification in this stage.
2. **Exploration:** Marked increases in receptivity to exploration and further consideration of emotional attraction.
3. **Deepening and Commitment:** Experiences crystallization of sexual identity as discovered through sexual, romantic, or intimacy-oriented exploration, a greater sense of fulfillment in relationships, and a positive perception of identifying with a new RAI.
4. **Internalization and Synthesis:** Achieved over time and successful demonstrations of internal conflict resolution, empowered exploration and self-love, and acceptance of one's RAI.

Bisexual Identity Development

Bisexuality describes a person who experiences emotional, romantic, and/or sexual attraction to, or engages in romantic or sexual relationships with more than one sex, gender, or gender identity. Weinberg and colleagues (1994) reported that many bisexual people describe their sexuality as an evolving process, although that is not always the case. Weinberg et al. (1994) developed a broad four-stage model to describe this identity development in bisexual people.

1. **Initial Confusion:** Individuals feel conflicted and confused by their attraction to other genders; this anxiety and confusion can last for years, and some might assume nonheterosexual attraction will erase their heterosexual attraction. In addition to confusion, many people limit their self-labeling options to only heterosexual or gay/lesbian rather than bisexual. This confusion and subsequent hesitation to use the bisexual label is more common in men.
2. **Finding and Applying the Label:** Individuals are engaging in sex and/or relationships with members of other genders that are enjoyable and fulfilling, which encourages them to apply the label *bisexual* to their RAI. Strong attraction to other sexes and receiving support and encouragement from others motivate some individuals to acknowledge their bisexual identity. Negative societal stereotypes can decrease confidence in their developing identity.

3. **Settling into Identity:** Individuals become more comfortable with their RAI, and some question if bisexuality is a temporary phase or transition. Some believe monogamous relationships could lead to adopting a monosexual identity, while others continue to align with their previously identified bisexual identity.
4. **Continued Uncertainty/Identity Maintenance:** Individuals highlight the normalcy of confusion about their bisexual identity. Lack of role models, social validation, and bisexual communities may contribute to uncertainty for some, while many still feel certain about their bisexual identity.

BOX 6.5 **PAUSE AND REFLECT: THE BISEXUALITY DEVELOPMENT MODEL**

The bisexuality development model highlights potential feelings of uncertainty while moving through an evolving process. How might you assist a client in managing these feelings? What therapeutic strategies would be helpful? How might you use advocacy to decrease barriers to social support?

RAI Model Gaps

Similar to many other IDMs, the gaps in the LGBTGEQIAP+ models highlight the need for intersectionality to be inclusive of all.

BOX 6.6 **FOCUS ON CLIENT CARE**

Robert, a 19-year-old male, comes to his counselor, Max, after being shamed by his parents for coming out as bisexual. Robert expresses feeling confused and conflicted about his sexuality and has been struggling with these feelings for years. Robert is hesitant to embrace bisexuality as an identity because he worries about societal stereotypes and backlash from his family.

Max begins by guiding Robert through the *initial confusion* stage. In this stage, individuals feel conflicted and confused, prompted by their attraction to both men and women; this anxiety and confusion can last for years. Max creates a safe space for him to explore his feelings and normalize his confusion. By validating Robert's experience and allowing him to lead the discussion, they help Robert process his thoughts and feelings.

Over time, Robert progresses to the second stage of the model, *finding and applying the label*. As Robert explores his sexuality and engages in fulfilling romantic and sexual relationships with people of various genders, he feels more comfortable identifying as bisexual. Max supports Robert by addressing the negative stereotypes surrounding bisexuality and providing resources to help him connect with the bisexual community. With this newfound confidence, Robert begins *settling* into his identity and accepts himself for who he is. Although he may experience some continued *uncertainty and identity maintenance* in the future, Robert now feels more secure in his bisexual identity and has the support he needs to thrive.

Religious and Spiritual Identity Development Models

Spirituality refers to the inherent human ability to transcend one's self and perceive the presence of the sacred, leading to increased compassion and love for both one and others. Religion is defined as a set of beliefs, practices, and experiences that are socially defined and institutionalized. Religion provides a structure for human spirituality and incorporates elements such as narratives, symbols, beliefs, and rituals rooted in ancestral and cultural traditions (Cashwell & Young, 2011. Further discussion on religion and spirituality can be found in Chapter 16.

Given the prevalence of many different religious/spiritual practices that exist, it can be useful for counselors to incorporate religion/spirituality development models within their practice to assist clients in identifying their own spiritual development (Association for Spiritual, Ethical, and Religious Values in Counseling [ASERVIC], 2021; Lownsdale, 1997; Young & Cashwell, 2014).

Fowler's Model

Fowler (1981) identified seven stages of faith development. Fowler constructed his stages based on the idea that faith development is a natural aspect of human growth (Foster & Holden, 2014). Each of these stages aligns closely with the theories of cognitive development by Piaget (1954) and Kohlberg (1963; Lownsdale, 1997; Runnels & Thompkins IV, 2020; see Table 6.4). Fowler viewed these stages as a framework to better comprehend individuals' strengths and weaknesses in relation to their faith, not as goals to achieve spiritual salvation (Lownsdale, 1997).

1. **Primal Faith – Infancy:** Parents/guardians in the infant's life shape pre-images of the ultimate environment. Trust and mistrust fluctuate through challenges that include inconsistencies, deprivations, and threats of perceived abandonment.
2. **Intuitive Projective – Early Childhood:** The ability to use language and symbolism gives rise to imagination and understanding relating to their faith.
3. **Mythic Literal – Middle Childhood:** Progressively adopts their family's religious/spiritual community's stories, beliefs, morals, and values. Conformity to community beliefs and practices is experienced at a higher level in this stage, as well as a strong influence related to traditions and authority. Due to neglect, abuse, or unfavourability from parental figures, individuals can embrace a denigrating sense of feeling as though they are *bad.*
4. **Synthetic Conventional – Adolescence:** An increased ability to self-reflect and take other viewpoints to explore one's meaning of life and important relationships.
5. **Individuative Reflective – Young Adulthood:** The individual begins to take responsibility for their own beliefs, attitudes, commitments, and lifestyle.
6. **Conjunctive Faith – Midlife:** The focus shifts from issues being seen as "either/or" to "both/and" in which paradoxes are now accepted in place of viewing problems as something to be solved.
7. **Universalizing Faith – Post-Midlife and Beyond:** Reaching this stage is rare. The individual traverses beyond the boundaries of the limits of their culture's religion and their own ego viewpoint.

TABLE 6.4 Comparison of Piaget, Kohlberg, and Fowler's Stages

Stages	**Piaget's Four Stages of Cognitive Development**	**Kohlberg's Stages of Moral Development**	**Fowler's Seven Stages of Faith Development**
Focus	Understanding and thinking about the world	Making moral and ethical decisions	Understanding and experiencing faith
Stages	(1) Sensorimotor (0–2 years) (2) Preoperational (2–7 years) (3) Concrete operational (7–11 years) 4. Formal operational (11–adulthood)	Pre-conventional (Self-Interest and Punishment Orientation) 2. Conventional (Good Child Attitude and Law and Order Morality) 3. Post-conventional (Social Contract and Universal Ethical Principle)	(1) Primal Faith-Infancy (2) Intuitive Projective – Early Childhood (3) Mythic Literal – Late Childhood (4) Synthetic Conventional – Adolescence (5) Individuative Reflective – Young Adulthood (6) Conjunctive Faith-Middle Adulthood (7) Universalizing Faith-Late Adulthood
Development	Building upon the previous stage to create a more advanced understanding of the world	Building upon the previous stage to create a more advanced sense of morality	Building on the previous stage to create a more advanced understanding of faith
Similarities All three theories propose that individuals go through a series of stages as they mature and develop their understanding of the world and their place within it. Both Piaget's and Kohlberg's theories posit that individuals build upon previous stages to create a more advanced understanding, while Fowler's theory suggests that individuals develop a deeper understanding of faith over time.			
Differences Piaget's theory focuses on cognitive development, while Kohlberg's theory focuses on moral development, and Fowler's theory focuses on faith development. Piaget and Kohlberg focus on the individual's internal processes and reasoning, while Fowler focuses on the individual's experience and relationship with faith.			

BOX 6.7 **FOCUS ON CLIENT CARE**

Laura is a 37-year-old Asian American woman who has been seeing her counselor, Annette, for 3 months for depression following the death of her partner, Linda. This loss has led to Laura struggling with her Buddhist faith, and she would like to explore this with her counselor. Annette is a 59-year-old Latinx counselor who practices Catholicism. Annette plans to use the seven stages of faith development to help Laura rediscover her connection to Buddhism.

Laura grew up in a Buddhist household and tries to adhere to the Four Noble Truths and the Eightfold Path. However, she feels disconnected from her faith and questions whether Buddhism is the right path. Annette begins her work with Laura by exploring her early experiences with Buddhism, helping her to reflect on her upbringing, her parents' teachings, and how this has shaped Laura's views on her own spiritual development.

Annette and Laura delve deeper into the stages of faith development, with Laura discussing her struggles with conformity and authority during middle childhood and how she has tried to reconcile these feelings with her faith, especially given her identity as a queer woman of color. Annette validates Laura's experiences and encourages her to continue to explore her beliefs and values. Annette helps Laura to self-reflect by encouraging the promotion of autonomy.

Annette helps Laura explore the stage of conjunctive faith, where she accepts paradoxes and sees issues as "both/and" rather than "either/or." Laura learns to embrace the complexities of her faith and understands that there is no single right answer. Annette helps Laura work through the loss of her partner through this stage. Through their work together, Laura gains a deeper understanding of her faith and feels more connected to her spirituality, while Annette feels grateful to have been a part of Laura's journey and hopes that she has helped her find peace and clarity.

Disability Identity Development Model

Disability is a fluid identity that is represented on a spectrum as anyone can become disabled at any point during their lifespan (see Chapter 12 for more about disability). The *disability identity model* (Gibson, 2006) provides insight into the perceptions and struggles of someone living with a disability in a world that does not accommodate their disability needs or identity. This three-stage model recognizes disability as an identity, allows for stage fluidity, and highlights and recognizes how society impacts disability identity (Forber-Pratt et al., 2017; Gibson, 2006). Importantly, this model does not try to change a person with a disability or insinuate that they should become able-bodied/non-disabled.

1. **Passive Awareness:** If the person's disability is congenital or acquired early in life, this stage can occur in childhood and continue into adulthood; their medical needs are met, but they are unable to recognize their disability due to having no role models with disabilities, no open conversations about said disability, and have been advised to ignore the social aspect of their disability.
2. **Realization:** This stage can occur in adolescence or early adulthood with persons with congenital disabilities. The person experiences an increase in their awareness of their

disability and how they are perceived by society. This realization often increases feelings of anger, resentment, and self-hate.

3. **Acceptance:** Occurs in adulthood for individuals with congenital disabilities. The individual begins to accept themselves and their disability, has less concern about how they are perceived by society, and focuses on advocating for themselves and others in the disability community. The person no longer views themselves as *less than* and embraces their disability identity.

Disability identity development occurs through personal and collective experiences within the disability community, a large community composed of people with different intersectional identities. For clients who have an acquired disability, Gill (1997) and Charmaz (1994; 1995) illustrated the movement through stages of understanding, adjusting to, and accepting the changes brought about by their acquired disability.

BOX 6.8 **FOCUS ON CLIENT CARE**

Shayla is a 22-year-old woman who seeks counseling because she is struggling to adjust to her new job. She was born with a congenital limb deficiency, which has required multiple surgeries and prosthetic fittings throughout her life. Despite this, she has never had any real conversations about her disability with anyone outside of her immediate family, and she never thought of it as an aspect of her identity. As Shayla shares her experiences with her counselor, Breann, Breann recognizes that Shayla is in the *realization* stage of the disability identity model. Breann helps Shayla explore her feelings of anger and frustration and encourages her to think about how society's views of disability have contributed to these emotions. Breann also validates Shayla's experiences and helps her see that her disability is not just a medical condition but an important aspect of her identity.

Through the counseling process, Shayla moves toward the *acceptance* stage of the disability identity model. Breann helps Shayla focus on accepting herself and her disability and encourages her to advocate for herself and others in the disability community. Shayla learns that it's okay to feel angry and frustrated, and that these emotions are a natural part of the disability identity development process. She also learns to accept herself and her disability and to embrace it as one aspect of her identity that she can be proud of. With Breann's guidance, Shayla can move toward a place of *self-acceptance and empowerment*. Shayla feels more confident in navigating her new job within the context of her environment.

Social Class

Liu (2001) proposed the social class worldview model (SCWM) to understand the function of social class and internalized classism in mental health (more on social class in Chapter 11). SCWM-Revised (SCWM-R) is the latest revision of Liu's model (Liu, 2011). The SCWM-R posits that an individual's worldview is shaped by their beliefs, attitudes, and values about their social class. This worldview is influenced by the individual's experiences and interactions with others, including friends, family, and peers, and the larger economic culture they are a part of (Liu, 2011).

In SCWM-R, economic cultures (EC; i.e., neighborhood, workplace, or town) set the individual's expectancies and requirements and give the standards by which individuals appraise their social class. Individuals attempting to uphold the expectations of their social class group are expected to develop, maintain, and use three types of capital: human, social, and cultural. Human capital is one's capacity and physical abilities or characteristics. Social capital refers to valued relationships in one's EC. Cultural capital is how individuals cultivate aesthetics that can be used as a form of *currency* within an EC to remain stable within their social class (Liu et al., 2013).

An individual's worldview helps them understand and interpret their experiences with classism, as well as how they perceive, respond to, and use classism to maintain a particular social class position (Liu, 2011; Liu et al., 2004). Socialization messages and social class consciousness influence how individuals interpret, perceive, and participate in classism. Implicit and explicit class-based messages come from family members, friends, peers, or groups of individuals who desire to be a part. These messages can be things like "hard work leads to success," "trust yourself, not anyone else," and "do not listen to people who earn less money than you." These messages can lead to attitudes and behaviors that favor materialism, certain social class-based behaviors such as etiquette or use of language, and how one spends their leisure time (Banerjee & Dittmar, 2008; Liu, 2011). Individuals may engage in downward classism in which they disparage individuals whom they consider *less than* them in terms of social class (Liu, 2001). Also, individuals may experience internalized classism, in which they develop anger, depression, and/or anxiety because of the inability to maintain their standing in their current social class or to obtain a higher-class status (Liu, 2001, 2013).

Areas of Identity Without Developmental Models

The integrity of the therapeutic relationship and the well-being of clients depends on using established models appropriately while acknowledging that additional work needs to be done in terms of creating IDMs that have not been prioritized. Additionally, the models highlighted in this section must be considered within the context of clients' other identities, such as education level, age, marital status, mental health status, professional identity, weight and attractiveness standards according to Western cultures, etc. It is necessary for counselors to have an awareness of how they perceive these identities and any biases that may accompany their perceptions.

Clients are impacted by how others and society view them; therefore, clinicians must be aware of the privileges and barriers society upholds based on intersectional identities that are not well-studied and advocated for through developmental models (e.g., individuals with disabilities, those who identify as bisexual, and individuals from lower socioeconomic status). Practicing allyship with clients not only strengthens the therapeutic alliance but also works toward eliminating barriers that impede successful treatment goals. Allyship can look like inclusive scheduling (e.g., holidays, less restrictive late/cancellation policies), broaching, and educating yourself through receptivity to new knowledge and unlearning harmful narratives. Taking a culturally humble approach can help to inform treatment options and the integration of elements of the client's identity that could increase the efficacy of overall treatment (see Chapter 3). Reflective work benefits the personal growth of the clinician as well as the therapeutic outcomes.

Conclusion

In this chapter, you have learned about a host of IDMs you can use to conceptualize and work with clients. While there are not developmental models for every individual identity or identity constellation, the models you have learned about offer a helpful starting place that you can build upon as you get to know the client and discern their specific therapeutic needs. Remember, there is no one-size-fits-all approach to conceptualizing and working with clients! Use your skills, discernment, and critical thinking to make the most of IDMs and to spur a positive working alliance. Remember what you have learned here to apply in upcoming chapters that are centered on specific identities.

Questions for Reflection

Consider what you learned in this chapter as you respond to the questions and prompts below.

1. Which of the IDMs aligned with your experiences? In what ways did they not fit your own development?
2. Which development models were new to you? What did you learn from reading about them in this chapter?
3. What are your thoughts on the identities that are without developmental models? How can that impact a counselor's work?
4. How do IDMs fit with what you have learned so far in this class?
5. What are the strengths of using IDMs with clients? Limitations?

Applying What You Have Learned

Complete each of the following activities, considering what you learned from this chapter.

Activity #1: Ethics and Identity Development Models

Pair up with a classmate and engage in a dialogue about culturally aware counseling! Listed below are American Counseling Association (ACA) Codes of Ethics that directly relate to the themes in this chapter. The objective of this activity is to apply tenets of the ACA code to fit the identity development model of your choice. Consider inclusive practices and potential challenges with your specific population highlighted in the model you chose.

A.2.c. Developmental and Cultural Sensitivity
D.1.a. Different Approaches
E.5.c. Historical and Social Prejudices in the Diagnosis of Pathology
E.8. Multicultural Issues/Diversity in Assessment
H.5.d. Multicultural and Disability Considerations

Activity #2: Introducing Identity Development Models to Clients

IDMs can be a helpful way to conceptualize clients and their needs, yet they can be used as part of the therapeutic process too. The question is, how do you introduce an identity development model to a client?

Using a case vignette or a fictional character from a TV show or movie, practice with a partner who is willing to embody the fictional character how you would introduce an identity development model to this fictional client. To prepare:

- Conceptualize the client using the chosen identity development model to determine its relevance.
- Determine why sharing the identity development model with the client could be helpful for them, specifically its therapeutic value related to the client's presenting concern.
- Plan how you will describe any technical terms or model jargon in a way the client can understand.
- Consider whether providing an informational handout about the model would be helpful to the client. If so, create one.

After you have prepared, have a go with introducing the model to the client! The "client" should have natural reactions and ask typical questions; afterward, the client will provide feedback about how the counselor explained the model (e.g., accessible language, explanation about therapeutic benefit) and any tweaks that could be helpful. After the counselor receives feedback, try again. Repeat the process as many times as you need to feel comfortable and confident.

Credit

Fig. 6.1: Jack D. Simons, Leeann Grant, and Jose M. Rodas, "Transgender People of Color: Experiences and Coping During the School-Age Years," *Journal of LGBTQ Issues in Counseling*, vol. 15, no.1, p. 37. Copyright © 2021 by Taylor & Francis Group.

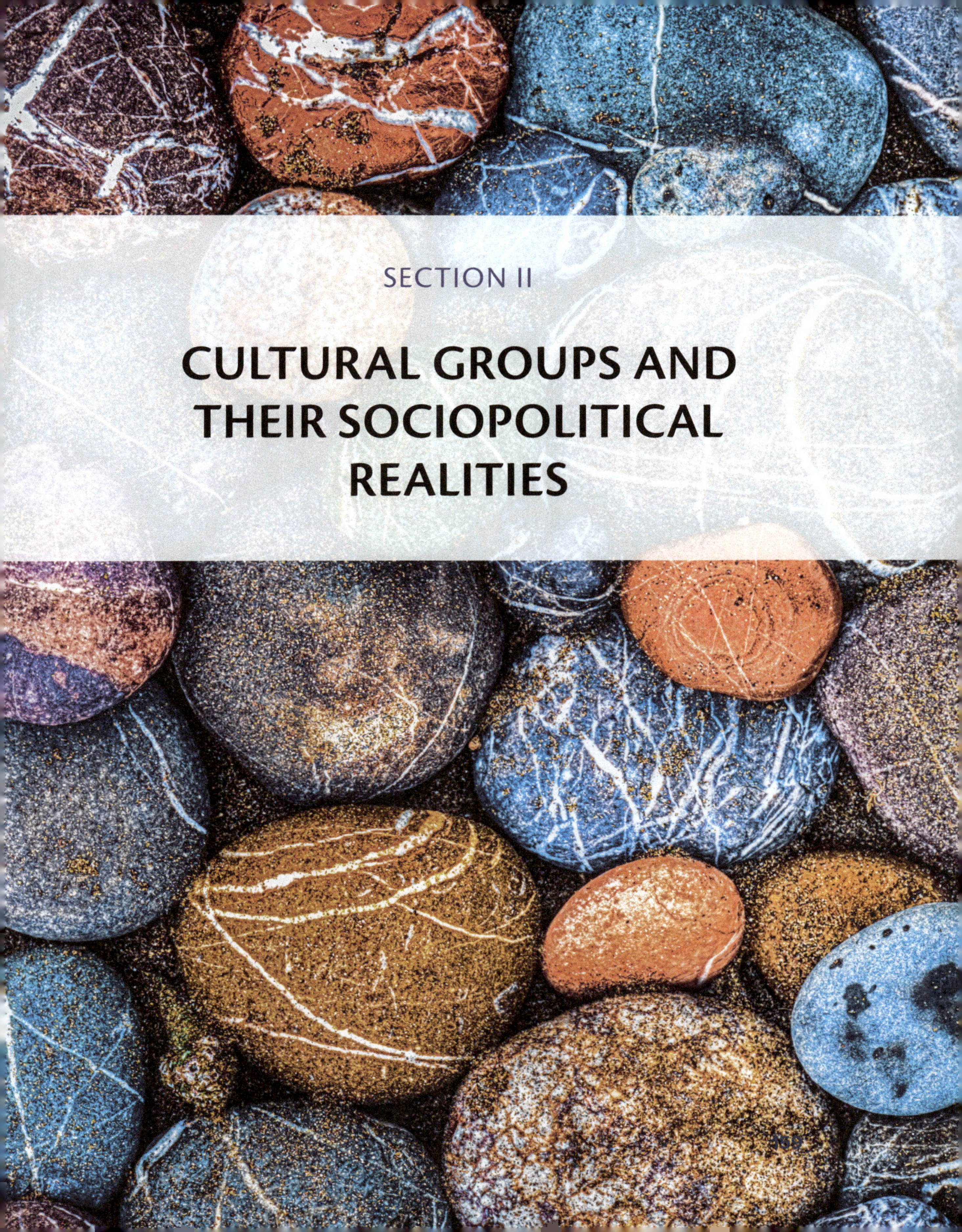

SECTION II

CULTURAL GROUPS AND THEIR SOCIOPOLITICAL REALITIES

CHAPTER 7

Race, Racism, and Colorism

Tanesha Rorie and Janice Byrd

In a racist society it is not enough to be non-racist. We must be anti-racist.

—Angela Davis

CHAPTER OVERVIEW

Exploring the topics of race, racism, and colorism in counseling and counselor education can be quite complex because there are many intricacies that contribute to the experiences and comprehension surrounding these concepts. In this chapter, we do not focus on the needs of one race over another, as that can continue to perpetuate the systemic oppression of the dominant culture over racially marginalized groups. Rather, the focus of this chapter is to challenge you to explore what these concepts mean in personal and professional contexts. Further, this chapter is meant to spark critical thought and action in how these concepts are experienced by the clients we serve. While reading through this chapter, please pause throughout to reflect on your own ideologies about race, racism, and colorism in order to foster introspection and individual growth.

Additionally, it is important to understand an important dialectic—race and racism are very real in terms of individual and group experiences—while also understanding that race is a social construct. This means that there is no scientific evidence to support racial distinctions; they have been created through power and privilege (i.e., White supremacist ideologies), leading to racism. Experiences of race, racism, and the process through which White supremacy racializes People of Color (POC) from various ethnicities are intricate, historically embedded, and uniquely individual. Further, race relates to, but is distinct from, ethnicity. ***Ethnicity*** is a term used to distinguish groups based on shared culture (e.g., country of origin, religion), characteristics, experiences, and background. Ethnicity can take on different meanings within different communities. ***Ethnocentrism*** is grounded in an ***us and them*** comparative lens (Isajiw, 1993) and results in dominant ethnic group superiority (see Chapter 8 for more information). For example, someone can identify as Black or African but ethnically identify as Latina/o/x or Hispanic (e.g., Afro-Latinx, Afro-Hispanic), while others could identify Latina/o/x as their race and their ethnicity. You will read more about ethnicity in Chapter 8, though as you read this chapter, consider the distinctions and overlaps between race and ethnicity and how they inform individual and group experiences of oppression and privilege.

LEARNING OBJECTIVES

By the end of this chapter, students will be able to

1. describe the relevant history of race, racism, and colorism and explain how it informs the current sociopolitical climate within the United States;
2. reflect on nondominant racial group experiences and apply awareness to counseling practice; and
3. discuss how race impacts counseling, including building and maintaining the relationship, practice, and advocacy.

CACREP 2016 STANDARDS

The information in this chapter supports the following standards:

- 2.F.2.a. multicultural and pluralistic characteristics within and among diverse groups nationally and internationally
- 2.F.2.c. multicultural counseling competencies
- 2.F.2.d the impact of heritage, attitudes, beliefs, understandings, and acculturative experiences on an individual's views of others
- 2.F.2.e. the effects of power and privilege for counselors and clients
- 2.F.2.f. help-seeking behaviors of diverse clients g. the impact of spiritual beliefs on clients' and counselors' worldviews
- 2.F.2.h. strategies for identifying and eliminating barriers, prejudices, and processes of intentional and unintentional oppression and discrimination
- 2.F.3.f. systemic and environmental factors that affect human development, functioning, and behavior
- 2.F.3.i. ethical and culturally relevant strategies for promoting resilience and optimum development and wellness across the lifespan

CACREP 2024 STANDARDS

The information in this chapter supports the following standards:

- 3.B.2. the influence of heritage, cultural identities, attitudes, values, beliefs, understandings, within-group differences, and acculturative experiences on individuals' worldviews
- 3.B.3. the influence of heritage, cultural identities, attitudes, values, beliefs, understandings, within-group differences, and acculturative experiences on help-seeking and coping behaviors
- 3.B.5. the effects of stereotypes, overt and covert discrimination, racism, power, oppression, privilege, marginalization, microaggressions, and violence on counselors and clients
- 3.B.9. strategies for identifying and eliminating barriers, prejudices, and processes of intentional and unintentional oppression and discrimination
- 3.B.10. guidelines developed by professional counseling organizations related to social justice, advocacy, and working with individuals with diverse cultural identities
- 3.C.7. models of resilience, optimal development, and wellness in individuals and families across the lifespan
- 3.C.11. systemic, cultural, and environmental factors that affect lifespan development, functioning, behavior, resilience, and overall wellness

Brief Historical Overview

The concept of race has been researched and discussed for centuries. Race is a social and political human classification system that is not scientifically or biologically based. Historically, race has been used to arbitrarily divide humankind into groups by skin tone and phenotype. This separation creates and maintains a social-political caste system that unfairly characterizes the target group (i.e., people who are darker skinned or with Afrocentric phenotypes) as inferior while the dominant group (i.e., those who are White, lighter skinned, and/or of European ancestry) is superior (Ray & DeLoatch, 2018; Tatum, 2001). Dating back to the 16th century, race was socially constructed in order to classify groups based on biological and phenotypic differences (Blakemore, 2019; Winant, 2006). There are a multitude of researchers who challenge the notion that racial categories are based on biological, evolutionary, and anthropological differences (Smedley & Smedley, 2005). Race was developed by those of European descent to categorize themselves as superior and anyone of other descent as inferior, specifically for the purposes of colonization and exploitation (Feagin, 2010; Guthrie, 2004). Race has been used to establish political and cultural power and continues to be redefined over the course of time and is part and parcel of *racism*.

Racism is an oppressive system of advantage based on race. Different from prejudice (e.g., preconceived judgment or opinion based on limited information), racism occurs when the racial group who holds power (i.e., the dominant group) carries out systematic discrimination through institutional policies/practices (e.g., local and national) within society that shapes cultural beliefs/values and institutionalize discriminatory practices that affect the target group (i.e., nondominant groups) across all facets of society (i.e., education, health care, justice system, and employment) (Ray & Deloatch, 2018; Tatum, 2001). Specifically in the United States, race has played a significant role in how the country was created, beginning with the land being stolen from Indigenous peoples and colonized to how power was established and functions in modern times. Also, race has had a key role in the development of capitalism. Capitalism can only be maintained with a class-based system, and monetary gains for the upper classes are dependent on individuals remaining in lower class groups. Chattel enslavement of Africans is a historical example of such dependence, and maintaining a large number of people in poverty is a present-day example.

Nondominant Group Identities

When discussing race, racism, and colorism in the United States, it is imperative that we discuss all communities of color, as there are similar and distinct experiences for nondominant racial groups. POC include all nondominant racial groups who are not classified as White; White is the dominant and privileged race in the United States. POC include African American and Black, Asian Americans, Native Hawaiians, Pacific Islanders, American Indians, Native/Indigenous Americans, Latinx, Hispanics, and multiracial people. One cannot fully understand these concepts without taking a significant dive into POC's unique experiences based on the communities/cultures in which their experiences lie.

For the remainder of this section, we discuss each racial group in greater detail. The following short subsections are simply an overview and do not represent the fullness and richness of each community. It is important to know some general experiences of groups while understanding people may have similar, divergent, or intersectional experiences related to their own unique identities! Readers are encouraged to take these cultural characteristics as general learning points to gain information about each community with the intention to learn about and honor everyone's experience who identifies with these cultures. Additionally, as mentioned earlier, race and ethnicity are often conflated. Someone can be Latinx and be White or White-passing, just as much as they can be darker skinned; the relationship between race and ethnicity does not always correlate with a person fully identifying as the dominant culture or fully identifying with the nondominant culture.

African American and Black Communities

Black communities include a wide range of ethnicities under the umbrella of the African diaspora. The African diaspora has many different meanings as it relates to the different experiences associated with Black people across history. The modern-day understanding of the African diaspora represents those of African descent who share in the historical and everyday struggles associated with race (Palmer 2018). Palmer (2018) discussed the emotional bond between Black people based on the oppressions they have endured, regardless of geographical location. There are Black people in countries all over the world, often in communities that have historical ties to enslavement, like the United States, Brazil, and the islands of the Caribbean. Black communities and the labor of Black people have been integral parts of the building and prosperity of those countries.

African Americans are responsible for many contributions and progress of the United States. For example, enslaved Africans advanced agriculture in areas such as cotton and tobacco. Additionally, they were forced to build many of the historical landmarks we know, such as the White House. Throughout history, African Americans have been innovators in areas such as STEM, the arts, and education. Black inventors have changed the lives of many in this country (and beyond) through monumental innovations such as the traffic light (George Washington Carver), the ironing board (Sarah Boone), and the clock (Benjamin Banneker), to name a few. African Americans continue to make contributions that advance the United States in all capacities.

Black and *African American* are distinct terms that depend on the person and their unique heritage. *African American* is often used to identify those living in the United States who are Black. Although they may classify themselves as Black, African American, or both depending on where they live and their individual experiences, not all people in the United States who identify as Black come from or identify with Africa. For example, there are many Black Americans who immigrated directly from countries such as Haiti, Jamaica, Trinidad and Tobago, or Brazil, or one of these countries is their ancestral home rather than Africa. As such, it is always important to ask an individual how they identify and not make assumptions.

BOX 7.1 TIPS FOR PROFESSIONAL PRACTICE: ASKING CLIENTS ABOUT THEIR RACIAL IDENTITIES

One way counselors ask clients about their identities is through *cultural broaching* (Day-Vines et al., 2007). Broaching race and ethnicity is essential for culturally relevant counseling. Counselors start conversations related to race/ethnicity with their clients to learn how they identify, to understand their experiences, to hear important information about their identities, and to uncover possible influences of race/ethnicity on their mental health. Below are sample questions that can be asked when broaching race:

1. "How do you identify your race?"
2. "What are some strengths you developed based on your identity as a [insert race client identified] person?"
3. "How do you think your race impacts your experiences of mental health?"
4. "As a White counselor, I recognize the differences in our experiences related to race. What are your thoughts about how this may impact our work together?"
5. "I understand as a POC that we may share similar experiences. How do you think this could impact our work together?"

One cannot discuss the Black experience in the United States without acknowledging the traumas endured by this group, including the period of enslavement (1607 to 1865) to current traumas associated with police brutality and ongoing systemic racism. The United States was founded and built off the traumas of POC (i.e., enslavement, Indigenous genocide), including Black folx. The transatlantic slave trade began in the 16th century and led to what we know today as the African-based institution of slavery (Taylor & Becker, 1999). Enslavement began generational trauma passed down over literal centuries for many Black people. Beyond the horrors of chattel enslavement, there have been further significant time frames that have included traumas experienced by Black people in the United States, such as the antebellum period, abolitionist movement, Jim Crow, and the civil rights movement. Furthermore, these traumas extend into present-day experience, with Black folx experiencing significantly higher rates of poverty, violence/abuse, educational gaps, and physical and mental health disparities compared to White populations.

Currently, Black people make up about 14% of the U.S. population (Moslimani et al., 2023; U.S. Census, 2020). Black people have greatly contributed to progress in the United States and have thrived immensely despite systemic racism and White supremacy (e.g., Black Wall Street, Harlem Renaissance, Historically Black colleges and universities). Some of the same movements that have been sparked and led by Black people, such as Black Lives Matter and the Civil Rights Movement, have frequently traumatized or retraumatized Black people. At the same time, they have demonstrated Black folks' strengths, resilience, brilliance, and creativity. As generational trauma has been passed down over the years, these positive qualities have been passed down generationally as well. One example is the thriving of Black women. While a numerical minority, Black women hold the top spot (17%) for starting and running new businesses (Kelley et al., 2021). Additionally, Black men have steadily increased their income and decreased their experiences of poverty (Wilcox et al., 2018). In the area of mental health, Black people have increased their utilization of mental health services (Terlizzi & Schiller, 2022; Wilson, 2001), especially since the COVID-19 pandemic (Walton et al., 2021). Black people are growing, striving, and thriving despite numerous structural inequities.

Intersectionality brings about specific challenges and triumphs that only add to the complexities of the Black experience. Race intersects with other identities such as gender, relational/affectional identity, and ability status, making for unique within-group experiences that highlight the oppressions and *-isms* that persist within the Black community. It is important to note that the basis of these issues stems from misogynistic, heterocentric, and White supremacist views that have been internalized by Black communities and continue to contribute to the traumas Black people and pushed forth by Black people, all of which contribute to mental health experience.

BOX 7.2 **FOCUS ON CLIENT CARE**

Charles is a 22-year-old, Black, gay, cis-male who has reported to counseling with symptoms of anxiety, including racing thoughts, broken sleep, and increased worry. He has recently graduated from college and has "no idea what I would like to do next." Charles comes from an affluent family in his community and is experiencing pressure from his parents about what his career path will be. He has shared with this counselor that, ideally, he would like to pursue a career in film. However, he does not think this would be a career that would meet the approval of his family. Charles shared with his counselor his previous experiences with his parents, including being high-achieving and always working to "please" them. However, he does not report being close to them and has not shared his "true self" with them out of fear of disappointment. Although he has other family and friends with whom he has chosen to share his sexual orientation, he has not had conversations with his parents because of the negative views they have about the LGBTQ+ community.

As Charles's counselor, how might the intersections of race and sexual orientation affect his current experiences of anxiety? How would you broach this with this client? Did you notice anything come up for you as you read the case, such as biases or assumptions?

Family plays a significant role in Black/African American culture; these families may have diverse family structures. The Black family has impacts on education, mental health, and overall wellness. Specifically, the Black family is often referenced when discussing the overall success of Black people in this country. Black family leaders have been highlighted as integral to Black individuals' success. For example, there has been much focus throughout the years on the role of the Black father. The cultural narrative of Black fathers being absentee parents has been ever present in media and society. However, that has been proven not to be the case. In 2013, the National Health Statistics Report found Black American fathers to be the most involved fathers across racial groups based on several markers, including helping their children with homework and talking with their children about their day.

The Black American family is typically matriarchal. As a result, the notion of the *strong Black woman* has emerged in terms of managing home and work responsibilities (Abrams et al., 2014; Jones, 1982). Families with females as the head of household make up about 39% of Black families (Moslimani et al., 2023). Particular expectations and pressures that accompany the strong Black woman persona have significant implications for the mental health of Black women (Jones & Pritchett-Johnson, 2018). As such, it's common for Black women to present for counseling with anxiety, depression, and low self-compassion (Donovan & West, 2015; Liao et al.,2020; Stanton et al., 2017).

Another important aspect of Black American culture is religion and spirituality. Approximately 66% of Black adults identify as Protestant, while about 21% are unaffiliated with a religion (Moslimani et al., 2023). What has come to be known as the *Black Church* has been instrumental for Black Americans, has been considered a strength as it creates a sense of community, and has been identified as a protective factor in overcoming difficult life experiences. With community comes support, relationships, and even allyship for some. However, there has been trauma associated with religion and the Black church in that homomisia and transmisia have been a part of these institutions historically. Therefore, counselors must be intentional about gauging the role that religion and spirituality may play in the lives of Black clients. Knowing the client's experience with religion and religious organizations can help counselors discern the overall impact it has had on their development and their mental health.

Colorism in the Black Community

Race and racism have led to separation, discrimination, and violence in many countries. The effects of racism have not occurred only between dominant and nondominant racial groups—it has created separation *within* communities of color because of *internalized racism*—the false belief that White/Eurocentric standards are the ideal. White supremacy has led to colorism, which historically and currently still has effects on communities of color.

Colorism is a term coined by Pulitzer Prize winner and Black American writer Alice Walker in her 1983 book *In Search of Our Mothers' Gardens*. Walker (1983) defined colorism as "prejudicial or preferential treatment of same-race people based solely on their color" (p. 260). More broadly, colorism is a form of discrimination that occurs within a racial or ethnic group whereby people of lighter skin are favored over those with darker skin (Burke & Embrich, 2008; Dixon & Telles, 2017). Colorism is also known as *skin tone bias* or *color-based discrimination*. Understandings of colorism continue to grow as various communities make meaning of this skin-hue-driven classification.

The origins of colorism are linked to the innate presence of White supremacy throughout European colonialism, American slavery, and class hierarchies in Asia (Hunter, 2007). Others have described colorism as "the allocation of privilege and disadvantage according to the lightness or darkness of one's skin" (Burke & Embrich, 2008, p. 17). As researchers continue to refine this definition to describe the phenomenon more astutely, we learn that colorism is bigger than color. Colorism delineates people within and across racial groups along a spectrum of Whiteness and Blackness that privileges skin, phenotype, and hair that is perceived to be more aligned with White/Eurocentric features (Dixon & Telles, 2017; Rosario et al., 2021). Therefore, colorism is not only a symptom of racism but also inherently anti-Black. It manifests in communities of color across the globe, including communities across Asia, Black people across the diaspora, Latinx communities, and Native American/Indigenous communities. POC are as likely to participate in colorism as people who are White. Notably, Hairston and colleagues (2018) shared that for many Black people in the United States, "colorism can be more hurtful than racism because colorism produces negative treatment not only from non–African Americans (inter-racially) but also from those of their own race (intra-racially) and sometimes even from immediate family members" (p. 171–172).

Color bias within the Black community is passed down from one generation to another and is a part of racial socialization (Crutchfield et al., 2022). White (2016) stated,

> The process of racial socialization then becomes an important process for Black adolescents because it helps to develop a positive ethnic identity, which throughout their life can be used to protect Black adolescents "against feelings of dissonance" and maintain healthy levels of stress. (p. 15)

Rosario et al. (2021) researched the ways Black girls combat negative messages about their dark skin to resist attacks on their self-esteem. One of their participants, Maya, shared, "[B] ecause of my skin color, um when I was younger, I often got picked on because I was darker than others but I learned to love my skin color as I got older, cuz dark skin is very pretty" (p. 514). While colorism persists in the Black community and other communities of color, darker skinned members of these communities have begun to resist this oppressive concept and find beauty and resilience in their own skin color.

Most research on colorism focuses on Black and Latinx communities. For this chapter, we focus on the history and ramifications of colorism within the Black community in the United States. These ramifications include darker skin contributing to discrimination, being associated with criminality and danger, increased chances of living in racially segregated neighborhoods, increased chances of being suspended from school, and dysmorphic beauty standards for girls and women (Jha, 2015).

Colorism is deeply ingrained in U.S. history. Colorism descends directly from racial slavery (Drake & Clayton, 1970; Hunter, 2007; Reece, 2020) when enslaved Black people were commonly divided by color (Davis & Gates, 1991). Billingsley (1968) shared that enslaved individuals who were lighter skinned were afforded easier household responsibilities and endured less violent treatment by their overseers compared to darker skinned individuals. This stratification of African ancestry led to a classification system reinforcing the *one-drop rule* (i.e., a person was classified as Black if they had any amount of African ancestry). Terms such as *quadroon* or *octoroon* were used to denote enslaved Black people with one-fourth or one-eighth African ancestry. Around the early 19th century, the term *mulatto* emerged to represent biracial/multiracial Black people with at least three-eighths African ancestry (Bowman et al., 2004; Reece, 2020). By 1910, after several state-level court cases debating how multiracial people would be classified, the one-drop rule gained legal legitimacy when Tennessee legislation established that a person with any Black racial ancestry is considered racially Black (Brown, 2014).

While individuals who are biracial/multiracial continue to face discrimination, lighter skinned Black people have historically been afforded privileges their darker skinned counterparts have not (Reece, 2020). Across history, some of these privileges included higher ranking political positions, landownership, or the ability to assume a White identity (i.e., *pass*; Jordan & Spikard, 2014).

Colorism has interconnected individual and systemic-level ramifications that are apparent across individuals' lifetimes. These ramifications disproportionally affect many areas, from mental health to experiences with the criminal justice system (Barideaux et al., 2021; Oh et al., 2021). Additionally, researchers have found that darker skinned Black people report higher incidences of discrimination in their day-to-day interactions (Seaton et al., 2008). Notably, Klonoff and Landrine's (2000) explored the experiences of 300 Black adults in the United States and found that those who are darker skinned were 11 times more likely to experience frequent, more stressful, and harsher occurrences of discrimination.

Anti-Blackness

A unique manifestation of racism, anti-Blackness, is experienced by Black people and those perceived to be of African ancestry (Wilderson, 2010). Anti-Blackness is defined as systematic discrimination, marginalization, and devaluing of Black people or those perceived to be of African descent. It affects Black people across all areas of society (i.e., educational, health care, justice system, and employment), and perpetrators can be White people and other POC (Dumas, 2016; Wilderson, 2010). Notably, Wilderson (2010) said, "Anti-Blackness manifests as the monumentalization and fortification of civil society against social death" (p. 90), which relegates Black humanity as a socially dead, nonbeing, and an antagonist in the story of the United States. Essentially, anti-blackness is a force that works to dehumanize Black people and their culture. Black people, their culture, and other productions are rendered inferior and/or inherently subject to commodification (Wilderson, 2010).

It is important to acknowledge that experiences of discrimination and prejudice can occur within any racial/ethnic group among Black, Indigenous, and People of Color (BIPOC). While the systemic racism Black people face at the hands of White people is persistent and ongoing, it is important to address the complexities of the unique manifestation of anti-Blackness within the Black community and the broader BIPOC community. Notably, Wilderson (2010) noted that anti-Blackness is a global phenomenon perpetuated by individuals from various racial/ethnic backgrounds and not limited to White people. Wilderson (2010) further asserted that anti-Blackness is deeply ingrained in the fabric of society and is a foundational component of the values that guide the racial hierarchies that maintain systems of oppression. As a result, many Black people can themselves perpetuate anti-Blackness and can also have a peculiar relationship with supposed unifying framings, such as POC and BIPOC (Bush, 2020), because of their experiences of discrimination and prejudice from other racially marginalized groups. There are many examples of anti-Blackness exhibited by other BIPOC communities, though we offer some for you to review in the appendixes for this chapter.

Asian American, Native Hawaiian, and Pacific Islander Communities

Asian American, Native Hawaiian, and Pacific Islander (AANHPI) are communities that come directly from or have ethnic ties to countries in Far East Asia, Southeast Asia, the Indian subcontinent, and the Pacific Islands. This group is incredibly diverse and encompasses multiple ethnicities (see Chapter 8) and Indigenous Tribal identities (see Chapter 10). While incredibly diverse and distinct (e.g., there are vast cultural differences between those who are Japanese, Korean, Indian, or Samoan, among others), the U.S. Census combines these groups into one category, eliminating country of origin and cultural nuances, insinuating homogeneity. According to the 2020 Census Report, about 6% of the U.S. population identifies as AANHPI (U.S. Census, 2022).

Historical Background

Historically, AANHPI populations have experienced racism and discrimination in the United States, including from the U.S. government. For example, the Chinese Exclusion Act was one of the first forms of discrimination against these populations in the United States. The Chinese Exclusion Act of 1882 was a ban placed on Chinese people immigrating to the United States in the 1800s. Additionally, Japanese people were forced into internment camps when the U.S. government implemented a policy that would isolate those of Japanese descent into isolated camps as a response to Pearl Harbor in the 1940s. Many individuals were made to leave their homes and forced into these camps with no regard to their current home life, situation, political ties to Japan, or whether they were born in the United States. These discriminatory acts have informed much of the discrimination that happens in present-day times. More recently, we have seen an increase in anti-Asian attitudes, racism, and violence in the United States, specifically related to the COVID-19 pandemic. Some examples include the 2021 mass shooting at an Asian-owned spa in Atlanta, increased verbal violence (e.g., *Wuhan Flu*, *China Flu*), and physical assaults. These anti-Asian incidents increased dramatically since the beginning of the pandemic (NPR, 2021). In May 2021, U.S. president Joe Biden signed the COVID-19 Hate Crimes Act in response to anti-Asian violence that occurred.

The COVID-19 pandemic heightened race-based trauma for many Asian Americans, which has led to many counseling considerations in treatment options for AANHPI individuals who have experienced such trauma. Litam (2020) suggested using microinterventions and mindfulness in addressing race-based trauma with this population to help address their unique mental health presenting concerns. Read more about these suggestions in the Professional Counseling Practice Applications section later in the chapter.

Colorism in AANHPI

Colorism affects the AANHPI community as colonialism penetrates all communities of color. Historically, the roots of colorism in Asian communities were directly influenced by European colonization and the acculturation into White ideology that occurs when immigrating (e.g., the Spanish colonizing the Philippines; Chen et al., 2022). Research continues to illustrate that colorism systemically affects individuals across Asian communities (Chen et al., 2022; Hunter, 2007; Khanna, 2020).

People of Asian ancestry are oftentimes lumped together and discussed as a monolithic culture. However, despite the cultural similarities they may hold, there are many cultural dissimilarities across these unique cultures that result in across-group and within-group discrimination. Notably, south Asian communities (i.e., Indian, Filipino/a, Thai) tend to have darker skin than those from East Asian communities (i.e., China, Korea, Japan). Colorism is pervasive. South Asian people are characterized as inferior/less desirable because of their darker skin tone, and the darker you are within Eastern and Southern Asian communities, the more social-political ramifications you face (Chen et al., 2023; Khanna, 2020; Marira & Mitra, 2013). Like in Africa, Latin America, and the Middle East, Asian communities have a huge economic market for skin-bleaching creams (Hall, 1994, 1995, 1997; Marira & Mitra, 2013) that are used to lighten their skin in response to this oppression. Hall (1994, 1995, 1997) coined the term *the bleaching syndrome* to describe the internalization of the White aesthetic among POC as a result of slavery and colonialism around the world. For example, Julie Chen Moonves, a well-known broadcaster best known for hosting the popular show *Big Brother*, revealed in an interview that she had surgery to slim her wide nose and enlarge her *Asian eyes* to conform to Eurocentric beauty standards.

Model Minorities

AANHPI populations are often considered to be the *model minority* because they are often associated with a high level of accomplishment and success (Ocampo & Soodjinda, 2016 Sue et al., 2022). This stereotype perpetuates the falsity that the American dream is achievable for all and alleges that those of Asian background will be successful; therefore, all minorities should follow them (Ngo & Lee, 2007). This status can affect how AANHPI individuals perceive themselves and can reinforce bias. Counselors must be aware of how the model minority concept may affect this population and their utilization of counseling services, which are often underutilized (Sue et al., 2019). Seeking mental health services has traditionally been a challenge for this community (Chang et al., 2014; Gee et al., 2010). However, there has been a steady increase in the use of mental health services for Asian American populations from 2019 to 2021 (SAMHSA, 2022).

BOX 7.3 **FOCUS ON CLIENT CARE**

Huang is a 40-year-old Chinese American ciswoman who has reported to counseling with the presenting problem of panic attacks. She mentioned she has suffered from panic attacks for a little over a year because of a traumatic car accident. Huang has shared her symptoms of panic attacks, including heavy breathing, heart palpitations, and sweaty palms. She only experiences these symptoms when she must drive on the highway, which is where her car accident occurred. She came to counseling wanting to be "cured," as she stated to her counselor, "I would like for you to tell me what to do to get better."

As Huang's counselor, what would be important to consider? How would you approach this case?

Familial Structure

Other characteristics of the AANHPI community include being collectivist, which means family is a major decision-making influence, and how each family member represents the family is extremely important (Sue et al., 2022). Parents and familial authority figures may make decisions for the family and individual members, and parents may use an authoritative parenting style. Families are often patriarchal and hierarchal in nature in that males and older people are considered of higher status and deserving of respect and consultation in decision-making. With the influence of family being so paramount, counselors must be cognizant of how this might influence the mental health experience of AANHPI individuals.

Latina/o/x and Hispanic Communities

One of the fastest growing populations in the United States is the Hispanic/Latinx community, which makes up about 19% of the population (U.S. Census, 2023; Office of Minority Health [OMH]), 2023). It is the largest U.S. racial minority group (OMH, 2023) and is expected to grow to 28% of the U.S. population by the year 2060 (Zong, 2022).

When discussing this community, it is important to distinguish between the terms Hispanic and Latina/o/x. Hispanic is an umbrella term that was created by the U.S. Census as an attempt to group all individuals who speak Spanish as their primary language together, which includes multiple countries around the world, including Spain, Cuba, Mexico, and most South and Central American countries (Sue et al., 2019). Because of its roots as a generalized, U.S. Census–driven term, some find this term pejorative and will not use it to describe themselves or others. *Latina/o/x* refers to individuals who are specifically from Latin American countries or have direct lineage tied to those countries (from Central or South America; Sue et al., 2019). For example, Brazilians are Latinx but not Hispanic because Brazilians speak Portuguese. Most people from Spain are Hispanic but are not Latinx. Further, many Latinx individuals may also identify with Indigenous tribes, while some may not. Knowing the difference between these terms can help counselors understand their clients' identities when they share their racial identity and/or ethnic identities. In some cases, people may identify as Latino (masculine) or Latina (feminine). Note: We have chosen to use the term *Latinx* in this chapter to be inclusive of all gender identities; however, as you learned in Chapter 1, identifying as Latino/a or using the term, *Latiné* is not wrong and is simply a personal preference! We recognize the term Latinx has been used in recent years. However, there has been debate and critical analyses of the use of the word and its fit in the Spanish language as "x" at the end of a word is not typical and causes pronunciation challenges (Miranda et al., 2023). It is critical to remember that while Latinx/Hispanic is a racial group, there are many ethnic identities within this racial designation. While experiences of racism can be similar across these groups, cultural values and identities often differ and are important within these communities (more on that in Chapter 8).

Historical Background

Hispanic and Latinx history is actually older than the United States itself, as many of the earliest Spanish explorers arrived in the early 1500s. Revolutions in countries such as Mexico (i.e., the Mexican Revolution in the early 1900s) forced a wave of Latinx individuals to migrate to what's now known as the United States in hopes of a better future. While Latinx individuals have made many contributions to agriculture, public policy, and the arts, there has been much racism and discrimination that has not ended. The Immigration Act of 1882 was one of the earliest pieces of legislation that targeted immigrants from Latinx and Hispanic countries by adding additional taxes on each immigrant coming into the country (US Citizenship and Immigration Services [USCIS], 2020). Other political actions, such as mass deportations dating back to President Eisenhower in the 1950s, have been taken against those of Latinx/Hispanic background. It has extended into present-day with the proposed political actions such as a U.S.-Mexico Border Wall (USCBP, 2023), moving undocumented people from one state to another, and opposition to the Dream Act (Miranda, 2010).

Common Characteristics

Characteristics of this population include collectivism with an emphasis on family that can reach beyond immediate family into extended family, including godparents. Latinx families are often hierarchical, with much respect and honor bestowed upon the eldest members of the family. This representation is reflected in media, such as the animated movies *Encanto* and *Coco*. High value is placed on loyalty and interdependence within the family. Religion and spirituality may be of high importance, with Catholicism being the most frequently practiced religion in this group. However, not all Latinx people practice Catholicism; some may be Protestant, practice Indigenous religious, or not be religious at all (Krogstad et al., 2023). Education is highly valued, as evidenced by the steady plummet of high school dropout rates (i.e., 34% to 10%; Gramlich, 2017) and the significant increase in post-secondary education—over a 200% increase over the past 2 decades in 4-year institutions (Mora, 2022).

Biracial and Multiracial Individuals

Being multiracial can often be a complex identity to navigate across the lifespan. Individuals who identify with more than one race often classify themselves as biracial or multiracial. However, there may be individuals who identify more with one race over another and choose to only identify themselves as one race. The individual is the one who determines how they identify and what that means for them, not anyone else. In the United States, bi- and multiracial individuals have a long-standing history that has been intertwined with racism and discrimination. Dating back to the *one-drop rule*, which originated during the time of enslavement and was perpetuated through the Jim Crow segregation era in the United States, those of more than one race have experienced many struggles related to their basic human rights and even their very existence. Under the one-drop rule, individuals were classified as Black based on having just one drop of African blood. The rule included those who had just one Black ancestor. This meant that individuals classified as Black under the rule could be enslaved or subjected to segregation and the violence and oppression associated with it. While the term *Negro* was used at the time to define race, Negro is now viewed as a pejorative and should not be used to describe Black/African people. What's confounding and something worth considering is that people who are White often encompass multiple ethnicities yet typically do not encounter similar struggles and discrimination as bi/multiracial individuals.

Identity development is important for multiracial individuals because they have two or more racial identities to understand. Sometimes there is a discrepancy between what someone's racial makeup is and what others perceive their race to be based on phenotypic and other physical traits; this can lead to identity confusion. Such confusion can result in an individual identifying with one race only to avoid internal and external conflict. Such experiences are shared in identity models which can be helpful in understanding what it may be like for some mixed-race individuals (more on those models can be found in Chapter 6).

BOX 7.4 **FOCUS ON CLIENT CARE**

Kayla is a 23-year-old, biracial (White mother, Black father) transwoman. She has recently come to counseling to "dive deeper" into identity issues she has been having. She shared that during her childhood, she identified as White, as she was closer to her mother and maternal side of the family. While she had contact with her father, she was not close to him or his family. She barely spent any time with her "Black side." While Kayla identified as White during her childhood, there were physical characteristics (e.g., kinky-curly hair) that were different from her family. Recently, Kayla has been wanting to explore her "Black side" more. As her counselor, how might you validate Kayla's experiences and help her develop her identity in a way that feels good to her?

The action of choosing one identity over another has been perpetuated even in the way we classify race and ethnicity. Historically, there has only been one choice allotted for race/ethnicity demographics on the U.S. Census. It was not until the year 2000 that the U.S. Census provided the option for individuals to choose more than one race for racial identity. As recently as 2020, there were still changes being made to the racial classifications on the Census. It is because of these changes we have discovered that the United States is much more multiracial than many people thought, with over 30 million people identifying with more than one race, a 276% increase since 2010 (U.S. Census, 2023).

With there being many different racial and ethnic identities associated with multiracial identity, it is important to acknowledge the uniqueness of each person's experience of being multiracial. Those experiences carry different strengths and different challenges. For example, any combination of racial makeup that results in someone being White-passing (i.e., having more Eurocentric phenotypic traits) may not endure the racism and colorism that another person might who has a darker skin tone or textured hair. It is important to give space for multiracial and biracial individuals to share what their experiences have been like and the complexities that are present.

Arab and Middle Eastern Americans

Arab Americans are individuals who are descendants or immigrants from Arabic-speaking countries in Southwest Asia and North Africa (Arab American Institute, 2023), whereas Middle Eastern Americans (MEAs) may or may not identify as Arab. Geographically, MEAs have roots in countries such as Lebanon, Jordan, Israel, Iran, and Iraq. Some MEAs may speak Arabic (like individuals from Jordan or Saudi Arabia), yet people from other countries may speak other languages (e.g., Israel (Hebrew), Iran (Persian), or Turkey (Turkish)). These individuals may ethnically identify as Arabic (like someone from Saudi Arabia), but many will not and prefer to identify with their country of origin, such as Lebanese or Jordanian. Additionally, there can be parallels in culture between Balkan, European, and Middle Eastern countries.

While many MEAs may practice Islam, often an assumption made by others, many religions are practiced in this religion, including Judaism, Christianity, and other minority religions, such as Druze and Zoroastrianism. It is important to understand how your individual client identifies while also knowing that because of their skin color, they are likely to experience similar oppressions to other Middle Eastern/Arab Americans.

There is a discrepancy in how many Arab Americans/MEAs live in the United States because the U.S. Census has had missing and deficient categories (Wintersmith, 2022). Historically, the earliest Arab immigrants had to classify themselves as White to gain U.S. citizenship (Stephan, 2021). This led to new efforts by President Biden and his administration to add new categories for race, including Middle Eastern and North African (Office of Management and Budget, 2023), to the U.S. Census. The Arab American Institution (2023 reports an estimated 3.7 million Americans with ancestry traced back to an Arabic-speaking country.

Ecological and Sociopolitical Contexts

As discussed earlier in the chapter, race has contributed significantly to the lived experiences of many racial minority groups. Systemically, race infiltrates the ways in which many institutions are run, as they are often structured to support the dominant culture and, in turn, reflect and enact White supremacy that keeps racial minorities marginalized. What is White supremacy? According to Blay (2011), White supremacy is defined as a "historically based, institutionally perpetuated system of exploitation and oppression of continents, nations, and peoples classified as 'non-White' by continents, nations, and peoples who, by virtue of their white (light) skin pigmentation and/or ancestral origin from Europe, classify themselves as 'White'" (p. 6). For example, in counseling, upholding White supremacy looks like holding Western, Eurocentric values (e.g., autonomy) as paramount without the flexibility and intentionality behind incorporating other values connected to collectivistic cultures (e.g., community).

BOX 7.5 **PAUSE AND REFLECT: WHITE SUPREMACY AND YOU**

How have you been impacted by White supremacy and systemic racism? Have you, your family, or your ancestors received benefits from White supremacy and systemic racism? Have you, your family, or your ancestors been marginalized by White supremacy and systemic racism?

Systems such as academia, health care, and law enforcement were designed with the intention of making it difficult for racial minority groups to advance (Yearby, 2018). Racial disparities have been identified across many institutions, including education (de Brey et al., 2019), health care (Schwartz & Blankenship, 2014; UNCF, 2023), law enforcement (e.g., policing and incarcerations; USDOJ, 2022, and housing (Quillian et al., 2020; Thomas et al., 2018), just to name a few. In these systems, POC have been the catalyst throughout history for raising important "Why" questions, leading to much research across these institutions.

Due to systemic racism, there is an impact on both internal and external locus of control in what is perceived to be within one's own capacity to control or change. POC can be mentally impacted about what is achievable based on messages portrayed in society, as well as the influence of the real barriers that make it difficult for POC to progress. Furthermore, their mental and emotional health can be impacted. Experiences of trauma, mental exhaustion, and overworking grounded in systemic racism are well-documented factors that contribute to the struggles clients of color experience (Josiah et al., 2023; Mulligan, 2021; Payne, 2022). In sum, the challenges associated with experiencing systemic racism can and will show up in counseling sessions with clients of color and all counselors must be prepared to adequately address these challenges in a culturally sensitive and affirming manner.

Colonialism continues to affect all races, as it is what drives the way in which we live our lives in Western society. Colonialism affects our standard ways of living, our day-to-day thinking, beauty standards, and so much more. It permeates how we conduct work and education, how we diagnose and prescribe, and how we monetize experiences that should be based on equity (e.g., health care; Bram et al., 2015; Jamtgaard & Lewis, 2023). It even impacts our political systems in terms of how we have structured democracy in the United States, including voting practices. To overcome White supremacy and colonial standards, we must acknowledge it exists. Further, we must make conscious, intentional decisions about how we combat the thoughts and ideas that drive our actions. Many of these thoughts and ideas are not in our consciousness or are outside of our awareness, which is where counseling becomes so crucial to the evolution of humanity. We, as counselors, must be open to what impacts our perpetuation of the status quo in how we navigate the mental health system. Practices such as the use of traditional counseling theories, limiting the work we do to one-on-one client contact, and even the traditional 9–5 work schedule are all examples of how we continue to reinforce colonized values. While it is not fair to state that these practices do not work for some, we must be willing to challenge them for those groups and clients they do not work.

BOX 7.6 **PAUSE AND REFLECT: ACCESSIBILITY OF SERVICES**

You receive a call from a potential client who desperately needs services but is not able to attend counseling due to the hours available (i.e., 9–5). This client works the same hours as the clinic operates and is further limited because there are only a few counselors in town who take their insurance. How can we adjust to meet this client's needs?

Professional Counseling Practice Applications

Race and racism are present in most systems. Mental health systems are not exempt. For example, clients of color are diagnosed with severe and persistent mental illnesses more often than White clients (MHA, 2023). Intentional efforts must be made to understand and increase cross-racial counseling interactions that are positive and effective.

The Counseling Relationship

The counseling relationship is important to the outcomes in counseling, with multicultural orientation having an influence on that relationship (Bathje et al., 2022; Ratts et al., 2015). Even with the increase in diversity among counselors, White counselors remain the dominant race in our profession, with around 60% of counseling students (CACREP, 2023) and close to 70% of the profession as a whole identifying as White (Data USA, 2023). Yet clients across specialty areas are much more racially diverse, and when you consider identity intersectionality, the likelihood of cross-racial and cross-cultural counseling experiences is more the rule than the exception.

Let's take, for example, counseling AAPI clients who have experienced race-based trauma; incorporating mindfulness can help promote self-love in the form of acknowledgment of one's needs in the moment (Litam, 2020). Additionally, empowering clients to use microinterventions in safe environments where power differentials are not seen as possibly harmful can invigorate AAPI clients (Litam, 2020). In practice, counselors should be mindful of the differences in communication patterns and expression of emotion since traditional counseling practices are based on the Western-driven practice of talk therapy. In AANHPI cultures, emotions may not be expressed directly or may be somaticized. Counselors can use a strength-based approach by acknowledging the client's ability to control emotions (Chang & O'Hara, 2013) while helping the client to build additional coping skills. Also, silence is a common part of communication that can be interpreted negatively in Westernized communication patterns (Chang & O'Hara, 2013). Counselors are often seen as being in an expert role within many Asian American communities, so operating from the stance of a consultant can be helpful in establishing an initial connection and building rapport (Atkinson et al., 1998). Additionally, self-disclosure can also be a tool to build connection (Sue et al., 2019).

There are times when clients of color may request same-race counselors for a number of relevant reasons. One primary reason is that clients may perceive that a same-race counselor will understand their culture without further explanation or education (Smith & Trimble, 2016; Sue et al., 2019) while still acknowledging their individual experiences. The burden of educating a majority (i.e., White) counselor can cause undue emotional labor, may be retraumatizing to the client, and could damage the counseling relationship.

Another reason is that same-race counselors can help clients feel more at ease in sharing their personal and private experiences that may be associated with their racial identity. Clients of color are frequently on the receiving end of bias, assumption, and discrimination from just a mere look at their outward appearance by White people (Walker & Bruns, 2022). Not only can this impact clients' comfort, but it can also influence how clients perceive their counselors' level of competence (Walker & Bruns, 2022). While there may be preferences for same-race counselors, there is no research that supports that counseling outcomes are more favorable with a same-race counselor. What has been proven to be more important is having a counselor who displays cultural humility and competence (see Chapter 3 for more on cultural humility).

Counselors who are culturally humble display several important behaviors. For example, they acknowledge the *-isms* associated with race (i.e., racism and colorism) and how those experiences intersect with clients' other identities. Additionally, they acknowledge the power, privilege, and marginalization associated with race and how they may affect the counseling relationship. Counselors intentionally apply and incorporate the multicultural and social justice counseling competencies (MCJCCs) when establishing and maintaining the counseling relationship.

MSJCC Application

The MSJCCs (Ratts et al., 2015) allow for clients and counselors of privileged and marginalized statuses to work together in a culturally competent way. With race, it is important to understand how this visible identity can have impacts in the areas of counselor awareness, client awareness, the counseling relationship, and advocacy efforts. Both counselors with dominant and nondominant racial identities can use the MSJCC model to understand their own status as privileged and/or marginalized as it relates to their client.

In the domains of counselor self-awareness, the counseling relationship, client worldview, and counseling and advocacy interventions, the competencies of attitudes and beliefs, knowledge, skills, and action are explored. The praxis is used to assist in this as the quadrants of counselor and client status can help focus the counselor's efforts in exploring these different domains. In the context of race, those with privileged status would be White counselors and White clients. White counselors can use this model to understand their privileged status in the context of the counseling experience when working with White clients and clients of color. For example, White counselors can examine their own self-awareness around their Whiteness using the domains and ask themselves the following questions:

- What is my belief about White privilege? Do I believe it to be a real experience for me and others?
- How much do I know about my Whiteness? What resources are accessible to me to increase my knowledge?
- What skills do I possess to increase my understanding of my White identity?
- Do I take action in regard to my White identity? Do I seek out opportunities to learn and understand more?

BOX 7.7 PAUSE AND REFLECT: MY RACE, MY PRACTICE

Ask yourself ...

As a White counselor, what awareness do I have regarding my Whiteness and my race-based privilege? How can I use my areas of privilege to advocate for my client?

If you struggle to identify your level of awareness, how can you explore this further? Who and what are resources for you?

Counselors of color can use the competencies in the areas of race to understand how same-race and cross-racial counseling dynamics are affected by privilege and marginalized statuses, as well.

Ask yourself ...

As a counselor of color, do I understand how race may impact the counseling relationship with a White client or a client of color? Do I understand the dynamics of intersectionality (e.g., race and social class, gender, ability, sexual orientation) that influence the relationship?

The MCSJCCs can be used as an intentional checkpoint to make sure counselors of color are not falling into the traps of cultural assumptions based on their own racial experiences and to acknowledge that they may have privilege that their clients do not have.

Counseling Recommendations

Much of establishing a strong therapeutic alliance is rooted in Rogerian practices. These approaches include maintaining the core conditions of unconditional positive regard, congruence, and empathy. Many of the theoretical approaches that have been found to work in cross-racial counseling relationships begin with a person-centered foundation.

For example, relational-cultural theory (RCT) uses healing practices by establishing empowering and empathic relationships (Comstock et al., 2008; see Box 7.14). Additionally, RCT can address the heaviness that is often experienced in today's political climate by many clients of color (Hartling & Lindner, 2016). Optimal theory is also a framework that can be used in counseling communities of color. The basic tenets of RCT are as follows (Jordan, 2001):

- People grow through and toward relationship throughout the lifespan.
- Movement toward mutuality rather than separation characterizes mature functioning.
- The ability to participate in increasingly complex and diversified relational networks characterizes psychological growth.
- Mutual empathy and mutual empowerment are at the core of growth-fostering relationships.
- Authenticity is necessary for real engagement in growth-fostering relationships.
- When people contribute to the development of growth-fostering relationships, they grow as a result of their participation in such relationships.
- The goal of development is the realization of increased relational competence over the lifespan.

BOX 7.8 PROFILE OF A PRACTITIONER: DR. CIARA DENNIS-MORGAN

IMG 7.1. Dr. Ciara Dennis-Morgan

I am a Black woman. I come from Black people. I have created life with my Black husband and our Black children. I am deeply in love with Blackness. I cannot ever recall not being Black. I was parented and socialized to honor the beauty and brilliance of Black people. I grew up experiencing the reality of the research on the power of racial socialization and Black racial identity development as protective factors for Black children and people. I learned African-centered values through lived love in church, rituals, education, neighborhood and beyond. My worldview continued to develop throughout my adolescent and early adult years, with my educational environments playing a significant role in my exploration of race-related factors in health and wellness. The insidious nature and impact of oppression of various forms, including racism, has continued to expand my consciousness. Death by racism (violence, health disparities, infant mortality, etc.) and internalized racism (colorism, suicide, interpersonal violence, etc.) are combated in my daily practice, along with many other Black counselors.

My service with a Black-owned mental health agency that adopts an alternative psychological theory and treatment approach, which is African centered has been a big part of my life. This informs my work with clients and in supervision, and it has informed my life. Breaking the psychological chains of slavery and returning to the truth of who people are, their purpose and liberation are essential to the mental health and wellness of participants in care, both client and provider, both supervisor and supervise.

While it is not homogenous, there is a distinct experience of being Black in this world. The relational-centered, holistic, African-centered approach to care is central to my work as a counselor. It is valuable to consider the deep structure of culture, historical context, spirituality, considering both/and self-knowledge, intrinsic worth, and extended self-identity within counseling and supervision practices. A phenomenological study of Black clinicians' experience developing cultural competency in working with Black clients is my dissertation focus from my PhD program. The findings highlighted themes of oppression, racial socialization, and self-knowledge. These themes are reality and are here to support us if we will allow them. The false concept of race will not be minimized, history/stories are important, and the magnificence of culture will be magnified to bring about liberation.

There is a familiar African concept: ubuntu, I am because we are; therefore, we are because I am. My ancestors, plus the commitment to supporting the full, abundant lives of Black and Brown people, have me curious and determined in this work.

"I have a life to garden, a multiverse to wake from sleep." Nayyirah Waheed

Dr. Ciara Dennis-Morgan is the clinical director at Minority Behavioral Health Group in Akron, Ohio. She is a licensed professional clinical counselor with a supervision credential, as well as a licensed psychologist.

BOX 7.9 **PROFILE OF A PRACTITIONER: DR. KRISTIN BRUNS**

IMG 7.2. Dr. Kristin Bruns

Learning about racial identity development has been one of the critical points of my development as a counselor. The lens through which we develop our own racial identity was something I had not thought about as a White woman prior to starting my master's degree. While I had learned and talked about White privilege before entering a counseling program, this was the first opportunity I really took a deep dive into the amount of privilege I, among others in my life, held.

It's interesting because I've been seeing clients for 14 years now, and I just keep learning about the complexity of race and privilege, among the many other intersectional identities we hold. Learning about privilege and racial identity development 15 years ago via textbooks, case studies, and class discussions was certainly an important part of my growth, but the pace at which I learned once I began working with clients was certainly different. Being in a space with clients where it was my responsibility to broach difficult topics, to own the privilege in that sacred client space, forced me to a level of transparency and reflection that allowed for a new depth of awareness. Using the image from the MSJCC that looks at the complexity of privileged and marginalized identities within the role of counselor and client has been such a useful tool for me in my work with clients. I've appreciated the increased diversity, equity, and inclusion focus within the counseling field, as well as a greater opportunity more broadly to learn about anti-racist practices.

While this is a journey that is ongoing, I'm grateful to have had mentors, colleagues, supervisors, and clients who have joined me in difficult conversations. These influences (both materials and persons) over time have undoubtedly aided in my work as a clinician. I am grateful for the challenges as well as the increased knowledge, awareness, and skills development to better serve the community in which I work.

Dr. Kristin Bruns is an associate professor at Youngstown State University. She is a licensed professional clinical counselor with a supervision credential.

Resiliencies, Strengths, and Fostering Wellness

Oftentimes, communities of color have traumas that have been endured and conquered over the generations. However, it is a disservice to communities of color to acknowledge the traumas that have been passed down over generations without acknowledging the gifts passed down as well. One of those gifts is the resiliencies developed because of the amount of pain endured over the decades of abuse and violence they have experienced. These resiliencies have come from survival, which gives way to thriving. Resiliency can be used in counseling that counselors can draw on when clients are struggling in various areas of their lives, as a tool that they already have at their disposal.

BOX 7.10 **TIPS FOR PROFESSIONAL PRACTICE: USING RESILIENCE IN COUNSELING**

Consider resilience and the sources that drive resilience in racial minority clients. As a counselor, it can be easy to focus on those sources and those stories. What might it look like to focus in on the strengths gained from those experiences? Further, how can we use tools to help our clients of color face the adversities that may come from systemic racism and oppression? Van Breda (2018) breaks down resilience theory to better describe the process of resilience and the outcome of being resilient. As counselors, we can focus on the mediating process and the outcomes to foster and highlight resilience as a strength.

From a wellness perspective, self-care can be seen as radical in a society that has been built on and emphasizes capitalistic values. Clients of color have traditionally been forced to an untenable level of exhaustion through work (and exploitation), with self-care being a privilege offered to few. Currently, there has been a shift in the embrace of self-care as a necessity and a right in many communities of color. One transformative wave that is currently circulating through communities is the concept of rest being a radical form of resistance to working to the point of exhaustion in White supremacist systems. Tricia Hersey, the self-proclaimed *nap bishop*, has cultivated a movement called the *Nap Ministry* that emphasizes rest for communities of color, specifically Black communities. In her book *Rest Is Resistance* (2022), Hersey discussed the need and right for communities of color to rest as a means of rebellion against the systems of capitalism and White supremacy. This work builds on the work of many other Black feminists such as Audre Lorde.

TABLE 7.1 Advocacy Across Systemic Levels

Advocacy Level	Example
Micro	Identifying the barriers that exist between clients of color and their practices of wellness
	Helping clients of color examine the practices that already contribute to their wellness and amplifying those practices
	Completing a wellness wheel to educate and encourage practices surrounding wellness
Meso	Assisting with coordination of care by communicating with providers who may be working with clients of color
	Being active in the communities that serve clients of color in regard to mental health and wellness
Macro	Reflecting on personal voting practices that may interfere with clients of color access to wellness
	Calling legislators regarding legislation that may impact the wellness of clients of color

Counselors can use wellness as an intervention in counseling to treat many of the presenting concerns that are brought forth by all clients of different races. Long et al. (2022) developed a model for integrating wellness into counseling practice that includes helpful strategies and tools. One of the key tools in promoting wellness is advocacy (Long et al., 2022), which can be crucial in the advancement of racially marginalized groups. Advocacy at the micro-, meso-, and macrolevels can help encourage and advance wellness for communities of color.

Working with clients of color can expose counselors to vicarious trauma, so wellness and self-care are essential in the prevention of burnout. Vicarious trauma is the secondary experience of trauma that can come in the form of traumatic symptoms or reactions as a result of hearing traumatic experiences that clients may go through (Trippany et al., 2004). Whether the counselor is of the same race or a different race, it is imperative to use self-care strategies. In the field of professional counseling, there is often an emphasis on wellness for clients and the need for adequate self-care for counselors; however, professional counselors have struggled with implementing these practices. One way to be intentional in doing so is to make sure those topics are being broached in supervision and consultation spaces as a necessary piece of the case conceptualization process, as it can have impacts on the counseling process and relationship.

Ethical Code Application

Multiple professional counseling organizations recognize race as an important factor in professional counseling as it is specifically addressed in many ethical codes. The American Counseling Association (ACA) *Code of Ethics* (ACA, 2014), National Board for Certified Counselors (NBCC) *Code of Ethics* (NBCC, 2023), American Mental Health Counseling Association (AMHCA) *Code of Ethics* (AMHCA, 2020), Commission on Rehabilitation Counselor Certification *Code of Ethics* (CRCC, 2016), and American School Counseling Association (ASCA) *Ethical Standards for School Counselors* (ASCA, 2022) all discuss race within their own respective areas. Specifically, race is discussed when referencing *nondiscrimination* along with other identity factors. However, some codes elaborate more on these identifiers, including race. The NBCC *Code of Ethics* (NBCC, 2016) discussed the need for counselors to demonstrate multicultural competence and directive 26 speaks to including techniques that are "based on established, clinically sound theory" (p. 3). However, the challenge with this directive is the lack of detail and direction pertaining to what this actually means and how this applies to clients with diverse racial identities. This critique supports the notion that additional research is needed in order in the area of race to understand how we can support racially underserved populations.

AMHCA goes a step further in code C.2.a by including the importance of mental health counselors taking responsibility to educate themselves on their biases in reference to different races. The CRCC includes race as part of their commitment to cultural diversity (CRCC, 2016) and ASCA mentions race several times in their ethical standards in reference to discrimination. However, in standard A.11.a, ASCA includes the fact that discrimination or bullying based on race is considered a violation of federal, state, and often local laws (ASCA, 2022), which is unique compared to all the other codes. There is also an entire section in the ASCA *Code*

(Section A10) focused on marginalized populations and the importance of advocacy work with marginalized populations.

While not all counselors are beholden to each code, depending on their specialization and organizational membership(s), it is clear race and effective counseling for persons of all races is an ethical mandate across counseling settings and codes. It is expected that counselors use these codes in their ethical clinical practice. However, these aspirational ethics are the very minimum of what is expected for counseling practice (Gladding & Newsome, 2018). The hope is that counselors will go beyond the level of nondiscrimination when it comes to race. For example, counselors might go beyond identifying the barriers that present challenges for many clients of color and their access to mental health services by advocating for change. Other behaviors may include using a sliding fee scale or incorporating pro bono work for those who do not have health insurance and/or those with inadequate coverage. We bet you can think of many others!

While there is a focus on race in each of the major professional counseling ethical codes, race is grouped with all identity markers, making it easy for its unique impact to get lost amid other identity markers. We acknowledge that all identities are of equal importance and it is not our intention to make race more important than the other identities; however, race is a visible identity that is often the basis for brutal actions of discrimination and violence toward marginalized racial groups. Counselors must acknowledge that reality and attend to it openly, appropriately, and consistently so that counseling work is effective and status quo systems can be dismantled.

Conclusion

The counseling profession acknowledges the importance of addressing social and cultural differences in our profession and in our communities, which includes identities such as race. Exploring race is crucial in our development and identity as counselors, as it has an impact on the work we do in all spaces. This chapter was intended to increase understanding and knowledge while sparking and enhancing critical thought as it applies to race and its impact on counselors. The hope is that all readers can use this chapter to go forth in their own personal and professional development with increased cultural understanding and cultural humility for all individuals of different racial backgrounds.

Questions for Reflection

Consider what you learned in this chapter as you respond to the questions and prompts below.

1. What new knowledge and insights have you gained about race since engaging with this chapter?
2. What has been your experience with your identified race?
3. How does your race intersect with your other identities?
4. How might race inform the mental health experience of your clients?
5. What are ways you can be intentional about including race in your case conceptualization process?
6. Identify the privileges you have and how you might use them to advocate for clients of color.

Applying What You Have Learned

Complete each of the following activities, considering what you learned from this chapter.

Activity #1: Identifying Your Race and Ethnicity

Understanding what concepts mean and how they differ is an important first step so you are able to apply them in multiple contexts. Write down the ways in which you identify yourself using race and ethnicity as separate identifiers. What are the differences? Now, practice explaining the difference between race and ethnicity to someone outside your class. It could be a family member, friend, or another peer in the program.

1. How well did the other person understand what you shared?
2. Were you able to answer any follow-up questions they asked?
3. How confident did you feel sharing this information?
4. How would you like to become stronger?

Activity #2: It's Still Hard to Be Humble

In Activity 2 in Chapter 3, you examined your reactions to being wrong and how you might want to become stronger. We are revisiting this activity with respect to race because many people, including counselors, are intimidated by discussing race because they are incredibly afraid of "getting it wrong" and "offending" someone.

To begin this activity, write down your concerns, fears, and/or anxieties related to discussing race with a client. No matter how small, record it. Next, jot down the people with whom you are comfortable discussing race. What is your relationship with each person? Is their race similar or different from your own? What makes them someone who is comfortable for you to discuss race? What if you made an error with one of these people? How would you feel? How would you react? Are your fears actualized in this context? Use this information to empower you through the next step and in your clinical practice.

It's natural to have concerns about "getting it wrong" when it comes to talking about race with clients, though that concern cannot stop counselors from discussing it. Most of the time, you will not make a mistake because you will ask open questions and reflect on what you hear; however, to put your anxieties to rest, it can be helpful to discern how you want to respond if you err. Think through how you would like to respond and feel when you slip up regarding race with a client—it can be similar, different, or a combination of the examples you listed above or in your responses in the prior chapter activity. How will you work to ensure this is your consistent approach with clients?

CHAPTER 8

Ethnicity, National Identity, and Ethnocentrism

Angelica M. Tello, Alena Pridhidko, and Jennifer M. Cook

> *Ethnicity should enrich us; it should make us a unique people in our diversity and not be used to divide us.*
>
> —Ellen Johnson Sirleaf

CHAPTER OVERVIEW

In U.S. society, ethnicity and ethnic identities are often discussed from a one-dimensional perspective: a group that shares a common national identity and traditions. Being socialized with this perspective of ethnicity can lead to stereotyping (e.g., all Mexican Americans speak Spanish and celebrate Cinco de Mayo) and marginalizing minority clients (e.g., telling an African American college student to work on anger management when discussing the microaggressions they experienced on their campus). Ethnicity is much more complex than a one-dimensional perspective.

Ethnicity is socially constructed—it is dynamic and evolves (Nagel, 1994). Ethnic identity is fashioned by how groups "shape and reshape their self-definition" and is influenced by "external social, economic, and political processes" (Nagel, 1994, p. 152). Therefore, those who hold dominant cultural identities and have social power influence the definition of ethnicity and moreover, the capacity to define what ethnicity means for groups to which they do not belong. An unfortunate result is often *ethnocentrism*—beliefs that one ethnicity is prized over all others—that can result in discrimination. As future counselors, it is important to intentionally reflect on the ways you have been socialized to view ethnicity. We invite you to reflect constantly while reading this chapter so you are prepared to be an ethnically responsive counselor who provides an affirmative counseling environment for clients with an array of national and ethnic identities. Throughout this chapter, you will learn more about what ethnicity is, how it functions in the United States, and some of the ramifications of ethnocentrism. Excitingly, you will learn skills to use with clients to affirm their ethnicities, the struggles they've faced, and how to bolster the strengths they already possess.

LEARNING OBJECTIVES

By the end of this chapter, students will be able to

1. describe the theories and models of multicultural counseling, cultural identity development, and social justice and advocacy;
2. explain the impact of heritage, attitudes, beliefs, understandings, and acculturative experiences on an individual's views of others;

3. discuss the effects of power and privilege for counselors and clients;
4. assess the help-seeking behaviors of diverse clients; and
5. explain the impact of intersecting identities on clients' and counselors' worldviews.

CACREP 2016 STANDARDS

The information in this chapter supports the following standards:

- 2.F.2.b. theories and models of multicultural counseling, cultural identity development, and social justice and advocacy
- 2.F.2.d. the impact of heritage, attitudes, beliefs, understandings, and acculturative experiences on an individual's views of others
- 2.F.2.e the effects of power and privilege for counselors and clients
- 2.F.2.f. help-seeking behaviors of diverse clients
- 2.F.2.g. the impact of spiritual beliefs on clients' and counselors' worldviews

CACREP 2024 STANDARDS

The information in this chapter supports the following standards:

- 3.B.1. theories and models of multicultural counseling, social justice, and advocacy
- 3.B.2. the influence of heritage, cultural identities, attitudes, values, beliefs, understandings, within-group differences, and acculturative experiences on individuals' worldviews
- 3.B.3. the influence of heritage, cultural identities, attitudes, values, beliefs, understandings, within-group differences, and acculturative experiences on help-seeking and coping behaviors
- 3.B.4. the effects of historical events, multigenerational trauma, and current issues on diverse cultural groups in the U.S. and globally
- 3.B.5. the effects of stereotypes, overt and covert discrimination, racism, power, oppression, privilege, marginalization, microaggressions, and violence on counselors and clients
- 3.B.6. the effects of various socio-cultural influences, including public policies, social movements, and cultural values, on mental and physical health and wellness
- 3.B.8. principles of independence, inclusion, choice and self-empowerment, and access to services within and outside the counseling relationship
- 3.B.11. the role of religion and spirituality in clients' and counselors' psychological functioning

Understanding the Historical Context

The origins of the construct of ethnicity can be traced back to the Greek notion of *ethnos* (Fenton, 2003). Ethnos evolved to *other* those who were considered non-Greek. When the word *ethnic* appeared in the English language, it was also used to describe *foreigners*—that is, people who came from another country. Today, ethnicity refers to a cultural identity associated with a sociocultural group that shares a common national origin and cultural traditions (e.g., cultural customs, heritage, language, and religion). Examples of ethnic groups in the United States include African Americans, Asian Americans, Arab Americans, and Latinx Americans. As you might notice in these examples, national identity is a component of ethnicity. Specifically, this term refers to one's national origin (e.g., Canada, Columbia, Germany) and can include their generational status (e.g., second-generation Asian American). Some individuals may also identify their national identity in terms of their cultural heritage or ancestry. For instance, some individuals in the United States who are of Mexican descent might identify as Mexican American. Other examples of the mix of cultural heritage and national identity include Korean Americans, Turkish Americans, and Nigerian Americans. These terms can be used with or without reference to generational status.

Ethnicity and race are often used interchangeably. However, as you learned in Chapter 7, these constructs are different. Race is a socially constructed designation grounded in physical characteristics and the perceptions of those characteristics (e.g., skin color, hair texture, prominent physical features). In many countries, race has been institutionalized. For example, in the United States, laws and public policies have created inequalities and fostered discrimination based on race.

Even in its origins, the term *ethnicity* had ethnocentric definitions. The United States has a long history of institutional oppression that is rooted in ethnocentrism. Ethnocentrism is a conscious or unconscious ethnic bias that one ethnic group is superior to all others. An individual who is ethnocentric views the world from their own ethnic cultural values, beliefs, and worldviews. Additionally, they judge other ethnic groups by using their ethnicity as the reference point because they believe their own ethnicity is ideal or superior to other ethnicities. Ethnocentrism can be experienced on a spectrum from placing value of one's ethnic identity over others to microaggressions, marginalization, and hate crimes. Ethnocentrism tends to foster an "us" versus "them" mentality (i.e., in-group versus out-group perspective). White European colonization of the Americas played a major role in the legacy of ethnocentrism and marginalization of people of color (Singh et al., 2020). Colonization is the

> visible and invisible attempts to socialize and resocialize those "at the margins" to fit into dominant cultural values and experiences. Thus, the dominant White, Eurocentric society maintains its sense of order, power, structural privilege, and supposed "normalcy" to which those from other cultures are supposed to accommodate, value, and acclimate. (Singh et al., 2020, p. 262)

For instance, Britain, France, Spain, and the Netherlands conquered lands and peoples in North America and claimed ownership of land for resources and religious conversion of Indigenous communities through missionary undertakings (Mark, 2020). Essentially, ethnocentrism was a guiding force in the colonization of Black, Indigenous, and People of Color (BIPOC) because European settlers saw their own ethnicity as superior to BIPOC persons' ethnic identities. This view of ethnic superiority allowed colonizers to inflict exclusion and harm on BIPOC communities, such as the enslavement of Africans and Indigenous peoples, the internment of Japanese Americans, and the forced relocation of Indigenous communities.

Laws and policies remain that have intentionally or unintentionally continued to foster the "us versus them" mentality of ethnocentrism. Some examples include the following:

- Jim Crow laws during the post–Civil War Reconstruction in 1877 that legalized racial segregation of Black Americans (Edwards & Thompson, 2010)
- The forced relocation and incarceration of 125,284 Japanese and Japanese Americans into internment camps by the U.S. government during World War II (Parker, 2004)

- The Family Separation Policy during the Trump administration in 2018 resulted in the forced separation of more than 2,000 children from their families of Central American origin who were seeking asylum at the U.S.-Mexico border (Todres & Villamizar Fink, 2020)

Ethnocentrism is not unique to the United States, nor is it only historic in other countries. Researchers have shown how it has evolved and progressed in Europe through multiple immigration waves over the last several decades (Aschauer & Mayerl, 2019). Aschauer and Mayerl argued that contemporary ethnocentrism in Europe is tied to societal malaise—a concept derived from medicine that describes significant discomfort and lack of well-being. When applied to social life it means that the society is in bad health, which signifies a lack of trust between people and toward social institutions, feelings of alienation and social pessimism. Societal malaise and a general feeling of ethnic threat coming from immigrants become the main factors that promote ethnocentrism.

Ethnocentrism, Discrimination, and Oppression

Because of the ethnocentric sociopolitical influences in U.S. society, it is likely that ethnic minority clients will have experienced discrimination and oppression (see Chapter 4). Discrimination manifests in violation of legal rights—for instance, a person of color is denied a job opportunity based on employers' prejudice toward their ethnicity, or a landlord denies signing a lease contract based on a person's ethnic group membership. Oppression refers to denying benefits or resources to members of nondominant groups that people of dominant groups readily and easily enjoy. For instance, a person who identifies as Latinx might face oppression in the classroom in terms of teachers having low expectations of their academic achievement and making jokes about students being in English as a second language classes (Córdova & Cervantes, 2010). This can lead to discrimination, like when students are not offered opportunities based on their actual abilities rather than perceptions and when Latinx students aren't encouraged at equal levels as their White counterparts.

With an ethnocentric perspective, individuals use their own culture as the ideal to which they compare other cultures. Counselors can inadvertently foster ethnocentrism if, for instance, they do not intentionally create space to understand the nuances of their clients' ethnic identities. For example, not all Eastern European clients are going to hold the same worldviews and cultural values. Clients from Ukrainian and Polish backgrounds may share some cultural values, but they will likely have more cultural values or customs that differ. To add to this example, an ethnocentric assumption would be to expect that a Ukrainian client speaks the Russian language, a common ethnocentric mistake Russians make regularly. In the former Soviet Union, everyone was required to learn Russian, and while many Ukrainians know it, it is impolite to begin speaking Russian with a Ukrainian person, and this has become even more offensive because of the Russian war in Ukraine. Rather than making assumptions about language, simply ask.

Generally, for clients who are immigrants, ethnocentrism related to language can be damaging, manifesting in *linguistic racism* and *accent discrimination* (Wang & Dovchin, 2023. Wang and Dovchin (2022) argued that linguistic racism is a form of symbolic violence. Symbolic violence can occur verbally when a person with a nondominant ethnic identity is accused of having an accent and nonverbally through what's called the *White gaze*. The *White gaze* is the phenomenon in which people from nondominant ethnic and racial groups feel compelled to take into account how people who are White will react or respond to them. The triad of racism, symbolic violence, and the White gaze reinforce racial hierarchy in the society. Dovchin (2021) showed that linguistic racism leads to depression and psychological trauma in persons who become its targets.

Some of the linguistic constructions used to scrutinize people who belong to nondominant racial and ethnic groups can include, "You speak English so well for a Russian person!" "You are German? Amazing. You do not have a German accent!" "You don't sound like a Mexican." People who use such statements might wholeheartedly believe they are complimenting the person while in reality, these are microaggressions that highlight the fact that the person does not belong to the dominant group and denigrate their linguistic abilities and ethnic-linguistic identities. Because language and culture are intertwined as a dimension of identity that interconnects with other cultural identity statuses (Arredondo et al., 2014; Trepal et al., 2019), counselors must go beyond simply translating documents from English to the client's first language to make the information accessible by paying close attention to their so-called compliments, encouraging clients based on the strengths the *client* identifies, and encouraging client expression; even if we don't understand every word they use, we must pay attention to the feeling being shared, the client's body language, and the explanations they provide.

Counselor Responses to Oppression and Discrimination

In order to provide counseling support that reflects multicultural and social justice tenets, it is the counselor's responsibility to understand oppressive experiences, not to replicate them in the counseling relationship, and to assist clients in their healing from such experiences (Ratts et al., 2015; Singh et al., 2020). If counselors do not create space in the counseling process to broach (i.e., openly discuss and acknowledge) these topics, the impact could be detrimental to the client's mental health (Burkard et al., 2015). Some counselors feel uncomfortable with discussions regarding race, ethnicity, and national identity because these topics are taboo in U.S. society (Burkard et al., 2015). This can lead some clinicians to hold a *colorblind perspective* that creates a therapeutic relationship based on color evasion and power evasion rather than acknowledging clients' ethnic and racial experiences and realities. A colorblind perspective not only diminishes or erases clients' experiences of oppression but also ignores the resources, strengths, and resiliencies they have based on their ethnic and racial identities. In short, counselors must engage in conversations with clients about their ethnic identities and their experiences of oppression.

The role of professional counselors is to acknowledge how social systems support ethnocentrism and work to dismantle oppression of people who come from nondominant ethnic groups and are suffering from discrimination. One of the ways to do so is to take a closer look at the counseling theories we use. According to Singh et al. (2020), classic counseling theories do not reflect the goal of dismantling oppression; instead, they represent dominant colonist ideologies unless we as counselors make an effort to focus on multicultural values and social justice perspectives. Counselors need to be aware that social stratification supports isolation of marginalized clients because Western society stratifies people based on social power. Power differentials are systemic and create imbalance, making people who come from nondominant social groups feel isolated. One of the goals of professional counselors is to help clients identify sources of isolation and find ways to overcome them.

Nondominant Ethnic Identities

Even though initial colonization in the United States occurred hundreds of years ago, the legacy lives on with the sociopolitical construction of people of White European descent being identified as the dominant ethnic group (Singh et al., 2020). BIPOC communities were socio-politically constructed to be minoritized as nondominant ethnic identities. In U.S. society, nondominant ethnicities include individuals of Latinx, African, Asian, Indigenous, and Arab descent.

The concept of nondominant identities is tied to the intersectionality framework. Intersectionality accounts for individuals' multiple identities (e.g., ethnicity, gender, affectual orientation, religion, and social class) and recognizes that their everyday lives are influenced by inequality that is grounded in social hierarchical power systems (Jackson et al., 2021). The intersectionality framework explains that one identity dimension (e.g., ethnicity, gender, relational/affectual orientation) cannot fully explain the inequality individuals experience without considering other intersecting identities. Therefore, when working with clients who represent nondominant ethnic groups, counselors must explore what other intersecting nondominant identities they have. For instance, you might be working with a client who identifies as Russian and gay. The level of oppression of LGBTQIAP+ people in Russia is exceedingly high, with people being prosecuted and killed because of their affectual/relational identity. The psychological traumas the client has endured may manifest in their self-perception and views about how they might be perceived by other people. Furthermore, they may struggle to trust the counselor and be fearful of them rather than see them as a source of support. This example demonstrates that it is essential to understand the client's ethnicity in tandem with their affectual/relational orientation because it captures their experiences more fully.

Individuals holding several nondominant identities experience unique microaggressions. Fattoracci et al. (2021) developed a measure—*Intersectional Microaggressions Scale*—and showed that the intersection of LGBTQIAP and nondominant ethnic identities predicts more variability in anxiety and social isolation scores compared to studies in which each identity was explored independently. These findings can reasonably be applied to other intersecting identities and support the importance of considering clients' intersecting identities and where the client is located within social structures of power and oppression.

Diversity Within Diversity

When it comes to ethnic and national identity, it is important for counselors to understand there is diversity within diversity. Society often discusses ethnic minoritized and BIPOC communities as homogenous groups (e.g., Latinx, African Americans, and Asian Americans). There is heterogeneity in all ethnic groups. For instance, there are ethno-specific groups within Asian Americans based on regional and national heritage, such as Chinese, Korean, and Japanese. These regional heritages can be seen across other ethnic groups as well, such as Latinx (e.g., Mexican, Puerto Rican, Cuban, and Columbian), Arab (e.g., Lebanese, Tunisian, Sadia Arabian, and Egyptian), and Eastern European (e.g., Romanian, Russian, Serbian, and Polish).

It is important to understand that clients define how they identify ethnically, not the counselor. For example, a client of Latin American heritage may be labeled as Hispanic by society and on demographic forms. However, many individuals are moving away from the term *Hispanic to Latina/o/x* because of the political origins of the term and may prefer to identify with their specific ethnicity (e.g., Puerto Rican/Boricua).

The term Hispanic is mostly used by governmental agencies and was first introduced in 1978 by the Office of Business and Management, an Executive Office of the President of the United States to label people who have a common ancestral language and culture (Jones & Castellanos, 2003). As a result, many scholars have argued the term *Hispanic* does not acknowledge the heterogeneity of Latina/o/x ethno-specific groups (Jones & Castellanos, 2003). Moreover, *Latina/o/x* or *Latiné* tends to be the preferred terms because it resonates with people from mestizo (i.e., a fusion of Native and European cultures) backgrounds rather than Spanish heritage (Jones & Castellanos, 2003).

Because the Spanish language is gendered (e.g., all nouns are assigned a gender: "o" for masculine and "a" for feminine), we are now seeing individuals identify as Latinx, a gender-neutral term for Latina/o (Castro & Cortez, 2017; Vélez, 2016). As such, Latinx is viewed as an inclusive term for individuals who are trans or nonbinary. However, this term is seen as purely *academic* by many Spanish-speaking people because of the challenges related to pronouncing *Latinx* when Spanish is one's first language. In fact, even first-language English speakers have struggled with uniform pronunciation of the term! To address this issue of pronunciation and gender inclusivity, some are choosing to use the term *Latiné* (pronounced *lah-teen-eh*). In sum, ethnic identity within groups can be complex (Garcia, 2020), and it is important for counselors to honor, explore, and understand how clients identify themselves; use the terms *they use* to describe themselves; and work diligently to understand their ethnic heritage.

Another facet of understanding clients' ethnic values, beliefs, and messages is exploring their spiritual and religious identities. This means going beyond simply identifying if the client *has* religious and spiritual beliefs and learning what they mean to them, how they are used, the strengths they gain from them, and how they are tied to their ethnicity. It is important for counselors to create space to understand how clients' religious and spiritual beliefs were shaped by their ethnic cultural messages and how this impacts their worldviews. There can be various ethnic cultural values that intertwine with religious and spiritual beliefs. For instance, Trevino (2006) used the term "ethno-Catholicism" to describe the "Mexican American way of being Catholic" (p. 4) – a mix of the colonized Spanish Christianity that is blended with Mexican Indigenous worldviews. An example of this is *Día de los Muertos* or Day of the Dead—a Mexican holiday that is a blend of Indigenous traditions and the European influences of Catholicism's All Souls' Day. The mix of culture is also seen in other ethnic groups, such as those of Arabic descent and Islam and those of Eastern European descent and Judaism.

Biculturalism

Nondominant ethnic groups often experience two cultures simultaneously: their ethnic culture (i.e., their cultural upbringing) and the dominant cultural values of the United States (i.e., White, European American culture), resulting in *biculturalism*. Biculturalism refers to individuals who are continuously exposed to two different cultures and develop "two cultural knowledge systems" (David et al., 2009, p. 211). LaFromboise et al. (1993) developed the model of bicultural competence to explore the psychological impact of being bicultural rather than to conceptualize experiences from "the linear model of cultural acquisition" (p. 395).

Bicultural individuals develop a cultural identity that incorporates characteristics and qualities from both cultures. According to David et al. (2009), challenges can arise for bicultural individuals because they are constantly negotiating two cultural identities within two sets of cultural norms, practices, and values. They found that when bicultural individuals are unable to successfully navigate these conflicts they are at increased risk for developing psychological difficulties, such as depression and anxiety (David et al., 2009). However, bicultural individuals with high levels of perceived bicultural self-efficacy had higher levels of psychological well-being and mental health (David et al., 2009). Counselors can help ethnic minoritized clients by fostering their bicultural strengths by using interventions that draw upon the ways in which they have been successful navigating both their cultures, identifying ways in which they feel connection and comfort within each culture, and validating their approach to their bicultural identities (rather than someone else's approach!) in order to help them bridge both cultures in a way that works for them (i.e., their cultural upbringing and the dominant U.S. culture; Tello, 2015).

Spectrum of Collectivism and Individualism

Each ethnic group tends to lean more toward being either individualistic or collectivistic. Individualism is the notion that one's behaviors and cultural values are guided by independence or self-determination. This can include self-promotion, agency, and competitiveness. Collectivism means that one's behaviors and cultural values are guided by relational interdependence. Decisions are made based on the betterment of others (e.g., family members, community) and are often made with input from others rather than by only one person. In the United States, the dominant culture favors individualism, the notion that one's behaviors and cultural values are guided by independence or self-determination. Individualism is rooted in colonial values and the *Protestant work ethic* and can include approaches to self-disclosure, self-promotion, agency, and competitiveness. Because the U.S. dominant culture favors individualism, members of nondominant ethnic groups can internalize messages that their collectivistic cultural values go against the *norm*. This can lead some ethnic minoritized clients to focus consciously or unconsciously on acculturating to the dominant cultural value of individualism.

Collectivism and individualism are often viewed as dichotomous. However, it is important for counselors to conceptualize them on a spectrum. Because clients hold diverse intersections of identities (e.g., race, gender, social class), their cultural worldviews and values may differ across the spectrum and not be solely collectivist or individualistic. For instance, a client who holds collectivist values regarding family could have an approach that leans more toward individualism in the workplace or at school. Tello and Lonn (2017) discussed the college experiences of Latinx students. There are times when family obligations may be placed above school. However, this does not mean Latinx families do not value education, despite beliefs that this is the case. Counselors must tailor their approaches to include Latinx clients' cultural expectations for assisting family in times of need (Tello & Lonn, 2017).

Another aspect of ethnic cultural values is communication style and emotional expression. This goes beyond how clients communicate their emotions (e.g., whether they openly express emotions to others) to include the cultural messages clients carry about expressing emotions with others. For some ethnic minoritized groups, communication is a way to build relational connections. For example, some clients of Native American descent may use silence when first building connections with others as a sign of recognition and respect (Garrett et al., 2011). Moreover, some clients may use less direct eye contact than the dominant culture expects and can be pathologized, even though some clients of Latinx and Native American descent may avert eye contact when listening as a sign of respect (Garrett et al., 2011). Finally, ethnic cultures that value collectivism may favor a communication style that is collaborative and focused on harmonious interactions (e.g., respectfulness and interdependence).

Maintaining positive relationships is central to some ethnic cultures that lean collectivistic in communication style and emotional expression. This can result in some clients wanting to maintain communication that is "harmonious and smooth" (Holloway et al., 2009, p. 1012). For instance, Latinos reported significantly higher *simpáctico*-related traits—a relational style that is personal, hospitable, and courteous—than White participants (Holloway et al., 2009). As a result, some clients who come from ethnic cultures that share this value may have a difficult time discussing emotionally unpleasant topics or problems they may be encountering, such as discrimination and microaggressions. Therefore, counselors must work to create a safe and trusting space for clients who hold this cultural value to feel comfortable voicing their concerns (Tello & Lonn, 2017).

BOX 8.1 **PAUSE AND REFLECT: YOUR ETHNIC IDENTITIES**

The societal legacy of placing individuals of White Western European descent as the dominant ethnic culture has resulted in some White individuals feeling they do not have an ethnic culture (Perry, 2001). For White counselors who share these sentiments, it is important to reflect on how your worldview has been shaped. Counselors who hold nondominant ethnic identities must engage in similar intentional self-reflection regarding the foundations of their worldviews and what they mean to them. We are all living and participating in systems that can often intentionally or unintentionally uphold ethnocentric views that support dominant cultural values—and many times, we don't realize it. As a result, clients with nondominant ethnic identities can internalize the messages coming from these systems.

To build awareness of your ethnic identities and how you were acculturated into dominate cultural values, you can

1. explore your family's immigration journey to the United States,
2. reflect on how your ethnic identity has provided benefits to you in terms of societal privilege, and
3. reflect on what impact societal oppression has on your worldview.

Being intentional in these areas of reflection can bring awareness of any unconscious bias within your worldview. The intent is not to shame your worldview or your life experiences, but rather to understand it better and to minimize any centering of your own worldview when working with diverse clients. This can help lead you toward the path of creating a therapeutic environment that is culturally affirming for your client, especially those who might hold cultural values that are very different from your own.

BOX 8.2 **PROFILE OF A PRACTITIONER**

Dr. Alena Prikhidko is a licensed marriage and family therapist in Florida. She holds a master's degree and PhD in social psychology from Lomonosov Moscow State University and a PhD in counseling and counselor education from the University of Florida. Dr. Prikhidko is ethnically Russian-Ukrainian and did not receive any education on diversity in Russia; thus, she is constantly working on developing her multicultural competencies in the United States and shares her journey of raising her multicultural awareness and skills.

Coming from Russia, where topics of diversity, race, and gender were not discussed while I was growing up nor when I studied psychology, my arrival to the United States was full of anxiety. I knew that I would be teaching a diverse group of students since my first day at the university. I was worried: what if I say something wrong to a person of color or someone who is gay? Among my first group of students whom I taught in an interpersonal communication skills course was a young woman who identified as Black and gay. This student taught me a lot by being open about her experiences. I remember that before I arrived in the United States, I read *The Help*, a book about the oppression of Black people. I was crying while reading it. I thought that America had conquered racism and homophobia. I realized that this was not the case when my student shared with me that she and her girlfriend did not feel welcome at a restaurant and were looked down on based on their sexuality. I was shocked and realized that I had idealized American culture.

Another colleague taught me about microaggressions. I had no idea that phrases that I considered a compliment were actually offensive. I learned that asking questions about a person's culture is appropriate and shows respect. However, it is important *how you ask* such questions and in what context. We, as counselors, need to keep in mind that everything we tell or ask our clients is an intervention; its ultimate goal is to help our client progress in therapy and enhance the counseling relationship. The concept of color blindness was totally new to me. I always thought that not noticing racial or ethnic differences made me a better person, but little did I know that saying, "all people are the same" is actually supporting oppression.

Multicultural counseling class transformed my mind. I realized that oppression is more alive than ever. I remember watching the movie *13* on Netflix and thinking about all the hardships Black people in the United States are going through. Since then, I am always looking for an opportunity to learn more about different cultures, asking questions, and acknowledging cultural, ethnic, and racial differences openly in my counseling practice. I am lucky to be surrounded by kind and warm colleagues who take the time to explain various complex concepts to me while understanding where *I* am coming from and seeing that I am eager to learn. I think that my desire to learn is one of my most helpful qualities when it comes to my multicultural awareness.

Another powerful concept I had no idea about is privilege. I constantly try to acknowledge my privilege. I think that, at times, communicating with people who come from dominant cultural groups is a challenging experience when there is a lack of awareness regarding their privilege. However, I know that people can change and learn if you are patient with them and are not attacking. It is not a person's fault they are not aware. The environment they come from shapes them, and once a person is placed in a different environment, whether within their community or far outside of it, they have the chance to change their beliefs and perceptions if they are willing and if others are patient and use the right words to explain difficult topics.

Ecological and Sociopolitical Contexts

One way counselors lay the foundation to incorporate clients' strengths into counseling is by understanding ethnocentrism within ecological and sociopolitical contexts. As you learned earlier, scrutinizing people with nondominant ethnic and racial identities has been societally sanctioned for centuries. To understand how this behavior has been maintained, we look to ecological systems theory (EST; Bronfenbrenner, 1994). EST accounts for how different systematic forces affect children's development, and it can be applied to clients of all ages. The macrosystem, the penultimate outer ring, encompasses societal norms that represent dominant cultural norms. To understand the macrosystem, counselors need to be aware that social stratification and social power are inherent to it. Social power is dependent on hierarchy—specific groups dominate while others are subordinate. The result is oppression and discrimination of *subordinate* or nondominant groups. While the chronosystem accounts for changes over time and there have been changes, the overall social structure and power hierarchy in the United States remains intact.

Ethnocentrism as a dominant ideology can manifest at all of the ecological system levels. Cultural values that support ethnocentrism are rooted in the societal structure endorsed by political discourse; children internalize such beliefs in their immediate circles at the Microsystem level. Even subtle reactions parents have toward a child's friends can form beliefs of superiority, let alone direct reactions or explicit instructions. For instance, a parent might convey to their child that it is not okay to be friends with someone who is Black through judgmental looks their parent gives Black people when they encounter them in the grocery store or at a school function. This can occur within the Mesosystem as well. For example, a child may overhear their parent and teacher talk disparagingly about students for whom English is their second language.

Within the Mesosystem, indirect experiences impact children. For example, a parent may come home from work outraged that a BIPOC was promoted over them and that they are experiencing *reverse racism*. The child internalizes a concept that is not real, yet it is promoted. Conversely, ethnic minorities might experience residential segregation and experience employment limitations and lower pay. Children are likely to hear about their caregivers' struggles and experience—for example, limited time with their parents because of working two or three jobs to make ends meet.

Let's explore reverse racism a bit more. You might have heard someone who is a member of the dominant culture (i.e., White) say that they have experienced *reverse racism*. They may use this term within the context of not being selected for a job, not earning a scholarship they had hoped for, or not being chosen as a first-string player on their sports team. Not only were they not selected, they learned that the person chosen has a nondominant racial or ethnic identity. Reverse racism is a term created by the dominant culture to explain such situations—when a White person perceives they were not selected based on their racial or ethnic identity.

As you have learned, all *-isms* are rooted in *systemic* power and oppression—only those who have the cultural power to discriminate (i.e., the dominant culture) can perpetrate racism, ethnocentrism, classism, etc. Reverse racism is an inaccurate term because nondominant cultural groups do not have the systemic and cultural power to discriminate. Further, it is an offensive term because it dismisses the oppressive and discriminatory experiences of BIPOC. As such, reverse racism is not a term that should be used to describe a White person's experience of not being selected when a BIPOC is—it is a disappointment, not racism. In fact, it's a term that should never be used at all.

The Chronosystem refers to life transitions and socio-historical events that can influence individuals. For instance, people who identify with non-dominant ethnic identities may be recent immigrants or may have family members who have recently immigrated and experienced how strict immigration policies are impacting and potentially separating their families. Even shared events, like the COVID-19 pandemic, as well as cohort milestones like graduating high school or having a child, are represented in the chronosystem. The important pieces for counselors to identify and understand are the impact these events have on clients based on their ethnic identities.

Professional counselors help clients identify sources of isolation and support their growth toward connection. See Box 8.5 for reflective questions you can use to stimulate conversation about clients' ecological experiences.

BOX 8.3 **TIPS FOR PROFESSIONAL PRACTICE: USING THE ECOLOGICAL MODEL TO UNDERSTAND CLIENTS' EXPERIENCES**

It may seem logical to apply the ecological model to understand clients' ethnicity, though what types of things might you explore? Below, we offer some areas to investigate. Based on these areas, what questions might you pose to understand clients' ethnic identities and ways of being?

1. How is the client's ethnic identity situated within the client's ecology? For instance, what is the process in which the client relates themselves to their ethnic group?

2. How does the client connect to their cultural communities and heritage (physically and interpersonally)?
3. What ethnic identities, cultural values, and roles appear salient to the client?
4. What ethnic and cultural messages (e.g., cultural values and life meanings) are salient to the client's presenting concern?
5. What are the client's experiences of navigating in society (i.e., experiences of oppression or privilege)?

How can clients use what they have learned through exploring the above topics to experience greater connection in their lives?

Adapted from Cook and Coaston (2015).

Professional Counseling Practice

The Counseling Relationship

When working with ethnically diverse clients, it is important for counselors to use a humanistic, person-centered approach. The main tenets of person-centered counseling—empathy, unconditional positive regard, genuineness, warmth, and trust—will help in working with clients with different ethnic identities. These skills have become core in almost any counseling relationship for a reason—they support humans' need to belong, feel accepted, and be heard. However, it's important to notice that these needs vary across cultures. For instance, there is evidence from a cross-cultural study performed in 63 countries that empathy is higher in countries with collectivistic cultures, high levels of emotionality, and subjective well-being (Chopik et al., 2017). The top 10 countries high in empathy include Ecuador, Saudi Arabia, Peru, Denmark, United Arab Emirates, Korea, United States, Taiwan, Costa Rica, and Kuwait. Although this *top 10 list* gives potential insight into values clients from these countries might possess, it is not an absolute.

We recommend you pay close attention to each client's reactions when you use person-centered counseling principles. For example, while unconditional positive regard is a way to demonstrate care for a person by fully accepting their emotions and feelings and respecting their autonomy, some clients may struggle with such acceptance. They may perceive it as disingenuous, or they could perceive it as a lack of guidance on the part of the counselor. The same may be true for a person-centered approach overall in which the counselor works to foster the client's autonomy and collaboration between counselor and client. For instance, I, Dr. Prikhidko, was born in Russia, immigrated to the United States, and work with clients from Eastern and Western Europe. A few times I encountered situations in which clients were upset when I suggested a few different routes of counseling and asked for their opinion. The reaction was not positive and basically translated as, "Why are you asking for our opinion and input? You are the professional, and you should figure it out and tell me what to do!" The history of oppression in Soviet countries formulated the perception of a counselor as an ideal caregiver *who knows better*, and if a counselor discusses the treatment with a client and asks for input, their position becomes devalued, which can result in aggression toward the counselor. This means that initially, clients might see the counselor as an expert and not expect them to ask for clients' opinions on treatment choices. Of course, this does not apply to all clients from the former Soviet Union, though it's something that can occur.

The Rogerian principle of congruence entails the counselor being their authentic self: Your inner experience matches the way you act without a façade. Being congruent related to ethnicity means knowing your ethnic identity, understanding the difference between you and your client's cultural values and beliefs that are grounded in ethnicity, and being open to dialogue about your similarities and differences. It is important for counselors not to shy away from asking questions about clients' ethnicity to understand their worldviews, values, and beliefs better, particularly as they relate to clients' ways of being, functioning, and presenting concerns.

Professional counseling practice requires constant work on developing *cultural intelligence* (CQ) and operating in the framework of *cultural relativism* (CR). CQ was introduced by Early (2002) and is defined as the capability to interpret someone's unfamiliar and ambiguous gestures the way that person's compatriots would (Earley & Mosakowski, 2004). CQ is a multifaceted construct comprised of three dimensions: cognitive, motivational, and behavioral. The cognitive dimension denotes knowledge about other cultures, the behavioral dimension corresponds with appropriate communication, and the motivational dimension captures the initiative individuals take to interact in cross-cultural settings and is tied to valuing these interactions. Developing CQ encompasses constant lifelong learning about the cultures of the clients you interact with. In sum, CQ conveys respect toward people who are different from oneself, including those who come from nondominant ethnic groups.

People with high CQ can work effectively with members of diverse cultures, avoid snap judgments, and seek to understand what occurs in communication. When working with clients who belong to nondominant ethnic groups, you can use "cultural check-ins" within yourself. For instance, if you identify as White American and your client identifies as Asian American and the client says something that annoys you, a cultural check-in about this annoyance might be asking yourself, "Is this annoyance related to our cultural differences?" If so, what are those differences that are leading you to feel irritated? Is it simply because you communicate differently, or maybe you are reacting to the facial expressions or tone the client is using? If you are unable to identify the difference, you can take steps to uncover it, such as conducting your own research, consulting with a colleague, or using supervision. Basically, when experiencing negative reactions, you always need to check in with yourself to figure out what evoked your reaction rather than passing the reaction on to the client.

CR is the opposite of ethnocentrism. CR means viewing and valuing other cultures by that culture's perspective rather than your own perspective of it. Using CR, counselors do not judge other cultures based on their own; they work to understand the other culture's uniqueness without making denigrating comparisons. CR is stressed in multicultural counseling as a way to explore enculturation and develop respect toward the cultural norms of people who come from nondominant ethnic groups. Client intake documents are the first step in learning what a client's ethnicity is, while the clinical interview and subsequent counseling sessions offer the opportunity to learn about how their ethnic identity shapes their worldview.

Communicating With Clients Whose First Language Is Not English

Clear and effective communication is the cornerstone of counseling practice, and working with clients for whom English is not their first language can challenge counselors' ability to communicate effectively. As we discussed earlier, ethnocentrism has many facets, and communication is one of them. Ethnocentrism in language can also contribute to "othering" or pathologizing clients. When clients are unable to express themselves in their language of choice, they might feel pressured to bring their own interpreters. This sometimes results in adults bringing their children to counseling. Researchers have labeled this behavior as *parentification of children*, particularly in immigrant families of Latinx, Asian, and African origin (Mercado, 2003). However, what is pathologized as parentification (i.e., ethnic minoritized clients having their children act as adults) is actually part of the systemic inequalities that clients who do not speak English face in the United States and is better understood as *language brokering*—a term used to describe situations when children who speak English better than parents serve as translators from English to the parents' native language (Mercado, 2003). Because of the language stressors imposed by ethnocentrism, children of immigrants are often forced to be language brokers to help their parents navigate educational, medical, and legal systems by translating documents and acting as their voice in responding to institutions. For children of immigrants, this can be an added stressor that impacts their mental health (Mercado, 2003).

Finally, counselors must consider how they will inquire about where a client is from, particularly if the client has an accent and it's seemingly evident that they were born somewhere other than the United States. For instance, people of European descent whose family origins are on the continent of Europe appear White; however, once they start talking, they are not perceived to be U.S. Americans, which is typically followed by the question, "Where are you from?" This question, even though it seems innocent, can evoke negative emotions because it is a microaggression. For instance, if the person was born in Russia, they might feel embarrassed to share that information because of Russia's invasion of Ukraine. Moreover, a person might have fled a country where they were suffering political, economic, social, or other oppression. Instead, ask an open question about the client's childhood that you would ask any client: "Tell me about your experiences growing up." Alternatively, during a broaching conversation, you might offer some about your geographic living experiences, for example, "I was born and raised in Florida, and as an adult, I have lived in Colorado, Virginia, and Wisconsin. What has your experience been?" The key is to use a tone that conveys interest rather than judgment or leads the client to feel as if they are being interrogated.

Attending to Acculturation

For clients who have nondominant ethnic identities who are recent immigrants, it is helpful to conceptualize their level of acculturation or the cultural changes they have experienced as a result of encountering a new, socially dominant group. Acculturation can include navigating communication styles, how affect is shown, and how time is perceived and used, as well as food, social activities, and even norms related to driving or queuing in a store! These are all differences that many, if not all, immigrants experience, some of which can be confusing and daunting, especially if they don't have close family or friends who have navigated the new culture before with whom they can discuss these experiences.

Counselors can use acculturation models (see Chapter 6) to examine the degree to which clients feel included in society. For instance, some ethnic minorized clients may experience acculturative stress, such as immigrants who experience an internal psychological reaction to learning and feel pressured to adapt to U.S. cultural values (Organista, 2007). Whatever the client may be experiencing related to acculturation, it is essential for the counselor to create space for them to share their experiences, normalize and validate their experiences, and be ready and willing to explain what they have encountered. Once a counselor shares why U.S. culture in their particular region seems to do something a particular way, they can inquire how the client did it in their country of origin and use what is learned to validate and normalize further what the client is experiencing.

Spiritual and Religious Informed Support

Spirituality and religion are powerful sources for navigating and overcoming oppression and discrimination. For some ethnic minoritized individuals, their religious views can help provide support and guidance when facing discrimination and oppression. Cultural resistance theory is one framework that can be used to understand how some ethnic minoritized groups have used religion to counter societal oppression (Duncombe, 2007; Trevino, 2006). Duncombe (2007) described cultural resistance as "the practice of using meaning and symbols—that is, culture—to contest and combat a dominant power, often constructing a different vision of the world in the process" (para. 1). Cultural resistance as religious practice can be seen in Hebrew scriptures that were cultural means to foster Jewish identity in the face of Roman oppression (Duncombe, 2007). Gibson (1988) described how Sikh high school immigrants used their religious beliefs when facing institutional oppression and discrimination during assimilation.

Another example can be found in how Mexicans and Mexican Americans honor the *Virgen de Guadalupe* (Virgin of Guadalupe). Cultural outsiders may see the reverence of the *Virgen de Guadalupe* solely as a religious symbol, yet cultural anthropologists have labeled this image as a source to symbolize gender roles (e.g., *marianismo*, a gender submissiveness of Mexican women similar to Catholic's view of the Virgin Mary; Navarro, 2002). Additionally, some Mexicans and Mexican Americans use the symbol of the *Virgen de Guadalupe* as a source of support and protection when facing oppression and discrimination (i.e., a social justice symbol; Trevino, 2006).

Many African Americans utilize their religious beliefs when facing various challenges, including systemic oppression such as racism (Avent & Cashwell, 2015). Avent and Cashwell (2015) described how liberation theology is one of the prevailing schools of thought in the Black church, the overall institution that encompasses predominately African American Christian congregations. The Black church is a place that "offered oppressed Blacks a sense of freedom rarely experienced in their day-to-day lives" (Avent & Cashwell, 2015, p. 85). Avent and Cashwell (2015) recommend that counselors use liberation theology in formulating client conceptualizations and treatment planning. Counselors can take a strength-based, optimistic approach that focuses on a holistic perspective and integrates religious strength and coping into treatment (Avent & Cashwell, 2015).

MSJCC Application

To better help clients who come from nondominant ethnic identity groups, Ratts et al. (2015) developed the multicultural and social justice counseling competencies (MSJCCs), which posit that counselors must develop four core multicultural counseling competencies while acknowledging the privilege and marginalization both counselors and clients hold. Exploring attitudes and beliefs begins with your own culture, particularly your ethnic identity. Reflections will differ between people who identify with dominant versus nondominant ethnic groups, which is the purpose of the reflection—to understand who *you are* so you are prepared to engage in cross-cultural counseling! Knowledge about your ethnic roots and background can help you to develop your ethnic identity further, particularly if you feel that it is not fully formed. It is not always possible to inquire about your ethnic roots, but try to find as much information as possible to shape your understanding of your ethnicity. Speaking with relatives, using services such as 23 and Me or Ancestry can be helpful; however, we recommend using them with caution as you may find hidden family secrets that you or your relatives might not be ready to bring to light.

Researchers have shown that students from nondominant groups considered didactic and experiential training beneficial to their development, while students from dominant groups reported that communication with ethnically diverse people was more beneficial for their multicultural growth. Additionally, students from nondominant groups shared that multicultural training made them an object of study for students from dominant groups (Cohen et al., 2022). This is important to reflect on as you continue to learn about ethnicity in a classroom context and engage with your peers, and eventually with clients. No one should be made to feel as if they are a *test case* or an *object* being used for someone else's development. This may be tricky to navigate at first, though don't avoid such interactions out of fear. Instead, rely on the core conditions and be willing to repair the rupture if a misstep occurs.

Developing knowledge and awareness about your client's ethnicity is a lifelong process. Sometimes, beginning counselors experience anxiety related to asking their clients about their ethnic traditions, values and beliefs. This anxiety stems from thinking that your questions might offend your client—this point of view is incorrect. Your clients will appreciate your willingness to learn about their ethnicity in order to understand them better and provide high-quality services. Here, your congruence and unconditional positive regard will help to ask such questions respectfully but always remember that each question is a counseling intervention. Counselors are not asking questions to satisfy their curiosity but to gain a deeper understanding of specific themes tied to the client's ethnicity that are connected to the client's goals in counseling. Day-Vines et al. (2007) asserted that professional counselors commit to exploring the issues of diversity with clients through broaching, which involves discussions of cultural differences, bias, and discrimination. A healing counseling relationship is possible when your client feels understood and does not feel ostracized. In order to provide validation, you need to know as much as possible about your client's attitudes, values, beliefs, biases, social identities, social group statuses, power, privilege, and experiences of oppression.

Individuals who belong to the dominant and nondominant ethnic groups develop a set of ideas regarding what they believe to be typical client behavior. Thus, when your ethnically diverse clients behave unexpectedly, you might feel confused or frustrated. Confusion stems from feeling lost and not understanding what is going on or how to respond. Frustration comes from seeing clients' behavior as an obstacle on the way to effective therapy. Developing CQ can help.

Professional counselors develop three dimensions of CQ—cognitive, motivational, and behavioral—by actively seeking multicultural education and applying it in their practice. How can we apply CQ and MSJCC framework to our everyday counseling work? One of the most important facets to focus on is the therapeutic alliance. Clients' and counselors' ethnicities intersect, and when counselors are reluctant to explore the intersections, difficulties may arise, yet exploring them can produce positive therapeutic outcomes. PettyJohn et al. (2020) offered a model to frame such discussions with clients (Figure 8.1). The therapeutic utility of discussing therapist/client intersectionality in treatment: how and when? model gives counselors guidance on how and when they engage in critical cultural discussions and positions it within the context of building the relationship and deepening the bonds between client and counselor. Importantly, the model highlights how counselors must self-assess and reflect in order to engage in these conversations effectively (Box 8.4). Intentional reflection and thoughtful process increase the potential for fruitful interactions with clients about their ethnic identities and beyond!

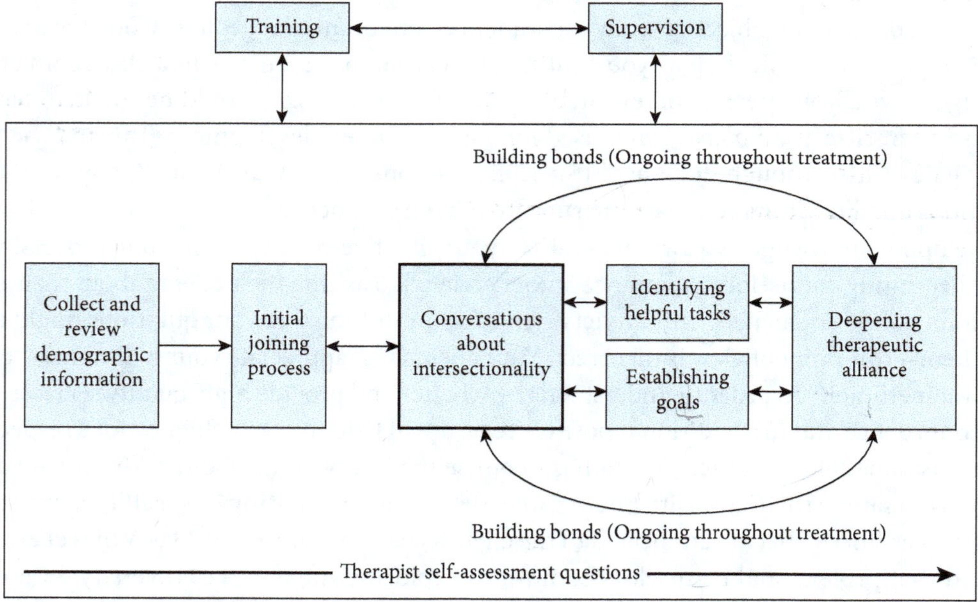

FIGURE 8.1 Therapeutic Utility of Discussing Therapist/Client Intersectionality in Treatment: How and When?

BOX 8.4 **TIPS FOR PROFESSIONAL PRACTICE: COUNSELOR SELF-ASSESSMENT (SALMON, 2017)**

As you have learned, counselors work to understand themselves so they are prepared to understand their clients. Below, we offer questions to help you reflect more deeply and to prepare you to work with a broader range of clients.

- On what dimensions of identity do I differ from the client(s) as indicated by the demographics collected? How might I unintentionally oppress the client(s) if I'm not careful?
- How will differences in my and the client's identity potentially impact the bond, goals, and tasks of treatment?
- How much knowledge/experience do I have with each aspect of the client's identity which differs from my own? What common stereotypes exist about the client's identity that could unconsciously influence my work with them?
- How comfortable/uncomfortable am I with addressing these aspects of intersectionality I have identified?
- What aspects of oppression are involved in the conceptualization of the presenting problem?
- What contextual factors going on in society at large need to be addressed based on my and the client's intersectionality?
- Based on my clinical judgment and interactions with the client(s), how do I believe they will respond to having a conversation about intersectionality?

Resiliencies, Strengths, and Fostering Wellness

Much of the literature on mental health support for clients with nondominant ethnic identities offers a deficit perspective. As counselors working with clients to foster mental health wellness, incorporating clients' cultural resiliencies and strengths is essential. Yosso's (2005) community cultural wealth (CCW) framework provides counselors with guidelines on fostering the client's cultural strengths throughout the therapeutic process.

Community Cultural Wealth

The CCW framework emerged from critical race theory and was derived to intentionally counter deficit narratives that are imposed on communities of color (Yosso, 2005). The CCW asserts that communities of color possess *capital* for navigating systems such as higher education, work environments, and community resources. Counselors can help clients identify the ways in which they have capital and the skills they possess in each area. Through this process, counselors encourage clients to continue to use their strengths and skills and to expand the ways in which they can apply them. Importantly, counselors draw out how clients use their skills and their multiple applications rather than naming them for them—they *empower* clients—and when there is an ethnic difference, they take special care not to reinforce ethnocentrism or dominant cultural values. Various types of intangible capital that are found within the CCW framework wealth include the following:

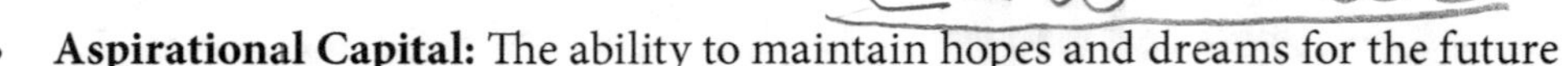

- **Aspirational Capital:** The ability to maintain hopes and dreams for the future
- **Familial Capital:** Cultural knowledge nurtured among familiar kin that carry a sense of community
- **Linguistic Capital:** The intellectual and social skills attained through communication in multiple languages and/or language styles
- **Navigational Capital:** Skills in navigating through social institutions not created with communities of color in mind
- **Resistant Capital:** Knowledge and skills fostered through oppositional behavior that challenge inequality
- **Social Capital:** Networks of people and community resources

For instance, BIPOC youth often use navigational, aspirational, social, and resistant capital in response to encounters of invalidation and microaggressions (Yosso et al., 2009). Given this, if you were working with a 17-year-old Black male who wants to become a nurse, you might engage him in the following ways about his capital within the CCW.

- **Aspirational Capital:** "How did you discover that you wanted to become a nurse?" "What helps you to keep your dream alive?"
- **Navigational Capital:** "I remember you telling me a few weeks ago how you stood up for yourself when your homeroom teacher refused to sign your schedule and said you weren't 'ready' to take honors trigonometry even though you have gotten straight As in math since middle school. How can you use this experience to fight the impostor syndrome you're feeling about applying to college?"
- **Social Capital:** "You have named so many people over the course of our sessions who want to see you succeed even though some of your teachers haven't. Who would you like to ask to support you as you apply to college? What kind of support would be most helpful for you?"
- **Resistant Capital:** "You have a track record of showing courage in the face of adversity, like the time you finally decided to confront the mall security who constantly accused you all of loitering and being involved in gang activity while saying nothing to the group of White kids you knew had stolen from stores in the past. I'm wondering how you can use this courage as you face the unknown in college?"

What do you notice in these examples? First, they use client evidence the counselor has gathered through their sessions together to name strengths they have already discussed. Using this method provides *evidence* for the strengths you note, giving them more power and eliminating the possibility that the client might perceive them as compliments. Second, they are conversational rather than a long string of closed questions that can be perceived as interrogational. Finally, they encourage the client to draw on experiences they've had already and apply them to a new situation. When using this type of method, the delivery method is critical. Your tone should be warm and convey an even affect, your body language open and mirroring the client, including matching eye contact. What are some other ways you can imagine drawing on clients' already established capital that elicits their strengths within their ethnic context and affirms their intersecting identities?

BOX 8.5 **PROFILE OF A PRACTITIONER: DR. JACQUELINE CONTRERAS**

IMG 8.1. Dr. Jacqueline Contreras

Dr. Jacqueline Contreras is a licensed professional counselor in South Texas. She holds a master's degree in clinical mental health counseling and a doctoral degree in counselor education and supervision. As a Latina first-generation college graduate, daughter of Mexican immigrants, and a gay woman, the lack of diverse representation in the counseling profession led her to become a professional counselor that serves diverse Latinx clients. Dr. Contreras shares how she uses culturally affirming counseling to support the cultural strengths of Latinx clients.

I identify as a Latina first-generation college graduate. I was born and raised on the West Side of San Antonio, Texas. I resided in one of the highest poverty rate neighborhoods in my city. As a first-generation college student (FGCS), my journey toward becoming a professional counselor has been a monumental experience filled with challenges, learning curves, and triumphs. I attended a high school that lacked college readiness. In addition, my parents, with no higher education experience, lacked knowledge about the resources that were available to apply to college. I quickly realized that if I wanted to earn a 4-year degree, I had to figure it out on my own. As I accessed higher education, my parents supported me emotionally and financially. However, I lacked guidance on how to succeed academically in an environment that was filled with microaggressions regarding my abilities to be successful. These negative experiences were the constant judgments I faced regarding the multiple marginalized identities I hold. Often, there were times I did not think I would graduate because these negative experiences made me question my worth. I needed mentorship. However, I did not know who to seek guidance from or how to ask for it.

It changed when I entered graduate school in clinical mental health counseling. That is where I discovered *communidad* (community) through informal mentorships. I finally had the support of knowledgeable Latinx faculty and staff members. My support group guided me to further academic success in a doctoral program. The mentors I gained validated the hardships I encountered as a Latinx FGCS by giving their own *testimonios*—sharing their own narratives. Meeting my mentors for a *plática* (conversation) confirmed I was not alone anymore. My mentors' shared experiences helped me become aware of my own resiliency. They also provided a key component to my confidence and perseverance: empowerment. Until then, I focused only on my weaknesses. However, my mentors consistently highlighted my strengths and achievements. They would often state that individuals where I hailed from, a low socioeconomic status neighborhood, often do not obtain a college degree. I am proud to say that I am part of the 2% of the population in the United States who hold a doctoral degree (USCB, 2022). I have crossed paths with multiple Latinx FGCS with similar experiences.

As a counselor, I work closely with Latinx FGCS to create a culturally affirming space that uplifts their resiliency. Using *testimonios*, such as narrative therapy approaches, with this population is essential because it emphasizes the struggles and resilience of BIPOC communities (Tello, 2020). This challenges the status quo that threatens to mask oppression within higher education and motivate students to seek social justice. Narratives may support educational empowerment and self-determination. I can attest to this from my own experiences. Upon entering and attending my undergraduate studies, I lacked confidence. However, my confidence level increased when my mentors called attention to my assets. Feeling empowered also increased my determination to set higher goals for myself in academia. Counselors can help build Latinx FGCS' empowerment and ignite their own academic resilience awareness. This builds coping skills for Latinx FGCS to overcome the negative experiences they might endure (Perez et al., 2009). Instead of using a deficit lens that deemphasizes BIPOC's abilities, I integrate Yosso's (2005) CCW model throughout my work, as this approach is congruent with my goal of focusing on the abilities, strengths, and knowledge of Latinx FGCS. My goal as a counselor is to help Latinx FGCS overcome the challenges that may arise in their academic journeys. I hope this strong and powerful group remembers to focus on the strengths they have acquired throughout their lives.

Ethical Code Applications

Ethical codes in counseling state directly the importance of counselors not imposing their personal values onto the clients they serve (see Table 8.3). Counselors must respect clients' autonomy; when counselors enforce their values, clients' autonomy is threatened, as they might feel *their worldviews* are devalued.

Sometimes, a counselor might be tempted to force clients toward change, disregarding a golden rule—meet your clients where they are. Being accepting of clients' values is crucial because its through acceptance and respect that clients grow, which aligns with the person-centered tradition discussed earlier in this chapter—showing unconditional positive regard. Additionally, recognizing the cultural differences in values through applying the MSJCC framework, we appreciate our clients' beliefs, which ultimately help them to cope with challenges they might be experiencing as members of nondominant ethnic groups.

TABLE 8.1 Code of Ethics: Avoid Imposing Personal Values

Code of Ethics Location	Description
ACA Code of Ethics A.4.a.	Counselors act to avoid harming their clients, trainees, and research participants and to minimize or to remedy unavoidable or unanticipated harm.
ACA Code of Ethics A.4.b.	Personal Values: Counselors are aware of—and avoid imposing—their own values, attitudes, beliefs, and behaviors. Counselors respect the diversity of clients, trainees, and research participants and seek training in areas in which they are at risk of imposing their values onto clients, especially when the counselor's values are inconsistent with the client's goals or are discriminatory in nature.

Code of Ethics Location	Description
AMHCA Code of Ethics I.A.4.d.	CMHCs are aware of their own values, attitudes, beliefs and behaviors, as well as how these apply in a society with clients from diverse ethnic, social, cultural, religious, and economic backgrounds. CMHCs do not impose their personal values on clients.
ASCA Code of Ethics A.1.h.	Respect students' and families' values, beliefs, sexual orientation, gender identification/expression and cultural background and exercise great care to avoid imposing personal beliefs or values rooted in one's religion, culture or ethnicity.
CRCC Code of Ethics A.1.e	Rehabilitation counselors respect the rights of clients to make decisions on their own behalf in accordance with their cultural identity, values, and beliefs. Decision-making on behalf of clients that limits or diminishes the autonomy of the client is made only after careful deliberation. CRCs/CCRCs advocate for clients to resume responsibility for their choices as quickly as possible.
CRCC Code of Ethics A.4	Avoiding value imposition. Rehabilitation counselors are aware of and avoid imposing their own values, attitudes, beliefs and behaviors. Rehabilitation counselors respect the diversity of clients and seek training in areas in which they are at risk of imposing their values onto clients, especially when the rehabilitation counselor's values are inconsistent with the client's goals or are discriminatory in nature.

To avoid imposing values, counselors must be reflective practitioners throughout their clinical careers. An area of reflection for counselors includes their ethnic and cultural messages. In particular, reflecting on where they fall on the spectrum of collectivistic and individualist worldviews and privilege and marginalization. This will help counselors to understand what worldview they bring into the counseling relationship and to create a culturally affirming space to support their clients.

There is, however, a set of values that counselors do share with clients—the value of the importance of mental health and wellness. Nonetheless, counselors consider clients' perspectives and understanding of mental health, and they accept that not every client values mental health in the ways you do. For instance, you might be working with a client who comes from an Asian American family in which seeing a counselor is considered a weakness, and the person who is seeking mental help is looked down on by their family. Even though your client is developing a set of values tied to appreciating what counseling can do for them, they still might have some values coming from their family of origin. In such a situation, the best way to proceed is to introduce the information and discuss it, understanding that changing values is a longtime process, clients move through various stages of change, and that they can only begin to fully value mental health services once they see benefits of them, which, again, might take time. Patience and acceptance are the key to successful change.

Conclusion

In this chapter, you have gained depth and breadth about ethnicity and how it connects to national identity, as well as its distinctions and overlap with race. Furthermore, you have had the opportunity to explore privilege and oppression related to ethnicity, particularly ethnocentrism, individualism, collectivism, and language differences. As you create a culturally affirming counseling practice with clients of all ethnic identities, you can apply key skills you have learned, such as the CCW model and Bronfenbrenner's EST. Continue to learn about your ethnic identities and how they may influence your practice and be open and curious about what is important to clients about their ethnic identities and realities.

Questions for Reflection

Consider what you learned in this chapter as you respond to the questions and prompts below.

1. Prior to reading this chapter, how did you understand ethnicity? How has your view expanded as a result of what you learned in this chapter?
2. What traditions, beliefs, ways of being, etc., are part of your ethnic identity? Which do you hold most dear? If you were unable to name any, how would you like to learn more about your ethnic identity?
3. If you are a person who identifies strongly with your ethnic identity, what is it like to be in a relationship with someone who does not have a strong ethnic identity? Conversely, if you are a person who does not identify strongly with your ethnic identity, what is it like to be in a relationship with someone who has a strong ethnic identity? What are ways in which you can gain more cultural comfort? Cultural humility?
4. What are ways in which you can apply cultural humility when working with clients who have a different ethnic identity from your own? What about clients who have the *same* ethnic identity as you have?
5. In what ways have you participated in ethnocentrism? Where are you in your journey of relearning in an effort to shed ethnocentric beliefs? What would you like to do to continue your journey so you can best serve clients?

Applying What You Have Learned

Complete each of the following activities, considering what you learned from this chapter.

Activity #1: Contextual Ethnicity

Some people know a great deal about their personal and familial ethnicities, though not everyone has that knowledge or the ability to learn that information. While our personal ethnic identities can be very important to who we are, our contextual or community ethnic identities can be just as important. What ethnic cultures form the neighborhood, city, or town in which you live? How are they present (e.g., community centers, elected officials, stores, restaurants, languages spoken, activities)? How have they made an impact on how you live your life? Is it different or similar to how you were raised? What do you value about the ethnic culture of your neighborhood, city, or town? What would you like to be different?

Activity #2: Expanding Your Professional Knowledge

As the counseling profession continues to grow, so does our knowledge related to working with specific ethnic groups. Take to your college or university's library database or Google Scholar and search specific ethnic groups and the phrase "counseling interventions." You can even modify the interventions search to represent your counseling specialization (e.g., school, rehabilitation, addictions)! Read the articles you find and compile a list of the similarities and differences you find. Dig further to learn more about the specific theories and interventions authors discuss. Consider how they fit with your theoretical orientation and how you will use what you learned to provide culturally affirming counseling.

Credit

Fig. 8.1: Morgan E. Pettyjohn, Chi-Fang Tseng, and Adrian Blow, "Therapeutic Utility of Discussing Therapist/Client Intersectionality in Treatment: When and How?," *Family Process*, vol. 59, no. 2, p. 319. Copyright © 2020 by Family Process Institute.

CHAPTER 9

Immigrants, Refugees, Diasporas, and Xenomisia

John J. S. Harrichand, Krista E. Kirk, Shreya Vaishnav, Joy M. Mwendwa, and Kevin C. Snow

No one leaves home unless home is the mouth of a shark

—Warsan Shire

CHAPTER OVERVIEW

Because persistent threats and racism impede immigrants', refugees', and asylum seekers' ability to seek help, counselors are tasked with identifying effective and culturally responsive strategies to support these populations. In this chapter, you will begin your journey of becoming a culturally relevant counselor for these populations including establishing foundational knowledge, increasing your awareness, and learning effective strategies. To begin, we offer term definitions, then a brief overview of historical and current literature on these populations, and finally, a conceptualization of multicultural and social justice counseling competencies (MSJCC; Ratts et al., 2015) within two model applications. Additionally, we provide a brief discussion on nondominant group identities, a discussion of constructs within ecological and sociopolitical contexts, a review of relevant ethical codes, and recommendations for professional counselors from a strengths-based perspective.

LEARNING OBJECTIVES

By the end of this chapter, students will be able to

1. identify the needs and challenges of immigrants and refugees relating to counseling,
2. apply the MSJCCs to immigrants and refugees,
3. examine culturally sensitive models that can be employed when counseling immigrants and refugees,
4. examine personal stories of immigrants and refugees and identify the challenges they face,
5. explore culturally sensitive strategies to meet the needs of immigrants and refugees, and
6. evaluate how counselor identity (e.g., student, clinician, educator, or supervisor) influences counseling with immigrants and refugees.

CACREP 2016 STANDARDS

The information in this chapter supports the following standards:

- 2.F.2.a. Multicultural and pluralistic characteristics within and among diverse groups nationally and internationally

- 2.F.2.b. Theories and models of multicultural counseling, cultural identity development, and social justice and advocacy
- 2.F.2.c. Multicultural counseling competencies
- 2.F.2.d. The impact of heritage, attitudes, beliefs, understandings, and acculturative experiences on an individual's views of others
- 2.F.2.e. The effects of power and privilege for counselors and clients
- 2.F.2.f. Help-seeking behaviors of diverse clients
- 2.F.2.g. The impact of spiritual beliefs on clients' and counselors' worldviews
- 2.F.2.h. Strategies for identifying and eliminating barriers, prejudices, and processes of intentional and unintentional oppression and discrimination

CACREP 2024 STANDARDS

The information in this chapter supports the following standards:

- 3.B.1. theories and models of multicultural counseling, social justice, and advocacy
- 3.B.2. the influence of heritage, cultural identities, attitudes, values, beliefs, understandings, within-group differences, and acculturative experiences on individuals' worldviews
- 3.B.3. the influence of heritage, cultural identities, attitudes, values, beliefs, understandings, within-group differences, and acculturative experiences on help-seeking and coping behaviors
- 3.B.4. the effects of historical events, multigenerational trauma, and current issues on diverse cultural groups in the U.S. and globally
- 3.B.5. the effects of stereotypes, overt and covert discrimination, racism, power, oppression, privilege, marginalization, microaggressions, and violence on counselors and clients
- 3.B.6. the effects of various socio-cultural influences, including public policies, social movements, and cultural values, on mental and physical health and wellness
- 3.B.9. strategies for identifying and eliminating barriers, prejudices, and processes of intentional and unintentional oppression and discrimination
- 3.B.10. guidelines developed by professional counseling organizations related to social justice, advocacy, and working with individuals with diverse cultural identities
- 3.B.11. the role of religion and spirituality in clients' and counselors' psychological functioning

Concepts, Terms, Models, and Definitions

Categorizing and defining the working terminology of immigrants and refugees can be complex because there are many terms for these groups, some of which are used interchangeably. The term *migrant* is defined as the movement of any person from their home/residence within and/or across countries, irrespective of their legal status, voluntary or involuntary, or length of stay, with the intent of improving their economic and social conditions. There are also different states of migration, including legal/regular, controlled, or free (Douglas et al., 2019). The term *migrant* can fit into categories that imply citizenship or residency (e.g., temporary or permanent, legal or undocumented) and/or modes of entry (e.g., asylum seekers, refugees, skilled workers, students; Douglas et al., 2019; Samers & Collyer, 2017). Some authors refer to *migrancy* as "the movement and process rather than stability and fixity across both space and time" (Harney & Baldassar, 2007, p. 192). In other words, the term *migrancy* not only describes a relocation to an area but also considers the impact of the given changes to the area over time. Globally, human migration is at an all-time high. Since the year 2000, there have been more than 258 million people who have migrated internationally, which is 3.4% of the global population (United Nations Department of Economic and Social Affairs, 2017).

Before moving into a detailed discussion of immigrants and refugees, it is necessary to make a distinction between the two terms based on the U.S. Department of Homeland Security (DHS; DHS, n.d.). This section provides language used by the U.S. government to identify/label immigrants and refugees and as such, we recognize that the language is dehumanizing and stigmatizing. It is important for counselors to understand these terms and the negative messages they embody, as clients/society may use them. We caution readers against using dehumanizing and stigmatizing terms to refer to immigrants and refugees in counseling; instead, we encourage you to employ less pathologizing terms. The term *immigrant* is a broad category under the Immigration and Nationality Act (INA) composed of any *alien* (i.e., individuals not born in the United States and/or not holding citizenship in the country), irrespective of status (i.e., legal vs. illegal). While the term *alien* is used to define an individual's citizenship status, this term is considered *otherizing* and problematic for individuals belonging to this community. The terms *documented* and *undocumented immigrant* are the preferred terms to identify an individual's legal immigrant status. Notably, immigrants may or may not be granted permanent resident status in the United States, even after residing for a prolonged time (DHS, n.d.).

The term *refugees*, according to the DHS, refers to individuals who are outside their country of nationality (i.e., home country) who cannot or will not return home because of persecution or a well-founded fear of persecution based on their race, religion, nationality, membership in a particular social group, or political opinion. The U.S. president, in consultation with Congress, determines annually the maximum number of refugees entering the country based on geographic area. In addition, refugees who complete 1 year of continuous presence in the United States are eligible to apply for lawful permanent resident status, which may or may not be granted (DHS, n.d.).

An important distinction is that refugees usually arrive in the United States for safety and/or political reasons, which often provides them with a greater probability of gaining legal permanent resident status in the United States compared to their immigrant counterparts. Typically, immigrants travel to the United States for educational and/or economic reasons, and as a result, tend to encounter a lengthier and sometimes more challenging process when seeking to become U.S. residents (Villalba, 2009). Importantly, one can immigrate to the United States because of political unrest yet not consider themselves a refugee, nor be recognized as a refugee because the U.S. government does not recognize their country of origin as one in which its citizens need refugee status.

Immigrants

Most authors discuss migration as both an internal (i.e., moving within one's own country) and international process (i.e., moving across international boundaries; Samers & Collyer, 2017). For the purposes of this chapter, the term *immigrant* represents those who reside in a country that is different from the one where they were born and are residents of the new country (i.e., temporary or permanent). In 2019, the most documented immigrant populations in the United States came from countries in Asia (350,000), Africa (110,000), and Mexico (155,000; Office of Immigration Statistics, 2019).

BOX 9.1 **PAUSE AND REFLECT: EXAMINING CULTURAL MYTHS**

What are some cultural myths you hold or might have heard? For example, many Americans believe Mexican immigrants are the only significant source of immigrants in the United States.

What beliefs do you hold about immigrants and refugees? Objectively, which of those beliefs are negative, which encapsulate stereotypes, and which convey seeing a holistic being who has strengths, hopes, and dreams?

What are some concerns or fears that arise as you think of working with immigrant and refugee clients?

Undocumented immigrants refer to noncitizens of a host country who did not obtain residence through the host country's policies. Undocumented immigrants in the United States accounted for 10.7 million people in 2016, according to a Pew Research Center report (Passel & Cohn, 2018). With these massive numbers, it is important for counselors to understand the driving force for people to immigrate and the implications of counseling these populations. For example, undocumented immigrants face unique challenges, and the stresses of immigration are exacerbated because of the ongoing fear of being detained or deported. Fear of being detained or experiencing deportation (e.g., personally, deportation of family or friends) often prevents undocumented family members from accessing health and government services. Those who are legal residents are often hesitant to seek service for fear of revealing the undocumented status of their loved ones. Together, both situations are cause for concern as they further compound immigrant families' stressors.

Refugees and Asylum Seekers

An *asylum seeker* is an individual who formally applies for refugee status in another country other than their own and whose legal status is still pending. Meanwhile, a *refugee* is an individual whose situation has been assessed, and the individual has been awarded either temporary or permanent permission to stay by the host country (McMahon et al., 2018). The refugee population has steadily declined in the United States since 2016 after leading the world in refugee admissions for 17 years (2003–2019). As refugee admissions continue to decline, undocumented immigration will likely rise, causing continual stress both at the economic and individual levels within refugee communities.

Diasporas

The concept of diaspora(s) is a term that has recently been used within multiple contexts connected to immigration and refugee populations but is more broadly related to notions of migration and the dispersion of populations beyond an original home territory or nation rather than someone's immigrant or refugee status. Specifically, *diaspora* refers to individuals whose heritage (e.g., ethnicity, culture) is historically rooted in certain geographical areas, nations, or territories but who now live in several different places around the world (Collins Online Dictionary, n.d.). Historically, this term was used to describe Jewish populations dispersed throughout Mediterranean countries beyond the ancient borders of the nation of Israel, with its usage rooted in the Torah going back to 250 BCE (Edwards, 2014).

Today, *diaspora* is used by some scholars and communities to describe their cultural group as they exist now—spread throughout the world. Within the United States, there are many examples of such diasporic populations, such as the Hmong diaspora, who settled in the United States following the Vietnam War; the large Muslim diaspora that exists in Illinois, Virginia, and Michigan, among other states; and the Cuban diaspora. Using the Cuban diaspora as an example, a large number of Cuban Americans live in Florida, especially in and around Miami. These Cuban Americans are as much a part of the Cuban culture as the citizens of the country of Cuba, as well as other people of Cuban heritage living in Canada, England, or any other country around the globe. Collectively, despite where they live, they make up the broader Cuban diaspora. This concept could be applied to many different cultural groups based on nationhood, ethnicity, religion, or other categories.

Xenomisia

Xenomisia is defined as negative feelings toward an individual or group because of their actual or perceived country of origin. It can be seen as a way in which some people try to distance themselves from ethnic and cultural groups different from their own by means of prejudice, discrimination, aggression, and oppression. A clear example of xenomisia is when 40% of Asian Americans reported that people acted uncomfortably around them since the onset of the COVID-19 outbreak, and over 30% reported they had been the target of racial slurs or jokes (Ruiz et al., 2020). We now turn to a discussion of acculturation models related to immigrants and refugees.

Acculturation Models

Acculturation is a process by which individuals, families, and groups encounter a shift in their cultural norms both at the institutional and interpersonal levels when they come into contact with a new or different culture from their original culture (Berry, 2019). Acculturation research originally emerged out of the concern for the effects of European colonization on Indigenous populations (Redfield et al., 1936), yet research on acculturation has grown to examine how immigrant and ethnocultural groups change and relate to each other while living in a pluralistic society (Haugen & Kunst, 2017). Berry (1997) discussed how in plural societies, cultural groups and their members must decide how to acculturate. Berry outlined four acculturation models: assimilation, separation, integration, and marginalization (see Chapter 6 for more information on this model). Notably, this model addresses the extent to which cultural identity is maintained and the extent to which the nondominant group and its individuals become involved with the dominant group. To further aid our understanding of Berry's model, we present the story of Nganuo.

BOX 9.2 **FOCUS ON CLIENT CARE**

Nganuo's Story

Nganuo is a 25-year-old woman who immigrated to the United States from India 7 years ago with the goal of attending a Christian college and seeking employment in the United States after graduation. Nganuo comes from a large family with 13 brothers and sisters, most of whom still reside in India. She indicated she has a strong relationship with her siblings and mother. Nganuo grew up in a home where her mother was safe for her, yet her father, who had an alcohol abuse problem, often threatened and physically abused her and her siblings. She has visible scars on her face and arms, and each has a story. The relationship with her dad was the catalyst for leaving India, although she stated that she misses her family deeply.

Nganuo speaks seven languages, several derived from the surrounding tribal areas in India. Each tribe has its own mother tongue, and often, there is much cross-over between tribal languages. Although she learned English in boarding school as a young child, Nganuo struggled with the intricacies that accompany the use of the language when she came to the United States. Accents, slang, and the speed at which Americans speak cause her a lot of anxiety when she communicates with others. Nganuo feels isolated and lonely because she does not have people in her life who "understand the struggle of using a language I only know on paper." She recalls going to the grocery store, and the store worker became irate because he was asking Nganuo a question she could not understand because of his southern accent and fast rate of speech. Additionally, Nganuo recalled becoming stressed when she encountered the drastic change in weather for the first time. She stated, "I came to the U.S. with one suitcase and a pair of flip-flops. It was quite scary to know that snow existed. I could not believe that some place could be so cold."

Now that Nganuo has lived in the United States for 7 years, she believes that she is adapting to American culture. She equally identifies with her Indian heritage and engages in traditional practices, such as cooking Indian cuisine, wearing Indian garb/clothing, and celebrating Indian holidays. When she first came to the United States, she began attending a church where a married couple invited all international students into their home and offered to cook for them while facilitating a place of friendship. She says that was her "lifesaver" for the last 2 years. She has entered counseling after discussing with her fellow international student friends that she fears for her younger siblings, who are still at home with her father, and her anxiety has affected her academic studies.

Processing the Case Through an Acculturation Lens

Applying Berry's (1997) acculturation model, one notices that Nganuo has *assimilated* into U.S. culture, adopting the dominant religion, Christianity, and "American culture." We can still see aspects of *separation* in the way Nganuo continues to wear Indian clothing, celebrate Indian holidays, and cook Indian food. Regarding *segregation*, one notices that Ngauno is anxious and "feels isolated and lonely" because of the way some Americans (like the store clerk) respond in relation to her English accent and their difficulty understanding her. Although subtle in Nganuo's case, segregation often results in immigrants and refugees minimizing contact with members of the dominant culture for fear of being "othered" or seen as less than. Regarding *integration*, we might say that Nganuo, after spending several years in the United States, is finding ways to honor both U.S. practices: engaging in counseling, attending church, spending time with a married couple, and retaining Indian practices (noted above). As counselors, we need to be aware of how acculturation might be expressed in the life of the immigrant or refugee client's overall health and well-being and in the process identify possible strengths and barriers.

Reflection Questions

1. What steps would you take initially to address Nganuo's concerns?
2. What resources exist in your area that could be helpful for Nganuo?
3. Based on the beliefs/biases you identified earlier, did you notice them arising as you read Nganuo's story?

Nondominant Group Identities

It is our hope that you have begun to understand the variability and complexity that comprise immigrant and refugee communities. The richness of these communities is made even richer and equally challenging when we factor in intersectional identities, especially identities like affectual/sexual identity, religion, spirituality, and gender. For example, challenges are compounded for LGBTQ+ immigrants and refugees—they already experience a set of unique challenges as immigrants or refugees, and in addition, they are further othered and oppressed because of their identity as members of the LGBTQ+ community. Similarly, those who are religious minorities in the United States (e.g., Muslims, Jews) often face added levels of discrimination in their daily experiences (see Chapter 16 for more on religious persecution).

Moreover, immigrants frequently encounter stereotypes linked to their racial and ethnic backgrounds. As an illustration, Asian immigrants and refugees are frequently labeled the *model minority* because of demonstrating high levels of integration into American society and perceived high productivity and intelligence over other racial/ethnic groups. In contrast, immigrants from Mexico, for example, have unjustly been branded as "criminals" or "lazy," exacerbating the differential treatment. Understanding these intersecting identities and their lived experiences creates opportunities for helpers to broach conversations around identity, as well as support individuals' mental health through an intersectional and holistic lens.

BOX 9.3 PAUSE AND REFLECT: THE IMPACT OF MIGRATION AND MOVEMENT

What is your story of immigration or refugee movement? What do you know about your family's migration heritage, if anything? Share your story with others (e.g., classmates, supervisees, colleagues, supervisor), and research it if you have not done so (see the activity at the end of the chapter). Even if you have moved from one U.S. state to another, that is part of your migration story and has potential counseling impacts. What might those impacts be?

Do you know anyone who has recently immigrated or been a refugee in another country? Seeking their consent, interview them about their experiences. Identify possible counseling implications related to their story. Did they seek counseling? Why or why not, and how did it go if they did seek it? Explore and share with others (e.g., classmates, supervisees, colleagues, supervisor).

BOX 9.4 PROFILE OF A PRACTITIONER: LISA (LISLE) SOSIN

IMG 9.1. Lisa (Lisle) Sosin

My name is Lisa (Lisle) Sosin, and I am an Israeli/Jewish American. I am a counselor educator and psychotherapist. My ethnic identity developed within the context of my family on Long Island, New York. Both sets of grandparents immigrated to New York at the turn of the 20th century and held to their orthodox Jewish faith in raising their children. Thus, my parents were raised in homes that celebrated Jewish holidays and feasts, kept kosher (dietary restrictions), and believed in the God of Abraham, Isaac, and Jacob of the Old Testament scriptures. My parents sought a more secularized form of Judaism that included celebrating the Jewish holidays and culture but not keeping kosher or abiding by the Jewish scriptures. Integrating my professional and ethnic identity is as organic as breathing. An aspect of Israeli culture is dance, music, and various other forms of creative and expressive arts. I integrated this aspect of my ethnic identity with my professional identity by developing and teaching a course called the Creative and Expressive Arts in Individual and Group Counseling. I also offer creative and expressive arts personal growth (CAPG) groups designed to promote multiculturalism, social justice, and peace. Moreover, I conduct ongoing research on the impact of the CAPG groups with diverse populations and created several manuals for the intervention to support recovery. As a person with a family history replete with immigrant/refugee narratives, my heritage provides a place of resonance with those I serve. Although each person's journey is unique, our shared humanity is authentic and provides a platform for meaningful collaboration.

Understanding the Historical Context of Immigration Regulation

Immigration regulation in the United States began after the United States received independence from Great Britain and laws were enacted to reflect the current political climate of the time (Cohn, 2015). Today, Republicans and Democrats express differing views regarding the U.S. immigration system (Oliphant & Cerda, 2022), and counselors need to be aware of how politics impact the lives and well-being of immigrants and refugees. As you will see, laws regulating immigrants and refugees entering the United States are based on systems of power and privilege that continue to perpetuate discrimination against some of our world's most vulnerable people. There are no definitive answers to solving these problems; however, we present this brief history to contextualize how people are impacted by the systems within which we *all* exist.

According to the U.S. Citizenship and Immigration Services (USCIS; 2020a), U.S. immigration during the 18th and early 19th centuries was a relatively open process, and it was not until the late 19th century that questions arose about the policies surrounding immigration. However, legal and immigration historians suggest that while the federal government did not assume responsibility for immigration until after the Civil War, individual states regulated entry. Neuman (1993) discussed five factors that influenced early immigration law in the United States: criminal resettlement, resettlement of persons living in poverty, public health, the presence of slavery, and other issues related to racial subordination. Prior to the end of the Civil War, free and enslaved Black citizens' movements were highly controlled, but laws varied by state. In 1875, the U.S. Supreme Court declared immigration regulations the responsibility of the federal government. See Table 9.1 for a time line summary of important immigration legislation in the United States.

TABLE 9.1 Historic Time Line of Significant Immigration Legislation in the United States

Prominent Immigration Legislation in the United States	Year	Facts (USCIS, 2020b)
The Immigration Act of 1917	1917	Required literacy for immigrants 16 and older, except in the case of those fleeing religious persecution.
The Quota Acts (Emergency Quota Act of 1921 and Immigration Act of 1924)	1921 and 1924	Limited the number of immigrants allowed from each country. Western and Northern Europeans were able to immigrate more easily and in greater numbers than immigrants from other parts of the world.
Displaced Persons Act of 1948	1948	After World War II, millions of refugees fled their home countries or were otherwise displaced. In an effort to address this issue in the United States, the U.S. Congress enacted the first refugee-specific legislation in 1948. The Displaced Persons Act facilitated the admission of over 350,000 refugees into the United States.

Prominent Immigration Legislation in the United States	Year	Facts (USCIS, 2020b)
INA	1952	Merged immigration and nationality laws into the same statute. The INA was passed by Congress in spite of President Truman's veto, and the act maintained quotas in the same way as the original Quota Acts. However, because there were no specific provisions relating to refugee admissions, many refugees "were later admitted under ad hoc programs outside of the quota system."
Refugee Relief Act of 1953	1953	In an effort to assist refugees fleeing communist countries, this act allowed the admission of almost 200,000 individuals. The act operated outside of the established quota system and assisted refugees, escapees, and expellees from countries and territories, such as China, the Soviet Union, and Eastern Berlin.
Hungarian Escapee Program	1956–1957	After the Hungarian Revolution of 1956, an uprising against the Soviet Union, thousands of Hungarians fled to Austria, and the United States agreed to help with their resettlement. An extension of the Refugee Relief Act of 1953, the Hungarian Escapee program admitted 6,130 Hungarian refugees. Furthermore, the attorney general used parole authority to approve the entry of another 30,000 Hungarians. Two years later, Hungarian parolees were afforded the opportunity to become permanent residents.
Azorean Refugee Act	1958	Another act that operated outside of the quota system, the Azorean Refugee Act permitted 2,000 visas for people seeking shelter from the natural disasters in the Azores Islands.
Fair Share Refugee Act of July 14, 1960	1960	At the end of the World Refugee Year (1959–1960), the Fair Share Refugee Act used the attorney general's parole authority to admit almost 5,000 refugees into the United States. These 5,000 refugees could obtain status as permanent residents after 2 years.
Cuban Refugee Influx Due to Fidel Castro and the Cuban Revolution	1959–1962	After the United States severed diplomatic ties with Cuba following the rise to power of Fidel Castro, the attorney general once again used parole authority to admit over 58,000 refugees who had fled Cuba.

(Continued)

TABLE 9.1 *(Continued)*

Prominent Immigration Legislation in the United States	Year	Facts (USCIS, 2020b)
Hong Kong Parole Program	1962	Similar to the preceding acts assisting those fleeing communist countries, the attorney general's parole authority authorized 15,000 Chinese refugees to enter the United States through Hong Kong and later obtain permanent resident status.
Migration and Refugee Assistance Act of 1962	1962	Provided monetary assistance to refugees, in addition to maintaining the expanded refugee admissions from the Fair Share Refugee Act.
Refugee Act of 1980	1980	Established a formal program for refugees and asylum seekers. The act instituted a neutral definition for refugees and gave the president the responsibility of determining the number of refugees who would be accepted each year and the number of refugees who would be accepted from each part of the world.
Department of Homeland Security	2002–2003	DHS was formed after the 9/11 terrorist attack in the United States. Organizations formed within DHS to address refugee and asylum programs (USCIS) and immigration (Immigration and Customs Enforcement). These organizations are still in place in 2021.

Ecological and Sociopolitical Perspectives

Drawing on the historical perspectives presented above, it is no surprise that immigrants and refugees have and continue to experience oppression and marginalization. Bronfenbrenner's (1979, 1994) ecological systems theory can help us understand how systems and the environment interact with an immigrant/refugee in ways that impact their overall well-being.

At the *microsystem* level, the immediate environment (e.g., family, school, peer group, neighborhood), immigrants/refugees may experience challenges with belonging, fear of deportation, racism, xenomisia, and being seen as the perpetual *foreigner* or *outsider*. In the *mesosytem*, connections between the immediate environment, immigrants/refugees might experience exclusion and othering at their place of employment or school because of their accent, challenges with written and spoken English, differences in how they interact with others, or even the food they eat during breaks. The *mesosystem* indirectly affects development. For example, hostility a parent experiences at work can impact the family at home.

Within the *macrosystem*, which refers to the larger cultural context, social systems must be examined (e.g., media, societal norms). For example, an immigrant or refugee may be lacking basic resources because their family is of lower socioeconomic status, yet because they feel pressured by society to prove they are *worthy* of residing in the United States, they believe they cannot

IMG 9.2.

ask for public assistance. As another example, a Muslim family who might settle in a Bible-belt state might feel pressured to hide their religious customs and practices for fear of being misunderstood or wrongfully targeted. Not having a local mosque, hearing biased comments about people who are not Christian when grocery shopping, or seeing billboards that communicate necessary salvation from Jesus can all be facets of the *macrosystem*.

Finally, the *chronosystem* accounts for the patterns and transitions over the course of time and development. For example, legislation and policies that have and continue to marginalize and systemically exclude immigrants and refugees in the United States present challenges to immigrants' overall health and well-being and their distrust in health providers as they work to navigate a system that consistently conveys they are *outsiders*.

With Bronfenbrenner's ecological system as a framework (1979, 1994), it is possible to see how trauma can exist for immigrants and refugees across multiple levels of their lives, often intersecting and compounding preexisting trauma or unique traumas present within the process of migrating to a new country and culture. Examples of these traumas include refugees fleeing oppressive and/or violent personal or societal events within their country of origin, such as someone fleeing because of severe crime, gang violence, or political persecution, or for more personal reasons such as sexual abuse or other forms of interpersonal violence (Goodman et al., 2017). Added to these traumas, which can have significant and long-term effects, are the traumas of arriving in a new country, possibly alone, and finding the new environment less than welcoming. This experience can lead to issues of identity loss or confusion, resistance to engaging in treatment or other social systems that may be necessary, and the many cultural shifts needed to interact with new ways of communicating, expressing emotions, and addressing psychological and other needs within a new culture (Marshall et al., 2016). There are also unique traumas to simply traveling to the United States for a new home, with many individuals coming through dangerous territories and terrain, often on foot or via other unsafe means—across deserts, through rivers, on makeshift rafts in treacherous seas, or arriving after spending years in refugee camps with unhealthy and poor living conditions.

Imagine a young person nicknamed Joe. Joe is from a war-torn country, and he experienced loss and firsthand violence from occupying forces. He sometimes used violence and sexual assault against civilians as a component of invasion. Joe was sent ahead by his family to a new country for safety. He arrives with his younger brother, and without parents, his other siblings, or other close relatives, in a country that does not fully welcome them and faces many barriers to accessing or accepting treatment for their needs, including their need for shelter, income, medical care, and mental health care (Goodman et al., 2017; Marshall et al., 2016). Additional barriers include being rejected and discriminated against in the new community that is hostile to immigrants and refugees (seen as a threat by local community members), poverty and unemployment, language learning, and cultural barriers. Consider, too, struggles with identity confusion/crisis and the challenges of embracing Western approaches to mental health. Social and health systems may be ill-prepared to meet their needs via a lack of resources and the absence of practitioners and other helpers who speak diverse languages or have training in intercultural communication and competency (Marshall et al., 2016). Through this example, it is apparent just how complex and interlinked trauma can be for many immigrants and refugees relocating to the United States and other countries.

Research on immigration conducted over the past 20 years by the U.S. National Academies of Sciences, Engineering, and Medicine (Blau & Mackie, 2017) found immigration had a positive impact on the economic growth in the United States over the long term. This finding is supported by Harrichand et al. (2022), and there appears to be little evidence that immigrants decrease the employment levels of their resident counterparts; instead, second-generation immigrants appear to be among the strongest contributors to the U.S. economy, both economically and financially (Blau & Mackie, 2017). Further, refugees who enter the United States before age 14 have similar graduation rates compared to U.S.-born students. On average, refugees arriving in the United States might exact an initial high cost stemming from relocation ($15,148) and dependence on welfare ($92,217); however, “over their first 20 years in the US refugees that arrived in the US aged 18–45 pay about $21,324 more in taxes [$128,689] than they take home in benefits” (Evans & Fitzgerald, 2017, p. 30). As we consider these points of difference between research findings and societal beliefs about immigrants and refugees and take into account Bronfenbrenner’s (1979) ecological systems theory, our hope is that you recognize the complex dynamics and how myths and misinformation about immigrants/refugees can perpetuate the oppression of these vulnerable groups in society.

Professional Counseling Practice Application

With certainty, counselors will work with immigrants and refugees. Counselors must engage in ongoing internal preparation in terms of their attitude and overall posture toward these groups while developing practical clinical skills. All counseling requires a strong therapeutic relationship (e.g., empathy, trust, attentive listening, advocacy, etc.), and clients who are immigrants, refugees, or members of a diaspora are no different; however, consider the following to strengthen the relationship with these populations.

- ***Learn what parts of my culture and customs are important to me.*** Clients who are immigrants, refugees, and/or members of the diaspora bring with them customs and cultures that are important to them (and maybe left some behind that were not important!). After gaining knowledge on your own, explore with clients the parts of their culture that are significant to them.
- ***My single story is important, so please listen.*** Counselors must use attentive listening skills to hear their clients' stories. For example, the nuances surrounding how two families escaped a war-torn country could be different if one family had personal bodyguards and security who helped them escape via a private plane, while the other family ran through an animal-filled forest to cross into a bordering country. In both cases, the trauma of leaving their home happened, but the specifics of how the escapes occurred were different. The counselor must allow space for each story to be heard and not assume similarities between clients' experiences. For the counselor, reflecting the client's content and checking for comprehension of the message is critical.
- ***Do you see the courage that it took for me to get here?*** The client who calls a counselor or agrees to a friend's suggestion to seek professional counseling displays a tremendous amount of courage, especially if there is stigma about counseling in their home country (remember, mental health stigma is alive and well in the United States, too!). Acknowledging this courage is paramount to the forward movement of their relationship. It's important to remember that the counseling profession continues to develop differently in various countries around the world (Hohenshil et al., 2015); thus, how the counseling profession has been introduced and is accepted varies across cultures. To this end, for a counselor working with a client who is an immigrant, refugee, or a member of a diaspora, learning what the client knows about counseling and honoring what is shared while inviting them to learn how the counseling relationship can unfold is critical to developing a strong therapeutic alliance. For example, an immigrant couple that comes for couples counseling may share the nuances of their journey in arriving to see you. Part of their story may include the initial efforts of formally calling on their parents, community elders, or religious leaders to help them work through their relationship difficulties. These calculated interventions that may be rooted in collectivist worldviews can be honored as informal counseling that may still have ongoing use as support systems and part of ongoing treatment for this couple. Thus, there's a need for counselors to genuinely honor their clients' help-seeking methods and use them to bolster the work they do together.
- ***Trust is layered.*** Clients seeking help about a personal matter from a stranger (i.e., the counselor) is not always common in many countries and cultures. Understand that for some immigrants, refugees, or a member of a diaspora, trust is mostly given to those who have earned it from years of being known by the client and their family, being a respected and experienced elder, and/or being named as trustworthy by community leaders. Your

title as a counselor, your graduate degree, or your state license are not always enough to build trust. These credentials can help clients acknowledge that you are a trained professional—that's one of the layers of trust—but for some, the deeper level of trust to share one's deepest personal life matters is seen as a sacred endeavor. Counselors must be present and display patience and genuineness to deepen trust. This kind of relationship might be the only relationship the client has ever formed where such personal matters were shared outside their family/community, so acknowledging its newness and unique structure is relevant for the counseling relationship.

Disregarding how *odd* the counseling relationship feels or displaying impatience can lead to the client feeling dismissed or the counselor wrongly assessing a client as noncommittal or unresponsive to counseling. While genuineness, patience, and curiosity are key to building the therapeutic alliance, counselors have a responsibility to find culturally competent support and resources.

- ***I didn't share that detail because I couldn't.*** Counselors are trained to be prepared to listen to difficult elements of clients' lives via the lens of unconditional positive regard and nonjudgment. However, just because counselors are prepared to hear challenging content doesn't mean clients are ready to discuss it. A key consideration in building the counseling relationship with immigrants, refugees, and members of the diaspora is to acknowledge that taboo topics exist (Harrichand et al., 2020). What makes some of the taboo discussion scenarios difficult is that the counselor might be unaware that a topic is taboo. Some of these topics may be related to certain practices within their religion, sexuality, rituals surrounding the end of life and dying, the birthing process, or unspoken elements of family visa status. The ongoing practice of the counselor to treat their client with dignity, compassion, and respect are paramount to carrying the embryotic counseling relationship to a mature stage at which the client might be open to sharing a private matter that they could not disclose initially. A client might leave out significant information in an intake and initial session because they find it challenging or inappropriate to communicate the taboo topic with their counselor. It does not mean that the client was lying to the counselor; it might simply be that this autonomous client chose to leave out significant information because it was not fitting to share at the time. If or when the taboo topic is finally uttered, a counselor's gratitude for being trusted by the client is necessary.
- ***Majority-turned-minority identity is confusing and complex.*** Clients who are immigrants, refugees, or members of a diaspora often come from being part of a majority cultural group in their home countries where they *fit* with those of their community as far as being citizens, sharing the same cultural values, and being known, accepted, and having a secure sense of belonging. Moving to a new country shifts their identity to a minoritized one in which, perhaps for the very first time, they are faced with discrimination based on race, socioeconomic status, religious expression, and/or language (Chacko, 2019). As such, clients might need to process the grief of their lost identity and work on navigating the need to prove their sense of worth and value, who they are, and what they

can accomplish. For example, it is not uncommon for trained professionals and experts, like engineers, counselors, or medical doctors who are successfully trained in rigorous academic programs in their home countries to be required to redo their graduate degrees partially or fully for their academic and work experience to be considered equivalent to their professional counterparts in the Americas. Therefore, it is important for counselors to infuse culturally responsive career counseling models in treatment, focus on adjustments linked to loss and grief of a past majority identity, and participate in ongoing advocacy initiatives for relevant community resources for these minoritized clients.

- ***Love is the greatest, but it is culturally defined.*** Empathy, support, and care are essential components in the counseling relationship. Counselors are trained to demonstrate these qualities to build a strong client-counselor relationship, yet how counselors deliver empathy, support, and care can vary culturally. For example, some clients may express feeling supported and normalized when the counselor names specific feelings they are experiencing, while others may find it off-putting. Pay attention to the client's nonverbal and verbal cues, and when in doubt, ask.

  Additionally, cultural definitions of love and care among family members and romantic partners are varied. It's important to respect and honor clients' autonomy and culturally bound expressions within relationships. Learn more about low-context and high-context cultures—this will inform you about whether direct verbal communication or body language is typically used. Additionally, hearing varied examples of how families and communities around the world express care for one another can broaden your knowledge and skills about different expressions of care.

Needs, Challenges, and Barriers Related to Counseling

The ongoing stress that most immigrants/refugees face is well documented. Migration stress can induce feelings of depression and anxiety, influence migration-related trauma (Perreira & Ornelas, 2013), and increase interpersonal violence (Page et al., 2017). Most refugees and asylum seekers are desperate to leave their countries of origin because of violence and lack of economic opportunity (Beltran, 2017; Donato & Perez, 2017); however, these challenges often remain even after arriving in the new host country. Persistent threats, fear of deportation, racism, and poverty isolate immigrants, refugees, and asylum seekers because barriers to assistance become too difficult to overcome.

According to Meyers (2016), many immigrants do not seek counseling simply because they are unaware of the services provided by professional counselors or because they lack an understanding of how mental health services work in the host country. Furthermore, language barriers, a shortage of bilingual counselors or language interpreters, and the lack of culturally competent counselors can add to the limitations of accessing counseling services for immigrants (Rogers-Sirin et al., 2015; Villalba, 2009). Some immigrants experience discrimination in the health-care system, which can lead to them avoiding or delaying the use of counseling services (da Silva Rebelo et al., 2018).

Ethical Considerations: Putting It Into Practice

Based on the numerous challenges experienced by immigrants and refugees, it is likely that mental health services will increasingly be used as these groups continue to grow and immigrants/refugees become more knowledgeable about what counseling can offer them (Snow et al., 2021); therefore, counselors will be required to tend to the varying needs of these populations and practice accordingly. Ethical considerations are paramount because many immigrants, refugees, or members of a diaspora group will enter counseling with a history of discrimination and barriers to accessing support (da Silva Rebelo et al., 2018). The American Counseling Association's (ACA) *Code of Ethics* (2014), American School Counselor Association (ASCA) *Ethical Standards for School Counselors* (2022), and the Commission on Rehabilitation Counselor Certification (CRC) *Code of Professional Ethics* (2023) all address the counselor's need to maintain awareness and sensitivity to the cultural meanings of counseling, confidentiality, and consent because differing views of disclosure may occur (*ACA Section B.1.a; ASCA Section A.2.b; CRC Section B.1.c*). Considering these groups will likely experience language, programmatic, and physical barriers, competent counselors must do the following:

1. Identify what barriers are occurring (ACA Section A.7.b; ASCA Section B.3.i; CRC Section C.2.c).

Many immigrants and refugees are unfamiliar with the services available in their new host country (Beltran, 2017; Donato & Perez, 2017). When entering the host country, discrimination and cultural incompetence can impede access to necessary services (da Silva Rebelo et al., 2018). Counselors must become aware of the different levels at which barriers occur to address them appropriately (e.g., immigration status, access to health care, language barriers, economic barriers).

2. Develop a plan to address barriers and increase access to services (ACA Section A.11a; ASCA Section C.b; CRC Section C.2.a).

In the United States, polarizing views on the U.S. immigration system continue to impact immigrants'/refugees' lives and well-being (Oliphant & Cerda, 2022). Counselors must continue to build connections at the micro and macro levels and advocate for an increase in access to education, medical and mental health services, and economic opportunity. Plans can include contacting policymakers, providing educational workshops to providers about this population's needs, and seeking consultation.

3. Sensitively and appropriately sharing information with clients about assessments (ACA Section E.3.a), attending workshops/trainings (ACA Section F.7.c; ASCA Section B.2.p; CRC Section L.1.d), diagnoses (ACA Section E.5.c; CRC H.3.a), and creating a culturally attuned counseling relationship (ACA Section A.2.c; ASCA Section B.3.k; CRC Section A.3.c).

As mentioned earlier in the chapter, terms used to label immigrants, refugees, and diasporas can be dehumanizing; therefore, counselors are tasked with using culturally sensitive language with immigrant/refugee clients. When selecting, administering, and interpreting assessments—especially assessments that involve a diagnosis—counselors must investigate who the assessments were normed on and whether they are appropriate for immigrants/refugees while administering them in a culturally informed way. By doing so, counselors create a welcoming therapeutic environment while building and maintaining the counseling relationship. Acceptable social interactions may also differ depending on cultural background, and counselors must be aware of how these interactions might affect the counseling relationship.

Additionally, because people of a diaspora group may be geographically settled in one area while their roots are still within their original culture, counselors need to (1) engage in relevant training/professional development opportunities to learn about the client's original culture, (2) use broaching skills to discuss such topics, (3) use supervision, and (4) seek consultation in order to ensure that clinical terminology is communicated in the most humanizing manner.

4. Provide necessary language services (such as a qualified interpreter or translator) to ensure the client comprehends their rights and can communicate fully with the counselor (*ACA Section A. 2.c; ASCA A.2.b; CRC A.1.e, A.3.c*).

In addition to the barriers that language may cause in accessing services (Rogers-Sirin et al., 2015), counselors are ethically required to self-reflect on their own experiences of counseling immigrants, refugees, and diasporas, and increase awareness of how those experiences might influence their work with clients (Harrichand et al., 2020; Harrichand et al., 2022). Then, counselors are better equipped to respect the rights of clients to make their own decisions based on their cultural identity and belief systems (*CRC A.1.e*) and to adjust practices accordingly. The counselor takes responsibility for using resources in counseling sessions to facilitate communication, such as family members or support systems for interpretation or by using verified interpreter services, in addition to engaging in ongoing discussions regarding client rights.

In addition to the ACA, ASCA, and CRC ethical codes for practice, other counseling organizations offer similar directions for counselors. The National Board for Certified Counselors (NBCC; 2023) and the American Mental Health Counselors Association (AMHCA; 2020) urge counselors to be actively involved in educating themselves about clients' cultural backgrounds (*AMHCA Section I.C.1.m*). Additionally, when counselors lack the knowledge and skills for competent counseling, they must seek consultation to promote the welfare of clients (*NBCC 31*). It is important that counselors and counselors in training invest the time and effort to learn the different ethical codes and standards required for their particular scope of practice. Concurrently, they must become increasingly aware of their own attitudes, beliefs, and biases that may stem from their own enculturation (Harrichand et al., 2020) and actively engage in systematic social justice initiatives to broaden access to mental health services and other health-care systems.

Multicultural and Social Justice Counseling Competencies

The MSJCCs (Ratts et al., 2015) provide a framework that can be applied to working with immigrants and refugees. As you learned in Chapter 5, counselors use the MSJCCs in four developmental domains: (1) counselor self-awareness, (2) client worldview, (3) counseling relationship, and (4) counseling and advocacy interventions (Ratts et al., 2015). Using culturally responsive evaluation skills, counselors seek to understand how socio-historical events and current social issues influence both counselors' and clients' beliefs, biases, cultural backgrounds, values, worldviews, and experiences of privilege and oppression (Harrichand et al., 2020).

When applying the MSJCCs (Ratts et al., 2015) with immigrant and refugee clients, counselors acknowledge their commitment to practice from a multicultural framework rooted in social justice. Regarding counselor self-awareness, it is important that counselors consider their own attitudes, beliefs, and biases. Counselor self-awareness may take the form of examining the beliefs of their own ethnic and national origins, for example, What privileges do I hold because of my ethnic and/or national origins? Alternatively, what forms of oppression do I experience, if any, because of my ethnic and/or national origins? Counselors may ask themselves, What are my beliefs and values with regard to working with immigrant or refugee clients? By practicing from a critically conscious framework, counselors are likely to be more sensitive to systems of oppression and privilege they experience as a result of their identities and the extent to which their beliefs influence their worldview.

When counselors are working with clients with whom they share ethnic or national origins, it is important for them not to assume that they have the same perspectives, worldviews, and beliefs based on their shared country of origin. For example, it must not be assumed that because the counselor and client are from Ukraine they share the same lived experience; it is likely that they differ in some way such as age, religion, sex, and education, to name a few—all of which may impact the counseling relationship at some level.

In relation to action, the counselor should be aware of how their prior counseling experiences working with immigrant and refugee clients might influence their communication with a current immigrant or refugee client (Harrichand et al., 2020). For example, counselors should not assume that because they have previous experience working with Syrian refugees that their knowledge will necessarily make prepare them to work with Ukrainian refugees. Similarly, each Syrian refugee has different experiences, so while there may be similarities, counselors cannot assume they *know* the client's experience based on prior clients' reports.

Counselors need to grasp the worldviews of immigrants and refugees, the ways in which they experience systems of privilege and oppression, and how these experiences shape their attitudes and beliefs. Overview knowledge can be accessed through research, such as intentionally learning about the challenges immigrants and refugees experienced in their home countries and how those challenges might exist and/or be magnified while living in another country. However, this is simply overview information. The best source of information regarding the *impact* will be each client's narrative. Counselors use critical thinking and analysis to understand the oppressive forces of power and privilege impacting the immigrant or refugee client and how those forces might be influencing the client's overall well-being (Harrichand et al., 2020).

Additionally, counselors must be sensitive to the privileged and oppressed statuses of both client and counselor and how they might influence the therapeutic relationship. Counselors must be mindful of their biases and expectations when working with immigrant and refugee clients, especially regarding acceptable cultural cues and customs. For example, as a male counselor, how might you respond to a female immigrant or refugee client who does not accept physical touch (including handshakes) from non-family members? Or a male immigrant or refugee client who greets with a physical embrace instead of a handshake? Counselors may choose to participate in continuing education opportunities such as immersion experiences, webinars, workshops, peer supervision, and consultation. Once the counselor gains insight and awareness regarding their beliefs and values related to working with immigrant and refugee clients and they address the dynamics of power, privilege, and oppression operating in the therapeutic relationship, they are then positioned to use culturally responsive interventions with their clients, with the focus of promoting social justice (Harrichand et al., 2020).

I-CARE Model

The I-CARE model of advocacy was developed to assist counselors with maneuvering challenges and barriers when working with clients living in poverty (Foss-Kelly et al., 2017). Despite its development for working with clients living in poverty, the I-CARE model can be applied to working with immigrant and refugee clients and communities as well.

I – Internal reflection
C – Cultivate a strong relationship
A – Acknowledge realities
R – Remove barriers
E – Expand on client strengths

Internally Reflect

Counselors are encouraged to understand immigrants' and refugees' diverse backgrounds, including socioeconomic positionalities, to assist them in exploring possible socioeconomic stress on their well-being. Foss-Kelly et al. (2017) encouraged counselors to recognize how bias can be a barrier to connecting and building a strong therapeutic relationship with clients and that counselors must actively seek to reconcile any discrepancies with the aim of meeting the needs of and caring for their clients. Counselors seeking to explore the economic heritage of their immigrant and refugee clients are encouraged to ask the following questions adapted from Foss-Kelly et al. (2017), which could inform the counselor of their own internalized classism and beliefs about immigrants/refugees:

- What did my caregivers teach me about immigrants or refugees living with poverty versus wealth?
- Was I excluded or rejected by social groups because of my social status as an immigrant or refugee?
- Was I denied or granted important life experiences or opportunities as an immigrant or refugee?

Counselors who explore the economic heritage of their immigrant and refugee clients might also collaborate with them in developing a financial status timeline that provides key information related to income-related events and accompanying emotions, beliefs, or symbols associated with the role income plays/played in each stage of the client's life (i.e., from home to host country).

BOX 9.5 **PROFILE OF A PRACTITIONER: CLAUDETTE BROWN-SMYTHE**

My name is Claudette Brown-Smythe, and I am Jamaican with American citizenship (Jam-Merican). I am a counselor educator, a licensed mental health counselor, national certified counselor, certified rehabilitation counselor, and an approved clinical supervisor. My ethnic identity was solidified before my migration to the United States. However, on arrival, it continued to be shaped through relationships with my extended family, which included blood and non-blood relationships. My family celebrates holidays and has random get-togethers. We bond over food specifically creating our traditional dishes and sharing stories. Important to all these relationships is our Christian faith. When I arrived here, one of my uncles would call me to check in, but the conversation never ended without encouragement and reminding me of the guidance and faith of my grandmother and mother. This remains true in conversations with my aunts and siblings to this day.

My ethnic identity informs my professional identity and is intertwined. My family for many generations were paraprofessional counselors serving their communities, so a lot of the techniques use of metaphors, humor, narrative styles, and advocacy are things I observed and learned from them. Advocacy and seeking justice for individuals who are marginalized is second nature, whether working alongside them or engaging in advocacy efforts on their behalf. Given the importance of faith, I integrate spirituality and explore this in all the courses I have taught as well as address spirituality in my counseling. My research is also centered on spiritual issues. As intricate as my intersections are, I am intentionally aware of not interpreting the narratives and life experiences of my clients based on my own beliefs and practices.

Cultivating Relationship

Widely regarded as the foundation of effective counseling, the counseling relationship is one of the common therapeutic factors associated with client change and the development of trust. The counseling relationship can be compromised based on the increased vulnerability that immigrant and refugee clients may feel in counseling. Because these populations are at a greater risk of experiencing discrimination, especially when navigating mental health and social service settings, they might have heightened sensitivity to feeling judged and/or rejected (Snow et al., 2021). Further, there is a high probability that immigrant and refugee clients may feel inferior to and/or uncomfortable with their counselor within the therapeutic relationship, which could be because of any number of reasons (e.g., language, ethnicity, immigration status, socioeconomic status, religion/spirituality, education level, shame, embarrassment). As a result of this potential power differential, the counselor is charged with the responsibility of broaching (i.e., acknowledging and monitoring) socio-cultural differences related to power. It is important for counselors to work collaboratively with clients in establishing mutually agreed-upon goals and to explore what it means to develop a therapeutic, professional counseling relationship.

Acknowledge Realities

Tt is important for counselors to understand and acknowledge immigrants' and refugees' lived realities. It is entirely possible for clients to arrive to counseling sessions hungry, and/or they might have also traveled long distances via public transit or by foot in various weather conditions. Immigrant and refugee clients may experience physical and emotional fatigue, in addition to insufficient housing and unsafe neighborhoods, limited health care, child- or eldercare struggles, limited access to quality education because of inadequate schools, limited career opportunities and job training, and limited access to transportation (Foss-Kelly et al., 2017). These barriers are further compounded by racism/xenomisia for immigrant and refugee families who are racial and/or ethnic minorities. Counselors must acknowledge these likely realities instead of dismissing their concerns as less relevant than mental health issues because basic needs *are* mental health concerns! Counselors can employ Maslow's (1970) hierarchy of needs as a form of psychoeducation (and learn from it themselves!) to understand how clients' lived experiences (i.e., challenges) can negatively impact other areas of functioning and aid in setting goals based on their specific economic and emotional needs (Foss-Kelly et al., 2017). It is by meeting the client where they are and validating their reality that the counselor is positioned to develop a strong therapeutic alliance and provide holistic treatment (Foss-Kelly et al., 2017).

Remove Barriers

It is only after the counselor and client acknowledge the realities of clients' lives that they can begin to identify the barriers to achieving success that are impeding growth and healing. According to Foss-Kelly et al. (2017), "barriers can be related to client attitudes or to larger system considerations" (p. 207). Access to treatment is part of these barriers that counselors can remove (e.g., limited transportation, lack of funding, conflicting schedules with work, and lack of childcare, among other issues). Counselors can help clients secure transportation to and from counseling (e.g., bus passes), offer in-home counseling or community counseling where the client lives, provide childcare options, and offer flexible scheduling of counseling sessions (Goodman et al., 2013). In this, counselors can alleviate stigma and shame by validating their clinical concerns and by infusing concrete interventions that focus on the problems of daily living they experience (Goodman et al., 2013).

Expand on Strengths

Harper et al. (2015) stated that clients who live in poverty, which can include immigrants and refugees, need to have a skill set superseding those needed by financially privileged individuals. It can be particularly challenging for immigrants and refugees to navigate public assistance systems because of language barriers and limited knowledge (Snow et al., 2021), which can be a "labyrinth of confusing documents, contradictory information, deadlines, and waiting lists" (Foss-Kelly et al., 2017, p. 208). Counselors are encouraged to carefully assess for strengths clients possess, especially those related to their survival and persistence, and use them as the foundation from which to dismantle other barriers they experience. One way counselors can empower clients is to have them discuss specific values related to living a meaningful life (e.g., values related to family, spirituality, and/or engaging in pleasurable activities) and encourage them to engage in activities that support meaning in their lives, if even only for a few minutes a day.

Resiliencies, Strengths, and Fostering Wellness: Stories and Counseling Implications

The following is a personal story of a refugee who came to the United States seeking safety from a war-torn country of origin. After the story, we explore counseling implications using a culturally sensitive model to foster resilience, strengths, and wellness.

BOX 9.6 **PAUSE AND REFLECT: BELIEFS ABOUT IMMIGRANTS AND REFUGEES**

Prior to reading the client vignette, pause and reflect:

What are your beliefs and biases about immigrants and refugees?
What do you believe about immigrants/refugees and their journey?
What do you suppose their background may be like (e.g., family, religion, education)?
Do you hold any beliefs or biases about the countries from which they come?

Note any strong beliefs that arise and explore whether any of these beliefs might be biased. If so, discern how you will address them so they will not impede your work. Who are trusted professionals you can speak with to help you in your process?

Story of Volodymyr

Volodymyr is a 16-year-old Ukrainian male who moved with his parents and younger sister to the United States from Ukraine following Russia's invasion of their home country. In the invasion, his family's home was destroyed, along with everything they owned. His parents, both of whom have siblings residing in different U.S. states, were encouraged to travel to the United States and seek refugee status on the grounds of fear of persecution and serious harm if they returned to Ukraine. Upon their arrival to the United States, Volodymyr shared that the immigration officer expressed little empathy for their situation and instead demanded "proof" that their home was completely destroyed. After hours of being held at the airport for questioning, Volodymyr and his family were finally released into the care of his mother's older brother who resides in Queens, New York.

Although Volodymyr and his family were granted permission to remain in the United States as refugees, he shared that he continues to experience frequent nightmares from witnessing his home destroyed by the Russian invasion. He recalls seeing neighbors and livestock severely hurt, and some people were reported missing and presumed dead because of the war. Both he and his sister were able to register in school, but Volodymyr stated that he finds it challenging to adjust to life in the United States, such as not being able to make new friends because his classmates keep telling him, "Your accent is funny and difficult to understand."

Volodymyr's parents are thankful for the support of his uncle; however, he is not able to provide much for the family, as he is the breadwinner for his own family. Volodymyr shared that his parents were experiencing difficulties navigating social services in New York; he recalled his dad expressing frustration with the process of obtaining resources to support his family and having an agent tell him, "You people keep benefiting from taxpayers' money, but you don't seem to want to look for meaningful work." This statement has become Volodymyr's motivation to rise above his challenges in hopes of a better future for himself and his family. Still, there are several challenges he and his family continue to experience as refugees.

Reflection Questions

1. What steps would you take initially to address Volodymyr's concerns?
2. What resources exist in your area that could be helpful for Volodymyr?
3. Based on the beliefs/biases you identified earlier, did you notice them arising as you read Volodymyr's story?

Counseling Implication for Volodymyr: I-CARE Model

Using the I-CARE model (Foss-Kelly et al., 2017) with Volodymyr, counselors must first reflect on their own experiences of witnessing the invasion of Ukraine (*internally reflect*). For example, "What did my parents teach me about a person's freedom (or lack of freedom)? How did that affect my reaction to the events that occurred in Ukraine? Did I have any personal experience with the tragedy that occurred?"

After reflecting, the counselor must recognize the vulnerability that Volodymyr might experience and any power differentials he may feel in the therapeutic relationship (*cultivate relationship*). For example, Volodymyr's father has been told that he is taking advantage of social services and they must "prove" they qualify for refugee status. Furthermore, seeking refugee status can bring several challenges for refugees when arriving in a host country. Volodymyr tells the counselor that his entire family has survived a traumatic event, Russia's invasion of Ukraine, which destroyed their home. Volodymyr is haunted by images of his neighbors and livestock being severely hurt and/or dying. It is vitally important to use a trauma-informed approach to work with Volodymyr. In brief, a trauma-informed counseling approach is marked by establishing safety in the counseling environment, maintaining trustworthiness, transparency, and collaboration in the therapeutic relationship, encouraging peer support, empowering the client(s), and recognizing/addressing issues of culture, history, and gender (Substance Abuse and Mental Health Services Administration, 2014). Murray and colleagues (2010) encouraged mental health providers to acknowledge but not overemphasize the trauma and trauma symptoms experienced by clients and instead work to understand clients' experiences and challenges with resettlement to their host country, seeking to foster strength and resilience.

It is important for counselors to use available research on counseling Ukrainian people (Bowen, 2011; Riabchuk, 2015; Van Lith et al., 2017) and cautiously apply it to Ukrainian refugees. Riabchuk

(2015) posited that the shift from the collectivist mindset that was forced during the Soviet era to more of an individualistic mindset is one that can create cultural identity confusion for Ukrainians. When Joseph Stalin came to power, the previous use of psychotherapy that was prevalent with Sigman Freud's influence was soon considered to be against the principles of the communist state that valued collectivism over individualism (Bowen, 2011). Subsequently, all forms of psychotherapy were banned, and even as recently as 2017, when Van Lith et al. (2017) explored art therapy with Ukrainian adolescents, identity confusion persisted (*acknowledge realities*), corroborating previous studies that highlighted help-seeking behaviors among the Ukrainian people were still quite low (Bowen, 2011; Yankovsky, 2011).

It is important for counselors to seek to understand family and cultural norms and expectations. For example, school counselors might consider helping Volodymyr secure additional support related to language skills and mentoring to aid in his adjustment to the U.S. educational system (*remove barriers*) while finding ways to celebrate his language and cultural heritage through educating his peers and teachers on cultural sensitivity, acceptance, and the motivation that helps Volodymyr and his family persist through tragedy and transition (*Expand on Strengths*). Clinical mental health counselors can work to advocate for Volodymyr and his family through social justice efforts seeking to minimize and dismantle racism and discrimination experienced by peers and professionals (e.g., social service agents) who are expected to provide support to families in need, like Volodymyr's, instead of criticizing and/or judging them for conditions beyond their control (Morrison et al., 2015).

Conclusion

Counseling can provide immigrants and refugees with a safe space to uncover, process, and resolve feelings of guilt and shame, leading to growth (Meyers, 2016). Counselors using approaches like the I-CARE model have the capacity to communicate value and respect for the humanity of the immigrant or refugee client and confidence in their ability to cope with challenging life circumstances more effectively. By actively engaging their clients throughout the counseling process, the counselor instills hope that they have the capacity to be successful in counseling (Foss-Kelly et al., 2017).

Questions for Reflection

1. What are some of the needs and challenges of immigrants and refugees related to counseling?
2. How might you apply the MSJCCs to a client who is an immigrant or a refugee?
3. What are some challenges or barriers that immigrants or refugees face? How might you work with those barriers in counseling?
4. What are some strengths or resiliencies that immigrants or refugees face? How might you work with those strengths and resiliencies in counseling?

5. Describe your counselor identity; how might that influence your counseling with immigrants and refugees?

Applying What You Have Learned

Complete each of the following activities, considering what you learned from this chapter.

Activity #1: Research and Discuss—Immigration in a Global Context

Although this chapter focuses on immigrants and refugees to the United States, the issues presented are not exclusive to one country, as migration is part of the story of nearly every nation. Research the topics of global immigration and the refugee crises around the world. Then, respond to the questions below. Be prepared to share the information you gather with others.

1. What did you find? For example, look at the current refugee crisis impacting Europe and detail what you find, in particular, related to counseling issues.
2. What resources for immigrants and refugees exist in your area? Research online to locate as many resources as you can, especially counseling resources.
3. If you cannot locate many resources, what resources would you create or wish to find in your community if you were a counselor working with these populations?

Activity #2: Identifying and Responding to Xenomisia

Xenomisia is not a new phenomenon in U.S. culture; in fact, it arrived on the Mayflower and has continued ever since. While different forms of xenomisia wax and wane depending on what events are happening at the time, the fact is that it continues to be pervasive and damaging.

Identify ways in which xenomisia is demonstrated within the contexts you inhabit. Examples might include school, work, places of worship, places of business, during your commute, or even in your home. Once you identify manifestations of xenomisia, determine what you want to do about it. How would you like to intervene to be part of eradicating xenomistic behaviors? What is one thing you can do *today*?

Credit

IMG 9.2: Copyright © by Quinn Dombrowski (CC BY 2.0) at https://commons.wikimedia.org/wiki/File:Jesus_is_Real.jpg.

CHAPTER 10 

Indigenous, Native, First Nations Groups, and Settler Colonialism

Christine Park, Brynn Luger, and Laurie "Lali" McCubbin

Not only are Indigenous people forced to shoulder the burden of colonialism; we are expected to celebrate it.

—Tanya Tagaq

CHAPTER OVERVIEW

Indigenous and Native persons are the original inhabitants of our lands. The history and culture of these original persons are essential to understanding the foundation of our modern society. In the United States, Native populations are diverse, yet there are common threads that connect Indigenous groups, including values, spirituality, land, loss, pain, trauma, and resilience. U.S. Native groups include Alaska Natives, First Nations, Native Americans, and *Kānaka'Ōiwi* (Native Hawaiian), along with Indigenous populations from Polynesia and the Pacific and Mariana Islands, such as Chamorro, Guam, and the Mariana Islands. We write this chapter from an Indigenous lens, mainly focusing on Native Hawaiian and Native American/American Indian cultures: *Kānaka 'Ōiwi*, *Kama'āina* (of the land-Hawai'i), and the *Očeti šakówiŋ* (The Great Sioux Nation). While we have our own ***lived experiences***, we recognize that our perspectives are not representative of all Indigenous persons and cultures as a whole. Native terms, concepts, and ideas are embedded throughout this chapter. Pronunciation is not included so that you can engage more fully with the material by researching the correct pronunciation of the words and language used. Additionally, Indigenous languages encompass a broad umbrella of peoples and geography spanning the U.S. nation and beyond into Oceania and thus represent multiple distinct languages and are outside the scope of this chapter. Aspects of Native and Indigenous history, models, practices, and considerations will be covered; however, there is much more to know and understand than what can be addressed in this chapter, so keep learning beyond it! We embedded stories and activities throughout, and we offer resources at the end of the chapter so you can embark on a deeper and richer learning journey.

In traditional Indigenous ways of practice, knowledge is passed on to stewards of knowledge and tradition. As the receiver of information, it is your ***kuleana*** (responsibility) to make meaning of the information presented and to seek further knowledge to transfer this information into your practice of being a culturally relevant counselor. As such, we will discuss the relationship between cultural/historical trauma and settler colonialism on mental health, which are central to the experiences of Indigenous and Native peoples. Additionally, you will learn about Native and Indigenous worldviews and values, and models of well-being associated with Indigenous peoples, including resilience and the resurgence of Native and Indigenous groups. Please note that because Native and Indigenous worldviews account for how systems interact at multiple levels and the impact that they have, we do not discuss Bronfenbrenner's ecological model like other chapter authors have. Finally, we discuss culturally relevant and sensitive healing strategies, practices, and implications.

LEARNING OBJECTIVES

By the end of this chapter, students will be able to

1. describe the relationship between historical trauma and settler colonialism on mental health,
2. list and apply Native and Indigenous worldviews and values in counseling,
3. discuss models of well-being relating to Indigenous peoples, and
4. use Indigenous, culturally relevant, and culturally sensitive healing strategies and practices.

CACREP 2016 STANDARDS

The information in this chapter supports the following standards:

- 2.F.2.a. multicultural and pluralistic characteristics within and among diverse groups nationally and internationally
- 2.F.2.b. Theories and models of multicultural counseling, cultural identity development, and social justice and advocacy
- 2.F.2.c. multicultural counseling competencies
- 2.F.2.d. the impact of heritage, attitudes, beliefs, understandings, and acculturative experiences on an individual's views of others
- 2.F.2.e. the effects of power and privilege for counselors and clients
- 2.F.2.g. The impact of spiritual beliefs on clients' and counselors' worldviews
- 2.F.2.h. Strategies for identifying and eliminating barriers, prejudices, and processes of intentional and unintentional oppression and discrimination

CACREP 2024 STANDARDS

The information in this chapter supports the following standards:

- 3.B.1. theories and models of multicultural counseling, social justice, and advocacy
- 3.B.2. the influence of heritage, cultural identities, attitudes, values, beliefs, understandings, within-group differences, and acculturative experiences on individuals' worldviews
- 3.B.3. the influence of heritage, cultural identities, attitudes, values, beliefs, understandings, within-group differences, and acculturative experiences on help-seeking and coping behaviors
- 3.B.4. the effects of historical events, multigenerational trauma, and current issues on diverse cultural groups in the U.S. and globally
- 3.B.5. the effects of stereotypes, overt and covert discrimination, racism, power, oppression, privilege, marginalization, microaggressions, and violence on counselors and clients
- 3.B.6. the effects of various socio-cultural influences, including public policies, social movements, and cultural values, on mental and physical health and wellness
- 3.B.7. disproportional effects of poverty, income disparities, and health disparities toward people with marginalized identities
- 3.B.11. the role of religion and spirituality in clients' and counselors' psychological functioning

Understanding the Historical Context of Indigenous and Native People's Experiences

The terms *Indigenous* and *Native* refer to the land's original inhabitants and their descendants. Indigenous peoples of the United States include (a) Native American/American Indians, (b) Inuit/Alaska Natives, and (c) Pacific Islanders, including Native Hawaiians. Indigenous populations worldwide are referenced by the names relevant to their cultures/nation of origin, including Aboriginal (Australia and New Zealand) and First Nations (Canada), among others. For the purposes of this chapter, we use Indigenous and Native interchangeably to refer to the original peoples of the United States. It should be noted that the boundaries of the United States and Canada come from processes of colonization that have and continue to impact Native peoples' lives and identities significantly while they continue to have thriving cultures, languages, governments/leadership structures, and ways of knowing prior to colonial contact. The United States has close to 600 federally recognized American Indian and Alaska Native tribes (Redmond & Gittelsohn, 2019); however, not all Indigenous people have federal tribal recognition, such as Native Hawaiians.

European colonization resulted in politics and practices of oppression and forced assimilation of Indigenous peoples (Nutton & Fast 2015). Additionally, it had detrimental impacts, including the introduction of infectious diseases from which Indigenous populations had no natural immunity. Epidemics of cholera, influenza, whooping cough, smallpox, Hansen's disease, measles, mumps, diphtheria, and tuberculosis swept through Native populations after contact and colonization (Kahol-okula et al., 2019; Nutton & Fast, 2015; Sotero, 2006). In North America and the State of Hawai'i, Indigenous populations declined by 90%–95% after 100 years of colonization, resulting in cultural genocide of Indigenous peoples. Other forms of oppression related to cultural genocide include the criminalization of Indigenous practices, policies forbidding Indigenous languages to be spoken/taught, outlawing cultural practices or culturally reappropriating customs in the name of Christianity, and forced geographic relocation of families (Brave Heart & Debruyn, 1998; Episkenew, 2009; Frideres & Gadacz, 2011; Lutz, 2009; Morse, 1985; Royal Commission on Aboriginal Peoples, 1996).

The historical traumatization that resulted from the loss and misuse of ancestral land carries weight as the land itself has cultural and spiritual significance to Indigenous populations (Duponte et al., 2010; Rezentes III, 1996). The holistic connection to environment, land, and spaces is woven into Indigenous perspectives (MacKenzie et al., 2007). The United States has an indelible history of forcibly removing Native Americans from their homes and relocating them to land that the American government had *set aside*—that is, *reserved* for them, resulting in the term *Reservation*. Often, this was land that was underdeveloped and far removed from original Native spaces. Additionally, for Native persons and communities, this loss of land paralleled a loss of identity. Indigenous lifestyles and practices are connected to the land, spaces, and environment. Therefore, some Native clients may not truly know where they are from or feel that their sense of connectedness has been lost.

Indigenous historical trauma (IHT) differs from other types of psychological trauma in four fundamental ways: (a) the colonial origins of the trauma, (b) the collective impact of this trauma on generations of Indigenous peoples, (c) the cumulation of events, and (d) the cross-generational effects on risk and vulnerability, including contemporary health status (Hartmann & Gone, 2014).

IHT results in health disparities among Native populations, including poor health status and indicators because of the accumulation of disease and social distress across succeeding generations (Sotero, 2006). This conceptualization of historical trauma was first developed by Maria Yellow Horse Brave Heart to describe the causal contributions of colonization on behavioral health among Native Americans/American Indians (Hartmann et al., 2019). Brave Heart (1998, 2003) classified historical trauma as the emotional and psychological wounding occurring across generations of people that results from a massive group trauma. According to Brave Heart and colleagues (2011), historical trauma theory frames trauma across the lifespan in the collective and historical context while indicating factors of how survivors at communal and individual levels reduce stigma and isolation. The subsequent response to historical trauma has been referred to as historical unresolved grief (Brave Heart et al., 2011), the soul wound, and intergenerational trauma (Duran, 2019). Using this framework, Brave Heart (1998) blended psychoanalytic theories of trauma with Indigenous cultural understandings of a loss of land, language, and culture.

By recognizing historical trauma, preventive efforts to mitigate its impact can help to improve the health of Native populations and allow for an expanded perspective of community interventions and protective factors (Hartmann et al., 2019). Sotero (2006) provided numerous examples of how historical trauma is connected to diseases, social determinants of health, and the interplay of ecological factors affecting health. They identified empirically supported pathways for how trauma might be passed on across generations (i.e., intergenerational trauma). According to Sotero, these include the following:

- Impairments in the capacity for parenting (Danieli, 1998)
- Impairments in genetic function and expression through in utero biological adaptations or environmental risk factors (Aboriginal Healing Foundation, 2004; Barker, 1992; Benyshek & Danieli, 1998; Emanuel et al., 1992; Feliit et al., 1998; McClellen et al., 2006; Ravelli et al., 1976)
- Disorders such as mental illness, depression, and PTSD can be genetically transmitted to secondary and subsequent generations (Eisenberg, 2001; McClellen et al., 2006; McMichael, 1999)
- Maternal malnutrition (Tulchinsky & Varavikova, 2000)
- Maternal care and depressive states as major determinants of endocrine and behavioral stress responses in offspring (Eisenberg, 2001; Lupien et al., & McEwen, 2000)
- Maladaptive behaviors and related social problems such as substance abuse, physical/sexual abuse, and suicide directly traumatize offspring and are indirectly transmitted through learned behavior, perpetuating the intergenerational cycle of trauma (Danieli, 1998; DeBruyn et al., 2001; Ehrensaft et al., 2003; Manson et al., 2005; Koss et al., 2003)
- Vicarious traumatization through collective memory, storytelling, and oral traditions
- Experiencing ancestral pain and issues of unresolved grief, persecution, and distrust
- Experience original trauma through loss of culture and language and proximal factors such as experiences of discrimination, injustice, poverty, and social inequality; this can reinforce historical trauma experience and response (Brave Heart, 1999; Williams et al., 2003)

BOX 10.1 **PAUSE AND REFLECT: THE IMPACT OF HISTORICAL AND CULTURAL TRAUMA**

1. In what ways do historical and cultural trauma affect Native and Indigenous persons in current times?
2. What are some of the impacts of intergenerational trauma?
3. How do culture and cultural oppression intersect with trauma as it relates to counseling?
4. What is important to understand about the impacts of cultural and historical trauma when counseling Native and Indigenous people?

Resurgence of Indigenous Peoples

Despite historical injustices, trauma, and attempts to diminish or extinguish Indigenous cultural ways of life, Native resilience is rooted in cultural strengths, values, and traditions (DuPonte et al., 2010). A resurgence of Indigenous culture and activism starting in the mid-20th century has taken root. The following sections provide examples of cultural genocide, exploitation, and appropriation to better understand the efforts of Native people, the importance of culture and values, and the resilience of Native communities. It is helpful for counselors to understand cultural oppression, progression, and stagnation to effectively grasp the lived experiences of Native persons and communities.

Hawaiian Renaissance

Two events exemplify the impact of colonization on Native Hawaiians: the banning of hula (Native Hawaiian dance) in the 1830s (Silva, 2000) and the prohibition of *ōlelo Hawai'i* (the Hawaiian language; Warschauer et al., 1997). In the 1960s and 1970s, a revitalization of cultural pride took place in Hawai'i. Interest in traditional practices, such as *hula*, voyaging and navigation, *mele* (music), and language, began to surge alongside activism and advocacy for sovereignty. Box 10.3 is a personal account of the contemporary impact of the Hawaiian Renaissance and emphasizes the value of connecting Native persons to their history, spaces, and culture.

Columbus Day—Indigenous People's Day

While exalted throughout history, actual historical accounts reveal Christopher Columbus to "arguably be one of the most brutal colonizers in recorded history" (Eason et al., 2020, p. 2). Over the past 3 decades, there has been a growing movement by Native Americans and allies to eliminate Columbus Day as a national holiday. In 1977, Indigenous people proposed to replace Columbus Day with Indigenous People's Day to acknowledge the experiences of Native Americans. In 1989, South Dakota became the first state to officially observe Indigenous People's Day, and as of 2022, 17 other states have followed (DeSilver, 2023; Eason et al., 2020). While still not a federal holiday, in 2021, President Joe Biden became the first U.S. president to issue a White House Proclamation recognizing Indigenous People's Day in October. Similarly, the second Monday in October in Hawaii is recognized as Discoverers' Day, which recognizes the Polynesian discoverers and voyagers who first arrived in the Hawaiian Islands.

BOX 10.2 **TIPS FOR PROFESSIONAL PRACTICE: ACKNOWLEDGING INDIGENOUS PEOPLES**

Below is a list of ways to get involved and acknowledge Indigenous people where you live. This will enhance your understanding and better prepare you to serve Indigenous peoples in a clinical setting.

1. Research the states that already celebrate Indigenous People's Day and determine what celebrations exist to recognize this day.
2. Many traditional tribal lands stretch across federal and state lines; what are the implications for that in how certain tribes and their respective state governments recognize Indigenous peoples?
3. One way of acknowledging and celebrating Indigenous peoples is by honoring ancestral land. Use the resource website Native Land Digital to research the tribal land on which your state resides.
4. What are the acknowledgment protocols for these tribal groups? How might that impact the way your state celebrates Indigenous people and ancestral lands?

Language Preservation

Language extinction is a global concern. It is estimated that half of the world's languages will disappear by the end of the 21st century (Carjuzaa, 2017). There is a significant relationship between language and culture. McCarty and Nicholas (2014) noted that language preservation is fundamental to tribal sovereignty and cultural protection. For many Native peoples, traditions are rooted in the generational dispersion of these practices that primarily occur through oral traditions and storytelling (McCarty & Nicholas, 2014). Because of the imminent threat to Native languages, Congress passed the Native American Languages Act in 1990 to preserve and protect Indigenous languages (Warhol, 2011). Indigenous language immersion schools have been established within many tribal and Native communities to address language preservation. Such schools have been shown to positively affect both students and the older generations of speakers who are typically involved in the instructional process (Carjuzaa, 2017).

BOX 10.3 **PROFILE OF A PRACTITIONER**

Aloha and *e komo mai* (hello and welcome) to my *mo'olelo* (story). My name is Dr. Laurie "Lali" McCubbin. My English name is Laurie, but my Hawaiian name is Lali. Even names have a story. At the time I was born, I could not be baptized without an English name. Therefore, I have two different names, with "Lali" as a direct English/Hawaiian translation of "Laurie." Names and places are intertwined, and my cousins went on to have beautiful Hawaiian names embedded in family history and place. My name reflects the times prior to the Hawaiian Renaissance, and I maintain it to remember my history and place. In my journey as a Western-educated Native Hawaiian, Japanese, and White cisgender female, the various intersectionalities associated with my name have evolved. This means I am, as always, a work in progress based on the *lōkahi* between my ancestors and humankind, the *'aina* and the *wai* (ocean). My identity is shaped by the colonization and genocide of my people and the *pewa* (cracks) in my family lineage.

Racism, discrimination, and social status had a heavy influence on my identity growing up. My grandfather, who was *kanaka 'oiwi* and Scottish, died at the age of 45. Prior to his death, he married a Japanese woman and had three children, including my father. My grandfather took in many of my grandmother's relatives. Unfortunately, at his funeral, racist comments were made that reflect the lateral oppression of *kanaka 'oiwi* on the islands by other racial groups. The legacy of lateral oppression permeated family relations as my father and his siblings were ignored by Japanese relatives. For example, on Christmas, no presents were given to my father and his sisters because they were not pure Japanese.

When my father married my White (German and English) mother, her parents, as represented in the social constructions of race during that time, stated that she would not marry "a colored man." These systemic layers of oppression in the 1960s saturated and shaped the nature of my parents' courtship, relationship, my mother's career, and their child-rearing practices. Despite these racial tensions, my parents were married in 1963. While we maintained relationships with all extended family members, my siblings and I had an interesting upbringing as individuals of mixed race and mixed faith (Buddhism and Christianity). Similar to the hypodescent phenomenon (Young et al., 2021), which refers to the automatic assignment of mixed-race people to the subordinate group because of the hierarchy of race in society, we identified more strongly with the *kanaka 'oiwi* side of the family. For me, this resulted in a deep commitment to *kanaka 'oiwi* and instilled a sense of *kuleana* (responsibility) to give back to the Native Hawaiian community.

My mother was a strong role model, fighting for injustice for Black, Indigenous, and People of Color (BIPOC) women throughout her life in health care and academia. She raised three children while having a chronic illness and obtaining her PhD. I inherited her rebellious spirit and, for a brief time, deviated from my family's tradition of helping professions and went into business. When the Mexican peso fell, I was promoted with a new office and a city view. Two weeks later, I quit, realizing that the exploitation of Indigenous peoples and global business endeavors perpetuated colonization and imperialism. I say these words now, though at the time, deep in my *na'au* (gutheart), I knew something was not right and I was not living my life congruent with my values. I decided to apply to graduate school and entered a clinical mental health counseling program at Boston College. Here I was able to collaborate with diverse clientele and chose a slightly different path, working with hospital patients and families, intertwining my father's commitment to BIPOC communities and my mother's passion for equitable health care. I learned that BIPOC folks sought treatment not from traditional Western mental health practices but more frequently through their religion and primary care physicians. In this capacity, I saw the intersection between societal systems of oppression, the cultural pathways for mental health services, and their impacts on physical and mental health. After completion of this degree, I pursued a PhD in counseling psychology at the University of Wisconsin-Madison. My commitment to stress, coping, and resilience in physical and mental well-being among BIPOC folks, with particular focus on Pacific Islanders, Asian Americans, and multiracial peoples, has not wavered. The opportunity to gain experience and develop as a scholar, clinician, and educator is deeply embedded in my Indigenous and family values and lived experiences. The gratitude that I have toward my *'ohana* and culture will continue in my commitment to healing and advocacy in health and well-being.

Reclaiming Spaces and Land Acknowledgment

Modernization and expansion have had devastating environmental consequences on Native lands. Environmental conservation is now a necessity because of the global impact of climate change. Contemporary movements can be seen through various actions to protect the environment, including sacred spaces, for example, the efforts to protect the sacred volcano Mauna Kea in Hawai'i (see Box 10.6) and resistance to the development of the Dakota Access Pipeline in North Dakota (see Box 10.7). Reclaiming Indigenous spaces also connects the land with its history through name restoration in which Western and English land identifiers are returned to their original Indigenous names. For example, in Minneapolis, Minnesota, the name of Lake Calhoun was restored to its original Lakota/Dakota name, *Bde Maka Ska*.

Land acknowledgment can be one step toward truth and reconciliation actions as seen in other countries (e.g., Truth and Reconciliation Commission of Canada and the Treaty of Waitangi in New Zealand). An Indigenous land acknowledgment is a statement that "recognizes the Indigenous peoples who have been dispossessed from the homelands and territories upon which an institution was built and currently occupies and operates" (Garcia & Anderson, 2018, p. 1). This is a way to partially indemnify centuries of misrepresented American history (Native Governance Center, 2019). These statements recognize the cultural value that exists in connection to one's homeland. Mary Lyons stated, "When we talk about land, land is part of who we are. It's a mixture of our blood, our past, our current, and our future. We carry our ancestors in us, and they're around us. As you all do" (Native Governance Center, 2019 para. 3).

Cases in Point

The Dakota Access Pipeline Conflict

During the summer of 2014 to the winter of 2017 at Lake Oahe near the Standing Rock Sioux Reservation in North Dakota, a natural gas pipeline company, Energy Transfer Partners, planned to construct the Dakota Access Pipeline (DAPL), which would connect the Bakken oil fields in North Dakota to oil refineries in Illinois via the Keystone Pipeline. The 2017 DAPL conflict captured global attention and remains one of many clashes between Indigenous communities and corporate/government agencies throughout history. With the DAPL protests, a younger generation of Americans was able to see how U.S. westward expansion and settler colonialism could still result in the suppression of Indigenous rights (Proulx & Crane, 2020).

Centuries prior to the DAPL conflict a series of treaties were made, and often broken, between the U.S. government and the Sioux. One particular treaty formed the base argument on behalf of the Sioux. In 1851, the Treaty of Fort Laramie created the Sioux Reservation, where the Sioux could live permanently. However, when gold was found in the Black Hills of South Dakota in 1874, the language of the treaty was changed without the consent of the tribes. With the changes, reserved land excluded the Black Hills, and the Indigenous people living there were forcibly removed. The resulting Sioux resistance ended in 1890 with the historic massacre at Wounded Knee Creek when the U.S. Army killed 300 Lakota men, women, and children (Proulx & Crane, 2020).

Over 175 years later, the Sioux were again faced with the prospect of an outside invasion of their protected land that had previously been sanctioned by the U.S. government. The DAPL protest centered on the *Očhéthi Šakówiŋ* (translated as Sioux Nation) camp in North Dakota.

IMG 10.1 & 10.2. Police officers used teargas against DAPL protesters on the Standing Rock Reservation

The protest camp itself was located on the land that was *given* to the Sioux in the Fort Laramie Treaty. On February 23, 2017, the U.S. National Guard forcibly evicted the *Očhéthi Šakówiŋ* protest campers, allowing the completion of the oil pipeline through Indian territory (Proulx & Crane, 2020). Since then, multiple leaks in the Keystone Pipeline have resulted in hundreds of thousands of gallons of crude oil spilling into adjacent land (Winsor, 2019).

Protecting Mauna Kea

Mauna Kea is a dormant volcano. It is the tallest mountain in the world and the highest point in Hawaiʻi. It has tremendous cultural significance to Native Hawaiians. As the home of *Wākea* (sky god) and the *piko* (summit), where the heavens and earth meet, and with hundreds of properties in the historic district of Mauna Kea, including ancient shrines, it is sacred (Hoʻomanawanui et al., 2019).

In the scientific world, Mauna Kea also holds significance. Since the early 1960s, Mauna Kea has been the home of many astronomical breakthroughs. With its unique position in the Pacific and its tall reach into the atmosphere, Mauna Kea is a prime position to look into the universe. It is above the inversion layer and with low-light ordinances on Hawaiʻi Island, light pollution is limited, helping to ensure the best views of the sky. The Hawaiʻi State Land Board issued the first lease to construct the first telescope in 1968 (Hoʻomanawanui et al., 2019). The University of Hawaii Institute for Astronomy has maintained the lease on the land approximately 3,700 meters and above. This was met with some controversy as land and cultural supporters and advocates maintain there is long-standing misuse and abuse of the land on Mauna Kea. The planning and construction of the Thirty Meter Telescope (TMT) have been hot topics among communities in Hawai'i and the scientific world. On one side is the consideration of the scientific benefits of TMT and on the other, the sacredness of Mauna Kea compiled with the repetitive misuse and loss of Native Hawaiian land, particularly that which has cultural significance and value.

IMG 10.3.

Essential Models

Counselors may question their role in helping Native clients promote Indigenous healing. As discussed above, health and healing for Indigenous persons must be approached through their historical context and an Indigenous lens. The following sections present Indigenous ways of knowing and healing as possibilities for counseling with Native populations.

Indigenous Ways of Knowing

Indigenous knowledge is a significant factor when providing culturally informed healing. Magni (2017) shared that *Indigenous ways of knowing*, sometimes referred to as Indigenous knowledge, comprise a system of generational teachings that reflect group members' skills, knowledge, and philosophies. While there are many shared aspects across Native and Indigenous cultures, remember that what is considered *Indigenous knowledge* varies depending on the nation or tribe. However, there are common qualities and characteristics across Indigenous Knowledge Systems (Joseph, 2018).

Native Models of Wellness

Indigenous relational well-being is acquired by remaining in harmony with the natural and spiritual worlds (McCubbin et al., 2013). A Native wellness perspective includes establishing one's connection and balance with nature, self, and spirit (Rybak & Decker-Fitts, 2009). Like the shared characteristics (Table 10.1) relating to intergenerational knowledge, Indigenous people are mindful of the future. The *Seven Generations* principle is a philosophy that the choices individuals make today will impact future generations (Moran & Bussey, 2007; Nutton & Fast, 2015). Similar to how the effects of trauma are passed from one generation to the next (Brave Heart et al., 2011), the generational transmission of healing also exists.

Ultimately, there is a shared perspective regarding the path of healing among Indigenous people; this is important for understanding the Indigenous healing process (Nutton & Fast,

TABLE 10.1 Qualities and Characteristics Found Across Indigenous Knowledge Systems

Adaptive	Invaluable
Cumulative	Irreplaceable
Dynamic	Moral
Holistic	Nonlinear
Humble	Observant
Intergenerational	Relative
Responsible	Unique
Spiritual	Valid

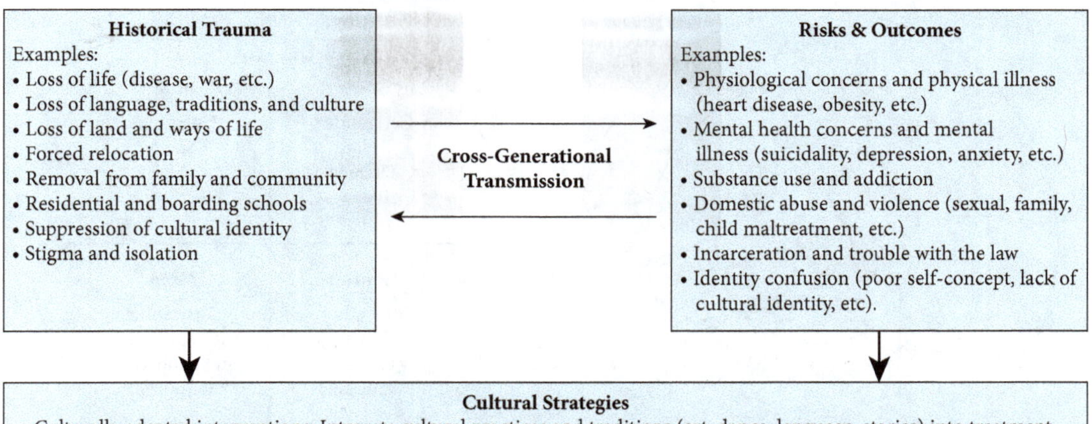

FIGURE 10.1 Culturally Adapted Health Interventions

2015). Protective factors emanating from individual or collective traumatic experiences must be considered to recognize Indigenous paths of healing. Protective factors can consist of (a) decolonizing strategies, (b) identity development, and (c) culturally adapted interventions. Trauma and healing do not exist in a vacuum. Rather, there is an interaction between historical trauma and/or cultural oppression and the subsequent health outcomes and risk factors of Indigenous people. Figure 10.1 depicts the relational and reciprocal nature of culturally adapted health interventions. Using culturally adapted health interventions may positively impact healing and decrease the transmission rate of traumas related to historical losses (Nutton & Fast, 2015).

Symbols and Pathways to Wellness: Balance, Harmony, and Unity

Other models of Native wellness may help counselors understand the unique nature of Indigenous healing. The shape of the circle reminds the Lakota Sioux that the Great Spirit, or *Wakȟáŋ-Tȟáŋka*, is like the circle itself; it has no end (Black Elk, 1953/1989) and represents the ongoing physical and spiritual journey of all living things. A significant element of Indigenous wellness is finding and maintaining one's balance and harmony, often represented by a circle or hoop (see Figure 10.2). This unending connection between the spirit, the body, the mind, and contextual factors represents the circle of life (Hodge et al., 2009). This epistemology is drastically different from linear notions of time, space, and healing found predominantly in Westernized medicine and healing protocols. Even the gold standard of empirical research for treatment effects is based on a linear framework.

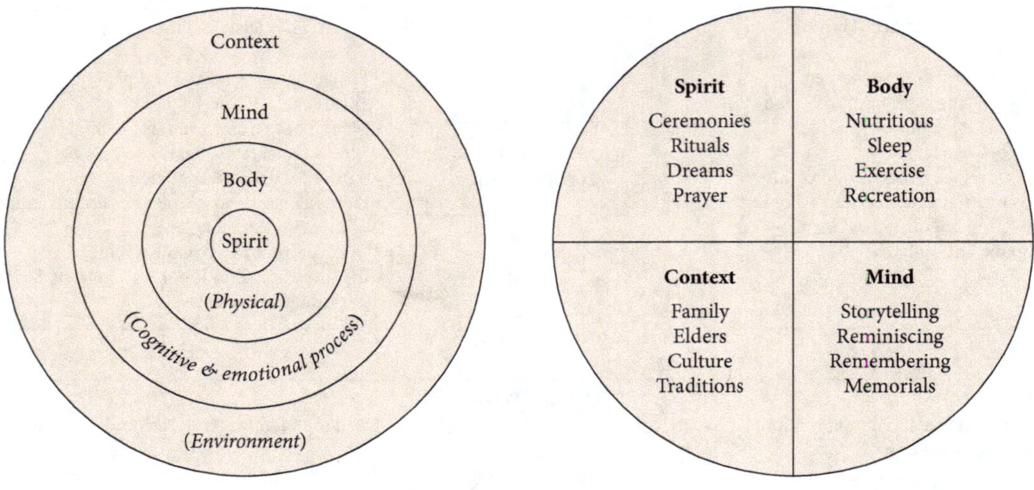

FIGURE 10.2 Circle of Life

The principles of balance, unity, and harmony (*lōkahi*) are components of the Native Hawaiian worldview (Hilgenkamp & Pescaia, 2003; Martin & Godinet, 2018; Pukui & Elbert, 1986). Harmony exists, or should exist, in all aspects of life on all levels: people, land/heavens/sea, spirituality, body, spirit, and thoughts/feelings (Martin & Godinet, 2018). Spirituality is grounded in *lōkahi* and is the connection to the past, present, and future (Paglinawan et al., 2020; see Figure 10.3). Maintaining a complete perspective on *the self* includes relationships with family/community, nature, and gods/spirits (Handy & Pukui, 1998; McCubbin & Marsella, 2009). Any disruption to this relational harmony could harm the self, community, nature, and spirituality (McCubbin & Marsella, 2009). While Western notions may view spirituality as an individual phenomenon

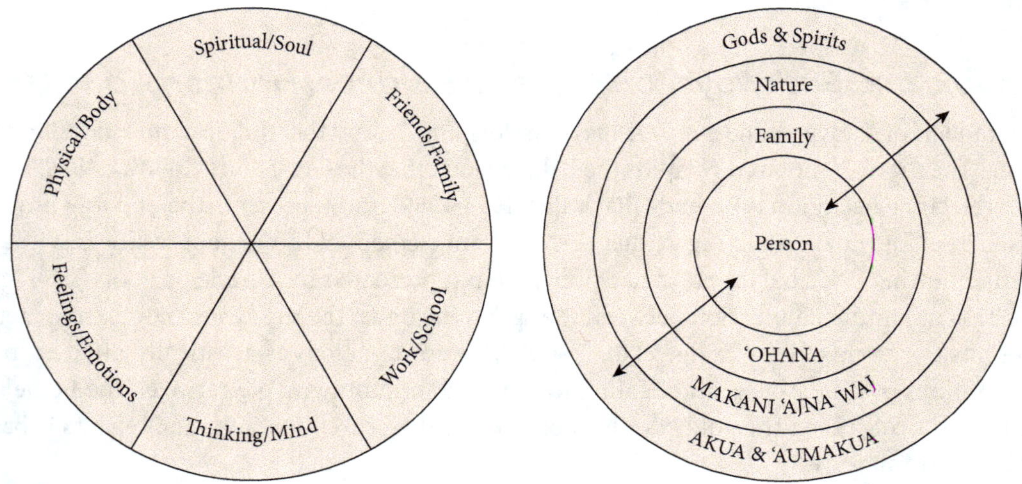

FIGURE 10.3 Representations of Balance, Unity, and Harmony

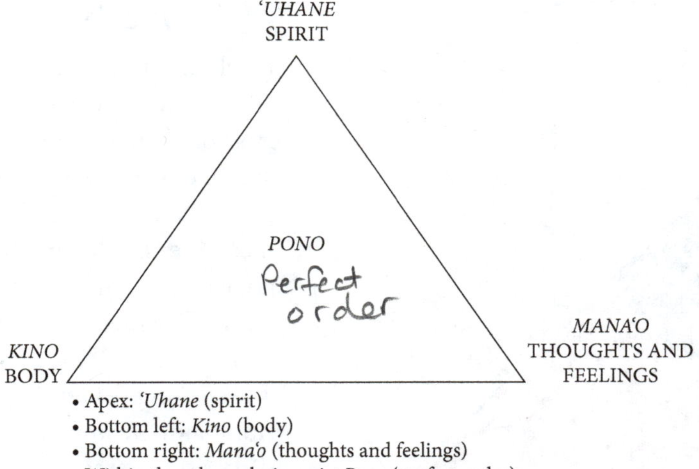

FIGURE 10.4 Hawaiian Worldview—Macrolevel

with the divine, spirituality in many Indigenous cultures is interwoven in everything and every relationship, including people, land, water, and inanimate objects.

The Hawaiian worldview is considered at micro- and macro-levels. While not a wheel or circle, Figure 10.4 illustrates the connection and balance needed between people, land/sea/heavens, and the ancestral gods.

Figure 10.5 illustrates the connection between the body, spirit, thoughts, and feelings. When balance occurs between these life aspects, one lives in *pono* or perfect order (Martin & Godinet, 2018).

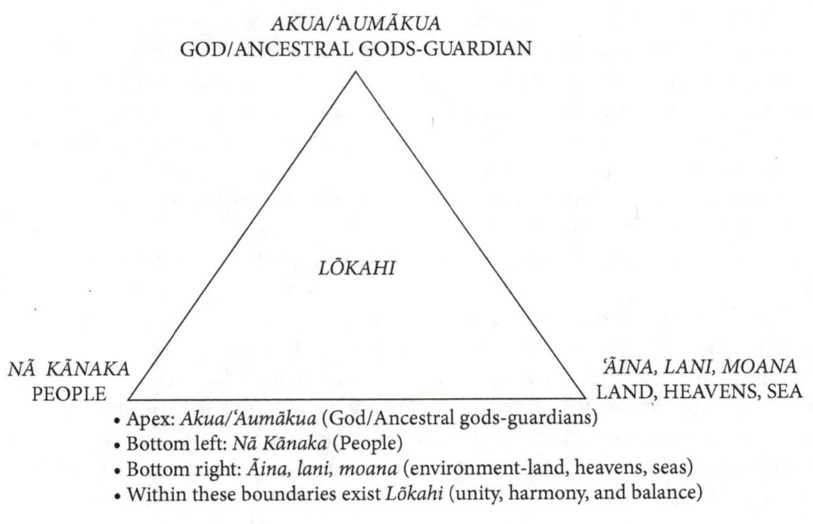

FIGURE 10.5 Hawaiian Worldview—Microlevel

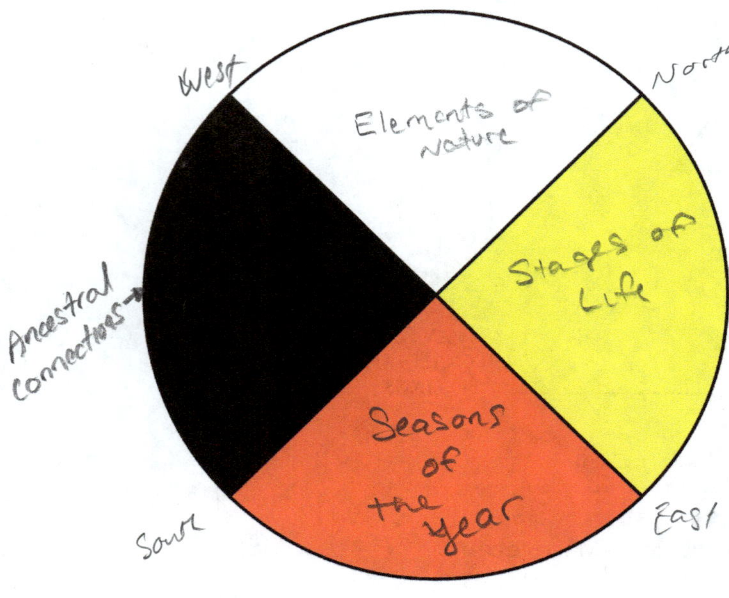

FIGURE 10.6 A Medicine Wheel

Medicine Wheel

Black Elk, an Oglala Sioux holy man, said, "Behold the circle of the nation's hoop, for it is holy, being endless, and thus all powers shall be one power in the people without end" (Neihardt et al., 2014, p. 22). The medicine wheel represents the value of balance and harmony that exists among the Sioux. The medicine wheel exists, in part, to orient the self to the cardinal directions. The spokes are identified as the four directions: north, south, west, and east. Each direction represents elements of nature, stages of life, seasons of the year, and ancestral connections (National Library of Medicine, n.d.; Rybak & Decker-Fitts, 2009; Wendt & Gone, 2016). Note that the specific interpretations of the medicine wheel often vary from tribe to tribe.

BOX 10.4 **FOCUS ON CLIENT CARE**

Linda, a 63-year-old Native American woman, has spent most of her life living in a small town on her tribe's reservation where she has worked as a counselor. Over the past year, her community has experienced a series of traumatic deaths by suicide, including, most recently, two teenagers from the local high school. There is a lack of mental health resources on the reservation, which makes Linda, the only other counselor who works there, overwhelmed with client needs and paperwork. She has considered retirement but feels a sense of responsibility to help her people. She is coming to see you for counseling because of feelings of sadness and being overwhelmed. Linda's husband of 24 years, Bruce, is White and works as a truck driver. He is a source of support for Linda, and they have a close relationship; however, there are times when she struggles to connect with him when talking about the cultural aspects of her wellness.

What are some possible cultural factors and how might they influence or impact Linda's well-being?

How might aspects of historical and other forms of trauma (e.g., vicarious trauma) be present in this case? What are the potential impacts of such trauma?

Considering an Indigenous framework for healing and wellness, how would you approach working with Linda? What aspects of the wellness models might apply?

Use the internet to do a quick search for the challenges and strengths of living on a Native reservation. What did you learn that was new? How can that information inform your practice as a counselor?

Multicultural and Social Justice Counseling Competencies

As mentioned throughout this text, the multicultural and social justice counseling competencies (MSJCCs) (Ratts et al., 2015) offer a framework for counselors to provide culturally sensitive and relevant counseling. The MSJCC can be applied to research, education, and supervision, as they address cultural competence and social justice by recognizing the intersections of "identities and the dynamics of power, privilege, and oppression that influence the counseling relationship" (Ratts et al., 2015, p. 3). The connections present in both the MJSCC and other socioecological models are not new concepts, nor are they known only through these models. These models parallel Native wellness models, which recognize the intersectionality of life and lived experiences.

The MSJCCs acknowledge privilege and marginalization, which are important to understanding and recognizing the impacts of oppression and colonization. However, it can also contribute to a separate consciousness that emphasizes marginalization and privilege rather than recognizing the strength and importance of interconnected relationships among culture and community. In applying the MSJCCs, we encourage you to go beyond the examination of the self, client, and counseling relationship in separate parts. Rather, to be culturally responsive, counselors must recognize the connection of self to others, culture, and community, which can be a source of strength. Counselors may inadvertently misunderstand the application of the MSJCCs and, in applying the framework, determine marginalization as a result of culture and identity. However, culture and identity are also a source of resilience and privilege. To say a client is marginalized because of their Indigenous identity can be akin to pathologizing a client because of their culture. Pathologizing and marginalizing perspectives are from a Western understanding and not from the Indigenous worldview. While oppression and marginalization do exist for groups of people (as is the case for Native and Indigenous communities that are marginalized as a result of the oppression of colonization), marginalization is not a result of culture or identities; it is present in spite of it. Rather than fit the Indigenous worldview into the MSJCCs, the MJSCCs can be viewed from an Indigenous lens, which identifies the interwoven nature of our existence and through culture and connection, which are healing rather than a source of marginalization. The MJSCCs can be applied to recognize that the self, others, community, environment, and culture are not separate. Rather, they are interconnected. With this understanding, the fourth domain of the MSJCCs (counseling and advocacy interventions) has particular importance. Advocacy interventions that decolonize and help culture and connection to move forward in a way that is healing stand not at the last domain but perhaps throughout all. Emphasizing connection to culture, instead of marginalization as a result of culture, is an important part of healing.

Indigenous models of wellness and healing practices have tremendous value to the health and well-being of Native and Indigenous persons. This is not to say that Western and contemporary approaches do not have a place. Contemporary medicine and traditional theoretical frameworks of counseling can be effective in helping Native and Indigenous persons, too. First, counselors should work to educate themselves by conducting their own research and attending training sessions, workshops, and learning opportunities. Aligning with the fourth domain of the MSJCCs, counselors should participate in cultural and community events and engage with experts and elders. The ultimate goal is to become a partner working for and in the community alongside

FIGURE 10.7 Integrating Traditional Healing Concepts (Adapted from Shore et al., 2015)

members of the community. To illustrate the path of integrating Western, contemporary, and Indigenous healing, the following process was adapted from Shore et al. (2015).

Projects and programs that emphasize traditional practices are particularly important for Native persons and communities. In the example of hula, the practice was banned; thus, the revitalization of such practices is a demonstration of cultural resilience (Baumhofer & Yamane, 2019). Incorporating Native practices that were once banned into the healing and treatment of Indigenous persons and communities empowers and strengthens not just the individual but also the community and culture. This approach aligns with the MJSCCs framework, which emphasizes advocacy interventions.

BOX 10.5 **PAUSE AND REFLECT: THE IMPORTANCE OF INDIGENOUS BELIEF SYSTEMS**

1. Why is it important to include aspects of traditional Indigenous belief systems in the counseling practice? What are some factors for practitioners to keep in mind when doing so?
2. How are "Indigenous ways of knowing" and the transmission of historical trauma similar? How are they different?
3. From a social justice and advocacy perspective, what role do counselors play in the healing of Native and Indigenous persons and communities?

Intersectionality

The points at which individuals' identities intersect must be considered to understand the complexity and their impact. Intersectionality provides context to understand how multiple identity factors impact a person's experiences of discrimination and privilege. According to Hopkins (2019), intersectionality is nuanced and about "relationality, social context, power relations, complexity, social justice, and inequalities" (p. 937). The paragraphs below explore just two aspects of identity; however, there are many more dimensions of identity and intersectionality.

Brown et al. (2016) studied the gender and sexual expression of Native and Indigenous persons. Two-spirit, or the embodiment of feminine and masculine spirits in one person, derives from the Northern Algonquin word *niizh manitoag*, meaning "two spirits" (Balsam et al., 2004). Native American two-spirit people are male, female, nonbinary, and intersex individuals. Traditionally, two-spirit individuals were highly respected and held as leaders within many tribes, dressing in men's and women's clothing and taking on special roles in the community such as advisors, counselors, and teachers (Mesa-Miles, 2018). However, not all Native cultures define *two-spirit* in the same way, with some regarding two-spirit as a modifier of one's sexual/affectual orientation. In contrast, other groups align the term with gender and nonbinary identification (Groot, 2019).

In the Hawaiian tradition, gender was not considered binary. Gender diversity was accepted and appreciated, and sexuality was not completely confined to male-female/husband-wife relationships (Snow, 2019). *Māhū* is a distinction for gender in the middle of male and female and refers to persons who embody both male and female spirits. They were valued, accepted, and considered beautiful (Snow, 2019). The *māhū* and diverse relationships were an integral part of Hawaiian culture; however, with the influence of Christianity and colonial values, the *māhū* tradition was seen as immoral. Through colonization and forced Christianity, the roles of two-spirit and *māhū* were threatened and, at times, forbidden (Balsam et al., 2004; Mesa-Miles, 2018; Snow, 2019). Presently, many two-spirit individuals face dual-sided homomisia and oppression from mainstream U.S. society, as well as their tribes and communities. Additionally, the intersection of race and culture with one's sexual/affectual and gender identities and expression creates unique health and risk factors (Balsam et al., 2004). In the face of the attempted erasure of two-spirit peoples throughout history, there is an empowered revival of two-spirit identity and community. In many parts of the country, local and national gatherings are intended to address community, belonging, tradition, and health disparities (Groot, 2019).

Professional Counseling Application

Colonization damaged generations. Despite a resurgence of culture, pride, and identity, and even with the allocation of resources and supportive programs, Native persons still struggle with insecurity about their traditions and authenticity, which is tied to unresolved cultural wounding, historical grief, loss, and trauma (Paglinawan et al., 2020). Receiving treatment can come with a stigma, and standard modes of care may not align with Native cultural values and traditional practices. It is counselors' responsibility to educate themselves on these wellness perspectives in order to have a more comprehensive understanding of Native wellness and healing (Rybak & Decker-Fitts, 2009). While this section will provide an overview of some concepts and strategies, we encourage you to seek additional knowledge and learning opportunities independently to continue to build your skill base for working with Native clients.

Deficit-Based Versus Resilience Focused

Early research on Native people and culture arose from a Western colonial perspective that was often pathologizing, deficit-based, and biased (McCubbin & Marsella, 2009; Tuck, 2009). Research narratives often depict Natives as deficient, that their problems and challenges result from being broken, and that they are responsible for their continued marginalization (Tuck, 2009). Failure to account for the impacts of colonization and cultural genocide has pathologized the Native experience and furthered the deficit-based narrative (Leigh-Osroosh & Hutchinson, 2019).

Additionally, treatment approaches are often rooted in scientific evidence from Western perspectives rather than through a Native lens. A common Western counseling method is cognitive behavioral therapy, which emphasizes maladaptive thoughts and behaviors (Hodge et al., 2009). This falls outside of the Native worldview and understanding of wellness that emphasizes the connection between mind, body, and spirit (Hodge et al., 2009; see Figures 10.1–4). Deficit-based approaches to health and healing do not account for the complex dimensions of well-being for Native populations. Pathologizing approaches focus on dysfunction and challenges, failing to recognize the strength and resilience of Native communities (Paglinawan et al., 2020; Tuck, 2009). It is important to approach counseling Native and Indigenous persons from a multidimensional and culturally sensitive framework that not only recognizes the barriers that Native communities face but also the strength and resilience of the people. Therefore, strengths-based strategies that build upon resilience are recommended as suggested in Table 11.2 and Nutton and Fast's (2015) recommendations focusing on decolonizing strategies, Indigenous identity development, and culturally adapted and Indigenous-based interventions.

BOX 10.6 **PROFILE OF A PRACTITIONER**

Mitákuyepi. Brynn Luger emáčiyapi kštó. Aŋpétu kiŋ lé wašté kštó. Greetings relatives, my name is Brynn Luger, and today is a good day. I am grateful to have the opportunity to share my journey to becoming a counselor. A journey starts with identifying the destination. However, this identification expands beyond that to include all facets of ourselves, our families, communities, professions, and passions. Like drawing a roadmap to find our way, tracing one's lineage can help us to understand ourselves. For Indigenous peoples, land, connection with the earth, and all that surrounds us are healing. Ancestral knowledge and pride are an integral part of my identity. My father's people are Hunkpapa Lakota Sioux from the Standing Rock Reservation, and my mother's people are from Norway and Scotland. After college, I needed to explore my roots. Therefore, I traveled to Stavanger, Norway, and the Isle of Mull in Scotland to stand where my maternal great-grandparents once stood. Exploring my paternal ancestry meant I didn't have to travel far, for I am fortunate to stand right where I am, in rural North Dakota on the Great Sioux Nation.

Being a graduate student working toward a master's degree in counseling is a journey. We start as novice learners, humble and eager to understand. We often put pressure on ourselves because we focus on helping people who have put their trust in us. It's important to meet that pressure with balance in the form of understanding ourselves and our role as helpers. This learning extends outside of the classroom and well beyond graduation. A certain amount of self-education is necessary when training in counseling. The development of a counselor as a professional and person never stops—we have to go out and do the work—the self-exploration necessary to learn. My journey included finding ways to use classroom teachings of established therapeutic techniques and theories and blending those with my culture's practices of healing mind, body, and spirit while honoring the ancestors. Unique to being a Native counselor is the concept of healing alongside. This occurs in a counseling setting when a practitioner engages in healing practices like traditional ceremonies alongside their client and, in essence, benefits from the ceremony themselves. Native and Indigenous healing is often community-focused; healing ourselves can help heal our people.

I believe there is great value in counseling; it explores a person's past, present, and future—while honoring emotion, family, community, and culture. When I think of the process of healing in the spiritual, mental, and emotional sense, I picture the role of a counselor as someone walking alongside another—being there to join them on their journey. As a counselor, one of the most important things for me is to be a support, a place of acceptance, for this is a sacred space on the healing journey.

Rapport, the Therapeutic Relationship, and Ethical Responsibility

A sense of trust and a positive working alliance must be established early in the counseling process. Trust takes time to build with those who have a history of oppression and injustice, and establishing rapport is a critical component of the counseling relationship. In a study by Thomason (2011), mental health practitioners who worked with Native American clients preferred a person-centered approach to counseling that emphasized warmth and authenticity. The National Board for Certified Counselors (2023), Section B.1.a of the ACA *Code of Ethics*, and Section D of the *Code of Ethics for Certified Rehabilitation Counselors* (CRCC, 2023) all emphasize the need for multicultural approaches in counseling. Person-centered concepts such as relationship building, trust, and non-judgment are important throughout the rapport building and therapeutic process. Additionally, Adlerian principles such as holism and social interest also align with Indigenous worldviews that emphasize connectedness with land, place, and family (living and nonliving).

Section A.4.b of the ACA Code of Ethics and Section A.1.h of the ASCA *Ethical Standards for School Counselors* call counselors to examine their personal values. Counselors are cautioned not to separate the client from their context and connection, nor should counselors impose their own worldviews or allow their worldviews to influence clients in ways that are not aligned with their worldview, such as individualist versus collectivist values. Additionally, counselors should be cognizant of their clients' pace, be patient, and mirror their clients (Thomason, 2011). Counselors may want to initiate sessions by warmly welcoming the client and offering hospitality, such as providing beverages like water or tea (Thomason, 2011). Introductions are important and can build a connection between the client and the counselor. They are often done through self-disclosure of where the counselor is from, including geographical and genealogical origins (Duponte et al., 2010). In general, opening sessions may look more like an inviting conversation in which clients are provided a space to share about the presenting concern (see Table 10.2). While intake procedures such as informed consent are necessary, counselors should be careful about starting with excessive formalities and paperwork.

TABLE 10.2 Strategies for Therapeutic Rapport

Person Speaking	**Example Conversation Text**	**Strategy and Notes**
Counselor:	Hi [Client], thank you so much for coming in today. Make yourself comfortable. Would you like water or juice?	Welcome and offer of hospitality
Client:	I'll take water. Thanks.	
Counselor:	Sure thing. So, I thought we could spend some time getting to know each other a little, and then we can decide if this is something that will work for you. Does that sound OK to you?	Soft opening, creating a comforting environment
Client:	Yeah, I guess so.	
Counselor:	Before we get started, I want to share about confidentiality [informed consent and confidentiality statement-limit jargon].	Mandatory informed consent and explanation of confidentiality
Client:	OK. Makes sense.	
Counselor	So, earlier on the phone, I shared a little about myself and what counseling might look like. It would be great to hear more about you. I noticed that you put that you live in _____?	Open dialogue without putting the client on the spot to share in an open-ended format. Refer back to the earlier introduction during the initial service inquiry. Connecting client to space and place (geographic)
Client:	Yeah, I live in ____ [current place] now, but I am originally from ____ [place].	Make note of geographic region (connection to place and space)
Counselor:	I have family in ____ [original place]!	Intentional self-disclosure to build connections with the client
Client:	Oh yeah? Small world! I'm sure we crossed paths at some point.	Make note of possible connections
Counselor	Yes, small world. So, what brought you to _____ [current place]?	Affirm connection, exploration of life events
Client:	Well, my grandparents are from here. I came to take care of my grandma. She was sick for a while and passed recently. It's been hard. That's why I was told to come see you.	Make note of family geography, client time line, possible family values (care for elder), presenting concern (possible grief and loss)

Culturally Sensitive Approaches

Despite advocacy and awareness efforts, literature and research surrounding counseling Native and Indigenous persons continues to be limited. Thomason (2011) found that mental health professionals who worked with Native Americans were unaware of any treatments or counseling methods specifically evidenced for working with Native Americans. Additionally, Moore et al. (2018) and Moullin et al. (2019) explored the attitudes among providers of substance abuse treatment for Native American clients. They found less favorable attitudes toward using evidenced-based practices (EBP) with Native clients than with non-native clients. These perspectives were partly because participants perceived that EBPs lacked consideration for Native clients' cultural norms, cultural relevance, and/or relevant evidence (Moore et al., 2018; Moullin et al., 2019).

More representation from Native and Indigenous professionals in the fields of counseling and counselor education is needed, and counselor education programs and state counselor licensure requirements do not adequately incorporate or recognize Indigenous healing, if it is incorporated at all. Moorhead et al. (2015) stated that most mental health systems do not recognize Indigenous healing practices, while Gray and Rose (2012) highlighted that many counselors do not receive specific training in working with Native clients. While state licensure requirements and standards set by the Council for Accreditation of Counseling and Related Educational Programs (CACREP, 2015) recognize the need for multicultural competence, education and training in Indigenous healing tend to be generic rather than specifically included in multiculturalism. All of this highlights the need for greater awareness, literature, training, and systemic/institutional change that addresses the needs of Native persons and communities.

From a community-based perspective, counselors may seek the support of Native and Indigenous community elders to develop culturally appropriate treatments for community members (Thomason, 2011), like integrating spirituality. Spirituality includes connections to gods, creators, relatives, higher powers, and other spiritual sources (Paglinawan et al., 2020; Thomason, 2011). In Native Hawaiian spirituality, connection to life and the world is known (felt) in one's *na'au* (gut, mind, heart) and is a guiding force that lives in each person. *'Aumākua* (a family or personal god or protector) is a guardian who provides help, guidance, and protection when needed (Paglinawan et al., 2020). Western approaches may view this as superstitious, irrational, or dissociative, and assessments may not take into consideration these beliefs. From a Native perspective, belief in spirits, guardians, and a connection to one's ancestors is necessary to one's worldview. In fact, a strong connection to ancestral lineage and spirituality may be a protective factor. Counselors should explore spirituality with clients as a resource for healing/health and take caution not to pathologize clients' beliefs unduly. The ACA *Code of Ethics* (2014) E.8. calls for counselors to recognize the impacts of multicultural and diversity issues with test administration and interpretation, and the *Diagnostic and Statistical Manual of Mental Disorders Fith Edition, Text Revision* (APA, 2022) calls for recognition that different cultures may experience and explain symptoms from a cultural worldview (APA, 2013).

IMG 10.4.

The Story of Kau'i

Dr. Kau'i Baumhofer is an Assistant Professor of Indigenous Health Sciences in Hawai'i. Her father is Norwegian and German from Minnesota, and her mother is Hawaiian, Korean, and Portuguese from Hawai'i. Her mixed ethnic identity is a large part of who she is. She was raised with a high level of confidence and identity as a Hawaiian child. In contrast, her mother grew up in a time in which it was hard to be Hawaiian because of the aftermath of annexation, yet she still had a strong sense of *kuleana* (responsibility) to Hawaiian culture and activism. Kau'i shares this value. She says proudly, "It's my responsibility. I've been given privilege because I'm Hawaiian." Like many other *kānaka maoli* (Native Hawaiians) and *kama'āina* (locals to Hawai'i), *kuleana* includes a responsibility to give back, be a leader, and take care of the *'āina* (land). She says many in Hawai'i are raised with that same sense and those values.

Another important value is *aloha*. Kau'i shares that the sense and meaning of *aloha* have been skewed over time. The meaning and significance of the word is deep. "*Alo*" means to face each other, "*Hā*" is the breath of life—to face each other and share the breath of life. The real meaning of *aloha* is reciprocal giving. They have a responsibility to you, and you to them. Hawai'is open to millions of visitors a year, and it seems that people just take, take, take, but there is no reciprocal giving back. She shared that the community has been violated for a long time. That *'eha* (pain) has started infiltrating the internal structure of the Hawaiian community. The income inequality is so great, and the sense of toxicity and animosity leaks into the fabric of society. A lot has been stolen, and people are trying to survive and make it in a system that is not made for them, which can lead to hopelessness. She adds that the Hawaiian youth struggle to find their place. They see that others are getting ahead, but they don't look the same as them or don't come from the same community. They often struggle with impostor syndrome and can feel as if they don't feel like they belong.

The younger generation of Hawaiians have a weight on their shoulders and can experience anxiety and pressure to excel in order to be competitive. Hawaiian kids have this *kuleana* to be Hawaiian, with more pressure and a heightened sense of anxiety. She says that many of her students are strong in their culture, but they still don't feel "Hawaiian enough." Kau'i struggled with this sentiment and shared her own journey, which she describes as a painful experience. She was advised to leave to further her education if she wanted to come home to work and help her community. She was the first Native Hawaiian and Pacific Islander to graduate with a doctoral degree from the university's School of Public Health. She gave 150% to prove she deserved to be there and spent 6 years away so that she could come home to help the Native Hawaiian community. However, this place was a source of missionaries with very conservative European values and the origins of the colonizers. She came home to pushback and rejection from her own Native community for "being away for too long" and not being "Hawaiian anymore." She left to gain legitimacy professionally, but by leaving, others saw a loss culturally of her legitimacy.

Generational Considerations

From a historical and socioecological perspective, there is a history of cultural suppression among Indigenous communities in the United States that has resulted in systemic barriers on many levels. While adopting approaches that align with Indigenous ways of well-being would seem to be the best approach, not all Indigenous persons align with Indigenous healing practices. In the late 1800s and early 1900s, Indigenous communities were barred from engaging in Native practices such as healing and ceremonial practices and speaking their language. As a result, many generations have lost connection with their traditional language and way of life. Having been stripped of all Native practices, many had no choice but to adapt to a Western way of life. In the case of residential boarding schools, Native American children were removed from their homes, often violently. Children were separated from their parents and siblings and from everything they knew. Residential boarding schools were designed to force Native children to adhere to mainstream Western U.S. culture, eliminating their access to traditional Native practices.

Still, younger generations of Natives may not feel connected to their culture; some are faced with the challenge of living in two worlds. They may feel connected to their Native roots but live in a Westernized world (Goebert et al., 2018). Contemporary society includes complex economic, technological, political, and cultural realities; for Native people, this can be even more complex. Finding a way to blend these perspectives is an ongoing personal journey, one that can benefit from culturally intelligent counseling.

BOX 10.7 **FOCUS ON CLIENT CARE**

Ms. Katie Portlock is a biracial, mixed White and Tsimshian Indian of the Eagle Clan in Alaska. Her ancestral roots connect to British Columbia, precontact, and Metlakatla, Alaska. She was born and raised in Anchorage and considers herself to be an "urban Native" with a strong connection to her Tsimshian culture as well as her White ethnicity. She shares her story of being raised by a Tsimshian mother and what her Native cultural identity means to her.

Katie was born and grew up in Alaska. Her father is White, and her mother is Tsimshian Indian. She was raised with Tsimshian values, fed traditional foods, and told traditional stories. When she was little, she didn't know the two sides of her family were different. As she got older, she realized that the way she acted around her Tsimshian side and White side were different. She shares she could switch her identity on and off. She noticed people would talk negatively to her about Alaska Natives because they would forget that she was Alaska Native. To them, Alaska Natives were the most extreme negative caricature they have seen. She has experienced microaggressions, and there are some who don't accept her because of her biracial identity. She heard a lot of comments like she was "another Dumb Native," or "you're just another Native" and "that ugly Native." She says even if you don't believe it or want that in your head, it burrows into your brain without you realizing it and creates defensiveness. She feels insecure about some of her physical features that are Alaska Native and not the mainstream definition of beauty; however, she has a lot of family, on both sides who love her no matter what, and this makes her resilient.

Family is an important value to her culture, and it extends beyond immediate family. If something happens to one of them, it happens to all of them. She shares that the trauma and pain that her great grandmother and grandmother experienced was passed down and she feels their pain. Katie shares that if counseling isolates them from family, it's harder for them to heal or recover. She has had experience with Native and non-native counselors. Ultimately, she shares that a counselor who understands the connection she has to her family and culture is much more helpful. Her Alaska Native counselor reminded her that her ancestors are with her and around her all the time and this gave her strength. In comparison, when she went to a counselor that didn't understand the comfort of having ancestors to walk with, she felt more isolated.

Cultural Connectedness

Cultural connectedness encompasses a person's relationship to their cultural traditions and values. With varying degrees of cultural identity and connectedness, counselors must attempt to understand aspects of their clients' culture in the ways they adhere to and engage in their culture (or not). A conversation, rather than an assessment, about clients' culture, background, and history can help counselors understand their clients' cultural identities, connectedness, and history (Shore et al., 2015). For example, counselors can engage clients in a discussion about values, beliefs, traditions, location, Native space, and genealogy. Assessments, such as the Awareness of Cultural Connectedness Scale (ACS; Mohatt et al., 2011) can be used to measure cultural connectedness. The ACS consists of 18 items targeted to assess self-awareness and connection to self in relation to a larger concept of humanity and nature/environment; it measures the degree to which an individual connects to the concept of interconnection between self, nature/environment, and family/community (Mohatt et al., 2011). Box 10.13 provides questions for consideration when exploring a client's cultural worldview.

BOX 10.8 **TIPS FOR PROFESSIONAL PRACTICE: SAMPLE QUESTIONS TO CONSIDER REGARDING CLIENT CULTURAL WORLDVIEW**

- How is this concern explained and understood from the perspective of the client's culture?
- How is mental health/wellness explained from the client's cultural worldview?
- What other explanations for the presenting concern are possible given the cultural and historical contexts?
- How strongly does the client align with their culture?
- How might cultural values, beliefs, and traditions influence the client's decisions, thoughts, and/or behaviors?
- What are some possible incorrect assumptions made about the client's culture?
- What, if any, spiritual, cultural, and/or traditional beliefs are important to the client?

Culturally Appropriate or Cultural Appropriation?

Elements of a culture can be divorced from their origin, resulting in marginalization by stealing another's cultural practices. *Cultural appropriation* occurs when aspects of one culture are taken without permission for the profit, gain, or personal use of another (Matthes, 2016). Traditional Native and Indigenous practices have entered the mainstream as trends for health and well-being. Practices such as *smudging* or participating in a sweat lodge ceremony can be harmful and reductive. Cultural approaches should *only* be used with proper training, permission (when appropriate), and from a complete contextual, historical, and cultural understanding. Counselors are advised to use care when incorporating traditional practices and to be aware of the harmful consequences of appropriation, including the marginalization of Native persons and communities.

Understanding culturally appropriate and traditional healing practices can provide a framework for working with Native and Indigenous clients. However, do not assume that all Native and Indigenous peoples align with traditional ways of knowing. Traditional practices and ceremonies must be respected. Counselors are cautioned not to use cultural ceremonies or practices without a complete understanding and in some cases, being granted permission. It is an honor and privilege to engage in Indigenous practices, yet engaging clients in cultural healing practices can be detrimental without fully understanding the practice and whether the client aligns with those beliefs.

Traditional Healing Practices

Culturally sensitive practices are not one-size-fits-all. Indigenous groups have shared elements of healing practices such as singing, storytelling, and dancing, but the actual traditions vary. There are hundreds of Indigenous tribes in North America and throughout the Pacific Islands; therefore, there are countless traditional practices. Two examples of healing ceremonies are presented from the Oglala Sioux. We present this information to give you a better understanding of such practices. As defined in the ACA Code of Ethics C.2.a., it is important for counselors to practice within the bounds of their competence. Thus, while counseling professionals will likely not use traditional practices, there is value in understanding them. Be advised that counselors may augment counseling by including cultural healers when appropriate.

Examples of Traditional Native Healing Practices

The Oglala are one of seven sub-bands of the Lakota Sioux, with a tribal headquarters located in Pine Ridge, South Dakota. According to Black Elk (1953/1989), an Oglala holy man, seven rites were given to the Oglala by the sacred White Buffalo Calf Woman. Two of the seven ceremonies are described below. Note that the Lakota terms and corresponding translations are included throughout the text.

The Rite of Purification (Inípi)

The *inípi* ceremony takes place in a sweat lodge. The frame of the lodge is made from 12 or 16 willow trees formed into a dome shape and covered with tarps and blankets. The door of the sweat lodge faces east, as this is the direction from which the light of wisdom comes. Outside of the lodge (approximately 10 paces to the east) is an external fire that is used to heat large rocks. Inside the lodge is a round altar where heated rocks, which represent all that exists in the universe, will be placed. Participants enter the lodge and moving sun-wise (clockwise), position themselves around the stone pit. Once the door is closed, it becomes completely dark inside the lodge. The darkness represents the darkness of the soul, which must be purified so that light may enter. Throughout the *inípi*, sage, sweet grass, and water are sprinkled on the hot stones while the individual who is leading the ceremony offers prayers and songs. The steam from the hot stones fills the lodge, causing it to become very hot. The heat allows for the purifying qualities of the *inípi* to work into the participants. Throughout the ceremony, the door to the sweat lodge is opened four times, letting in the light. During these times, water is passed around sun-wise, allowing each participant to drink or rub the water over their body. These symbolic actions allow participants to reflect on the first time that they received the light from *Wakȟáŋ-Thánka* (the Great Spirit). At the completion of the *inípi*, participants have left all that is impure behind and may now live as the Great Spirit wishes (Black Elk, 1953/1989).

The Sun Dance (Wiwáŋyaŋg Wačhípi)

Every year, in either June or July, the *wiwáŋyaŋg wačhípi* (dance looking into the sun) takes place. This sacred rite is an offering of the bodies and souls of the sun dancers to *Wakȟáŋ-Thánka* (the Great Spirit). Each detail of the sun dance lodge construction represents a part of creation. When it is viewed as a whole, the lodge becomes a symbol of the entire universe. Twenty-eight posts form a circle; attached at the tops of these posts are 28 corresponding forked sticks, all of which meet at a cottonwood tree that is ceremoniously placed at the center. Just as the cottonwood tree stretches from earth to heaven, so will the dancers' prayers reach the Great Spirit. The dancers engage in an initial *inípi*, after which the objects to be used during the ceremony, such as buffalo hides and sacred symbols cut from rawhide, are also purified. It is believed that through the sun dance ceremony, dancers are doing a sacred thing; they are giving their bodies to the Great Spirit, creating a closer relationship with all things of the universe. As the sun dance progresses, the backs, chests, or shoulders of the dancers' bodies are pierced with a sharpened stick. For some dancers, buffalo hide thongs are tied to their piercings and attached to either the center pole or a dried buffalo skull, and they dance until the thongs break loose from the flesh. For the dancers who vowed flesh offerings, small pieces of flesh are cut from their bodies. These sacrifices serve as a symbol of the dancers being freed from the bonds of the flesh. Then, after a final *inípi*, the dancers are met by people bearing food and a joyous spirit where they all rejoice in the great thing that has been done (Black Elk, 1953/1989).

Conclusion

Native populations have a unique and rich history filled with culture and tradition as well as tremendous loss, suffering, and pain. Movements to advance the rights of Indigenous people have empowered them to reclaim pieces of their culture and protect their land and spaces. However, challenges regarding cultural oppression and appropriation, climate change, and environmental destruction continue to threaten the Native way of life. As more is known and understood about the challenges Native persons and communities face, the importance of a multidimensional approach comes to the forefront. The recognition of cultural sensitivity and the appropriate use of traditional healing practices are important for the future of counseling Native clients. Prevention and intervention programs that use a cultural component through the integration of and respect for traditional values, ways of knowing, and practices have been found to be effective (Baumhofer & Yamane, 2019; Kaholokula et al., 2019).

Questions for Reflection

1. How does what you learned through reading this chapter influence your worldview regarding Native and Indigenous peoples?
2. What is the relationship between historical trauma and settler colonialism on mental health?
3. How might you apply Native and Indigenous worldviews and values in counseling?
4. How do models of well-being for Native and Indigenous peoples differ from other models of wellness?
5. How does your counselor identity impact how you may work with a Native and/or Indigenous client?

Applying What You Have Learned

Complete each of the following activities, considering what you learned from this chapter.

Activity #1: Reflection on a Personal and Contemporary Account of Cultural Emergence

Christopher "Chris" James Kuʻuhaku Blake, head of the Office of Pacific Innovations, which looks at traditional knowledge such as *oli* (prayer), *mele* (song), and *moʻolelo* (stories), weaving them into a contemporary context. Since 2014, he has been connected to Hōkūleʻa (a 62-foot, double-hulled, deep-water sailing canoe), the Polynesian Voyaging Society, and navigators Nainoa Thompson and Bruce Blankenfeld. Hōkūleʻa was a critical piece of cultural revitalization. An icon of the Hawaiian Renaissance, Hōkūleʻa helped usher in cultural connection. Launched in 1975, it was built for one voyage; however, it continues to voyage decades later.

Chris talked of Pūnana Leo, a Native Hawaiian language immersion school modeled after Kōhanga na Reo, a Maori language immersion school in Aotearoa, New Zealand. The prevailing thought was if preschoolers learned their Native tongue, it would allow for even more cultural growth. Youth are now a generation or two removed from when the ʻōlelo Hawaii was banned. The Hawaiian language continues to grow to all levels of education, connecting Native Hawaiians and Hawaiʻi to traditional culture and ways of life. Cultural connection is also made through the water and the land. It is the way for us to connect to the language of nature, which is key to Indigenous culture. To this point, Chris asks, "What are their winds? What are their rains? What kind of things are happening in their community or the places they live?"

From a counseling perspective, many Native Hawaiians do not trust a system that was not built for them or with them in mind. Chris wonders, "How do we show them that our situation has changed in a way that is hopefully more productive?" He believes there has to be systemic change; the best way is to treat everyone fairly but not equally. Empathy and genuine connectivity can help them understand that your role is to help and support them. We must understand the need to be agile and possess multiple tools to find different ways that equate to success. Also, we must be grounded in our past while having a firm footing in the present to shape us into our future. Our *kūpuna* (elders) and ancestors stored the information away, waiting for us to engage with it when the time was right.

Questions

1. How have past efforts shaped the future for Native and Indigenous persons and communities, and what are the implications for counseling?
2. What are some considerations regarding cultural connectedness and the role counselors might play in helping Native clients connect to their culture or formulate their identity?
3. What historical movements had and continue to have contemporary impacts? Why is it important for counselors to know about these movements and outcomes?

Activity #2: Cultivating Awareness of Cultural Appropriation

As you have learned in this chapter, cultural appropriation happens regularly and is damaging. It is important to identify when cultural appropriation is occurring and to take steps to stop these behaviors.

What are contemporary examples of cultural appropriation?

How might cultural appropriation be harmful to Native and Indigenous persons and communities?

What can you do when you witness cultural appropriation? What steps are you willing to take to advocate for Native and Indigenous communities so that their traditions remain sacred to them and not usurped by others?

Credits

IMG 10.1: ABC News, "The end of the Standing Rock standoff between authorities, protestors," https://www.youtube.com/watch?v=BqXlLudFQa0&t=174s. Copyright © 2017 by American Broadcasting Company.

IMG 10.2: ABC News, "The Seventh Generation: Youth at the Heart of the Standing Rock Protests | ABC News," https://www.youtube.com/watch?v=1Rz_TkpysKk&t=290s. Copyright © 2017 by American Broadcasting Company.

IMG 10.3: Big Island Video News, "Mauna Kea Update - 11 a.m. - News Teleconference (July 15, 2019)," https://www.youtube.com/watch?v=LcsWuD8d_Gs&t=180s. Copyright © 2019 by Big Island Video News.

Fig. 10.1: Adapted from Jennifer Nutton and Elizabeth Fast, "Historical Trauma, Substance Use, and Indigenous Peoples: Seven Generations of Harm From a 'Big Event'," *Substance Use and Misuse*, vol. 50, no. 7. Copyright © 2015 by Taylor & Francis Group.

Fig. 10.2: David R. Hodge, Gordon Limb, and Terry Cross, "Moving from Colonization toward Balance and Harmony: A Native American Perspective on Wellness," *Social Work*, vol. 54, no. 3, pp. 214-215. Copyright © 2009 by Oxford University Press.

Fig. 10.3a: Adapted from Tammy Kahalaopuna Kaho'olemana Martin and Meripa Godinet, "Using the Lōkahi Wheel: A Culturally Sensitive Approach to Engage Native Hawaiians in Child Welfare Services," *Journal of Indigenous Social Development*, vol. 7, no. 2, p. 28. Copyright © 2018 by University of Calgary.

Fig. 10.3b: Laurie D. McCubbin and Anthony Marsella, "Native Hawaiians and Psychology: The Cultural and Historical Context of Indigenous Ways of Knowing," *Cultural Diversity and Ethnic Minority Psychology*, vol. 15, no. 4. Copyright © 2009 by American Psychological Association.

Fig. 10.6: Copyright © by Littlejohn657 (CC BY 4.0) at https://commons.wikimedia.org/wiki/File:Medicine_Wheel.png.

Fig. 10.7: Adapted from Jay H. Shore, et al., "Traditional Healing Concepts and Psychiatry: Collaboration and Integration in Psychiatric Practice," *Psychiatric Times*, vol. 32, no. 6. Copyright © 2015 by MJH Life Sciences.

CHAPTER 11

Social Class and Classism

Madeline Clark, Jennifer M. Cook, and Susan M. Long

The closest most folks can come to talking about class in this nation is to talk about money.

—bell hooks, *Where We Stand: Class Matters*

CHAPTER OVERVIEW

As bell hooks aptly noted, people in the United States are not terribly eager to discuss social class; everyone has *class*, yet few people want to talk about it. When social class is discussed, it's often relegated to income-only conversations, and counseling professionals are not immune to this phenomenon because it is deeply embedded in U.S. culture. Social class is about so much more than income! In this chapter, you will learn the depth of what social class is, how it impacts people's lives—clients and counselors alike—and how it intersects with other identities. Further, you will explore your social class identity, how it can impact the counseling relationship, and how you can work ethically with clients from all social class backgrounds.

LEARNING OBJECTIVES

By the end of this chapter, students will be able to

1. define and describe social class and socioeconomic status, including their overlap and differences;
2. identify one's own socioeconomic status and social class group(s) and how they may influence the counseling relationship;
3. name the ways social class bias and discrimination manifest, the impact on individuals, and strategies to effect positive change;
4. explain how poverty is measured in the United States and how it relates to individuals' ability to receive services;
5. apply various social class and poverty counseling models in a multicultural context;
6. develop assessment skills to examine social class related to client well-being; and
7. name social class interventions and strategies that can be used in practice.

CACREP 2016 STANDARDS

The information in this chapter supports the following:

- 2.F.2.a. Multicultural and pluralistic characteristics within and among diverse groups nationally and internationally
- 2.F.2.b. Theories and models of multicultural counseling, cultural identity development, and social justice and advocacy
- 2.F.2.c. Multicultural counseling competencies
- 2.F.2.d. The impact of heritage, attitudes, beliefs, understandings, and acculturative experiences on an individual's views of others
- 2.F.2.e. The effects of power and privilege for counselors and clients
- 2.F.2.f. Help-seeking behaviors of diverse clients
- 2.F.2.g. Strategies for identifying and eliminating barriers, prejudices, and processes of intentional and unintentional oppression and discrimination

CACREP 2024 STANDARDS

The information in this chapter supports the following standards:

- 3.B.1. theories and models of multicultural counseling, social justice, and advocacy
- 3.B.2. the influence of heritage, cultural identities, attitudes, values, beliefs, understandings, within-group differences, and acculturative experiences on individuals' worldviews
- 3.B.3. the influence of heritage, cultural identities, attitudes, values, beliefs, understandings, within-group differences, and acculturative experiences on help-seeking and coping behaviors
- 3.B.4. the effects of historical events, multigenerational trauma, and current issues on diverse cultural groups in the U.S. and globally
- 3.B.5. the effects of stereotypes, overt and covert discrimination, racism, power, oppression, privilege, marginalization, microaggressions, and violence on counselors and clients
- 3.B.6. the effects of various socio-cultural influences, including public policies, social movements, and cultural values, on mental and physical health and wellness
- 3.B.7. disproportional effects of poverty, income disparities, and health disparities toward people with marginalized identities
- 3.B.9. strategies for identifying and eliminating barriers, prejudices, and processes of intentional and unintentional oppression and discrimination
- 3.B.10. guidelines developed by professional counseling organizations related to social justice, advocacy, and working with individuals with diverse cultural identities

Unpacking Social Class Terminology

Labels such as *upper, middle, lower,* and *working class*, and terms such as *socioeconomic status, classism*, and *poverty* are commonly associated with *social class.* In fact, many terms you have likely heard and even used, like socioeconomic status, are important components of understanding social class, yet do not capture the depth and breadth of social class. In this section, we explain the various terms used to describe social class, social class groups, and related phenomena, and how professional counselors can apply these correctly.

Socioeconomic Status and Social Class

Social class is a complex construct, so much so that many people, including counselors and counseling scholars, frequently reduce social class to *socioeconomic status* (SES; Clark et al., 2019; Cook & Lawson, 2016). SES is comprised of three components: income, education, and occupation. These components are discrete and measured easily. While SES is foundational to understanding social class, it is not social class in and of itself. Below is a list of SES components and how each is defined.

- **Income:** The amount of money a person earns and/or has access to use (e.g., family financial resources, government monetary benefits). Measured in local currency and understood in terms of daily, weekly, monthly, or annual earnings.
- **Education:** The amount of formal education a person has completed, ranging from grade school through graduate degrees (e.g., masters, doctoral, medical). Typically, does not include informal education like on-the-job training.
- **Occupation:** The jobs or careers one has. There are multiple ways to measure occupation, with some measures including occupational *prestige*: the culture-specific respect and value placed on each occupation. The Standard Occupational Classification system (see U.S. Bureau of Labor Statistics; https://www.bls.gov/soc/) is a structure for organizing occupational information without integrating prestige. Duncan's Socioeconomic Index (https://usa.ipums.org/usa-action/variables/SEI#description_section), an occupational rating scale used since the 1950s, includes prestige in its occupational rankings (see Caston, 1989, and Stevens & Featherman, 1981, for more information and critique).

As you read the definitions for income, education, and occupation, you likely began to make connections between these factors. A person's educational attainment can influence their occupation, and their occupation may give you an idea of their earnings. However, there is not always a positive correlation between income, education, and occupation. Increased education *can* lead to increased income, though not always. Similarly, increased education does not necessarily lead to a *prestigious occupation*. These are important connections to consider because they are priming you to understand social class.

SES factors (i.e., income, education, and occupation) are indivisibly linked to social class but are not *in and of themselves* social class. Most simply defined, social class is one's experiences and interactions with SES or how they *do* their SES. A person's experiences and interactions with SES can be individual or as part of groups (e.g., family, neighborhood, school, religious organizations). These experiences contribute to one's beliefs, values, attitudes, expectations, and behaviors, as well as how one understands the world. Additionally, SES influences one's access to resources, social capital, systemic power and privilege, and the amount of advantage or oppression they experience based on their level of social class privilege (Cook et al., 2021). Social class is more nuanced and influential in a person's life than discrete SES variables. The beauty of social class lies in its complexity and its inherent ability to convey far more than what people do for a living or have obtained financially. Clients' stories and experiences with social class help to describe who they are, what they value, and how they understand their world.

How much a person earns or how much money they have access to use is incredibly important, though a social class perspective about income offers far more information. For example, if a person earns $50,000 per year, how do they interpret or perceive their earnings? Consider the following questions:

- What is the person's perspective about their annual earnings? Do they view $50,000 to be a *good living*, or are they embarrassed that they do not earn more?
- Are their needs and their family's needs met earning this salary?
- How many jobs does the person work to earn this salary? How much free time does the person have?
- How many people are supported by this salary, both inside and outside their household?
- What is the cost of living based on the person's geographical location?
- Does earning this amount allow the person to live in a neighborhood that feels comfortable and safe for them?
- How do they use their income? Are they able to live comfortably and without worry engage with pleasures they enjoy?
- Do they have conflict with their family of origin about their income?

These are only a few questions that begin to uncover how a person understands their income and their *social class perspectives* about their income. To understand social class more deeply, it is important to explore questions regarding the individual's education and occupation too.

Although there are similarities between individuals who belong to specific social class groups, there are differences as well. In this chapter, we are intentional about not providing a taxonomy by social class group that defines typical behaviors, beliefs, values, etc. Such descriptions, such as Payne's (2005) *hidden rules of social class*, are not grounded in empirical evidence and have caused harm by perpetuating social class bias, stereotyping, prejudice, and institutional discrimination (Biles et al., 2012; Dworin & Bomer, 2008). Instead, we provide you with tools, like the aforementioned questions, to explore your own social class identity and the social class identities of your clients.

It is important to acknowledge that a person's social class identity is part of the constellation of their other identities such as gender, sex assigned at birth, race, ethnicity, religion/spirituality, disability, and sexual/affectional orientation, just to name a few. The dominant and nondominant social statuses associated with a person's identity influence how they understand themselves and others, as well as how others may perceive them. We will explore this topic further when we discuss social class bias.

Classism

Classism is an overarching term that includes bias, prejudice, discrimination, and/or oppression based on an individual's actual or perceived social class or SES group membership (Cook, 2017; Smith, 2006). While members of all social class groups can hold bias and prejudiced beliefs about other groups, only the dominant culture (i.e., individuals who are middle social class or higher) holds the cultural power and privilege to restrict others from valued resources, such as jobs and housing (Brown et al., 2005). This is key because some may posit that *upward classism* (i.e., people in low social class groups discriminating against people in middle and upper social class groups) is possible. It is not. Just as the authors in Chapter 8 explained that *reverse racism* is an inaccurate concept, *upward classism* is just as erroneous because people in low social class do not have the systemic power to discriminate.

BOX 11.1 **PAUSE AND REFLECT: YOUR SES AND SOCIAL CLASS IDENTITIES**

Have you ever thought about how your experiences with SES have shaped your social class identity? In the *multicultural and social justice counseling competencies* (MSJCC), Ratts et al. (2015) called counselors and counselors-in-training to identify and understand their cultural identities, both privileged and marginalized, and how their identities may align or differ from their clients.

To understand your social class identities, consider your SES experiences in your family of origin and while you were growing up **AND** your SES experiences as an adult. Take a moment and consider your answers to one or more of these questions:

- What messages did you learn in your family about money? What "value" was placed on money? How was it spent? Was it saved? How do you view money now?
- What messages did you receive in your family about education? Did everyone in your immediate family finish high school, attend college, or trade school? Was it assumed you would go to college? What do you believe about education now? If you have children, will you expect them to attend college?
- What messages did you receive at school and what messages did you receive at home about occupation?
- What was your access to resources like in your family of origin and now?
- What were your personal and professional experiences with class bias when you were growing up and as an adult?

As you review your answers, where do you notice overlaps and differences between your family of origin and now? What social class group do you identify with based on these experiences? Do you belong to one social class group or more than one?

Nondominant Group Designations: Social Class Stratification

Social class group designations tend to be grounded in SES rather than social class. Even when groups are coined *social class groups*, they are likely determined by SES and are more aptly called *SES groups* rather than social class groups because they were created based on education, income, and occupation. SES groups are determined in a hierarchical fashion based on the social stratification inherent to capitalistic societies like the United States (see Table 11.1). Social stratification refers to how valued resources are distributed and who has access to them based on their place in the economic hierarchy (Beeghley, 2000).

TABLE 11.1 *SES Groups* (Adapted From Cook, 2017)

Overarching Term	Groups Included in Each Overarching Term (adapted from Warner et al., 1960)
Low Social Class	Poverty, Lower-Lower, Low, Upper-Lower
Middle Social Class	Lower Middle, Middle, Upper Middle
High Social Class	Lower Upper, Upper, Upper Upper

There are many colloquial terms used to describe SES groups, many of which contain implicit and explicit bias about how such groups are perceived based on their social class. For example, the terms *blue collar* and *white collar* are tied to individuals' occupations and are derived from what people traditionally wore to perform the jobs in those categories. In middle-class and higher jobs, employees wore white collar shirts, like dress shirts, to work. Individuals in blue-collar jobs, like a mechanic or a plumber, typically wore blue-collar work shirts or coveralls. While work environments have changed significantly in terms of dress in the 21st century, the terms *white* and *blue collar* are still used frequently to describe the social status of individuals in different jobs.

Additionally, terms such as *trailer trash*, *the poor*, *squatters*, and *the underclass* are clear examples of terms rooted in disparaging societal perceptions of individuals who are part of low social class. In stark contrast, idioms for people in high social class include the *upper crust*, *one-percenters*, *the ruling class*, and *high society*. There are no colloquial terms listed for people who are middle social class because middle social class is the dominant culture within the United States, and such terms do not exist.

When considering intersecting identities, particularly race and social class, additional terms are added to the list. *White trash*, *cracker*, and *hillbilly* are often used to describe White people in low social class, particularly in the southern United States. Although terms such as *welfare queen* and *ghetto* are almost unilaterally applied to People of Color (POC) who live in low social class, Wray (2006) noted that there are no terms equivalent to *White trash* to apply to POC because the default cultural assumption is that POC are members of low social class. Such cultural assumptions about race and social class are inaccurate, harmful, and prejudicial, and should not be used to describe any social class group.

Because of social stratification, 70% of people born into low social class will remain in low social class throughout their lives (Pew Charitable Trusts, 2013); however, individuals can and do change SES groups in terms of higher educational attainment, increased income, and obtaining occupations that are considered socially prestigious. A colloquial term used to refer to individuals who were reared in low social class and are now members of middle social class or higher is *class jumper*, akin to *claim jumping*, which means stealing from someone else. Despite the ubiquitous U.S. belief in the *American dream* and the idea that all persons can and should aspire to more, *class jumping* seems to indicate that the American dream is not intended for people who live in low social class. What is interesting to consider in tandem is the cultural trope that individuals living in poverty need to *pull themselves up by their bootstraps* and improve their financial circumstances. Such societal messages assign blame to individuals for causing and maintaining their economic circumstances, while calling someone a *class jumper* implies they ought not change economic groups. It is a cultural catch-22.

When exploring SES with clients or about your own experiences, it is important to note that SES changes do not automatically lead to *social class* changes. Although a person's SES may shift, their values, worldviews, behaviors, and perspectives may remain consistent with their social class group of origin. Additionally, people who have changed SES groups may hold social class perspectives that align with two social class groups simultaneously. Consider Tasha's experience (Box 11.2). As you read about Tasha's experience, consider what it would be like to be her counselor and how you would explore her identities with her.

BOX 11.2 **FOCUS ON CLIENT CARE**

Tasha is a White first-generation college graduate who was raised by her father in a single-parent household. They lived in a modest apartment in a neighborhood that felt mostly safe to her. Her father worked in a nursing home maintenance department for most of her upbringing. Tasha attended public school, did most of the household duties, and babysat to earn extra money for her family from ages 12 to 16 years old. At 16, she became employed in the kitchen at the same nursing home where her father worked. After college, Tasha earned a master's degree in counseling and, upon graduation, obtained employment in a hospital setting. She earns a reasonable income, far more than her father ever did when she was growing up, and lives alone in a safe, urban neighborhood.

Tasha has had experiences with two social class groups: low social class and middle social class. She noticed that her values, views, and behaviors differed from her classmates when she was in her counseling program despite sharing a racial identity with most of them. When she went on practicum at a suburban hospital that mainly served clients from middle social class and higher, she continued to notice value and behavioral differences, like those she noticed with her classmates. Her awareness was heightened when she would return home and hang out with friends who opted for direct-entry employment after high school. Tasha began to believe she did not fit in with either environment. Through work with her counselor, she came to terms with value clashes related to holding values from both social class groups simultaneously.

How would you work with Tasha to validate her experiences with two social class groups? How might her racial identity play a role in your discussion? How would you empower Tasha to identify the strengths she gained within both of her social class groups?

Understanding the Historical Context of Social Class

Social class is a complex sociopolitical structure (Clark et al., 2019). Social class and related topics (e.g., poverty, classism) are presented throughout recorded history in religious texts and Eastern and Western philosophy. Beyond experiential differences, the opinions of those in different social classes have shifted through time, largely influenced by sociopolitical events that shape the collective history and memory of cultural groups (e.g., the Great Depression, the Great

Recession; Mink & O'Conner, 2004). Also, social class differences and systemic oppression of those marginalized by social class (e.g., persons experiencing poverty) are influenced by cultural values and political policies, such as individualism versus collectivism, economic systems, social safety, and welfare benefits.

The history of social class in the United States is complex and strongly influenced by colonization, both of land and of people, and the way social class is conceptualized varies by geographic region, such as race and class intersections in the southern United States because of African enslavement, the Midwestern *work ethic*, or east coast wealth (Pimpare, 2008). Also, these regional differences are greatly influenced by national events and political movements. For example, Thomas Paine's *Rights of Man* (Paine, 1791/2012) and the American Revolution, the social welfare movement of the 19th century, the Great Depression and the New Deal of the 1930s, the War on Poverty of the 1960s, the Welfare to Work policies of the 1990s, and the Great Recession in the early 2000s all influence not only how we have conceptualized class in the United States but also the ways in which people in different social class groups experience their worlds (Mink & O'Conner, 2004). These varied experiences may produce unique, individual social class understandings and values, impacting how, when, where, why, and *if* clients seek counseling services.

Social class continues to be influenced by current events. For example, the impact of COVID-19 on the economy and employment had a significant impact on the experiences of many U.S. individuals and worldwide. The pandemic greatly disrupted the global workplace, and one in five persons in the United States was unemployed (Mackrael & Cameron, 2020). Financial, housing, and health-care instability became increasingly commonplace. As previous historical events have influenced our conception of social class, undoubtedly, future events will do the same. Further interest in social policies such as living wage requirements, student debt erasure, affordable housing, childcare, and health care will all continue to inform and reinforce social class experiences in the United States. Ultimately, professional counselors will need to understand these ever-evolving social class issues and advocate with and on behalf of clients to ensure dignity, welfare, and wellness for all we serve.

Classism in Systemic and Ecological Contexts

Social class is present and influential in each level of Bronfenbrenner's ecological model (i.e., micro, meso-, exo-, macro-, and chronosystems) and with that, the level of social class privilege or marginalization the person has influences their experiences and worldview. For people with marginalized social class identities (i.e., those who identify within the spectrum of low social class), social class bias and classism are not only present and persistent but can have an indelible impact on them in terms of access to resources, mental health struggles (e.g., self-worth, depression, anxiety), and what they believe about their capabilities. *Social class biases* are beliefs that all persons should be middle social class, and if they aren't, it's because of their own failings. *Classism* denotes ways in which individuals, groups, and systems enact their social class bias through words and/or actions that restrict others.

As you learned earlier, SES and social class are inextricably linked yet are distinct concepts. Classism can be rooted in SES just as much as it can be rooted in social class. For example, take Joe. Joe is a 35-year-old single parent who works full-time as an assistant manager at a fast-food chain. He knows he has decreased access to housing based on his income as a result of his occupation (SES), yet he goes to see an apartment that he can just afford in a neighborhood that has a better school for his 12-year-old son. At first blush, it may seem that when Joe is turned down for the apartment it's about his income; however, social class may play a role too. Imagine that just after Joe was told he did not meet the income requirements for the apartment he viewed, he is standing outside the building scrolling through his phone to determine where he will look next when he overhears the apartment manager say to a tenant, "We don't need *that* type of person living in our building, he would bring it down." This type of comment highlights classism—that presumption Joe would not be a good tenant based on the limited information the apartment manager has about him (really, only his occupation, income, and some small talk while viewing the apartment) and that he is somehow vastly different from the other tenants who live in the building and would contribute negatively. The apartment manager's statement is not a one-off but rather a deeply embedded belief system developed within a cultural context that prizes people who are middle social class and as a result, he restricts Joe and his son from a valued resource: housing in a neighborhood with a good school.

Regarding the ecological model, this example is multidimensional and complex in terms of its impact. It may appear that Joe is only interacting with the exosystem, yet the macrosystem (i.e., widely shared values, beliefs, customs) is likely leading to his experience with this system. Furthermore, this experience does not affect only Joe but his son as well at the micro- and mesosystem levels. Consider the following points about how this experience might impact them.

- The school the son will attend and the opportunities he will have
- The neighborhood in which they will live
- Their relationship as a family unit
- Their relationships with others outside the family
- Beliefs about themselves, what they can achieve, and what they *deserve*
- Feelings of safety
- Local and unencumbered access to resources such as healthy foods, clean drinking water, mental health and medical care

Remember, too, that Joe and his son are in the midst of distinct chronosystem stages. Joe is approaching midlife and tackling meaning making within his developmental life stage, while his son is an early adolescent who is working to understand his identity and who he wants to become as an adult.

In the next two sections, we discuss two important topics that have implications within an ecological approach: (a) poverty and (b) classism and microaggressions within counseling. As you read these sections, we invite you to reflect on your beliefs about and your experiences with social class.

BOX 11.3 **PAUSE AND REFLECT: CLASS, CLASSISM, PRIVILEGE, AND MARGINALIZATION**

1. How do you identify your social class? Is your identity privileged or marginalized?
2. How has social class impacted your experiences? Has it been something you have been confronted with throughout your life or something you've never given much thought to?
3. What beliefs do you hold about social class groups different from your own?
4. What do you want to learn more about in terms of social class and classism?

Poverty

Persons experiencing poverty are a unique social class group who are particularly impacted by classism and other structural inequalities, such as access to food, housing, health care, education, and employment, among other sociopolitical concerns. Because of these financial, social, and environmental challenges, persons experiencing poverty often have higher rates of mental, physical, and social health concerns compared to higher social class groups (Kraus et al., 2012; Long et al., 2019; Weissman et al., 2015). Poverty is an intersectional experience that interacts with other identities, all of which have distinct and interrelated effects on well-being (Kim & Cardemil, 2012). Overlapping oppressions may lead to increased stress, various physical and mental health concerns (i.e., social determinants of health; see Chapter 4), and even trauma and violence; this can be understood as *multiple minority stress* (Meyer, 2003; Wong et al., 2014). For example, a Black transgender woman experiencing poverty may simultaneously confront the stressors of racism, cissexism, transmisogyny, and classism. In contrast, an individual who holds privilege as a White, cisgender male may still experience the barriers and stressors associated with poverty but does not face racism or sexism.

Defining Poverty

Globally, poverty is defined within the following domains:

a. *housing poor* (inadequate or barriers to housing);
b. *health poor* (inadequate or barriers to health care); and/or
c. *time poor* (when an individual spends most of their time working to support financial needs without time for avocational activities; UNESCO, 2020).

Individuals may experience one or all of these challenges associated with poverty. In the United States, poverty is typically defined socially as *relative poverty* and formally *as income poverty*. Socially, poverty is conceptualized *relatively* in that individuals are perceived to be experiencing poverty if their standard of living falls below the expected or relative standards in their "given social context" (UNESCO, 2020, p. 1). In the United States, this may mean a person does not have access to health care, safe or stable housing, food, clean water, and/or clothing.

In contrast to social perceptions of poverty, most governing bodies use *income poverty* to determine if individuals and/or families are experiencing poverty and meet standards to receive government assistance (UNESCO, 2020). The U.S. income poverty measure is the *federal poverty level (FPL)*. The FPL is updated yearly and issues income cutoffs for access to social safety net programs, such as TANF, WIC, SNAP, childcare, and subsidized housing (see Table 11.2). While the FPL is helpful in that it establishes a means for accessing services, if an individual earns even one cent greater than the FPL, they do not qualify to access numerous social programs. Further, this measure does not address *relative poverty* and may deflate yearly poverty statistics in that a person who earns just slightly higher than the FPL is still experiencing poverty without having access to needed governmental resources. This is necessary to remember when reviewing federal poverty statistics because many more individuals are experiencing relative poverty than statistics report.

The Federal Poverty Level

The FPL is an income-based measure used to determine who is and is not experiencing poverty in the United States (see Table 11.2). You can find information regarding the FPL from the Department of Health and Human Services: https://aspe.hhs.gov/poverty-guidelines.

Beyond these resource-based poverty definitions, it is important to consider that poverty and poverty experiences differ by circumstances and duration. Poverty may be episodic, chronic, or generational (Chopp, 2017). Episodic poverty is poverty that lasts for less than 2 months and is typically associated with short-term financial constraints (e.g., job loss, health concerns). Poverty experiences that last longer than 4 years are deemed *chronic* (U.S. Census Bureau, 2023). A case in which poverty is experienced for two or more generations is called *generational poverty* (Chopp, 2017). Persons experiencing chronic and generational poverty can face challenging social, emotional, and political experiences. These are important factors for counselors to consider because they can result in worldviews, values, and beliefs that differ from people who are

TABLE 11.2 2024 Federal Poverty Guidelines

Household/Family Size	Income/Year
1	$15,060
2	$20,440
3	$25,820
4	$31,200
5	$36,580
6	$41,960
7	$47,340
*8	$52,720

Guidelines are for the 48 contiguous states and do not include Hawaii or Alaska.

**Add $5,380 for each additional household member.*

middle social class—all of which extend beyond SES factors. What people in poverty have or do not have material-wise is important to acknowledge; counselors must go beyond that. Counseling is an interpersonal, relationship-based experience, so counselors must explore clients' beliefs, ways of being, values, and worldviews in order to work from a person-centered perspective and not fall prey to imposing their values.

There are several things that are common for people in middle social class that are uncommon or unlikely for people who live in poverty. People experiencing chronic/generational poverty are unlikely to own property, complete higher education degrees, and may have significant barriers to employment and/or employment mobility (PSU, 2020). These barriers may include a lack of access to safe or stable housing and health care, including mental health care, meaning clients may have unique needs and presenting concerns in the counseling setting, which must be addressed as part of their treatment plan. Furthermore, counselors must be cautious not to make assumptions about what clients in poverty need or want and must take exceptional care not to shame or blame clients.

Classism, Microaggressions, and Counseling

Researchers have discovered that counselors have biases about people in low social class that may manifest in the counseling relationship. Smith et al. (2013) uncovered that counselors believed that poverty caused mental illness and that people in low social class were "dirty, lazy, or violent" (p. 141); could not hold a job; and lacked decision-making skills. Cook (2017) found that study participants expressed social class privilege, misconceptions about social class, and social class microaggressions. Social class microaggressions included using otherizing language (e.g., *those people*, *SES challenged*, *poor people*) to speak about people in low social class and denying clients' social class as a relevant cultural variable. Participants exhibited similar class-denying behaviors via their own social class privilege by stating that they did not need to think about their own social class position or experiences. Finally, participants expressed misconceptions about social class by endorsing the belief in meritocracy and equating being economically poor with being happy (Cook, 2017).

Social class microaggressions are subtle, covert, commonplace comments or behaviors based on perceived or actual social class or SES group membership that convey to the recipient that they do not belong (O'Hara & Cook, 2018). Social class microaggressions, whether intentional or unintentional, can cause harm. O'Hara and Cook (2018) investigated the experiences of counselor education doctoral students who had experienced social class microaggressions and found that they had negative relational, emotional, and cognitive impacts on participants. Additionally, Cook and O'Hara (2019) developed a data-driven theory that social class microaggressions likely persist to preserve the status quo, that is, for those in the middle social class to maintain the power and privilege that benefits them. Theory components include social class invisibility, privilege and unawareness about social class, perceptions and assumptions about social class, and unequal societal structures that explain how social class microaggressions and classism serve a distinct societal purpose. However, these components point to concrete areas in which counselors can increase their knowledge and awareness so they can develop affirmative social class skills and advocacy actions.

Counseling Applications

Ethical Responsibility

Understanding the impact of social class as both a separate and intersecting identity is imperative for counselors to provide ethical and effective services to diverse clients (ACA, 2014; AMHCA, 2020; ASCA, 2023; CRCC, 2023; NBCC, 2023). While *social class* is only mentioned specifically in the ASCA *Code of Ethics*, SES is named in ACA (C.5) and AMHCA (I.C.2.a) nondiscrimination codes; this absence could be related to the complexity and misunderstandings of social class, along with the simplicity and comfort many have with the term *SES*. The CRCC (2022) and ACA (2014) *Codes* are the only ones to specify attention to SES regarding assessment: "A client's socio-economic and cultural experiences are considered when diagnosing mental disorders" (G.3.b and E.5.b, respectively), while ACA is the only code to call counselors to recognize the impact SES may have on assessment and interpretation (see code E.8). These are important considerations given the empirical evidence that counselors hold bias about clients in low social class.

Counselors must acknowledge that access to counseling and mental health care is a social class experience insomuch as many individuals may not have access to counseling due to economic, transportation, and childcare barriers. Additionally, social stigma and internalized stigma perpetuated by classism can be barriers to mental health treatment, further exacerbating mental health concerns (Goodman et al., 2012; Kudrna et al., 2010; Rubin & Stuart, 2017; Toporek, 2013). Mental health concerns such as depression, anxiety, posttraumatic stress, and substance use disorders can be amplified or mitigated based on how a person perceives their social class, with lower social groups viewing mental health concerns as more severe than higher social class groups (Liu, 2004; Martiny & Rubin, 2016; Rubin & Stuart, 2017). Counseling ethical codes (i.e., ACA, AMHCA, ASCA, CRC) call counselors to advocate at individual, institutional, and societal levels, including removing barriers and fighting stigma. Counselors must find ways to live these codes to benefit clients and society.

Multicultural and Social Justice Counseling Competencies

Counselors are expected to be self-aware and possess the knowledge, skills, and actions to support the wellness of clients from diverse social class backgrounds and to understand how their identities are similar and different from their clients in service to providing competent care (Ratts et al., 2015). Counselors can use the MSJCC framework to explore simultaneously their social class identities and their class privilege and marginalization, while discerning how social class impacts clients' lives in direct and indirect ways.

Broadly, counselors should seek to understand clients' unique social class identity and address the sociocultural systems that affect client well-being; this enables counselors to determine—in collaboration with clients—appropriate counseling and advocacy interventions to enhance their lives (Ratts et al., 2015; Trott & Reeves, 2018). Counselors should have deliberate conversations about social class differences and similarities with clients early in the therapeutic relationship (i.e., broaching) so they can explore how their collective privileged and marginalized identities can enhance or impede the counseling relationship. When social class is broached, clients may feel more positively toward the counselor and the counseling process, leading to increased client well-being and treatment efficacy (Trott & Reeves, 2018). Additionally, counselors may experience an increased ability to offer empathy and display unconditional positive regard when they attend to clients' diverse identities (Coma & Hunter, 2018). However, when social class is left unexamined, clients may feel misunderstood, judged, and disconnected from their counselor (Trott & Reeves, 2018). Limited attention to social class in counseling may reinforce middle-class values and perpetuate systems of oppression and powerlessness for clients in lower social class groups (Trott & Reeves, 2018; Vontress, 2011); counselors have a responsibility to dismantle such systems to best serve clients. Furthermore, not attending to social class can lead to premature termination and counselors blaming clients for this action (Vontress, 2011). This lack of attention poses clear ethical issues; counselors are expected to provide effective services to diverse client populations and avoid imposing their values (ACA, 2014; AMHCA, 2020; ASCA, 2023; CRCC, 2022).

BOX 11.4 **TIPS FOR PROFESSIONAL PRACTICE: BEING PART OF CHANGE**

Cook and O'Hara (2019) identified several components that contribute to social class microaggressions and classism, and counselors are in a unique position to make a difference. The activity below is designed to help you identify, reflect on, and respond to issues related to class and classicism.

1. First, read each brief explanation.
2. Then, read the points under *What can I do*, considering how each connects to what you learned in this chapter and the MSJCCs.
3. Last, in the space provided, write one or two questions you could use in a counseling setting as you work with a client.

Social Class Invisibility

Many people believe that the United States is a *classless society* because they believe that opportunities are equally distributed and available to all. This leads people to deny social class and to be *class blind*.

What Can I Do?

- Acknowledge there are differences in individuals' experiences, beliefs, actions, etc., related to their social class identities and that social class exists.
- Speak out when people deny class and its impacts on clients and help educate others about class differences.
- Ask about and validate clients' social class worldviews and experiences.

My Broaching Questions:

Privilege and Unawareness About Social Class

When one holds dominant culture group membership, it is natural not to examine the privileges one is afforded because of one's social class status. Such privilege can lead to unawareness about the lives and experiences of people in other class groups, particularly those who live in low social class. Unawareness can result in bias, prejudice, discrimination, and oppression based on social class and can manifest negatively in the counseling relationship.

What Can I Do?

- Increase your awareness about your social class identities by examining how you have privilege and how you do not.
- Increase your knowledge about individuals from other social class groups and challenge your pre-established beliefs about who they are.
- Broach social class differences with clients and demonstrate willingness to understand their experiences.

My Broaching Questions:

Perceptions and Assumptions About Social Class

A common U.S. belief is that of meritocracy—if you work hard, you can achieve whatever you want. Tied to the belief in meritocracy is that if people are economically poor, it is a result of what those people have or have not done, that their economic reality is their fault. These are two examples of perceptions and assumptions about social class (see Cook, 2017; O'Hara & Cook, 2018; and Smith et al., 2013 for more examples). Although these beliefs can stem from social class privilege, they are embedded deeply in U.S. culture and are considered *acceptable*.

What Can I Do?

- Learn the common assumptions applied to social class groups and examine your own belief systems. Challenge others when they make assumptions about people in low social class. For example, if someone says, "Everyone on public assistance is lazy and working the system," ask them for the references used to support this idea.
- Prepare yourself with reliable data to refute such sweeping claims.

- Refuse to use disparaging colloquial terms for social class groups and challenge those who do.
- Engage in public policy advocacy to fight discriminatory laws such as mandatory drug testing for individuals who receive SNAP and other public assistance benefits.

My Questions for Gathering Data and Learning More:

Social Class Counseling Framework

There are limited theoretical models used to understand and address social class and poverty in counseling (see Chapter 6), yet the CARE model (Foss et al., 2011) and the updated I-CARE model first presented in Chapter 9 (Foss-Kelly et al., 2017) can help counselors working with clients who are experiencing poverty.

The I-CARE model subsumed the CARE model and added an internal reflection component essential for counselors' development and practice. The I-Care model provides specific questions to assist counselors in exploring their social class experiences:

- "What did my caregivers teach me about people in poverty?"
- "Was I excluded or rejected by social groups because of my social status?"
- "Was I denied or granted important life experiences or opportunities?"
- "What sorts of pressures were related to my family's income level?"
- "When have I engaged in the classist United States?" (Foss-Kelly et al., 2017, p. 204)

In addition to applying the MSJCCs, these frameworks provide methods for counselors to better understand the client's lived experiences related to social class (Cook & Lawson, 2016).

Readers can revisit the full description of the I-Care model on p. 000.

Best Practice for Working With Clients Experiencing Poverty

Five best practices have been identified for counseling clients experiencing poverty: (a) awareness, (b) training, (c) knowledge, (d) skills, and (e) advocacy (Clark et al., 2020). This five-point model provides data-driven best practices for working with clients experiencing poverty, while it is appropriate to apply more broadly to understand social class.

Awareness relates to counselor self-awareness of social class identity, power, and privilege within the counseling relationship. *Training* is developing social class competency from both formal and informal educational experiences, such as graduate education, reading books, attending conferences, and attending cultural events. *Knowledge* indicates that specialized knowledge is needed when working with clients who have poverty experiences, including knowledge of barriers, intersectionality, and the impact of power and oppression on clients' experiences. The *skills* best practice names four skills: poverty-sensitive assessment, person-centered and relational skills, cultural broaching, and recognition of client strengths and empowerment. Finally, *advocacy* is for and with clients experiencing poverty to empower clients and reduce barriers (Clark et al., 2020).

Person-Centered and Humanistic Strategies

A strong counseling relationship is foundational for successful interventions and client change. However, social class bias, social class microaggressions, and classism can stand in the way of building a strong counseling relationship. Because the vast majority of counselors identify as middle social class in their family of origin and currently, counselors may hold social class bias and enact social class microaggressions and classism without even knowing it. Similarly, many counseling theories were developed by people with middle social class identities for working with people with middle social class identities. The reality of present-day counseling practice is that more and more counselors and clients are from low social class, so our awareness, knowledge, and skills must shift.

BOX 11.5 **PROFILE OF A PRACTITIONER**

We (the chapter authors: Maddie, Jenn, and Susan) have our own social class stories and various experiences working with clients from various social classes because, as we have come to know, everyone has social class experiences! Social class is an identity factor that every person has, with influence across an individual's lifespan and how they interact with and experience the world around them, yet it is rarely discussed in mental health and therapeutic spaces.

When I (Maddie) was a counselor in training and a pre-licensure resident, I worked in a community mental health setting. In that setting, I worked with a variety of clients, most of whom were adults, with various presenting concerns and diagnoses. At that time in my life, I was a graduate student, either in my master's program or my doctoral program, and not very wealthy. But, because of my race (White), my educational level, family, educational background, and access to parental resources if I needed them (I never EVER asked my parents for money, although I definitely could have if necessary!), I experienced social class privileges. In many ways, my social class was reinforced by my role as the "expert" counselor in the community mental health setting, and it was something I did not realize I needed to manage actively when I started my work as a beginning counselor.

I am not a person from "means." My grandparents grew up in the Depression in mining towns in Appalachia or on rural farms in central Ohio. I was raised in a working-class suburb of Toledo, Ohio. My father was a single dad and a nontraditional first-generation college student who began his career as a teacher in my early childhood. I did not grow up without my basic needs being met, yet the first decade of my life was certainly lower middle class by definition. Most of my clothes were hand-me-downs or thrifted. I grew up in a two-bedroom house in a small Midwestern town. I don't remember going out to eat very much, and we only went on a handful of vacations (only by car, of course) in the first decade of my life.

My life changed dramatically in terms of social class throughout my childhood. My dad went to graduate school and became a principal and then superintendent of a school district. He was able to buy and sell his first house for a profit and paid off his student loans. We moved to a nicer, bigger house. He married my stepmom, so the household then became dual income. As our household finances changed, my family's standard of living changed. My later adolescent years were different: I had new clothes, and I even had my own car! While some things changed, my family's *wealth* did not. I was fortunate to get my undergraduate degree fully funded by academic scholarships; otherwise, I would have student loan debt from that experience.

All in all, I thought I was a pretty "average" person who was firmly middle class. I thought that I somehow could communicate that down-to-earth vibe to my clients in this community mental health setting without addressing it. I found when I started my counseling work that clients, many of whom were often older than I, POC, or men, were not as warm to me as my Midwestern, working-class upbringing would lead me to expect. I was a privileged (in reality and in client perception), Midwestern-sounding White woman working in a coastal southern city. I was different, and my clients didn't know my background or story. Thus, in my early counseling experiences, I was challenged to connect with and build rapport with clients who were different than me, maybe less so in reality than they perceived, but in that time and space, we were quite different.

As a practicum student, I brought these concerns to my supervisor, feeling uncertain and incapable in my own skills as a beginning counselor. It was helpful for me to process with my supervisor what my class experiences were, what my class expectations were, and how I perceived my class was apparent in counseling sessions. She challenged me directly, asking me something like, "How would clients know any of that about you?" and of course, she was correct. Without engaging in any cultural broaching, I had completely ignored social class in my own counseling relationships. I began to discuss social class and perceptions of class (as well as other identities) with my clients. Practically, it allowed our relationships to grow in an open and vulnerable way. Clinically, it allowed me to learn a great deal about clients' experiences and worldviews and how that might impact their presenting concerns. I learned that what I thought I was, or what I perceived I was, was not necessarily what clients perceived or understood about me because of the power structure that is inherent to the counseling relationship. It became critically important for my own genuineness and congruence in the counseling relationship and to navigate complex power structures to engage in open conversations with my clients regarding social class along with other important facets of my identity and theirs.

The first step toward social class inclusive counseling is to identify your values, beliefs, worldviews, and actions that are grounded in your social class. What and who do you value? How do you spend money? What are *acceptable* places to live, clubs to belong to, and activities to engage in during your leisure time? How easy is it for you to access what you need? Is your neighborhood safe? Can you get to school or work easily and in a short period of time? Do you go on vacations that do not include visiting relatives? Are you afraid of people who are homeless or have fewer resources? These are just a few questions to get you thinking about your social class worldview.

The next step is to reimage the core conditions (i.e., unconditional positive regard, warmth, empathy, genuineness, congruence) and key humanistic components that are essential to professional counseling. This step is about continually examining your values and beliefs, while it is about perspective taking too—how does your *client* understand these concepts? How will you display the core conditions so they jibe with your client? Will they feel a connection, or will they feel dismissed? Table 11.3 is a guide to get you thinking about and taking social class affirmative actions that align with person-centered and humanistic concepts.

TABLE 11.3 Reimagining Person-Centered and Humanistic Components

Component	Definition and Purpose	Examples
Empathy	Demonstrating that you are feeling with the client with the intent to normalize and validate the client's emotions	"I can imagine how scary it feels to be working so many hours and still have such a fragile housing situation."
Unconditional Positive Regard	Displaying a nonjudgmental, affirming stance of clients' personhood that allows them to be who they are and to express themselves freely without negative repercussions	"I am sensing that you feel shame related to these financial issues; these challenges don't reflect the quality of who you are as a person."
Congruence/ Genuineness	Being your true self in the role of counselor without putting on airs or pretending to be someone you are not. Counselors who are congruent and genuine are *comfortable in their own skin* and demonstrate ease with all clients, thereby allowing clients to feel more comfortable and less inhibited	"It might be frustrating that I don't have that same experience as you. I know that I don't know everything and I really want to understand your experience in whatever way you want to share it."
Warmth	Creating an inviting and hospitable environment, both in terms of physical space and counselor presence, that allows clients to feel welcomed and relaxed	"Would you like some water before we begin?"
Meaning Making	Identifying value, purpose, and motivation for life choices and the activities in which clients engage	"I know you're working multiple jobs right now, and it is difficult, but you've also shared how these sacrifices are important to support your children and family."
Strengths and Resiliencies	Naming and drawing on ways in which clients have persevered, triumphed, and done their best in a variety of circumstances so clients know the tools they have already at their disposal	"You have shared so many barriers that you are facing but I am noticing how well you are navigating these challenges with your resourcefulness, persistence, and using your support system."

Social Class Assessment

Counselors should assess clients' social class at the outset of the therapeutic relationship; this enables counselors to broach the subject early and gain a better understanding of the clients' social class experiences (Kim & Cardemil, 2012; Trott & Reeves, 2018). During intake, counselors should ask about income, educational and occupational attainment, housing, transportation, neighborhood characteristics, financial savings, health care, experiences of oppression, and values, beliefs, strengths, and resiliencies they have developed from their social class identity(ies) (Cook & Lawson, 2016; Kim & Cardemil, 2012; Liu et al., 2013). Although frequently excluded, social class markers can easily be added to any intake and/or biopsychosocial interview. Counselors should explore what social class means to the client and its relationship to the presenting concern (Liu, 2001; Liu, 2011). The initial assessment is an opportunity to broach differences and similarities and establish a stronger therapeutic relationship (Kim & Cardemil, 2012; Liu et al., 2013; Ratts et al., 2015; Trott & Reeves, 2018; Vontress, 2011).

BOX 11.6 **TIPS FOR PROFESSIONAL PRACTICE: ADDRESSING SOCIAL CLASS**

The following questions, when asked directly in a session, can help counselors explore how social class impacts clients:

- "How do you describe your social class?"
- "How did your social class influenced your life growing up?"
- "What thoughts and feelings do you have about your social class, past and present?"
- "Has your social class impacted opportunities in your life (e.g., work, education, relationships)?"
- "Do you have access to resources such as food, shelter, transportation, and health care?"
- "We share/do not share a social class background; however, I do not presume to understand your experience, and I want you to know that I am willing to talk about class as it is relevant to you."

Based on the client's responses, counselors can work with clients to implement advocacy interventions and referrals for additional support, if needed.

Social Class Genogram

A genogram is a practical assessment and therapeutic instrument counselors can use with clients to construct a visual representation of their cultural background (Hardy & Laszloffy, 1995). One way a genogram can be used is by focusing on one or more sociocultural dimensions that influence the client's life (Ivey et al., 2018; Hardy & Laszloffy, 1995), including gaining a better understanding of struggles and resiliencies related to their social class experiences (Ivey et al., 2018). Genograms can be created in session or may be given as homework and then discussed in subsequent counseling sessions. Clients may represent their social class genogram in a variety of ways, such as drawing, photography, or in digital formats, based on client interest and access (Ivey et al., 2018).

BOX 11.7 TIPS FOR PROFESSIONAL PRACTICE: CREATING A SOCIAL CLASS GENOGRAM

The following steps can assist clients in developing their own social class genogram:

- Identify your social class; this can be your social class of origin and/or the social class you currently occupy.
- Choose the format that appeals to you. Be creative!
- Select a significant symbol or icon to represent yourself, and place it in the center of your genogram.
- Choose symbols or icons to represent kin and influential relations.
- Select symbols and shapes to represent social class statuses and use these to illustrate social class experiences across generations.
- Create a legend to refer to your chosen symbols, icons, and shapes and what is represented by each.

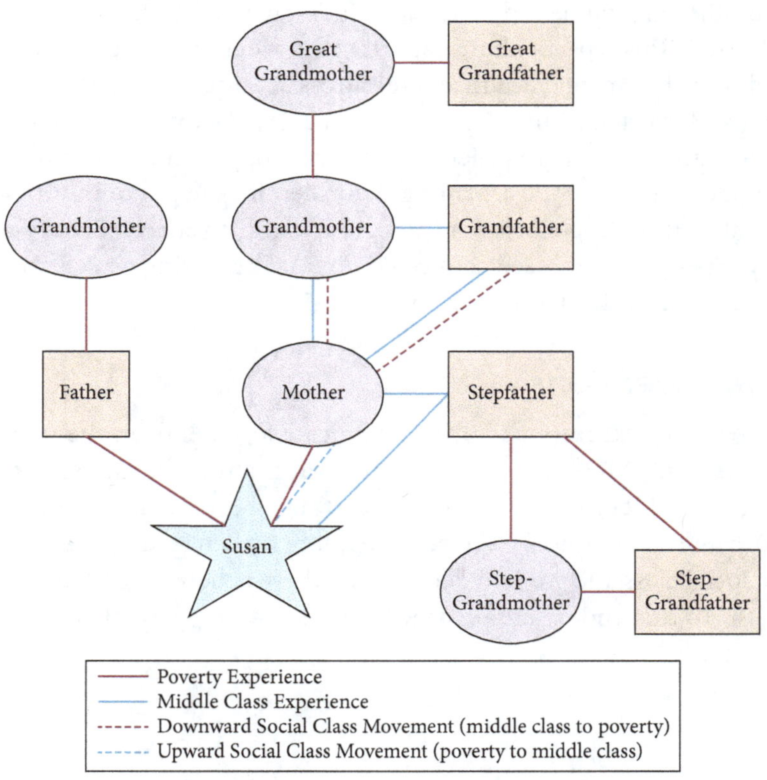

FIGURE 11.1 Social Class Genogram Example

BOX 11.8 **TIPS FOR PROFESSIONAL PRACTICE: DEBRIEFING A SOCIAL CLASS GENOGRAM**

The following questions can be used to enrich the meaning of a social class genogram with clients:

- What images, memories, or stories came up for you during and after creating your genogram?
- What barriers or hardships have you faced because of your social class? What are the strengths and assets you have developed because of your social class?
- How useful was your genogram in understanding your social class?
- What do you want to do in your life to enrich your family's social class story?

Wellness and Social Support Strategies

Social support (e.g., family, friends, community) can buffer against stress, feelings of isolation, depression, and other mental health concerns (Hansson et al., 2005; Myers & Sweeney, 2008; Rubin & Stuart, 2017). This is particularly important for people in low social class groups because they may have diminished mental health and resources because of social stigma, discrimination, and oppression (Kudrna et al., 2010; Trott & Reeves, 2018; Vontress, 2011). Drawing on current systems of support and encouraging clients to seek new opportunities to expand positive connections can support clients while affirming their identities (e.g., community-based support groups; Long et al., 2019). People in lower class groups who positively identify with their social class group may experience increased connectedness and belonging, which are important wellness factors (Kudrna et al., 2010; Rubin & Stuart, 2017).

Advocacy Interventions

Counselors have an ethical responsibility to advocate for clients on the micro-, meso-, and macrolevels (Ratts et al., 2015; Sue et al., 1992). On the microlevel, counselors address clients' social class and other identities to better understand their clients' barriers and strengths (Ratts et al., 2015; Sue et al., 1992). Counselors explore if clients have internalized oppression related to their social class and work to deconstruct these beliefs to generate alternative stories (Ivey et al., 2018). To this end, a self-advocacy plan is a strategy for client empowerment and resiliency building.

BOX 11.9 TIPS FOR PROFESSIONAL PRACTICE: CREATING A SELF-ADVOCACY PLAN

The following questions can be used to support clients in building a plan for self-advocacy:

- What are my strengths and current resources?
- What are my goals and how can I express them clearly?
- What resources, information, and skills do I need to advocate for myself?
- Who can help me with meeting my goals? How do I care for myself?

Now, transition the answers into a plan that includes when, how, and for what purposes they will use the strategies they listed. If any self-doubts arise, work through them with the client and teach tools to combat these doubts. Listen carefully for any systemic barriers the client mentions—those could be opportunities to advocate with and/or on behalf of the client, and at the very least, they can be a time to strategize how to navigate these barriers with as little impact as possible to the client's sense of self.

Interventions at the micro-level can include increasing client access to resources such as employment, housing, transportation, job training, and health care, and locating accessible resources in the client's community. Systems of positive support can increase connectedness and emotional and practical resource sharing. Interventions at the macrolevel may include lobbying at local, state, and national levels for relevant policy changes that affect people in low social class groups (e.g., increasing the minimum wage, access to health care, fair and equitable housing, clean water access, eliminating food deserts, and educational and employment opportunities to improve client mental health and well-being for all). Finally, counselors must address classism and intersecting "-isms" to enact social change with and on behalf of clients at every systemic level.

There are great opportunities for social class advocacy at the meso- and macrolevels. These can include advocacy within the systems counselors are embedded, such as schools and agencies, or even at the local, state, and national levels. There are multiple policies and sociopolitical structures that do not adequately support persons of low social class and/or experiencing poverty. These can include agency policies related to payment, reimbursement, or client attendance. Other examples of these policies may relate to attendance in schools. At the local, state, and national levels, many policies, such as lack of fair, safe, and affordable housing; the FPL; and that gap many individuals fall into by not qualifying for social safety programs, such Medicaid, TANF, and WIC. Other examples and opportunities for counselor macrolevel advocacy include universal health and mental health care, raising the minimum wage, affordable higher education, and access to affordable childcare. As these sociopolitical issues continue to evolve, counselors must pay close attention to their implications for our most marginalized clients.

Conclusion

Diversity, inclusion, and equity in counseling continue to evolve. How professional counselors define and enact multiculturally focused counseling has changed since its inception, and we will continue to adapt to clients' needs within their social contexts, including how counselors attend to social class. We expect that our understanding of social class and different social class groups will change and develop over time, just as the understanding of social class has been shaped by history. Counselors' understandings of social class, how their social class presents to others, and the social class experiences of others are lifelong growth areas, as is identifying how social class microaggressions and classism present and persist. There are concrete actions that professional counselors can integrate into their practices. This includes using a class-conscious counseling practice and class-affirming skills, which we hope to have communicated to you in this chapter.

Questions for Reflection

1. How do you believe history has influenced how we understand social class in the United States? Identify which historical moments and/or policies have informed your own social class understanding.
2. How might you explain the concepts of SES and social class to someone who has never heard the terms before?
3. Describe social class privilege and indicate what some social class privileges are. Now, describe social class oppression and provide examples. Can you identify social class privilege and/or oppression in your own life? How might you explore this with a client?
4. Describe some steps you may take in an intake interview to assess a client's social class. How might you broach social class with a client?
5. Counselors are advocates at the micro-, meso-, and macrolevels. Describe how you might engage in social class advocacy at each of these levels. What form of advocacy would be easiest for you? Which might be more challenging?

Applying What You Have Learned

Complete each of the following activities, considering what you learned from this chapter.

Activity #1: Best Practices for Counseling Persons Experiencing Poverty

For this activity, work individually and then discuss your answers with a group or a partner. Take time to answer/assess your capabilities in the following areas: awareness, training, knowledge, skills, and advocacy. Identify your strengths and growing edges; determine with your partner or group the best way to remedy your growing edges to ensure you are ready to practice competently with clients experiencing poverty.

AWARENESS

Self-Awareness of Social Class Identity:

- What is your awareness of your own social class identity?
- How would you describe it to someone else?

Client Worldview of Social Class Identity:

- How might you know your client's own social class worldview?
- How might you help a client articulate their social class identity for your own understanding?

Counselor Boundaries and Wellness:

- When working with clients experiencing poverty, how might you keep yourself well and set clear boundaries with clients?

TRAINING

Formal Training:

- What are formal training opportunities you could take advantage of to learn more about poverty and poverty experiences?

Informal Training:

- What are informal ways in which you can learn more about poverty and poverty experiences?

KNOWLEDGE

Poverty Barriers:

- Can you identify common barriers that are associated with poverty?
- How might you learn from your clients what their barriers are?

Privilege, Oppression, and Intersectionality:

- How would you define social class privilege? Oppression? Intersectionality?
- How do these issues impact individuals who experience poverty and those who counsel them?

Systems Theory:

- Define systems theory.
- How do collectivism and individualism impact the counseling relationship with persons experiencing poverty?

Severe and Persistent Mental Illness (SPMI):

- What do you know about the diagnosis and treatment of people with SPMI?
- How would you navigate an SPMI diagnosis with someone experiencing poverty?

Crisis and Trauma:

- What is your knowledge of crisis and trauma?
- How would you use a trauma-informed approach with someone experiencing poverty?

SKILLS

Poverty Sensitive Assessment:

- Describe how you will assess clients for needs, such as housing, employment, or food security.
- What might you ask clients to learn this information from them?

Person-Centered and Relational Skills:

- Why are person-centered and relational skills important to use with clients experiencing poverty?
- Provide examples of useful skills and how you would apply them.

Cultural Broaching:

- How would you culturally broach your own social class and other identities with a client experiencing poverty?

Recognition of Strengths:

- What is the importance of recognition of client strengths?
- How will you identify strengths in clients experiencing poverty?

ADVOCACY

Assist Clients With Problem-Solving:

- What are the problems you could assist clients experiencing poverty with?
- How might you help clients establish solutions to challenges they are experiencing?

Increase Client Access:

- How would you increase your clients' abilities to access services in your agency, office, or school?

Challenge Poverty Stereotypes:

- In what ways can you challenge poverty stereotypes in your family, friendships, and social circles?
- What are some ways in which you can correct common misconceptions about persons experiencing poverty?

Activity #2: Proactive Discussions About Social Class

As you learned in this chapter, social class is not a topic many people in the United States want to discuss, including within professional counseling. Why do you think this is the case? What are we afraid of? Why does it make us uncomfortable? Do you think structural oppression might play a role? Is it possible that not talking about social class keeps privilege and privileged systems intact?

Advocacy actions can take many forms. One form of advocacy action is to speak to the unspoken with the goal of bringing attention to that which is usually hidden or absent. Armed with what you have learned about social class in this chapter, commit to engaging in conversations about social class. Start by talking with a classmate or close friend, then expand your reach by talking with others about it. Determine some starter questions you could ask such as the following:

- Which of your values came from your social class upbringing?
- How important is your social class identity to you?
- What do you think accounts for why there is so much poverty in our country? What do you think can be done about it?
- Do you think that everyone should go to college?
- How do you think people in the upper 1% are able to stay there?

As you consider the questions you might ask, discern your viewpoints on these topics, including how you might respond to any biases your conversation partner expresses. How will you continue to engage with them? How will you provide accurate information that opposes their biases? How will you remain open to the other person's viewpoint?

CHAPTER 12

Disability and Ableism

Melissa D. Deroche and Elizabeth K. Mautz

My disability exists not because I use a wheelchair, but because the broader environment isn't accessible.

—Stella Young

CHAPTER OVERVIEW

In this chapter, we offer a foundational understanding of the disability experience and the diversity that exists within the disability community, including other intersecting identities for people with disabilities (PWD). The information we provide is meant to increase your knowledge about disability and to extend your understanding of historical markers and the systems that shape the perception of disability and PWD, the structural inequities present in society that limit access for PWD, and culturally relevant practices that promote cultural competence, cultural humility, and social justice advocacy.

LEARNING OBJECTIVES

By the end of this chapter, students will be able to

1. describe historical markers that have shaped societal perceptions of disability;
2. define terms and discuss the intersection of disability, ableism, and other nondominant cultural identities;
3. discuss how classification, onset, course, and visibility of disability impact the individual experience;
4. compare and contrast the different models of disability;
5. explain systems perspectives for counseling practice with persons with disabilities;
6. discuss potential ways to integrate disability considerations in counseling practice; and
7. analyze how counselor professional codes of ethics provide limited guidance for working with PWD.

CACREP 2016 STANDARDS

The information in this chapter supports the following standards:

- 2.F.1.e advocacy processes needed to address institutional and social barriers that impede access, equity, and success for clients
- 2.F.2.c multicultural competencies

- 2.F.2.d the impact of heritage, attitudes, beliefs, understandings, and acculturative experiences on an individual's views of others
- 2.F.2.h strategies for identifying and eliminating barriers, prejudices, and processes of intentional and unintentional oppression and discrimination
- 2.F.3.i ethical and culturally relevant strategies for promoting resilience and optimum development and wellness across the lifespan
- 2.F.5.b a systems approach to conceptualizing clients

CACREP 2024 STANDARDS

The information in this chapter supports the following standards:

- 3.A.4. the role and process of the professional counselor advocating on behalf of and with individuals receiving counseling services to address systemic, institutional, architectural, attitudinal, disability, and social barriers that impede access, equity, and success
- 3.B.2. the influence of heritage, cultural identities, attitudes, values, beliefs, understandings, within-group differences, and acculturative experiences on individuals' worldviews
- 3.B.4. the effects of historical events, multigenerational trauma, and current issues on diverse cultural groups in the U.S. and globally
- 3.B.6. the effects of various socio-cultural influences, including public policies, social movements, and cultural values, on mental and physical health and wellness
- 3.B.8. principles of independence, inclusion, choice and self-empowerment, and access to services within and outside the counseling relationship
- 3.B.9. strategies for identifying and eliminating barriers, prejudices, and processes of intentional and unintentional oppression and discrimination
- 3.B.10. guidelines developed by professional counseling organizations related to social justice, advocacy, and working with individuals with diverse cultural identities
- 3.C.7. models of resilience, optimal development, and wellness in individuals and families across the lifespan

A Contextual Framework for Understanding People With Disabilities

There are myths and misconceptions about PWD and the disability experience, particularly the notion that individuals with chronic illness or disability are irresponsible, unlucky, and make poor decisions that resulted in their conditions. In fact, disability is a natural part of the human experience, and no one is immune to temporary or permanent disability. According to the Centers for Disease Control and Prevention (2020), approximately one in four adults in the United States reports at least one disability; women, individuals of lower social class, people over 65 years of age, Native American Indians/Alaskan Natives, and those living in rural areas are more likely to experience disability. Additionally, 14% of public school students ages 3–21 received services through the Individuals with Disabilities Education Act (IDEA) in the 2019–2020 school year (National Center for Education Statistics [NCES], n.d.). Additionally, 19% of undergraduates and 12% of postbaccalaureate students have disabilities (NCES, n.d.). Given the prevalence, it is probable that all counselors, regardless of specialization or work setting, will encounter PWD.

Therefore, it is essential to develop an understanding of different disability characteristics and the ways in which disability is defined and described.

Though there are a myriad of ways in which disability can be defined and described, the most common definition is derived from the Americans with Disabilities Act (ADA) of 1990:

> A person with a disability is someone who has a physical or mental impairment that substantially limits one or more major life activities, has a history or record of such an impairment, or is perceived by others as having such an impairment. (U.S. Department of Justice, n.d.)

Major life activities can include actions (e.g., speaking and breathing), movements (e.g., walking, standing, lifting), cognitive functions (e.g., thinking, concentrating), sensory functions (e.g., seeing, hearing), tasks (e.g., working, reading, communicating), and the operation of internal bodily functions (e.g., circulation, individual organs). This definition provides the initial context for understanding models of disability.

Models of Disability

Models of disability are theoretical frameworks used to define and describe the disability experience. These models hold power based on their influence on public perception of disability, their capacity to shape the self-identity of PWD, and their potential influence on the therapeutic alliance (Smart, 2009). Each model provides a unique perspective regarding the causes of and so-called *solutions* for the disability experience, yet no model provides the *correct* perspective or a comprehensive view of the disability experience. These models coexist alongside one another, and at times, one model becomes more dominant depending on the situation or context. We urge you to attend to the varied ways in which PWD discuss their disability experiences. Such an approach can facilitate greater understanding of how your client experiences their disability, and it enables you to recognize the daily experiences and the structural inequalities faced by PWD.

Moral Model

The oldest model of disability is the moral model. The moral model uses religious-laden language and contends that disability results from moral lapse or sin, is a failure or test of faith, or is punishment for negative actions by the individual or their family. From this perspective, PWD are held morally responsible for their disability, asserting the idea that people *get what they deserve* because of the choices they've made. Therefore, the solution is for PWD to adjust to or transcend their disability (Olkin, 1999).

Alternatively in this model, disability can be seen as a sign of faith or strength. For example, someone with a strong faith may believe that they were chosen to have a disability based on God's faith in them or as a sign of survival of a life challenge (e.g., surviving a plane crash with a spinal cord injury; Olkin, 2022). In either case, the views held by religious/spiritual communities regarding disability have the power to create inviting or unwelcoming environments for PWD. This means that a PWD with a religious/spiritual identity may feel isolated from or betrayed by their religious/spiritual community, or they may receive ongoing support from their religious/spiritual community.

Medical Model

The medical model of disability defines disability as a medical illness or impairment of the mind or body and is the primary way the public understands disability. The medical condition or illness is diagnosed by physical and mental health professionals who use evaluative, standardized, objective criteria and categorical systems to diagnose disability (e.g., *International Classification of Diseases* or *Diagnostic and Statistical Manual of Mental Disorders*) with a focus on rehabilitation, treatment, or cure. From this vantage point, disability is seen as abnormal and viewed as a deficit located within the individual, resulting in PWD needing to find ways to adjust their disability to their environment rather than the environment providing necessary accommodations. While an appropriate and accurate diagnosis is necessary to guide treatment and allows PWD the capacity to assert their civil rights through the ADA, including access to governmental programs and services such as vocational rehabilitation, social security, and adaptive or assistive aids, PWD cannot be reduced to their diagnosis. When PWD are seen only as their diagnosis, limited attention is given to their individual needs, the environmental and societal barriers they encounter, their life struggles outside of their disability, and the importance their other identities hold for them.

Functional and Environmental Models

Although the functional and environmental models are sometimes discussed as separate frameworks, we, like Smart and Smart (2006), conceptualize these models as interactional and discuss them alongside one another. Both models consider the biological factors of disability (i.e., impairment). The difference is that the functional model describes disability as an interaction between the PWD's impairment (e.g., limb paralysis) and the role or function they need to perform (e.g., reaching or grabbing; playing a violin), whereas the environmental model describes disability as an interaction between the impairment the PWD has and *the environment* (e.g., inability to open a door that does not have an automated sensor or button). Disablement, therefore, resides external to the PWD and is associated with the lack of adaptive aids, accommodations, and inaccessibility of their environments. The solution to disablement, at least in part, is the responsibility of society, and it entails providing accommodations or adaptations and removing environmental barriers.

Sociopolitical or Minority Group Model

In contrast to the moral, medical, and functional/environmental models, the sociopolitical or minority group model of disability is said to have more explanatory power in describing the daily experiences of PWD (Smart, 2009). The minority group model of disability is a product of the Disability Rights Movement, in which PWD began to challenge negative societal attitudes and structural barriers that impeded their access to and participation in educational, employment, and community environments. From a minority group model perspective, disability is not a result of the individual's impairment but rather impairment is the result of stigma, stereotypes, negative attitudes and biases (i.e., prejudice), barriers to access (e.g., inaccessible physical and digital spaces), and denial of accommodations and opportunities (i.e., discrimination). In fact, PWD report that negative attitudes are more problematic than the disability itself (McCarthy, 2003). Therefore, the solution to disablement requires collective action on the part of people with and without disability identities to advocate for a more inclusive society and to participate in the creation of policies and practices that promote greater equality.

Biopsychosocial Model

Considered a multifactorial approach to disability, the biopsychosocial model implies that it is the negative attitudes of others toward PWD that prevent them from realizing their individual potential rather than what has been assigned to them because of an impairment or condition (Shakespeare et al., 2017). This model explores the intersection of biological, psychological, and social effects of the disability experience and argues that how we attend to each of these areas influence the impact of the condition. Proponents of this model claim to have enhanced the treatment for individuals with chronic conditions by recognizing that symptomology is as much psychological and social as it is biological. By managing the complex reactions people have to disability, treatments can more effectively address disability holistically without differing the treatment approach (Shakespeare et al., 2017). While the approach itself seems to take a comprehensive look at care and treatment of disability, some argue that this model unfairly suggests that impairment of one kind (e.g., physical versus psychological) equals impairment overall. Shakespeare et al. (2017) concluded that consideration needs to be given to how such models can stigmatize PWD and minimize treatment progress.

Classification, Onset, Course, and Visibility of Disability

While we discuss disability as a singular cultural identity, we urge you to conceptualize disability as a multifaceted construct because there is a range of human diversity within the disability community. The range of human diversity specific to ability status is grounded in category or type of disability, onset and course of disability, and visibility of disability, yet keep in mind that each of these constructs intersects with one another, as well as with other cultural identities, contributing to varied life experiences.

One disability classification system is based on symptomatology with three broad categories of disability: (a) physical disabilities (e.g., sensory loss, orthopedic impairments, amputations, paralysis, chronic illness), (b) cognitive or neurodivergent disabilities (e.g., intellectual, learning, developmental), and (c) psychiatric disabilities (i.e., mental illness and substance use disorders). As a categorical system, it uses biological terms and provides a common language for describing disability, yet it does little to explain the varied iterations or level of severity across a single disability category or the differences experienced by PWD with the same disability.

TABLE 12.1 Examples of Types of Disabilities

Physical Disabilities	*Neurodivergent or Cognitive Disabilities	Psychiatric Disabilities
Blindness or low vision	Autism spectrum disorder (ASD)	Posttraumatic stress disorder (PTSD)
Deafness or hard of hearing	Down syndrome	Major depressive disorder (MDD)
Cancer, Diabetes, HIV/AIDS	Dyslexia	Substance use disorders (SUD)
Paraplegia or Quadriplegia	Cerebral palsy	Schizophrenia
Spinal cord injury	Intellectual developmental disorder	Bipolar disorders
Multiple sclerosis	Alzheimer's disease	Anxiety disorders

**Note: Neurodivergence and substance use disorders are discussed in greater detail in Chapter 17.*

The *onset* and *course* of disability extend our understanding of disability beyond a discrete categorical system; it provides further context for understanding individual disability characteristics and developmental considerations. Disability onset captures a moment in time and refers to the age at which the disability is present or diagnosed. *Congenital* refers to disabilities that occur within the first year of life, while *acquired* denotes disabilities that develop after 1 year of age. For example, congenital disabilities may include blindness, deafness, spina bifida, or cerebral palsy. Acquired disabilities encompass a range of diagnoses that are typically the result of injury or aging, such as traumatic brain injury (TBI), spinal cord injury, arthritis, and vision/hearing loss.

The *course* of disability describes the progression of symptoms, which may be stable, episodic, degenerative, or a combination of the three. These constructs are presented in discrete terms yet a PWD can be diagnosed with a disability at birth and later develop an acquired disability or experience progression of impairment associated with a congenital disability. Each disability has its own onset and course, and each may impact the other. Together, onset and course of disability may differentially impact physical, cognitive, and socioemotional milestones throughout the lifespan (Smart, 2019), as well as one's disability identity.

Visibility of disability refers to the degree to which a disability is apparent to others or whether it is nonapparent or concealable from others. A person's disability is often visible because of the use of adaptive aids, such as a cane, service animal, hearing aid, or wheelchair, or it is noticeable by one's physicality (e.g., unusual gait, prosthetics, missing limbs). Nonapparent or concealable disabilities are generally not readily known or apparent to others, like learning or psychiatric disabilities or chronic illnesses such a Crohn's disease. Essentially, the visibility of disability influences one's ability to *pass* as able-bodied and not having to disclose one's disability; however, this does not mean that a non-apparent disability is preferable to a visible disability. Instead, these differences translate to people with visible and nonapparent disabilities encountering marginalization from different vantage points.

It's important to consider how the terms used to conceptualize this category impact a specific individual or client with a disability. While the disability literature uses all of these terms to discuss disability, individuals and specific disability groups may prefer one term over another. For example, a client who is blind may not appreciate you referring to their blindness as a *visible disability* and would prefer you speak about it as an *apparent disability*. Alternatively, a client with a chronic heart condition may prefer *nonapparent disability* rather than *hidden disability* because they feel the latter term is disempowering—it makes them feel as if people are insinuating their disability is not real if it is referred to as *hidden*. The goal is to use language clients prefer rather than imposing academic labels they may find troubling or inappropriate.

PWD constantly navigate their disability disclosure. People with nonapparent or concealable disabilities continually negotiate their own disability *coming out* processes (Lingsome, 2008), which entails determining contexts in which hiding one's disability would be advantageous or how, if, when, and to whom to disclose disability-related information. Alternatively, individuals with visible disabilities have little choice in their disclosure simply because of the apparent nature of their disability, and as a result, they encounter ableism more readily. For people with visible disabilities, ableism can occur in the form of infantilization, unwanted help, and invasion of privacy, whereas people with hidden or concealable disabilities encounter ableism in terms of invalidation and accusations of fraud (Nario-Redmon et al., 2019). For example, a person who is blind may encounter assistance from others when it is unwanted or harmful to their safety or be asked personal questions about the cause of their blindness (e.g., how long they have been blind, how much they can see). In contrast, someone with a chronic illness who only uses a wheelchair during illness flare-ups is questioned about the validity of their disability or if they are *faking* their disability. Consequently, persons with visible and nonapparent disabilities must navigate a society that values able-bodiedness, lacks an understanding of the disability experience, and often views disability in stereotypical ways, yet these experiences of ableism are often experienced differently based on the visibility and nature of one's disability.

While classification, onset, course, and visibility of disability are helpful classifications we use to describe diversity within the disability community, PWD possess other relevant cultural identities. We must recognize that both similarities and differences across these characteristics, as well as other cultural identities, impact the everyday experiences of PWD. For example, PWD can hold both privileged and marginalized identities in terms of race, ethnicity, gender identity and expression, relational/affectual identity, religious/spiritual affiliation, socioeconomic status and social class, and additional marginalized cultural identities may compound the oppression experienced by PWD with multiple minoritized identities (Chowdhury et al., 2022).

Chronic Illness and Spoon Theory

Christine Miserandino (n.d.) is the founder of www.butyoudontlooksick.com, and she is credited with the idea of spoon theory. Christine used spoons as an analogy to describe her everyday experiences as someone who lives with lupus. She explained that everyone begins their day with a specified number of spoons, and they cannot get more spoons for the day. Each spoon represents a unit of energy. Unlike healthy individuals, people with chronic illnesses must carefully manage their spoons. They are confronted with making daily decisions about the tasks and activities they can complete or participate in based on their level of energy and the amount of energy it takes to complete a said task or participate in any activity (e.g., getting out of bed, getting dressed, showering, preparing a meal, shopping, visiting with friends, etc.).

For example, someone who is undergoing cancer treatment may experience daily symptoms related to their diagnosis, as well as side effects specific to their treatment. On particularly symptomatic days, it may take two spoons just to get out of bed, another three spoons to get dressed, and two spoons to fix some cereal for breakfast. At this point, they may have used half of their spoons and haven't left their house or tended to their children's needs or household chores. Consequently, they must be economical with their use of spoons and are faced with making decisions about what they can and cannot accomplish based on the number of spoons (i.e., energy) they have remaining for the day. Essentially, people with chronic illness, unlike able-bodied individuals, are continually making decisions, altering plans, and negotiating life-based activities based on the number of spoons they readily have available.

BOX 12.1 **PAUSE AND REFLECT: INTERSECTIONALITY AND DISABILITY**

Consider the following scenarios and your responses to these questions: What are your initial emotional, cognitive, and behavioral reactions to each of these individuals? What conceptualizations do you begin to develop about these individuals based on the descriptions? What messages have you received that shape your reactions?

> You are assigned a new client who is an African American man with a physical disability because of a gunshot wound, and he uses a wheelchair as a mobility aid.
>
> You read initial intake paperwork about a new client and learn you will be working with a biracial lesbian woman who has a progressive eye disease.
>
> You are referred a 36-year-old single White woman who has received a diagnosis of cancer and was referred by her employer because she has missed too much work.
>
> You are referred a 10-year-old Latino boy who has a learning disability and lives with his parents and six older siblings in a lower socioeconomic status neighborhood.
>
> Your supervisor assigns you a new client who is a 65-year-old Hispanic male with a long history of substance abuse who has been court-mandated to counseling.

As you read each client's description, to what extent did the person's disability shape your perception? Did you have different emotional or cognitive reactions based on the person's type of disability? For example, did you notice any differences among your reactions to clients with physical disabilities versus those with neurodivergent disabilities or mental health disabilities? How might the presence of other cultural identities influence your reactions or conceptualizations?

These questions are meant to inform you about the attitudes, beliefs, and assumptions you may hold about PWD, as well as the additional cultural identities they possess. We encourage you to use this information to guide you in the process of developing your multicultural disability competence. What steps might you take to aid in combating any biases or assumptions you hold?

Ableism and Ableist Microaggressions

To better understand the relationship between disability and ableism, we must situate our discussion within the context of society, the individual, and the intersection between the two. In U.S. society, being able-bodied is a valued identity (i.e., privileged identity), whereas having a disability is perceived as an undesirable or devalued human characteristic (i.e., nondominant, marginalized identity). The outcome of this dominant narrative translates to unconscious (i.e., implicit) and conscious (i.e., explicit) bias that can result in prejudice (i.e., negative attitudes and biases) and discriminatory behaviors toward PWD. Together, prejudice and discrimination toward PWD become embedded into the fabric of society and its systems, resulting in ableism and impeding PWD's full participation in society (Scuro, 2018).

Ableist thinking tends to further the ideology that the goal of public policy is to accommodate the needs of *normal*-functioning individuals, which can have an adverse impact on groups and individuals with disabilities (Cherney, 2019). In effect, ableism promotes placing the needs of able-bodied people over all others and leads to the perceived reality that PWD cannot attain an equal level of functioning. In working with PWD, it is critical that counselors understand the ways in which the client views the world and their role in it and not rely only on an able-bodied understanding. Most importantly, we gain a better understanding of the client with a disability if we examine how the barriers they experience relate to their feeling of worth in society and the extent to which they believe they have the capacity to reach their full potential.

One form of ableism that is sometimes overlooked yet persists in the everyday lives of PWD is ableist microaggressions. Ableist microaggressions are subtle and often unconscious ways in which people verbally and nonverbally communicate negative attitudes and biases, stereotypes, and stigmatization toward PWD. According to Keller and Galgay (2010), some common forms of ableist microaggressions include the following:

- Denial of personal identity. An overemphasis on disability or failure to acknowledge other salient identities PWD hold.
- Denial or minimization of the disability experience. A failure to recognize attitudinal or access-related barriers.
- Denial of privacy. Insensitive, intrusive, and personal questions about one's disability, as well as denying body autonomy, personal space, and freedom to act without interference.
- Perceived helplessness. The belief that PWD are incapable and require the assistance of others.
- The disability spread effect. The assumption that a limitation in one area results in limitations in other areas.
- Patronization. Praising PWD for the accomplishment of any task, particularly those that are not noteworthy.
- Second-class citizenship. The rights of equal access are viewed as unreasonable, unjustified, or bothersome.
- Desexualization. PWD do not have sexual needs, wants, or desires.

These initial eight types of ableist microaggressions are experienced across the disability community and are experienced differently based on a PWD's visibility of disability. For example, Deroche et al. (2023) found that people with visible disabilities experienced more helplessness and otherization types of ableist microaggressions, whereas people with nonapparent disabilities experienced more minimization types of ableist microaggressions. People with both visible and nonapparent disabilities experienced more denial of identity types of ableist microaggressions. Additionally, these same researchers found that PWD who possess other nondominant sociocultural identities, such as nondominant racial and ethnic identities, may differ in their experiences of ableist microaggressions.

When PWD are faced with ableist microaggression experiences, they are left with trying to interpret the intentions of the perpetrator and how or if to respond to the ableist microaggression (e.g., educate others, ignore the microaggression, express real emotions). Regardless of the response, ableist microaggressions can result in feelings of frustration, anger, invalidation, embarrassment, and alienation (Gonzales et al., 2015; Keller & Galgay, 2010). Counselors must be aware of the impact of ableist microaggressions and avoid perpetrating them in the counseling relationship that may take the form of

- assuming that presenting problems are directly related to the client's disability;
- failing to acknowledge a client's disability or not inquiring about ability status;
- overlooking clients' ableism experiences or diminishing them;
- asking, out of curiosity, irrelevant and intrusive questions about a PWD's disability; or
- overlooking romantic/sexual relationships in the lives of PWD.

While avoiding ableist microaggressions within counseling, counselors must allow clients the space to process their microaggressive experiences and their impact. Meanwhile, counselors must continually identify how they have contributed to ableism, knowingly and unknowingly, and work to dismantle ableism within their communities.

Understanding the Historical Context of Treatment of Persons With Disabilities

To understand the context of ableism and the experiences of disability, it is important to know how environmental, social, and political factors have shaped the experience of PWD historically. This section is not a complete discussion of events; rather, it provides a summary of major eras of thinking and offers context about how the meaning assigned to disability has evolved.

From the earliest recording, societies have interpreted disabilities as functional limitations and, at times, were less tolerant and more suppressive toward PWD who naturally exhibited such differences. For example, an individual's worth has historically been equated to their ability to contribute to society in a meaningful way, which has created a challenge for PWD when employment practices have limited their participation in work. Attitudes toward PWD are shaped by society's perception of their ability to contribute, which in turn, can influence religious, cultural, social, and political practices, creating a bidirectional relationship between these forces. For counselors to ensure opportunities exist for PWD, it is important to understand how such perceptions have formed and influenced decisions that impact the individual and their place within larger systems. Historically, societal perceptions of PWD as *less able* than others have shaped the treatment they have endured. For example, early Spartan societies left weaker individuals in the countryside to die during wartime. Greek and Roman societies believed all PWD, particularly children, should be abandoned and left to die. Romans made exceptions if the condition was not physical or noticeable; however, they expected the individual to show gratitude and complacency in return.

In early religious practices, like those in Europe during the Middle Ages, many referenced disabilities as a symbol of God's displeasure but did not consider the individual universally condemned. Blindness, for example, was caused by the sins of parents, while mental illness was caused by the possession of spirits (Shakespeare, 2018). Frances Bacon, a well-known religious scholar, was among the first to express disability as acceptable *if* acquired over one's lifetime. As history progressed, many advocates spoke against disability being divine punishment and promoted the idea that disability was the exception and deserving of charity. For example, a congenital disability was thought to be an atrocity, while adventitious disorders (i.e., those occurring by accident) were more acceptable. Blindness bore a higher status because prisoners of war were blinded by captors, implying the individual had sacrificed for a cause (Shakespeare, 2018). Further, popular religious thought of the time considered conditions originating from disease as favorable because they were believed to earn the individual eternal salvation.

While religious dogma highly influenced attitudes about PWD through the Middle Ages and Renaissance periods, an increase in scientific understanding did not necessarily improve these attitudes. Following the publication of Charles Darwin's theory of evolution, thinkers of the time promoted a scientific approach to improving human genetics through the process of eugenics. Eugenics, a technique designed to *purify* society through the disposal of PWD, emerged and was accepted as a way to eradicate disabilities. Practices such as forced sterilization of PWDs were instituted to control the population for possible births with disabilities. As recently as 1924, *Buck vs. Bell* legalized sterilization of individuals with cognitive disabilities (Cohen et al., 2020). Eugenicists did and still do believe that PWD are defective, which is clearly very problematic and cruel.

Continuing into the 1800s, PWD were mostly seen as unfit, tragic, or subhuman. Such beliefs were supported by the thought that these developmental outcomes came from evil spirits and, thus, were believed to be a penance for sin (Shakespeare, 2018). In early folktales and stories, individuals categorized as mentally ill appeared as animalistic or savage-like, sometimes depicted as feral creatures or as changing from human to animal upon experiencing symptoms. The D/deaf were often equated to animals because they lacked spoken language. People with physical or medical abnormalities, such as leprosy, were sometimes described as monster-like and referred to as elephants, foxes, lions, or reptiles because of the condition of their skin. Likewise, people with developmental or intellectual disabilities were seen as incomplete or biologically deficient (Covey, 1998).

Depictions of PWD in books, films, and other popular media sources, whether true depictions or not, have the power to reinforce beliefs about disabilities. Table 12.2 lists examples of popular media that potentially perpetuate misperceptions of PWD.

TABLE 12.2 Examples of Popular Fictional and Nonfictional Depictions of PWD

Story Title	**Media Source**	**Problematic Themes**
Snow White and the Seven Dwarfs	A fictional Disney movie and popular children's book	Represents PWDs as being separated from society, characterized as laborers, and dependent on a person of privilege to rescue them.
Hunchback of Notre Dame	A fictional Disney movie, original novel published in the 1800s by Viktor Hugo	Explores themes of morality and the consequence of public perception when the main character, living with a congenital disability, is subjected to cruelty by society that he must overcome to express his romantic feelings that have developed for a person without a disability.
The Elephant Man	A nonfictional account of Joseph Merrick, who was a famous "freak show" performer in the 1800s	Explores themes of deformity and humanity when the main character, who is born with a rare congenital disability, becomes the subject of abuse and ridicule as a circus performer.
Split	A 2016 film based on the true story of the first person diagnosed with dissociative identity disorder (DID)	Depicts PWD as unpredictable or dangerous, which has the potential to unfairly and inaccurately represent disabilities by definition and diagnosis.

As negative attitudes toward disability persisted over time, the propensity to search for cures or relief became an accepted resolution. Painful procedures like trephining were developed to rid the body of the unwanted condition by boring holes into the skull to release spirits. Such harsh practices perpetuated a growing indifference toward disability. From the 1800s forward, many societies held the opinion that the PWD must be confined to be cared for, leading to the eventual institutionalization of PWD (Fleischer & Zames, 2001). Institutionalization became common practice, a form of isolation when PWD needs exceeded the family's ability or the community's willingness to support them. Over time, facilities or asylums that housed PWD were operating under such poor conditions that many were eventually closed. By the early 1960s, PWD in the United States who were thought to be facing lifetime institutionalization began to leave those institutions and enter the community, ultimately increasing the number of individuals seeking to live independently and exercise their rights (Fleischer & Zames, 2001). This increased freedom helped support the Disability Rights Movement.

The Disability Rights Movement

Beginning as early as the Industrial Revolution in the 1800s, society placed great importance on one's ability to work. This ideal led to further devaluation of PWD when it was determined erroneously that the individual did not possess the ability to be a producer. As a result, the notion of PWD in the workplace was met with a sense of objectification and marginalization. Capitalism, in essence, became a justification for overlooking the potential worth of PWD in the workplace, further perpetuating ableism as laws did not exist at the time to protect the right to work.

Following World War I, veterans organized to appeal to the U.S. government to provide rehabilitation programs, including support for college, owning a business, and accessible housing, in exchange for their military service. In 1935, the League of the Physically Handicapped was developed to protest job discrimination for PWD. Also, they made resources available to create government jobs for PWD (Fleischer & Zames, 2001). From the 1940s to 1960s, additional advocacy efforts for PWD began to form, and activists drew connections between individuals with disabilities and other minority groups. This effectively prompted conversations of discrimination and oppression in the areas of accessibility to work, wealth, and individual equality. Suddenly, the civil rights movement began to include PWD who being subjected to discrimination and lacked opportunities in ways similar to People of Color. Nonetheless, it would be decades before U.S. policy would begin to correct the injustices experienced by PWD exclusively.

As PWD petitioned for the right to work, the focus on laws and protections changed from charitable to confrontational in nature. In the 1970s, disability advocates like Edward Roberts fought to establish opportunities for PWD to live independently, remove barriers that inhibited their freedoms, and seek formal education. Roberts was the first student with a severe disability to attend the University of California, Berkley. Roberts's efforts launched the Center for Independent Living in 1972 for PWD and operated by PWD to leverage funding and political capital to support PWDs' ability to self-govern (Fleischer & Zames, 2001).

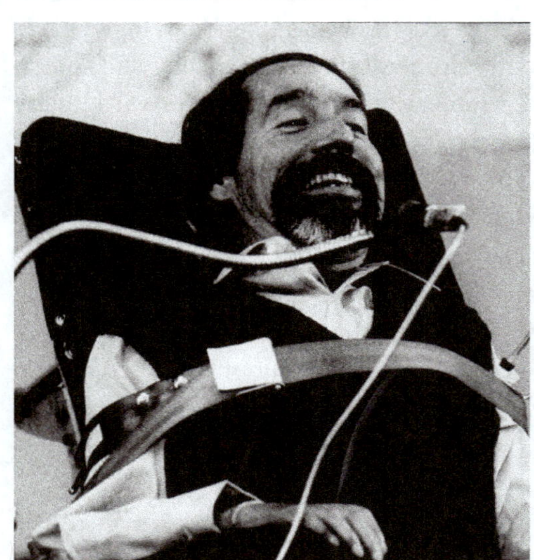

FIGURE 12.1 Who Is Ed Roberts?

In 1973, President Richard Nixon signed the Rehabilitation Act, the first legislation to protect the civil rights of PWD, supporting their right to work and prohibiting discrimination based on physical or mental disability. Perhaps most importantly, the legislation provided Section 504, which initially mandated equal access to government-associated businesses and programs and allocated funding for vocational training, and today is represented in K–12 and college settings as well.

Section 504 Today

At this time, Section 504 covers all persons with a disability who seek education at a covered institution, which refers to any agency, school, or institution that receives federal financial assistance. The goal is to eliminate barriers that would prevent a student from participating fully in programs or services that are offered to the school population generally.

The impetus for this important milestone in history highlights the rise of organized advocacy efforts for disability rights. Protesters like Judith E. Heumann gathered with 80 protesters on Madison Avenue in New York City in October 1972, staging the longest sit-in protest of the time, lasting 25 days. These and demonstrations in other parts of the country, like San Francisco and Washington, DC, rejected notions that PWD were unemployable or otherwise feeble.

Attention to disability rights for children began early in the 1800s with the founding of schools for deaf-blind communities and the development of Braille as a form of communication. However, there was no specific policy to support this education, and most of these settings were created for specific

FIGURE 12.2 Judy Heumann in a Scene From "Crip Camp: A Disability Revolution." Photo Credit: HolLynn

FIGURE 12.3 Signing of the ADA

populations were often racially segregated and funded by private charities. It was not until the development of the Education for All Handicapped Children Act in 1975 (today referred to as the IDEA) that public education was guaranteed for all children with disabilities beginning at birth and mandated that all children must be integrated into K–12 educational settings. Such efforts changed the learning experiences for children by providing a mechanism for public schools to create accessible and supportive learning environments for all children. Prior to these changes in the 1970s, even receiving a public education was a challenge for children with disabilities.

Perhaps one of the single biggest achievements of the Disability Movement to date has been the signing of the ADA of 1990 by President George H. W. Bush. Disability advocates of the time believed the consolidation of various disability legislation would broaden protections for individuals, like those that had been achieved by the civil rights movement. The Civil Rights Act of 1964 had not included PWD, and the ADA extended those protections, providing for the necessary accommodations to access employment and public services, and mandating the full inclusion of PWD in all parts of society prescribed in five titles within the legislation (Table 12.3).

While policies like IDEA and ADA began to correct the mistreatment PWD endured for centuries, the fight for equality continues because what society promotes as equality for all people does not fully align with actions that increase accessibility and positive representation of PWD. For instance, PWD still appear as stereotypes in media and entertainment, businesses and communities continue to overlook barriers that prevent accessibility for PWD, and public policies often fail to include language that would allow PWD to realize complete independence. In the end, such ableism results in communities that are not funded nor skilled enough to appropriately accommodate PWD. Lack of funding and appropriate accommodations ultimately excludes PWDs from many public spaces and places (e.g., ramps, accessibly marked paths, widened doorways).

TABLE 12.3 The Five Titles of the ADA of 1990

Title I	Employment – helps PWD access the same employment opportunities and benefits available to people without disabilities.
Title II	Public Entities and Transportation – prohibits discrimination against qualified individuals with disabilities in all programs, activities, and services of public entities.
Title III	Public Accommodations – prohibits discrimination against individuals with disabilities in privately owned, leased, or operated facilities like hotels, restaurants, retail merchants, doctor's offices, golf courses, private schools, day-care centers, health clubs, sports stadiums, and movie theaters.
Title IV	Telecommunications – requires interstate and intrastate telecommunications relay services that allow individuals with hearing and speech disabilities to communicate over the telephone.
Title V	Miscellaneous – relates to the ADA's relationship to other laws, state immunity, its impact on insurance providers and benefits, prohibition against retaliation and coercion, illegal use of drugs, and attorney's fees and provides a list of certain conditions that are not to be considered as disabilities.

To overcome issues of inadequate policy and language that address the representation of PWD, efforts such as the following serve as helpful examples:

- Implement programs and practices that demonstrate knowledge of the experience of PWD.
- Provide education that targets decision-makers and policymakers about the differences among PWD.
- Build collaborations that include consumers, in addition to representatives of the organization and other partners.
- Use common methods of evaluation and reporting that incorporate accessibility standards.

Today, multiple countries have laws that reflect a greater emphasis on disability rights and inclusion. According to the United Nations (un.org), the *Convention on the Rights of Persons with Disabilities* was implemented as part of the pledge of the 2030 Agenda for Sustainable Development with the goal of leaving no one behind. More than 160 countries and regional integration organizations signed the Convention or optional protocol in May 2022. For more information, visit https://bit.ly/UNCRPD-Status. These policy efforts are changing attitudes and approaches to addressing the rights and protections of PWD around the globe.

Overall, as time has shown, perceptions can have a cumulative effect on both society and the individual. Figure 12.4 illustrates the evolution of societal perceptions beginning from the 1800s to 2000s to emphasize changes over time and the collective influence of those perceptions on society and the individual. As discussed in this section, perceptions have changed over time and new perceptions have led to the development of policies and practices promoting the inclusion of PWD in all aspects of society. However, despite these advances, advocates continue to argue that PWD have not reached full inclusion nor independence, indicating that a gap still exists in our understanding of disability and its impact on PWD's lived experience.

Systems and Intersectional Perspectives

For purposes of understanding the impact of ableism among PWD, Bronfenbrenner's ecological systems theory (EST) has unique applications. In terms of the microsystem, disability can negatively impact and/or limit relationships because of interpersonal barriers that prohibit the development of meaningful relationships (e.g., biases about PWD, ability to form and maintain equitable relationships, infantilization, perceived helplessness). Within mesosystems, PWD may experience lower expectations from teachers or employers, while individuals, groups,

Unfit; Evil spirits; Sin (Early Civilization)	+	Weak; Disfavored; Abandoned (9th-12th Century)	+	Dependent; Pitied; Cures (13th-15th Century)	+	Institutions; Sterilized (18th-19th Century)	+	Charitable; Noble (19th-20th Century)	+	Deserving; Civil Rights (20th Century-from 1960s)	+	Protections; Access (Today)	=	**Perception** **(Society and Self)**

FIGURE 12.4 Impact of Changing Perceptions of PWD

and policies within the exosystem can impact PWD's freedom (e.g., ability to complete daily tasks without assistance because of environmental barriers), mobility (e.g., public transit), and overall independence. As you might notice, all three systems are impacted greatly by *others' perceptions and actions* rather than those of the individual with the disability. Such interactions can have a negative impact and be difficult to overcome. The individual with a disability may begin to adopt and respond to others' impressions (macrosystem) and make decisions based on the restricted opportunities that persist, particularly community, national, and international events that impact large groups tend to impact PWD more (chronosystem). For example, PWD experienced increased barriers during the height of the COVID-19 pandemic that few sought to rectify or accommodate (e.g., masks being a barrier for those who read lips, people who are blind being unable to social distance as indicated by signs they could not read). In the end, the pressures of the system can influence the individual's ability to realize and actualize their full potential.

Other researchers have used EST to study human behavior in the context of the environment and draw distinctions regarding which influences have the greatest impact on a person's development. For example, Ungar et al. (2013) studied resilience in children, examining their interactions with multiple reciprocating systems and determined that they were more influenced by environmental qualities than by individual qualities such as cognitive ability. Such research on the influence of the ecological systems suggests that the locus of change in terms of growth and improvement of a child is in the multilayered environmental factors (e.g., micro-, meso-, and macrosystems), not solely the child themself (Ungar et al., 2013). When working to understand a client's experience of disability, it can be helpful to focus on environmental aspects with which they are connected to identify contexts that contribute to resilience, adjustment, and abilities, as well as those that foster beliefs about their inabilities.

Intersectionality acknowledges that there are multiple systems of oppression (e.g., racism, sexism, ageism) and that ableism may not be the only form of oppression PWD experience. Multiple identity oppressive experiences warrant additional consideration and attention within counseling to understand the unique lived experiences and their impact on the client. Specific historical, environmental, and societal factors must be considered, as well as the client's personal qualities and factors (Brinkman et al., 2023).

Brinkman et al. (2023) offered such an approach. They adapted a multiple-level framework for conceptualizing PWD's experiences using a contextual approach to racial trauma exposure. They asserted that attempting to categorize people into discrete groups while failing to highlight diversity within disability underscores the disadvantage and marginalization that is compounded when PWD identify with multiple nondominant identities, so multiple categories need to be considered simultaneously. Example categories include (a) sociohistorical events (e.g., institutionalization, medicalization, eugenics); (b) broader societal factors (e.g., ableism, accessibility, mass media, the criminal justice system); (c) education, employment, and neighborhood experiences (e.g., exclusion, special education, discrimination); (d) family dynamics (e.g., isolation, abuse, neglect, emotional support); and (e) individual factors (e.g., age, race, religion).

As a counselor applying these concepts, you might consider, for instance, how PWD often have trouble integrating into religious or spiritual services because of curricula and physical structures favoring able-bodied and neurotypical people and not accounting for the different ways people learn, access, and use group spaces. Similarly, as PWD age, their functional needs are often compounded and their caregiving needs increase. In terms of race/ethnicity, consider that there are a disproportionate number of students of color who have a disability, which may further exacerbate experiences of segregation and underutilization of supportive resources in the classroom, leading to higher rates of dropout and increased risk of contact with the juvenile justice system (Harper, 2017). Thus, PWD who possess another marginalized identity may endure additional barriers as they seek personal fulfillment and to achieve or maintain independence.

Professional Counselor Practice Application Considerations

As counselors in training, you are well acquainted with the notion that developing cultural awareness, knowledge, and skills is central to a successful counseling relationship. Researchers have found that counselors report limited or inconsistent training specific to disability or PWD (Deroche et al., 2020; Rivas & Hill, 2018). Therefore, we provide you with some practical strategies grounded in the research literature, professional codes of ethics, multicultural and social justice counseling competencies (Ratts et al., 2015), and the American Rehabilitation Counseling Association (ARCA) disability-related counseling competencies (Chapin et al., 2018) to help you develop your disability cultural awareness, knowledge, skills, and advocacy actions.

Self-Awareness

Counselors are expected to respect diversity, avoid imposing personal values, refrain from referring clients based on personal values, and seek training in areas in which they are at risk of imposing their values (ACA, 2014 Section A.4.b; AMHCA 2020 Section I.A.4.d; ASCA, 2022 Section B.3.j; CRCC 2023 Section D.2.a). Only AMHCA and ASCA reference specific aspects related to client and counselor diversity (e.g., religion, culture, race, ethnicity, and socioeconomic status) and none of the ethical codes refer to how personal values intersect with disability. Therefore, we recommend you examine any able-bodied privilege you hold, acknowledge any adherence to dominant narratives about disability or PWD (i.e., internalized ableism), and examine your attitudes, beliefs, values, and biases that may influence your behaviors or interpretations about the lives of PWD (Chapin et al., 2018). These recommendations hold true for both counselors with and without disabilities, as all people are susceptible to believing the stereotypes, myths, and misconceptions about PWD and/or adopt these beliefs about their own disability or others' disabilities.

BOX 12.2 **TIPS FOR PROFESSIONAL PRACTICE: WAYS TO COMBAT DOMINANT NARRATIVES ABOUT PWD**

Because exposure to and interactions with PWD are known to help combat dominant narratives about PWD and to promote cultural development (Deroche et al., 2020; Lawson et al., 2017), engage in one or more of the following activities:

Read research literature that includes the voices of PWD (e.g., Hunt et al., 2006; Keller & Galgay, 2010).

Seek opportunities to listen to the voices and stories of PWD via autobiographies, podcasts, and vlogs about disability or the disability experience, and TedTalks featuring PWD (e.g., Brady, 2019; Young, 2014; Zayid, 2013).

Directly interact and create meaningful relationships with PWD.

Volunteer with an organization that serves PWD.

List the myriad of abilities and other characteristics PWD hold.

Participate in trainings and workshops.

It is essential that counselors use their self-awareness to continuously self-monitor and examine their perceptions, reactions, and behaviors toward PWD. This process is not meant to produce guilt or shame; rather, it is intended to bring awareness, heighten your cultural sensitivity, and increase culturally relevant behaviors. Although feelings of guilt or shame can sometimes be a natural part of self-examination, we encourage you to recognize that the development of cultural sensitivity and cultural competence are ongoing processes and that you have the power to alter your attitudes and perceptions.

BOX 12.3 **PAUSE AND REFLECT: YOUR DISABILITY PRIVILEGE**

Inspired by Peggy Mcintosh's (2003) work, "White Privilege: Unpacking the Invisible Knapsack," we ask you to consider the following statements and write down your "yes" and "no" responses.

I can easily arrange to be in the company of people of my physical or mental ability status.

I can assume I will have physical access to any building.

I am reasonably certain that assumptions about my mental capabilities will not be made based on my physical ability status.

I can do well in challenging situations without being told what an inspiration I must be to other able-bodied people.

I can plan my day without considering potential physical or mental fatigue because of my ability status.

If I am fired, not given a raise, or not hired, I do not question if it has anything to do with my physical or mental ability status.

I can plan activities, appointments, and errands without consideration of public transit schedules or the availability of accommodations.

I do not have to be concerned about others asking personal questions about my illness or disability because of my visible disability status.

Whether you are able-bodied or have a disability, you may have responded "yes" to all of the above statements, responded "no" to all of the statements, or had a mixed set of "yes" and "no" responses. "Yes" responses signify able-bodied privilege, which translates to an advantage gained by people solely based on the fact that they do not have a physical or mental impairment or that their disability does not impact them in a specific way. For example, not all PWD need to consider physical or mental fatigue when planning their daily tasks or routines.

Remember from the first section of this chapter, PWD experience disability characteristics based on type, onset and course, and visibility of disability—all of which intersect and impact one's experiences. Again, this activity is intended to heighten your awareness of the ways in which PWD must navigate the world that is not inherently designed with them in mind and for you to develop some perspective around the day-to-day attitudinal and access-related barriers PWD encounter.

BOX 12.4 **PROFILE OF A PRACTITIONER: DIANA RHYNE, MBA, MS, LPC-IT, NCC, CRC, CTP**

IMG 12.1. Diana Rhyne, MBA, MS, LPC-IT, NCC, CRC, CTP

Growing up in a relatively traditional South Korean family, I had little exposure to anything "mental health" related, especially not psychosis. My only knowledge of people living with psychosis came from movies, TV, and media. I learned to associate psychosis with unpredictability, aggression, paranoia, and, to be blunt, danger. Movies like *Psycho* portrayed psychosis as terrifying hallucinations and delusions, and violence. I was in my late thirties and the first year of my master's program when I first learned to define and diagnose psychotic disorders. My first exposure, or so I think, to psychotic disorders was during my practicum.

Providing behavior management and psychoeducation to prison inmates for years and working with more acute individuals was uncommon. Primarily, I dealt with trauma disorders, personality disorders, mood disorders, cognitive developmental impairments, and substance use disorders. I learned a lot about the link between mental health and criminality, and it was a reminder that things are not always as they seem. It taught me to look beyond the label to see the individual. Interestingly, I was comfortable working with inmates but was nervous when placed in a psychiatric facility for crisis stabilization serving clients with psychosis during my practicum and internship.

In my practicum, I met "Lisa," a tall, slim, Black woman in her 50s diagnosed with psychosis and on an involuntary Chapter 51 hold. Lisa was deemed a safety risk to herself and others and court-ordered to engage in treatment and take medication. She was under the long-term care of an intensive case management team who worked to keep her housed, attended to her physical and mental health needs, managed her finances, and ensured her personal needs were met. Without knowing anything about her beyond her diagnosis, Lisa was the image the media had created in my mind. At times, she was loudly arguing and aggressively gesturing toward something/someone others could not see, and at other times, she quietly wrote in her journal. I found myself avoiding her because I bought into the misconception that she was dangerous, which was unfair. So, one day, I introduced myself.

I listened with empathy as she described her life, family, and the circumstances that brought her to the facility. Later that day, she stopped by my office during a staff meeting, quietly placed her journal on my desk, and quickly walked away. I was stunned. It was like I had unlocked a secret door, and she was inviting me into her world. I learned a lot about Lisa and the impact of her psychosis from her journal. The words she chose, the colors she used (when she used color), the direction and placement of the text, the doodles, and the patterns were all clues. I don't know if it was a chronicle of actual events or a product of her psychosis. But did it matter? It was real to her. From then on, we continued to build rapport and worked through her hallucinations by playing games.

Nearly 2 years later, I am a licensed counselor and certified vocational rehabilitation counselor in compensated work therapy at the Department of Veterans Affairs, providing supported employment for veterans with mental health disabilities. My experiences with Lisa and others like her have taught me the importance of *listening* and building rapport in the *context of the clients' lived reality*. Taking the time to build rapport with clients, observe, and listen to their concerns from *their* perspective can tell you a lot about their most salient identities (race, sexuality, etc.), values, attitudes, and motivation for change, giving context to the clinical information found in their medical charts. Lisa taught me to work *with* clients to identify their presenting concerns rather than relying solely on clinical assessments.

As a mental health professional, I don't challenge clients' realities or tell them what their concerns *should* be. My job is to give clients a space that is as safe as possible to talk through their concerns, validate their experiences as their truth, advocate for them, and encourage them to use their strengths to minimize the impact of their symptoms on their quality of life. All clients, especially those labeled as "disabled" (physical or mental), deserve to be seen, heard, and validated in their experiences. They are not their diagnoses or symptoms. They are human beings.

Skills

Depending on your area of counseling specialization or work setting, you may receive information about a person's cultural identities via educational, medical, or vocational records, or you may have obtained said information via initial intake paperwork or an initial interview. Whatever the case, it is vital to develop an understanding of your client as a unique, multidimensional cultural being (ACA 2014, Preamble; ASCA 2022, Preamble; CRCC, 2023 Preamble p. 1), which includes acknowledging ability status as a cultural identity and using cultural broaching skills to better understand PWD's experiences. In practice, *acknowledgment* translates to counselors including open-ended questions about chronic illness and disability on intake forms and initial counseling interviews. Questions may include, "Do you have a chronic illness or disability? If so, please elaborate." "Is there anything I can do to make your counseling experience more accessible?" "What accommodations, if any, might be helpful to you during the counseling process?" These questions communicate an interest in a cultural identity that is often overlooked (Cook et al., 2020) and opens the door to further inquiry about the client's experiences as a PWD.

PWD often take on the responsibility of making others comfortable in their presence, so we list some general guidelines counselors can use when interacting with PWD. These guidelines are not meant to be an exhaustive list or to be applied uniformly to all PWD; rather, they are designed to inform you about some common areas of disability etiquette.

- Be sensitive to how PWD refer to their disability. PWD may use person-first or identity-first language (see Box 12.5). If you're unsure, ask them how they prefer you reference their disability.
- Direct your conversation that is meant for the PWD to them and not to a personal assistant, companion, or interpreter.
- Avoid automatically helping a PWD. Ask first. Wait for your offer to be accepted, listen for further instructions, or inquire how you can be of most assistance to them. Keep in mind a PWD may decline your offer and recognize they enjoy their independence, just like able-bodied individuals.
- Do not touch a PWD's assistive aid (e.g., cane or crutches), mobility equipment (e.g., wheelchair), or service animal. These aids are an extension of the PWD and part of their personal space. If a service animal is present, do not speak to, pet, or otherwise interact with the service animal—they are working and should not be distracted.
- For people who are hard of hearing, it may be helpful to first gain their attention before starting a conversation (e.g., tap the person gently on the shoulder or arm). Face the person, speak in a normal tone and avoid shouting.
- For people with speech disabilities, listen attentively and avoid speaking for the person or completing their sentences. Instead, give them time to communicate with you; ask them to repeat anything you don't understand; verify your understanding of their communication. If necessary, consider asking questions that require only brief responses.
- For PWD with mental illness, avoid pathologizing their psychological or psychiatric symptoms.

BOX 12.5 **TIPS FOR PROFESSIONAL PRACTICE: PERSON-FIRST VERSUS IDENTITY-FIRST LANGUAGE**

It is generally accepted to use person-first language until you know the person's preference. Listen closely to how folks describe themselves and follow suit. When in doubt, ask! Likely, the person will feel respected because you asked.

Person-first language refers to the person first, followed by their disability.
Examples: Person with a disability, person who is blind, person with autism

Identity-first language refers to the person's disability first.
Examples: Disabled person, blind person, autistic person

Cultural Broaching

Early in the counseling relationship, counselors use cultural broaching to explore disability among clients' cultural identities. Questions such as "What do you think is important for me to know and understand about your chronic illness or disability?" "What would you like me to know about your experiences as a PWD?" are helpful starting points. Throughout the counseling relationship, counselors listen for client themes or stories that convey prejudice or discrimination based on ability status or other marginalized identities, and they use cultural broaching to validate or to further explore the sociocultural realities of the PWD. For example, a 25-year-old White female client who uses a wheelchair for mobility expresses frustration because she has interviewed for over 20 jobs for which she is well qualified, directly addressed her disability in the job interview, and believes most interviews went well. However, no employer has offered her a job. A counselor might respond, "I wonder if you think there may be any disability discrimination taking place?" to validate and invite further conversation about the topic.

While these strategies align with culturally relevant practices (Day-Vines et al., 2021), counselors must be cognizant of the multiple intersecting identities of PWD and be cautious about exclusively focusing on a client's disability. Instead, counselors attend to the multiple intersecting identities of their clients and recognize there are instances in which certain identities hold more salience than others. For instance, a 19-year-old Latinx gay male with a learning disability describes feeling apprehensive about disclosing his affectual identity to his friends. In this scenario, the PWD's affectual identity may hold more salience than his disability identity.

We recognize you may feel challenged by the seemingly contradictory messages to (a) attend to disability identity and (b) avoid overly focusing on disability. Like working with any student or client, it is vital to consider their multiple intersecting identities, the various contexts in which they live, and the range of strengths and abilities they possess. These inherent complexities are best understood through a lens in which disability is seen as an important part of one's identity, yet it is not the *only* aspect of who they are as a cultural being. Consequently, counselors listen for the ways in which PWD refer to their disability and their other cultural identities (e.g., race, ethnicity, gender), recognize the supportive and nonsupportive contexts in which they live (e.g., home, school, work, community), and identify the strengths, abilities, and resources they possess. In practice, this translates to counselors giving attention to repeated themes mentioned in the above areas, directly addressing said themes in an empathetic manner, and helping the client to piece together these complexities in a way that fosters internal strengths, resilience, external resources, and self-advocacy skills.

Use of Assessments

Counselors rely upon a wide range of assessment strategies and interviewing techniques to conceptualize client issues and to determine appropriate forms of treatment and intervention. When conducting biopsychosocial assessments and other assessments, counselors recognize PWD as individuals with both strengths and limitations and consider them as whole persons. By doing so, counselors can prevent overlooking certain topics that are sometimes viewed as irrelevant to PWD (e.g., sexuality, relationships) or unjustifiably assuming that an issue is relevant when it is not at that time (e.g., disability, vocation/career; Kemp & Mallinckrodt, 1996). Additionally, counselors should recognize there can be significant and ongoing adaptation to a disability that may shape one's disability identity development process; this adaptation process should not be conceptualized as abnormal adjustment, psychopathology, or delayed adjustment (Chapin et al., 2018).

When using more formalized assessment measures, counselors need to take into account a PWD's developmental age (ASCA, 2022, Section A.13.d), recognize that adaptation or accommodation provisions may be warranted (ACA, 2014 Section E.7.a; CRCC, 2023 Section H.6.a), consider accommodations and norm groups when making interpretations (ACA 2014, Section E.9a; CRCC 2023, Section H.7.b; NBCC, 2016 Sections 48-49), and explain results in a developmentally appropriate manner (ACA 2014, Section E.3.a; CRCC 2023, Section H.1.a). Also, counselors need to ensure treatment planning is an individualized, collaborative endeavor that supports the worth, dignity, and autonomy of the PWD to the highest extent possible (ACA 2014, Section A.1.a; AMHCA, 2020 Section I.b.1.a; ASCA, 2022 Section A.10.g). Ultimately, all counselors view their students, clients, and consumers as multidimensional individuals and strive to empower them.

Fostering Individual Resilience, Strengths, and Wellness

When protective factors exist to support development and adaptation, some individuals demonstrate great resilience, even in the face of severe adversity. The inverse is also true: When support systems are impaired, adversity has been shown to increase the risk for developmental problems and weaken one's ability to be resilient (Masten, 2001). Determining what factors contribute to clients' competence and, ultimately, to their resilience is an important focus for counselors. Masten (2001) suggested that resilience is not a unique phenomenon but rather an ordinary process. This introduces the idea that constructs such as psychological well-being and support from family and/or community foster the development of resilience. Counselors take active steps to recognize and nurture resiliencies, strengths, and wellness in their clients, and clients with disabilities are no different; to do otherwise is to accept the cultural narrative that PWD are incapable and to perpetuate sociocultural ableism.

Access and Accessibility

Though ACA, AMHCA, ASCA, CRCC, and NBCC state that counselors should not engage in discriminatory behavior, specific guidance is limited. For example, only AMHCA (2016 Section I.a.5.a) addresses creating an accessible counseling environment for PWD. Keeping in mind that both individuals and systems can either impede or promote access, counselors, counselor educators, and counseling organizations need to be attuned to any discriminatory policies, practices, procedures, or access-related barriers within any system. To learn more about the accessibility of different spaces, consult the Institute for Human-Centered Design ADA checklist, which can be found at https://www.adachecklist.org/doc/fullchecklist/ada-checklist.pdf.

BOX 12.6 **TIPS FOR PROFESSIONAL PRACTICE: CREATING ACCESS AND ACCESSIBILITY**

Inspect your building and office space for physical accessibility. This translates to building entrances and office spaces having flat surfaces and/or ramps; elevators being easily available to someone using a wheelchair or some other type of assistive aid or who experiences physical fatigue because of a chronic illness; and availability of disabled parking.

Place furniture in ways that allow a PWD with an assistive aid (e.g., wheelchair, walker, service animal) the ability to easily maneuver around the physical space.

Recognize that office décor, such as a rug, may impede ease of navigation for someone using a mobility aid or may be a tripping hazard for some PWD. Include lamps as part of office décor, so overhead lights can be turned off if a PWD is sensitive to bright lights.

If your building or office space is ADA accessible, include this information in any advertising or marketing materials.

Upon initial contact with a client, inquire about any disability-related needs or accommodations that may be helpful.

Include questions about ability status, history of ability status, and/or impact of disability on intake forms and in initial assessment.

When creating or altering a website, enlist the aid of an information technology specialist who is knowledgeable about and has experience with creating websites that meet Web Content Accessibility Guidelines (WCAG).

To help ensure digital accessibility of documents, use 12- to 14-point sans serif font styles (e.g., Arial, Comic Sans, Verdana, Tahoma, or Calibri) and use accessibility checkers in software programs.

When selecting telehealth platforms, inquire about accessibility for individuals using assistive technology. Ask if the platform is WCAG compliant and if the platform has been tested using assistive technologies.

With appropriate experience or training, offer telehealth options when PWD experience transportation difficulties or are unable to participate in in-person counseling because of disability-related ailment or fatigue.

https://www.adachecklist.org/doc/fullchecklist/ada-checklist.pdf

Advocacy and Allyship

Counselors are called to engage in advocacy efforts at individual, group, and systemic levels to address potential barriers and to promote individual and community welfare (ACA, 2014; AMHCA, 2020; ASCA, 2022; CRCC, 2023). Interestingly, only ASCA (2022) provides specificity regarding advocacy actions (e.g., home and school safety, equal access to education and technology, equitable school counseling programs, student learning needs), while CRCC (2023) is the only code of ethics that refers to providing information to promote client self-advocacy (C.1.b). Additionally, we encourage counselors to consult Section B of the ARCA disability-related counseling competencies, which includes guidelines for counselors to advocate on behalf of PWD and support their self-advocacy.

We provide a few examples to illustrate the ways in which counselors can be agents of change. At an individual level of advocacy, counselors can inform PWD about their rights and mechanisms for reporting discrimination or unfair treatment (Chapin et al., 2018 B.5), and they can provide opportunities for students, clients, and consumers with disabilities to develop self-advocacy skills (e.g., problem-solving, communication, and assertiveness skills) through observation and role play. At the group level, counselors may create a list of American Sign Language certified interpreters and counselors in their state, and they can distribute this list via social media and to organizations, agencies and groups that serve individuals who are hard of hearing or D/deaf. On a systemic level, counselors can spearhead advocacy efforts and act as allies with PWD in their schools, agencies, and organizations by evaluating the accessibility of physical and digital spaces (ACA 2014 Section H.5.b; AMHCA, 2020 Sections I.a.5, I.a.5.a; ASCA, 2022 Section A.14.f; CRCC, 2023 Section K.2.a) and assess policies that may inadvertently discriminate against PWD.

Allies are members of dominant groups who are committed to and work on behalf of and alongside individuals with nondominant identities to address prejudice and discrimination, and to combat systemic inequities. Becoming an ally requires one to recognize their privilege, examine the systems in which they benefit from said privilege, and strive to understand the ways in which nondominant groups are oppressed. Forber-Pratt et al. (2019) suggested able-bodied individuals demonstrate allyship by *showing up* in the following ways: (a) understand intersectionality, (b) ask about and respect the language and terminology choices of PWD, (c) embrace principles of universal design, (d) recognize problematic representation of disability in the media, (e) become aware of current disability rights issues, and (f) honor the experiences and perspectives of all disabled people.

Additional Practice Considerations

Counselors work with clients to help them realize their full potential. In doing so, one objective is to guide the client to explore their values, attitudes, and self-perceptions that lead to the development of self-affirming goals. Professional codes of ethics operate on the assumption that they can fit every counseling situation. However, in working with PWD, it is apparent that certain codes may reflect negative attitudes toward PWD. In these situations, it is fair to assess whether certain codes are outdated and in need of revision. For instance, a counselor may disclose and be justified in their disclosure of a student's or client's communicable disease status when warranted (ACA, 2014 Section B.2.c; ASCA, 2022 Section A. 2.h; CRCC, 2023 Section B.2.b). When these codes were added, they were directed at individuals with an HIV/AIDS status, which could qualify someone as disabled. Given the treatability of HIV/AIDS, as well as the recent COVID-19 pandemic and the proliferation of other communicable diseases, the question remains whether these codes could be viewed as discriminatory and unduly violate clients' right to privacy.

BOX 12.7 PROFILE OF A PRACTITIONER: MELISSA W. FLEMING, PHD, LPC-S, NCC

IMG 12.2. Melissa W. Fleming, PhD, LPC-S, NCC

I am a 37-year-old White heterosexual female counselor who owns a private practice in southern Louisiana. I specialize in treating anxiety, depression, and general mental health issues in adolescents and adults. This is my journey of working with clients who struggle with a disability.

Life experiences can inform your work with clients. I did not have specific training on how to work with clients who live with a disability. However, I have some insight into this world based on my personal background. I grew up as a physically normal, neurotypical child. A car accident at age 15 suddenly changed that, triggering an onset of symptoms I had not previously experienced before. I found myself stumbling down the rabbit hole of specialists, medical tests, and hospitals in a search for answers amid misdiagnoses. What became clear in the confusion was there may never be clarity or a "silver bullet" that would perfectly permeate the pain or adequately address the wide spectrum of neurological symptoms. I arrived at four diagnoses but no perfect prognosis on how to "feel good" again.

Through my own experience, I charted a path back toward having a better quality of life again. I would make peace with the "good days, bad days" reality of chronic illness. I would make accommodations to preserve my quality of life and better define when I could push through and when I need to honor my limitations and rely on a restorative regimen. Self-care was no longer a psychological, luxurious coping skill; it was imperative to allow my body to function at its maximum capacity. Goals could still be accomplished, but steps would need to be taken in a more creative, less linear fashion. Expectations were adjusted to be realistic. Unknown variables were factored into time lines. "Health permitting" will determine my day.

Transitioning from a "healthy" person to someone who could be perceived as "disabled" is life-altering. I factored my experience with disability and chronic illness into my work as a counselor. I have primarily worked in private practice settings, where I have seen a broad spectrum of clients, including children, adolescents, individual adults, couples, families, and groups. Along the way, I have worked with many clients who are disabled or struggle with compromised health. When working with clients who struggle with a disability, here are some strategies to keep in mind.

Learn from your client. Despite my insight into the world of disability, it is important to monitor my own assumptions and beliefs. Clients should be cast in an expert role, and the counselor as a pupil learning about their specific experience of health. It is likely their health and disability have significantly colored their perspective. However, I cannot assume my reality mirrors their experience. I cannot predetermine significant themes based on my own.

Solve the solvable problems. When working with clients who struggle with a disability, it becomes apparent that some dilemmas cannot be resolved. However, some issues do have solutions. For example, a rug in my office may bring together the décor but can also be a barrier for someone with an impaired ability to walk. I cannot alleviate a client's physically painful symptom, but I can remove an obstacle in my office space when I provide counseling to my clients.

Process the grief. Grief is a common framework for clients with disabilities. Many depressing triggers are based in a harsh reality that may or may not change. Acknowledging difficulties that stem from a disability is not an irrational thought but a truth that must be accepted.

Research. Disabilities vary, and it is important to become educated about a client's specific diagnosis. Here are some questions to consider. Is cognitive decline a factor? What is physically possible within the diagnosis, and what is not? How painful is the diagnosis? Are there resources available to assist with this disability?

Validate. Validation of a client's experience is critical. Disabled clients struggle with overwhelming circumstances, which can cause people in their lives to minimize or discount their experience to alleviate their own negative feelings about such harsh realities. Others may problem-solve, albeit with good intentions, but invalidate the client's feelings in the process. Many clients seek help from other health professionals who have insulted, dismissed, or misdiagnosed them. As counselors, we can offer a healing atmosphere where clients can be validated and empowered.

Intentionally learning about and honoring disability as a cultural identity can inform your work with disabled clients and provide meaningful, effective therapy. The need for more understanding of this marginalized population is significant. A commitment to become a more multiculturally competent counselor who is adept at working with a disabled population is well worth the attention of our profession.

Conclusion

PWD are an often-overlooked minority group who continue to encounter societal oppression, whether through individual negative attitudes, biases, or structural inequalities. As such, counselors need to understand the collective ways in which PWD are marginalized, recognize the diversity within the disability community and how these differences are experienced on individual and societal levels, and acquire competencies to help promote the worth, dignity, and respect of PWD. We hope this chapter has both challenged you and sparked an interest in becoming an advocate and ally for PWD.

Questions for Reflection

Consider what you learned in this chapter as you respond to the questions and prompts below.

1. How will you take a strength-based perspective and use resiliency-focused actions with PWD?
2. What are your experiences with ableism? How have you contributed to ableism? If you are a PWD, have you internalized ableism? What are some ways in which you want to work toward a non-ableist identity?
3. What does it mean to you to contribute to creating a society that embraces and is accessible to people with different abilities?
4. How will you attend to disability within the counseling relationship without making disability "the problem" while remaining open to the possibility that the client may name their presenting problem as a disability?
5. What are some ways that the disability movement overlaps with other identity advocacy movements? In what ways are you involved currently in advocacy, and how would you like to get more involved? How can your advocacy actions contribute positively to your counselor identity and the counseling services you provide?

Applying What You Have Learned

Complete each of the following activities, considering what you learned from this chapter.

Activity #1: Case Scenarios

Read the following case scenarios and identify which model or models are represented in the case descriptions.

Case 1: Anna is a 24-year-old White lesbian female who experienced a moderate TBI 3 months ago from a car accident, resulting in visual field deficits. She has returned to school and has been advised to change majors to something less challenging than her chosen field of architecture.

Case 2: Darius is a 17-year-old African American male who lives with his family in a middle-class neighborhood and who was recently diagnosed with generalized anxiety disorder (GAD), prescribed an anti-anxiety medication, and was told to schedule a return visit to his doctor in 4-weeks to determine medication efficacy. After his diagnosis, Darius felt angry and questioned his masculinity because "real men" can manage their stress without medication. Also, he noticed his family and friends began to treat him differently.

Case 3: Sophia is a 35-year-old Latina female with a spinal cord injury who uses a wheelchair. She experiences significant difficulty entering her office building each day because of the heavy weight of the door, upper limb atrophy, and the nonexistence of an automated door opener. Consequently, she either must call a colleague to come and open the door for her, or she has to wait for someone else to enter or exit the building and request their assistance.

Case 4: The Rivers are a devout Christian couple who just learned that their 6-month-old boy, Dominic, has congenital bilateral hearing loss, resulting in a diagnosis of deafness. With no medical explanation for Dominic's deafness, Mrs. Rivers believes God is punishing both her and her husband for their previous drug and alcohol addictions.

Case 5: Tameka is a 40-year-old single African American female who is a mother to two teenage girls and who is a well-respected civil rights attorney in Chicago. She generally works 50–60 hours per week and seems to have boundless energy. Over the past few months, however, she has experienced episodic instances of overwhelming fatigue, blurry vision, and difficulty with balance. Her primary care physician didn't think Tameka's complaints were significant and attributed her symptoms to being overworked and not getting the proper amount of sleep. Tameka continued to experience these episodic symptoms and noticed occasional tingling sensations in her right hand. As a result, she pursued a second opinion, which led to an MRI and a diagnosis of multiple sclerosis.

Check Your Answers

In case 1, the sociopolitical or minority group model of disability is represented in the failure of Anna's advisor to provide her with information about accommodations or a more manageable plan of study, thereby denying her access to full participation in her chosen field. In case 2, the biopsychosocial model of disability is represented in Darius's diagnosis of GAD and the resulting psychological impact on his identity and the way others treat him differently because of his mental health diagnosis. In case 3, the functional/environmental model of disability is represented in the interaction between Sophia's disability, the function being performed (i.e., opening a heavy door), the environmental barriers (i.e., nonexistence of automated doors), and her need to request assistance from others to enter her office building. In case 4, the moral model of disability is represented in the Rivers' belief that their child's deafness is a punishment for their previous alcohol and drug addictions. In case 5, the medical model of disability is represented in Tameka's encounters with medical professionals evaluating and diagnosing her symptoms.

Activity #2: Identifying Microaggressions

Identify the type of ableist microaggressions expressed in each scenario. Keep in mind that there may be more than one that is applicable.

A D/deaf woman is told that she speaks well for someone who cannot hear.

A middle-aged African American man in an airport using a seizure alert service dog is told that he is lucky he can bring his dog everywhere he travels.

A young mother using a wheelchair experiences a stranger saying to her children, "I hope you take good care of your mom."

A Latina woman with a chronic illness and a disabled parking ID is yelled at by a stranger who claims she does not look disabled and is taking the spot away from real PWD.

Someone in an elevator asks a middle-aged blind woman what happened to her.

Activity #3: Advocacy Activity

For the purpose of engaging in advocacy work with or on behalf of members of the disability community, we draw upon the advocacy action plan developed by Cook (2020). Below are steps to consider when developing your advocacy action plan.

Identify a group of PWD whom you may need to develop your cultural sensitivity toward or to whom you feel passionate about. Be specific with your choice. In other words, avoid simply focusing on people with physical, cognitive, or mental health disabilities because people who have different types of disabilities within these categories experience systemic inequality differently.

Research the ways in which your group of PWD encounter systemic inequality/issues. Research may entail reviewing scholarly works on disability or PWD, reading autobiographies written by PWD, interviewing PWD in your community, visiting social media groups and pages directed toward PWD, following PWD on social media, connecting with disability advocacy organizations, etc.

Make a list of themes or "hot button" issues for your group of PWD. Do you feel passionate toward a particular issue or form of systemic inequality?

Select one issue to focus your advocacy efforts and ask yourself the following questions.

What do I want to see improve/change?
Who will my goal impact?
How will I know I've met my goal?
What do I need to work toward my goal (e.g., other people, resources, materials)?
How much time will I need to meet my goal?

Credits

Fig. 12.1: William Bronston, https://commons.wikimedia.org/wiki/File:Edward_V_Roberts_(1981)_(1).jpg, 1981.

Fig. 12.2: William Bronston, https://commons.wikimedia.org/wiki/File:Judy_Heumann.jpg, 1981.

Fig. 12.3: Source: https://commons.wikimedia.org/wiki/File:Bush_signs_in_ADA_of_1990.jpg, 1990.

CHAPTER 13

Age and Ageism

Matthew Fullen, Jordan B. Westcott, Mary Chase Mize, Lisa M. Boyd, Julianna Williams, and Nicole Castagna

Age is just a number. Life and aging are the greatest gifts that we could possibly ever have.

—Cicely Tyson

CHAPTER OVERVIEW

All people experience aging. In fact, many of the concerns that bring people to counseling are explicitly related to developmental matters. For example, a client who is looking to make a career change may come to counseling to discern direction; in this case, their age and stage of life are likely to influence their decisions. Additionally, age can be experienced as a sociocultural identity that coincides with privilege or a lack thereof, and people may experience ageism at various points in their lives. Counselors are wise to recognize aging as a salient cultural factor that should be attended to as we implement social justice and multicultural counseling competencies. In this chapter, we discuss the aging process, ageism, and cultural considerations for working with clients across the lifespan.

LEARNING OBJECTIVES

By the end of this chapter, students will be able to

1. recall and identify developmental theories, key concepts, and terms related to biopsychosocial aspects of aging;
2. apply psychological theories to discuss the impact of ageism across the lifespan and use strategies to combat ageism as a professional counselor;
3. critically examine the need, interest, and access to professional counseling, and distinguish related federal systems and legislation as they relate to mental health care with older adults;
4. organize strategies for culturally competent counseling skills and develop awareness of multicultural and social justice counseling competencies as they pertain to working with age-diverse clients; and
5. assess and evaluate counselor self-awareness and the counseling relationship to develop interventions and promote client advocacy.

CACREP 2016 STANDARDS

The information in this chapter supports the following standards:

- 2.F.1.a. history and philosophy of the counseling profession and its specialty areas
- 2.F.1.b the multiple professional roles and functions of counselors across specialty areas, and their relationships with human service and integrated behavioral health care systems, including interagency and interorganizational collaboration and consultation
- 2.F.1.e. advocacy processes needed to address institutional and social barriers that impede access, equity, and success for clients
- 2.F.2.a. multicultural and pluralistic characteristics within and among diverse groups nationally and internationally
- 2.F.2.b theories and models of multicultural counseling, cultural identity development, and social justice and advocacy
- 2.F.2.c. multicultural counseling competencies
- 2.F.2.d. the impact of heritage, attitudes, beliefs, understandings, and acculturative experiences on an individual's views of others
- 2.F.2.e. the effects of power and privilege for counselors and clients
- 2.F.2.f. help-seeking behaviors of diverse clients
- 2.F.2.h. strategies for identifying and eliminating barriers, prejudices, and processes of intentional and unintentional oppression and discrimination
- 2.F.3.a. theories of individual and family development across the lifespan
- 2.F.3.i. ethical and culturally relevant strategies for promoting resilience and optimum development and wellness across the lifespan

CACREP 2024 STANDARDS

The information in this chapter supports the following standards:

- 3.A.1. history and philosophy of the counseling profession and its specialized practice areas
- 3.A.2. the multiple professional roles and functions of counselors across specialized practice
- 3.A.3. counselors' roles, responsibilities, and relationships as members of specialized practice and interprofessional teams, including (a) collaboration and consultation, (b) community outreach, and (c) emergency response management
- 3.A.4. the role and process of the professional counselor advocating on behalf of and with individuals receiving counseling services to address systemic, institutional, architectural, attitudinal, disability, and social barriers that impede access, equity, and success
- 3.B.1. theories and models of multicultural counseling, social justice, and advocacy
- 3.B.2. the influence of heritage, cultural identities, attitudes, values, beliefs, understandings, within-group differences, and acculturative experiences on individuals' worldviews
- 3.B.3. the influence of heritage, cultural identities, attitudes, values, beliefs, understandings, within-group differences, and acculturative experiences on help-seeking and coping behaviors
- 3.B.4. the effects of historical events, multigenerational trauma, and current issues on diverse cultural groups in the U.S. and globally
- 3.B.5. the effects of stereotypes, overt and covert discrimination, racism, power, oppression, privilege, marginalization, microaggressions, and violence on counselors and clients

- 3.B.6. the effects of various socio-cultural influences, including public policies, social movements, and cultural values, on mental and physical health and wellness
- 3.B.8. principles of independence, inclusion, choice and self-empowerment, and access to services within and outside the counseling relationship
- 3.B.9. strategies for identifying and eliminating barriers, prejudices, and processes of intentional and unintentional oppression and discrimination
- 3.B.10. guidelines developed by professional counseling organizations related to social justice, advocacy, and working with individuals with diverse cultural identities
- 3.C.1. theories of individual and family development across the lifespan
- 3.C.7. models of resilience, optimal development, and wellness in individuals and families across the lifespan
- 3.C.11. systemic, cultural, and environmental factors that affect lifespan development, functioning, behavior, resilience, and overall wellness

What Is Aging?

Over the lifespan, people experience physiological, psychological, and social changes that are dynamic in nature in a process called aging (National Institute on Aging, n.d.). There are several developmental theories—Freud's psychoanalytic stages of development, Erikson's theory of psychosocial development, Piaget's periods of cognitive development, Bronfenbrenner's bioecological model, and Kohlberg's stages of moral development—all of which help counselors understand the aging process and the impact on individuals and groups. In this chapter, we focus on Erikson and Bronfenbrenner.

Let's examine Erikson's model (we will explore Bronfenbrenner's model later in the chapter). Each of Erikson's eight stages of psychosocial development are defined by a central challenge or basic conflict, wherein individuals face new decisions that prompt the development of one of two opposing forces: a positive strength or a negative maldevelopment (Orenstein & Lewis, 2022). As individuals progress developmentally, they may or may not resolve the conflicts presented by each psychosocial stage. Resolution typically results in the development of strengths associated with the syntactic or positive force in the conflict, whereas failure to resolve the conflict may lead to later challenges. Notably, resolution happens over the life course; stage outcomes are not fixed, allowing individuals to resolve maldeveloped belief systems later in life.

TABLE 13.1 Erikson's Stages of Development

Approximate Age	Stage	Important Event(s)	Virtue
Infancy (0–12 months)	Trust vs. Mistrust	Feeding, abandonment	Hope
Toddlerhood (1–3 years)	Autonomy vs. Shame/Doubt	Toilet training, clothing oneself	Will
Early Childhood (3–6 years)	Initiative vs. Guilt	Exploring, using tools, making art, play	Purpose

(Continued)

TABLE 13.1 *(Continued)*

Approximate Age	Stage	Important Event(s)	Virtue
Late Childhood (6–11 years)	Industry vs. Inferiority	School, sports	Competence
Adolescence (11–19 years)	Identity vs. Role Confusion	Social relationships	Fidelity
Early Adulthood (20–44 years)	Intimacy vs. Isolation	Romantic relationships	Love
Middle Adulthood (45–64 years)	Generativity vs. Self-Absorption	Work, parenthood	Care
Late Adulthood (65 years and older)	Integrity vs. Despair	Retirement, reflection on life	Wisdom

It is worth noting that developmental models are fallible and subject to influences of ageism. For example, a limitation of Erikson's model is that it doesn't acknowledge the developmental needs that occur once someone turns 65. More recently, scholars have proposed additional stages specific to later adulthood, arguing that older adults (people over the age of 65) have specific developmental needs and considerations (Ortman et al., 2014). This is particularly relevant given that people are living longer than ever before! Three specific developmental stages have emerged: young-old, middle-old, and old-old. The young-old stage begins at age 65 and continues until individuals begin to experience changes to their physical, emotional, cognitive, and social development that may be more limiting (Barnes, 2011). People in this life stage generally experience relatively good health, social engagement, decreased responsibility, and increased freedom to pursue hobbies, interests, and recreational activities. The age at which people transition to middle-old or oldest-old is contested. Some suggest the young-old stage includes ages 65 to 74, and the middle-old stage begins at age 75 (e.g., Lee et al., 2018); others argue the middle-old stage starts at age 85, and the oldest-old category is composed of centenarians, or people aged 100 years and older (Ortman et al., 2014). In either case, many people begin to experience new and often age-related health problems between 80 and 85 (Okoro et al., 2018). However, there are people in this category who experience positive health and counselors should be cautious not to assume that health problems, including mental health problems, are present for an older person simply due to age. There is great heterogeneity that accompanies growing older, which makes working with older adults both invigorating and incredibly rewarding!

Cultural Diversity in Aging

Aging is a culturally unified experience that all people share, regardless of other social and cultural identities. However, there may be cultural differences related to perceptions and values of the aging process. For example, there is some evidence for more positive perceptions of aging and older adulthood in Eastern cultures compared to Western cultures (Vauclair et al., 2017), and these perceptions may impact the aging process. For example, older adults in Japan reported they experienced more personal growth than adults in midlife, but the opposite was true in the United States (Karasawa et al., 2011), demonstrating how different cultural values around aging may influence individuals' experiences and perceptions of their aging processes.

There is far more evidence for similarities across cultures in how some aspects of aging are perceived. Vauclair et al. (2017) found that Taiwanese members of their sample perceived older adults as more competent and experienced more admiration toward older people than did members of their sample in the United Kingdom. However, the United Kingdom and Taiwanese samples did not differ in other key areas, such as pity, ambivalent perceptions of aging, and negativity. A study of college students in 26 different cultures demonstrated more similarities than differences across cultures regarding how people perceived the aging process (Löckenhoff et al., 2009). Specifically, across cultures, younger people had shared perceptions of age-related declines (e.g., attractiveness, cognitive ability), age-related increases (e.g., wisdom, knowledge, received respect), and stability in family authority. Therefore, we should interpret potential culture differences related to aging with caution, as they may be less stark than previously believed.

Additionally, aging experiences are related to how people understand themselves socially, and aging contributes to a distinct cultural identity. Later life presents unique life transitions in which age becomes an increasingly important element of people's identities (Barnes, 2011). Furthermore, older adults are the fastest growing demographic in the United States: 54.1 million older adults currently reside in the United States (Administration on Aging, 2022), and that number is projected to increase by 173% to 94.1 million by 2060 (Vespa et al., 2022). Just recently, older adults outnumbered young children globally for the first time ever (United Nations, n.d.). Historically, counseling professionals had limited opportunities to work with older adults, in part because of exclusion from the Medicare program (Fullen et al., 2019), which is the largest insurer of people over the age of 65 (Kaiser Family Foundation, 2019). However, because of Medicare policy changes in 2023, counselors now have greater opportunities to provide services to Medicare beneficiaries, including older adults (Consolidated Appropriations Act, 2023).

Counselors must be prepared to work with older adults. Although there are many stereotypes of older adults as a monolithic population, there is evidence of social and cultural diversity among people over the age of 65 in the United States. In their 2021 "Profile of Older Americans," the U.S. Administration on Aging (USAA; 2022) found roughly 30.8 million women and 24.8 men were over the age of 65. Over 10 million older adults reported they were still in the workforce, with five million people over the age of 65 living below the poverty line in 2020 and another 2.6 million near the poverty line (Administration on Aging, 2022). Additional relevant demographic characteristics, such as select information about marital status (which has bearing on social support), racial/ethnic identity, disability status, and LGBT identification, are included in Table 13.2.

TABLE 13.2 Older Adult Demographics (Administration on Aging, 2022)

Population	Percentage
Relationship Status Men who are married	69%
Women who are married	47%
Members of LGBT community	2.4%
People living with a disability Race/Ethnicity	40%
White	76%
Black or African American	9%
Hispanic/Latinx Asian American	9% 5%
American Indian or Alaska Native	0.6%
Native American or Pacific Islander	0.1%
Two or more Races	0.8%

Note: These percentages may not add to 100% because of rounding errors or unreported data.

These demographic data provide a snapshot of cultural diversity in later life. More importantly, they illustrate that many may encounter additional forms of oppression (e.g., racism, heterosexism, ableism) that intersect with ageism. A helpful framework for understanding how systems of power impact older clients is intersectionality theory, which posits that people occupy several social-cultural positions and have intersecting social and cultural identities that expose them to multiple, intersecting forms of oppression (Crenshaw, 1988, 1992; Collins, 2015). Simply put, intersectionality acknowledges that occupying a social position at the intersection of multiple oppression forces has specific impacts on well-being, safety, and health. For example, a 70-year-old Black woman encounters the intersection of misogyny and racism, or misogynoir; that misogynoir intersects with ageism such that the ageism she encounters is informed by misogynoir, and the misogynoir she encounters is informed by ageism.

Indeed, there is a wealth of evidence that multiple marginalized older adults face unique challenges borne out of that intersectional experience of oppression. Among LGBTQIA+ older adults, for example, housing is a concern. More than half of LGBTQIA+ older adults express concerns about needing to hide their identities when seeking housing out of fear of discrimination (AARP, 2022). Long-term care settings also present challenges for LGBTQIA+ older adults; 43% reported mistreatment or discrimination from other residents or staff based on their LGBTQIA+ identity (Justice in Aging, 2015).

Intersectional oppression impacts healthcare, too. Latinx/Hispanic and Black older adults reported being treated unfairly based on their racial or ethnic identity when seeking healthcare, and more than one in four older adults who experienced discrimination based on their racial/ethnic identity did not receive the care they needed as a result (Doty et al., 2022). Older women are more likely than older men to experience discrimination in employment related to their age and disability (McLaughlin & Neumark, 2022). Taken together, these examples illustrate the impact of intersecting oppression on diverse older adults in the United States.

Understanding Aging Within the Ecological Framework

Intersectionality has implications for how systems affect aging. As people age, their environments impact their development and wellness, both directly and indirectly. Bronfenbrenner and Morris (2006) recognized that people's characteristics and their environments interact, impacting how people develop over the lifespan. Systems include everything from family and friends, the home, schools, neighborhoods, churches, and community laws and policies, all of which impact how people age. Bronfenbrenner identified five interconnected systems that describe how people, environments, and social contexts interact to affect development. Normal life changes affect what/who is present in a person's system; those changes lead to differences in how people develop (Bronfenbrenner & Morris, 2006). For example, graduating college may lead to a person entering the workforce. The people in their microsystem change, which shifts the mesosystem around them, leading to a new range of influences.

Within the microsystem, one's most important relationships, as well as the events that influence people in those relationships (i.e., mesosystem), impact development (Schafer & Shippee, 2010). Other things that impact the microsystem include important individual events, relationship dynamics, and individual characteristics (e.g., age, personality). When people have access to social resources (e.g., peer/family support) and they know how to use them, they experience healthier development (Eriksson et al., 2018). As people age, the people and interactions in their microsystems change. What was once limited to family, teachers, and classmates evolves to include romantic partners, coworkers, adult friendships, and children. For some, the microsystem gets smaller as they age. Things like retirement, new mobility limitations, and death shrink the number of relationships available to them. For others, older adulthood may coincide with an expanded social network because of growth in their family (e.g., grandchildren, children partnering), volunteering, and added social experiences (e.g., sports, clubs).

Depending upon a person's chronosystem, which refers to major historical or life events that impact a person's development, the importance of different resources in the microsystem may change. These can include individual life events such as graduating high school, getting married or divorced, or experiencing the loss of a loved one. But an individual's chronosystem is also influenced by the broader societal context in which development is occurring, and these societal shifts can influence microsystems as well. For example, technology has expanded the scope of the microsystem across the lifespan as people use phones and computers to connect (Navarro, 2022). Contrary to popular belief about older people's use of technology, the Pew Research Center (PRC; Faverio, 2022) found 92% of older adults have a cell phone. The importance of technology in the microsystem expanded during the COVID-19 pandemic when many people relied on technology to connect with loved ones. Some elements are impacted more by life stage than social changes. Direct social services, for example, are most important in childhood and adolescence (i.e., childcare, school) and again in later life (i.e., nutrition services, home health supports) but matter less during early and middle adulthood due to greater physical and financial independence (Cvitkovich & Wister, 2001).

The mesosystem accounts for how interactions within a person's microsystem impact their development. For example, a person who is happy at work comes home with less stress. Additionally, the mesosystem can help people expand their point of view and deepen their self-understanding (Newman & Newman, 2020). Consider a recent retiree who begins attending a busy neighborhood recreation center for older adults. Seeing other older adults be active might prompt that retiree to start walking every day. In this case, her interactions with peers at the recreation center are a part of her spouse's mesosystem; when she invites her spouse to walk with her every day, her spouse's mesosystem has exerted influence to enhance their own wellness.

The exosystem accounts for how broader societal factors affect development and is especially relevant in later life, as a primary goal of aging services is to develop more "livable" communities. For example, AARP's (n.d.) Age-Friendly Communities Network is focused on policies, programs, and services that enhance people's ability to age in place and thrive in their communities.

Another important part of the exosystem is the media. Regardless of age, people internalize messages from popular media about what is considered normal or acceptable. Seeing few examples of positive representation of aging in movies or TV shows contributes to negative perceptions of aging (MediaSmarts, n.d). Given that adults 60 and older now spend over 4 hours a day watching TV or videos (Livingston, 2019), understanding the impact of media is especially important in later life. For example, exposure to negative stereotypes about older adulthood can negatively impact people's aging experiences.

The Golden Girls was a sitcom on NBC from 1985 to 1992 that depicted four women navigating the aging process through their relationships (and a lot of laughter). With 68 Emmy nominations and 11 wins (Emmy's, n.d.), it's no surprise that *The Golden Girls* is perhaps the most critically acclaimed show focused on later life. But what made this show so special? For one, this show challenged negative stereotypes about aging by depicting four women in later life who were able to grow and develop. Critics pointed out the way the show embraced all aspects of aging and explored challenging topics, including age discrimination, sexuality in later life, visibility of disability, gay rights, and racism in America (Ross, 2015).

The exosystem includes national and state-level programs and policies impacting social welfare, public safety, and healthcare systems. At the federal level, the U.S. Department of Health and Human Services oversees multiple public health and human services agencies such as the Centers for Medicare and Medicaid Services, the Centers for Disease Control and Prevention, and the Administration for Community Living, which support community resources for older Americans and people with disabilities. Other resources available to people in later life include Medicare, the federal health insurance program for people aged 65+ and for people with disabilities. It's important to know that all parts of Medicare are not without financial cost. While there are programs to help low-income adults pay for Medicare, many encounter gaps and financial burdens related to medical expenses. Social Security, a system to ensure workers earn retirement benefits after the age of 65 (on average—the age at which one can receive Social Security varies based on birth year), is another resource. Additionally, Social Security provides income to individuals who cannot work due to disability and supports dependents (i.e., spouse, children, or parents) with benefits in the event of a family member's death. In 2020, nearly 90% of older

IMG 13.1.

adults received Social Security benefits, 27% of whom relied on Social Security for 90% or more of their income (Social Security Administration, 2023).

The macrosystem and chronosystem have more diffuse impacts on development: These systems impact broader groups of people but have a less direct impact on each individual person. Social norms influence what we think is appropriate and how we think we should behave at different life stages. Therefore, the macrosystem has an important impact on people's understanding of their own aging process, as well as how they treat people at different stages of aging (Cvitkovich &

IMG 13.2.

Wister, 2001). Similarly, major life events that comprise the chronosystem are important to individual development (Eriksson et al., 2018), as well as specific cohorts of people. The Vietnam War had a significant impact on the cohort of men drafted to fight in the conflict, as well as their families. Similarly, the more recent COVID-19 pandemic affected people across the globe and will define cohort experiences based on the developmental stage when it occurred. In a bit, we will discuss the age-period-cohort model, which further elucidates how these systems intertwine in the lives of older adults.

Environment and Aging

As we discussed previously, people's behaviors, thoughts, and feelings can be the result of risk and protective factors in a given environment. As individuals age, home environments can profoundly impact their purpose, social connection, and safety. This is especially true in later life, given that most older adults spend about 80% of their time at home (Iwarsson et al., 2007). Almost 90% of adults over the age of 70 live in home settings as opposed to retirement communities or communities that provide care assistance (Freedman et al., 2021). However, long-term care or housing with care options for older adults with greater support needs can enhance people's quality of life. These options include assisted living communities, communal residential environments with support services (e.g., meals, transportation assistance), and long-term care options that provide medical care.

Environments have a significant impact on people's ability to function, especially as we age (Cvitkovich & Wister, 2001). For example, an older person who has a newly acquired disability would have a greater risk of health decline living alone in a third-story walk-up apartment compared to someone in the same situation living with a caregiver on the first floor. People prefer to age *in place* (i.e., remain in their homes), but social services may not provide adequate support to allow them to do so (Greenfield, 2012). Access to services that can enable someone to stay in their home is financially inaccessible for many older adults, and paying out of pocket might increase financial strain for those who can afford it (Greenfield, 2012). When working with older clients, it is important for counselors to consider these environmental influences.

Understanding Generational Differences: The Age-Period-Cohort Model

An important component of working with people at different stages of the lifespan is understanding how unique life experiences shape their perspectives. Although people around the world understand time differently (Graham, 1981), we are all shaped in numerous ways by forces of time. Our lives are shaped by the historical time in which we are born and by the group of people with whom we experience major life events. Given their centrality in shaping our lives, time factors inevitably influence how we view ourselves, other people, and groups.

One of the consequences of viewing others through a temporal lens is we tend to group people by age and stage, such as by the generation they belong to—the Greatest Generation, the Silent Generation, Baby Boomers, Generation X, Millennials, Gen Z, and Gen Alpha. Although generations are not tied to any objective metric aside from birth year, they have become the primary way we think about differences across age groups in the United States. The concept of generations is appealing because it allows for easy categorization of people into groups, one of the human brain's built-in tendencies (Rhodes & Baron, 2019). Also, generations represent an organizational structure most of us are familiar with from our own families, making them an intuitive way to view the broader social world. Additionally, shared generational events and experiences partly explain the chronosystem, as we discussed above. However, these shortcuts can obscure the enormous diversity that exists within generations and risk flattening our understanding of people who differ from us in age.

For example, political party affiliation is often framed by age, with young adults perceived as more liberal than older adults. The reality is more nuanced. In a survey of 30 political views across demographic groups, the largest between-group differences in views were observed by political party (39%) and race (17%; PRC, 2019). Only a 10% difference was observed between those aged 18 to 49 and those aged 50 or older, which is equivalent to the difference observed by education level (college graduate vs. non-college graduate; PRC, 2019). Looking at political party membership, there are some meaningful differences by generation: among Millennials, 59% are Democrats/lean Democratic, whereas 32% are Republican/lean Republican, proportions that represent dramatic shifts from Baby Boomers and Gen X (PRC, 2018). However, this is an incomplete picture. Not only is racial identity a much more powerful predictor of party membership than generation—attesting, in part, to the influence of the increased diversity of the U.S. population over time—but gender plays a powerful role, too. Millennial women are much more likely to lean Democratic than Millennial men: 70% compared to 49% (PRC, 2018). Clearly, generation must be considered alongside other identity factors.

As the prior example illustrates, drawing broad generalizations about large groups of people based on one factor (i.e., age) obscures important parts of their story. A more informative way to think about this is by using the concepts of *age*, *period*, and *cohort*. These factors allow us to understand how various temporal factors impact people within context. The three central concepts of the Age-period-cohort model are in the name. Age is familiar to us: it refers to an individual's chronological age, which tells us where they are in the lifespan. Period refers to a span of historical time, including a stretch of time defined by events (e.g., the postwar period) or any year or set of years (Hobcraft et al., 1982). Cohort, which may be the least familiar concept to most readers, refers to all the people experiencing a specific event at the same time (Hobcraft et al., 1982). For example, a birth cohort refers to everyone born in a given year (e.g., everyone born in 2004), yet *cohort* can also be applied to all persons who experienced the COVID-19 pandemic or all those who started their graduate counseling program at the same time.

Let's apply these concepts to an example. The economy is an institution affecting people's well-being. When the economy enters a period of significant change—experiences a crash, for instance—everyone in the economic system is affected (*period effect*). However, how and how much people are impacted will vary by a range of factors: whether they are students, on the job market, in the workplace, or retired, for example, with each factor influenced by *age* and *cohort effects*. The impact of the crash will vary across groups of people based on the resources they started out with and the downstream impact of the crash on their future earnings. A college senior in the job market might be more severely impacted—unable to find a job and pay off loan debt—than a well-established senior manager whose earnings remain steady during the crash. Another senior manager, however, may have to postpone her retirement due to concerns about being able to maintain financial independence in the face of economic uncertainty.

Applications to Counseling

As a counselor, having a basic familiarity with social forces that have shaped individuals' lives over the past several decades—economic recessions, major pieces of legislation, U.S. involvement in wars and armed conflicts, and traumatic events like the 9/11 terrorist attacks—will allow you to better understand your client's life circumstances and help prevent overattributing people's decisions and choices to personal tendencies. In general, recognizing the role of period, cohort, and age in your clients' outlook and life circumstances, alongside the influence of systems such as Bronfenbrenner's framework, will provide insight into their life experiences and help you serve them better.

Consider *Game of Thrones*' Lady Olenna Tyrell, the matriarch of the Tyrell family and a formidable political force, was the only older adult woman to occupy a position of high political power across 72 popular TV shows in the 2016 to 2017 season (Smith et al., 2017). Although 17% of the U.S. population is over the age of 65 (Administration on Aging, 2022), only 9.4% of television speaking roles go to characters who are 60 or older, and series regulars who are older adults account for only 8.2% of roles (Smith et al., 2017). In this context, Lady Olenna's character was a true standout in modern television. One might argue that this is an example of workplace ageism in the entertainment industry.

Ageism

The World Health Organization (WHO; n.d.) defines ageism as "the stereotypes (how we think), prejudice (how we feel) and discrimination (how we act) toward others or ourselves based on age" (para. 1). The term *ageism* was first coined by Robert Butler. In *Why Survive? Being Old in America,* Butler (2002) wrote:

> Ageism can be seen as a process of systematic stereotyping of and discrimination against people because they are old. ... Ageism allows the younger generation to see older people as different from themselves; thus they can subtly cease to identify with their elders as human beings. (p. 12)

This process of seeing older adults as "different" is a key factor in understanding the potential origins of ageism.

Stereotypes of aging play a critical role in understanding the origins of ageism. Psychologist and epidemiologist Becca Levy created a field of study exploring how negative age stereotypes impact longevity among older adults called stereotype embodiment theory. This framework posits that assimilated aging stereotypes from one's culture impact how a person views themselves as they age, which influences health, functioning, and longevity (Levy, 2009). In other words, the beliefs we hold in childhood toward older adults will turn into the attitudes we hold toward ourselves as we age; if we have negative beliefs about aging and older adults, we will embody those negative beliefs as we age. In fact, Levy's extensive research shows older adults who have more positive attitudes and beliefs toward aging and growing older live over 7 years longer than those who hold negative beliefs toward aging (Levy et al., 2002).

Another theory of understanding ageism is terror management theory. Terror management theory, based on the writings of Ernest Becker, suggests humans have unique knowledge of their impending deaths; this knowledge creates unconscious anxiety that must be managed at all times. According to the theory, cultural belief systems and self-esteem are psychological defenses to combat this terror (Martens et al., 2005). Psychological defenses to manage death anxiety, alongside fears of aging, may result in discriminatory behavior. Martens et al. (2005) suggested,

> [A]geism exists ... because [older adults] represent a future in which death is certain, physical deterioration probable, and the loss of current self-worth-enhancing characteristics a distinct possibility. Negative attitudes and behaviors directed toward [older adults] can be explained in large part by people's own fears about aging and death. (p. 223)

In other words, terror management theory may explain why some younger adults view older persons as *other*; to combat the fears of their own mortality, they turn to unconscious negative age stereotypes to separate themselves from those who are older in age.

Ageism Across the Lifespan

Developing age-related stereotypes in childhood, as described by stereotype embodiment theory, may profoundly impact one's longevity as a future older adult. Let's consider an example of how age beliefs are assimilated in childhood. In many elementary schools in the United States, to commemorate the 100th day of school, students dress up like *old people*. For an entire day, kindergarteners transform into caricatures of how they envision a centenarian. How many children in this situation think of an older adult as compassionate, wise, resilient, lively, or fun? Or, more likely, how many delight in dressing up and pretending to be cranky and hard of hearing?

Although older adults are argued to be most negatively impacted by the effects of ageism at macro- and microlevels, age discrimination occurs across the lifespan given that the *privileged age* in the United States lasts for only a relatively short period of time (approximately 35–55). Westman (1991) defined institutional juvenile ageism as discrimination that occurs "when social systems ignore the interests of children ... and the developmental interests of a child are not respected" (p. 237). Westman (1991) also posited that while older adults may remind individuals, especially in the United States, of the inevitability of death, children may also be reminders of dependency and vulnerability, resulting in ageist behaviors and beliefs.

Alongside stereotype embodiment theory is social identity theory, or a person's sense of who they are based on their group memberships (Tajfel, 1979; Mcleod, 2023). Social identity theory may help explain the origins of ageism across the lifespan. Ageism toward children and youth may be a function of cohort biases, such as negative attitudes toward younger adults based on their generational affiliation (Van Vleck, 2021). For example, in a recent poll, 31% of Millennials and 32% of Gen Z workers reported experiencing workplace ageism driven by a perceived lack of experience (Meyer, 2021). Ageism toward younger adults by older adults does not negate the harmful impacts of ageism toward older adults, and vice versa; ageism is a form of prejudice that is harmful at any stage of the lifespan. However, compounding instances of discrimination can lead to more detrimental outcomes among older adults.

BOX 13.1 **PAUSE AND REFLECT: EXAMPLES OF AGEIST BELIEFS**

Read through the following list and note what comes up for you. Do you believe these things apply to all older adults?

1. "You can't teach an old dog new tricks." Older adults are unwilling to learn and grow.
2. All older adults are religious.
3. Older adults do not have sex or do not have fulfilling sex lives.
4. Older adults need others to help them complete daily living tasks.
5. Most older adults prefer to stay at home rather than lead active lives.
6. Addictions do not happen to older adults; when they do, there is little hope for change.

Intersectionality and Ageism

Nelson (2005) described ageism as "prejudice against our feared future self" (p. 207). Indeed, old age is likely the one aspect of our possible identities that all people hope to attain one day. The double-jeopardy hypothesis suggests being an older adult, as well as holding an underrepresented ethnic identity, has an impact on health, life satisfaction, and adjustment to aging (Markides & Gerst-Emerson, 2014). We see the impacts of multiple jeopardies among older adults, particularly older women of color in the context of career and wage discrepancies. Older women in the United States are likely to earn lower wages, have lower total payroll tax contributions, earn less Social Security income, engage in more unpaid care work, and live longer—therefore, older women are much more likely to live in poverty (Justice in Aging, 2018). Finally, ageism impacts health outcomes for older adults regarding healthcare, including more hospitalizations and delayed or inadequate care (Mohammed et al., 2019).

Combating Ageism: Strategies for Counselors

Although ageism is a widespread and damaging systemic issue, counselors have opportunities to combat ageism and promote positive experiences for children, young people, and aging and older adults. In a meta-analysis of ways to reduce ageism, Burnes et al. (2019) found ageism interventions strongly reduced negative attitudes toward older adults, including education and having intergenerational contact. Raising awareness is key to combating ageism. For example, by reading this chapter, you are combating ageism by learning more about its origins and effects, as well as how that may impact your work as a counselor.

Combating ageism can be connected to the theories we discussed to understand the origins of ageism. From a stereotype embodiment theory perspective, one way to combat ageism is to advocate for and create positive age beliefs in childhood. This may change your self-directed attitudes toward aging and growing older, too. Rather than using the 100th day of school to create parodies of older adulthood, what if that day was focused on celebrating older adults' wisdom and experience, and exploring how exciting it would be to live to be 100 years old! For counselors who work with children, what would it look like to provide positive age beliefs in the therapeutic environment (e.g., asking the child to describe an older person in their lives and all the things they admire about them)?

Using terror management theory, one approach to combat ageism is tending to death anxiety. Bodner et al. (2015) found both aging and death anxieties contribute to ageist attitudes—in other words, the more death anxiety you have, the more likely you are to have ageist attitudes. Therapeutic interventions for death anxiety, such as existential therapy (Yalom, 2008), cognitive behavioral therapy, and death acceptance, have been found to reduce death anxiety (Furer & Walker, 2008). The therapeutic relationship provides a powerful opportunity to discuss death anxiety and fears of aging.

BOX 13.2 **PAUSE AND REFLECT: CHECK YOUR OWN AGEIST BELIEFS**

Our task as counselors is to attend to our ageist beliefs and personal death anxiety so we can hold space for others.

What beliefs do you hold about older adults? Children, adolescents, and young adults? What proportion of your beliefs are positive? Negative?

Where do your beliefs about different age groups come from?

On a scale of 1–10, how high is your death anxiety?

What ideas do you have about how you can work through your ageist beliefs and death anxiety?

Another strategy to combat death anxiety (which may, in turn, combat ageism) is to attend a Death Café. Death Cafés are events in which individuals gather to eat cake, drink tea, and discuss death, with the goal of increasing awareness of death to help people make the most of their lives (Death Café, n.d.). These and other interventions focused on combating ageism—such as life review and reminiscence therapy—are some of the many ways counselors can address the professional needs related to aging and working effectively with older adults.

Understanding the Historical Context of Aging and Counseling

Access to health care based on age has a unique history in the United States. In 1965, after decades of debate, the Social Security Amendments of 1965, also known as the Medicare and Medicaid Act (National Archives, n.d.), were signed into law (Oberlander, 2013). Regarding mental health care access, the psychiatry community recognized the passage of Medicare as a pivotal moment in the provision of mental health care (Frank, 2000). As a result of the amendment, a greater proportion of older people began to seek care from specialized mental health care providers, and the field of mental health care underwent *transinstitutionalization*, or a significant shift in the settings where mental health care was delivered (Frank, 2000; Primeau et al., 2013). As part of this process, utilization of public mental hospitals decreased markedly and many former patients were moved to prisons or, in the case of older patients, to nursing homes. These facilities were often poorly equipped to provide the level of care required by older adult patients with mental disorders (Primeau et al., 2013). This was due in part to counselors being unable to serve older adults under Medicare—their care was provided by physicians, psychologists, and social workers only. The field of gerontology, or the study of the aging process, ageism, and specific concerns of old age, expanded from 1970 to 1980, reflecting growing awareness of the unique needs associated with growing older in the United States.

Despite these developments, inclusion of lifespan and aging issues in the mental health professions remains incomplete. For example, as of 2013, more than half of geriatric psychiatry residencies go unfilled each year, and only 4.2% of practicing psychologists focus on older populations (Bartels & Naslund, 2013). Meanwhile, 17.2% of social work faculty reported an interest in aging, and only 8.2% reported regularly teaching an aging class (Wang et al., 2013). In addition, only 9% of social workers identified aging as an area of practice (Wang & Chonody, 2013). These trends reflect the consequences of ageism: Older adulthood is devalued in society, resulting in few specialists able to teach and train students in helping professions, which results in fewer individuals entering the workforce who can provide specialized care for older adults.

How has the counseling profession fared when it comes to serving older adults? For most of its history, counselors were excluded from participation in the Medicare program, making it difficult, albeit not impossible, to work with older adults on a consistent basis. In the 2000s, counseling advocacy organizations began supporting legislation to address this gap by expanding Medicare coverage to licensed counselors and marriage and family therapists. Because these professions comprise approximately 225,000 members of the U.S. mental health workforce, their exclusion from Medicare represented a substantial barrier to mental health care for older adults (American Counseling Association, 2022). After decades of advocacy, Medicare law was changed in 2022 (Consolidated Appropriations Act, 2023), adding licensed counselors and marriage and family therapists to the list of mental health care providers eligible to participate in the Medicare program. It remains to be seen how counselor education programs will adapt training standards so people of all ages have consistent access to quality mental health care (Fullen, 2018).

BOX 13.3 PAUSE AND REFLECT: VALUES AND AGING

What does this history tell us about the values we hold related to aging?

How can counselors promote age-based inclusivity and advocate for the continued expansion of older adult mental health care?

Professional Counseling Related to Aging: Needs, Interest, and Access

Let's try a quick thought experiment. Imagine you are a counselor getting ready to meet Tara, a new client who asks to speak with a counselor about relationship stress, questioning her purpose in life, and wrestling with a flare-up of depression symptoms she thought were under control. You learn about this new client from the office assistant and begin to form a mental picture of who this person is and what they will be like to work with. As you started to think about Tara, roughly what age was she? If you learned that Tara is 75 years old, would you think differently about her and her case? Why or why not?

Many people, when asked to think about mental health care, assume it is primarily for people in the first half of their lives. Key theorists like Sigmund Freud and Erik Erikson spent a lot of time thinking about the aspects of psychological and relational development in the earlier years of life without providing the same degree of nuance in older adulthood. As you have learned thus far in this chapter, older adulthood is far more complex than most people realize, and this impacts how people in later stages of life experience mental health and access mental health care. Broad stereotypes about older adults and mental health, such as the notion that all older adults are depressed (*False!*) or disinterested in mental health care (*False!*), should be replaced with greater appreciation for the heterogeneity within the older adult population, as well as greater recognition of how ageism shapes the discourse around mental health in older adulthood.

But first, let's start with some basics. Overall, older adults tend to have high levels of life satisfaction (George, 2010); some scholars argue that psychological well-being follows a U-shaped curve over the course of the life span (Blanchflower & Oswald, 2008), with higher well-being among young adults and older adults, while a dip occurs during middle adulthood. Overall, older adulthood is a phase of the life span that has a great deal to offer, assuming basic needs are met. Just like any age group, older adults also face legitimate challenges, and these can result in mild, moderate, or serious mental health problems. According to a recent study (Gerlach et al., 2021), an estimated one in five older adults is experiencing anxiety, depression, substance use, insomnia, or another mental health disorder. Of note, 18% of respondents said their mental health was worse than it had been prior to the COVID-19 pandemic. Suicide rates among older adults are higher than the national average (Drapeau & McIntosh, 2021), with White males 85 or older consistently having one of the highest rates of suicide per capita in the United States (Drapeau & McIntosh, 2021).

BOX 13.4 TIPS FOR PROFESSIONAL PRACTICE: THE CORE CONDITIONS AND WORKING WITH OLDER ADULTS

By now, you have learned that the core conditions of person-centered approaches to counseling (i.e., unconditional positive regard, genuineness, warmth, and empathy) are incredibly important. That is no less the case when working with older adults! The following questions are aimed at helping you consider how to promote these core conditions in your clinical work with older people:

How might you convey unconditional positive regard to an older adult counseling client? What would you say? What about genuineness?

Do you have personal experiences with older people that you would characterize as warm? If yes, how might that impact the way you communicate warmth to older clients? If no, could you think of an opportunity to dedicate time to getting to know people who are older, or much older, than you?

In your estimation, how do you tap into empathy when you are getting to know someone who has very different life experiences than you? What are your go-to empathy strategies when this happens, and how might you apply that to working with clients who are older, or much older, than you?

What about rates of neurocognitive disorders or mental disorders commonly associated with memory? A recent study found almost 10% of older adults had dementia, with another 22% meeting the criteria for mild cognitive impairment (MCI; Manly et al., 2022). The study authors found rates of dementia shifted from only 3% of people between 65 and 69 years of age to around 35% for people 90 years or older. Notably, the authors found that compared to White, non-Latinx older adults, dementia was more common among Black older adults and MCI more common among Latinx individuals.

So, what happens when older adults face mental health concerns that might warrant talking to a professional? Does it surprise you to find out that in one recent study (Gerlach et al., 2021), 87% of older adults reported feeling comfortable talking about their mental health? Notably, 71% of this sample declared they would not hesitate to see a mental health professional in the future. It should be noted that the study cited here included individuals ages 50 to 80, and it is entirely possible there are differences between the average 50-year-old respondent and 80-year-old respondent when it comes to perceptions of mental health and help-seeking. This is an important opportunity to reflect on the age-period-cohort approach described earlier in the chapter. According to this approach, why might a person in their 50s be more open to discussions of mental health than someone in their 80s? As far as age, a person in their 50s is more likely to be employed, which may coincide with health insurance through their employer. The employer might have a workplace wellness program or an employee assistance program, making the notion of counseling more fitting for this individual. Now consider the contrast with the person who is 80. Prior to legislation that was passed in 2022, Medicare excluded a significant proportion of the mental health workforce, making it difficult for this individual to access care if they wanted it (Larson et al., 2016). Rather than receiving messages that mental health support is available, like the hypothetical 50-year-old may have received, the 80-year-old individual may not receive the same sort of messaging.

There are similar differences that can be attributed to *period* and *cohort* as well. Meeting with a mental health professional is different than other forms of mental health care that may have been the norm in the past (e.g., psychiatric hospitalization), and psychiatric medications are more ubiquitous and reliable than they used to be (i.e., period effects). Depending on when a person came of age, they may have different attitudes toward the acceptability of mental health care, both in general and for themselves (i.e., cohort effects). For example, Baby Boomers have had more exposure to psychological explanations for life challenges than individuals born earlier (Knight, 2009). These factors impact how much a person perceives mental health is a core aspect of their lives and whether they believe resources are available, acceptable, and accessible (Stewart et al., 2015).

BOX 13.5 **PAUSE AND REFLECT: WORKING TOWARD INCLUSIVITY FOR ALL**

Consider what you are learning about multicultural counseling and its application to various groups of people. What can counselors do to communicate to their communities and clients that mental health care is *for* me and people like me? In previous chapters, you learned about what this might look like when race, ethnicity, and social class identity are considered, but what about when it comes to age?

What should mental health professionals know about counseling best practices when it comes to serving older adults? One expert, Bob Knight (1996), described what he calls a contextual, cohort-based, maturity, specific challenge model (CCMSCM). Although this is far from the only distinctive approach to counseling older clients, the CCMSCM demonstrates how someone might adapt their counselor training to maximize its effectiveness with older adults. *Contextual* refers to the social-environmental context that influences where older clients are receiving care. Do they call your office manager directly in hopes of setting up an appointment at your private practice, or are they referred for a depression assessment by the social worker employed at an assisted living facility? The wide range of contexts inhabited by older adults may tell you more about their needs than age or birth year alone. Next, the reference to *cohort* should be familiar to you by now! By roughly estimating which age cohort represents the individual older adult, you may begin to form working hypotheses about previous exposure to mental health services or messages the individual may have received regarding help-seeking as they grew up. Don't hesitate to check out these hypotheses with your older clients; there are always exceptions and individual differences that emerge.

Maturity recognizes that, broadly speaking, older age may coincide with developmental changes such as slowing down or the use of simpler language, as well as increased emotional complexity and broader life experiences. Finally, Knight points out that in working with older adult clients, mental health professionals should be aware of *specific challenges*, specifically a greater prevalence of chronic health conditions, including neurological disorders, grief work, and caregiving concerns. This does not mean all presenting issues will be focused on these domains, yet culturally adept counselors are prepared for these issues to emerge and are willing to discuss their impact on the client's goals, relationships, and well-being.

Finally, it is important to remember there are developmental transitions and specific challenges that can affect the well-being of older adults. Life role transitions is the state in which a person passes through different stages in life that involve changes in identity, role, and responsibility (Sue et al., 2021). Among older adults, these can include a wide variety of experiences. For example, an older adult around age 65 may be experiencing retirement and being an "empty nester" as their adult children leave their home while simultaneously serving as a primary caregiver for their aging parents. Skerrett et al. (2022) coined the term *emerging elderhood* to conceptualize "the perception of and reaction to the realities of the aging process" (p. 378). The realities of the aging process—physical, emotional, and contextual—are nuanced and complex.

Death, dying, and loss impact individuals at all stages of their lifespan, yet there are circumstances unique to older adulthood. Older adults may have smaller social networks because of the deaths of family, friends, and peers (Kemperman et al., 2019). Grief and bereavement may be circumstances for which an older adult seeks counseling. End-of-life decisions and care are also challenges that may be unique to older adulthood. Planning an advanced directive, a legal document providing instructions for medical providers if you are unable to make decisions for yourself, is an important part of preparing for end-of-life care. As we enter the later stages of the lifespan, having plans in place to advocate for preferences in death and end-of-life care, such as the decision to have a DNR (do not resuscitate) order, to enter hospice care, or to enter palliative care, may be an important and challenging task to complete.

If this seems like a lot to consider, it is, and don't worry. You are learning the skills needed to help people who represent a wide variety of social identities, and in many ways, age can be considered as one more intersection that adds complexity and nuance to the work you're doing already. That is part of what makes counseling work so unique! Each of us has a perception of aging that is influenced by the social forces you read about earlier in this chapter. Given that ageism is prevalent in American society, it is important for the counselor to consider how their own assumptions about aging impact the process of forming a therapeutic relationship, assessment and diagnosis of clients who are at different ages and life stages, and the formation and execution of a treatment plan.

BOX 13.6 **PAUSE AND REFLECT: YOUR EXPERIENCE WITH OLDER ADULTS**

This is an appropriate time to reflect on your own history, including past personal or professional experiences involving interactions with individuals who were much older or younger than you. In the context of working with older adults, you might reflect on past or present relationships with grandparents or parents. How did (or does) their aging process/changing needs impact you? What is your comfort level in working professionally with older people, and what might you do to enhance that comfort level?

Just as you would with other cultural identities, broaching (Day-Vines et al., 2021) can be a powerful technique that invites differences/similarities into the room and communicates to the client that their identities (in this case, age/aging) are a valued aspect of the therapeutic dialogue. For counselors who may feel intimidated by the prospect of working with a client who is several decades older or younger than they are, broaching has the potential to shift the tone from apprehension to openness. Below are some specific statements/questions that may be used to broach age differences:

- Based on your intake information, it looks like there is a sizable age difference between us. What, if any, concerns/questions do you have about how that age difference might impact our work? What are some ways that this difference might be helpful to each of us?
- Will you describe how your age impacts the presenting problem(s) you shared? I don't want to make any assumptions about how age may influence concerns you're having, and it would be helpful to me to hear your perspective.

BOX 13.7 **PROFILE OF A PRACTITIONER**

Matthew Fullen, PhD, MDiv, Associate Professor, Virginia Tech, LPCC

My counseling work with older adults began shortly after I graduated from my master's degree program and received my provisional license. A community mental health agency had an opening to work with long-term care settings where I would conduct intake assessments and provide weekly counseling services. I thoroughly enjoyed getting to know my clients, most of whom were navigating old age, medical challenges, or a combination of both, and much of the focus of the staff in those buildings centered on the physiological deficits experienced by these individuals. As I became more acquainted with my clients, I realized their self-perceptions were far more complex; they described needs and hopes that weren't just physical or medical in nature but relational, spiritual, psychological, and existential. My clients were multidimensional people, but they resided in a context that was hyper-medicalized, perhaps due in part to their advanced ages. Likewise, my clients had strengths and virtues, but most conversations with staff focused on how their bodies were breaking down. The tenor of these conversations seemed short-sighted at best, ageist and ableist at worst.

Thanks to these clients, I began experimenting with holistic wellness and **resilience** and how these constructs might apply to older adulthood. I designed a mental health program focused on resilience and piloted it within an adult day health center (Fullen & Gorby, 2016). Among our participants—most of whom qualified for support services due to medical conditions, socioeconomic status, or both—we found discussions of the whole person were well-received, serving as a subtle antidote to the fixation on the body that oftentimes accompanies our understanding of older age. Further, these participants came out of their shells when resilience, or the ability to "bounce forward," was discussed, resulting in a new vocabulary they could apply to their own self-concepts. I'll never forget one participant, a woman in her 80s, who, when asked to identify who came to mind when the word "resilient" was used, looked across the room and gently pointed at another older woman in the room. Quietly yet eloquently, she described how this woman navigated many challenges and hardships but always managed to attend their center, offer a smile to the other participants, and ask how they were doing. In this simple, accessible definition of resilience, it struck me that so many of my older adult clients over the years were also resilient but were unlikely to hear this sort of message from professionals or family members.

I'm very grateful to have encountered so many older adult clients whose strengths were obvious if you had the eyes to see them. I have since had the privilege of developing a wellness model that is distinctively focused on older adulthood (Fullen, 2019) and a curriculum to support older adult wellness that is currently being used in retirement communities (Fullen et al., 2023). As a counselor and counseling researcher, I hope these efforts allow older adult clients to experience their worth at a time when ageism looms large. I also hope these frameworks and interventions provide counselors with tools to shift the conversation with older adults from one that is narrow, medicalized, and deficits-oriented to one that is broad, holistic, and focused on client strengths.

Multicultural and Social Justice Counseling Competencies

Counselors have professional standards that can help guide age-aware practice. The multicultural and social justice counseling competencies (MSJCC; Ratts et al., 2016) acknowledge counselors and clients occupy positions of both privilege and marginalization in relation to one another. Rather than reducing either party to a single identity, the MSJCC ask counselors to consider the intersectional forces of oppression shaping clients' lives as well as the counseling relationship. In the context of aging, these influences address how the aging process intersects with other forms of marginalization clients and counselors experience, in addition to examining age as its own cultural identity. The MSJCC empower counselors to address systemic barriers and inequities that affect clients of all ages by combating ageism, supporting client autonomy, and promoting a holistic wellness framework across the lifespan. Below, we explore considerations in each of the four MSJCC domains for counseling clients across the lifespan and integrating aging considerations into the counseling process.

Counselor Self-Awareness

Counselor self-awareness around aging includes the counselor's attitudes and beliefs about aging, recognition of how their approach integrates aging considerations, and awareness of strengths and weaknesses in their skills related to counseling people of different ages. By exploring their own thoughts and feelings about age and aging, counselors can mitigate ageist beliefs (ACA, 2014, A.4.b; NBCC, 2023, Professional Responsibilities 7, p. 2, 17, p. 3; CRCC, 2023, D.2.c) and promote positive attitudes toward aging for themselves and their clients. Counselors may use resources such as holistic wellness frameworks for later life (Fullen, 2019) and gerontological counseling competencies (Myers & Schwiebert, 1996) to enhance their knowledge. Knowing more about experiences with aging may help counselors take action to help clients navigate life transitions and develop coping skills to deal with the challenges of aging and to embrace aging well.

Client Worldview

Client worldview related to aging, their own age, and how their age intersects with other salient identities impacts the counseling process. Counselors may consider exploring these topics in early sessions to better understand how clients experience their own age and aging process. Importantly, the client's cultural and historical background, as well as the social climate that has shaped their life, are likely to impact their age-related worldviews. For example, the current cohort of older gay men experienced the HIV/AIDS epidemic and associated heterosexism, which may inform their experience of aging today. Assessing how clients' historical context intersects with current experiences, their beliefs about aging, and their own intersectional identities is an important way counselors can act to better understand client worldviews. Additionally, using age-informed assessments and evaluations can enhance how counselors understand the client's worldview.

Counseling Relationship

The counseling relationship is informed by the client's and the counselor's worldviews about aging and ageism, as well as their own ages in relation to one another. Broaching similarities and differences related to age and aging experiences can enhance the counseling relationship. Acknowledging the objectives and strengths of different age cohorts can help counselors better understand and relate to clients from age groups that are not their own. To provide effective counseling for clients of all ages, counselors should seek training and continuing education about age groups with which they may be less familiar or comfortable working (see Bartels et al., 2005; Fullen, 2018). By integrating these strategies, counselors can provide more effective and culturally sensitive counseling, ultimately leading to improved outcomes for clients of all ages.

Counseling and Advocacy Interventions

Finally, counselors can employ counseling and advocacy interventions that integrate age and aging processes. The MSJCC highlight six target areas of intervention: intrapersonal, interpersonal, institutional, community, public policy, and international/global (Ratts et al., 2016). In each of these, the age of both the client and the counselor may be relevant, as is the aging process and related intersections. At the intrapersonal level, discussing how age impacts the counseling relationship and assisting clients in unlearning ageist stereotypes by providing evidence-based psychoeducation may enhance the counseling process. Interpersonally, clients may experience microaggressions and discrimination related to their age; therefore, exploring the impact of such experiences and consciousness-raising around ageism may help externalize oppression.

To intervene institutionally, counselors can explore client experiences within their workplaces, schools, and other organizations. This process may illuminate ways in which institutional environments support or oppress the client based on their age. Counselors engage at the community level by learning and acknowledging age-related societal values and how norms and attitudes influence their clients' self-perceptions and perceived wellness. Public policies impact clients too. Counselors advocate with and for clients to promote equitable laws and policies, such as the Mental Health Access Improvement Act discussed earlier in this chapter. Similarly, counselors stay informed of international and global events that may impact clients. For example, the rhetoric surrounding the COVID-19 pandemic often devalued older adults, causing some to feel expendable and forgotten (Webb & Chen, 2022).

BOX 13.8 **PAUSE AND REFLECT: YOUR EXPERIENCE WITH AGEISM**

- How have you experienced ageism?
- What steps will you take to increase self-awareness to combat ageism in your personal and professional life?
- What ways do you see yourself advocating for older adults?

Ethical Considerations

Counselors can find help navigating their work with clients by referring to professional codes of ethics and key ethical principles associated with counseling. The following discussion is not exhaustive, though it should help you begin to develop skills to apply various ethical codes to concepts, such as aging and ageism, that are not explicitly detailed within the codes.

A key principle in counseling practice is autonomy, or "fostering the right to control the direction of one's life" (ACA, 2014, p. 3; ASCA, 2022, p. 10; AMHCA, 2020, A.1.a; CRCC, 2023, A.1.e.; NBCC, 2023, 39, p. 6). Ageism can directly impact and interfere with the autonomy of older and younger people. However, counselors must have knowledge of developmental theories and research that contradict ageist assumptions and support client autonomy, particularly when it relates to their scope of practice and ethical decision-making (ACA, 2014, C.2.a; ASCA, 2022, F.g; CRCC, 2023, Defining the Profession, p. 3; NBCC, 2023, 1, p. 2). Counselors honor client autonomy through the presumption that clients are the experts of their own lives and can define, pursue, and attain their own optimal wellness at all ages.

Another essential ethical consideration is client welfare. ACA's (2014) *Code of Ethics* states that "the primary responsibility of counselors is to respect the dignity and promote the welfare of clients" (A.1.a., p. 4; see also ASCA, 2022, A.1.a, A.2.d; CRCC, 2023, A.1.a; NBCC, 2023, 8, p. 3). We are responsible for respecting clients' dignity and promoting their welfare, regardless of age. When clients are physically or legally unable to provide informed consent, we seek assent and involve clients in decision-making and treatment planning (ACA, 2014, A.2.d; ASCA, 2022, A.2.h; AMHCA, 2020, A.2.k; CRCC, 2023, A.3.d.; NBCC, 2023, 38, p. 6). For clients experiencing cognitive impairment or for minors, which may make consent legally impossible, it is still important to seek assent and ensure that we involve them as much as possible in the decision-making process. Similarly, we should work to be sensitive to the developmental needs of clients across the lifespan to best support clients' growth and development free from ageist assumptions.

It may be necessary to consider additional strategies to maintain confidentiality and privacy as well. In some cases, older adults may have caregivers or loved ones involved in their care

(ACA, 2014, B.5.b; CRCC, 2023, B.1) or live in integrated care communities. Clinical and school counselors working with minors balance ethical obligations to the client or student with the parent's and guardian's right to access information about their child's care (ASCA, 2022, A.2.g; AMHCA, 2020, B.2.b; NBCC, 2023, 38, p. 6). We diligently ensure clients have informed consent regarding the scope and limitations of confidentiality within the counseling relationship (ACA, 2014, B.1.d; ASCA, 2022, A.2.b; CRCC, 2023, A.3.a; NBCC, 2017, 32, p. 5) specific to their context. For example, adults living in assisted living communities should be made aware of the members of the team and the types of information that may be shared among team members (ACA, 2014, B.3.b; CRCC, 2023, B.3; NBCC, 2023, 28, p. 5) while counselors ensure they make only minimal disclosures (ACA, 2014, B.2.e).

Counselors do not discriminate on the basis of age (ACA, 2014, C5; AMHCA, 2020, C.2.a) and must recognize and respect unique age-related needs and concerns. In addition to theories and models of development and counseling, ethical codes provide a framework for addressing issues related to aging and ageism in counseling practice. By honoring autonomy, obtaining informed consent, maintaining confidentiality, and centering client welfare, counselors can provide effective care that promotes wellness for clients across the lifespan.

When working with older adults, consider any additional ethical codes you would intentionally apply to aging and ageism. Thoughtfully plan your response to a situation in which you see someone in a professional setting struggling to apply the code of ethics in relation to age. Consider how you would use the code of ethics to promote wellness among people of all ages.

BOX 13.9 **PROFILE OF A PRACTITIONER: NICK GOWEN, MA, LPCC, BOULDER, COLORADO**

I was 29 when I began my master's in clinical mental health counseling, and I was quickly drawn to work with older adults. Since entering adulthood, I have maintained friendships across the lifespan; when I began my master's, I realized that my ability to foster intergenerational relationships came in handy when connecting with clients of all ages, especially older adults.

Knowing this, I helped develop an internship site at a senior living community. It was the first time the community had a mental

IMG 13.3. Nick Gowen, MA, LPCC, Boulder, Colorado

health counselor, and many people were skeptical about whether the residents would even seek out my services. Critics said, "Oh, you won't get older people to open up. They're of a generation that doesn't like to talk about their feelings. It's a sign of weakness!" And yet, within a month, my schedule was completely full. My clients ranged in age from 55 to 103—all of whom were ready and excited to show up and do the hard work of mental health counseling.

Some of the topics of conversation were familiar from my work across the entire lifespan: Clients were anxious or depressed, worried about their long-term relationships, and wondering what their life's calling might be. However, I also began noticing concerns that seemed particular to older adulthood. For example, I realized a lot of our conversations revolved around death and what it might look and feel like—when it might happen and whether they were scared of it. Now, if I were having conversations like that with a 20-year-old, I might be concerned, but speaking with a client with terminal cancer, I realized conversations about death actually empowered her. The client was facing an inevitability, and she craved a safe space to discuss the reality of her future. It took bravery for this client to face the future, and talking about it made it less scary and made her feel less alone in her thoughts. So many other people were afraid to talk to her about death, and counseling was the one place where she could freely wonder what it might be like. I learned to be less afraid of the topic too.

Leaning on Erik Erikson's stages of development, I also realized many clients were battling with the stage of "integrity versus despair." They were asking themselves, "Did I live a meaningful life?" This kind of reflective work required a lot of wisdom on the part of my clients. They were reviewing the entire lifespan and calculating what all their actions, relationships, beliefs, and values added up to. Not only was this valuable for the client, but selfishly, it has given me questions to ponder on myself: Have *I* lived a life I am proud of?

Nowadays, I work in private practice and see a range of clients from ages 22 to 85. My work in senior living shapes my approach to counseling every day. I have witnessed clients at the end stage of life grappling with whether they have lived a meaningful life, and I try to help my clients of all ages consider this question ahead of time so that the answer doesn't surprise them later in life.

My early critics had a valid concern: Some older adults are less likely to receive mental health services, which fuels the stigma that they are unwilling or uninterested in help. But if you dig deep and get a little creative, you can seek out these clients and learn from them. Their experiences are the culmination of the lifespan. It is vital to know their stories.

Conclusion

In this chapter, you learned about the experience of aging as a key social identity that intersects with other identities that make us human. Through our discussion of theories related to aging and the systems that influence it, the role of ageism in shaping how people experience their lives, and the many ways aging shows up in the work of counseling, we hope you have a more nuanced understanding of what it means to be a person who is aging. By linking these concepts to multicultural counseling and social justice, you have the opportunity to promote mental health and well-being among clients and students of all ages.

Questions for Reflection

Consider what you learned in this chapter as you respond to the questions and prompts below.

1. What does growing older mean to you? When you think about becoming an older adult, what thoughts and emotions come up for you?
2. What feelings do you have about entering into a therapeutic relationship with someone who is significantly older than you? How do you conceptualize adults who are 10, 20, 30, or 40 years older than you? How do you think they feel about you and your age?
3. How does the meaning of aging change across the life course? For example, how is aging as a teenager viewed differently than aging as a middle adult or older adult? What kinds of images and ideas do you relate to aging at different stages? This question can be answered from your personal perspective or by reflecting on social messages around the meaning of aging.

Applying What You Have Learned

Complete each of the following activities, considering what you learned from this chapter.

Activity #1: Create Your Own "Age, Period, Cohort" Profile

1. Steps to create your profile. Individually:

    a. Write down your age. What stage of life do you consider yourself to be in? Do you think of yourself as a teenager, young adult, adult, or something else? Write down descriptors that come to mind.

    b. Write down the year you were born. Think about milestones in your life, both past and future. What year did you graduate from high school? When will you graduate from college or from your graduate program? Write down important dates that come to mind, as well as any groups of people you are a part of that are important to you.

    c. Looking at the dates in (b), think about national or global events in your lifetime. Who was the first president you voted for, and what social policies has their administration enacted? What social trends or shifts have you noticed since you were a kid? What natural disasters or other catastrophes have impacted your city or country? Write down a few events or changes that have shaped your world.

2. After time for students to think and jot down their responses, the class can create a larger class representation that includes all of the individual student profiles.
3. Then, as a class or in small groups, students can create an age-period-cohort case conceptualization of a fictitious client (someone of a different age than the majority of the class—perhaps one client who is an older adult and one who is younger to show that ageism can occur across the lifespan).

Activity #2: Write Your Obituary

1. Take 10–15 minutes to write what you would hope to read in your own obituary. Aim for about 250–300 words. What was it like to write this?
2. Death anxiety has a relationship to ageism and how we think of older adults. When you write your obituary, what are your thoughts/feelings about growing older? How high is your death anxiety? Can you draw connections between your death anxiety and how you think about older adults or growing older?

Credits

CHAPTER 14

Sex, Gender, Patriarchy, and Transmisia

Lena Salpietro, Jacob Perez, and Kassie Terrell

We are born as who we are. The gender thing is something that is imposed on you.

—Laverne Cox

CHAPTER OVERVIEW

How much have you thought about how you "do" your gender? Is your gender expression what culture and society promotes and expects, or are you blazing your own gender identity path? How much have you considered how much sex and gender impact our experiences and how society functions? What about gender inequality and patriarchy? These are just a few topics you will learn about and explore in this chapter. As you interact with this chapter, we invite you to examine how your life and the lives of those around you are impacted by gender identity, patriarchy, and inequality. Search for avenues for advocacy and decide how you can make a difference in the lives of others by working to mitigate the negative impacts of patriarchy.

LEARNING OBJECTIVES

By the end of this chapter, students will be able to

1. describe the historical social, cultural, and political influences on gender equality and gender identity and expression in the United States;
2. name how gender intersects with other identities;
3. explain, using ecological and sociopolitical contexts, how patriarchy and transmisia are maintained in society;
4. apply concrete strategies specific to gender identity to promote strong therapeutic alliances, integrate humanistic and person-centered perspectives, and foster strength and wellness; and
5. understand and apply relevant ethical codes and ethical decision-making to situations related to gender identity and expression.

CACREP 2016 STANDARDS

The information in this chapter supports the following standards:

- 2.F.1.e advocacy processes needed to address institutional and social barriers that impede access, equity, and success for clients
- 2.F.2.a multicultural and pluralistic characteristics within and among diverse groups nationally and internationally

- 2.F.2.b theories and models of multicultural counseling, cultural identity development, and social justice and advocacy
- 2.F.2.c multicultural counseling competencies
- 2.F.2.d the impact of heritage, attitudes, beliefs, understandings, and acculturative experiences on an individual's views of others
- 2.F.2.e the effects of power and privilege for counselors and clients
- 2.F.2.f help-seeking behaviors of diverse clients
- 2.F.2.g the impact of spiritual beliefs on clients' and counselors' worldviews
- 2.F.2.h strategies for identifying and eliminating barriers, prejudices, and processes of intentional and unintentional oppression and discrimination
- 2.F.3.i ethical and culturally relevant strategies for promoting resilience and optimum development and wellness across the lifespan
- 2.F.5.d ethical and culturally relevant strategies for establishing and maintaining in-person and technology-assisted relationships
- 5.B.2.c the unique needs and characteristics of multicultural and diverse populations with regard to career exploration, employment expectations, and socioeconomic issues
- 5.C.2.j cultural factors relevant to clinical mental health counseling
- 6.B.1.f ethical and culturally relevant counseling in multiple settings
- 6.B.5.j models and competencies for advocating for clients at the individual, system, and policy levels

CACREP 2024 STANDARDS

The information in this chapter supports the following standards:

- 3.A.4. the role and process of the professional counselor advocating on behalf of and with individuals receiving counseling services to address systemic, institutional, architectural, attitudinal, disability, and social barriers that impede access, equity, and success
- 3.B.1. theories and models of multicultural counseling, social justice, and advocacy
- 3.B.2. the influence of heritage, cultural identities, attitudes, values, beliefs, understandings, within-group differences, and acculturative experiences on individuals' worldviews
- 3.B.3. the influence of heritage, cultural identities, attitudes, values, beliefs, understandings, within-group differences, and acculturative experiences on help-seeking and coping behaviors
- 3.B.5. the effects of stereotypes, overt and covert discrimination, racism, power, oppression, privilege, marginalization, microaggressions, and violence on counselors and clients
- 3.B.7. disproportional effects of poverty, income disparities, and health disparities toward people with marginalized identities
- 3.B.9. strategies for identifying and eliminating barriers, prejudices, and processes of intentional and unintentional oppression and discrimination
- 3.B.10. guidelines developed by professional counseling organizations related to social justice, advocacy, and working with individuals with diverse cultural identities
- 3.B.11. the role of religion and spirituality in clients' and counselors' psychological functioning
- 3.C.7. models of resilience, optimal development, and wellness in individuals and families across the lifespan
- 3.E.6. ethical and legal issues relevant to establishing and maintaining counseling relationships across service delivery modalities

- 3.E.7. culturally sustaining and responsive strategies for establishing and maintaining counseling relationships across service delivery modalities
- 5.B.2. the unique needs and characteristics of diverse clients with regard to career exploration, employment expectations, and socioeconomic issues
- 6.B.1.d. scholarly examination of culturally sustaining counseling practice across multiple settings, contexts, and across service delivery modalities
- 6.B.1.f. legal and ethical issues and responsibilities in counseling across multiple settings and across service delivery modalities
- 6.B.5.j. models and competencies for advocating for clients at the individual, system, and policy levels

Terminology and Concepts

We begin by defining terms that are essential for you to know as you embark on this chapter. You may notice that this chapter begins with an extensive term list while other chapters have not. This is intentional. With the topics of gender and sex identity, as well as with relational and affectual orientation in the next chapter, how we talk about these concepts and the terms we use are incredibly important, particularly in terms of social justice and advocacy. It is important to note that some of these terms may be defined differently among different groups of people. Terminology evolves as we learn more about gender and how it is experienced, so these definitions are contextually accurate when we wrote this chapter. Counselors always ask clients how they prefer to identify and what that identity means to them.

Agender
A person who identifies without a gender (Ginicola et al., 2017).

Androgyny
A form of gender expression in which gendered appearance is ambiguous or not clearly identifiable as culturally defined as feminine or masculine (Ginicola et al., 2017).

Assigned Sex
The biological sex a person is given at time of birth based on external anatomy. Also referred to as sex assigned at birth or biological sex assigned at birth.

Cisgender
A person whose gender identity is congruent with the sex they were assigned at birth (Ginicola et al., 2017; e.g., a person whose assigned sex is female and they identify as a woman).

Cisnormativity
The assumption that all people are cisgender or identify with the gender they were assigned at birth. The implicit assumption that cisgender is superior to other gender identities (Ginicola et al., 2017).

Cissexism
"Behavior that permits preferential treatment of cisgender [people] and discrimination and prejudice against" (Ginicola et al., 2017, p. 361) individuals with transgender and other gender-expansive identities. Often used interchangeably with the term *sexism*.

Coming Out

The process in which individuals choose to disclose their identities. This process should be initiated by the individual, but there are times in which people are *outed*, which is when one's identities are disclosed without their consent.

Gender Binary

A system in which woman and man are the two distinct categories of gender (Human Rights Campaign, n.d.). This binary is reinforced through various individual, social, and political systems.

Gender Dysphoria

A mental disorder defined by the *Diagnostic and Statistical Manual of Mental Disorders Fifth Edition, Text Revision* (*DSM-5-TR*; APA, 2022). Symptoms encompass a person's clinically significant distress because of a "marked incongruence between one's experienced/expressed gender and assigned gender" (APA, 2022, p. 512). Previous iterations of this diagnosis consisted of *transsexualism* in the third edition (APA, 1980) and *gender identity disorder* in the fourth edition (APA, 2000) of the *DSMs*. The diagnosis is controversial because some believe it pathologizes gender-expansive identities as a mental disorder (Ginicola et al., 2017), while others recognize its ability for individuals to obtain services, and oftentimes, this diagnosis is needed for gender confirmation surgeries.

Gender-Affirming Medical Care

Surgical, hormonal, or other medical interventions or procedures used to change one's body to align with their gender identity or desired expression. Also known as gender-affirming surgery, gender affirmation, gender-confirming surgery, gender-confirming medical care, and gender confirmation (HRC, n. d.).

Gender Expression

A person's external representation of gender identity through clothes, hairstyle, demeanor, body language, behaviors, and interests (Ginicola et al., 2017).

Gender Fluidity

Gender identity is not fixed and can change across time and space.

Gender Identity

A person's internal concept and experience of gender. This influences how a person perceives themself and what they call themself (name and pronouns) and can be reflected in their expression of gender through physical presentation.

Gender-Expansive

A person whose gender identity and/or expression do not align with cultural and social expectations of masculinity and femininity (i.e., the gender binary). Sometimes referred to as gender non-conforming; this term is typically avoided because of the idea that non-conformity is viewed as a negative, while gender-expansive is an inclusive, positive term.

Gender Roles
Culturally and socially created norms that dictate accepted behaviors associated with being male or female. It is based on a binary understanding of gender (Ginicola et al., 2017).

Feminism
Ideologies and movements aimed to identify and change social, political, and economic inequalities that are rooted in patriarchy.

Intersex
A person who has one or more sex characteristics that do not align with traditional, singularly male or female characteristics. This may include hormones, internal/external sex organs, chromosomes, or other secondary sex characteristics (Ginicola et al., 2017).

Microaggressions
Verbal, behavioral, or environmental slights that are hostile, derogatory, and/or negative attitudes toward people with nondominant or marginalized identities. Microaggressions can be intentional or unintentional and subtle or overt (Sue et al., 2007).

Misgender
To refer to a person using pronouns or gendered language that do not align with the person's gender identity.

Nonbinary
The classification of gender into more than two distinct categories (i.e., man and woman) that are not "separate and distinct" (Ginicola et al., 2014, p.365). Also describes an individual who does not identify with binary gender identities, identifies somewhat with one or more binary identities, or identifies completely outside of binary categories.

Passing
A term used to describe when a transgender person is assumed to be a cisgender person based on their external gender expression.

Patriarchy
Attitudes, beliefs, values, and actions that reinforce the notion that men are and should be in control of all things (e.g., decision-making, families, people, systems). Patriarchal tenets are embedded into many systems, including economic, political, and social systems, and function in ways that ensure men stay in power, often by oppressing others. Patriarchy is frequently maintained by the actions of all people, not only men. Patriarchy oppresses women and gender-expansive people in significant ways and can also be upheld through internalized patriarchy, which is a subconscious adherence or belief of patriarchal tenets (e.g., a woman believing that it is her *job* to take care of the house).

Pronouns
The words used to refer to a person when not using their name that are associated with their gender identity. Pronouns may change over time based on one's identity. *They* is commonly used as a singular pronoun for those who do not identify within a binary (e.g., he/him/his or she/her/hers).

Neo-pronouns are gender neutral and include xe/xyr, (pronounced zee/zeer) ze/zir or ze/hir (pronounced zee/zeer or zee/heer), among others. There are many resources that can provide updated information on pronouns (e.g., https://pronoun.fandom.com/wiki/Pronoun_Wiki).

Transgender
Used to describe a person whose gender identity differs from their sex assigned at birth.

Transsexual
Historically, this term has been used to describe persons who transitioned from male to female or female to male, and typically those who have had gender-affirming surgery. Sometimes, transsexual is used to describe persons who identify with a gender other than the sex assigned at birth, whether or not they undergo gender-affirming surgery. This term is considered outdated, as it was used in medical and mental health settings to pathologize gender-expansive people. Some clients may use this term to describe themselves—it is important to use the language your client uses (GLAAD, n.d.), yet this is not a term that should be used on paperwork or initiated by the counselor.

Transition
The processes a person takes to better align their gender expression with their gender identity. Transitions can include social transitions (e.g., appearance, pronouns, and name), legal transitions (e.g., changing name and/or gender on legal documents like driver's licenses and bank accounts), and/or medical transitions (i.e., gender-affirming surgeries). Some individuals transition in several areas, while others may transition in only one.

Transmisia
The systematic oppression and discrimination toward gender-expansive people rooted in internalized hatred and desire to maintain the gender binary. Transmisia is used in place of *transphobia* in this chapter. Transmisia uses the Greek suffix '-misia' derived from the Greek word for hate or hatred, while '-phobia' comes from the Greek word for *fear of.* Phobias are mental health disorders, and using the phobia suffix equates anti-trans prejudice with mental health disorders and reinforces ableism (more on ableism in Chapter 13). *Misia* more accurately portrays the etiology and effects of oppression and discrimination (Simmons University, 2022).

The Distinct Concepts of Sex and Gender

The concepts of sex and gender, while often related, have notable differences. Sex, often known as *assigned sex*, is the biological sex a person is given at time of birth based on external anatomy and/or chromosomes. Assigned sex consists of two culturally created categories, male and female; however, some people do not fit into one of two categories, as there can be variations in how biological attributes are comprised and expressed (i.e., intersex individuals).

Gender is defined as the socially constructed categories that represent how society perceives people of a specific sex should behave, think, feel, and express themselves. People who are cisgender experience an alignment between their assigned sex and their gender, while those who are gender expansive do not. How gender is understood and expressed, and how people of different genders are treated is influenced by personal, societal, cultural, and political factors. This often leads to the oppression of cisgender women and gender-expansive people, as opportunities for power, control, and influence are limited by the social roles and expectations that have been assigned based on the binary system of sex assigned at birth and associated gender identity. While predominantly benefiting cisgender men, these roles and expectations have negative consequences for men too (e.g., the concept of masculinity leaves little room for emotional expression outside of anger).

Sex, gender, and sexual/relational/affectional identity are often conflated despite being three distinct concepts. Contributing to this confusion is the inclusion of transgender persons in the acronym LGBT (lesbian, gay, bisexual, and transgender). While the first three identities are sexual/relational/affectional identities, transgender is a gender identity and is unrelated to one's sexual/relational/affectional identity. Just because someone is transgender or gender-expansive does not mean they identify as LGB.

Socially or culturally constructed concepts are categories, thoughts, ideas, and beliefs that have been created and accepted by society or specific groups within society. Binary gender designations are socially/culturally constructed based on biological attributes, behaviors, attitudes, and emotions. If they were not created by people, they would not exist. These categories were created to try to make sense of the world around us, yet can be limiting for people who do not identify within the designated categories.

Person-First and Identity-First Language

Person-first language puts the person before their disability, identity, disease, or other health condition in an effort to avoid language that is stigmatizing or dehumanizing (Wooldridge, 2023). An example of this is "people with disabilities" versus "disabled people." In the former, we describe what a person has, not who a person is. However, there are many people who prefer to use identity-first language, like D/deaf people, because they want to emphasize a core aspect of who they are (Wooldridge, 2023). There are no steadfast rules to follow when deciding to use person- or identity-first language, and practitioners are empowered to research multiple sources (e.g., advocacy groups, organizations) created or led by the communities about whom you are communicating to determine what language they use. With clients and communities, it is respectful and prudent to ask how they would like to be referred to (Wooldridge, 2023).

Understanding the Historical Context of Sex and Gender

Gender has had a dominant role in social, cultural, religious, and political systems throughout history. The origins of patriarchy can be hard to pinpoint. Some theorize that agriculture created a hierarchical system in families and society so resources and property could be accumulated. Therefore, the paternity of heirs became important, contributing to the subjugation of women, especially as resource competition and social hierarchy began to emerge (Lerner, 1986). Others suggest there are both social and biological influences, arguing that motivation to dominate and control women's sexuality is evolutionary (Smuts, 1995), which has been met with significant critique (McCaughey, 2008).

Gender roles include the emotions, behaviors, and attributes that are expected of a person based on their sex assigned at birth. This often leads to stereotypes, like the belief that women are more emotional and men are more logical. *Gender socialization* is the process of how individuals learn to *do* gender, often through observation and reinforcement. Messages about what society expects, based on assigned sex, are communicated at a very young age and reinforced throughout the lifespan. Children are often reprimanded or punished for engaging in behaviors that violate these expectations (e.g., a young girl wanting to play football and being told football is for boys, a boy wanting to play with dolls is told if he does, he is a *sissy*) and this continues into adulthood (e.g., a man being told to "man up" if he cries, women being dissuaded from the assertiveness that men are praised for).

BOX 14.1 **PAUSE AND REFLECT: YOUR EXPERIENCE WITH GENDER ROLES**

How were gender roles enforced in your home growing up? Consider the emotions that you were allowed to express, the toys you played with, etc. How might this impact your ability and willingness to listen to a client's feelings and understand their experiences?

The emergence of gender equality and gender-expansive identities are often cited as a relatively new phenomenon, but challenges to traditional gender roles and gender-expansive people have existed across time and cultures. For example, Indigenous populations around the world have long celebrated people who identify as a third gender and shift fluidly within and beyond binary gender (Beemyn, 2014). Examples include the Mapuche of Chile, who have gender-fluid religious healers and leaders known as machi (Bacigalupo, 2007), and the gender-fluid nádleehí of the Navajo/Diné (Robinson, 2020). However, it is important to note that not all Indigenous communities acknowledge and celebrate gender diversity, sometimes as a direct result of colonization and Western ideology related to gender and gender roles (Robinson, 2020). As we explore the history of gender equality and visibility, it is important to acknowledge and attend to the fact that with each stride toward equality, those with intersecting minority identities and gender-expansive people were often excluded and continue to be excluded.

The Time Line of Gender Equality and Visibility in the United States

1848 Women's suffrage movement formally begins with the Seneca Falls Convention, where women took a stand against the patriarchal power structure in the United States (Yang, 2020). This is often considered the first wave of feminism. This first wave of feminism can be considered a movement not for all women but for White women, as Black women were often excluded (no Black women attended the Seneca Falls Convention—they were not invited). There was a notable discrimination in how White women and Black women were perceived and treated at the time.

1851	Sojourner Truth addressed the discrimination White women expressed toward Black women in her 1851 speech *Ain't I a Woman?* White suffragettes dismissed the disenfranchisement of Black women as a race issue, not a gender issue, effectively excluding them from the movement's agenda.
1870	Black men gained the right to vote with the 15th Amendment; however, many people of color were unable to exercise this right until the Civil Rights Act of 1965, which removed barriers such as poll taxes and literacy tests (Yang, 2020).
1920	Women earned the right to vote and hold political office with the 19th Amendment.
1952	Christine Jorgensen, a former army private from the Bronx, transitioned publicly and brought the concept of what was then called a *sex change* into everyday U.S. conversation and altered narratives about gender-affirming medical care (Beemyn, 2014).
1960s–1980s	This era is often considered the second wave of feminism. Movements, laws, and political and social narratives during this time focused on the role of women in the workplace and home and family environments, as well as women's sexual liberation (Malinowska, 2020). Feminists of this time fought for more work opportunities and representation in the media.
1963	The Equal Pay Act prohibited pay discrimination based on sex.
1964	Civil Rights Act expanded protections for discrimination based on race, color, national origin, religion, and sex (Quffa, 2016).
1966	Harry Benjamin, an endocrinologist, published *The Transsexual Phenomenon*, which explored gender-affirming medical care for transgender people. Benjamin argued that gender-affirming medical care was vital to the wellness of transgender people, and he openly prescribed hormone treatment therapy and referred his patients to other countries for affirmation surgery (Meyerowitz, 2002; 2008). Soon after publication, Johns Hopkins University opened the first gender identity clinic to provide medical care and conduct research (Beemyn, 2014).
1970	Street Transvestite Action Revolutionaries (STAR) was created by Sylvia Rivera, a Puerto Rican transgender woman, and Marsha P. Johnson, a Black transgender woman. They were active in the movements that led up to Stonewall and worked tirelessly to create safe spaces for transgender and gender-nonconforming people; STAR offered shelter, food, and clothing to gender-expansive youth. Although gender-expansive people were integral in the Stonewall riots and the organizing of LGBT people, they were ostracized by the larger LGB rights movement in the years that followed. Transgender people were banned from participating in Pride celebrations in many cities, and gay and lesbian activist groups often excluded them in an "attempt to appear more acceptable to mainstream society" (Beemyn, 2014, p. 23).
1972	Title IX of the Educational Amendments (1972) and Title VII of the Civil Rights Act (1964) banned discrimination based on sex, among other identities, in workplace and educational settings that receive federal funding (Quffa, 2016). This forced employers and institutions to address and be proactive about discrimination, harassment, and violence. However, these protections were not allotted to gender-expansive people until 2020 (See *Bostock v. Clayton County*).

1973 Roe v. Wade was heard by the Supreme Court, resulting in the right to legal abortion. This was later overturned in 2022 (see *Dobbs v. Jackson Women's Health Organization*).

1979 Janice Raymond's book *The Transsexual Empire: The Making of the She-Male*, was published. Raymond's book promoted prejudice through false and transmisic rhetoric that was shared by some in the medical profession, resulting in many gender-affirming medical clinics closing as misleading scientific evidence about the outcomes of gender-affirming medical care was published and distributed among the medical community (Beemyn, 2014). This book was harmful and supported hateful and violent rhetoric, harming the advancement of rights for gender-expansive people.

1990s-2000s Third wave feminism arose and built on the political and economic gains secured by their predecessors. Unlike the first and second waves, the third wave of feminism did not have a defining goal or purpose but instead focused on various areas of society, including violence against women, reproductive rights, sex positivity, maternity leave, and representation of women in music and technology (Malinowska, 2020; Mohajan, 2022). Additionally, third wave feminists acknowledged the intersection of feminism with class, race, and heteronormativity (Malinowska, 2020).

1994 *Transsexualism* is changed to *gender identity disorder in the DSM-IV* in an effort to reduce stigma, but advocates emphasized that the diagnosis still pathologized gender identity.

1999 First Transgender Day of Remembrance was held 1 year after the murder of Rita Hester in Massachusetts to honor those lost to transmisic violence. It is observed internationally every year on November 20.

2010s The fourth wave of feminists leveraged social media like Twitter, Facebook, Instagram, and Tumblr to empower women and draw attention to gender inequality (Mohajan, 2022). Personal stories of gender harassment, discrimination, and inequity drew attention to the treatment of women (as well as gender-expansive people and men) in media and the workplace and advocated for justice and accountability.

2013 *Gender dysphoria* replaced *gender identity disorder in the DSM-5*, citing a focus on gender-identity-related distress that some individuals experience; however, it could still be interpreted as conflating identity with a mental illness. There is debate on the utility of this diagnosis; for some, it is marginalizing, while for others, this diagnosis can help support them in getting gender-affirming medical care (World Professional Association for Transgender Health [WPATH], 2022).

2013 The United States Armed Forces lifted the Combat Exclusion Policy, allowing women to serve in combat positions from which they were formerly excluded.

2017 The #MeToo Movement, created by Tarana Burke in 2006, went viral in 2017 following the sexual abuse allegations against film producer Harvey Weinstein. #MeToo aimed to raise awareness of sexual abuse and assault in society and normalized discussions about gender inequity and invisibility/silencing of survivors and victims.

2020 Supreme Court ruling in *Bostock v. Clayton County* and subsequent executive orders in 2021 protected gender identity and expression under Title IX.

2021 Kamala Harris was sworn in as the vice president of the United States as the first woman and first woman of color to hold such the position.

2022 In a historic ruling on *Dobbs v. Jackson Women's Health Organization* (2022), the Supreme Court of the United States overturned *Roe v. Wade* (1973), which had guaranteed the constitutional right to abortion. Abortion access is now determined by each state, many of which had trigger laws that were created to take effect immediately or shortly after the appeal of *Roe v. Wade*. Many states have proposed, and in some cases passed, restrictive abortion legislation. Post-Roe repercussions are far-reaching on people who can become pregnant but disproportionally affect people of color, who are more likely to get abortions and die from pregnancy-related causes (Hoyert, 2022; Kortsmit, 2021), and gender-expansive people who experience significant barriers to accessible and affirming health care (James et al., 2016).

2023 U.S. lawmakers introduced 427 pieces of legislation that would restrict the lives of LGBTQ people, including gender-expansive people—the highest rate than at any other time in history. These bills restrict access to affirming medical care, limit discussion of gender and sexuality in K–12 classrooms, and ban people from participating in sports teams and using facilities that align with their gender identity (American Civil Liberties Union, 2023).

Ecological and Sociopolitical Contexts

The influence of patriarchal values and beliefs on current systems are significant, influencing how people function on micro-, meso-, and macrolevels. Patriarchal systems dictate who is in control and were constructed to ensure that those individuals stay in power, often by oppressing others. Patriarchy is maintained by the actions of many people regardless of gender, not just men. Examples of the pervasiveness of the patriarchy in society include codified gender roles and unequal pay between men and women (which is even more prominent for women of color).

The perpetuation of patriarchy and transmisia must be considered in their full ecological contexts to understand how they are reinforced by sociopolitical systems. While patriarchy and transmisia cause detrimental effects at an institutional level, like gender-based violence on college campuses, or at a legislative level, for example, challenges to reproductive and gender-affirming health care, the effects of patriarchy and transmisia occur within interactions between individuals and their immediate ecological and sociopolitical settings. We break down these interactions and systems using the lens of Bronfenbrenner's ecological systems theory (Bronfenbrenner, 1986; Bronfenbrenner, 2005).

Microsystem

Daily, individuals' interactions may contain language or behaviors based on patriarchy and transmisia. Examples of this include assumed pronoun usage, association of names with specific genders, and the use of gendered language, such as assumptions about the makeup of another person's family (e.g., assuming a person has a mother and father rather than asking about their parents, guardians, or caregivers). Regardless of their intention, these statements and actions, which may be microaggressions or overt hostility, send messages that uphold the rigidity of patriarchy and cisheteronormativity and reject a conceptualization of gender roles and gender expression beyond the gender binary. Particularly, microaggressions may lead to internalizing negative self-beliefs and the projection of these negative beliefs onto others who share the same or similar identities (Haines et al., 2017; Nadal et al., 2012).

For gender-expansive individuals who come out, the coming out process and any rejections of their identity occur at a microsystem level. The coming out process, which typically occurs multiple times for individuals (Bockting & Coleman, 2016), can be a highly vulnerable experience in which they may directly encounter transmisia and patriarchy from people involved in their daily affairs. People who identify as gender-expansive and/or queer may experience stages of the coming out process for multiple identities as well. For example, an individual might first begin identifying as nonbinary or genderqueer before identifying as transgender, or vice versa. The coming out process is intersectional and will likely vary for each individual experiencing it.

Mesosystem

At a mesosystem level, such as at a neighborhood gathering, school open house, or religious service, the microsystems that affect any given individual interact with one another. For instance, consider the microsystem between a trans adolescent student and their supportive parent interacting with the mesosystem of the adolescent's relationship with their teacher in the Florida public school system. Legislation in 2022 reduced the discussion of LGBTQ+ topics in school settings (American Civil Liberties Union, 2023); thus, an interaction such as a parent-teacher conference, which connects both the school and home settings of the student, would affect the student at the mesosystem level in that topics about identity cannot be discussed legally. The teacher's lack of expressed acknowledgment of the adolescent's gender identity could send the message to the parent that it is unimportant to the teacher or be perceived as a microaggression; new tensions and a lack of cohesion may directly influence their attitudes and actions toward one another, negatively influencing the child. Additionally, such legislation can reduce teachers' capacity to be authentic with students and hinder students' ability to feel safe to express their gender identity (Bockting & Coleman, 2016).

Microaggressions against families or individuals who do not subscribe to a patriarchal family structure or gender roles (Haines et al., 2017) may occur through interactions with other families, such as how each family refers to their children or their job aspirations when speaking with other families. For instance, a woman studying pre-med in college who is struggling in some of her classes might be prompted by her partner's family to consider studying nursing instead. In another example, a trans man using he/him/his pronouns who transitioned after beginning parenthood may find that other families refer to him only as a parent and refrain from using his preferred, more affirming titles such as *father* or *dad.*

Exosystem

Patriarchy and transmisia operate at the exosystem level, which is the level at which interactions among an individual's microsystems intersect with institutions of society at large. Patriarchy is inextricably linked to the intersections of gender with race, sexuality, ethnic background, and social class. Combating patriarchal institutions that marginalize people based on these stated identities requires an intersectional perspective that acknowledges colonialism, imperialism, and White supremacy (Patil, 2013).

> BOX 14.2 **PAUSE AND REFLECT: WOMEN'S WORK?**
>
> As a result of gender roles and stereotypes, there are some jobs that are deemed "women's work." What jobs do you think have been labeled as "women's work"? What do you think contributes to this stereotype?

The effects of patriarchy can be seen in economic data. Societal gender roles for women have reduced their opportunities for employment and education and have encouraged caretaker or family-oriented roles, limiting work opportunities to part-time or low-skill positions (Gharehgozli & Atal, 2020). The wage discrepancy between men and women rose from 53% to 67% between 1986 and 2016, and there is not strong evidence that this is because of reduced wage inequality (Gharehgozli & Atal, 2020).

The Gender Pay Gap

In 2009, U.S. Congress passed the Lily Ledbetter Equal Pay Act, which allows workers facing pay discrimination to seek justice under federal anti-discrimination laws. Despite this, the gender pay gap remains and disproportionally affects women, women of color, and gender-expansive people. According to the Pew Research Center, in 2002, cisgender women earned 80 cents for every dollar earned by a cisgender man (Aragão, 2023). Little progress has been made in the past 10 years, as the Pew Research Center reported that in 2022, cisgender women earned 82 cents for every dollar earned by a cisgender man. The pay gap has narrowed for younger cisgender women, as cisgender women ages 25–34 earned an average of 92 cents for every dollar earned by a cisgender man in the same age group (Aragão, 2023). Women of color fare far worse across the board. For every dollar earned by White men in 2022, Hispanic women earned 65 cents and Black women earned 70 cents (Kochhar, 2023). Asian women earned 93 cents per dollar, an example of the *model minority* phenomenon you read about in Chapter 9. In an analysis of data collected from private and government agencies, Baboolall et al. (2021) found that transgender employees make 32% less than their cisgender counterparts, even when they have similar or higher levels of education.

Macrosystem

At the level of the macrosystem, social structures are replicated in themes in media, education, and political discourse. For instance, queer people have been portrayed in literature and theater as monsters or villains; their existence in contrast with typical patriarchal themes has lent to an *otherness* in queer characters, and patriarchy sets a stage for such characters to be ostracized or be perceived as threatening to the status quo of societal standards (Vrtis, 2022). This portrayal, while associating the characterization of queer stereotypes with an evil character, can be interpreted as also associating moral goodness with the concepts of heterosexism and cisheteronormativity.

Exclusion of queer people, particularly trans people, extends to counseling literature and practice as well. Current multicultural counseling and counselor education practices tend to be written from dominant perspectives, with marginalized students reporting that they learn less than their dominant culture peers. A review of current research over the last 2 decades found that this is consistent in counselor education for individuals identifying as LGBTQ+ and that they experience stereotyping, tokenization, erasure, and isolation within their educational programs (Thacker & Minton, 2021). Tokenization of queer identities has a political dimension; societal rejection of gender outside of the gender binary may cause queer identities to be perceived as politically radical and ultimately othered. This *otherness* lends to preconceived notions about political identity and social standing based solely on one's queer identity, and queerness might be viewed as a sociopolitical catch-all that allows for the stereotyping and weaponization of politics against queer identities.

The effects of patriarchy and transmisia at the macrosystem level negatively affect all genders, including the dominant culture. Rigid gender roles upheld by social structures—such as in the examples of education and media—not only reject gender identity and expression beyond the gender binary but also restrict the gender identity and expression of those individuals who identify with gender within the binary. Such restrictions may discourage particular interests and careers based on an individual's gender, as well as influence biases about counseling, such as men's lower utilization rate of mental health services (Sagar-Ouriaghli et al., 2019). The negative impacts of gender roles perpetuated by patriarchy and transmisia affect individuals of all genders.

BOX 14.3 **PAUSE AND REFLECT: THE IMPACT OF PATRIARCHY**

Although this chapter focuses primarily on how marginalized groups are affected by patriarchy, we would be remiss not to highlight that patriarchy negatively impacts *everyone*—including cisgender men. Patriarchy demands that men abide by strict gender roles; otherwise, men risk deviating from what it is to be perceived as a man in society at large. Displays of vulnerability and emotion may be perceived as weakness or an obstacle to masculinity, and this may translate to lower utilization of mental health services (Sagar-Ouriaghli et al., 2019).

Imagine that you are counseling a cisgender man who states in the first session that "this feels stupid," that he hopes you can help him "fix having feelings," and repeatedly describes himself as "too soft."

How might you broach the topic of gender roles or patriarchy with this client, if at all?

Chronosystem

Historically, the diagnosis of gender identity disorder has pathologized gender expansiveness despite efforts to mitigate stigma in newer *DSM* editions. The current edition's diagnosis of gender dysphoria is only given to those gender-expansive clients who experience distress as a result of their gender (APA, 2022). These diagnoses may place undue responsibility on gender-expansive people to adjust to a cisheteronormative standard of wellness. Consideration of the history of oppression in health care and beyond is vital for understanding gender-expansive clients through an ecological systems lens.

Federally protected rights to autonomy (e.g., *Obergefell v. Hodges*, *Bostock v. Clayton County*) have been threatened by recent legislation such as *Dobbs v. Jackson Women's Health Organization* (2022), negatively impacting clients' identity development, expression, and safety. Public support and reproductive health education may be lifesaving for some women and gender-expansive people. As counselors, it is our ethical duty to be advocates for our clients' autonomy.

Nondominant Group Identities

As we have already discussed in prior sections, those with nondominant gender identities experience the effects of the patriarchy, sexism, and transmisia within multiple systems, which leads them to have an increased risk for violence, poverty, psychological distress, and barriers to accessing health care; however, the intersection of gender with other nondominant identities, like race, ethnicity, or social class, creates intersecting and overlapping identities that may privilege or further oppress. People are best understood and served within the context of the totality of their salient identities, and counselors must attend to intersectionality in order to provide effective and competent treatment. There are infinite ways identities can intersect and impact a person, and while we will discuss a few of these intersections, it is not exhaustive. As we have iterated many times in this chapter—and within this textbook itself—how each client experiences their identities varies. Counselors must prioritize the worldview of the client and their interpretation of their identities overgeneralized knowledge or common experiences of a population.

BOX 14.4 PROFILE OF A PRACTITIONER

Anonymous Author, MA, LPC

All my life, I knew something was "wrong" with me. I never felt right in my body; I never felt at home in my own skin. I spent most of my young life feeling as if I was someone's idea of a cruel joke. My natural loves and talents like football and military affinity, science and the outdoors, were largely off-limits to me as a biological female. My mother was a military brat raised in several countries by a career in the army and a very strict father. One is not allowed to voice much of their own opinion in such an environment. In turn, she carried on that view. I wasn't very good at conforming. I had the wrong blend of my father's progressive and gentle nature and my mother's intensity and fierceness. This ended up causing so many problems for me over my lifetime, especially as the only child growing up in her home. Fairness, justice, and equity are terms I grew up understanding but that I rarely experienced or witnessed.

I wanted to join the military like much of my family, but as a biological female, I was not allowed to do any of the things I really wanted to do. I was only able to consider logistics, administration, intelligence analyst, and other similar positions, but nothing remotely combat related. In my civilian life, I wanted to play sports—football, baseball, etc. These were also forbidden to me. Back then, everything I loved was kept away from me, or I was discouraged for being "too tomboy." I eventually identified as a very butch lesbian in my early 20s to 30s. I still did not understand or have a name for being transgender, and I was still unaware of the ability to transition. I simply lived in this strange existence filled with feelings of injustice and inequities. It nearly killed me for so many reasons and in so many different ways.

I believe it was due, in no small part to these experiences, that I grew my overinflated sense of justice. I wanted nothing more than equitable treatment. I was already treated unfairly because of my sex. People could look at me and tell that there was something "other" about me racially, and I was too butch to fit much of anywhere traditional. I don't know how many times I wished my breasts would just fall off so I would feel better and people would treat me more fairly. It felt like a cruel joke that I hadn't been born a man. When I finally discovered that transition was a possibility, I was filled with immense joy and, simultaneously, complete dread. Here was this amazing possibility at my fingertips to be (finally!) my authentic self from the inside out, but if I were to take it, I would be even more of a family and social pariah than ever. I was absolutely certain that my family, especially my mother, would disown me. Eventually, I was so unhappy in my existence that if I didn't jump at transition, I would likely take my own life or at least speed up the inevitable, so to speak. I began my transition at age 40, and I did not tell my mother for nearly 5 years.

As clinicians, we are often taught to focus on a specific theory or modality as our lens. My integrative techniques lean person-centered, holistic, and strength-based. I believe, upon reflection, that this is largely because of my sense of justice and equity. It feels like the most appropriate way to treat people, and it feels to me like it brings out the best in people while honoring who they are at their core. My goal is to help others find their most authentic selves, whatever and whomever that may be, in the same way I wish I could have known much earlier in life. It isn't up to me, as a therapist or a person, to judge that authenticity; I simply make space for them to find it for themselves. It is incredibly hard work to consistently make that space for people while helping them navigate their own lived experiences of injustice. I am a person, after all, and it is hard to turn yourself off when in concert with others the way therapists often are. I think my life experiences help me in unique ways in this work. They certainly influence and drive my social justice work, my research interests, and my advocacy.

I think employers often ignore how difficult it is for some of us to do the work we do in the face of constant discrimination and hatred. So often, as trans folks, we are told to leave our identities out of our workplace. It isn't professional to "flaunt" our views and lives. But my experience as a trans person, as a multiracial person, as an "other" of various kinds absolutely influences my lens and my work in all arenas. It is very much a part of my professional experience as well. People treat me differently once they know I am trans or not entirely White. I once told a manager that I didn't feel safe as an employee, and rather than responding with any level of empathy, I was asked to prove it by listing the reasons why. My life as a trans person is the embodiment of resilience.

A reason I was drawn to the counseling field was its ability to look at individuals' struggles through a holistic lens. I found myself interested in the systems in place that impact a person's abilities to reach overall wellness. Growing up in a household where there were very traditional expectations of gender and practices, I found it to be very constricting. In adulthood, allowing myself to unwind and unpack these traditional restrictions that society and my family had placed on me was so freeing. I aspire to do that every day with my clients. I challenge their traditional expectations and allow space for the possibility of new ways of thinking that were not previously given to them. The acknowledgment of the oppressive systems, values and roles forced upon them puts clients in the position to evaluate their personal values separate from the systems that sculpted them. This allows clients to lean into their personal autonomy and agency to achieve change in their lives and live more authentically. I have found it to be so important to be sensitive to the range of intersections of identity, such as gender, race, sexual identity, sexual expression, and religion. The relationships between these identities and how they interact provide vital information that aids in treatment planning and building rapport with clients.

Cisgender Women and Race

Sexism and patriarchy form a deeply ingrained network of attitudes, beliefs, and structures that have profound systemic and sociocultural influences, resulting in many challenges that disproportionately affect women. Women are influenced by these systems in their occupational, economic, and interpersonal lives. Because of preconceived notions about their abilities in the workplace, women experience discrimination related to hiring, promotions, professional development, and leadership. This discrimination also extends to unequal pay, causing a gender pay gap and perpetuating financial disparities for women. Women are subjected to high rates of violence (e.g., intimate partner violence and sexual assault) that have lasting impacts on their mental, physical, occupational, and financial wellness. Compounding these challenges are persistent gender stereotypes that often dictate the choices women make and the opportunities available to them (e.g., the judgment placed on women with children who work and the belief that women are more emotional than men). When someone identifies with more than one nondominant identity, they experience more complex forms of oppression that compound on each other. One example of this compounding oppression is the experience of women of color.

Neither race, ethnicity, or gender fully encapsulates the experience of women of color whose oppression is at the intersection of racism and sexism (Yang, 2020). This creates additional barriers for women of color as they experience multiple types of oppression at systemic levels. As a result, women of color have an increased risk of victimization, discrimination, and mental health issues, and they experience significant barriers to accessing health care, making them disproportionally impacted by restrictions and bans on reproductive health care (Artiga et al., 2022).

Overall health and access to care are determined by several social and economic factors, including employment, housing, education, and personal and community safety (Hill et al., 2022). As a result, women of color experience greater barriers to accessing health care than White women. Women of color are less likely to have health insurance, and Indigenous, Black, and Hispanic women are 1.5–2 times more likely to live 200% below the poverty line than White women (U.S. Census Bureau, 2019).

Disparities in health-care access translate to worse health outcomes and are compounded by the chronic stress of racial discrimination, which has been linked to poorer birth outcomes (Alhusan et al., 2016). Women of color are more likely to have pregnancy risk factors that contribute to infant mortality and long-term consequences for the health of their children (Osterman et al., 2022). Disparities in maternal health and birth outcomes are disproportionally experienced by Black women, who are 3 times more likely than White women to die during pregnancy or within a year of pregnancy (Petersen et al., 2019). Women of color are more significantly impacted by limitations in reproductive health care, such as abortions, as more than half of abortions are provided to women of color (Kortsmit et al., 2021).

Transgender People

Transmisia affects transgender people's ability to access health care, obtain education and employment, and exist safely in social and public places. They are at an increased risk of experiencing violence, as transgender people are 4 times more likely to be victims of violent crimes than their cisgender counterparts (Flores et al., 2021). What causes transgender people to be more subjectable to violence is complex, as it involves not only transmisic discrimination and oppression but the failure of multiple systems to protect and support transgender people. A study conducted by the Human Rights Watch (2021) reported,

> Data suggest that the compounding effects of discrimination significantly limit transgender people's opportunities and ability to keep themselves safe. When transgender people face family rejection or are kicked out of their homes at a young age, are unable to get an education or find employment, find work in informal and unregulated economies where violence is rampant, grapple with homelessness and housing insecurity, are unable to obtain gender-affirming health care or accurate identification, rely on public transportation and facilities where they are scrutinized by others, and are turned away from antiviolence resources and emergency services, they may be repeatedly exposed to violence with little ability to escape it, often running from one form of violence to find themselves faced with another. (p. 2)

Violence against transgender people is rampant, and people of color are disproportionally at risk. In a study of U.S. transgender people, 46% reported being verbally harassed, and 9% were physically attacked within the past year; 47% reported that they had been sexually assaulted within their lifetime (James et al., 2016). Gender-expansive people of color report far worse. Those who identified as Middle Eastern, multiracial, Black, or Indigenous reported higher rates of verbal harassment, public physical assaults, and lifetime incidences of sexual violence than those of other racial/ethnic identities (James et al., 2016). Fatal violence against transgender people has been deemed by the American Medical Association (AMA, 2019) as an epidemic, with Black transgender women targeted most. In 2022, 38 transgender people were victims of fatal violence; 76% were people of color (Human Rights Campaign [HRC], 2022a). Since the HRC (2022a) began collecting data in 2013, 85% of murdered transgender people were people of color, and 63% were Black transgender women.

Nonbinary People

As a result of cisnormativity, nonbinary people experience unique challenges, as their identities may be less visible or recognized both socially and legally. There is not a clear definition of what it means to be nonbinary. The term encompasses a range of gender identities, as nonbinary people may identify somewhat with men or women or identify outside of these categories (Ginicola et al., 2014). Additionally, this can change depending on the day or circumstance.

In one survey, 88% of nonbinary people reported that none of their IDs or personal documentation had their gender marker because they did not identify with the available gender markers (James et al., 2016). Only 22 states have the option for a nonbinary gender marker (X) for driver's licenses, and only 16 states have this marker on birth certificates (Movement Advancement Project, n.d.). As of April 2022, people can select X as their gender marker on their U.S. passport application (U.S. Department of State, 2022). This not only leaves nonbinary people with few options to legitimize their identity on official documents, it can negatively impact their mental health and put them at risk for harassment and discrimination. Nonbinary and gender-expansive people who do not have accurate IDs reported higher rates of psychological distress and suicidal thoughts (Scheim et al., 2020). Thirty-two percent of gender-expansive people who presented documentation that did not match their gender expression have been harassed, denied access to services, and/or physically attacked (James et al., 2016).

Nonbinary people may be forced to carry the extra burden of having to educate others about their gender identity. The gender of nonbinary people is often assumed by others based on their gender expression, and nonbinary people often do not correct others. Nearly two-thirds of nonbinary people reported that others assumed, based on their gender expression, that they identified with their assigned sex at birth (James et al., 2016). Of the binary people surveyed, about half (53%) reported that they sometimes tell others that they are nonbinary if they are assumed to be a cisgender man or woman, and 44% do not correct others when they assume (James et al., 2016). The most common reasons for not telling others that they are nonbinary are because they do not think others will understand, it is *easier* to not say anything, and the fear is that it will be dismissed as not being a *real* identity (James et al., 2016). Nonbinary people are almost twice as likely (66%) to avoid asking people to use their pronouns compared to transgender people (34%), adding to the *erasure* of their identities (Skaistis et al., 2018).

Professional Counseling Practice Applications

Person-Centered Perspectives

Person-centered counseling is closely aligned with the fundamental ideology that drives the counseling profession—that people have the potential to be their most authentic selves when provided with genuine, empathic, and nonjudgmental relationships. Influences of patriarchy, sexism, cisnormativity, and transmisia create a culture in which there is a biased understanding of what gender should be, even though it is an incredibly individualized experience (Ginicola et al., 2017). By using post-modern philosophies like person-centered therapy (PCT) and relational-cultural therapy (RCT), counselors can help clients develop a deeper understanding of their gender, understand how societal standards have influenced their gender, and empower them to create more authentic ways of living.

One of PCT's facilitative conditions is congruence, in which counselors have a deep understanding of themselves, are genuine in their interactions with others, and live authentically—meaning their internal and external experiences are consistent (Kress et al., 2021). A goal of PCT is to help clients self-actualize and become more congruent by exploring the ways in which they have been disingenuous and by identifying more authentic values, attitudes, and beliefs (Kress et al., 2021). Clients may experience incongruence between their internalized understanding of gender and their behaviors or authentic feelings of who they are. Men, due to early gender role socialization and hegemonic masculinity, may be unable to authentically express emotional distress and instead act out in destructive or violent ways (Weikert, 2010). Gender-expansive individuals may present in ways incongruent with their gender identity to avoid rejection or transmisia, resulting in distress and invalidation (Knutson & Koch, 2022). Women may shy away from their natural tendency to connect with others for fear of being perceived as dependent (Clark et al., 2018). PCT techniques such as modeling congruency, immediacy, and appropriate self-disclosure can strengthen the counseling relationship and promote client self-awareness and growth.

BOX 14.5 **TIPS FOR PROFESSIONAL PRACTICE: PCT AND GENDER-EXPANSIVE CLIENTS**

Knutson and Koch (2022) offered concrete strategies for implementing PCT with gender-expansive clients:

Creating an open environment: Use visual and verbal cues that communicate acceptance and support. This could include displaying Pride flags, using inclusive intake paperwork, introducing yourself with your name and pronouns, and broaching.

***Counselor self-awareness*:** Counselors explore their own gender identity and gender experiences. Counselors are cautioned not to use their own insight as a foundation for understanding their clients—your experience of gender is different than someone else's.

***Bracketing*:** Recognize how personal biases, values, and expectations may manifest when working with clients and separate them from the counseling process.

***Client-guided process*:** Let the client guide the direction of counseling, resisting the urge to provide unsolicited interpretations. Focus on unconditional acceptance and positive regard.

***Taking an immersive-centered stance*:** Make efforts to truly empathize with the client by immersing in the client's world and experience instead of passively engaging with them.

***Avoiding a problem-centered focus*:** Acknowledge that diagnoses, like gender dysphoria, are pathologizing and focus more on the client than the problem. Consider that symptoms may be a result of underlying incongruence (e.g., isolation from others may be a symptom of an underlying fear of rejection).

Which strategies do you feel confident that you could implement? Which strategies do you think you would struggle to implement?

The Counseling Relationship

The counseling relationship is one of the most important predictors of counseling outcomes (Norcross & Lambert, 2018). There are common factors, or Rogers' core conditions, that are known to promote the counseling relationship regardless of theoretical orientation or client population, including empathy, unconditional positive regard, and congruence. In addition to the core conditions, attending to the privileged and marginalized identities held by both the counselor and client is foundational to creating meaningful counseling relationships (Ratts et al., 2016).

BOX 14.6 **PROFILE OF A PRACTITIONER: ROSALYN ZACARIAS, MS, RMHCI (FL)**

IMG 14.1 Rosalyn Zacarias, MS, RMHCI (FL)

A reason I was drawn to the counseling field was its ability to look at individuals' struggles through a holistic lens. I found myself interested in the systems in place that impact a person's abilities to reach overall wellness. As a cisgender Hispanic female and child of an immigrant, I grew up in a household where there were very traditional expectations of gender and practices; I found it to be very constricting. In adulthood, allowing myself to unwind and unpack these traditional restrictions that society and my family had placed on me was so freeing. I was finally able to live more authentically, and I grew an appreciation for my identities as a minority, a woman, and a bisexual. I was able to construct what that meant to me as an individual. I aspire to do that every day with my clients.

I challenge clients' traditional expectations and allow space for the possibility of new ways of thinking that were not previously given to them. The acknowledgment of the oppressive systems, values and roles forced upon them puts clients in the position to evaluate their personal values separate from the systems that sculpted them. This allows them to lean into their personal autonomy and agency to achieve change in their lives and live more authentically. I use skills such as self-disclosure, when appropriate, to connect with clients and to make the space safer. I explore the relationships with power and how it has impacted the client's behaviors and choices. Reframing and challenging are helpful, as they normalize some thoughts, feelings, and behaviors within the lens of the larger social environment as well as push clients to look beyond that. Working with clients I have found it to be so important to be sensitive to the range of intersections of identity, such as gender, race, sexual identity, sexual expression, religion, etc. The relationships between these identities and how those identities interact provide vital information that aids in treatment planning and building rapport with clients.

Gender accounts for a large portion of individual identity, so gender can greatly impact a client's ability and willingness to engage in the therapeutic process; however, research is unclear about the impact the gender of the counselor and client have on the quality and effectiveness of the therapeutic relationship. Studies have found a *female effect* in which clients paired with female counselors, regardless of client gender, reported stronger or more effective counseling relationships (Bhati, 2014), while others found mixed results (Schmalbach et al., 2022). Few researchers have explored the relationship between a counselor's gender and gender-expansive clients. Compton and Morgan (2022) analyzed 10 studies on the experiences of gender-expansive clients in counseling and found that although clients may seek LGBTQ+ counselors, findings suggest that the counselor's visibility in the community and openness to exploring gender and cisnormativity was determined to be more important than the gender identity of their counselor. These findings, and findings from metanalyses of therapeutic effectiveness (e.g., Norcross & Lambert, 2018), suggest that counselor competency impacts the counseling relationship most, and this is something all counselors can develop to promote the counseling relationship.

BOX 14.7 **PAUSE AND REFLECT: YOUR GENDER IDENTITY IN YOUR PRACTICE**

How would I feel about working with a client who doesn't share my gender identity? What about a client who does share my gender identity?

What barriers might prohibit me from connecting with a client who does not share my gender identity? What can I do to address and overcome these barriers?

What has been proven repeatedly is the effectiveness of broaching clients' salient identities and how they have impacted their experiences (Norcross & Lambert, 2018). Because gender identity is a large part of our experience, it is vital we attend to gender in counseling. One skill that can achieve this is broaching. *Broaching* is a skill used by counselors to specifically discuss relevant sociocultural and sociopolitical factors that influence clients' presenting concerns (Day-Vines et al., 2007). This involves broaching the identities of the counselor and how they are similar and different from the client's (Day-Vines et al., 2021). This is known as the *intracounseling broaching dimension*, where the counselor explicitly

- explores the client's feelings and reactions about shared and differing identities between the counselor and the client;
- acknowledges the limitations of their ability to fully understand the client's experience; and
- reduces the power imbalances by treating the client as the expert and asking them to explore their experiences and identities, all of which
- strengthens the counseling relationship (Day-Vines, et al., 2021).

When broaching, a cisgender counselor may ask a gender-expansive client, "The privilege my cisgender identity has afforded me has protected me from the hurtful experiences you have described. I have experienced a lot of privilege as a cisgender woman. What is it like sharing your experiences with me?" They could also acknowledge how their privileged identities may reflect their client's oppressors, "I realize that I share an identity with those who have caused you harm. I wonder if this might impact our ability to connect with one another?" The goal is to acknowledge your identities and what they may represent, and express openness to understanding the client's experiences and point of view.

MSJCC Application

The multicultural and social justice counseling competencies (MSJCC; Ratts et al., 2015) were established to guide multicultural counseling work. The MSJCC encourage counselors to discuss the intersections of marginalization and privilege between clients and counselors, and in the case of gender to explore the effects of patriarchy and transmisia. Individuals may experience privilege in one dimension of their identity while simultaneously experiencing marginalization in another dimension of identity, and these two experiences are inextricably linked. For instance, a Black cisgender woman counselor working with a White transgender man will experience unique intersections of their privileged and marginalized identities that must be explored within the context of their unique relationship. Also, it cannot be assumed that transmisia will only affect the gender-expansive person in this counseling relationship, nor can it be assumed that patriarchy will only influence the woman in this counseling relationship. Patriarchy and transmisia demand their own norms of gender identity, roles, and expression that affect all people. Each dimension of one's identity interacts with other dimensions, making intersectionality vital for multicultural and social justice praxis (Moradi & Grzanka, 2017).

BOX 14.8 **PAUSE AND REFLECT: YOUR INTERSECTING IDENTITIES**

Consider your own identities. In what ways are you privileged and marginalized? In what category is your gender identity? How might the counseling relationship be impacted based on the privileged and marginalized identities of both counselors and clients? What strategies can you use to address this?

The MSJCC task counselors with attaining essential knowledge related to how clients experience the world and essential issues that impact them; for some gender-expansive clients this may mean social, legal, or medical transition. Counselors should be prepared to have discussions with clients about the process of transitioning, potential barriers they may encounter, and strategies to establish coping skills and support (Ausloos & Salpietro, 2022). Social transitioning may involve visible changes, such as how they dress or express themselves, or it can be more interpersonal, like coming out to family, friends, or coworkers. At times, this may involve the counselor and client assessing the safety of the client's social and environmental circumstances, as transgender people face high rates of discrimination and violence, and a client may not feel safe with some forms of gender expression. It can be a financial burden to change legal documents like a driver's license or birth certificate, and not all states allow for changes to be made.

Navigating the legal system can also be a complicated process; counselors can help support their clients through this process, as having documentation that affirms one's identity can have positive impacts on one's mental health and feelings of acceptance. Medical transitioning may involve gender-affirming care, like surgeries or hormone replacement therapy. The World Professional Association for Transgender Health (WPATH, 2022) created standards that provide guidance to health professionals to help gender-expansive clients "maximize their overall health, psychological well-being, and self-fulfillment" (p. 55). Some medical professionals and insurance companies may require a letter from a mental health professional before providing gender-affirming care, creating an inherent power dynamic. Counselors should be prepared to advocate for their clients and should have access to referrals for gender-affirming care (Ginacola et al., 2017).

Resilience, Strengths, and Wellness

Counselors are tasked with engaging in practices that promote the mental well-being of clients (ACA, 2014), which involves focusing on not only areas of distress but also resilience, strengths, and wellness. There are a few gender-informed theoretical frameworks and approaches that counselors can use to integrate clients' strengths and resources.

TRIM

Matsuno and Israel (2018) created the transgender resilience intervention model (TRIM) to help mental health practitioners identify interventions that target specific resiliency factors for gender-expansive people. TRIM emphasizes the impact of distal and proximal stressors (Meyer, 2003) and how group and community resilience factors and interventions often have a direct impact on individual resilience factors. *Distal stressors* include gender-related discrimination, rejection, victimization, and nonaffirmation of gender identity. *Proximal stressors* develop because of distal stressors and include concealment of gender identity, expecting rejection, and internalized transmisia. While Matsuno and Israel (2018) used synthesized literature on the resilience strategies of transgender people to expand the minority stress model (Meyer, 2003), no research has been conducted on the effectiveness of TRIM.

TABLE 14.1 TRIM Model

Level	Resilience Factors	Interventions
Individual	Self-worth Identity pride Hope Positive and self-defined identity Gender-affirming medical care	Counselor knowledge and attention to gender-expansive considerations (e.g., personal biases, impact of discrimination and oppression), Hope-based or positive psychology interventions Self-compassion interventions (with acknowledgment of the impact of minority stressors and societal stigma) Exploration and validation of gender identity and expression (affirmative counseling) Resources (*The Gender Quest Workbook*, *Queer and Transgender Resilience Workbook*) Providing knowledge and referrals for gender-affirming medical care
Group and Community	Social support Community belonging Involvement in activism Family acceptance Positive role models Being a role model to others	Group therapy Local/online support groups Mentoring programs Family and couples counseling intervention

Relational-Cultural Therapy

RCT is an effective (Lenz, 2016) post-modern approach that aims to understand the unique phenomenological perspectives of a client through empathy and connection (Clark et al., 2018). RCT practitioners understand that people strive for connection and develop a sense of self through their relationships. Like PCT, RCT emphasizes relational authenticity and congruency and believes that clients are the experts. Unique to RCT is its roots in feminism and how it explicitly explores how sociopolitical and sociocultural issues, particularly those related to gender, impact clients' lived experiences. RCT practitioners help clients identify how oppressive systems have influenced their development and sense of self and provide opportunities to deconstruct their identities to create new ones (Clark et al., 2018). Clark et al. (2018) proposed the following RCT therapeutic techniques that help foster growth and deepen client-counselor connection:

- Show respect and curiosity for the client by exploring and appreciating their unique journey by asking questions about their lives. Emphasize client strengths and areas of their lives where they are doing well.
- Openly address and analyze counselor-client power differentials by exploring how the client perceives the counselor and how the counselor perceives the client. Power can be diminished by demystifying counseling by clearly explaining the process and purpose of therapeutic work.
- Facilitate discussions about how discrimination, oppression, and marginalization have impacted their individual identities and relationships with others.
- Encourage empowerment, high self-esteem, assertiveness, and emotional identification and expression.

RCT can be used to identify strengths and promote new ways of living through *encouragement techniques* that empower and foster growth (Clark et al., 2018). RCT helps women enhance their desire for connection and seeks to "change the manner in which women are viewed by uplifting women and depathologizing those behaviors that were traditionally seen as negative" (Clark et al., 2018, p. 526). Clark et al. (2018) identified four types of encouragement:

- ***Encouraging Empowerment*** by exploring client strengths and stories of empowerment and encouraging them to experience these more often.
- ***Encouraging High Self-Esteem*** by facilitating conversations on how societal expectations and cultural norms have dictated their sense of value and worth. Counselors can help clients recognize that they have the power and ability to establish their own measures of worth and success.
- ***Encouraging Assertiveness*** by teaching assertiveness skills and deconstructing the pressures and expectations that have led to passivity and silence.
- ***Encouraging Emotional Identification and Expression*** by increasing the client's ability to identify, sit with, and express a range of emotions.

BOX 14.9 **FOCUS ON CLIENT CARE**

Nia, a White cisgender woman counselor, is working with Shay, a 25-year-old Muslim, Black, cisgender woman. Shay has been unhappy in her current relationship, reporting that her partner lives in another state, and therefore, it is difficult for them to spend time together. She shared that she is feeling lost in life, without direction. When Nia asked her about her goals for counseling, Nia shared that she wants advice on what she should do with her life, sharing that she struggles with *making decisions* for herself, feeling like she never makes the right choices. Nia *demystifies the counseling process* and explains to Shay that her role is not to tell Shay what to do, *emphasizing* that she is not an expert, and explains how counseling can be used to help Shay better understand herself and her goals in life.

Nia spends the first few sessions demonstrating curiosity by asking Shay questions about her life so that she can better *understand* her experiences and what is important to her. She discovers that Shay recently got a new job after being miserable at her last job for many months. Shay reported that she grappled with the decision for weeks and is really happy at her current place of employment. Nia helped *empower* Shay by having her expand on her opinion that she is unable to make the "right" decision and pointing out that she has made good choices in the past, like leaving her last place of employment. Nia also reminds Shay that she made the decision to leave her assignment in the military 4 years ago because she was unhappy, and because Shay had shared that she never regretted that decision.

As trust in the relationship builds, Shay shares that she has been fantasizing about having sex with her coworker. She explains that this makes her feel like a bad partner. Nia encourages Shay to *identify and experience her emotions*; Shay expresses that she feels ashamed. She shared that she and her partner do not have sex often since he lives in another state. She often feels sexually frustrated but is too embarrassed to ask her partner to engage in long-distance sex, like phone sex, stating, "Men are supposed to be the sexual ones!" To *encourage self-esteem*, Nia helps Shay identify the factors that influence her perceptions of sex, including the influences of her religion, society, and gender roles, helping Shay to work through the shame she expressed.

Shay begins to feel more comfortable with her sexual desires and decides that she wants to talk to her partner about it. Nia emphasizes Shay's decisiveness and *encourages her assertiveness* by teaching Shay different strategies she can use to communicate her needs and roleplaying Shay's partner so that she can get practice and *receive* feedback.

Additionally, RCT can be used to promote healthy masculinity and interpersonal connection in men by helping men identify the impacts of hegemonic masculinity and gender role socialization to create new ways of being that promote vulnerability, connection, and compassion (Di Bianca & Mahalik, 2022). RCT underscores the repercussions of patriarchy and rigid gender roles, and although men may not be directly exploited or oppressed by their gender identities, their ability to express emotions and connect interpersonally and socioculturally may be stifled (Frey, 2013; Di Bianca & Mahalik, 2022). Hegemonic masculinity is learned and maintained socially and relationally, and therefore, the framework proposed by Di Bianca and Mahalik (2022) suggests that it must also be deconstructed through connection. In addition to the foundational relational tenets of RCT (e.g., mutual empathy, empowerment), they suggest other relational interventions, including those that increase connection for young boys in their most influential environments, such as social connections at school (e.g., school-based programs that address masculinity and encourage relationships among peers and mentors) and within their families (e.g., psychoeducation for families on promoting social-emotional development). Interpersonal process groups for men provide the opportunity to deconstruct sociopolitical pressures with their peers and promote universality. Hegemonic masculinity maintains systems that oppress and dehumanize others, so Di Bianca and Mahalik (2022) advocate that through RCT, men have the ability to create social change and prevent violence. They suggest encouraging men to become involved in programs that combat violence against women, such as psychoeducation on topics like rape culture and bystander intervention training.

Ethical Code Application

The counseling profession is governed by codes of ethics. These codes protect clients and clinicians, standardize clinical practice, set minimum expectations, and unify practitioners. Clinicians practicing within different sectors and those who hold licensure and certifications must honor relevant codes of ethics (e.g., ASCA, CRCC). While ethical codes are meant to provide best practice guidelines and are often useful in providing guidance for solving ethical dilemmas, ethical codes are inherently flawed. Codes are often dated, don't include current inclusive language or cultural considerations, fail to keep up with the ever-evolving social and political challenges clinicians face in their practices, and do not provide answers for many clinical dilemmas. These limitations result in practitioners interpreting and applying codes subjectively in their practice. While some subjectivity is expected and necessary, it is not blanket permission for counselors to interpret the codes in ways that do not protect clients. It is important that consumers of ethical codes be mindful of these limitations within professional codes and approach decision-making and clinical practice with an inclusive, culturally sensitive lens.

Additional challenges can arise when social and political movements are in direct conflict with professional codes. In these cases, clinicians are called to integrate and honor codes of ethics while also working to dismantle systems that are discriminatory and oppressive. Toward this end, clinicians must take a critical look at the flaws within the codes that might subjugate people or give way to discriminatory practices. House Bill 1557 is one example that can be used to explore this dilemma.

House Bill (HB) 1557: Parental Rights in Education

HB 1557: Parental Rights in Education is an act that protects parents' rights to control their child's upbringing and information they are exposed to in public schools. The act requires school boards to notify parents at the start of each school year to inform them of health-care services and specific content within the curriculum that will be shared with their children. Parents then have the option to withhold consent for services and education. One such designation in the act notes that "classroom instruction by school personnel or third parties on sexual orientation or gender identity may not occur in kindergarten through grade 3 or in a manner that is not age-appropriate or developmentally appropriate for students" (Florida Senate Education Committee, 2022). HB 1557 was first proposed to the Florida Governor in January of 2022, was approved in March of 2022, and took effect in July of 2022. The state was required to update all policies and procedures around parent consent and educational materials by June of 2023.

Critically Examining and Applying Codes of Ethics

Using HB 1557 as an example, we consider the American Counseling Association *Code of Ethics* (2014) and the American School Counseling Association *Code of Ethics* (2022) and examine codes that might serve to protect and those that might support discriminatory practices.

To start, the mission of the ACA Code of Ethics (2014) is to "enhance the quality of life in society by ... using the profession and practice of counseling to promote respect for human dignity and diversity" (ACA, 2014, p.1). A similar commitment is noted in the preamble for ASCA: "[S]chool counselors are advocates, leaders, collaborators, and consultants who create systemic change by providing equitable educational access" (p. 1). In addition to these pillars, there are similarities regarding advocacy directives, non-discrimination, responsibilities to parents and legal guardians, and continuing education. While these directives communicate a great platform for mental health providers to carry out their work, bills such as HB 1557 directly violate what is considered necessary for clinicians to accomplish such missions. For example, the ASCA preamble includes a statement indicating that all students have the right to

> have access to a comprehensive school counseling program that advocates for and affirms all students from diverse populations including but not limited to: ethnic/racial identity, nationality, age, social class, economic status, abilities/disabilities, language, immigration status, sexual orientation, gender, gender identity/expression, family type, religious/spiritual identity, emancipated minors, wards of the state, homeless youth and incarcerated youth (p. 1).

Additionally, students have a right to "receive the information and support needed to move toward self-development and affirmation within one's group identities" (ASCA, 2022, p. 1). When confronted with a conflict between laws and ethics—such as between the ethical codes about providing comprehensive and inclusive instruction and support around sexual orientation and gender identity to children in public schools and the restriction of such in HB 1557—clinicians are forced to either break the law or violate their professions ethical code. This decision is multifaceted and complex. As such, it is important to review specific codes to guide clinical practice and decision-making.

TABLE 14.2 Comparing Ethical Codes

Topic	ACA	ASCA
Advocacy	A.7.a When appropriate, counselors advocate at individual, group, institutional, and societal levels to address potential barriers and obstacles that inhibit access and/ or the growth and development of clients.	A.10.b Advocate for and collaborate with students to ensure students remain safe at home and at school. A high standard of care includes determining what information is shared with parents/ guardians and when information creates an unsafe environment for students. A.10.f Advocate for the equal right and access to free, appropriate public education for all youth, in which students are not stigmatized or isolated based on their housing status, disability, foster care, special education status, mental health or any other exceptionality or special need. B.2.m Promote cultural competence to help create a safer more inclusive school environment.
Non-Discrim-ination	C.5 Counselors do not condone or engage in discrimination against prospective or current clients, students, employees, supervisees, or research participants based on age, culture, disability, ethnicity, race, religion/spirituality, gender, gender identity, sexual orientation, marital/ partnership status, language preference, socioeconomic status, immigration status, or any basis proscribed by law. C.7.c Harmful Practices: Counselors do not use techniques/procedures/modalities when substantial evidence suggests harm, even if such services are requested.	A.10.a Strive to contribute to a safe, respectful, nondiscriminatory school environment in which all members of the school community demonstrate respect and civility. A.10.e Understand students have the right to be treated in a manner consistent with their gender identity and to be free from any form of discipline, harassment or discrimination based on their gender identity or gender expression.

(Continued)

TABLE 14.2 *(Continued)*

Topic	ACA	ASCA
Responsibility to Parents and Legal Guardians	B.5.b Responsibility to Parents and Legal Guardians: Counselors inform parents and legal guardians about the role of counselors and the confidential nature of the counseling relationship, consistent with current legal and custodial arrangements. Counselors are sensitive to the cultural diversity of families and respect the inherent rights and responsibilities of parents/guardians regarding the welfare of their children/charges according to law. Counselors work to establish, as appropriate, collaborative relationships with parents/guardians to best serve clients.	B.1.b Respect the rights and responsibilities of custodial and noncustodial parents/guardians and, as appropriate, establish a collaborative relationship with parents/guardians to facilitate students' maximum development.
Continuing Education	C.2.f Continuing Education: Counselors recognize the need for continuing education to acquire and maintain a reasonable level of awareness of current scientific and professional information in their fields of activity. Counselors maintain their competence in the skills they use, are open to new procedures, and remain informed regarding best practices for working with diverse populations.	A.1.g Are knowledgeable of laws, regulations and policies affecting students and families and strive to protect and inform students and families regarding their rights. B.3.e Engage in professional development and personal growth throughout their careers. Professional development includes attendance at state and national conferences and reading journal articles. School counselors regularly attend training on school counselors' current legal and ethical responsibilities. B.3.i Monitor and expand personal multicultural and social justice advocacy awareness, knowledge and skills to be an effective culturally competent school counselor. Understand how prejudice, privilege and various forms of oppression based on ethnicity, racial identity, age, economic status, abilities/disabilities, language, immigration status, sexual orientation, gender, gender identity expression, family type, religious/spiritual identity, appearance and living situations (e.g., foster care, homelessness, incarceration) affect students and stakeholders.

When confronted with legislation such as HB 1557, it is essential to consider how these policies can impact the application of ethical codes. For example, when working with gender-expansive minors, ASCA's *Code of Ethics* (2022) includes explicit directives for clinicians to create a safe space within the school system. However, the means by which clinicians are called to create that safe space (e.g., providing access to inclusive services, not isolating or stigmatizing clients, being respectful of individual differences) are compromised and restricted under such laws. For other clinicians, who might interpret the language in the code in favor of their personal values, they may use the *Code of Ethics* to carry out discriminatory practices, citing the law as justifying the implementation of their personal beliefs.

From a guardian's perspective, the interpretation and application of the codes can also create friction. ACA (2014) and ASCA (2022) indicate a responsibility to work collaboratively with parents and legal guardians; this includes being mindful of diversity, establishing a collaborative relationship, and respecting parents' rights. While these directives serve as a platform for creating an alliance with guardians, there are parents who have vociferous beliefs about removing comprehensive sex education or affirming services from public school systems. These guardians may have a different interpretation of what constitutes respect and collaboration when serving their children.

The children being served in school systems, or those who are being denied these services, are the most impacted by the ambiguous interpretation and application of these codes. Regardless of the clinician's and parents' personal beliefs, children need safe spaces and resources to aid in self-exploration and acceptance. Gender-expansive children face an incredible amount of alienation and discrimination; for those practices to be built into our legal systems and enacted by public school personnel who are meant to educate, mentor, and support children is inhumane and can be detrimental to gender-expansive youth.

Clinicians must think critically about how to bracket personal values and practice aspirational ethics in the face of oppressive policies and systems. To best support and affirm gender-expansive youth, clinical practice and ethical decision-making must align with the spirit of the ACA (2014) and ASCA (2022) codes. Clinicians must honor the values of the profession, promote and respect human dignity and diversity, refrain from and advocate against discriminatory practices, recognize personal limitations, and seek to educate and expand personal knowledge and cultural competence. These principles allow clinicians to embark upon advocacy work and create social change, much like the work that is needed to address HB 1557 and similar bills, within our communities that ultimately serve as a platform to create an inclusive and affirming space for all people.

In addition to using respective codes of ethics and decision-making models, it is essential that counselors-in-training are invested in social advocacy and change in their local communities. There are several ways to become involved in your community. Counselors can join listservs to stay abreast of local legislation that impacts their community and work, write letters to their local representatives, attend open meetings to voice concerns and brainstorm inclusive legislation, publicly share about the harmful nature of discriminatory legislation, ask to meet individually with local representatives to share case studies and examples of the potential impact of discriminatory legislation; and create new or join existing alliances with local advocates to strengthen the message and reach of inclusive legislation.

Conclusion

In this chapter, you have learned about sex, gender, patriarchy, and transmisia, likely adding to your awareness, knowledge, and skills about these topics. Gender, gender inequality, and gender oppression cannot be ignored. As professional counselors, we look for ways our clients are resilient just as much as we identify systems and structures that represent barriers to their wellness—and we take action. We began this chapter by inviting you to search for avenues for advocacy and to decide how you can make a difference in the lives of others impacted by patriarchy. What have you identified? What steps will you take? Your clients and community need your culturally attuned skills and your advocacy—they're waiting for you and what you have to offer.

Questions for Reflection

Consider what you learned in this chapter as you respond to the questions and prompts below.

1. Consider what you learned from this chapter; how has it changed how you understand gender and gender identity?
2. What are some ways that counselors can work with clients from oppressed gender identities directly in individual counseling sessions (microlevel)?
3. What are actions that you could take within your immediate community to advocate for people from oppressed gender identities (mesolevel)?
4. What are policies, laws, or issues that directly impact individuals with oppressed gender identities at the national and global levels (macrolevel)?
5. Consider gender identities and gender roles. Which gender that is different from your own do you need to learn more about to be effective with that population?

Applying What You Have Learned

Complete each of the following activities, considering what you learned from this chapter.

Activity #1: Queer Coding

One example of a *queer as villain* portrayal is evident in "Him" from the animated children's show *The Powerpuff Girls*. The character "Him" is portrayed as an androgynous villain expressing both stereotypically masculine and feminine features (Thompson & Lowry, 2016). The association of Him's gender expression with evil acts, such as "manipulation plots" and "demonic powers" throughout the course of the show, supports societal norms that associate moral deviance with gender expansiveness (Thompson & Lowry, 2016).

Where have you seen "queer coding" in the media you have consumed? What impacts do these media examples have on people's perceptions of LGBTQ+ people? How might it impact your clients?

CHAPTER 15

Romantic and Affectional Identity and Queer Oppression

Clark D. Ausloos, Stacy Pinto, and Chase Morgan-Swaney

Hope will never be silent.

—Harvey Milk

CHAPTER OVERVIEW

You might have heard someone say, "Why do romantic and affectual identities matter? I don't care what people do in their bedrooms." While the person who says this likely does so with positive intent, this is an off-putting and inaccurate statement. Relationships, no matter the type, are foundational to who we are as humans. Relationships shape us, facilitate growth, teach us things about ourselves, and are places in which we express ourselves and allow us to feel connection. Our relational identities, including our romantic and affectual identities, are a part of who each of us is and must be understood within each person's unique context. In this chapter, you will learn about these identities, the oppressions people with nondominant romantic and affectual identities experience, and how to address these topics within counseling, including ways in which you can advocate for individuals and communities.

LEARNING OBJECTIVES

By the end of this chapter, students will be able to

1. describe historical context of oppression related to romantic and affectional identities in the United States;
2. define concepts and terms critical to RAIs, their oppression, and context within counseling settings;
3. interpret contextual implications among diverse RAIs and attend to unique intersections among identities;
4. apply foundational concepts (e.g., history, definitions) to the practice of professional counseling consistent with relevant ethical standards and guidelines; and
5. learn and apply ethical, affirmative, and liberatory counseling principles in work with individuals who identify with nondominant RAIs.

CACREP 2016 STANDARDS

The information in this chapter supports the following standards:

- 1.F.1.d the role and process of the professional counselor advocating on behalf of the profession
- 2.F.1.e advocacy processes needed to address institutional and social barriers that impede access, equity, and success for clients
- 2.F.2.a multicultural and pluralistic characteristics within and among diverse groups nationally and internationally
- 2.F.2.b theories and models of multicultural counseling, cultural identity development, and social justice and advocacy
- 2.F.2.c multicultural counseling competencies
- 2.F.2.d the impact of heritage, attitudes, beliefs, understandings, and acculturative experiences on an individual's views of others
- 2.F.2.e the effects of power and privilege for counselors and clients
- 2.F.2.f help-seeking behaviors of diverse clients
- 2.F.2.g the impact of spiritual beliefs on clients' and counselors' worldviews
- 2.F.2.h strategies for identifying and eliminating barriers, prejudices, and processes of intentional and unintentional oppression and discrimination
- 2.F.7.m ethical and culturally relevant strategies for selecting, administering, and interpreting assessment and test results
- 5.A.2.g culturally and developmentally relevant education programs that raise awareness and support addiction and substance abuse prevention and the recovery process
- 5.A.2.j cultural factors relevant to addiction and addictive behavior
- 5.C.2.j cultural factors relevant to clinical mental health counseling
- 5.C.3.e strategies to advocate for persons with mental health issues
- 5.D.2.s cultural factors relevant to rehabilitation counseling
- 5.E.2.j the influence of institutional, systemic, interpersonal, and intrapersonal barriers on learning and career opportunities in higher education
- 6.B.1.f ethical and culturally relevant counseling in multiple settings
- 6.B.5.j models and competencies for advocating for clients at the individual, system, and policy levels

CACREP 2024 STANDARDS

The information in this chapter supports the following standards:

- 3.A.4. the role and process of the professional counselor advocating on behalf of and with individuals receiving counseling services to address systemic, institutional, architectural, attitudinal, disability, and social barriers that impede access, equity, and success
- 3.A.5. the role and process of the professional counselor advocating on behalf of the profession
- 3.B.1. theories and models of multicultural counseling, social justice, and advocacy
- 3.B.2. the influence of heritage, cultural identities, attitudes, values, beliefs, understandings, within-group differences, and acculturative experiences on individuals' worldviews
- 3.B.3. the influence of heritage, cultural identities, attitudes, values, beliefs, understandings, within-group differences, and acculturative experiences on help-seeking and coping behaviors
- 3.B.4. the effects of historical events, multigenerational trauma, and current issues on diverse cultural groups in the U.S. and globally

- 3.B.5. the effects of stereotypes, overt and covert discrimination, racism, power, oppression, privilege, marginalization, microaggressions, and violence on counselors and clients
- 3.B.6. the effects of various socio-cultural influences, including public policies, social movements, and cultural values, on mental and physical health and wellness
- 3.B.9. strategies for identifying and eliminating barriers, prejudices, and processes of intentional and unintentional oppression and discrimination
- 3.B.10. guidelines developed by professional counseling organizations related to social justice, advocacy, and working with individuals with diverse cultural identities
- 3.B.11. the role of religion and spirituality in clients' and counselors' psychological functioning
- 3.G.5. culturally sustaining and developmental considerations for selecting, administering, and interpreting assessments, including individual accommodations and environmental modifications
- 3.G.6. ethical and legal considerations for selecting, administering, and interpreting assessments
- 3.G.7. use of culturally sustaining and developmentally appropriate assessments for diagnostic and intervention planning purposes
- 5.A.10. culturally and developmentally relevant education programs that raise awareness and support addiction and substance use prevention and the recovery process
- 5.C.8. strategies to advocate for people with mental, behavioral, and neurodevelopmental conditions
- 5.E.6. the influence of institutional, systemic, interpersonal, and intrapersonal barriers on learning and career opportunities in higher education
- 6.B.1.d. scholarly examination of culturally sustaining counseling practice across multiple settings, contexts, and across service delivery modalities
- 6.B.1.f. legal and ethical issues and responsibilities in counseling across multiple settings and across service delivery modalities
- 6.B.5.j. models and competencies for advocating for clients at the individual, system, and policy levels

Terminology

As we begin this chapter, like Chapter 14, we start with terminology because how we talk about romantic and affectual identity (RAI) and queer oppression is essential to how we understand it. It is important to recognize that terminology, language, and concepts continue to advance and evolve. As such, terms that appear here may someday be replaced by more affirming, person/client-centered language. Note that while these definitions provide general guidelines, it is *best practice* to use the language clients use to describe themselves.

Affectional Orientation
One's emotional, mental, physical and/or sexual attraction or bond (or lack thereof) with another person/people (Ginicola et al., 2017).

Affirmative Therapy
A pan-theoretical framework for conducting counseling that involves normalizing and validating stress, facilitating emotional awareness and regulation, using empowerment and liberation, and facilitating supportive relationships (Proujansky & Pachankis, 2014).

Alloromantic
A person who experiences romantic attraction to other people.

Allosexual
A person who experiences sexual attraction to other people (Ginicola et al., 2017).

Aromantic
A person who experiences little or no romantic attraction to other people.

Asexual
The asexual or *ace* identity spectrum, traditionally understood as a lack of sexual attraction, is inclusive of many identities/positionalities related to an individual's sexual disposition that are inconsistent with allosexuality, such as gray-a, a/sexual-ish, demi-/semisexual, fray-/ignota-sexual, and cupiosexual (Pinto & Blueford, 2022, p. 124).

Biromantic
Someone who may be romantically interested in more than one gender/sex (see Chapter 14 for gender/sex definitions).

Bisexual
Physical, romantic, and/or emotional attraction to people of more than one gender/sex (GLAAD, n.d.).

Coming Out
Disclosing one's sexual orientation or gender identity to others (Cass, 1979). **Coming out** occurs again and again throughout the lifespan of queer people.

Consensual Nonmonogamy
An umbrella term for relationships in which all partners give explicit consent to engage in romantic, intimate, and/or sexual relationships with multiple people.

Demiromantic
Someone who feels romantic feelings for someone only after a strong emotional connection is built.

Demisexual
Someone who feels some degree of sexual feelings for someone only after a strong emotional connection is built.

Fraysexual/Ignotasexual
Describes people who more easily feel sexually attracted to people they have just met rather than those with whom they have built an emotional connection.

Gay
Individuals who are primarily attracted to members of the same-gender/sex; it can be an umbrella term similar to queer (Killermann, 2017).

Gray Asexual (Graysexual; Gray-A)
Someone who experiences a limited to no degree of sexual attraction and is generally under the umbrella term of asexuality.

Heterosexism
The assumption that all people are heterosexual, which can result in microaggressions, oppression, and/or discrimination.

Heterosexual
Individuals who are primarily attracted to people of a gender/sex different from their own (colloquially, the term *straight* has been used; Killermann, 2017).

Homonegativity
Any prejudicial, discriminatory, or stigmatizing attitude, behavior, or response toward people who experience same-sex attraction (SSA), same-gender attraction (SGA), or who are, or perceived to be, lesbian, gay, queer, or questioning ([LGBQQ], Ausloos, 2023a).

Homophobia/misia
Historically, the term *homophobia* has been used to describe fear of queer people. *Homomisia* better describes aversion to and disgust of queer people, which more accurately describes the phenomenon (Simmons University, 2019).

Homosexual
Historically, this term has been used to describe a person who experiences attraction toward persons of the same-gender/sex. However, it has since become a pathologized term and should not be used to describe queer people unless in specific contexts or specified by individuals.

Internalized Homophobia/Homonegativity
Stigmatizing attitudes, feelings, and behaviors (e.g., self-hatred, disgust, shame) queer people have toward themselves (Ausloos, 2023a).

Lesbian
A woman/femme who is primarily attracted to other women (Killermann, 2017).

LGBTGEQIAP+
An umbrella acronym used to capture a broad range of queer identities, including lesbian, gay, bisexual, transgender, gender-expansive, queer, intersex, asexual, aromantic, pansexual, panromantic, polysexual, and beyond (LGBTIC LGBQQIA Competencies Taskforce, 2013).

Panromantic
Romantic attraction to others regardless of their gender identity.

Pansexual
One's sexual, romantic, and/or emotional attraction toward others, regardless of their gender identity.

Polyamory
Ethical, honest, and consensual nonmonogamous relationships (Killermann, 2017).

Polyromantic
Someone who has various degrees of romantic attraction to many, but not all, genders.

Polysexual
Sexual attraction to multiple gender identities.

Queer
A reclaimed term used as an umbrella term for individuals who identify with non-cis/-hetero/-allo/-mono sexual, romantic, and gender identities.

Romantic Identity/Orientation
Romantic attraction based on a person's gender, regardless of one's sexual orientation. Romantic orientation may or may not align with sexual orientation (can include aromantic, biromantic, panromantic; LGBT Center, UNC-Chapel Hill, 2022).

Semisexual
Describes someone who experiences sexual attraction but does not have a desire to act on it.

Sexual Identity
An individual's personal perception of their sexuality; it is generally representative of their gender identity, gender role(s), biological sex, and sexual orientation (Andler, 2021; Lev, 2004).

Sexual Orientation
A component of sexual identity that represents an individual's patterns of *sexual* attraction, behavior, fantasies, emotional preferences, and self-identification (Klein, 2014). Related terminology has included heterosexual, gay, lesbian, bisexual, pansexual, and queer (GLSEN, ASCA, ACSSW, & SSWAA, 2019). This term differs from affectional orientation, a holistic term that may include one's emotional, mental, romantic, physical *and/or* sexual attraction to others.

Sexual Orientation Change Measures (SOCE)
A harmful practice that involves psychotherapeutic work to change, reorient, or *repair* one's affectional or sexual identity (Ausloos, 2023a).

Sexual Prejudice
Negative attitudes and/or judgments toward someone based on their affectional, romantic and/or sexual orientation(s).

Sexuality
Sexual feelings, thoughts, attractions, bonds, and behaviors toward other people.

Sexually-Fluid
Describes a sexual orientation that is not fixed in nature. This term may be used to describe someone who identifies as pansexual.

Straight
A stigmatizing term historically used to describe heterosexual people. Using this term is considered oppressive to same-sex or same-gender loving people, as it implies non-straight people are crooked and/or abnormal (Ausloos, 2023a). The preferred term is heterosexual.

Skoliosexual
Someone who experiences sexual attraction toward transgender, nonbinary, and/or gender-diverse people.

Zsexual
Individuals who experience sexual attraction to people of any gender.

Affectional, Romantic, and Sexual Identity Development

Affectional identity is a holistic term used to describe one's emotional, mental, and/or physical attraction or bond with another person. *Affectional identity* is the preferred term over *sexual orientation* because sexual orientation does not account for the diversity within emotional, mental, spiritual, and romantic bonds. Affectional identities include people who identify as asexual, those who experience varying degrees of sexual attraction, or no sexual attraction at all, all of which, historically, sexual orientation has not captured or included.

While we examine foundational identity development models, it is important to keep in mind the context of their development, the populations on whom they were based/normed, and their alignment with current social, cultural, and identity standards. To begin, Cass (1979) identified a homosexual identity formation model with several stages, including Pre-stage 1, Stage 1: Identity Confusion, Stage 2: Identity Comparison, Stage 3: Identity Tolerance, Stage 4: Identity Acceptance, Stage 5: Identity Pride, and Stage 6: Identity Synthesis. Cass (1979) conceptualized identity synthesis to include acceptance, a positive attitude toward one's identity, a desire for disclosure, and more frequent contact with other gay males or lesbians. Similarly, Meyer and Schwitzer's (2008) model included several steps, including recognizing a difference within oneself, reflective observing, internalizing reflective observing, self-identifying, coming into proximity, and networking and connecting. You can read more about affectual identity development models in Chapter 6 of this text.

While these identity development models provide some structure to RAI development, it is important to highlight some critiques. First, as language has shifted and evolved, we are intentional in using less stigmatizing, more person-centered language (e.g., the use of the word *tolerance* in these models may not be as widely used today). Additionally, models that represent a linear identity development process can be limiting to the unique, nonlinear identity development journeys individuals take. For example, if using these models explicitly with a client, they may feel their journey is invalidated or incongruent with developmentally *normal* milestones within the model. Additionally, most of these models focus on binary sexual identities (e.g., gay, lesbian), lacking attention to a spectrum of affectional, romantic, sexual, and/or asexual identities, such as bisexuals, demisexual, or other marginalized RAIs. Further, these models lack specific attention to factors of intersectionality (Crenshaw, 1991), including gender identity and/or expression and race/ethnicity, and how these factors impact RAI development (Goodrich & Brammer, 2021; Kenneady & Oswalt, 2014). Additionally, the concept of *coming out*, which often happens at later stages of identity development, can be further complicated by sociopolitical and other contextual factors, and may be less about the person themselves than the systems in which they are embedded. So, while we encourage readers to explore RAI development models, we urge counselors to use the models in an informed and nonprescriptive way.

Minority Stress, Intersectionality, and Internalized Homophobia/misia

Individuals who identify with marginalized RAI populations in addition to other marginalized cultural identities (e.g., Queer People of Color (QPOC), people with disabilities) may experience greater marginalization and stigma, as proposed by the minority stress model (Meyer, 2003). Minority stress results from harmful and stressful social environments based on one's nondominant identities and may cause extreme anxiety and hyperarousal because of anticipating future stress. More recent terminology, *marginalization stress*, properly locates this problem within the *experiences* of marginalization itself rather than the marginalized *person* (Hope et al., 2022). People who experience minority/marginalization stress can have increased negative physical and mental health consequences including anxiety, depression, PTSD, body-image issues, self-harm, suicidality, substance use disorders, and risky sexual behaviors (Ausloos, 2023a).

People with nondominant RAIs may experience intense self-hatred and negative internalization because of marginalization stress, called *internalized homophobia*. Internalized homophobia occurs because of a general lack of social acceptance, microaggressions, and discrimination against queer people, resulting in a strong hatred toward and disgust for oneself and one's own sexuality. Internalized homophobia can result in distress, poor self-esteem, increased anxiety and depression, and poor overall well-being (Newcomb & Mustanski, 2010). The externalization of internalized homophobia might include substance use and/or risky sexual behavior (Ausloos, 2023a). Historically, *homophobia* has been used to describe negativity toward people with nondominant RAIs. However, using this term could further stigmatize legitimate mental health conditions, such as clinical phobias. Additionally, the term removes a sense of responsibility from the person, as if they have no control over their *fear* (Simmons University, 2019). Alternatively, *homomisia* is the preferred term, squaring the responsibility of the hatred with the individual who holds those views.

BOX 15.1 **PROFILE OF A PRACTITIONER: MICHAEL P. CHANEY, PHD, LPC, ACS, OAKLAND UNIVERSITY, DEPARTMENT OF COUNSELING**

I just lay there on the lawn of my front yard as 9-year-old me was kicked and verbally assaulted with, "Faggot!" from the neighborhood bully. I felt helpless and worthless. It was experiences like this throughout my childhood and adolescence that guided me to the counseling profession. From a young age, I knew I wanted to make a difference in the lives of LGBTQ+ people. Since then, my gayness has influenced every professional path I have taken and every decision made, and it intersects with every aspect of who I am as a queer clinician and counselor educator.

I didn't start my undergraduate education until I was 23 years old because I grew up in a family that was government cheese and food stamp poor, and education wasn't valued. It wasn't until I started to explore my queerness that I realized I didn't feel safe to be out in my hometown. Attending college in a city a few hours away allowed me to earn an undergrad degree and gave me the anonymity I needed to come out and live authentically as a gay man. Being gay also influenced where I went to graduate school. I intentionally sought a master's program where there was faculty conducting research on LGBTQ+ issues. I moved from Columbus, Ohio, to Atlanta, Georgia, to work on my master's, and eventually earned my EdS and PhD at the same institution. Upon earning my doctorate in 2004, I began the search for a tenure-track faculty position. Again, my gayness influenced this process in positive and negative ways. Because my dissertation, scholarship, and service involvement at that time was LGBTQ+ focused, I was invited for many interviews because of the "diversity" that I would bring to a department. Conversely, I felt like I could only interview in geographic locations where LGBTQ+ diversity was valued, where I would have a queer community with whom to connect, and where I wouldn't have to worry about getting gay-bashed. I remember feeling the need to come out during interviews as a way to gauge if a particular department was gay-affirming or not. The truth is, no institutions or people are free from heterosexism, including the most liberal universities, well-intentioned counseling departments, and fellow counselor educators. When I went up for tenure, I was told by someone above me with more power that my scholarship and service were "too gay" and that I should consider exploring other areas of scholarship. I have been confronted by a cishetero male counselor educator who asked me, "What do you really know about counseling issues besides *gay things*? In these moments, I again felt helpless and worthless. However, instances such as these just bolstered my resolve to continue to explore LGBTQ+ issues in counseling in scholarship, service, and teaching, and further solidified my development as a counselor educator who happens to be gay. My own experiences with heterosexism, personally and professionally, have allowed me to be a more cultural-responsive and empathic professional counselor and educator. Given that I do not conceal my gay identity in the classroom and in counseling contexts, students have felt comfortable asking difficult questions that have enhanced their competence to work with queer clients, and my LGBTQ+ clients tend to trust me and open up to me rather quickly. Additionally, over the years, I have had students and clients come out to me when they have not yet told others about their identities; they felt shielded. And as I write this narrative and reflect on how my gay male identity has intersected with my identities as a counselor and counselor educator, the researcher in me can't help but pull out themes. A primary theme that emerges at the intersection of my gayness and my professional development is that all of the negative things I have experienced associated with being a gay man empowered me to excel as a scholar, clinician, and counselor educator. Though I am still a faggot, and although I still experience heterosexist kicks and assaults at various systemic levels as a counselor educator, I no longer feel helpless or worthless; instead, I am empowered and unyielding.

IMG 15.1 Michael P. Chaney, PhD, LPC, ACS, Oakland University, Department of Counseling

Understanding the Historical Context of RAI

RAI Across Time, Space, and Culture

Throughout recorded history, there is evidence that diverse RAIs were regarded as commonplace within many cultures. Indeed, ethnographic literature described facets of romantic and affectional expansiveness as embedded within cultural customs, traditions, and rites (Tskhay & Rule, 2015). Examples have been documented across time, geographic location, and culture, such as the mentoring relationships among men in ancient Greece (Bertosa, 2009; Hoffman, 1980) and among Basotho women in South Africa (Gay, 1986). Considering their cultural relevance, the nature of these mentoring relationships was not questioned, as they were situated within their respective cultural contexts and, therefore, not subjected to pathologizing.

European colonization and the privileging of Western, Judeo-Christian values and practices fostered prejudicial attitudes and beliefs toward nondominant RAIs. For instance, folks across the African diaspora who were trafficked to parts of South America during the transatlantic slave trade were predominantly affirming of a broad range of RAIs because they were believed to possess an enhanced connection to ancestral spirits (Tskhay & Rule, 2015). Nevertheless, because of the preeminence of Catholicism across colonized South America, nondominant RAIs became regarded as iniquitous among the settlers, non-native and native peoples alike. Throughout the centuries that followed, as Western Judeo-Christian societies continued their forced expansion throughout the Americas, attitudes, beliefs, and behaviors toward the diversity of RAIs grew increasingly pathologizing and oppressive in nature.

TABLE 15.1 Examples of the Impact of Colonization on RAI

Precolonization	Nondominant Culture	Colonization
Two-spirit[a] individuals were often revered within their tribes for their masculinity and femininity of spirit, regardless of sex, gender, and RAI. Two-spirited folks could be found officiating ceremonies, engaging in healing work, serving as mediators, or educating youth.	Native American peoples	Two-spirited persons must contend with the dualistic nature of colonized society. As a result, some two-spirited individuals may feel pressured by the dominant culture to align with the gender and romantic and affectional norms and expectations of their designated sex at birth.

Precolonization	Nondominant Culture	Colonization
Babaylanism[b] was a female-dominated career, though it was not exclusive to female individuals. Regarded as women in society, men were permitted to become male *babaylanes* so long as their gender expression was akin to that of a femme cis woman. Moreover, male babaylanes shared many of the societal norms and expectations of women, including taking on a husband.	Southeast Asian peoples	The contemporary *babaylan*, commonly known as the *bakla*, no longer retain their privileged status in society because of Spanish Catholic colonization, which labeled babaylanism as "demonic and immoral."[c] Once regarded as spiritual healers and leaders, the bakla have been subjected to stereotypes that have seemingly confined them to careers in cosmetology and fashion design.

a Refers to folks with Native American heritage who are expansive in their RAI and gender identities and expressions in a manner that transcends categorization, binary or otherwise (Ginicola, 2017)

b Refers to a form of shamanism, rooted in religious animism, reserved for folks who possessed masculinity and femininity of spirit (Inton-Campbell, 2021)

c Inton-Campbell, 2021, p. 29

Dismantling Queer Oppression in Postmodern America (1960–Present)

Because of the religious underpinnings of colonization and the needs of the post-World War II American populace, the oppressive forces of heterosexism, heteronormativity, and monosexism, among others, were pervasive within social institutions. What constituted a *normal* relationship (i.e., a monogamous dyad consisting of a heterosexual cisgender man and cisgender woman) fostered explicit and implicit troubling attitudes toward diverse RAIs. Throughout the 1960s and '70s, postmodern and critical lines of inquiry, which were influenced by and emerged from various civil rights and countercultural movements, inspired a collective effort among nondominant RAIs and their allies to work toward eradicating these oppressive social forces. However, as a counter-response to these largely secular movements of thought, Christian evangelicalism became a potent political force throughout the 1980s and '90s, influencing anti-LGBTGEQIAP+ policy agendas of U.S. presidents Ronald Reagan and George H. W. Bush (Wilcox & Lida, 2011).

While most Christian evangelicals were ideologically conservative and affiliated with the Republican Party, the societal influence of their values toward nondominant RAIs transcended political ideology and party affiliation (Wilcox & Lida, 2011). For example, U.S. president Bill Clinton, a Democrat, signed the Defense of Marriage Act (DOMA, 1996), limiting access to marriage to heterosexual couples and granting states permission not to recognize the legality of same-sex marriages conducted in other states. Throughout the 1990s to the 2020s, queer people continued to experience oppression. Despite the Matthew Shepard and James Byrd Jr. Hate Crimes and Prevention Act (2009), which expanded existing federal hate crime laws to

Queer Oppression in Postmodern America: Strides & Setbacks

1969

The New York Police Dept. raided the Stonewall Inn, leading to a four-day uprising of its RAI patrons, arm-in-arm with many of their trans and gender expansive co-conspirators. This event is widely considered to have ignited the modern LGBTGEQIAP+ civil rights movement

1987

The AIDS Coalition to Unleash Power is founded in New York City with the aim of using civil disobedience to increase visibility surrounding the devastating impact of the HIV/AIDS epidemic on RAI and to ensure access to both effective and emerging treatments

1997

Ellen DeGeneres, and her fictional character of the same name, came out as gay on primetime TV. Ellen became the first show to feature an RAI lead character. The sitcom was cancelled the following year, but DeGeneres would return in 2003 to host her acclaimed talk show until 2022

2011

The Obama administration ended "don't ask, don't tell" (DADT), permitting soldiers to serve openly in the military regardless of their RAI. When DADT required soldiers to conceal their RAI beginning in 1994, RAI civil rights activists were enthused that soldiers would finally have the opportunity to serve despite their RAI

2022

The Respect for Marriage Act (H.R. 8404) was passed on a bipartisan basis in both chambers of the U.S. Congress. Signed by President Biden, the act codified into law the federal government's requirement to recognize same-sex marriages in the U.S.

FIGURE 15.1 Timeline of Queer Oppression in the United States

include crimes motivated by *sexual orientation* (among other identities), the Federal Bureau of Investigation reported that 1,127 hate crimes motivated by sexual orientation were perpetrated in 2021. Figure 15.1 contains a brief timeline of several key events central to queer oppression in postmodern America.

Dismantling Queer Oppression in the Counseling Profession

As society has grown more affirming and liberation-minded regarding diverse RAIs, mental health professions have done the same. The American Psychological Association (APA) Board of Trustees passed a resolution which both urged an end to discrimination based on RAI and recommended that homosexuality be declassified as a mental health disorder within the second edition of the *Diagnostic and Statistical Manual of Mental Disorders* (APA, 1968, 1973). Yet, it took 40 years for the APA to completely remove all vestiges of pathologizing RAIs (i.e., diagnoses of sexual orientation disturbance and ego-dystonic homosexuality) from the DSM (Ginicola et al., 2017). In the decades that followed, this delay cost the mental health field in terms of its trustworthiness and reputability among the queer community, as even a modicum of pathologization gave rise to further societal proliferation of disaffirming and dangerous sexual orientation change efforts (SOCE).

Although professional counselors have contributed substantial effort and made noteworthy strides toward the eradication of lawful SOCE, especially as it pertains to queer youth, the counseling profession faces unparalleled challenges considering the current state of anti-queer and anti-trans legislation throughout the nation (see Figure 15.2).

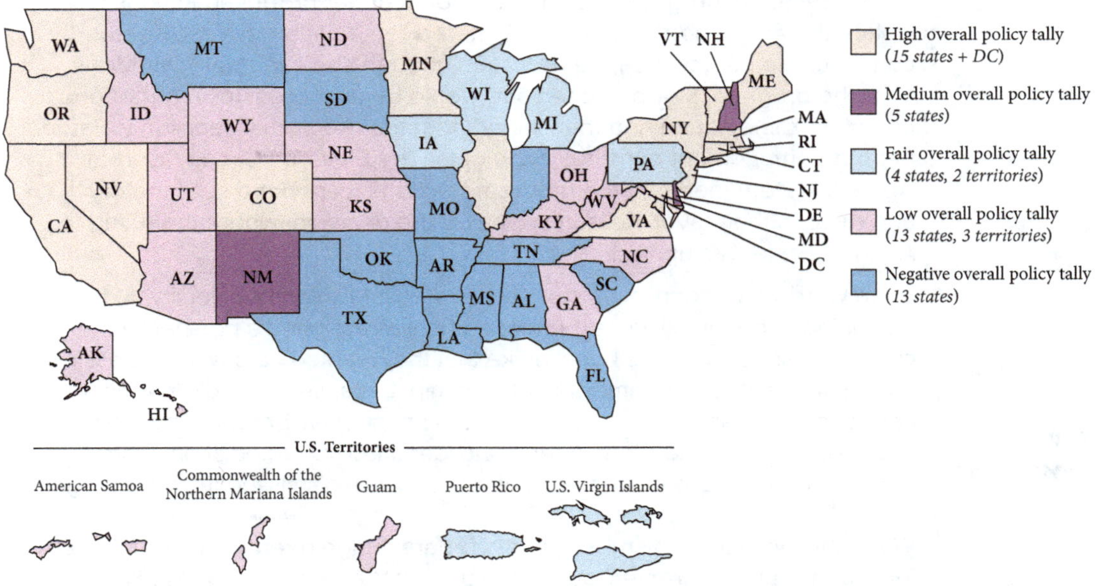

FIGURE 15.2 Anti-LGBTGEQIAP+ Legislation in the United States, 2023

Within the counselor's roles as clinician and advocate, the counseling profession has grown markedly in its collective competence and humility to serve marginalized RAI populations through an anti-oppressive framework. With much of the necessary foundation having been laid during the period when diverse RAIs were still partially pathologized within the DSM, professional counselors' roles when serving this population have become more defined, informed, and fortified. Yet despite decades of progress toward affirmative, liberatory counseling frameworks, we must not forget that our profession exists within the context of the greater society and is therefore influenced by oppressive beliefs and values that are antagonistic to people with nondominant RAIs. The American Counseling Association (ACA) *Code of Ethics* (2014), while not without its challenges (e.g., Keeton v. Anderson-Wiley, 2010, 2011; Ward v. Polite, 2012; Ward v. Wilbanks, 2010; see Table 15.2 for case details), has been a vital resource in ensuring that individuals who identify with diverse RAIs retain access to professional counseling services despite counselors' personal beliefs and values.

TABLE 15.2 The Cases of *Keeton* and *Ward*: Cases in Point

Keeton (2010, 2011)	Jennifer Keeton was a counseling student at Augusta State University. Throughout her time in the program, Keeton was unambiguous concerning her view that one's RAI was a choice and that the romantically and affectionally diverse were experiencing identity issues. When a counselor educator engaged Keeton with a hypothetical question involving a student in crisis who was questioning their RAI, she responded that she would inform the student that same-sex relationships were wrong and attempt to change their behavior. If unable to do so, Keeton stated she would refer the student to engage in some form of SOCE. In response, the program informed Keeton that her proposed actions would violate the ACA *Code of Ethics* and offered remediation. At first, Keeton consented to participate in remediation, though she eventually withdrew from the program. Keeton stated she would be unsuccessful in her efforts to complete remediation and that she felt that the program's decision violated her First Amendment constitutional rights. The Eleventh Circuit Court of Appeals determined that the program's actions were not discriminatory and ruled in their favor. Keeton appealed the decision, where the ruling for Augusta State was upheld.
Ward (2010, 2012)	Julea Ward was a counseling student at Eastern Michigan University. At the beginning of her practicum experience, she was assigned a prospective client who stated in their phone intake that they wanted help with depression and issues related to a same-sex relationship. Because of Ward's inability to condone such relationships, she consulted her supervisor regarding the best course of referring the client. After being identified for remediation, Ward declined to adhere to the remedial efforts and was dismissed from the program. Ward challenged the dismissal, and a federal judge ruled in favor of Eastern Michigan, citing Supreme Court precedent that afforded responsibility to programs for determining standards of professional training to which students of the program must adhere. Prior to any additional legal action, Eastern Michigan engaged Ward privately with a monetary settlement.

Models of Affirmative and Liberatory Counseling

Affirmative counseling is a pan-theoretical approach that involves affirming and validating diverse RAIs using a holistic, strength-based framework. Important to this framework is the counselor's knowledge of internal and societal biases and forces of oppression that impact life functioning for clients with marginalized RAIs. Additionally, it is imperative that counselors engage in critical self-reflection and introspection about their own biases and RAI views, including their own identities. Affirmative counseling requires collaborative problem-solving, empowerment, advocacy for and with clients, and crisis planning and management (Ausloos, 2023b; Ginicola et al., 2017).

Liberatory counseling involves removing structures and systems that have long enabled the mistreatment and discrimination against nondominant RAIs (Phillips II et al., 2022). A liberatory framework is not reactionary in nature; it asks counselors and clients to embrace dialectic thinking and challenge themselves and others to see how they may be part of the problem while also being part of the solution (Scharrón-Del Rio, 2017). Counselors engage in frequent self-reflection and self-challenging of biases, as well as working with clients to change oppressive systems (e.g., legislative advocacy). Often, there may be limits and challenges within typical psychotherapy and counseling approaches when working with marginalized individuals. Traditional counseling approaches, such as cognitive behavioral therapy, may assume the client has maladaptive thinking and not consider the influence of a discriminatory society on the client. Therefore, counselors must continue to work to change oppressive systems *for* and *with* their queer clients using foundations of affirmation and liberation therapies.

It is essential that counselors do not generalize the experiences of clients with marginalized RAIs based on assumptions or those of previous clients with whom they have worked—*even if those clients share identities.* Counselors must be mindful that there are differences within the queer spectrum, particularly with the type of oppression individuals experience. For example, a gay person may experience more discrimination from a heterosexual person than a bisexual-identifying person; however, within queer communities, bisexual people are often stigmatized by nonbisexual queer people (e.g., gay, lesbian) and invalidated in their attractions, experiences, and desires. The human instinct to categorize and *other* remains active within marginalized populations. Everyone's experience must be understood in context.

Counseling Standards

Ratts and colleagues (2015) refined the multicultural counseling competencies and standards (MCCS; Sue et al., 1992) to include social justice and advocacy domains. The expanded multicultural and social justice counseling competencies include the counseling relationship as an important part of culturally responsive counseling, alongside counselor self-awareness, client world view, and, importantly, culturally sensitive advocacy and interventions (Ratts et al., 2015). Advocacy is an important addition to counselors' work with clients who have nondominant RAIs. Counselors who advocate for clients increase the strength of the therapeutic alliance and positive therapeutic outcomes (Zilcha-Mano et al., 2016). Counselors must continue to enhance their multicultural and social justice competence by developing attitudes and beliefs, knowledge,

TABLE 15.3 Examples of Relevant Standards

Association	Competencies	Published
Association for Lesbian, Gay, Bisexual, and Transgender Issues in Counseling (ALGBTIC; now the Society for Sexual, Affectional, Intersex, and Gender Expansive Identities (SAIGE)	Counseling With Lesbian, Gay, Bisexual, Queer, Questioning, Intersex, and Ally Individuals	2013
American School Counselor Association (ASCA)	The School Counselor and LGBTQ+ Youth	Adopted 1995, Revised 2000, 2005, 2007, 2013, 2014, 2016, 2022
APA	Guidelines for Psychological Practice With Sexual Minority Persons	2021
The American Association for Marriage and Family Therapy (AAMFT)	Clinical Guidelines for LGBTQIA-Affirming Marriage and Family Therapy	2021

skills, and actions when working with this population. Particularly important is the component of *action* whereby counselors advocate with and on behalf of clients at the micro (individual), meso (communities and schools), and macro levels (public policy).

Since the inception of the MSJCC, many professional counseling organizations and entities have created, adapted, and updated standards for working with clients who hold nondominant RAIs (see Table 15.3).

Professional counseling organizations continue to update standards related to best practices in working with diverse RAIs, and it's counselors' responsibility to intentionally integrate them into counseling practice. Additionally, we encourage counselors to use a trauma-informed lens to acknowledge and validate clients' life experiences and foster a space for healing and growth (Chang et al., 2018). Read the short case of Toni (Box 15.2) and reflect on your thoughts related to the case.

BOX 15.2 **FOCUS ON CLIENT CARE**

You are a new counselor at an agency and are working with a new client, Toni. You are conducting an intake interview with Toni, and when asked about their affectional/sexual identity, they say, "Not quite sure." You make sure to re-address this later in the session, asking, "I heard you say you weren't sure about your identity. I'm wondering if you can tell me more about that." Toni replies they have been exploring their sexuality and believe they are bisexual. Using a humanistic, person-centered, affirmative and liberatory framework, you begin to explore this with Toni. You explain your experiences in working with diverse

RAIs and review limits to confidentiality. You share resources for a queer-affirming group you know meets each month in the local community. You validate Toni's experiences with identity-based discrimination and empower them to use their strengths to collaboratively build goals for future treatment. Toni agrees to return for future sessions.

In reflecting on this session with Toni, ask yourself these questions:

1. What did this counselor do that demonstrates an affirming environment?
2. What kinds of questions would you want to make sure you ask at this initial intake after learning of the client's bisexuality?
3. Is it appropriate to refer the client to a community peer support group at intake? Why or why not?
4. How can you frame your intake/initial assessment in a humanistic way to better understand the clients' experiences?

Nondominant Group Identities

When reflecting on the many identities our clients hold, it is important to note the unique identity intersections related to power, privilege, and oppression. QPOC experience unique, layered discriminatory experiences (e.g., educating White queer people about race or being sexualized by other queer people because of their race; Woulfe & Goodman, 2020). Multiple layers of societal discrimination, including White supremacy, racism, heterosexism, and homonegativity, impact QPOC (Mosley et al., 2021). For example, a cisgender male client who is queer, Black, and able-bodied has intersecting identities that hold different degrees of power and privilege. He may hold privilege as cisgender and male, yet experience marginalization related to his queer and Black identities, compounded by pervasive cultural biases that Black men are *scary* and *violent*. These intersections highlight the uniqueness and importance of honoring clients' experiences and having knowledge of the various barriers they may face at the individual, structural, community, and societal levels (Mitchell et al., 2021). Not only can this phenomenon be conceptualized via intersectionality (Crenshaw, 1991) but also through Bronfenbrenner's (1979) ecological systems theory. Note that this theory will be discussed in additional detail in the "Ecological and Sociopolitical Contexts" section of this chapter.

An additional consideration to note when working with this population is the intersection of diverse relationship structures. For example, polyamory is a relationship and familial form, practice, and identity that translates into *many loves* (Anapol, 2010). Polyamorous relationships are those in which people engage in meaningful, ongoing, loving, and/or sexual relationships with more than one partner (who may or may not be queer). Polyamory is a type of nonmonogamy, specifically consensual nonmonogamy, in which people within relationships fully consent to include additional partners through various relationship structures. As these types of relationships deviate from the mono-normative, heteronormative, dominant cultural paradigms, polyamorous people are often discriminated against and stigmatized by society.

Religiosity/Spirituality and RAIs

Counselors must be attuned to religion and/or spirituality and their intersections with RAIs in counseling. For some clients, religion may have had a negative impact on their development, while other clients may find the connection to spirituality to be a protective factor (Suprina et al., 2019). Suprina et al. (2019) recommended exploring the client's spiritual development to encourage development beyond a strict, dichotomous view of spirituality and to support building congruence with one's RAI. This might involve a counselor and client exploring and processing previously learned religious ideologies from childhood or assigning the client to journal about their spirituality. Additionally, a client's embrace of both religious/spiritual identities and marginalized RAIs may involve various levels of disclosure or coming out. For example, a gay client may be comfortable being out at work but is not out at church for fear of rejection. As such, it is important to support clients as they navigate non-affirming contexts (Killian et al., 2019). Last, when working with diverse RAIs in relationships, partners may hold differing spiritual and/or religious identities, and it's important for counselors to recognize these intersecting identities and be able to hold space for this in session (Killian et al., 2019).

BOX 15.3 **PAUSE AND REFLECT: THE IMPACT OF SPIRITUALITY AND RELIGION**

Consider how you might use the following reflection questions with clients in session.

How does spirituality and/or religion impact your psychological and social functioning, if at all?

Tell me about your spiritual development and how spirituality and or religion was communicated to you when you were young.

Are the goals we set together consistent with your spiritual and/or your religious perspectives?

BOX 15.4 **PROFILE OF A PRACTITIONER**

David Julius Ford, Jr, PhD, LCMHC, LPC, NCC, ACS, Monmouth University, Professional Counseling Department

Growing up in a small town in North Carolina with a strict Baptist upbringing and being raised by my grandmother, I had no frame of reference regarding my feelings toward other boys in my neighborhood and in school. I just knew that I found them attractive and dreamed of being with them. As I reflect upon my childhood, I am a walking contradiction of people who say a child has no clue about their affectional identity. I did and had my first "boy crush" in the first grade. I grew up being called gay slurs, having people assume that I was gay, and being bullied for my mannerisms. I hated high school and did not have a good experience. I was ready to get out of that small town and away from those people. I never wanted to go back either.

I went away to college right out of high school and had no inclination to affirm who I was. I also had no clue about mental health and seeing a licensed mental health professional. I just knew that the feelings I had growing up followed me to college, a small, private, predominantly White institution in urban North Carolina. While at college, I found a group of friends who had the same feelings I did and were "wrestling" with their identity like I was.

While I was an undergrad, I was the pianist for the school's Gospel choir and was employed as a church musician. I also involved myself with the school's LGBTQ+ organization and became president. I began to wrestle with my affectional identity and my spiritual/religious identity. I believed that I could not be both and an internal struggle ensued. Both organizations seemed to be at odds, but I felt the need to be a part of both. They were both a part of my identity. The devil on one shoulder started fighting with the angel on the other, but I knew that the peace I needed did not rest in my pastor or any other religious figure.

I had a long conversation with the director of the Office of Multicultural Affairs, a strong Black woman who was a prayer warrior. She was like a mother to me and really cared about me and my well-being. She did not judge me or throw scriptures at me. Instead, she embraced me and helped me to find solutions. She suggested that I make an appointment with the university counseling center. There was a Black female counselor that she highly recommended. I made an appointment with the counselor, but I did not know what to expect. My family never talked about mental health in a positive light.

Looking back on that experience, the counselor helped me work through the pain and stress I was having and provided me a space to say, "I am gay." She assisted me in beginning the process of affirming and accepting who I was. She did not judge me. She gave me the tools to be who I was and to be who and what God made me to be. I became more comfortable with myself and the skin I was in. She helped lay the foundation for me being the bold person I am now and to be an advocate for others. I want to be for others what she was for me. Thank you, Joyce.

Ecological and Sociopolitical Contexts

Homonegativity refers to discriminatory, marginalizing, and stigmatizing attitudes, beliefs, and/or behaviors toward nondominant RAIs. Homonegativity results from the societal belief that heterosexuality is normal and acceptable (i.e., heteronormativity), while nondominant RAIs are not. Individuals with marginalized RAIs may experience pervasive discrimination, marginalization, and stigma in many parts of their lives, which can range from microaggressions to overt physical, verbal, and/or sexual assault or abuse. This includes at home, where youth are particularly at risk for struggles related to homonegativity. Youth who hold nondominant RAIs may face unaccepting families and are often forced to be unhoused.

RAIs, Homelessness, and Youth

In one study of homeless adults, researchers found that 17% of those with nondominant RAIs who were adults reported they experienced lifetime homelessness, which is twice the general population (Wilson et al., 2020). Disproportionately higher rates of those with marginalized RAIs who are Black experience financial instability and being unhoused. In another recent study, researchers found 28% of youth-identifying RAI experience homelessness or instability in their housing at some time in their lives (The Trevor Project, 2022). In turn, youth who experience homelessness report higher rates of health challenges, mentally and physically. Therefore, it is imperative that professional counselors are equipped with the resources necessary to work with this unique population.

Consider these sources for additional reading:

- https://youth.gov/youth-topics/lgbtq-youth/homelessness
- https://nche.ed.gov/lgbtq-youth/
- https://williamsinstitute.law.ucla.edu/publications/lgbt-homelessness-us/
- https://www.lambdalegal.org/know-your-rights/article/youth-homeless
- https://www.ncbi.nlm.nih.gov/pmc/articles/PMC6695950/

Consider these reflection questions when working with unhoused RAI:

- What community resources do I know of that I can refer my client/student to for housing?
- What possible supports might the school offer for the student, if applicable?
- How can we collaborate to create a safety plan that honors my client's/student's autonomy?

In schools and in communities, youth with marginalized RAIs are at higher risk for poor mental health and educational outcomes. Youth and adolescents must often navigate hostile and unaccepting environments in which they are often made to feel different and are often "othered." In the workplace, they often face higher rates of discrimination when compared with their heterosexual counterparts. They are less likely to get a job interview and report experiences of harassment, identity-based termination, and not receiving commensurate financial advances (Singer & Deschamps, 2017). Because folks with marginalized RAIs can experience discrimination in most spaces they occupy, they develop higher rates of depression, anxiety, PTSD, self-harm, and suicidality.

Micro- and Mesosystems

In the next few sections, we examine queer oppression framed in an ecological and sociopolitical context using Bronfenbrenner's (1979) ecological model. The microsystem is the system with which people have direct contact: their immediate environment. This could include partners, parents/guardians, close family, teachers, peers, and colleagues. While microaggressions occur within all levels of Bronfenbrenner's (1979) ecological model, they are most often experienced in interpersonal relationships and settings. Researchers have determined several categories for these types of microaggressions (Nadal et al., 2011), which are articulated alongside associated examples in Table 15.4.

TABLE 15.4 Microaggressions and Discrimination

Category of Microaggression	Example
Using heterosexist terminology	Saying "faggot," "dyke," or "that's so gay"; assuming a man is married to a woman
Endorsement of heteronormative culture	Someone telling someone to not "act so gay" in public; invalidating bisexuality as an identity
Assumption of universal RAI experience	Stereotyping that all gay men are fashionable or all lesbians must act and look "butch"
Exoticization of RAI	Dehumanizing RAI, for example, stereotyping the gay man as "comic relief"
Discomfort/disapproval of RAI experiences	Staring at a lesbian couple with disgust
Denial of societal heterosexism	Telling a coworker who identifies as RAI and experiencing unfair treatment at work that they are "overreacting" about their perceived discrimination
Assumption of sexual pathology	Assuming that all gay men are "child molesters"
Denial of individual heterosexism	"I'm not homophobic; I have a friend who is gay!"
Threatening behaviors	Ranging from micro-assaults to hate crimes, including verbal, physical and sexual assault and harassment

**Adapted from Sue et al., 2007*

In schools, students can experience discrimination and marginalization by peers, teachers, administration, and staff. Microaggressions in these settings could include heteronormative examples in textbooks and classroom activities, lack of attention to celebrations of important historical days or days of remembrance related to diverse RAIs, and harmful school policies that ban same-gender couples at school dances.

In the workplace, folks with nondominant RAIs often face discrimination based on a lack of clear policies that protect them and targeted treatment related to hiring, job assignments, promotions, and firing procedures. As of 2020, the U.S. Supreme Court ruled that people in all states can seek recourse for discrimination based on RAI through the Federal Equal Employment Opportunity Commission. However, 16 states and 3 territories still do not have explicit state laws protecting RAIs (Movement Advancement Project (MAP), 2023). Therefore, individuals with marginalized RAIs may have to navigate confusing and contradictory legislation when dealing with employment-based discrimination.

In addition to workplace discrimination based on RAI, members of this population often have other marginalized identities, such as being people of color, younger or older, undocumented, and in a lower income bracket, which are associated with experiences of lower overall wellness (MAP & NLGBTQWC, 2018). Research has found that individuals with marginalized RAIs who *come out* in the workplace are more likely to experience discrimination (i.e., 33% vs. 25%; Sears & Mallory, 2011). This illustrates the need for this population to navigate whether to come out at work and potentially experience increased discrimination or remain discrete and experience mental distress. The coming out process for RAIs is not a one time isolated event, but often something they navigate *many times* throughout their lifespan, with a variety of different people, and in a variety of settings (e.g., home, work, school, community). This can cause continual stress and issues with broaching and safety—important components to consider when working with RAIs in counseling settings.

The mesosystem involves the interactions between and among people in the client's life. For example, the mesosystem might involve a parent and a teacher or a peer and another peer. These exchanges greatly influence well-being and sense of self. For example, if a client continues to see negative interactions within their family, this may impact their viewpoint of themselves and of the world, particularly their affectional, romantic, or sexual identities.

Exosystem and Macrosystem

The exosystem includes extended family and neighbors, government agencies, social services, and mass media. These formal and informal social structures may or may not directly impact the client but can affect their development. First, at the legislative level, bills continue to be introduced that impact diverse RAI safety and protections in the workplace, school, adoption and assisted reproduction, housing, public accommodations, and in the criminal justice system (MAP, 2023). These bills, even if not passed, demonstrate a strong heteronormative sentiment.

Another example of the exosystem in action is the role of popular culture and social media. Historically, RAIs have been censored and either not represented or represented stereotypically in media. In our current media-saturated culture, television and movies are ways for people to make meaning of their life experiences through representation (Reed, 2018). Therefore, the lack of representation and visibility of RAIs in the media negatively impacts the lived experiences of RAIs. Additionally, the internet and social media (e.g., Discord, Twitter, Instagram) impact the lives of those with nondominant RAI by providing a broad range of functions for exploration, connectedness, and acceptance, including increasing self-awareness, learning about and communicating with identity-based communities, finding comfort and acceptance, and facilitation of the coming out process (Harper et al., 2016). Concurrently, the internet can be a source of discrimination and bullying, contributing to poor mental and social health outcomes, leading students to feel unsafe and even skip school. Lack of representation in a variety of settings (e.g., media, within communities and schools, in literature, and in leadership roles) can lead to increased isolative feelings and a myriad of mental health concerns for RAIs.

The macrosystem refers to how sociocultural elements impact development and functioning. This includes many cultural factors, like social class, geographic location, race/ethnicity, gender, and overall ideologies of the culture in which the client lives. For example, those who live in rural areas may experience unique, increased discrimination compared to those who live in urban or suburban areas. This differs from the previous systems, as it does not attend to direct interactions but more so the world and culture in which clients live.

TABLE 15.5 Heteronormativity in Childhood and Adolescence

Examples of Microaggressions	Inclusive Language
Will you bring this home to your mom and dad?	*Will you bring this home to your parents/guardians/family/caretakers?*
Are you bringing a girl to the dance with you?	*Are you attending the dance with anyone?*
Who is the "man" in the relationship?	No suggested alternative. Avoid asking intrusive questions about RAI partnerships.
How can you be bisexual when you're dating a girl?	No suggested alternative. Avoid asking intrusive questions about RAI partnerships.
If you don't enjoy sexual experiences, you must have experienced abuse.	Do not assume allosexuality or other experiences. Be mindful of a continuum of asexual identities.

Chronosystem

The chronosystem refers to changes that occur over one's lifetime that influence development and functioning. These changes include typical childhood transitions and changes, nontypical environmental changes, and impactful historical events. It is important to be aware of how pervasive heteronormativity is in society. See Table 15.5 for examples of this in childhood and how you can reframe your language.

Until very recently, some mental health professionals used approaches aimed at changing or *converting* a client's RAI. It is recognized, professionally, that within affirmative therapy, any work to reorient or repair one's affectional, romantic, and/or sexual orientation (SOCE) in any way is ineffective and harmful.

Professional Counseling Practice Application

The Counseling Relationship

The counseling or therapeutic relationship is recognized as one of the most important factors for counseling success (e.g., Burlingame et al., 2018; Friedlander et al., 2018; Norcross & Lambert, 2018). Founded on congruence, unconditional positive regard, and empathic understanding (Rogers, 1957), the relationship is understood as a shared therapeutic factor across theoretical perspectives (Duncan, 2010). The counselor's goal of building a productive, comfortable therapeutic relationship must be approached from a variety of perspectives. Because the relationship begins before a client ever enters the session, counselors must be mindful of precounseling practices, such as marketing and client scheduling, through the formal counseling relationship toward curating and fortifying the relationship. Young (2021) articulated four *relationship enhancers* counselors can use. Table 15.6 illustrates these enhancers and their potential applications to individuals with diverse RAIs.

TABLE 15.6 Relationship Enhancers and RAI Application

Relationship Enhancer (Young, 2021)	RAI Application
Nonverbal skills such as physical closeness, posture, and warmth – in addition to in-session nonverbal skills, these can be applied via internet presence, voicemail greeting, email signature, office décor, lobby set-up and greeting, etc.	RAI-specific affirming artwork, literature in the waiting room, Pride flags, inclusive intake paperwork
Adapting to your client's unique characteristics – learn about and adjust your approach based on the qualities and identities of your client; consider systematizing how you gather information related to key areas (e.g., family/personal health/history; communication preferences/patterns) and identities (e.g., romantic, affectional, religious, ethnicity)	RAI-affirming and inclusive assessments, with nonheteronormative assumptions; use of more qualitative assessments to gather a holistic picture of the client (as RAI is just one part of their identity)
Presence – fully engage with the client during your time together by listening intently with full attention to be as present as possible	Using person-centered, affirmative and liberatory counseling principles
Empathy – work to experience and communicate an understanding of of your client's experience	Knowledge of historical and current anti-RAI social and political topics, barriers to access/treatments to better understand client experience

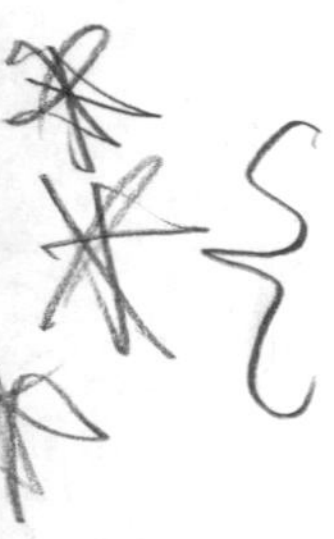

The importance of empathy cannot be overstated when working across RAIs. As counselors grow, they know it is not necessary to share circumstances or identities with a client to demonstrate empathy. As we are reminded by the tenets of intersectionality, we will never hold the same identity intersections as another individual—so we are *always* engaging in cross-cultural counseling. When confronted by identities or experiences with which you are not familiar, the aforementioned *relationship enhancers* will allow you to continue building the counseling relationship without necessitating specific familiarity with circumstances.

Further, counselors must consider queer oppression as it relates to human development, inclusive of identity development. The power dynamics inherent in the counseling relationship can lead clients to engage in high levels of *cultural concealment* (Drinane et al., 2018). The counselor can promote openness and honesty to help to mitigate cultural concealment. These efforts can be supported through active *broaching* (Day-Vines et al., 2020). By developing an integrated/congruent broaching orientation, counselors are equipped not only to address identity differences but to support clients in connecting their presenting issues with their cultural identities, as appropriate. This can deepen the application of relationship enhancers and minimize potential cultural miscommunications.

BOX 15.5 **PAUSE AND REFLECT: BROACHING SEXUALITY**

Am I ...

1. avoiding broaching with my clients?
2. defensive when asked about broaching by my supervisor?
3. using culturally appropriate interventions while broaching in a way that meets my client where they are?
4. recognizing and acknowledging the potential impact of RAI on clients presenting issues while broaching?
5. aware of my own biases and assumptions during the process of broaching?

Humanistic and Person-Centered Perspectives

The application of humanistic (e.g., Maslow, 1968) and person-centered (e.g., Rogers, 1957) perspectives to the practice of counseling with individuals who carry diverse RAIs is essential. Seeing clients as experts of their own lives and experiences is important for forming a strong therapeutic relationship. Additionally, a humanistic framework allows us to see our clients as holistic beings and to focus on strengths, empowerment, and growth. Goodrich et al. (2016) described the overlap of Queer Theory with tenets of humanism to guide culturally responsive practice with individuals of marginalized RAIs, including promoting self-exploration and holistic integration, validating all our clients' human potential, and decentering and deconstructing dominant cultural narratives. With a focus on the here and now, as well as the counseling relationship rather than pathology, these perspectives are positioned to offer the support and judgment-free environment that facilitates growth within and across diverse identities.

The Harm of SOCE

SOCE, also referred to as conversion therapy, reparative therapy, and sometimes ex-gay ministries, can include heterosexual-focused interventions, the use of shame for SGA, and even physical shock to "change" one's RAI. SOCE are extremely ineffective and harmful, and they can increase guilt, avoidance of intimacy, anxiety, depression, self-harm, and suicidality (Blosnich et al., 2020). As of 2023, only 20 states and DC have laws that ban SOCE for minors (Movement Advancement Project, 2023). SOCE are condemned as harmful practices by major health and medical professional organizations, as well as counseling organizations like the ACA. In 2017, ACA passed a resolution on reparative therapy/conversion therapy/SOCE as a significant and serious violation of the ACA *Code of Ethics* (ACA, 2017b).

MSJCC Application

The counseling relationship is inherently informed by intersectionality (Crenshaw, 1991), which helps to conceptualize the complex relationship of power, privilege, and oppression within and between individual identities and the distinct social locations where identities intersect. As illustrated by the MSJCC conceptual framework (Ratts et al., 2015), counselor self-awareness and client worldview are essential to the creation of a productive counseling relationship and the subsequent successful implementation of interventions. This is true regardless of the nature of privilege or marginalization of identities carried by either—and both—the counselor and the client. Further, the MSJCC requires that counselors invite clients to explore how their varied intersecting identities and associated oppression and/or privilege impact the counseling relationship. Similarly, counselors reflect upon and broach their own salient identities with clients. Counselors who avoid self-reflection or processing/broaching sexuality or RAI in sessions are doing their clients a disservice that is likely to lead to a weak or fractured therapeutic alliance.

We have discussed the significance and roles of self-awareness, client worldview, and the counseling relationship. With a foundation built by these formative developmental domains, a privileged or marginalized counselor is equipped to intervene and advocate on behalf of their privileged or marginalized client. Counselors must consider how the client is impacted at seven levels: intrapersonal processes, interpersonal processes, institutional inequities, community norms, values and regulations, public policy, and international and global events.

Resiliencies, Strengths, and Fostering Wellness

While people with marginalized identities can and do experience various types of oppression across contexts, they also forge resilience and strength—providing opportunities to foster wellness. While there are commonalities between the terms *strength* and *resilience,* they are distinct concepts. That distinction is illustrated by the ways in which each construct manifests within the queer community.

Resilience is an individual's ability to withstand or *bounce back* from adversity. It is a complex construct because of the responsibility placed on the individual to overcome challenges with which they are confronted based on their marginalized identities. Within that context, resilience develops uniquely based on the nature of an individual's challenges and, as such, is categorized by different constructs for different communities within the larger LGBTGEQIAP+ population. For example, Black queer communities find resilience through engagement in collectivism and activism, and in using their relationships for wellness (Mosley et al., 2021). Resilience for queer youth has been associated with peer-level social support (Lardier et al., 2020; McConnell et al., 2015), school-based LGBTQ support groups (Heck et al., 2011), school belongingness (Lardier et al., 2020), and positive media representations (Craig et al., 2015). More generally, researchers have found that those with marginalized identities may be better equipped to navigate their additional marginalized identities or marginalization based on their experience and understanding of challenges associated with such an identity (Parks et al., 2004; Schmitz & Tyler, 2019); This suggests that resilience may be sparked by the presence of multiple minoritized identities and has been seen within domains such as housing status (Schmitz & Tyler, 2019) and race (Parks et al., 2004; Singh et al., 2017), illustrating the strength-building properties of *positive* adaptation to adverse life experiences. Beyond resilience, queer identities have been found to foster unique strengths within community members. These include networks of support created by *families of choice*, general community connectedness with other queer-identified individuals

(Wardecker & Matsick, 2020), resource sharing, and collective action and advocacy (Hudson & Romanelli, 2020).

Empowered by awareness of the queer community's assets, services can be delivered in a way that is positioned to meet clients *where they are.* Counselors can support and fortify wellness in queer individuals through affirmative practice (Goodrich & Luke, 2016) that is grounded in attention to the sources of strength and resilience garnered from the queer community itself, such as fostering connectedness through queer communal spaces and group services or facilitating opportunities for activism through empowering queer clients to become engaged with their communities.

Ethical Code Application

In Chapter 2, you learned about the cultural relevance within our ethical imperatives as exemplified by applying the MSJCC (Ratts et al., 2015) to the major ethical codes guiding our profession (e.g., ACA, 2014; American Mental Health Counselors Association (AMHCA), 2020; ASCA, 2022; Commission on Rehabilitation Counselor Certification (CRCC), 2017; National Board for Certified Counselors (NBCC), 2016). Equipped with our understanding of the intimate relationship among our cultural and ethical responsibilities, we recognize that it is one thing to be aware of and know the codes as they exist *regardless* of cultural context, and it is another to possess the skills necessary to consider the codes *within* cultural context by applying your cultural awareness and knowledge. As ethical codes are contextually applied, note that most codes were constructed in an atheoretical and acontextual manner, guided only by our professional values and foundational ethical principles. As you will see in the following example, the application of ethical codes to situations involving RAI requires maintaining a keen awareness of queer oppression.

The ACA *Code of Ethics* (2014) addresses counselors' ethical responsibilities concerning confidentiality and privacy if clients were to disclose that they live with any disease commonly known to be communicable and to possess an elevated lethality potential if contracted (Section B.2.c.). Counselors must be mindful of the potentially problematic implications of applying this code without consideration of the history of how those with marginalized RAIs experienced maltreatment and neglect by many in the U.S. health-care system during the HIV/AIDS epidemic of the 1980s and '90s. Moreover, the code states that "counselors may be justified in disclosing information to identifiable third parties, if the parties are known to be at serious and foreseeable risk of contracting the disease" (ACA, 2014, p. 7). There are several factors that must be considered when formulating one's justification in this example, including the advancements in HIV/AIDS prevention and treatment that have markedly reduced disease transmission and mortality rates. If a client is HIV+ and reports they are informing any current and prospective romantic and affectional partners of their HIV+ status in accordance with any relevant laws, counselors may not be justified in disclosing information to such parties. Importantly, one must consult the laws pertaining to counselors' disclosure of clients' disease status, as any legal imperatives would need to be factored into the ethical decision-making process.

The intent of the prior example was to highlight that applying cultural context to ethical considerations involves not only awareness and knowledge of nondominant groups but also an understanding of the relevant current and historical power, privilege, and oppression dynamics.

Please note that this section is not designed to provide a comprehensive guide to applying ethical codes within the context of RAI and queer oppression. Rather, the intent is to serve as a primer to the innumerable ways we may apply our ethical codes within this chapter's cultural context while considering both counselors and clients from the perspective of their distinct social locations. For the remainder of this section, we will focus on the contextual application of relevant codes to a case vignette concerning our ethical and professional obligations when engaging in advocacy, seeking consultation, and pursuing continuing education.

Cases in Point: Tremaine and Julianne

Tremaine (he/him) and his family recently relocated from a major city where they had resided all of Tremaine's life to a predominantly White, rural community. Tremaine's stepmother, Shai (she/her), who is employed by a large health-care system whose main hospital is in the city, was recently promoted to nursing director of a satellite hospital located in this community. Shortly following the move, Tremaine began his senior year at the local high school, which would not be without its challenges. As a Black gay kid entering his senior year at a new school in a predominantly White rural community, Tremaine thought it was a recipe for disaster. As such, Tremaine decided he was going to keep to himself so as not to draw any unwanted attention and focus solely on his studies to see him off to college. Soon enough, one of his teachers, Madame Barrow (she/her), witnessed him sitting and eating alone in the hallway every day of the first semester during his lunch period. At the end of the semester, Mme. Barrow requested a parent-teacher conference with Tremaine's stepmother and father, Viktor (he/him). Mme. Barrow shared how pleased she was with Tremaine's stellar performance in her French class, as well as how concerned she was with Tremaine's lack of engagement with his peers. Upon the insistence of his parents following their conference with Mme. Barrow, Tremaine started attending weekly outpatient counseling sessions with Julianne (she/her) at the local community mental health agency.

During their most recent appointment, Tremaine informed Julianne that he was continuing to struggle with his family's recent move, as he had been looking forward to graduating alongside his childhood best friends, Rae (she/they) and Holly (she/her), as salutatorian of his former senior class. Julianne, who was keen on further assessing Tremaine's social isolation from all angles, inquired if Tremaine had ever experienced any bullying by other boys on account of having platonic friendships with girls. Tremaine disclosed to Julianne that he is gay, and, because of stereotypes, he assumed that guys at his old school expected these friendships of him and left him alone. For future reference, he thought it was important to add that Rae identifies as nonbinary, so Julianne is less likely to misgender them moving forward. At the end of the session, Julianne felt compelled to disclose that she has not worked with a gay, lesbian, or "transexual" client across the span of her 30-year career, but she enjoys working with him. Tremaine replied that his identity as gay is a source of pride for him, yet it is but one of many identities from which he derives a sense of pride. He added that it is likely Julianne worked with queer and trans clients who had decided not to come out to her, had not yet begun the process of disclosing their gender and/or RAI, or for some other valid reason. Julianne replied that any of those reasons would have been fine by her because she still had a lot to learn. She added that she is grateful to Tremaine for being such a good teacher because continuing education can be expensive, she joked. He hesitated to respond, opting for a strained smile and a slight nod.

Feeling a bit out of her depth, Julianne sought out her peer consultation group. When she presented her case conceptualization of Tremaine, Julianne found that her colleagues never had more questions for her than they had about this case. One of her group consultants suggested she consult with a counselor of a younger generation. As a result, Julianne consulted with one of her junior colleagues, who suggested that she consider contacting the nearby branch campus of a public university to schedule an agency-wide safe space training. Following the safe space training, Julianne's office was adorned with various pride flags, safe space stickers, and pronoun pins. At Tremaine's next appointment, Julianne was concerned and confused as she followed his gaze from flag to sticker to pin and repeat, with no eye contact to be had between them. Toward the end of their session, Tremaine shared with Julianne that although he appreciated her intention, all he felt he was to her was a gay person, especially considering that these items were not inclusive of folks of color. Though visibly shaken from Tremaine's perspective, Julianne gave an encouraging nod for him to continue as she suspected he had more to share. Tremaine told Julianne that he was unsure if they could proceed in their work together if she were to continue this surface-level display of being an ally. Julianne asked if Tremaine could explain what he meant by "surface-level display," as she was anticipating that he would be heartened to see the lengths that she and the agency had gone to increase their awareness and knowledge for him. Tremaine replied that he never asked for this.

Advocacy

As discussed in Chapter 2, counselors are directed by our ethics to engage in multi-level advocacy work on behalf of and alongside our clients. As it pertains to RAI, advocates seek to redress societal injustices and inequities, eliminate barriers and obstacles related to oppressive forces (e.g., homomisia, monosexism, heterosexism, heteronormativity, homonormativity), and expand access to affirmative, liberatory, and celebratory care (ACA, 2014, Section A.7.a.; AMHCA, 2020, Standard I.F.2. Introduction; CRCC, 2023, Section C. Introduction). While Julianne, upon the suggestion of her more novice colleague, engaged in a mesolevel advocacy intervention by holding a safe space training at her agency (Estrada et al., 2017), it is apparent based on Tremaine's reaction in session that she did not exercise cultural sensitivity regarding the potential impact of this undertaking, nor did she consider the potential negative ramifications of this effort, which we are called by the AMHCA (2020, Standard I.F.2.a.) to be aware of and avoid.

During the former session with Julianne, Tremaine made a point to share how he derives a sense of pride from many of his identities and not solely his identity as a gay person. Counselors would be wise to consider this an invitation from their clients to begin to explore their additional cultural identities and how they are experienced by clients both intrinsically (e.g., identity pride, internalized homomisia) and extrinsically (e.g., RAI-centered support networks, institutionalized heterosexism). Tremaine's statement highlights the need for Julianne to increase her cultural awareness and knowledge of the lived experiences of possessing multiple minoritized identities and the unique strengths and challenges that exist at their intersections.

Lastly, we want to refrain from placing the onus of responsibility of furthering our cultural awareness and knowledge of RAIs and queer oppression onto our clients. Tremaine, a member of multiple nondominant cultural groups (e.g., gay, Black), cannot and should not be expected to speak on behalf of identities for the purpose of educating Julianne, as this could reasonably be considered exploitative. Though the ethical codes do not explicitly name clients as among those with whom we are to avoid exploiting while engaged in a professional relationship (ACA, 2014, Section C.6.d.; AMHCA, 2020, Standard 3.A.1; CRCC, 2017, Section D.5.e.), the ethical principle of avoiding maleficence supports this interpretation.

Seeking Consultation

While consultation with colleagues to promote client welfare is appropriate and encouraged, consultees are directed to seek professionals who possess the requisite attitudinal awareness, knowledge, and skills to address the subject matter competently and authoritatively (NBCC, 2024, Directive 51). In the case of Tremaine and Julianne, it was evident that Julianne possessed a dearth of competence working with diverse RAIs, and she realized her lack of competence would present an issue for Tremaine's care and sprang into action by presenting her case to her peer consultation group. During consultation, though, Julianne realized that her consultants held a similarly low level of LGBQIA+ counseling competence.

Though she was eventually advised to consider safe space training by a younger agency colleague, it would have been appropriate to inquire if this colleague specialized in or had familiarity with counseling LGBQIA+ clients rather than presuming competence. A final consideration, to Julianne's credit, is even if she had first sought out an LGBQIA+ competent consultant, metanalytic data on health care for RAIs in rural communities (see Rosenkrantz et al., 2017) suggest it is unlikely such a professional would be readily available for her to consult. In this case, it would likely serve Julianne well to search electronic professional membership directories such as ACA or SAIGE to assist her in locating an appropriate consultant. Some membership directories highlight members' specialty areas (e.g., LGBQIA+), indicate their interest in peer consultation or supervision, and specify whether other members have permission to contact them.

Pursuing Continuing Education

A constant across various counselor specializations is recognizing the need for continuing education to keep current on the clinical, scholarly, ethical, and cultural advancements and trends within their area of professional concentration (ACA, 2014, Section C.2.f.; AMHCA, 2020, Standard I.C.1.n.; ASCA, 2022, Standard B.3.e.; CRCC, 2017, Section D.1.f.). In most, if not all, cases, the accrual of a minimum amount of approved general and specialized (e.g., focused on diversity, ethics, supervision) continuing education is required to renew one's counseling license and/or certification. The importance of continuing education when working with diverse RAIs cannot be overemphasized, especially for more seasoned counselors, like Julianne, who were trained in counseling graduate programs several decades prior to the establishment and curricular infusion of LGBQIA+ counseling competencies (see Association for Lesbian, Gay, Bisexual, and Transgender Issues in Counseling (ALGBTIC), 2003; ALGBTIC LGBQQIA Competencies Taskforce, 2013).

Since the publication of the last iteration of the competencies a decade ago, the lexicon surrounding RAI has continued to evolve to such an extent that revision will require quite an undertaking, which suggests that even the most LGBQIA+ competent among us must be diligent in seeking continuing education opportunities. In 2016, the Council of the District of Columbia enacted the *LGBTQ Cultural Competency Continuing Education Amendment Act*, which requires any health professional licensed or certified in Washington, DC, to obtain continuing education to further their LGBTQ+ cultural competence. While it is our hope that more credentialing bodies will follow their example in requiring LGBQIA+ continuing education, it is important to highlight the distinction between safe space training and continuing education. Julianne's pursuit of safe space training likely resulted in a more aesthetically welcoming environment for those with marginalized RAIs as well as a generally more aware clinical and administrative staff, which have merit; however, safe space trainings are, in most cases, not approved as continuing education for counselors, as their content is intended to be broadly applicable and generalizable across settings. In light of this, many counselors will seek out LGBQIA+ continuing education opportunities by contacting their state's licensing authority, which is the entity most often responsible for approving continuing education programs, as well as relevant professional counseling organizations (e.g., ACA, Association for Multicultural Counseling and Development [AMCD], Counselors for Social Justice (CSJ), SAIGE). An example of areas to expand one's understanding is to know days of importance for clients with diverse RAIs.

TABLE 15.7 Days of Importance Clients With Diverse RAIs

January	
third week	No Name-Calling Day
February	
week after 14th	Aromantic Awareness Week
7th	National Black HIV/AIDS Awareness Day
28th	HIV Is Not a Crime Awareness Day
March	
full month	Bisexual Health Awareness Month
varies	National LGBT Health Awareness Week
10th	National Women and Girls HIV/AIDS Awareness Day
20th	National Native HIV/AIDS Awareness Day
31st	International Transgender Day of Visibility (TDOV)
April	
varies	Day of Silence
6th	International Asexuality Day
10th	National Youth HIV/AIDS Awareness Day
18th	National Transgender HIV Testing Day
18th	Nonbinary Parents Day
26th	Lesbian Visibility Day

(Continued)

TABLE 15.7 *(Continued)*

May	
17th	International Day Against Homophobia, Transphobia and Biphobia
18th	World AIDS Vaccine Day
19th	National Asian and Pacific Islander HIV/AIDS Awareness Day
22nd	Harvey Milk Day
24th	Pansexual and Panromantic Visibility Day
June	
full month	LGBTQA+ Pride Month (United States)
1st	LGBTQ Families Day
12th	Pulse Nightclub Remembrance
26th	LGBT Equality Day/Anniversary of Same-Sex Marriage Legalization in the United States
27th	National HIV Testing Day
28th	Stonewall Riots Anniversary
30th	Queer Youth of Faith Day
July	
14th–21st	Nonbinary Awareness Week
14th	International Nonbinary People's Day
16th	International Drag Day
August	
14th	Gay Uncles Day
20th	Southern HIV/AIDS Awareness Day
September	
18th	National HIV/AIDS and Aging Awareness Day
23rd	Celebrate Bisexuality Day, followed by Bisexual Awareness Week
27th	National Gay Men's HIV/AIDS Awareness Day
October	
full month	LGBTQ History Month
3rd Wednesday	International Pronouns Day
3rd Thursday	Spirit Day
8th	International Lesbian Day
11th	National Coming Out Day
15th	National Latinx HIV/AIDS Awareness Day
19th	National LGBT Center Awareness Day
22nd–28th	Asexual Awareness Week
26th	Intersex Awareness Day
November	
1st Sunday	Transgender Parent Day
8th	Intersex Solidarity Day
13th–19th	Transgender Awareness Week
20th	International Transgender Day of Remembrance

December	
1st	World AIDS Day
8th	Pansexual/Panromantic Pride Day
10th	Human Rights Day
14th	HIV Cure Research Day

(GLAAD; n.d.; University of Nebraska-Lincoln, 2023; Wright State University, 2023)

Conclusion

As we conclude this chapter, we summarize several of the foundational elements of working with individuals with marginalized RAIs. Using the tripart model of multicultural and social justice counseling (Ratts et al., 2016), counselors must explore their attitudes and beliefs. Remember, language is important. It is important to recognize the constant flux and development of language and identity terminology. It is equally important to remember that you should use the language of the client. If you make a mistake in your language, or incorrectly address your client, simply apologize and move forward in the session. Continue to learn from your mistakes and seek consultation and supervision. It is our sincere hope that this chapter better informs your work with the range of RAIs in counseling. We hope you better understand the historical context of queer oppression, can better define concepts and critical terms, can better interpret contextual implications among diverse identities, and can apply foundational concepts to the professional practice of counseling, including ethical, affirmative, and liberatory counseling principles.

Questions for Reflection

Consider what you learned in this chapter as you respond to the questions and prompts below.

Counselors and counselors-in-training reflect upon our own biases, values, and worldviews throughout the counseling process with RAIs. Below are some questions for reflection (Ausloos & Salpietro, 2022).

1. When did I first become aware of my affectional/romantic/sexual identity?
2. What do I first remember about experiencing attraction (if any) and expressing it (if at all)?
3. What are my earliest memories of adhering or not adhering to heteronormative roles in society?
4. How might my perceptions of my and others' affectional/romantic/sexual identities be influenced by my upbringing, parents/guardians/caregivers, and family?
5. How might my perceptions of my RAI be influenced by my social history, friends, religious/spiritual affiliation, and, if applicable, romantic partners?
6. How do other cultural factors (e.g., race/ethnicity, age, ability/disability status) influence the privilege, power, and oppression I experience because of my RAI?

7. Do I know nondominant RAI people in my personal or professional life? How do I perceive them and engage with them?
8. How can I continue to work on my own biases and prejudices throughout my life? Professional career?

Applying What You Have Learned

Complete each of the following activities, considering what you learned from this chapter.

Activity #1: Advocacy and SOCE

SOCE is recognized as harmful and ineffective, yet as of 2023, only 20 states and DC have laws that ban SOCE for minors. Why do you think there has been resistance or delay in more states adopting these bans despite the stance of major health and counseling organizations? What can counselors do to advocate against the use of SOCE and for more protective legislation? With a peer or small group, identify where your own state stands. Draft a letter to representatives regarding the harm of SOCE.

Activity #2: Accessing Empathy

Considering the importance of the counseling relationship and the role of empathy in it, discuss the challenges counselors might face when counseling across RAI differences, especially when they do not share the same identities or experiences with their clients. How can the relationship enhancers presented in the chapter help counselors navigate these challenges? Share an example from your own experience or hypothetical scenario to illustrate your points. How might a counselor use these in a session?

Credits

Fig. 15.1a: Copyright © by Gryffindor (CC BY 3.0) at https://commons.wikimedia.org/wiki/File:Stonewall_Inn_New_York_001.JPG.

Fig. 15.1b: NIH History Office, https://commons.wikimedia.org/wiki/File:ACT_UP_Demonstration_at_NIH_(14336262776).jpg, 1999.

Fig. 15.1c: Copyright © by Images Alight (CC BY 2.0) at https://commons.wikimedia.org/wiki/File:Ellen_DeGeneres_(210976072).jpg.

Fig. 15.1d: Copyright © by Nancy Pelosi (CC BY 2.0) at https://commons.wikimedia.org/wiki/File:Don%27t_Ask,_Don%27t_Tell_Repeal_Act_of_2010_(5283984750).jpg.

Fig. 15.1e: White House, https://commons.wikimedia.org/wiki/File:President_Biden_signed_the_%22Respect_for_Marriage_Act%22_into_law.jpg, 2022.

Fig. 15.2: Adapted from Movement Advancement Project, https://www.lgbtmap.org/equality-maps.

Fig. 15.2a: Copyright © 2020 Depositphotos/kyryloff.

CHAPTER 16

Spirituality, Religion, and Religious Persecution

Erik Braun, Christie Nelson, and Tabitha Fabin

> *If Jesus, Buddha, and Confucius were all alive and gathered in the same place, would they argue over who is right? Or would they respect and admire one another's teachings?*
>
> —Haemin Sunim

CHAPTER OVERVIEW

Spirituality and religion are aspects of culture that all counselors must be well-versed in to be effective and culturally relevant (Young et al., 2007). Religion and spirituality (R/S) are sometimes intertwined with specific ethnic groups, such as Judaism, which is both a religion and an ethnic identity. R/S can heavily influence one's values and worldview, so R/S can impact how counselors express empathy, demonstrate care, and even their level of engagement with clients of diverse R/S backgrounds. The *World Population Review* (2023) estimates that there are between 4,000 and 4,300 different R/S groups worldwide. This highlights the need for counselors to understand the diversity of R/S groups, as it is inevitable that they will encounter R/S diversity within the communities they serve. Like other aspects of culture, counselors cannot simply ignore clients' spirituality or religion and deem it a topic not to be discussed; to do so may alienate or even harm clients. Counselors are encouraged to discuss spirituality/religion with their clients, as it can be an important part of individual and group identity, and for many clients, it is a source of community, comfort, coping, and healing. In this chapter, we define terms and concepts and offer a brief overview of the world's religions and spiritual identities. We explore religious persecution and the oppression clients with nondominant identities may experience, as well as how to engage in advocacy actions. Finally, we discuss how to incorporate spiritually based interventions into counseling practice and integrate knowledge about R/S into one's developing cultural skill set.

LEARNING OBJECTIVES

By the end of this chapter, students will be able to

1. articulate concepts and theoretical models relevant to spirituality and religion,
2. use awareness of the ecological and sociopolitical contexts of spiritual and religious identities to discuss the privilege and oppression related to these identities,
3. explore the lived experiences and paths of counselors in the field regarding spirituality and religion,
4. apply awareness of how religious and spiritual differences affect the counseling dynamic and relationship,

5. apply techniques related to spirituality and religion to the practice of counseling diverse populations in a multicultural society, and
6. become prepared to respond to legal and ethical issues related to religion and spirituality in the field of counseling.

CACREP 2016 STANDARDS

The information in this chapter supports the following standards:

- 2.F.2.a multicultural and pluralistic characteristics within and among diverse groups nationally and internationally
- 2.F.2.b theories and models of multicultural counseling, cultural identity development, and social justice and advocacy
- 2.F.2.c multicultural counseling competencies
- 2.F.2.d the impact of heritage, attitudes, beliefs, understandings, and acculturative experiences on an individual's views of others
- 2.F.2.e the effects of power and privilege for counselors and clients
- 2.F.2.f help-seeking behaviors of diverse clients
- 2.F.2.g the impact of spiritual beliefs on clients' and counselors' worldviews
- 2.F.2.h strategies for identifying and eliminating barriers, prejudices, and processes of intentional and unintentional oppression and discrimination
- 2.F.3.i ethical and culturally relevant strategies for promoting resilience and optimum development and wellness across the lifespan
- 2.F.5.d ethical and culturally relevant strategies for establishing and maintaining in-person and technology-assisted relationships

CACREP 2024 STANDARDS

The information in this chapter supports the following standards:

- 3.B.1. theories and models of multicultural counseling, social justice, and advocacy
- 3.B.2. the influence of heritage, cultural identities, attitudes, values, beliefs, understandings, within-group differences, and acculturative experiences on individuals' worldviews
- 3.B.3. the influence of heritage, cultural identities, attitudes, values, beliefs, understandings, within-group differences, and acculturative experiences on help-seeking and coping behaviors
- 3.B.4. the effects of historical events, multigenerational trauma, and current issues on diverse cultural groups in the U.S. and globally
- 3.B.5. the effects of stereotypes, overt and covert discrimination, racism, power, oppression, privilege, marginalization, microaggressions, and violence on counselors and clients
- 3.B.6. the effects of various socio-cultural influences, including public policies, social movements, and cultural values, on mental and physical health and wellness
- 3.B.9. strategies for identifying and eliminating barriers, prejudices, and processes of intentional and unintentional oppression and discrimination
- 3.B.10. guidelines developed by professional counseling organizations related to social justice, advocacy, and working with individuals with diverse cultural identities
- 3.B.11. the role of religion and spirituality in clients' and counselors' psychological functioning
- 3.C.7. models of resilience, optimal development, and wellness in individuals and families across the lifespan

- 3.E.6. ethical and legal issues relevant to establishing and maintaining counseling relationships across service delivery modalities
- 3.E.7. culturally sustaining and responsive strategies for establishing and maintaining counseling relationships across service delivery modalities

Distinguishing Religion and Spirituality

In this chapter, two important terms are used throughout: *religion* and *spirituality*. These two terms are similar but not interchangeable. In this chapter, the authors will refer to both at the same time by saying *religion/spirituality* or *R/S* when the topic applies to both. However, it is important to understand the differences between these concepts. Religion refers to the organized communal aspects and social practices in which people practice spirituality together beneath a given ideological framework (Geertsma & Cummings, 2004). Religion applies to activities such as attending group meetings (e.g., weekly religious services, studying religious texts as a group), studying to become a spiritual leader, going on a mission trip, or participating in religious-based rituals. Spirituality refers to the personal and individual aspect of working toward enlightenment or some approximation of enrichment, fulfillment, and/or meaning making (Geertsma & Cummings, 2004). Spiritual practices can be part of organized religious practices yet can and may be practiced separately and outside the auspices of religion.

For those who identify as spiritual, some may believe in some form of a Higher Power and/or divinity, while others may not. However, even atheists, agnostics, and existentialists who may not believe in a Higher Power may still consider themselves spiritual people. For example, a person who identifies as an atheist may not believe in divine forces or beings but may be committed to self-improvement and mindfulness through practices such as yoga, meditation, and/or martial arts, all of which can have spiritual aspects to them. Conversely, someone who practices meditation, attempting to gain control over their mind and find inner peace, may or may not associate their practices with spiritual beliefs.

Some individuals may believe in *forces* that cannot be explained by science and may or may not believe that these forces are sacred or divine—they are simply unexplainable. However, whether the person identifies as spiritual based on these beliefs varies from person to person. It might be clear that they are not religious because they do not have any formalized social practices or rituals related to their beliefs, yet nonetheless, this is the individual's way of understanding the universe.

Another important term is *worldview*, which refers to one's ideas about how life and/or the universe works, their estimation of the best way to approach life, and their values. This may or may not be associated with religion and/or spirituality, but certainly has some bearing on the individual's view of morality and ethics. For example, someone who is a devout Catholic will likely have approaches to life and sense of self that differ from, say, someone who practices Zen Buddhism. Additionally, one's worldview may be *secular* rather than *sacred* (or vice versa!)—that is, instead of being influenced by R/S, their worldview may be shaped by specific philosophies such as existentialism or stoicism. Everything from career decisions to opinions on political issues can be influenced by the individual's religion and/or spirituality, and the word *worldview* refers to that influence. As counselors, it is our job to understand the client's worldview without judgment and to incorporate it consistently into the counseling process.

Spiritual Well-Being

Culturally relevant counselors understand how the client's spiritual or religious worldview influences them—positively, negatively, and everything in between. R/S worldviews are connected to overall well-being and play a role in various aspects of wellness (Fatima et al., 2018). In a general sense, spiritual well-being is connected to well-being dimensions such as physical, psychological, intellectual, emotional, social, and vocational wellness. Spiritual well-being can be conceptualized with two factors: *religious well-being* (RWB) and *existential well-being* (EWB). Ellison (1983) described RWB as an individual's feeling of connectedness to God. An extended version of this term, to go beyond a Judeo-Christian lens, can include cosmic energies, higher powers, mindfulness practices, folk practices, and other spiritual beliefs that are not necessarily related to the concept of a God, gods, or deities. For example, there are people who may not believe in a god yet believe in communicating with deceased relatives or ancestors. As such, RWB can refer to a connectedness with divinity and/or spiritual practices.

EWB refers to the individual's life satisfaction and sense of purpose and meaning. EWB, like RWB, is connected to all aspects of well-being but can be strongly connected to vocation for some people and therefore is especially relevant in the realm of career counseling (Ellison, 1983). When an individual's job is aligned with their personal sense of purpose, work/career can be a source of joy in one's daily life and help ease one's suffering. For example, imagine having a job that paid extremely well, but your boss and the company made decisions that you found morally reprehensible. You might feel like you were contributing to and aiding such behavior as a result of your employment, and you might be able to imagine how keeping that job might come at the expense of your psychosocial well-being. Compare that to working for a company that pays a livable yet modest wage, but you whole-heartedly believe in the company's morals and ethics; perhaps it is a nonprofit that contributes something positive to society. You can imagine how this job, while it might not pay as much, could feel a lot better in some ways than the other higher paying job. If you keep the high-paying job, you might feel conflicted and perhaps your self-esteem might decrease because of the incongruity you feel. With a lower paying job, while it might be more challenging to pay bills, the sense of purpose might make it worth it.

Morals and Values

Two additional factors to consider are morals and values. Morals are one's beliefs about right and wrong, while values represent one's standards and behaviors related to their morals. Morals and values often develop from religious and/or spiritual belief systems, and are shaped by family of origin, lived experiences, and personal exploration.

Some people's morals dictate that there are clear lines between good and evil, which can potentially make decision-making quite straightforward. One could imagine that those who are highly religious might view morality this way because their religion defines their morals and values. You might notice both advantages and disadvantages to this view. One advantage is that decisions are clear and purely driven by deeply held beliefs rooted in religious teachings; however, this view can result in oversimplifying issues that are more complex and missing important contextual nuances.

Others believe that the difference between good and evil is murkier and that there is some good and some evil in nearly every action. This belief can make decision-making more challenging. This view might resonate with those who lean more toward the spiritual side of the spectrum. This latter view aligns with the case Albert Ellis (2005) made in his book, *The Myth of Self-Esteem*, in which he asserted that all decisions individuals make are inherently nuanced and that trying to calculate the *goodness* or *badness* is impossible and a path to misery. This view comes with both advantages and disadvantages as well. An advantage may be the ability to navigate more complex dilemmas with nuance, while a disadvantage may be possible indecision, leading to failure to take a strong stance when one is required.

> BOX 16.1 **PAUSE AND REFLECT: THE SOURCE OF *YOUR* CORE VALUES**
>
> Spiritual and religious backgrounds can have a great influence on the morals and values of an individual. If you had to choose three core values, what would they be? How do they connect to your religious and/or spiritual identity? How might these differ within the populations you serve?

Understanding the Historical Context of Religion and Spirituality in Counseling

Prior to 1940, psychodynamic approaches were considered the standard for counseling and therapeutic methods were drawn from the ideas of psychoanalysts, such as Sigmund Freud and Carl Jung (Lovinger, 1984). Freud was not accepting of religion, and as a result, anti-religious notions were present in psychotherapy for decades. Clinicians avoided therapeutic content involving religion in favor of more scientific thinking (Gockel, 2011). However, in the 1940s, existential therapy arose, which provided a space for counselors to include discussions of a more spiritual nature, such as one's place in the universe, transcendence, and meaning making to address emotional well-being.

Viktor Frankl

Viktor Frankl, a Jewish neurologist and psychiatrist born in 1905 in Austria, suffered extreme religious persecution and unspeakable acts at the hands of the Nazis during World War II. In 1942, Frankl and his family were imprisoned in a concentration camp; only he and his sister survived. Because of his medical background, he was assigned to help new arrivals assimilate to the conditions of the camp and established a special suicide unit. From his personal experiences and witnessing the experiences of others, he drew several conclusions regarding the nature of suffering within a psychological and spiritual context.

IMG 16.1. Viktor Frankl

Frankl determined that even while experiencing severe suffering, one's psychological reactions are based on the freedom of choice they have and hope in the future. He believed that one survives such brutal environments because of a spiritual self: a province of inner freedom that persists despite all conditions, without which one is doomed. According to Frankl, even in the most horrific and dehumanizing environments, life is still meaningful, and therefore, suffering is meaningful too. This conclusion served as the foundation for his therapeutic approach, logotherapy, which he describes in his book, *Man's Search for Meaning* (Frankl, 1946). Humans' primary motivation is their *will to make meaning* or their desire to find meaning in life and that life is unconditionally meaningful, no matter what happens.

Existential thinkers such as Frankl and Rollo May in *The Art of Counseling* (1939) offered a humanistic view of the human condition as an alternative to psychoanalytic approaches. Humanism posits that people are inherently able to address their internal needs and make appropriate changes when given the space and freedom to do so. Building upon the early existential thinkers, Carl Rogers (1951) took humanism a step further and developed person-centered therapy, which looked at the whole person through a phenomenological and value-neutral lens.

Other influential thinkers like Joseph Wolpe (1958) and Benson and Klipper (1975) made significant contributions to the field by introducing Eastern spiritual practices and incorporating practices such as yoga, meditation, and alternative healing modalities into counseling. Benson and Klipper published the *Relaxation Response* (1975) after conducting research on practitioners of Transcendental Meditation, popularizing ancient Indian forms of spiritual wisdom-seeking as a method of reducing autonomic arousal, lowering blood pressure, and improving well-being. With these spiritual practices part of the zeitgeist, counselors were given permission to integrate spiritually related practices into counseling (Worthington & Sandage, 2002). However, the argument can be made that the use of the tools from Eastern religions could be cultural appropriation if used by clinicians of other cultural backgrounds who do not hold these spiritual beliefs.

Later in the 1970s, *eclecticism* or an integrated approach to counseling arose, making it more acceptable for counselors to incorporate spirituality into sessions with client consent. There was an increased demand for spiritually oriented interventions and for counselors who could address such needs. At this time, clergy did most of the counseling involving R/S matters, and most of the research relied on Christian samples only (Worthington & Sandage, 2002). By the 1980s, there was an increase in published articles related to spirituality and counseling. Notably, Bergin (1980) published an article calling for a more systematic approach to incorporating spirituality into the field of mental health and for counselors to be more open to discussing spirituality within counseling and therapeutic settings.

The mindfulness movement began gaining momentum in the 1990s, drawing on Eastern philosophy and spirituality. Secular counseling integrated more spirituality-based concerns while remaining largely nonreligious. Clients began to feel more comfortable asking for religiously focused approaches, and there was a greater demand for them (Worthington & Sandage, 2002). There were several major books published, which signaled that integrating both R/S into counseling was becoming mainstream (Miller, 1999; Richards & Bergin, 1997; Shafranske, 1996). By the 2000s, R/S were more common in clinical practice, and some practices partnered with churches to help reduce costs, with the church subsidizing some of the cost for the client (Worthington &

Sandage, 2002). The United States has continued to become more religiously and spiritually diverse, so counselors must be well-versed in therapeutic approaches that include and reach beyond Judeo-Christian perspectives to best meet client needs.

Major Religious and Spiritual Belief Systems

A culturally attuned counselor can describe the similarities and differences between spirituality and religion and knows the basic tenets of various spiritual systems and major world religions (ASERVIC, 2009). Religious and spiritual practices go as far back as human civilization; one of the earliest known ceremonial burial grounds was discovered in the Middle East, dating back to 100,000 BCE (Pettitt, 2010). While it is beyond the scope of this chapter to provide a detailed account of all religious and spiritual beliefs, an overview of the common religious and spiritual groups and practices provides you with helpful information to become oriented to the major world religions. It is important to recognize that the descriptions we offer are general and it will benefit you to engage in further research. No R/S background is a monolith, as all individuals are different. The descriptions here are simply typical commonalities for people who identify with each of these groups. No description can accurately account for all individual differences within groups, so client accounts of their experiences with their faith will be the most useful when integrating R/S into counseling with specific clients.

Christianity

There are at least 99 Christian denominations present in the United States under the umbrellas of Roman Catholicism, Eastern Orthodoxy, and Protestantism (PRC, 2022). Because of the many denominations, there is a broad range of beliefs and practices within Christianity, yet people who are Christian hold a number of beliefs and practices in common. Christianity is monotheistic, yet most Christians believe in the Holy Trinity: the Father, Son, and Holy Spirit. Christians tend to believe that God created the universe and that Jesus Christ is His son, who is both human and divine. Jesus Christ is said to be without sin, and he suffered crucifixion so that humanity

TABLE 16.1 Major Religious Categories and Estimated Number of Followers Pew Research Center (PRC, 2022)

Christianity	2.38 billion
Islam	1.91 billion
Unaffiliated	1.19 billion
Hinduism	1.16 billion
Buddhism	507 million
Indigenous Religions (e.g., African traditional, Native American, Chinese folk)	430 million
Other Religions (e.g., Taoism, Sikhism, Wicca)	61 million
Judaism	14.6 million

Source: Pew Research Center, "Religious Composition by Country, 2010-2050," https://www.pewresearch.org/religion/interactives/religious-composition-by-country-2010-2050/.

could be forgiven for their sins (Cashwell & Young, 2011). The sacred text within Christianity is the Bible, which is made up of a collection of 66 books. Depending on the sect of Christianity a client belongs to, they will understand the Bible in different ways, ranging from believing that the Bible is the inerrant word of God to it being a document written by multiple authors that must be interpreted. Additionally, Christian values can range from conservative to progressive to very liberal, and this can transfer to political views, though not necessarily. Protestant Christianity is the dominant religious identity group in the United States and experiences the power and privilege associated with that sociocultural designation.

Judaism

Judaism is a monotheistic religion. One of the core beliefs of Judaism is that there is an all-powerful, omniscient God who created the universe and continues to rule over it. In Judaism, it is also believed that the Jewish people were chosen by God. As they believe themselves to be recipients of divine law, people of the Jewish faith see it as their responsibility to act as an example of moral living (Morrison & Brown, 1991). Judaism is rich in tradition and rituals. Some of the most notable of these practices include *keeping kosher* (not eating certain animals that are considered unclean) and observing the sabbath (a day of rest and reflection each week). The Torah is the main sacred text of Judaism, but there is also the Talmud, which includes writings that explain the Torah, and the Midrash, which includes rabbinical sermons. As with Christianity, there is not just one version of Judaism. Orthodox, Conservative, and Reform are the three major types of Judaism, all of which hold varying worldviews ranging from conservative to progressive. Additionally, some may identify as being religiously Jewish while others may only identify as being culturally Jewish. Another important consideration for counselors when working with clients who identify as Jewish is that they may have ancestors who survived the Holocaust. As such, they may be experiencing generational trauma or current trauma based on anti-Semitic rhetoric that the Holocaust did not occur. Anti-Semitism, or the hatred of Jewish people, hit an all-time high in 2021 and has not decreased since that time (Associated Press, 2023; more on anti-Semitism later in the chapter). Counselors must acknowledge the historic and current prejudice and discrimination Jewish people experience and be prepared to support and advocate for their rights.

Islam

People of the Islamic faith believe that Allah is the one true God and that Muhammad is His messenger. Individuals who identify with Islam are referred to as *Muslim*, and their connection to Islam, much like those who are Jewish, can be religious and/or cultural. The Five Pillars are the foundation of Islamic practice. *Shahada* is the declaration of the belief in the divine unity of Allah as the one and only God. *Salah* is the ritual prayer in which the *Shahada* is repeated five times every day. *Zakat* is giving a portion of one's wealth to those in need. *Sawm* refers to fasting during the Holy month of Ramadan. *Hajj* is done at least once in a person's lifetime if it is within their means to do so, and it is a sacred pilgrimage to the sacred site called Mecca (Al-Azhari, 2023). There are two sacred texts within Islam: the Qur'an and the Sunna. The Qur'an is considered the infallible word of Allah, whereas the Sunna contains the teachings and traditions of the Prophet Muhammad (Rahman, 1993). One of the most important considerations with regard to working with people who identify as Muslim in the United States is the likelihood that they, their families, and/or community members have experienced Islamomisia and/or discrimination. Since the terrorist attacks on September 11, 2001, Muslim people in United States have been stereotyped and targeted as extremists and terrorists. The presence of this discrimination, more than 20 years since September 11, may act as a major barrier for people who are Muslim in navigating through life in the United States (Aljazeera, 2022; more on Islamomisia later in the chapter). Like with clients of the Jewish faith, counselors who work with Muslim clients need to be prepared to acknowledge their realities and provide support and advocacy to increase their quality of life and their ability to move freely without fear and violence.

Hinduism

Hinduism is a polytheistic religion with three deities at its core: Brahma, Shiva, and Vishnu. *Puja* refers to the daily worship of these deities, often through offerings of incense, food, flowers, or other small gifts (Cashwell & Young, 2011). In Hinduism, *karma* is an important concept. *Karma* is a relationship between cause and effect and is shared by those who follow Buddhism. Actions done with a peaceful and loving intention will yield peaceful energy back, while actions done with anger and spite may have less pleasant returns (Cassaniti, 2015). Another important concept in Hinduism is that one's physical and mental body is reincarnated in subsequent lives. Hinduism proposes that there are multiple paths or *yoga* that one can take in life. It is common for people who practice Hinduism to refrain from eating meat, especially beef, out of a sacred reverence for cattle. The sacred texts of Hinduism include the Ramayana, the Mahabarata, the Upanishads, and the Puranas. An important consideration is that an estimated 72% of people in the United States who are Indian American identify at least partly as Hindu. Nikalje and Çiftçi (2023) discussed that many people who are Indian American experience internalized cultural shame and colonization mentality (i.e., seeing one's own culture as inferior to the culture of the colonizers) because of the British colonization of India. Results from Nikalje and Çiftçi's (2023) study on colonization mentality with Indian American participants ($N = 198$) indicated that cultural shame was higher in non-Hindu-identifying participants than in the Hindu-identifying group. This may suggest that those who identify as Hindu may draw from their R/S as a source of resilience.

Buddhism

Buddhism shares a number of beliefs with Hinduism, particularly the concepts of *karma* and reincarnation. However, Buddhism is not attached to any particular God or deity. Instead, Siddhartha, a human who ruled as an emperor, imprisoned from the outside world, is the central figure. When Siddhartha came of age, eventually, he was able to venture out to learn about the world. After learning of the world's suffering, he experimented with different ways of living and achieved enlightenment or *nirvana*. Buddhism is based on his teachings, which were passed down through oral tradition, and outlined an eightfold path to enlightenment: Right understanding, right thought, right speech, right action, right livelihood, right effort, right mindfulness, and right concentration. To reach enlightenment is to end one's suffering forever. Meditation is an important tool for those who follow

Buddhism, as it contributes significantly to the eightfold path that leads to enlightenment. Lee and Tang (2023) developed the *note, know, choose* model as a three-phase psychospiritual treatment approach based on Buddhist teachings to train the mind in a way that may help clients who are Buddhist in their eightfold path toward enlightenment. Because many aspects of Buddhism are deemed *acceptable* by other U.S. religious groups, and perhaps because Buddhism is not tied to a specific God or deity, people who practice Buddhism in the United States have not been subjected to the same kind of hate speech and discrimination as people who are Jewish or Muslim have.

The Religiously Unaffiliated

Of those who identify as religiously unaffiliated, there are three distinct subgroups: atheists, agnostics, and no religion (PRC, 2014). As of 2014 estimates, about 12% of the unaffiliated describe themselves as atheist, 17% as agnostic, and 71% describe their religion as nothing in particular. The religiously unaffiliated are an important group to understand, as they are the second largest group in the United States at an estimated 22%.

Atheism refers to a belief that there are no gods nor divine entities. Some atheists may believe in energies in the universe, but they are unlikely to describe them as a divine force or by the name god (Coleman et al., 2018). Agnosticism is defined as not knowing whether a god or a divine entity exists. Typically, a person who is agnostic believes either that humans are not capable of knowing whether a god or divine entities exist or that knowledge related to cosmic mysteries is not important enough to pursue (Coleman et al., 2018). Individuals in these three categories often have experiences that make them feel like *outsiders* in their communities, particularly in U.S. regions with high religiosity. While they may not experience hate crimes and discrimination as people who are Jewish or Muslim do, microaggressions and *othering* are common. As such, it is important for counselors to understand clients' atheist, agnostic, or nonreligious worldviews without bias and to incorporate their individualized meaning-making processes into the counseling process.

Religious Trauma

Some people grow up with interpretations of R/S traditions that are abusive or traumatic. This is called religious trauma. Religious trauma can come from being part of a cult, or it can be a result of religious extremism in their family of origin. Cults have been loosely defined and difficult to distinguish clearly. For the purposes of this chapter, the word *cult* refers to *groups of psychological abuse* grounded in religious principles (Castaño et al., 2022).

Key Features of Cults

Castaño et al. (2022) stated that some features of a cult can include the following:

- Isolation from people outside of the cult
- Working toward a common goal with no regard for members' wellness
- Excessive devotion to the movement and/or leader

For example, one organization that fits the definition of a cult is the ***Fundamentalist*** Church of Jesus Christ of Latter-day Saints (FLDS), not to be confused with the Church of Jesus Christ of Latter-day Saints (LDS) from which the FLDS was excommunicated because the FLDS still endorses the practice of polygamy, which has not aligned with LDS values since 1890 (the Church of Jesus Christ of Latter-day Saints, n.d.). The LDS has made efforts to distance itself from the FLDS. As such, they created a policy that anyone who enters into a plural marriage is excommunicated (Church of Jesus Christ of Latter-day Saints, n.d.).

In the FLDS, women may be forced into marriage during adolescence to a man who may be much older than they are, and ongoing sexual assault is not uncommon. Members are expected to strictly adhere to certain rules (e.g., prohibition of listening to rock music, dancing, specific dress based on gender) under penalty of being excommunicated (Rios, 2011). To many of us, being kicked out of such an organization may sound like a good thing and ultimately an end to being subjected to religious trauma, but to a person who grew up in such a group with no outside resources and no knowledge of how to survive elsewhere, the prospect of being out on one's own without community can be terrifying. Counselors need to take care not to impose their values on clients or dismiss their lived experiences.

Cult leaders have the power to use the threat of such isolation, abuse, and damnation to bend members to their will. Of course, not all fundamentalist or dogmatic religions are cults. A cult is grounded in dogma and fundamentalism taken to the point of ongoing psychological, sexual, and/or physical abuse.

People who survive and escape cults do so with great difficulty and often have massive trouble adapting to the world on their own. They may have no money or resources, and depending on the level of isolation they were subjected to and for how long, they may not know anyone in the outside the religious group. This can result in homelessness or poor living conditions and no employment opportunities, restricting their autonomy and well-being. Furthermore, because of the abuse they endured, they are likely to suffer from mental health struggles, particularly symptoms of posttraumatic stress disorder, and may be at risk for sex trafficking and addictions.

BOX 16.2 **PROFILE OF A PRACTITIONER**

Erik Braun, PhD, NCC

In grade school, I was Catholic because it was what was most accepted in my community. In high school, feeling the world was not what I wanted it to be, I rebelled and declared that I was an atheist. In college, I refined that view and felt that I did not truly know whether or not there was such a thing as the Divine. In graduate school and upon getting my training as a counselor, I began to look more toward existentialism and mindfulness and experienced the benefits of a daily meditation practice. When I became a professor, I realized my life lacked a focused purpose and meaning, so I began searching for something else.

One spring, I went to New Orleans for an academic conference, and while I was sightseeing, I came to a spirituality store that had spiritual tools, candles, incense, books, and there was even a tarot reader. Even though I knew little about it, I felt drawn to it, like it fit my identity. I looked through their books, and I noticed a big blue book called *Buckland's Complete Book of Witchcraft* (Buckland, 1986). On a whim, I bought it and began reading it and was deeply moved by the individual and customizable nature of pagan spirituality. I thought to myself: "Most of what I'm reading here is how I have always seen the world anyway!" It was so validating, and it felt like I had come home. That was how I decided to be a witch, to form a relationship with the Morrigan, and to follow the path of Wicca.

Through Wicca, I have made my meditation more meaningful to me personally, and I have clarified my life's purpose: "To make the weak strong, and to make the strong gentle." We are all weak, and we are all strong. I now know that I live to foster these qualities in others both in my practice of martial arts and as a counselor educator, and life feels more vibrant.

During a ritual on Samhain years ago, I was initiated into a Wiccan coven, and as of Samhain 2022, I have been inducted as a high priest in the coven. In my new leadership role, I hope to help others refine their practice of meditation and sorcery and find their own life's purpose.

Nondominant Group Identities Related to Spirituality and Religion

When considering religious and spiritual identity, it is important to remember that spiritual and religious groups do not exist in isolation. As with other aspects of culture, such as race or ethnicity, there is diversity within diversity. The beliefs, practices, customs, and traditions of a given spiritual/religious group are helpful to know, especially if you have a client of that group. However, prepare to be wrong. It may be tempting, even for those who are culturally aware, to make assumptions based on the client's group membership. These assumptions or biases may come from prior personal experiences. For example, a counselor who is atheist may have had prior experiences with people who were Christian and may have felt judged for not believing in God. That counselor, if they do not reflect and bring this into awareness, may make the assumption that because their client is Christian, they are not open-minded. This is a judgment that may or may not be correct. Below (see Box 16.3) is the lived experience of a counselor who experienced discrimination and exclusion from their Christian church because of their LGBTQIA+ identity and then found a new church that was accepting and affirming.

BOX 16.3 **PROFILE OF A PRACTITIONER**

Anonymous Contributor, PhD, LPC

I identify as a Black AFAB (assigned female at birth) individual. I currently work as a counselor educator and own a small private practice aimed at supporting members of the LGBTQ community. My faith journey begins in my childhood in the Midwest. I grew up in a home with a Baptist father and a COGIC (Church of God in Christ) practicing mother. My parents were very active in their respective churches (praise team member/deacon) and instilled in all their children the principles that they espoused.

Entering my practicum/internship experience during my master of counseling training program, I began to reflect on my religious beliefs. If I could reflect back, there was one encounter with a client that changed my faith trajectory. I was working with a client who displayed great bravery against opposition in their family and community as they lived out their lives as a member of the LGBTQ community. As I sat with the client for the first time hearing their story, I felt an internal change come on. I didn't have the biased thoughts noting that to be gay or queer was a sin. Instead, I believed in my heart that God created us all and that there were no mistakes. From that day on, I had a more open mind when it came to affectional orientation and gender expression.

With a new outlook on the concept of "love," I began to explore my own attractions. During my doctoral studies, after a few years of contemplation, I came out as a lesbian to my close family. I was met with a lot of the staunch dogma that I fed into as a child and adolescent. As a part of my spiritual journey, I changed my dress options to ones that helped imbue me with more confidence (male presenting). I also decided to leave the church I was attending, as they held very rigid beliefs about being a member of the LGBTQ community. It was quite striking that, at times, they would say such harsh things about members of the LGBTQ community. It didn't feel like love. I also didn't want to attend church as a closeted member while listening to sermons that denounced the LGBTQ community. I didn't believe that it was healthy for my self-concept to be in a nonaffirming environment. Leaving the church was a bit tough, as I was receiving commentary from a close family member who stated that a Bible-based church would never be okay with my "lifestyle" choice. I sought out a faith group that was affirming and Bible based. I also got input from people while on the dating scene, as my faith was noted in my dating profile and an important topic for me. A few women mentioned attending affirming churches in the city. I was able to find a predominantly Black LGBTQ-affirming church affiliated with the United Church of Christ. I also sought out organizations that offered LGBTQ-focused peer support groups. The support groups gave me an opportunity to be around other individuals who shared a similar gender presentation. I would also note that my experiences helped spark a desire to ensure that I offered a safe space for clients who identify as members of the LGBTQ community who want to infuse spiritual practices into their clinical work.

This narrative is part of an originally published Illinois Mental Health Counselors Association's Spring 2023 Newsletter. Reprinted with permission by the author.

An additional consideration for counselors is that a person's R/S background is often a hidden or nonapparent identity. That is, many people can choose whether or not to reveal their religious or spiritual background if they do not have outward signs of their faith (e.g., head coverings, religious jewelry). This has implications for both counselor and client; both can choose whether or not to reveal their cultural identity, and both can influence the counseling relationship! For example, imagine a client who considers themselves to have a strong faith who believes that someone who is religiously unaffiliated is immoral. In this specific case, the client's relgious identity is hidden. If the counselor did not ask about R/S on the intake or broach it during the intake interview, they may not be aware of their client's faith. They may assume that the client is not religious or spiritual, or they might assume they are part of the dominant group. During the third session, the counselor asks the client how they make meaning and is caught off-guard and doesn't know how to respond when the client says, "The way all Evangelical Christians do, through my relationship with Christ." The counselor struggles to respond and is silent a little too long, so the client fills the space and asks the counselor if they have been saved by Christ. The counselor says curtly that they are not religious. No further discussion ensues. The counselor attempts to return to their initial line of exploration, and the client gives one-word answers and leaves the session 10 minutes before it's over. The client does not return.

Cross-cultural religious/spiritual relationships are not uncommon in the counseling profession. Because R/S are often deeply connected to clients' personhood, identities, and worldviews, it is essential that counselors broach R/S with clients, are prepared with what they would like to share about their R/S, and engage with clients about meaningful differences and similarities in their R/S when it impacts the counseling relationship/process. The purpose is not to have a theological discussion or to convince the other of your views but rather to build the relationship and to use what you learn in a meaningful way to bolster the client's healing processes. Recall what you learned in Chapter 3 about the multicultural orientation model. Cultural humility, comfort, and opportunities are essential to the counseling relationship, including those with clients who identify as religious and/or spiritual.

BOX 16.4 **FOCUS ON CLIENT CARE**

Beth begins counseling with Dino and early on explains that her connection to her church is important to her and that her values are guided by her religion. Her counselor, Dino, is an atheist and has a much different perspective on the world.

Should Dino disclose his hidden cultural status to Beth?
What benefits and/or disadvantages do you see in such a disclosure?
How might this disclosure hurt or benefit the counseling relationship?

Spirituality and Religion Within Ecological and Sociopolitical Contexts and Oppression

In this section, we discuss R/S through the lens of Bronfenbrenner's (1979) ecological systems theory framework (EST). R/S can have sociocultural and political implications, which we address along with dominant religious group privilege and the oppression of nondominant religious and spiritual groups.

Ecological Context

Bronfenbrenner's EST focuses on explaining the influence of social environments on human development. More specifically, this theory argues that the environment one grows up in and the social factors one experiences can impact how one thinks and feels. Within EST, the microsystem, mesosystem, exosystem, macrosystem, and chronosystem all impact each individual's development and how they understand the world. This theory can be used to illustrate how oppression can affect religious minorities on different levels of social influence.

The microsystem refers to the groups with which one has direct contact. For instance, family, friends, peers, school, work, or even religious gatherings. According to Bronfenbrenner (1979), this is the most influential system in terms of impacting human development. At this level, oppression is executed through social interactions between people in their everyday lives. These may include microaggressions and other forms of individual discrimination ("Bioecological Systems Theory," 2022). The mesosystem includes interactions between environments closely surrounding the individual. The relationship between parents and schools, for example, will indirectly affect a child and how the family system functions (Ballard et al., n.d.). Oppression from multiple relationships in the microsystem or mesosystem can, according to Bronfenbrenner, deter people from exploring other parts of their environment; in turn, this can lead to antisocial behavior, lack of self-discipline, and inability to provide self-direction ("Bioecological Systems Theory," 2022).

The exosystem involves larger institutions, such as the mass media or the health-care system. These have an impact on individuals, families, peers, and schools that operate under policies and regulations found in these institutions (Ballard et al., n.d.). The macrosystem involves the larger cultural context. For instance, it may include Western cultural values, the national economy, and the political culture ("Bioecological Systems Theory," 2022). Oppression, on greater scales, operates within social institutions, including education, media, government, and the judicial system, among others. Also, it operates in the social structure itself, which organizes people into hierarchies based on ethnicity, gender, and religion, just to name three (Ballard et al., n.d.). For example, consider the oppression Muslim women face in some parts of the United States for wearing hijabs. While this is a form of oppression they experience in Western cultures, many Eastern cultures see hijabs as an important part of cultural identity, so oppression is an unlikely experience. Another example is the First Amendment of the U.S. Constitution. It states that "Congress shall make no law respecting an establishment of religion, or prohibiting the free exercise thereof" (U.S. Const, amend. I). This means that the U.S. Constitution protects freedom of religion; however, in practice, not all states have laws that prohibit religious hate crimes, and even those who have them may not enforce them equitably. This means that those who are members of R/S minority groups may not be protected when hate crimes and discrimination occur. The exo- and macrosystem levels affect the larger population as a whole and, therefore, can cause stress on social development.

The final level is the chronosystem. This level encompasses the historical context of all previous levels discussed. In other words, this system refers to the patterning of environmental effects as well as the transitions of values and policies over time (Bioecological Systems Theory, 2022). Religious milestones during childhood or adolescence like first communion (Catholicism), bar/bat mitzvah (Judaism), or the first Ameen (Islam) are part of the chronosystem. Historical events and specific cohort experiences are part of the chronosystem, too. Earlier, we mentioned the terrorist attacks on September 11, 2001. This was an historical event that had religious meaning to many and resulted in religious persecution for those with nondominant religious identities who lived through this time period and in the decades that followed. Therefore, when examining the chronosystem and integrating R/S, consider the impact events had on specific spiritual and/or religious groups, including how they made meaning. Overall, each system contains roles, norms, and rules that can powerfully shape development, especially in terms of oppression.

Oppression Within Sociopolitical Contexts

Religion has a complicated relationship with oppression and marginalization. Religiosity and authoritarianism have a modestly positive correlation with one another (Hansen et al., 2017); in other words, as religiosity increases, so do authoritarian views. Zhong et al. (2017) found that religiosity tends to strongly correlate with conservative political views and policies, which is linked to a more authoritarian view.

Nations where religious conflict occurs are more likely to experience religious oppression (Henne & Klocek, 2019). Perceived religious oppression, which is when a group believes they are being oppressed based on their religion, can sometimes lead to radical mobilization in religious minority groups (Moyano & Trujillo, 2014). White Christians, for instance, tend to believe they are being oppressed with the rise of *cancel culture* when in reality, it is the feeling that they are losing their privileged status rather than oppression (Joshi, 2020).

Religious minorities in the United States experience discrimination for several reasons. Marks et al. (2019) conducted a qualitative study of U.S. religious minority families ($N = 131$) that included 30 Jewish families consisting of Orthodox, Conservative, and Reformed traditions, 25 Muslim families (Sunni and Shia), 26 LDS/Mormon families, and 20 Asian American Christian families, with the remaining percentage comprising minority Christian faiths including, but not limited to, Quaker, Seventh-day Adventist, Jehovah's Witness, and Christian Scientist. The results illuminated struggles related to several factors: difference and minority status, relational tension from other religious people, misunderstanding and ignorance, demands of the faith community, and animosity and rejection (Marks et al., 2019). Marks et al. (2019) found that religious minorities experienced far more religious bias, prejudice, and violence compared to those in the majority group. Specifically, in 2015, 20% of the 5,818 hate crime incidents were motivated by religious bias. The overall results of the study concluded that having a nondominant religious identity is associated with increased religious struggles (Marks et al., 2019). On one hand, religion can be a source of coping, and on the other hand, it can be a source of oppression. Below, we explore common forms of oppression religious and spiritual minorities face, though first, we explain an important backdrop—White Christian privilege.

White Christian Privilege

Eastern, shamanic, and folk religions are usually not included in discussions about religious and spiritual diversity and inclusivity, and at the same time, Christian privilege is often overlooked, specifically White Christian privilege. The dominant religion in the United States is Christianity, specifically Protestant Christianity, and the dominant racial group is White. Combined, their numerical majority and long-standing political power have resulted in White Christians having more power than all the minority religious groups combined (Schlosser, 2003).

BOX 16.5 PAUSE AND REFLECT: CONNECTING POLITICS AND RELIGION

What are some current U.S. political issues? How much or how little of a role does religion play in these issues? In what ways does White Christianity play a role? How can counselors help clients who are impacted?

Christian religious dogmatism contributes to the cultural devaluation of nondominant religious groups and often results in discrimination and oppression (Schlosser, 2003). One major example of White Christian privilege is the formal structure of the calendar. Work and school calendars are set from Monday through Friday, with Sunday designated as a rest day (Seifert, 2007), aligning with many Christians' day of worship. Additionally, it is not a coincidence that the day on which most businesses are closed is Christmas, one of the central Christian holidays (Seifert, 2007; see Table 16.2). These privileges, in turn, lead to other religious groups being overlooked and excluded.

TABLE 16.2 A Selection of Religious Holidays by Month

Month	Holidays				
January	Makar Sankranti (Hinduism)				
February	Maha Shivaratri (Hinduism)				
March	*Ramadan (Islam)	Lunar New Year/Yugadi (Hinduism)	**Ash Wednesday (Christianity)		
April	Eid al-Fitr (Islam)	Good Friday (Christianity)	Passover (Judaism)	Holy Saturday (Christianity)	Easter (Christianity)
May	***Shavuot (Judaism)	Declaration of Bab (Baha'i)	Ascension of Baha'u'llah (Baha'i)		
June	Eid-al-Adha (Islam)				
July	Ashura (Islam)				
August	Ganesh Chaturthi (Hinduism)				
September	Rosh Hashana (Judaism)	Navaratri Begins (Hinduism)			

(Continued)

TABLE 16.2 *(Continued)*

Month	Holidays				
October	Vijaya Dashami (Hinduism)	Yom Kippur (Judaism)			
November	Diwali (Hinduism)				
December	Hannukah (Judaism)	****Christmas (Christianity)			

**Ramadan is listed in March for representation purposes, yet it does not always occur in March—it occurs at different times each year because the Muslim calendar is shorter than the Gregorian calendar used today. The same is true for Eid al-Fitr, Eid-al-Adha, and Asura.*

***Ash Wednesday is listed in March for representation purposes, yet it can occur in either February or March depending on the lunar cycle. The same is true for Maundy Thursday, Good Friday, Holy Saturday, and Easter—they are listed in April yet can occur in March.*

**** Shavuot is listed in May for representation purposes, yet it can occur in May or June. Similarly, Rosh Hashana and Yom Kippur can occur in September or October.*

*****The only holiday in which the majority of businesses are closed nationwide.*

Forms of Oppression

Homomisia

As you learned in Chapter 15, homomisia is hatred toward people who are part of the LGBT+ community. Such hatred can be expressed as prejudice and discrimination in areas as employment, housing, and legal rights. The LGBTQ+ population has been oppressed by some religious institutions and, in some cases, may have experienced religious trauma. Heterosexism dominates some religious communities, particularly those that are fundamentalist, rigid, or dogmatic (Garrett-Walker & Torres, 2017). Religiosity has a positive correlation with negative self-identity, and anti-LGBTQ+ religious messages that have been internalized can cause incongruity in a person's identity (Huffman et al., 2020; Liboro, 2015). Further, people from the LGBTQ+ community have been threatened with and experienced physical violence because of others' religious beliefs (Garret-Walker & Torres, 2017). Many LGBTQ+ individuals who are members of religious communities that condemn their affectual and/or gender identities are left with the harrowing choice between being excluded and alienated from their religious community, friends, and family or denying their authentic selves (Clark et al., 1990).

Sexism

The APA (2023a, para. 1) defined sexism as "Discriminatory and prejudicial beliefs and practices directed against one of the two sexes, usually women. Sexism is associated with acceptance of sex-role stereotypes." Religion can create rigid gender roles (Gu, 2015). For example, in Thailand, Theravada Buddhism is the predominant religion. It is a widely held belief among Theravada Buddhists that only men can achieve enlightenment. This belief, in combination with gender-based beliefs about how women should behave in marital relationships, contributes to gender inequity in Thailand and, in some cases, even to sexual slavery (Vejar & Quach, 2013). Another example is religious beliefs held by some Islamic sects that require women to wear a niqab, an interpretation of hijab, in which women must cover their faces (O'Neill et al., 2015). Christianity in the United States is no stranger to sexism either. Some Christian denominations tend to place women at an inferior status to men (Küng, 2001). Additionally, there are prohibitions related to contraception, abortion, and divorce, all of which have higher consequences for women than for men (Küng, 2001), as well as prohibitions in some Christian organizations from women serving as clergy.

Anti-Semitism

Anti-Semitism refers to "prejudice against or hatred of [Jewish people]" U.S. Holocaust Memorial Museum, n.d.). People who are ethnically and/or religiously Jewish have long been subjected to oppression and discrimination, including their enslavement during ancient times, the Spanish Inquisition, pogroms in Russia, the Holocaust, and modern anti-Semitic hate groups. Anti-Semitism still exists in the current era. As one example, there are anti-Semitic conspiracy theories that promote the idea that Jewish people have organized and control the world's banks (Kofta et al., 2020). In a report released by the FBI, people who identify as Jewish were the most targeted group of religious hate crimes from the years 1991 through 2019 ("Hate Crime Statistics," n.d.). Some of these hate crimes included destruction of property, assault, and even shooting incidents ("Hate Crime Statistics," n.d.). Additionally, Jewish people have had to endure attempts to minimize their oppressed status and history of oppression through claims that the horror of the Holocaust was fabricated and never happened. Furthermore, it is common for Jewish people to experience microaggressions, including derogatory names and biased tropes (e.g., to "Jew someone down"), as well as more direct forms of aggression, such as displaying a swastika or making jokes about the Holocaust (Berkovski, 2022).

Islamomisia

Islamomisia, or hatred and discrimination against Muslim people, is a common problem in the United States. Marks et al. (2019) explored the struggles faced by religious minority families in the United States. When speaking with Muslim families, some spoke of misunderstanding and ignorance following the events of 9/11. Specifically, one individual said, "After September 11th, you can feel it ... they ... question you sometime[s], not with words but with their eyes" (Marks et al., 2019, p. 251). It is estimated that there are at least 74 special interest groups in the United States that in some way contribute to Islamomisia, 33 of which were said to promote Islamomisia and anti-Muslim causes as their primary purpose.

Anti-Muslim sentiments have inspired over 300 known attacks on mosques since 2005, including threats, vandalism, arson, and physical assault of people who identify as Muslim (Anti-Muslim Discrimination, 2022). Additionally, Muslim women, in particular, "have been harassed, fired from jobs, denied access to public places, and otherwise discriminated against because they wear a hijab" (Anti-Muslim Discrimination, 2022). In public places, such as schools, shopping centers, swimming pools, and amusement parks, Muslim women have been denied the right to enter. In other cases, such as with law enforcement, Muslim women have been denied the right to wear a hijab and have been harassed by police officers (Anti-Muslim Discrimination, 2022).

BOX 16.6 **PAUSE AND REFLECT: THE IMPACT OF YOUR SPIRITUALITY AND/OR RELIGION**

Consider your spiritual and/or religious background.

- Has the religious/spiritual identity that you identify with been historically marginalized or privileged? Maybe its been both? In what ways?
- What are some ways you see religious privilege in your day-to-day life?
- How can you support nondominant religious/spiritual identities at school or work?

Recommendations for Counselors

Ninety percent of Americans believe in some kind of Higher Power (PRC, 2014). Despite this, counselors may still be hesitant to discuss R/S in clinical settings and may assume these conversations are unethical or prohibited. They are not unethical or prohibited! However, a critical question facing counselors is how to best use R/S to inform the counseling process, the therapeutic relationship, and the assessment of presenting issues (Cashwell, 2017). For clients, the invitation to explore R/S meaning can be a vital source of healing and growth.

To support clients in their spiritual journeys toward wellness, resilience, and strength, counselors can begin by reviewing the Association for Spiritual, Ethical, and Religious Values in Counseling (ASERVIC, 2009) competencies for addressing spirituality and religion within the counseling relationship. The ASERVIC competencies offer 14 guidelines organized into six areas that embrace a cross-cultural perspective to promote the overall development of R/S values concerning the person, society, and the counseling profession (please see appendix for the link to the ASERVIC competencies). A core tenet of the ASERVIC competencies is to appreciate the many facets of diversity and honor the individual nature of each person's spiritual growth and transcendence.

In the spirit of professional collaboration, ASERVIC endorses the counseling competencies that have been established by the Association for Multicultural Counseling and Development (AMCD) and the Association for Lesbian, Gay, Bisexual and Transgender Issues in Counseling. In so doing, these three divisions seek to enhance the counseling of clients and the training of students by intentionally focusing on honoring the many facets of diversity.

The Multicultural and Social Justice Counseling Competencies

When integrating R/S in counseling, counselors should implement the multicultural and social justice counseling competencies (MSJCC) in addition to ASERVIC competencies because the

MSJCC highlight the intersection of multiple identities and the dynamics of power, privilege, and oppression that influence the counseling relationship. Within the MSJCC framework, there are four developmental domains (Ratts., et al., 2016) that reflect different layers that contribute to multicultural and social justice competence. The domains include (1) counselor self-awareness, (2) client worldview, (3) the counseling relationship, and (4) counseling and advocacy interventions align well with person-centered counseling and can serve as a framework to support clients in addressing R/S content and in recovering from spiritual or religious persecution. Let's look at how each domain can serve as a point of reference for counselors to increase their efficacy in conceptualizing R/S-informed interventions.

Counselor Self-Awareness

Counselors must self-reflect and gain awareness as to how their personal values affect their ethical decision-making (Kocet & Herlihy, 2014), especially in relation to spiritual/religious concerns (Nelson, 2021). The ASERVIC competencies suggest that counselors actively explore their personal attitudes, beliefs, and values about spirituality and religion and continuously evaluate the influence their spiritual/religious beliefs may have on the client and the counseling process. This includes how the counselor has experienced privilege or marginalization based on their religious/spiritual identity. Accordingly, as counselors develop their self-awareness, they simultaneously develop knowledge, skills, and social justice actions that give them the ability to identify the limits of their understanding of clients' spiritual and/or religious perspectives and tailor their actions and interventions responsibly.

BOX 16.7 **PAUSE AND REFLECT: SPIRITUALITY, RELIGION, AND DECISION-MAKING**

- What are the main tenets of your personal beliefs and values about spirituality and religion?
- How do your personal spiritual/religious beliefs impact your ethical decision-making?
- In what ways do your religious/spiritual beliefs impact your status as a privileged or marginalized counselor?

Client Worldview

Each client has a unique worldview because it is their personal conceptualization of their relationship with the world and the universe. The ASERVIC competencies hold that professional counselors recognize that clients' beliefs (or absence of beliefs) about R/S can be central to their worldview and influence their psychosocial functioning. The MSJCC support this notion and further stipulates that counselors are called to be aware, knowledgeable, and skilled in understanding clients' worldviews. In so doing, counselors are better equipped to respond to clients' R/S with acceptance and sensitivity. This stance supports counselors in living out the ASERVIC standard that calls counselors to use spiritually oriented concepts that are acceptable to the client and consistent with their R/S perspectives.

However, in cross-cultural counseling, especially in instances where the counselor holds majority status and the client is from a historically oppressed or marginalized group, clients may be concerned about the counselor's ability to be sensitive, unbiased, and understanding of their presenting concern, identities, and worldviews. In this respect, empathy, a central tenet of person-centered counseling, can aid a counselor in more fully understanding a client's worldview. Rogers (1961) described empathy as the counselor's ability to perceive the client's private world as if it were their own while communicating the *as if* quality. In this way, the counselor demonstrates interest and appreciation for the client's beliefs (or absence of) beliefs about R/S with a willingness to adjust their understandings as the relationship evolves.

BOX 16.8 **PAUSE AND REFLECT: CULTIVATING UNDERSTAND AND EMPATHY FOR THOSE WITH DIFFERENT VIEWS**

- What beliefs do you hold based on your privileged or marginalized R/S worldview that might interfere with understanding a client's differing worldview?
- Think about a different religious or spiritual group from your own. What might get in the way of having empathy for someone from this group? How can you use empathy to understand and connect with such a client?

The Counseling Relationship

There is nothing more fundamental to counseling than the counseling relationship. Rogers (1961) believed that in a warm, genuine, empathetic, and congruent relationship, the client could discover the ability to heal and grow from within. Rogers proposed six necessary and sufficient conditions for counseling, which include psychological contact, client incongruence, counselor congruence, unconditional positive regard, counselor empathy, and the communication of empathy.

Psychological contact highlights that the experiences of the counselor and client together occur within the context of a *genuine* relationship. Client incongruence, the second condition, refers to how a client may feel when entering the counseling relationship; a lack of alignment between their perceived self and their ideal self (i.e., the self they wish they could be). For example, if a lesbian client was raised in an environment with high religiosity and anti-LGBTQ+ messages, they may experience negative self-identity if they have internalized these messages (Huffman et al., 2020; Liboro, 2015). Because clients come to counseling in a state of incongruence, it is essential for counselors to be congruent. Congruent counselors are in touch with what they are thinking, feeling, and experiencing moment-to-moment, and at the same time, they express genuine empathy and unconditional positive regard toward the client. Unless the counselor is congruent, the client will find it difficult to be themselves in the counseling relationship, connect with their counselor, and work through their incongruence.

According to person-centered counseling, counselor congruence goes hand in hand with genuineness; without both, the client will find it difficult to truly be themselves in the counseling relationship. In addition to genuineness, the fourth necessary condition is for the counselor to express unconditional positive regard to the client. This means that the counselor has a warm demeanor and a positive, accepting attitude toward the client. It is within this accepting relationship that the client learns to accept themselves. With regard to R/S, this will come in the form of supporting the client's R/S cultural lens. While, at times, the counselor may challenge pieces of that lens that may be inhibiting their growth and development, they only do so once the relationship is strong and the counselor has earned the right to challenge.

The fifth necessary and sufficient condition is counselor empathy, which has already been described in the previous section as a method to aid in understanding client worldviews, yet the final necessary condition for counseling is the communication of empathy. The client will need to perceive the counselor as someone who can listen and truly understand them. To communicate empathy to a client who is of a different R/S background than you, being proactive in learning the client's background (perhaps by reading about it between sessions) may aid you in speaking from the client's frame of reference. Also, paying close attention to and using the words the client uses is a proactive approach for reflecting clients' worldviews. Remember, counseling is about the client's R/S, not the counselor's R/S.

Clients need to experience a non-threatening, safe relationship to fully recognize the counselor as someone who can appreciate their worldview without judgment. From an MSJCC perspective, understanding how client and counselor privilege and marginalization influence the counseling relationship is vital. This means that counselors are aware of how client and counselor experiences with power and oppression influence the counseling relationship. As such, culturally attuned counselors recognize spiritual and/or religious themes in client communication and broach these themes with the client when they are clinically relevant (ASERVIC, 2011).

Counseling and Advocacy Interventions

Once a supportive relationship has been formed, the client is in a better position to recognize and express their needs. The person-centered approach maintains that within every client is the innate ability to self-actualize and to develop their potential. The primary goals within this approach are to close the gap between the client's perceived and ideal selves, to increase their sense of self-worth, and to assist them in becoming more fully functioning as the client defines it within *their* worldview. The person-centered counselor is growth oriented and views the client as an equal partner within the relationship. Because beliefs about R/S influence psychosocial functioning, counselors set goals with the client that are consistent with *the client's* spiritual and/or religious perspectives.

The ASERVIC competencies encourage counselors to gather information during the intake and assessment processes to understand the client's spiritual and/or religious perspectives. In addition, counselors follow the lead of the MSJCCs and EST to assess the degree to which historical events, current issues, power, privilege, and oppression contribute to the client's worldview, presenting problems, and their ability to take action. Once the counselor has a fuller picture of the client within a multicultural context, they can begin to draw out the client's strengths and abilities in light of their spiritual/religious beliefs. For example, the ability to construct personal meaning, to find purpose in one's experiences, and the capacity to master one's life purpose are sources of spiritual/religious strength that can be explored with clients.

Person-centered counseling employs techniques aimed at raising consciousness to help clients free themselves from living out the expectations of others, which might be challenging for a client to accomplish in the face of religious persecution or oppression. However, if the counselor can be fully present and accessible and can meet the client on a moment-to-moment experiential basis, the client can engage in self-exploration. As the counselor provides a supportive environment, the client uses the relationship to gain self-understanding, and their natural self-healing abilities are activated. Spiritual/religious information, such as the capacity to perceive transcendent dimensions of self, others, and the physical world, can further support self-exploration, ultimately leading to a restructuring of the self and an increased ability for the client to make choices consistent with their desire to live their best lives.

R/S values can play a major role in people's lives and thus should be viewed as a potential resource in therapy (Corey, n.d.). Counselors can encourage clients to embrace their spiritual and/or religious values to benefit multiple aspects of their lives. Religious faith or some form of personal spirituality can act as a powerful source of meaning and purpose (Corey, n.d.). There is growing empirical evidence that spiritual values and behaviors can promote physical and psychological well-being. Additionally, involvement in religion can create a feeling of belonging and a caring connection with others (Corey, n.d.). Exploring these values with clients can enhance the therapeutic process.

A study done by Dolcos et al. (2021) examined the impact of religious coping strategies on those facing adversity and distressing emotions. The results indicated that those who had strong religious and/or spiritual beliefs had increased resiliency, reduced symptoms of distress, and were better able to maintain emotional well-being (Dolcos et al., 2021). Evidently, research indicates that religion and spirituality can be a form of resilience and support for many individuals.

Clients from both privileged and marginalized religious and/or spiritual backgrounds who are experiencing external barriers to wellness with regard to their R/S may benefit from advocacy interventions at the intrapersonal, interpersonal, institutional, community, public policy, or global affairs levels (Ratts et al., 2016). For example, at the *intrapersonal* level, counselors might challenge thoughts related to internalized prejudice experienced by clients who identify as atheist (e.g., "I am immoral," or "I am a bad person because I do not believe in God") and help them reframe those thoughts to help empower them.

At the *interpersonal* level, perhaps a client who identifies as Buddhist has been searching for a counselor who is able to work within the specific framework of Buddhism. The counselor may consider learning and using the *note, know, choose* model (Lee & Tang, 2023) to help them on their eightfold path to enlightenment. At the *institutional* level, consider a Muslim client who is experiencing discrimination preventing them from engaging in their daily practice of prayer at their workplace. The counselor might help them identify trusted individuals within that institution who might support them in changing policies that act as barriers. At the *community* level, a counselor who is working with a client who is Christian and feels she does not have permission to express unpopular beliefs within her community might help her explore how her beliefs and the norms in her religious community both help and hinder her growth and development.

Counselors may act on the *public policy* level by advocating for public school lunch policies that provide kosher options for students who are Jewish. At the *international and global affairs* level, culturally alert counselors might identify religious or spiritual groups that they are likely to serve in their community and be proactive in learning about the historical and geopolitical events that may have influenced people from these groups.

Spiritual Genograms and Ecomaps

A spirituality-focused genogram can help clients identify religious/spiritual resources within their family (Dunn & Dawes, 1999) and provide greater insight into how spirituality informs their worldview. A spiritual genogram is a map of one's religious and spiritual affiliations, events, and conflicts, which helps clients make sense of their religious and spiritual heritage and explore the ways in which their experiences impact current issues, beliefs, and values (Frame, 2000). Spiritual ecomaps are similar to spiritual genograms, but instead of focusing on the previous generations of a client's spiritual journey, spiritual ecomaps focus on the client's current spiritual story and their relationships with various ecological structures (e.g., rituals, communities, and spiritual leaders; Hodge, 2000). Spiritual genograms and ecomaps can be applied during the intake process to assess client spiritual beliefs and how these beliefs inform their worldview, or they can be used later in the counseling process as an intervention.

Spiritual genograms are similar to traditional genograms but are focused on spirituality, spiritual connections, and how that spirituality affects family dynamics. To create a spiritual genogram, the client draws a family tree, typically including the two previous generations of their family. Then, the client draws lines representing notable relationships. Solid lines represent strong connections, dotted lines represent weaker connections, and jagged lines represent a strained relationship. Usually, a genogram will include information like the family members' ages, careers, mental health history, and any other information that might suit the needs of the client. In a spiritual genogram, the emphasis will be on spiritual information, such as each family member's religious affiliation and spiritual path. The genogram can be taken a step further by having the client add ecomap elements.

A spiritual ecomap is a more free-flowing approach in which deities, spirits, gods, and other nonhuman entities can be included. For a spiritual ecomap, the client draws circles around the genogram, with each circle representing a spiritual domain. Some examples of spiritual domains include rituals and practices, god and transcendence, faith communities, spiritual leaders, parents' spiritual traditions, and transpersonal beings (saints, angels, deities, spirits, etc.). Others can be added or subtracted as desired by the client. Finally, the client draws lines to represent connections between various family members and these domains (Cashwell & Young, 2011).

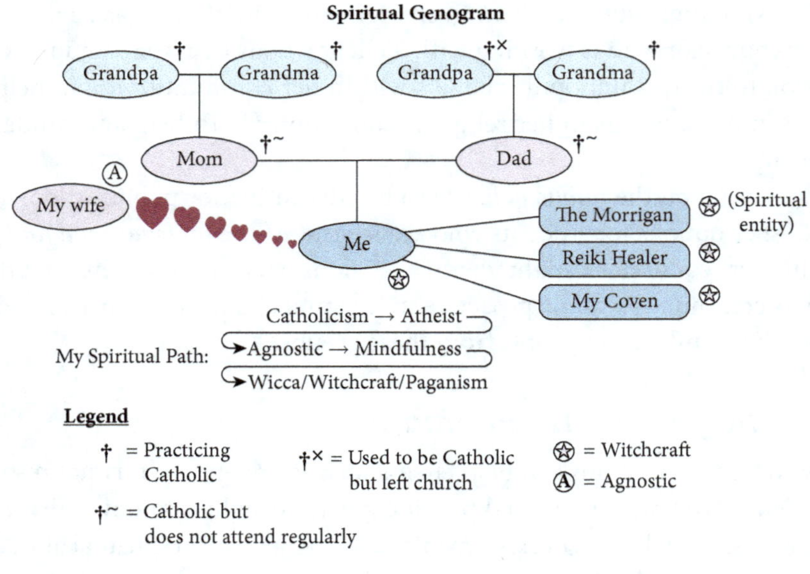

FIGURE 16.1 Spiritual Genogram Example

Music Chronology

Duffey (2005) discussed music chronology, or the *Emerging Life Song*, as a way to help clients clarify and make sense of the spiritually/religiously defining moments in their lives, to recall joyful memories, and to give meaning to past suffering from a spiritual perspective. Music chronology can be adapted into a spiritually based intervention whereby the client gathers the songs they find meaningful and uses them to discuss related spiritual/religious experiences with the counselor in session in a four-step process.

Steps for Creating the Spiritual Emerging Life Song

Step 1: Client selects songs that illustrate their personal story and spiritual life themes. Though some of these may also be the client's favorite songs, they should have some emotional value and spiritual meaning to the client. However, this can be interpreted as liberally as the client likes or that the counselor feels is appropriate for the client's needs. Perhaps the selected piece reminds the client of a specific memory, a meaningful time in their life, or maybe it captures a certain feeling from a significant spiritual event. The lyrics, the sound, or both can be considered in the client's song selection. The counselor may instruct the client to select any number of songs or may ask them to select songs that relate to a particular area of their life or spiritual journey.

Step 2: Songs are used as a vehicle for revisiting the client's memories and experiences. The client listens to the music with the counselor and reexperiences hearing the song in the present moment, allowing thoughts and feelings to arise. As the client reminisces, the counselor helps the client to identify limiting beliefs, attitudes, and parts of the narrative that continue to impact the client's current emotions, thoughts, and behaviors in a negative way. The counselor helps the client to reevaluate these memories and see them through a different lens.

Step 3: The client selects a song to express their current spiritual worldview. Duffey (2005) noted that this stage should act as a reality check. As the client and counselor discuss the experience, the counselor helps the client consider changes that the client may wish to make in their life and at this current stage of their spiritual journey.

Step 4: The process is repeated but with a song that represents the client's spiritual future.

Music chronology interventions like the *Emerging Life Song* can be used for a variety of populations and applications, particularly for clients who may benefit from changing the narrative they have constructed for their lives. Music chronology can be applied as a spiritual intervention, as it deals in meaning making, transcendent experience, and one's path in life.

Religion and Spirituality as a Form of Resilience

Using a strengths-based lens, counselors can view the client's religious and/or spiritual background as a source of strength and resilience. People use religion and spirituality to make meaning in their lives. Counselors can help clients explore their values through their R/S lens to resolve dilemmas or to make important life choices. If a client is experiencing suicidal ideation, the counselor may help them explore where there is meaning in continuing to live from the perspective of the client's religious and/or spiritual background. With enough rapport, difficulties, such as the loss of a job, can be reframed, if appropriate, as challenges that are part of the client's spiritual path. Meditation (spiritual) or prayer (religious) might be used as a coping skill for clients who are experiencing anxiety. Culturally alert counselors adjust interventions to fit the client's religious and/or spiritual worldview. For example, clients of some religious backgrounds may prefer not to meditate as it may not be aligned with their faith. However, prayer may serve a similar purpose. Counselors should collaborate with clients and draw on their R/S as a resource of resilience.

Ethical Code Applications

There are several important ethical considerations regarding R/S in counseling. Counselors must be aware of their own values, biases, and beliefs and determine how they could affect the counseling relationship negatively—and intervene before they do. The ethical codes of the American Counseling Association (ACA; A.4.b), the American Mental Health Counselors Association (AMHCA; I.A.4.d; I.C.2.c), the American School Counselor Association (ASCA; A.1.f), and the Certified Rehabilitation Counselors (CRC; A.4) agree that counselors do not impose their values on clients. This is particularly germane within the context of R/S and counselors who identify as highly religious or strongly as nonreligious/nonspiritual. They must be particularly cautious in this area.

Additionally, culturally adept counselors actively attempt to understand their clients' diverse spiritual and religious backgrounds and how their own values and beliefs might affect the counseling process (AMHCA; I.C.1.g; I.C.1.g). For example, culturally alert counselors who are Christian will be aware of the privilege they have in the United States because of being part of the dominant religious group when working with clients who identify with other spiritual identities. Those who are part of the dominant religious group can sometimes make others feel alienated if they are not careful. For example, asking the client which church they belong to when they have not told you their religious background may make a person feel otherized or subtly judged if they do not belong to a religious group that has "church" or if they are not religious or spiritual. Let's take a look at a case example to consider the potential impact of dominant culture religious values on the counseling relationship (see Box 16.9).

BOX 16.9 **FOCUS ON CLIENT CARE**

Molly is a counselor at a clinical mental health agency. She is Christian and believes all life is sacred. She and her husband tried for many years before they were able to conceive. Molly had a miscarriage and believed that she had to accept that she would never have a child of her own. This was devastating to Molly, but after going to a fertility clinic, Molly eventually became pregnant and gave birth to her son. Molly's client, Perry, a 37-year-old man who is religiously unaffiliated and unemployed, has been struggling to find a job. He used to be an entrepreneur, but years ago, his business failed, and he is now deep in debt that feels insurmountable. Perry has mounting anxiety about his ability to provide for his family and reports increasing levels of depression. Perry reports in a dejected tone that his wife is pregnant. "What a blessing!" says Molly.

What are your initial thoughts about Molly's response to Perry about his wife's pregnancy? In the case above, Molly was operating under the assumption that everyone's perspective is the same and that others are always happy about pregnancy news. However, Molly failed to consider that this may have been a product of her the beliefs and values that are foundational to her religious background. When the counselor assumes the client is part of the dominant group when they are not or, like in this case, that the client has the same values and beliefs as the counselor, this can result in microaggressions; the client is potentially reminded of their minority status. Similarly, it could potentially trigger guilt or shame in the client for not following familial or societal expectations. Instead, the counselor might say, "Tell me how you're feeling about your wife's pregnancy." Then, the counselor might explore the client's values and beliefs, any expectations they feel like they aren't meeting, and any struggles Perry is having in his relationship.

Working With Clients Whose Beliefs Differ From the Counselor

It is likely that counselors will work with clients who have unfamiliar and opposing belief systems from their own. As such, it is necessary to have a plan for how you will learn about specific religions/spiritualities, engage in ongoing learning, as well as develop methods to manage instances when your beliefs conflict with clients' beliefs. Because religious and spiritual beliefs are an integral part of one's cultural makeup, we recommend that clinicians embrace learning about world religions and spirituality as an ongoing part of their professional development.

It's not uncommon for the counseling process to uncover connections between clients' religious and/or spiritual upbringing and their presenting problems that can become an area of clinical focus. Through exploring and evaluating these beliefs and values, the client can move from an externally given belief system to an internally chosen belief system, thus giving them the opportunity to own their R/S. Counselors must be ready to and capable of working with all people, and they must be willing to work toward the client's stated goals, even if this is antithetical to the counselor's personally held values/beliefs. This may be difficult for some counselors who have strongly held religious beliefs and values, so it is especially important for counselors to seek additional training, supervision, consultation, and support. Remember, all decisions the client makes about their life must be discussed through the lens of the client's worldview, not the counselor's (ACA, A.4.b.; AMHCA, I.A.4.d, I.C.i.m; ASCA, B.3.j, A.1.f; CRC, A.4).

Topics like sexual/affectual orientation or gender identity, the client's salvation, and the decision of whether or not to stay in a marriage may be religiously/spiritually influenced. Counselors explore these topics fully with clients, highlighting the client's values and where they might be experiencing discord, ambivalence, or distress. Counselors do not, for example, try to convince or influence clients to *save their marriage* simply because that is the counselor's personal opinion that aligns with their religious/spiritual belief that divorce is wrong. Additionally, counselors do not terminate or refer when their values differ from their clients' values. Continuing with the divorce example, a counselor who has the opinion that divorce is wrong cannot simply terminate counseling or refuse services to those who wish to discuss divorce. This holds true no matter the counseling context (e.g., clinical mental health, school) or the belief/value difference (ACA, A.11.b; AMHCA, C.2.a; ASCA, A.1.d).

Inclusive Language

Counselors strive to use inclusive language so that the counseling environment is as welcoming as possible (ASCA, B.2.p; B.3.i, A.10.a). For example, in schools, it is best practice to say "Happy Holidays" when addressing all students who may be of a variety of religious/spiritual traditions. "Merry Christmas" or "Happy Chanukah" can be appropriate if you know that you are addressing people of those specific religious identities. Otherwise, as with the assumption that everyone is of the dominant group, it may be alienating to students of other groups to use specific phrases, so it's wise to take note of which religious holidays you highlight and to which groups individuals belong. Consider: Do you offer well wishes for only Christian or Jewish holidays, or do you include Islamic and Hindu holy days as well?

Culturally relevant counselors are aware of the factors that may impact clients and students. For example, Islamic students might be fasting for Ramadan, which may have an impact on their behavior or cognition in the classroom. Counselors should be prepared to provide extra support or advocacy for those students if needed. Additionally, some students may have dietary restrictions related to their religious/spiritual traditions. In the interest of equity, school counselors may advocate for such students if the school cafeteria does not provide reasonable options for them. For example, Islamic dietary restrictions prohibit the consumption of pork (Derani & Reynish, 2020).

Conclusion

Spirituality and religion are important aspect of culture that have historically been avoided by counselors. However, if we as counselors wish to treat the client in a holistic manner, we must understand religious and spiritual backgrounds and identities as well as how they impact the counseling dynamic and relationship. From a multicultural and social justice perspective, counselors must have an awareness of the privilege that applies to the dominant religious and spiritual groups as well as the oppression that is endured by nondominant groups. Counselors benefit from learning methods for integrating R/S into counseling interventions in a culturally sensitive way. Finally, culturally alert counselors understand and reflect on how R/S apply to counseling codes of ethics so that they avoid doing harm by imposing their own biases, assumptions, and values onto the client.

Questions for Reflection

Consider what you learned in this chapter as you respond to the questions and prompts below.

1. What are some ways in which you want to become stronger in your ability to broach religion and spirituality?
2. In what ways could your personal spiritual or religious beliefs/values interfere with your work as a professional counselor? In what ways could they bolster it?
3. What are your thoughts on the necessary and sufficient conditions for counseling as they apply to clients' religion and spirituality?
4. How important is the *quality* of the counseling relationship when addressing power and oppression in the context of spirituality/religion?
5. How can you demonstrate the core conditions to provide spiritually/religiously affirming counseling?

Applying What You Have Learned

Complete each of the following activities, considering what you learned from this chapter.

Activity #1: A Deeper Dive Into the ASERVIC Competencies

The ASERVIC (2023) Competencies have six areas in which counselors consider and potentially integrate religion and spirituality into their work with clients: culture and worldview, counselor self-awareness, human and spiritual development, communication, assessment, and diagnosis and treatment. Compare and contrast the ASERVIC competency areas and specific competencies with the *Code of Ethics* under which you will practice. Then, examine the ASERVIC competencies within the context of the AMCD and SAIGE competencies. How do all of these guiding documents work together? Where are their conflicts? Discuss with a colleague how to apply the competencies ethically and strategies for resolving conflicts.

Activity #2: Meaning Making isn't Only for the Religious and Spiritual

As you have learned in the chapter, religion and spirituality are two ways in which people make meaning and understand their lives within a broader context of purpose. As you learned, too, there is a great deal of bias about those who are not religious or spiritual, not to mention those who do not identify as Christian. As professional counselors, we know that having a sense of meaning and purpose is essential for well-being, yet those concepts do not have to be tied to religion or spirituality.

For this activity, devise a plan for how you can explore meaning and purpose with clients from a nonreligious/nonspiritual perspective. What questions would you ask? Are there established interventions that might be appropriate? Are there interventions you would create? As you create your plan, don't be afraid to be creative! Sometimes words work well, yet you might find that using pictures, movement, or song might be more effective!

Notice what comes up for you as you create your plan and how your worldview is reflected in your plan. How can you use your experiences and values to help you create your plan without imposing your experiences or values on the client? What can you do to open up your plan more so you can use it with clients who are not religious or spiritual?

Credit

IMG 16.1: Copyright © by Prof. Dr. Franz Vesely (CC BY 3.0) at https://commons.wikimedia.org/wiki/File:Viktor_Frankl2.jpg.

CHAPTER 17

Emerging Topics in Diversity

Fatmisia, Neurodivergence, Incarcerated Populations, Individuals With Substance Use Disorders, the Individuals Coping With the Climate Crisis

Susan M. Long, Jennifer Rio, and Kaitlyn M. Forristal

Honesty and openness is always the foundation of insightful dialogue.

—bell hooks

CHAPTER OVERVIEW

We have developed this chapter to address five areas we believe are emerging areas that need to be addressed directly and regularly within diversity training and culturally informed clinical practice: fatmisia, neurodivergence, incarcerated populations, individuals with substance use disorders, and the climate crisis. We chose to highlight these areas because they are rarely considered within diversity literature despite the oppression and discrimination these groups often experience, the cultural identity diversity within these groups, and the resource and treatment disparities members of these groups tend to experience.

This chapter is organized differently than the ones you have read up to this point because we address five distinct areas. Each section will have its own learning objectives and is written by a different author. While you might not have expected to learn about these specific populations as part of this textbook, we invite you to free your mind and expand the ways in which you understand the identities, oppressions, privileges, and lived experiences you have learned about so far to include even more than you imagined.

OVERARCHING LEARNING OBJECTIVES

By the end of this chapter, students will be able to

1. understand what fatmisia is and how it can impact clients from different intersecting identities inside and outside of counseling;
2. understand the nuances of neurodivergence, how it is like yet differs from disability, and how a paradigm of neurodivergence can be applied within the counseling setting;
3. remember and apply the cultural components of substance use disorders and how that may intersect with diverse identities for people with addiction; and
4. conceptualize how climate crisis and change impact mental health and the impact that this will have on clients, especially those from intersecting oppressed identities.

CACREP 2016 STANDARDS

The information in this chapter supports the following standards:

- 2.F.1.e advocacy processes needed to address institutional and social barriers that impede access, equity, and success for clients
- 2.F.2.a multicultural and pluralistic trends, including characteristics and concerns within and among diverse groups nationally and internationally
- 2.F.2.c multicultural counseling competencies
- 2.F.2.f. help-seeking behaviors of diverse clients
- 2.F.2.h. strategies for identifying and eliminating barriers, prejudices, and processes of intentional and unintentional oppression and discrimination
- 2.F.3.e. biological, neurological, and physiological factors that affect human development, functioning, and behavior
- 2.F.3.f. systemic and environmental factors that affect human development, functioning, and behavior
- 2.F.5.b. a systems approach to conceptualizing clients
- 2.F.5.k strategies to promote client understanding of and access to a variety of community-based resources

CACREP 2024 STANDARDS

The information in this chapter supports the following standards:

- 3.A.4. the role and process of the professional counselor advocating on behalf of and with individuals receiving counseling services to address systemic, institutional, architectural, attitudinal, disability, and social barriers that impede access, equity, and success
- 3.B.3. the influence of heritage, cultural identities, attitudes, values, beliefs, understandings, within-group differences, and acculturative experiences on help-seeking and coping behaviors
- 3.B.4. the effects of historical events, multigenerational trauma, and current issues on diverse cultural groups in the U.S. and globally
- 3.B.6. the effects of various socio-cultural influences, including public policies, social movements, and cultural values, on mental and physical health and wellness
- 3.B.9. strategies for identifying and eliminating barriers, prejudices, and processes of intentional and unintentional oppression and discrimination
- 3.B.10. guidelines developed by professional counseling organizations related to social justice, advocacy, and working with individuals with diverse cultural identities
- 3.C.10. biological, neurological, and physiological factors that affect lifespan development, functioning, behavior, resilience, and overall wellness
- 3.C.11. systemic, cultural, and environmental factors that affect lifespan development, functioning, behavior, resilience, and overall wellness
- 3.E.17. principles and strategies of caseload management and the referral process to promote independence, optimal wellness, empowerment, and engagement with community resources

Fatmisia

Kaitlyn M. Forristal

Section Overview

Fatmisia is the systemized discrimination against fat people (Simmons University Library, 2022) that encompasses beliefs that fat people are annoying, unhealthy, lazy, unfriendly, unintelligent, unhygienic, and uncreative (Bacon et al., 2001; Puhl & Heuer, 2010). Discrimination against fat people is generally acceptable in Western societies (Brochu, 2020), so both implicit and explicit biases continue unimpeded, even when the perpetrators are attentive to other social justice and equity causes (Campbell, 2022). One of the ways fatmisia thrives is by the use of fear: The fear of becoming marginalized because, unlike other oppressed identities, body size is changeable, and it is possible that thin people may become fat. The consequences of being fat in a fatmisic society are seemingly endless; fat people experience financial hardship because of their size; relational issues; often avoid seeking medical care, which impacts physical health; and barriers to wellness because of the indignities they suffer. Professional counselors are susceptible to the biases expressed by members of the general public since there is currently no training for examining fatmisia in counseling students or practitioners, which puts clients at risk of unintentional harm in the counseling relationship. In this section, you will learn about indicators of fatmisia, their impact on clients, and how you can work with clients of all sizes and affirm their worth and dignity.

Learning Objectives

By the end of this section, students will be able to

1. define *fatmisia* and other key concepts;
2. discuss the history of fatmisia and its lasting effects on diverse individuals and communities;
3. identify the intersectional mental, emotional, physical, financial, sociopolitical, and wellness impacts of fatmisia for fat individuals;
4. describe the potential impacts fatmisia and body politics have on the professional counseling relationship for clients and counselors; and
5. determine counseling skills and interventions for use with fat clients and others struggling with body image, etc.

Power of Language

The use of the term *fat* to describe individuals living in bigger bodies in this section is intentional; activists call for reclaiming the word rather than using terms such as *overweight* or *obese*, which are used by the medical industrial complex to vilify and demonize fat bodies (NAAFA, 2011). Identity-first language, such as *fat people*, is used rather than person-first language throughout this section to align with activists' argument that identity-first language is a way for marginalized people to claim identity and promote pride (Dunn & Andrews, 2015).

Misia (Greek for *hatred of*) is used instead of *phobia* (Greek for *fear of*) to describe instances of hate-based antagonism, to cease the use of clinical terms to describe nonclinical phenomena, and to accurately describe the disdain for fat people that upholds oppression. Indeed, fatmisia is not a phenomenon carried out by people of average size and those who are thin; fat people can and do participate in fatmisia, which is called *internalized fatmisia*.

BOX 17.1 **PAUSE AND REFLECT: FEELINGS ABOUT "FAT"**

Reflect on the way we're socialized to feel about fatness. What is your reaction to the word *fat*? How can you/we reframe *fat* as a neutral word and descriptor of bodies, like we do for the term *thin*?

Lived Experiences of Weight Stigma

Fat people report facing discrimination in employment, promotion, and salary decisions (FairyGodBoss, 2017; Flint et al., 2016; Ji et al., 2021); social ostracization (Amlund, 2021; Lenz, 2017); and often report the most significant instances of fatmisia come from loved ones (Lawrence et al., 2022; Lenz, 2017; Plummer et al., 2022; Puhl et al., 2008; Thomas et al., 2008). Society is inundated with messages that fat people are inherently unhealthy and susceptible to a myriad of diseases because of their body size. These messages can cause fat people to constantly feel under siege, activating the body's acute stress response and the production of stress hormones to deal with the threat. The release of cortisol, the human body's stress hormone, can cause changes in cardiovascular, immune, and neurological systems and lead to arteriosclerosis, insulin resistance, metabolic conditions, high cholesterol, and cardiac illness (Udo et al., 2016). Researchers assert that many scientific studies purporting fatness causes poor health fail to control for the lived experiences of fatmisia and the detrimental physiological responses it creates (Fryhofer, 2013; Schvey et al., 2014; Tomiyama et al., 2014; Udo et al., 2016).

Microaggressions

Pierce (1970) described *microaggressions* as verbal and nonverbal exchanges that are subtle, stunning, often automatic, and cause harm to marginalized people. Anti-fat microaggressions are unique in that they have disciplinary intent; if fat people are shamed and ridiculed enough, there is hope they will become thin and can leave the marginalized group (Reiheld, 2020). Below are common fatmisic microaggressions.

Spatial Discrimination

Spatial discrimination describes the intentional exclusion of fat people from public spaces that were not designed for their bodies. We see this in many public gathering spaces (e.g., booths and small chairs in restaurants, inaccessible seating in courtrooms and other public offices, stadiums, arenas) and most especially on airplanes and other modes of travel (Rinaldi et al., 2020). Modes of travel commonly govern fat bodies in ways that do not affect thin people and result in fat people being excluded, including refusal to participate to avoid shame and embarrassment (Evans et al., 2021).

Encouraging Weight Loss

Since 1959, research has shown that 95% to 98% of attempts to lose weight fail and that two thirds of dieters gain back more than they lost within 3 years (Spreckley et al., 2021). Researchers demonstrated that dieting for weight loss does not work long-term (Mann et al., 2015) and in fact can cause additional weight gain (Bacon, 2010) and severe health problems (Bosomworth, 2012; Groven et al., 2010) for dieters, but many people still pursue intentional weight loss to better fit in and avoid the social consequences of being fat. Fatmisic stigma and shame can cause physical illness (Schvey et al., 2014; Tomiyama et al., 2014; Udo et al., 2016; Westermann et al., 2015) and mental distress (Gerend et al., 2022). Examples of weight loss encouragement include an overabundance of targeted advertisements (e.g., print, television, social media) for weight loss products and processed "healthy foods," the underrepresentation of fat people in the media, and scads of weight loss systems with "before and after" pictures.

Backhanded Compliments

Backhanded compliments are statements made with good intent that have a harmful impact: What they give with one hand, they take back with the other (Reiheld, 2020). These so-called *compliments* may be used with fat people to subtly imply the person could be so much prettier, more handsome, etc., if they just lost weight. While these are intended to be flattering to fat people, the impact is often a hurtful reminder that their closest friends and family members do not accept their body which in turn, leads individuals to feel unaccepted completely. For example, a woman who is fat might be told that they have "such a pretty face," indicating that if they were to lose weight, then she would *really* be pretty. Men receive similar "compliments," yet they are usually focused on strength rather than beauty, such as, "I bet there is a lot of muscle hiding under there!"

Concern Trolling

Concern trolling describes the phenomenon of someone feigning sympathy for a perspective, such as fat people living freely without shame and stigma, while advancing a view that is antithetical to the cause (DiFranco, 2020). Masked as simple concerns for the health of fat people, people who make these comments rely on commonly held beliefs that fat people are inherently unhealthy and frame their fatmisic rhetoric into a more socially acceptable form of fatmisia (Holi, 2019). Concern trolling can occur face-to-face between people who know each other well, yet it happens frequently in multiple internet spaces (e.g., message boards, social media posts, comment threads). Western medicine reinforces this idea in various ways, including stigmatizing language (obese and overweight), reliance on the body mass index (BMI) despite its lack of reliability, and the American Medical Association's questionable decision to classify obesity as a disease in 2013.

Fatness in Media

Watching television or engaging with any popular media demonstrates the disgust our society has for fat people (Puhl et al., 2013); studies show that 72% of media images and 77% of videos that show fat people stigmatize them (Amlund, 2021). Common tropes are that fat people exist purely for comedic relief, are funny sidekicks, or are vilified as antagonists (Byers & Williams, 2022; Justin, 2021). News programming often contains warnings of the *obesity epidemic*, which is thought to be the result of (a) people self-reporting their weight more accurately than they have in the past and (b) the average change in weight per person has pushed more people into the "overweight" and "obese" BMI categories (Campos et al., 2006).

BOX 17.2 **PAUSE AND REFLECT: RECOGNIZING YOUR OWN POSSIBLE MICROAGGRESSIONS**

Have you engaged in any of these microaggressions discussed in the preceding passage? If so, can you think of how you could have handled the situation better or reframed a potentially harmful thought or words you used about a fat person?

Intersecting Identities

Body size is an intersectional identity; fatness does not exist in a vacuum and intersects with individuals' other marginalized identities to compound the oppression they face (Crenshaw, 1988). The intersection of fatmisia and gender identity affects women more than men when it comes to their working lives and earning potential (Flint et al., 2016; Newcomb, 2022), public scrutiny (Schmalz, 2021), and mental health impacts (Rinaldi et al., 2020). Fatmisia and internalized weight bias affects girls as young as 3 (Harriger et al., 2019), and research shows that by age 5, 34% of girls have intentionally restricted their food intake to lose weight (Damiano et al., 2015).

Anti-Blackness and Racism

The neutral or even positive view of fat bodies that existed before the Enlightenment Era changed when fatness was intentionally intertwined with beliefs that Black people were inferior, overly sexual, and disease-ridden (Strings, 2019). Strings (2019) argued that fatmisia is a White supremacist tool used to assert that fat people are deviant and inherently immoral and perpetuate the *savagery* of Black people. The belief that fatness was a distinctly Black trait persisted throughout the 18th and 19th centuries and was reified by the transatlantic slave trade. Fatness and body size, like skin color, became a symbol of who was allowed bodily autonomy and freedom, laying the groundwork for the fatmisia and public ownership of fat bodies we see today.

Professional Counseling Practice Application

The Counseling Relationship

Professional counselors have a unique opportunity to combat fatmisia with clients and as part of larger scale social justice advocacy because of our use of the wellness model. Other mental health disciplines have called on their members to prioritize behavioral changes with clients to "reduce their obesity," asserting the faulty claim that fatness is a result of individual choices and behavior (Johnson, 2012, p. 5). Counselors can better meet the needs of all clients by examining and reflecting on their own biases, shifting language away from pathology, integrating social justice perspectives, and honoring all bodies as they are.

BOX 17.3 **PAUSE AND REFLECT: RECOGNIZING THE INTERNALIZATION OF FATMISIA**

How can you determine if a fat client has internalized fatmisia that is affecting their mental health? What are some questions to add to a questionnaire or to add to your intake interview to assess new clients' relationships with their bodies?

Person-Centered Perspectives

Professional counselors are ethically mandated to treat clients with dignity and respect regardless of body size, and one way to effectively do this is to integrate person-centered techniques into counseling with fat clients. Counselors can demonstrate empathy, unconditional positive regard, and congruence with fat clients by being open about their own experiences with and gaps in knowledge regarding fatmisia, seeking training in this area to develop a fat-positive politic which can be shared with clients, and listening to client concerns (e.g., struggling with a desire to lose weight or love their body as-is) without passing judgment or offering suggestions.

Who Is Fat?

Counselors have a responsibility to gather information about clients' identities and align their language and questioning to each client's descriptors (e.g., gender, relational/affectual identity, race). Counselors can easily incorporate information on how each client describes their body type. While there is no way to definitively state who qualifies as *fat* and who does not, counselors can use their discretion to differentiate those who have faced marginalization because of their body size (i.e., not being able to find clothes that fit in a local store, not fitting into seats at a theater, being publicly ridiculed or humiliated about their size) and those who have low self-esteem, do not like their body, or are suffering from an eating disorder and/or body dysmorphia.

Fostering Wellness in Fat Clients

Fostering wellness practices with fat clients should be liberation and social justice-informed and more nuanced than with thin clients. Fat people often report being uncomfortable in public exercise facilities because of overt fatmisia (Rinaldi et al., 2020), so physical wellness and joyful movement for these clients will look different. Clients can work to find size-inclusive exercise groups, identify people in their lives to participate in movement with them, or participate in movement in their own homes and/or communities. Playing with children, going on an evening bike ride, or swimming in the lake at a picnic are all forms of movement that can bring joy to clients and accomplish their exercise goals without the pressure they may feel in traditional exercise settings.

Social justice advocacy as self-care is another tool for fostering wellness in fat clients. Navigating unjust systems can cause burnout and psychological distress (Shewan, 2021), but actively working to combat fatmisic systems has been effective in reframing oppression in fat individuals. Broadening one's lens to contextualize individual suffering within systemic fatmisia will help to understand and describe the client's problems in the larger oppressive system rather than individual pathology (Shewan, 2021). Counselors can provide psychoeducation on diet culture, intersectional oppression, and work with clients to unlearn fatmisia in themselves to allow for increased mental peace and wellness.

Ethical Code Applications

There is no current mention of body size as an area of human diversity or fat people as a protected class in any professional counseling codes of ethics or training and supervision standards. Counseling ethics call on professionals to advocate for social justice initiatives to best serve clients and communities (ACA, 2014; AMHCA, 2020; ASCA, 2022), so failing to address complex sociopolitical issues such as fatmisia could make us complicit in fat oppression. Fatmisia is directly intertwined with anti-Blackness, racism, and misogyny, so it is impossible to effectively advocate for or treat, for example, Black fat women in counseling ethically without acknowledging anti-fat bias (Shewan, 2021).

Counselor Scope of Practice

Counselors are at risk of violating ethical codes addressing scope of practice if their own beliefs about body size, weight, and health remain unchecked (ACA, 2014, C.2.a.; AMHCA, 2020, I.C.1.b.; CRCC, 2023, E.1.a.; NBCC, 2024, Sec. 17). Despite socialized beliefs that thinness is inherently correlated with positive health outcomes, there is no evidence to support this. If a client wishes to discuss weight loss or other medical issues in counseling, professional counselors need to refrain from providing medical advice to protect the client and themselves. Counselors can process a client's reasons for wanting to engage in weight loss efforts and the social implications of these goals, but counselors must not work outside their scope of practice.

TABLE 17.1 MSJCC Application

MSJCC Domain	Anti-Fatmisic Tenets	Skills and Interventions
Counselor Self-Awareness	Counselors actively examine their own interpretations of body size, fatness/ obesity, and health and wellness.	Counselors reflect on their own attitudes, beliefs, and biases regarding body size diversity, fatness and fat people, health, and wellness. Counselors examine their own body type/size through the lens of social power, privilege, and oppression. Counselors engage in professional development opportunities to learn more about fatmisia as a phenomenon and its potential impacts on clients.
Client Worldview	Counselors acknowledge their own limitations and defer to the lived experiences of their fat clients.	Counselors recognize that learning about fat clients' experiences and worldview may be an uncomfortable or unfamiliar experience. Counselors study historical events and current issues that shape the experiences of fat clients. Counselors articulate the social structure of fatmisia. Counselors apply intersectionality to understand how being fat impacts clients' other identities (e.g., racial, gender, religious, sexual, social class, ability status).
Counseling Relationship	Counselors are aware of how differences in body size may influence the counseling relationship.	Counselors create accessible and affirming therapeutic spaces for fat clients. Counselors explore identity development theories and how they influence the counseling relationship with fat clients. Counselors directly and empathically communicate with fat clients if discussions of weight/ body size create a conflict in the counseling relationship. Counselors collaborate with fat clients to determine whether individual counseling or systems advocacy is needed.
Counseling and Advocacy Interventions	Counselors empower fat clients to embrace a body-neutral or pro-fat identity.	Counselors assist fat clients in the development of self-advocacy skills that promote a fat-is-neutral stance of bodies and/or a fat-positive outlook. Counselors assist fat clients in developing communication skills to discuss issues of fatmisia, thin privilege, healthism, and related power and privilege with others. Counselors engage in social action to eliminate fatmisic systems Counselors advocate for legal and social protections for fat people in their communities.

Neurodivergence

Susan M. Long

Section Overview

Neurodiversity applies to the entire human species because no two brains are the same, even monozygotic (identical) twins! Counselors must understand the meaning of neurodiversity as an important dimension of human diversity and explore this concept with the individuals and communities they serve. By understanding the neurodivergence and neurodiversity paradigm, counselors can approach counseling through a neurodivergence-informed lens. You will notice a shift from person-first language when discussing neurodivergent populations; this is intentional. Neurodivergent people, such as autistic individuals, prefer autistic, autistic person, or autistic individual rather than person-first language (e.g., person with autism) because autism cannot be separated from a person's identity (Autistic Self Advocacy Network (ASAN), 2022). Keep in mind that language and perspectives shift over time and culture, and it is important to ask each person to self-identify and use the term(s) they provide.

Learning Objectives

1. Define neurodiversity and related terms.
2. Identify the neurological conditions under the neurodiversity umbrella and understand neurodiversity as a component of diversity.
3. Understand the models of disability in relation to the neurodiversity movement.
4. Identify how neurodiversity may influence the counseling relationship and the delivery of counseling services.
5. Identify the counseling skills and interventions that can be used in practice with neurodivergent individuals within a multicultural context.

Neurodiversity

Neurodiversity refers to the natural and infinite variations in the human brain (Singer, 1998). The concept of neurodiversity was coined in the 1990s by Judy Singer, an autistic sociologist who advocated for the inclusion of neurological minorities within disability rights activism (Chapman & Botha, 2021; Singer, 1998). As a dimension of biodiversity, neurodiversity describes the uniqueness of every human nervous system and mind (Dwyer, 2022; Singer, n.d.). For example, graduate students enrolled in a counseling program are *neurodiverse*. Within any group, different *neurotypes* are represented between and among individuals; in this way, neurodiversity includes everyone. Recognizing neurodiversity broadens our understanding of human diversity along with other categories, such as race, ethnicity, gender, sexuality, social class, and disability, and how these factors overlap and influence a person's unique experience (Singer, n.d.).

BOX 17.4 **PAUSE AND REFLECT: NEURODIVERSITY AND INTERSECTIONALITY**

How can neurodiversity inform your understanding of intersectionality? Is it important?

How would you explain the concept of neurodiversity to clients?

What are the multicultural and social justice considerations when including neurodiversity in your counseling approach?

How can neurodiversity relate to experiences of privilege and nonprivilege for clients?

How would you explore the idea of person-first language with neurodivergent clients?

Neurodivergent and Neurotypical

Within any neurodiverse group, there are individuals whose brain functions within a standard range of *normal* as defined by societal and cultural norms. So, what is typical and what is divergent? Attention, learning, memory, communication, language, socialization, sensory processing, and motor movements are domains used to compare neurotypicality and neuroatypicality (Walker, 2014). Characteristics of normality must be examined within a sociocultural, environmental, developmental, and relational context (Chapman & Botha, 2021; Dwyer, 2022). Individuals are *neurotypical* (NT) when their brain development and functioning are within the normal/expected limits (Hughes, 2013; Walker, 2021). Individuals whose brain *significantly* diverges from the dominant standards of *normal* are labeled as *neurodivergent* (ND) (Walker, 2021).

Forms of Neurodivergence

Some of the more familiar forms of neurodivergence include the following:

- Autism Spectrum Disorder (ASD)
- Attention Deficit-Hyperactivity Disorder (ADHD)
- Learning Disorders (e.g., dyslexia, dyscalculia, dyspraxia, dysgraphia)
- Tourette's Syndrome
- Sensory Processing Disorder

Neurodivergence is innate/congenital, and people may be born with two or more types of neurodivergence. People with two or more neurodivergences are considered *multiply neurodivergent.*

The Neurodiversity Paradigm and Models of Disability

The *neurodiversity paradigm* is an emerging framework that provides a philosophical foundation for the *neurodiversity movement* (Walker, 2021). To understand neurodiversity as a paradigm, it is important to analyze two opposing models of disability and the conceptualization of neurodivergence. The medical model of disability traditionally understands disability as a pathology to be cured (more on this in Chapter 12). We see this perspective in the classification of neurodevelopmental disorders in the *Diagnostic and Statistical Manual of Mental Disorders, Fifth Edition,*

Text Revision (*DSM-5-TR*; American Psychiatric Association (APA), 2022). Conversely, the social model of disability does not view disability as pathology but rather as dominant social values of neurotypicality and a failure to accommodate neurodivergence (Hughes, 2020). Both the social model and medical models have merit in supporting the wellness of ND/disabled people. The critical distinction is related to the power these perspectives hold in shaping what it means to be ND and/or disabled in society (Chapman, 2021; Chapman & Botha, 2022).

Understanding the Historical Context of the Neurodiversity Movement

A complete history of the neurodiversity movement is beyond the scope of this chapter; however, there are a few key points to highlight. First, the neurodiversity movement is led by ND self-advocates and emerged from the autistic self-advocacy movement (Singer, 1998). This movement is grounded in social justice activism with the purpose of challenging the inequitable social structures, policies, and laws that historically and currently exclude ND people from having a stake in the decisions that impact their well-being. The neurodiversity movement intersects with the larger disability justice movement and shares the perspective that neurodivergence and disability are not deficits within the individual but that distress and disablement occur in the context of an unaccommodating and ableist society (Hughes, 2020). Finally, the neurodiversity movement acknowledges the intersectional factors that further shape the ND experience, such as race, queerness, gender, social class, ability, and their relationship to privilege and oppression (Hughes, 2013). The neurodiversity paradigm is essential to increasing the awareness of neurodivergence and the nuanced experiences of ND populations. This is especially important in a society that historically and currently fails to examine and challenge its stigmatizing perceptions. This leads to microaggressions toward ND/disabled people, furthering misunderstanding and marginalizing this population. Some examples of ND/disabled microaggressions are listed below. After reading these specific examples of microaggressions, can you identify instances when you have heard microaggressions used toward ND/disabled people?

ND/Disabled Microaggressions

You don't look autistic. You must be high functioning.
I thought autism only affected males.
Everyone has ADHD.
Some sounds, textures, and smells bother me too sometimes, but I ignore it.
You like to read? I thought you were dyslexic.
Everyone is neurodivergent now. They just want attention.

Professional Counseling Applications

Neurodiversity is not widely recognized or integrated into counseling theory and praxis, which has traditionally limited professional counselors' ability to work effectively with ND/disabled clients and families (Chapman & Botha, 2021). Counselors have an ethical responsibility to be aware of themselves and others and to gain knowledge and skills to effectively intervene with and on behalf of diverse clients, including neurodiverse/disabled populations (American Counseling Association (ACA), 2014). The multicultural social justice counseling competencies (MSJCC) outline specific strategies counselors can use to engage in multicultural and social justice praxis in terms of neurodiversity alongside other privileged and marginalized identities (MSJCC; Ratts et al., 2016). In addition, a proposed model of neurodivergence-informed therapy offers a conceptual basis for counselors to approach the therapeutic relationship, counseling processes, and advocacy interventions with ND/disabled clients (Chapman & Botha, 2021). Table 17.1 presents the main tenets of neurodivergence-informed therapy (Chapman & Botha, 2021) and integrates these concepts with the MSJCC (Ratts et al., 2016) framework to guide strategies to support ND/disabled client populations. As you review the integrated strategies column in Table 17.2, list strategies that you could implement with clients.

TABLE 17.2 Neurodivergence-Informed Therapy

Neurodivergence-Informed Tenets	Aligned MSJCC Domain	Integrated Strategies
Reconceptualizing Dysfunction: Examine one's interpretations of neurodivergence, disability, and the utility of the medical model.	*Counselor Self-Awareness*	Counselors proactively learn about their attitudes, beliefs, and biases regarding neurodivergence/disablement. Counselors reflect on their neurotype and how this relates to privilege and nonprivilege. Counselors engage in opportunities to expand their current knowledge and understanding of neurodivergence/disablement.
Cultivate Epistemic Humility: Acknowledge the limitations of one's experiences, education, and training regarding neurodivergence/disability and center the expertise of ND/disabled clients.	*Client Worldview*	Counselors broach neurodivergence/disability with clients. Counselors intentionally explore and infuse the ND/disabled affirming language determined by the ND/disabled client. Counselors explore how neurodivergence/disability, race, ethnicity, gender, sexuality, class, etc. shape the client's worldview and experiences.

Neurodivergence-Informed Tenets	Aligned MSJCC Domain	Integrated Strategies
Neurodivergent Flourishing: Respect the autonomy of ND/disabled clients, accept and embrace the client for who they are, and proactively explore resources and supports for optimal well-being.	*Counseling Relationship*	Counselors assess for ND/disabled clients' communication styles, information processing supports, environmental and social needs, and sensory needs, and partner with ND/disabled clients to cocreate an accessible and affirming therapeutic space. Counselors integrate the ND/disabled clients' strengths, skills, and resources into the entire counseling-related process. Counselors invite ND/disabled clients to share positive images, stories, and messages about neurodivergence/disablement.
Reclamation, Pride, and Community: Empower ND/disabled clients to develop and embrace a positive self-identity.	*Counseling and Advocacy Interventions*	Counselors assess how social systems impede on ND/disabled clients' well-being. Counselors assist ND/disabled clients with building and practicing self-advocacy skills and identifying groups that share a positive ND/disabled identity. Counselors engage with and on behalf of ND/disabled clients to eliminate stigmatizing and ableist policies and practices.

Advocacy Interventions

Neurodivergence and disability must be conceptualized within a social, cultural, and political context (den Houting, 2018; Hughes, 2013). To this end, it is imperative for counselors to examine the dominant views of normativity and its influence on the mental health and wellness of ND/disabled people through Bronfenbrenner's ecological perspective. At the microlevel, counselors must acknowledge and prioritize the wants and needs of ND/disabled people, including the various strengths, supports, and resources. On the mesolevel, counselors draw upon the collective and communal supports available to ND/disabled clients to increase a sense of belongingness and a positive, shared group identity. At the macrolevel, counselors engage in opportunities for advocacy with and on behalf of ND/disabled clients; this includes tracking current issues, policies, and practices that impact this group and contacting legislators to advocate for systems-level change.

Incarcerated Populations

Jennifer Rio

Section Overview

More and more people in the United States experience incarceration or are a family member of a person who is incarcerated, particularly people of color and individuals from low social class. In this section, you will learn who constitutes incarcerated populations, cultural groups who are most effected, the historical context of incarceration, and ways to provide effective counseling. In this section, pay close attention to any beliefs or biases that might arise for you surrounding topics, such as biases about people who are incarcerated, what you believe about their life trajectory may be because of incarceration, or stigmatized beliefs you may have about their ability to engage in counseling and to create a meaning-filled life.

Learning Objectives

1. Define the incarcerated population and related concepts.
2. Explain the historical context of mass incarceration.
3. Identify interventions counselors can use with the incarcerated population through a multicultural and social justice lens.

The Incarcerated Population

The incarcerated population, or persons who are confined to a correction setting like a prison or jail, is a marginalized population that presents with higher rates of mental health and substance use disorders when compared to the general population. This population is further marginalized once involved in the criminal justice system, facing disproportionate poverty, homelessness, and chronic health-care conditions upon release from carceral settings. These systemic issues can exacerbate untreated mental health and substance use disorders and increase the likelihood that individuals will recidivate and face repeat arrests and subsequent reincarceration. When considering the lived experiences of the incarcerated population, intersectionality is important to consider, as persons of color and those in poverty are incarcerated at higher rates.

The incarcerated population refers to persons who are confined to a correction setting. Such settings include jails, which are administered by local law enforcement agencies and used for short-term incarceration, and prisons, which are within state and federal correctional systems and used for long-term incarceration (24 months or more). This population presents with higher rates of mental health issues and substance use disorders when compared to the general population. When released from carceral settings, they often face further marginalization through disproportionate poverty, homelessness, and chronic health conditions.

These systemic issues can exacerbate untreated mental health and substance use disorders and increase the likelihood that individuals will recidivate and thus face repeat arrests and subsequent reincarceration. When considering the lived experiences of this population, it is important to take intersectionality into account as well, as persons of color and those living in poverty are incarcerated at higher rates.

Understanding the Historical Context of Incarcerated Populations

The deinstitutionalization of mental health facilities and the War on Drugs are contributing factors to mass incarceration in the United States and the disproportionate rates of substance use disorders (SUDs) and co-occurring disorders (CODs) among the incarcerated population. Deinstitutionalization refers to the closing of state mental health hospitals during the 1960s and 1970s, which shifted treatment to the community (Felton & Shinn, 1981). However, as this occurred, the number of individuals entering correctional facilities increased substantially; this is attributed to a lack of adequate mental health treatment in the community, homelessness, and lack of social support for individuals with mental health disorders (Lamb & Weinberger, 2005). The national War on Drugs campaign that arose in the 1980s is another systemic factor that contributed to incarceration growth. As opposed to rehabilitation for SUDs, the federal government implemented disciplinary measures for drug-related crimes and focused efforts on supporting and funding drug enforcement agencies (Alexander, 2012). Sentencing laws implemented during the War on Drugs included harsher penalties for substances such as crack cocaine versus powder cocaine, disproportionately affecting the African American population (Mauer & King, 2007).

Sociopolitical Influences on Incarceration

Persons who are incarcerated are overly represented by culturally marginalized groups, specifically racial minorities and those in poverty (Alexander, 2012). Implicit racial bias within the criminal justice system and socioeconomic inequality contribute largely to this overrepresentation (The Sentencing Project, 2018). African Americans are 5.9 times more likely to be incarcerated compared to White Americans and, on average, serve longer sentences for similar crimes (The Sentencing Project, 2018). Individuals of lower social class are also more likely to face incarceration (Alexander, 2012). The criminal justice system perpetuates poverty, as individuals with a history of incarceration face disproportionate poverty and homelessness once released from carceral settings (Tobin-Tyler & Brockmann, 2017). This is due in part to housing and employment discrimination that previously incarcerated individuals face upon release from correctional settings (Alexander, 2012). The effects of incarceration on marginalized populations highlight the need for multiculturally competent and effective treatment for the incarcerated population, as well as advocacy for this population related to sentencing, treatment availability, and post-incarceration success initiatives.

Counseling Applications

Person-centered approaches, which include demonstrating empathy, a nonjudgmental stance, and unconditional positive regard, can improve treatment outcomes in correctional settings (Marshall et al., 2003). Unconditional positive regard with persons who are incarcerated may be difficult for counselors to practice because of the nature of clients' criminal histories. However, many clients in correctional settings have experienced traumatic lives, and counselors have an ethical obligation to support clients and demonstrate empathy, regardless of their histories. Because of the inherent power differential that exists when working with clients who are incarcerated, building a trusting therapeutic alliance is essential (Rio et al., 2022).

MSJCC Application

Awareness

An essential component of the MSJCC is counselors having awareness of their own worldview, identities of power and oppression, and how biases affect their work with clients (Ratts et al., 2015). When working with clients who are incarcerated, professional counselors must consider clients' worldviews and how they may have been shaped by the prison or jail setting in addition to their cultural realities prior to incarceration (Carrola & Brown, 2018).

Knowledge

There are several areas of specialized knowledge that counselors should have when working with clients who are incarcerated. This includes knowledge of structural barriers in correctional settings, including lack of access to effective mental health treatment (Rio et al., 2022). Mental health treatment is not accessible across correctional settings, and existing treatment programs do not adequately address the complex needs of the population (Gonzalez & Connell, 2014). Often, counselors must implement crisis management interventions instead of growth-oriented interventions (Carrola & Brown, 2018). Furthermore, correctional culture and mental health are rooted in differing philosophies, and as a result, correctional staff can serve as a barrier to treatment (Rio et al., 2022). Counselors can address this barrier by building collaborative relationships with correctional staff.

Counselors must have knowledge of carceral oppression, including how status as an *offender* or *felon* perpetuates marginalization. Previously incarcerated persons often face housing and employment discrimination because of their criminal records and are denied public benefits (Alexander, 2012). Subsequently, the incarcerated population can cycle between prison and jail settings and social service systems. Incarcerated persons with CODs are at higher risk of facing systemic issues (Peters et al., 2012), highlighting the need for effective mental health and SUD treatment.

TABLE 17.3 Types of Stigma and Effects on Incarcerated Population

Stigma Type	Examples
Systemic stigma	Reduced access to resources Lack of voting rights Lack of access to public benefits
Public stigma	Labeling language (i.e., criminal, felon, offender) Employment and housing discrimination
Internalized stigma	Internalization of criminal stereotypes Increased mental health concerns

Interventions

There are several interventions specific to working with incarcerated clients that can promote social justice, including trauma-informed care and cultural broaching. Trauma-informed care is essential in correctional settings, as most incarcerated clients have experienced trauma, including childhood abuse, violence (Anderson et al., 2016), and vicarious trauma. Incarceration itself can also be a traumatic experience because of the often violent nature of correctional settings (Cima et al., 2008). Trauma-informed care in correctional settings includes protecting the physical safety of clients, creating a safe therapeutic relationship to process trauma, and resisting re-traumatization by fostering a sense of trust and mutual respect (SAMHSA, 2014). In correctional settings, counselors can use broaching (Day-Vines et al., 2007) to address intersecting identities, including race, ethnicity, gender identity, and cultural identities; additionally, professional counselors should address incarceration as an intersecting identity and how this affects the client's worldview (Rio et al., 2022).

Advocacy

According to the ACA, advocacy is defined as the "promotion of the well-being of individuals, groups, and the counseling profession within systems and organizations. Advocacy seeks to remove barriers and obstacles that inhibit access, growth, and development" (ACA, 2014, p. 20). Professional counselors have an ethical obligation to advocate for clients at the individual and

TABLE 17.4 MSJCC Application to Incarcerated Population

MSJCC Domain	Skills and Interventions
Counselor Self-Awareness	Counselors examine the inherent power differential that exists with their clients in carceral settings. Counselors reflect on how stigma affects the incarcerated population and their own biases.
Client Worldview	Counselors reflect on incarceration as an intersecting identity and how it shapes the attitudes and beliefs of their clients. Counselors acquire knowledge of correctional culture (e.g., prioritization of safety) to work effectively in carceral settings. Counselors reflect on how race, ethnicity, and socioeconomic status intersect, and broach these intersecting identities with incarcerated clients.
Counseling Relationship	Counselors remain aware of how mandated treatment impacts the power differential and therapeutic relationship in correctional settings. Counselors use person-centered approaches (i.e., practicing empathy, congruence, and being genuine) when working in carceral settings.
Counseling and Advocacy Interventions	Microlevel (i.e., individual level): connect clients to resources and serve as a liaison between clients and the criminal justice system Mesolevel (i.e., organizational and community level): collaborate with the criminal justice system and provide education to correctional staff. Macrolevel (i.e., systemic level): promote rehabilitative legislation and advocate for mental health and SUD treatment.

societal levels (ACA, 2014, Standard A.7.a). Professional counselors can advocate for the incarcerated population at (a) the micro or individual level, (b) the meso or community level, and (c) the macro or sociopolitical level (Toporek & Daniels, 2018). On a microlevel, counselors can engage in case management strategies, including connecting clients to resources within the community, such as employment and housing. Counselors can also build allies in correctional settings, including correctional officers and psychiatric providers, to minimize clients' barriers to wellness (Rio et al., 2022).

On a mesolevel, counselors can offer mental health and SUD training for correctional staff, as correctional staff often play a role in responding to crisis situations (Appelbaum et al., 2001). Counselors can build collaborative relationships with court systems, as well as partner with employment agencies, that can enhance successful reentry. Macrolevel advocacy includes advocacy on a systems level, including analyzing sources of power within the system and identifying potential stakeholders (Toporek & Daniels, 2018). Counselors should be aware of legislation that impacts their clients and advocate for policies that enhance successful rehabilitation, like advocating for an approach to justice that is preventive rather than punitive (McLeod, 2015). Prison abolitionists argue that the current system perpetuates systemic oppression of marginalized groups, including persons of color and those in poverty, and neglects underlying systemic issues (McLeod, 2015). Counselors can serve as a positive presence in impoverished communities to increase education and provide mental health and substance abuse services to those who are at risk of entering the carceral system (Rio et al., 2022).

Substance Use Disorders

Jennifer Rio

Section Overview

Substance use disorders (SUDs) affect individuals across cultural groups in the United States, and use patterns vary widely by gender and cultural groups, as do cultural values, beliefs, and norms (SAMHSA, 2017). SUD may also be a COD, with an individual experiencing both the SUD and a mental health disorder (SAMHSA, 2015). Furthermore, access to treatment for SUDs varies, and counselors must have awareness, knowledge, and skills of how SUDs manifest across different cultural groups while also being aware of the stigma that surrounds SUDs and how this affects treatment.

We included SUDs in this chapter because cultural identities play a substantial role in addiction development and treatment and because culture needs to be considered more regularly and robustly when working with clients who have addictions. Further, both people who are in active addiction and those who are in recovery often understand their group membership as a culture within itself with specific norms and ways of being. You may notice that this section of the chapter is a bit shorter—that is intentional. Most students will take an entire course in addictions during their course of study, so we encourage you to use what you learn in this section to bolster what you learned (or will learn!) in your addictions course.

Learning Objectives

1. Define SUDs and related concepts.
2. Explain the historical context of SUD treatment.
3. Identify interventions counselors can use when working with clients with SUDs through a multicultural and social justice lens.

Understanding the Historical Context of SUDs

Moral and Medical Models of Addiction

The etiology of substance use has been explained through several models, including the moral model and the medical model. There has been debate whether SUDs are a moral failing or a biological brain disease. The moral model, which dates to preindustrial times, suggests that persons with SUDs have a choice and willfully make the decision to continue using substances despite negative consequences (Frank & Nagel, 2017). Addictive behavior is viewed as a moral failing, and those who engage in substance use are viewed as having the ability to make alternative choices.

The medical model explains addiction as a treatable medical condition. According to the American Society of Addiction Medicine (ASAM), a SUD is a chronic biological disease that involves interactions between genetics, brain circuity, the environment, and an individual's unique experiences (ASAM, 2022). Despite research advances demonstrating that SUDs are a biopsychosocial condition, the moral model continues to influence public policy and treatment.

Temperance Movement

Treatment for SUDs in the United States began with alcohol, as it has been consumed by Americans since colonial times. In the late 1700s and early 1800s, individuals with an addiction to alcohol were housed in various institutions, including jails and hospitals. However, both types of institutions failed to provide adequate treatment for SUDs (Rosenberg, 1995). The Temperance Movement, which began in the United States in 1808, heavily shaped public opinion of alcohol addiction. This movement began in response to societal issues resulting from alcohol use; proponents of the movement viewed alcohol addiction as a moral failing and supported an abstinence approach (Lemanski, 2001). The Washingtonian Total Abstinence Society emerged in 1840 and was key to shaping current self-help groups such as Alcoholics Anonymous, which support an abstinence-only approach to treating addiction.

In 1870, the American Association for the Cure of Inebriation arose, which purported that alcoholism was a medical disease and should be treated as a medical condition rather than a criminal offense (White, 1998). This organization arose largely because of the ineffectiveness of the Temperance Movement. Treatment centers began to emerge for alcohol addiction; however, because of a lack of funding, they disappeared by 1920.

Criminalization of Substance Use Disorders

The Harrison Act of 1914 criminalized possession of illicit substances, including opiates and cocaine. After the passage of this act, treatment for SUDs shifted to a criminal justice model (White, 1998). The War on Drugs, enacted by President Nixon in the 1970s, further criminalized SUDs, led to the militarization of police departments, and allocated increased funding for drug law enforcement (Alexander, 2012). This movement led to a tenfold increase in the number of individuals incarcerated for drug offenses from 1980 to 2020 (Mauer & King, 2007).

Disparities in SUD Treatment

SUDs disproportionately impact marginalized populations, including persons involved in the criminal justice system, those in poverty, the homeless population, and racial and ethnic minorities. According to Pear et al. (2019), opioid overdoses are more prevalent in areas with higher rates of poverty, lower education, and lower median household incomes. Race, poverty, and SUDs intersect within the criminal justice system, and incarceration reinforces oppression of marginalized populations. The criminalization of drug use impacts treatment as clients are often mandated to attend treatment or risk facing punitive consequences, including incarceration. Professional counselors work in various settings to provide SUD treatment, including outpatient, residential, and prison-based settings.

BOX 17.5 **PAUSE AND REFLECT: SUDs AND STIGMA**

What are some initial thoughts that you have regarding working with individuals who have a history of addiction?

How do you think the stigma associated with being an "addict" rather than a "person with SUD" affects treatment for SUDs?

SUDs and Disability

According to the American Disabilities Act (ADA), SUDs are considered a disability because they affect the brain on a physiological level and can impair major life activities (Whaley & Williamson, 2023). Thus, it is unlawful to withhold care or to discriminate based on addiction history. There is an exception to this law for individuals who are still actively using illicit substances (e.g., cocaine, heroin). Because of the stigma and biases that often accompany SUDs, there has been resistance to viewing individuals with addiction as having a disability, and many still face discrimination in health-care settings, yet the fact remains that SUDs are included in the federal definition of disability.

Biases toward those with SUDs specifically impact the treatment of opioid use disorder (OUD). There are two approaches to treating OUD: an abstinence-only approach, based on the moral model, and treatment using medication-assisted treatment (MAT). MAT includes the use of buprenorphine (i.e., Suboxone) and methadone, which are prescribed in controlled settings to help reduce misuse of other opioids (Madden, 2019). Despite the effectiveness of MAT in reducing cravings, mitigating withdrawal, and reducing overdoses, clients are often denied MAT because of biases toward this approach, particularly in criminal justice treatment settings. Professional counselors working with clients who have SUDs must have knowledge of the various approaches to treating SUDs and advocate for best treatment practices.

Counseling Applications

MSJCC Application

The MSJCC (Ratts et al., 2015) provide a framework for serving diverse clients and promoting social justice. They can serve as a guideline for how counselors can work with clients with SUDs. There are several facets of the MSJCC that are relevant to counselors' work with clients with SUDs, including self-awareness, client worldview, and interventions.

Awareness

Prior to engaging in work with clients who have SUDs, counselors should examine their worldviews and develop self-awareness of how their values and biases affect their work (Ratts et al., 2015). Professional counselors working with clients who have SUDs should examine how their own biases may serve as a barrier to treatment (Ratts et al., 2018). Because of the stigma that often accompanies a SUD diagnosis, clients may feel reluctant to engage in the treatment process. Counselors should be aware of their clients' worldviews, including how resistance to treatment may manifest in the therapeutic process due to this stigma. Finally, counselors should remain aware of their own biases toward addiction and how these biases can impact the treatment process.

Person-Centered Approaches

According to the ACA *Code of Ethics* (2014), counselors should gain knowledge, awareness, and skills to be culturally competent and work effectively with a diverse client population (Standard C.2.a). In the past, training for counselors treating SUDs has been less rigorous than training for mental health counseling. Historically, addiction counselors received training through personal experience, seminars, and workshops (Kerwin et al., 2006). Currently, not all 50 states have addiction counseling licensure, and subsequently, mental health counselors often have the responsibility of treating individuals with SUDs (Astramovich & Hoskins, 2013). Thus, counselors in training should have knowledge of how to treat clients with SUDs.

Person-centered counseling approaches align with the MSJCC and are valuable when working with clients with SUDs. Many clients who are in treatment for an SUD are mandated to treatment by the court system or social services agencies. The counseling relationship is particularly important when working with mandated clients. In any counseling relationship, there is an inherent power differential between counselors and their clients; however, when working with mandated clients, counselors have added institutional power (Carrola & Brown, 2018). Professional counselors should strive to build a trusting therapeutic relationship and remain aware of the inherent power differential. Furthermore, counselors can use a collaborative approach to minimize the power differential by engaging clients in the treatment process. For instance, if a client is mandated to treatment because of a DUI charge, the counselor can work with the client to identify other areas of their life they may want to address and engage the client in the goal setting process. While abstinence is often the goal of the legal system, the counselor can ensure that the client establishes other goals that are meaningful to them and can be addressed collaboratively through treatment.

Counselors are aware of the importance of language and using person-first language when discussing clients. This includes avoiding labeling their clients as "addicts" or "alcoholics." For instance, counselors can refer to their clients as a "person with a substance use disorder" or "a client struggling with methamphetamine use." By viewing clients through a humanistic lens and being intentional about language, counselors can build collaborative relationships with clients and avoid further marginalization.

Climate Crisis and Mental Health

Susan M. Long

Section Overview

The climate crisis is a reality for people and the planet. Naturally, this includes the clients and communities that we serve. Further, the state of the climate crisis is expected to worsen over the coming years in various ways. Counselors can reasonably expect to see an increased concern related to climate change in their clients in the future. In this section, you will learn why it is necessary for counselors to have foundational knowledge of local, national, and international impacts of climate change and be prepared to address the impacts on holistic health and wellness.

Learning Objectives

1. Define climate crisis and related terms.
2. Understand the relationship between the climate crisis and mental health.
3. Identify counseling interventions to assist individuals and communities with coping with the mental health effects of the climate crisis.
4. Understand climate change as a social justice issue.
5. Identify advocacy strategies to address the climate crisis.

Climate

Climate is defined as the long-term average type, frequency, duration, and intensity of weather variables in a specific area (National Oceanic and Atmospheric Administration (NOAA), n.d.). *Weather* is the short-term state of the atmosphere and includes temperature, precipitation, wind, and clouds (EPA, 2022a). As you can see, climate and weather are related yet distinct concepts.

You can visualize the differences between climate and weather by your clothing choices. For example, the weather conditions where you live inform what you wear each day, whereas the climate influences the entirety of your wardrobe. *Climate change* refers to the significant shifts in the earth's climate over a long period of time (years, decades, or centuries) and has profound effects on the planet and its inhabitants (EPA, 2022c). *Global warming* is just one component of climate change and refers to the average rising surface temperature of the earth (EPA, 2022b; NASA Global Climate Change, n.d.).

Climate Crisis and Well-Being

Shifting the language from *climate change* to *climate crisis* is necessary to capture the magnitude of harm it has on people and the planet (Strum et al., 2020). Climate change has been declared the "defining crisis of our time" (UN, n.d., para 1.) and the "single biggest threat to humanity" (WHO, 2021, para. 1). The climate crisis is escalating more rapidly than scientists initially predicted, adversely affecting human health, ecosystems, food production, and infrastructure worldwide (Intergovernmental Panel on Climate Change (IPCC), 2022). Adverse impacts such as air pollution, allergens, wildfires, temperature extremes, precipitation extremes, disease carried by vectors, food and waterborne diarrheal disease, food security, and mental health and stress related concerns will intensify or emerge (Strum et al., 2020; CDC, 2022). Mental health concerns such as depression, anxiety, post-traumatic stress disorder, acute stress disorder, substance use, schizophrenia, and suicidality, aggression, and violence are expected to sharply rise in response to the climate crisis (Strum, 2020). Further, 25% to 50% of people exposed to a climate-related disaster (e.g., flood, fire, displacement) will experience poorer mental health outcomes (Trombley & Chalupka, 2017).

Eco-Anxiety

Clearly, the climate crisis is a global risk factor for mental and physical health illness; it is a human health crisis (EPA, 2022g). The concept of climate anxiety or eco-anxiety has recently emerged in the literature to describe the broad distress experienced in response to climate change (Coffey et al., 2022; Whitmarsh et al., 2022). Symptoms associated with eco-anxiety include cognitive, affective, and somatic symptoms, persistent fear of living in dangerous environmental conditions, chronic worry, depression, sleep disturbance, guilt, irritability, hopelessness, grief, dread, and panic attacks (Coffey et al., 2022; Ogunbode et al., 2022; Whitmarsh et al., 2022). According to a poll distributed by the American Psychological Association (APA) in 2020, 67% of Americans reported feeling somewhat or extremely anxious about climate change, and 55% of respondents reported feeling somewhat or extremely anxious about the impact of climate change on their mental health. Further, poll results were consistent among respondents across race (Hispanic/Latino, Black, White, Native American, Asian, and other) and gender (APA, 2020).

Symptoms related to eco-anxiety may be better explained by another mental health condition (e.g., generalized anxiety disorder) or the exacerbation of preexisting psychological distress (Whitmarsh et al., 2022). Still, the concept of eco-anxiety is relevant to better understand the impact of climate change on overall well-being and to develop strategies to assist individuals and communities to cope with the adverse impacts of climate change and guide pro-environmental activism such as avoiding food waste, limiting household energy outputs, and increasing sustainable practices across sectors (IPCC, 2022; Ogunbode et al., 2022; Strum et al., 2020; Whitmarsh et al., 2022).

BOX 17.6 **PAUSE AND REFLECT: CLIMATE CHANGE AND YOU**

- What influence has climate change had on your overall well-being, if at all?
- Do you believe eco-anxiety is a distinct disorder? Is it adaptive or pathological?
- How does your experiences of privilege and nonprivilege influence your perspectives and experiences with climate-related anxiety?
- How could you assist a client presenting with eco-anxiety with respect to their privileged/marginalized experiences?

Environmental Justice

Environmental justice is the equitable, meaningful inclusion and participation of all people in the development and implementation of environmental laws and policies regardless of race, ethnicity, gender, social class, or country of origin (EPA, 2022h). However, an estimated 3.3 billion people are living in contexts that are highly vulnerable to climate change (IPCC, 2022). Factors such as geographical location, race, ethnicity, gender, age, sexuality, social class, Indigenous identity, migrant status, and disability affect the level of exposure and vulnerability to climate hazards (IPCC, 2022). People living in poverty, communities of color, children, pregnant women, older adults, disabled persons, immigrants, refugees, and individuals with preexisting health issues are especially vulnerable (Strum et al., 2020). Other factors such as colonialism, capitalism, governance, and violent conflict exacerbate climate and health inequities, marginalization, and injustice (IPCC, 2022). Climate change is a complex issue, and the socioecological impacts of climate-related hazards require intersectional analysis (Strum, 2020). For example, refugees and other displaced people are highly affected by climate hazards (IPCC, 2022). More than 20 million people a year are displaced because of extreme weather events (e.g., flooding, rising sea levels, cyclones, and desertification) (United Nations High Commissioner for Refugees, [UNHCR], 2022). For more information on immigrants and refugees, please see Chapter 9.

Black, Indigenous, and People of Color (BIPOC) are disproportionately harmed by climate hazards (IPCC, 2022). Disparities in climate-related health outcomes are grounded in environmental racism, defined as discriminatory policymaking, practices, regulations, and laws (e.g., redlining, racial segregation) based on race or color (Berberian et al., 2022; Brulle & Pellow, 2006; Kaufman & Hajat, 2021). BIPOC adults and children are overburdened by environmental injustices such as poor air quality, water contamination, proximity to landfills, noise pollution, residential crowding, substandard housing, exposure to chemicals and toxins, less access to green spaces, and other environmental injustices (Brulle & Pellow, 2006). Environmental injustices

BOX 17.7 **PAUSE AND REFLECT: EXPERIENCE, KNOWLEDGE, ADVOCACY**

Questions to ask yourself:

What do I know about climate change? Where has my knowledge of climate change come from?

How important is climate change to me personally? Why?

How do my own cultural background and experiences of privilege and marginalization influence my views of climate change?

How would I work with a client impacted by the climate crisis?

What more do I need to know about climate change?

How can I best advocate for climate justice within my community?

closely interact with and are compounded by poverty (Berberian et al., 2022). Communities of color suffer from health inequities such as higher rates of infant mortality, cardiovascular disease, stroke, renal illness, respiratory illness, mental illness, reproductive complications, adverse perinatal outcomes, infectious diseases, heat-related illness, and overall higher rates of mortality compared to White people (Berberian et al., 2022; Brulle & Pellow, 2006; IPCC, 2022). Environmental justice is an issue of diversity, equity, and inclusion for all people, especially the most marginalized.

Counseling in the Climate Crisis

Counselors have a responsibility to address the mental health needs of clients and communities affected by the climate crisis and "advocate at the individual, group, institutional, and societal levels to address potential barriers and obstacles that inhibit access and/or the growth and development of clients" (ACA, 2014, Section A.7.a., p. 5).

BOX 17.8 **TIPS FOR PROFESSIONAL PRACTICE: COUNSELING IN CLIMATE CRISIS**

When broaching subjects such as climate change, well-being, and eco-anxiety with clients, the following questions can be helpful conversation starters.

How does your environment affect your health and well-being?

Have you been exposed to a frightening weather event like a flood, fire, or tornado? Do you have any concerns about your environment?

How would you describe your relationship with nature? What would a safe and harmonious climate mean to you?

Many techniques that are effective in alleviating anxiety and depressive symptoms are transferrable to eco-related distress, such as mindfulness, guided meditation, progressive muscle relaxation, and deep breathing exercises (Feder, 2022; Strum et al., 2020; Whitmarsh et al., 2022). Additionally, counselors can support clients by providing psychoeducation about climate change and processing the injustices experienced by the client and other communities (Feder, 2022; Reese & Myers, 2012). From here, counselors can integrate the seven components of EcoWellness (Reese & Myers, 2012) to foster climate resilience with clients and communities (Meyers, 2020; Reese & Todd, 2019; Strum et al., 2020). Table 17.5 provides an overview of the seven components of EcoWellness and example strategies (Reese & Myers, 2012).

TABLE 17.5 EcoWellness Strategies

Dimensions of EcoWellness	EcoWellness Counseling Strategies
Physical Access: *Spending time in a natural environment*	Do you have regular and safe access to nature or green spaces? How much time do you spend in nature? Do you experience barriers to interacting physically with nature?
Sensory Access to Nature: *Engaging the senses without physical access to a natural environment*	What nature sounds, sights, smells, and other senses are soothing to your system? Do you have access to these sensory modalities? Are there sensory elements of nature that are distressing to your system?
Connection: *Reflecting on the images, memories, and positive feelings experienced when in a natural environment*	What is the importance for you to feel connected to nature? When you imagine nature, what feelings and thoughts happen for you? Where do you feel most connected to nature?
Protection: *Integrating elements of nature to support safety and well-being*	How do you promote your safety and well-being while in nature? In what natural environments do you feel the safest?
Preservation: *Partaking in environmental activities*	How important is it to you to make a positive difference to the natural environment? What activities, if any, do you regularly participate in to preserve nature?
Spirituality: *Feelings of connectedness with oneself and beyond oneself while in nature*	How is nature related to your sense of spirituality, if at all?
Community Connectedness: *Experiencing a sense of belonging with other people while in nature*	Does nature influence your sense of community with others? How does nature affect your sense of connectedness with all living beings?

Ecological Advocacy and the Climate Crisis

The climate crisis is a global threat; however, this threat disproportionately impacts socially and culturally marginalized populations (IPCC, 2022). To best employ effective advocacy interventions with and on behalf of clients and communities, counselors must acknowledge the urgency of the climate crisis (Meyers, 2020; Ratts et al., 2016; Strum et al., 2020). Counselors should assist clients in identifying the factors that contribute to eco-anxiety and the existential elements that influence their cognitive, affective, and behavioral responses to the climate crisis (Strum et al., 2020). It is important for counselors to acknowledge that access to safe greenspaces may be inequitable for clients; counselors should assist clients in engaging in alternative modalities of nature such as through storytelling, artwork, writing, music, and photography (Baudon & Jachens, 2021; Reese & Myers, 2012). Counselors can provide opportunities to explore environmentally meaningful activities that align with the clients' values, such as reducing single-use plastics and limiting energy use at home (Baudon & Jachens, 2021; Reese & Myers, 2012). These strategies may be useful for managing eco-anxiety by empowering clients to build a pro-environmental identity (ACA, 2018; Ogunbode et al., 2022; Whitmarsh et al., 2022). Further, fostering a pro-environmental identity within the counseling relationship may motivate clients to engage in other levels of climate advocacy (Bauchon & Jauchons, 2021). Examples could include clients joining local or national advocacy groups and organizations that encourage collective action and support (Baudon & Jachens, 2021; Feder, 2022; Reese & Myers, 2012).

At the community level, counselors should consult with community members to determine community resources that may reduce climate-related harms, including the need for counselors to provide crisis response following a climate-related event. Collaborating with stakeholders is imperative to assess the diverse needs of the community, including their strengths and resiliencies (Meyers, 2020). To promote EcoWellness at the community level, counselors should conduct a needs assessment of current and impending climate hazards and strategize solutions with community stakeholders (Strum et al., 2020). Attention to community action should be focused on the urgent needs of its members, especially vulnerable persons. For example, counselors can advocate with or on behalf of a community to increase access to safe drinking water, community gardens, and safe access to parks.

Both nationally and internationally, counselors must recognize their positions of privilege and nonprivilege with respect to climate change and how this may influence their roles as advocates for environmental justice (Ratts et al., 2016). Many leaders in larger environmental justice organizations are White and middle-class (Yale Sustainability, 2020). This is important to emphasize because the experiences of BIPOC and other socially vulnerable groups should be represented and centered in the lobbying efforts that disproportionately affect them (Meyers, 2020; Strum et al., 2020). The climate crisis is a social justice issue, and counselors must acknowledge and examine the intersectional factors that compound climate risk exposure for individuals and communities globally and prioritize advocacy efforts to mitigate the overburdening of climate change (IPCC, 2022). This could include participating in professional panels on mental health and climate change, meeting with national and/or global authorities, voting for representatives who are committed to climate equity, and participating in national and/or international protests and activist campaigns to promote environmental justice worldwide.

Conclusion

In this chapter, the authors have illuminated five emerging areas critical for culturally relevant and ethical practice: fatmisia, neurodivergence, incarcerated populations, individuals with substance use disorders, and the climate crisis. While these are separate, discrete topics, they have a great deal of overlap when considering who they impact most frequently and what counseling strategies are most appropriate. As you continue to grow in your counselor identity and define your practice, be alert to new areas of culturally relevant practice. As our communities, country, and world continue to change, we, too, will adapt to our clients' changing needs.

Questions for Reflection

Consider what you learned in this chapter as you respond to the questions and prompts below.

1. What do you believe will be the pressing, emerging issues for counselors to learn to address? Were they explained in this chapter or something else?
2. Which cultural groups are most susceptible to the emergent areas discussed in this chapter?
3. Of the areas discussed in this chapter, which did you have the most biases about or feel less compelled to serve the individuals who represent these groups? From where do these biases stem? How would you like to work through them?
4. How do you plan to increase your knowledge and skills about new areas of concern clients are experiencing?
5. Have you been impacted by any of the emerging areas discussed in the chapter? If so, how will it impact your counseling practice? If not, how will you learn more about the lived experiences of others who are?

Applying What You Have Learned

Complete each of the following activities, considering what you learned from this chapter.

Activity #1: Advocacy Video

The areas discussed in this chapter are new in terms of considering them within a multicultural context within professional counseling, yet they have been quietly affecting individuals and communities for decades. With a partner or small group, create a 90 second video that focuses on how professional counseling can help regarding one of the areas discussed in this chapter. Then, post the video on social media so others can learn how counseling can be beneficial.

Activity #2: See Your Community in a New Way

Every community, no matter how large or small, has indicators of the areas discussed in this chapter. Choose one of the areas discussed in this chapter, and with a partner, go out into your community and record what you see. You can do this by walking, driving, or taking public transportation. Before you go, discern what types of things might indicate support for the group you are examining, as well as what might be detrimental. Pay attention to stores, billboards, advertisements, the overall environment, people, and conversations, and record your observations. Afterward, discuss what you encountered, what clients' impressions might be, and how what you observed can be integrated into the counseling process. Bonus: If you identify more detrimental indicators than supportive ones, decide on an advocacy action you can take (which could be the advocacy video in Activity 1!).

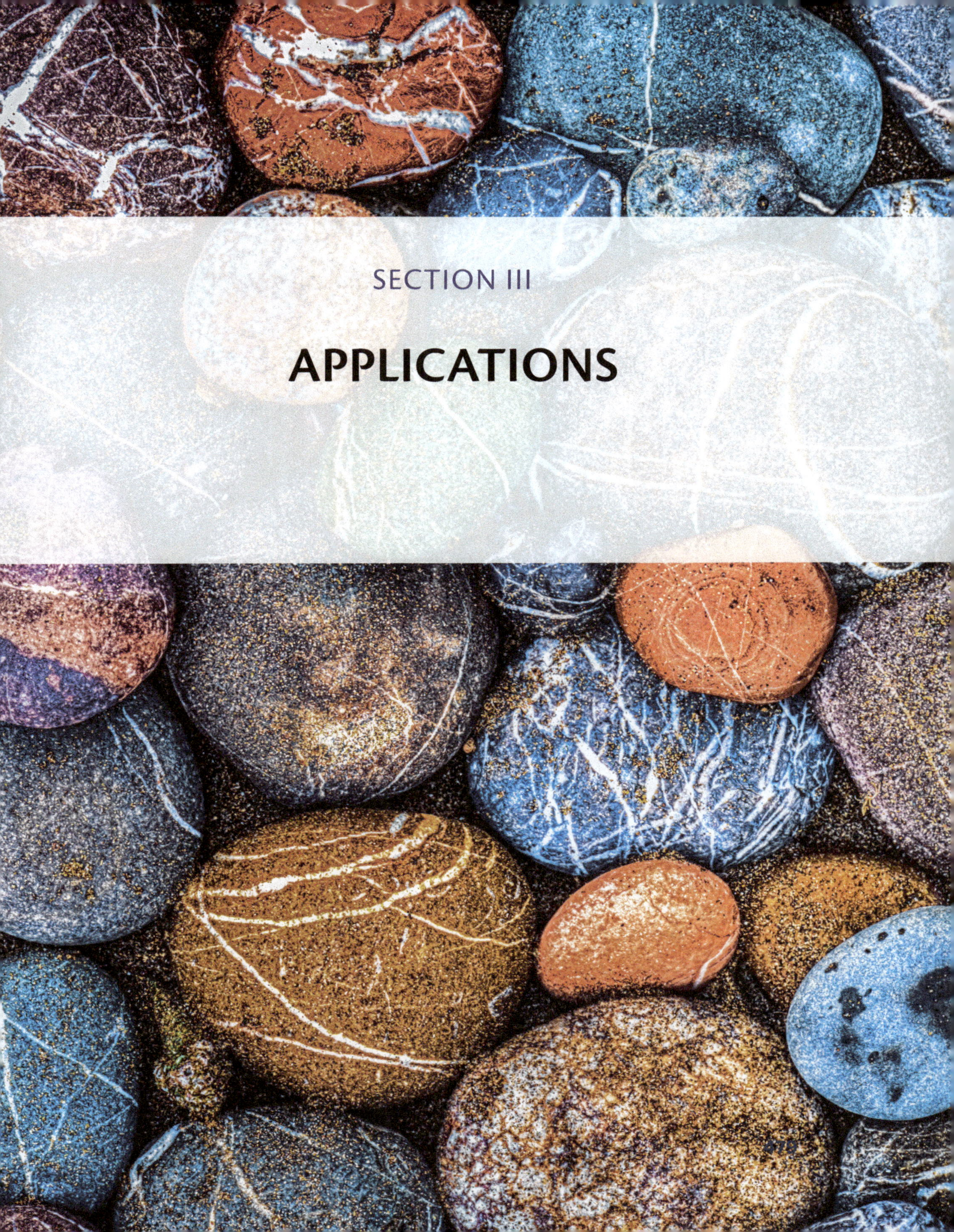

SECTION III

APPLICATIONS

CHAPTER 18

Applying Culturally Competent Skills Across Counseling Settings

Intake, Assessment, Diagnosis, Case Conceptualization, and Treatment Planning

Madeline Clark, Gwendolyn Hooks, Kathleen Klein, and Renee Stack

Healing is a matter of time, but it is sometimes also a matter of opportunity.

—Hippocrates

CHAPTER OVERVIEW

In this chapter, we discuss the applications of the content that you learned throughout this textbook, specifically as it relates to key counseling processes: intake, assessment, diagnosis, case conceptualization, and treatment planning. Ultimately, we aim to give you concrete examples of what you might do in various counseling settings as a culturally relevant practitioner and social justice advocate when working with clients, consumers, and/or students. We focus specifically on inpatient, outpatient, and school counseling settings, though counseling settings are not limited to those three. Counselors work in a variety of settings, and diversity, equity, and inclusion in the counseling process are paramount in all. We hope you will consider this chapter within the context of your own counseling identity, whether that is as a school counselor, clinical mental health counselor, marriage and family counselor, rehabilitation counselor, or addictions counselor in training. First, we introduce you to common terms, diversity models, and ethical considerations in various settings. Next, we discuss diversity, equity, and inclusion in the counseling process from intake to termination. Finally, we provide case studies to apply the skills you've learned throughout this text in a variety of counseling settings.

LEARNING OBJECTIVES

By the end of this chapter, students will be able to

1. explain the basic stages of the counseling process (e.g., intake, assessment, diagnosis) in various counseling settings and how they can make them culturally relevant for each client,
2. identify the differences in counseling processes and diversity applications across various professional counseling settings (e.g., school counseling, clinical mental health counseling, rehabilitation counseling) and levels of care, and
3. apply cultural competence across the counseling relationship, including intake, assessment, diagnosis, case conceptualization, treatment planning, interventions, and referral/termination.

CACREP 2016 STANDARDS

The information in this chapter supports the following standards:

- 2.F.1.e advocacy processes needed to address institutional and social barriers that impede access, equity, and success for clients
- 2.F.2.h strategies for identifying and eliminating barriers, prejudices, and processes of intentional and unintentional oppression and discrimination
- 2.F.5.h developmentally relevant counseling treatment or intervention plans
- 2.F.5.i development of measurable outcomes for clients
- 2.F.7.a historical perspectives concerning the nature and meaning of assessment and testing in counseling
- 2.F.7.b methods of effectively preparing for and conducting initial assessment meetings
- 2.F.7.m ethical and culturally relevant strategies for selecting, administering, and interpreting assessment and test results

CACREP 2024 STANDARDS

The information in this chapter supports the following standards:

- 3.A.4. the role and process of the professional counselor advocating on behalf of and with individuals receiving counseling services to address systemic, institutional, architectural, attitudinal, disability, and social barriers that impede access, equity, and success
- 3.B.4. the effects of historical events, multigenerational trauma, and current issues on diverse cultural groups in the U.S. and globally
- 3.B.6. the effects of various socio-cultural influences, including public policies, social movements, and cultural values, on mental and physical health and wellness
- 3.B.7. disproportional effects of poverty, income disparities, and health disparities toward people with marginalized identities
- 3.B.9. strategies for identifying and eliminating barriers, prejudices, and processes of intentional and unintentional oppression and discrimination
- 3.E.11. strategies for adapting and accommodating the counseling process to client culture, context, abilities, and preferences
- 3.E.12. goal consensus and collaborative decision-making in the counseling process
- 3.E.13. developmentally relevant and culturally sustaining counseling treatment or intervention plans
- 3.E.14. development of measurable outcomes for clients
- 3.G.1. historical perspectives concerning the nature and meaning of assessment and testing in counseling
- 3.G.10. use of structured interviewing, symptom checklists, and personality and psychological testing
- 3.G.5. culturally sustaining and developmental considerations for selecting, administering, and interpreting assessments, including individual accommodations and environmental modifications
- 3.G.6. ethical and legal considerations for selecting, administering, and interpreting assessments
- 3.G.7. use of culturally sustaining and developmentally appropriate assessments for diagnostic and intervention planning purposes

Essential Terms and Models

Assessment: The process by which a counselor gathers information about a client to make decisions about their needs and to inform treatment planning (Leppma & Jones, 2013). Assessment is a critical step in the counseling process and occurs not only at the beginning of the relationship but throughout it. Assessments can be formal or informal, formative or summative, and qualitative or quantitative. Information gained through assessment includes client relationships and perceived support; presenting concerns and the impact (e.g., symptoms, functioning); client identities and associated worldviews, values, and ways of being; and client environment, experiences with oppression, resources, and strengths. Assessment is on-going, and one might say that the entire counseling process itself is assessment because the counselor learns new information about the client constantly.

Case Conceptualization: Using the totality of the data counselors gather about clients, they devise a full picture of the client, their context, and why the problem is a problem for them. This process begins by building a mental map of the client's experiences, needs, access to resources, barriers, privileges, oppressions, presenting concerns, and other variables that impact the client's case (Sperry & Sperry, 2020) and then transfers the mental map to a formalized conceptualization that is used to devise a treatment plan. Essentially, case conceptualization is how you understand the client and their problems and how you will work with them to meet their needs. Case conceptualization is highly influenced by counselors' own cultural values and development, as well as their theoretical orientation.

Diagnosis: Diagnosis is the process by which a counselor uses the data gathered through assessment to determine a named mental health disorder using established diagnostic criteria (typically through the *DSM-5-TR* or *ICD-11* in medical settings). Diagnosis is used in many but not all counseling settings for the purposes of guiding treatment providing clients with a name for their presenting concerns and symptoms, and typically is necessary for third-party payment (Banks-VanAllen, 2023). Diagnosis has a complicated history in the mental health professions; diagnostic procedures and outcomes were often leveraged without consideration for clients' identities and contexts, raising several multicultural and social justice issues. This means that in some cases, the act of diagnosis itself can be oppressive for some clients. While improvements have been made, social justice concerns and challenges with cultural competency in diagnosis remain (e.g., accurate diagnosis, norming groups, symptom variations across groups).

Evidence-Based Practices (EBPs): EBPs are critical in mental health treatment and help counselors know if the interventions they are using have specific research backing to determine their efficacy. EBP is a common buzzword used in physical and mental health settings. Unfortunately, there is significant confusion about what EBPs actually are. EBPs are interventions and/or programs that have established efficacy through research in a controlled setting (e.g., clinical trial; Melnyck et al., 2010). This means that not every intervention or program with empirical support is an EBP because of the rigorous process interventions must undergo to receive EBP status. While empirical support is a necessary condition, it is insufficient. EBPs must be aligned with client values and be delivered by competent professionals. Combining all three EBP components increases the likelihood of quality treatment that will help clients without causing harm. The history and creation of EBPs is fraught with hazards. In many cases, EBPs were not developed with diverse and or minoritized populations. This means that what might be an EBP with a White, Eurocentric, heterosexual male population is not an EBP for all.

Interventions that are supported by research but do not meet the criteria for EBPs are called evidence-supported practices (ESPs) or evidence-supported treatments (ESTs). Whether counselors use EBPs, ESPs, or ESTs, it is important to engage in a counseling process that uses culturally appropriate and affirming interventions that infuse the core conditions.

Intake: An intake, intake interview, and biopsychosocial interview, among others, is the initial step of the assessment process. In many settings, the intake begins with clients completing paperwork. The intake interview is typically conducted during the first meeting with the client and may include other relevant stakeholders like parents or caregivers. During intake, counselors collect background information, personal history, and information about their presenting concern (American Psychological Association, 2023) and follow up with information recorded in the intake paperwork during the intake interview. The intake and intake interview are the first steps of assessment and influence the subsequent counseling process, so counselors must remember that relationship building is essential during this first session! It is critical that counselors suspend judgment and bias in order to actively listen and assess the client without prejudice; a lack of cultural competency, counselor awareness, or poor awareness of client culture can negatively impact this initial assessment and therefore the rest of the assessment, case conceptualization, and diagnostic process.

Multi-Tiered System of Supports (MTSS): MTSS is a prevention-based framework that uses data to inform instruction and intervention through direct and indirect services in educational settings (ASCA, 2021; Belser et al., 2016; Betters-Bubon et al., 2022; Edwin et al., 2021) that has three identified tiers (Tier 1-Universal, Tier 2-Targeted, Tier 3-Intensive). Additionally, there are four elements of MTSS—data-driven decision-making, EBPs, school-wide systems, and student outcomes (Edwin et al., 2021).

Referrals: The process by which counselors make recommendations to clients to access other health-care professionals, either to augment current counseling services or to begin treatment with another counseling provider. Referring a client to another source for assessment, care, or other healing practices is an important ethical responsibility (Natwick, 2017). The counselor is tasked with ensuring that the source the client has been referred to not only meets their needs but is also a culturally competent and affirming resource. Notably, counselors do not refer based on clients' cultural identities.

Treatment Planning: Treatment planning is establishing, in collaboration with the client, what will occur in the counseling process based on the counselor's assessment, diagnosis, and case conceptualization to help the client reach their goals. There are various models that can be used for treatment planning, some being more general (e.g., ICANSTART) and those that are grounded in counseling theoretical orientations (e.g., cognitive behavioral therapy (CBT), RCT; Gutierrez et al., 2018). Treatment planning includes client contextual factors, client expectations, client attributes, counselor attributes, and cultural factors (Wampold, 2015).

Ethical Considerations by Setting

When we consider the role of the counselor in diverse counseling relationships and contexts, we must first understand our scope of practice, relevant models (e.g., MSJCC; Ratts et al., 2015), and our charges via our ethical codes. As outlined in Chapter 2, our professional codes of ethics require us to be engaged in the work of multicultural orientation, ethics, and inclusion throughout the counseling relationship and in all areas of practice. Table 18.1 summarizes some relevant codes from the American Counseling Association (ACA), American Mental Health Counseling Association AMHCA, American School Counseling Association (ASCA), Commission on Rehabilitation Counselor Certification (CRCC), and National Board for Certified Counselors (NBCC) related to intake, assessment, diagnosis, treatment planning, interventions, and referrals. For a refresher on ethics and ethical codes, please review Chapter 2.

Each professional counseling body has delineated the responsibilities of counselors in the domains we will address in this chapter. While not every counseling specialization has the same scope of practice, the same principles typically apply. Broadly, the ACA (2014) outlines that counselors should convey information to clients in a culturally competent way across the counseling relationship (A.2.c), does not allow counselors to refer clients on the basis of values or cultural differences (A.11.b), and reinforces that counselors must consider client culture and the history of oppression in client assessment, testing, diagnosis, and treatment planning (E.5.b, E.5.c, E.8). Similar to ACA, the NBCC (2023; another profession-wide body) requires counselors to consider culture across the counseling relationship (7) and specifically how cultural identity impacts client presentation and the use of testing and assessments (61).

When we examine the ethical codes for different counseling specializations, we also see consistency. The AMHCA (2022) focuses on cultural competence in treatment planning (B.1.a), how cultural values shape the counseling relationship (C.1.g), cultural sensitivity in diagnosis and assessment (D.1.a), and cultural considerations for interpretation and reporting assessment results (D.2.b) specific to the work setting of clinical mental health counselors (CMHCs). The ASCA (2022a), the organization for professional school counselors (PSCs), lists these same topics but in a school setting. The ASCA *Code* (2022a) names culturally competent appraisal and assessment of students (A.1.d and A.14.a), appropriate and culturally sensitive interventions (A.1.j), and requires that PSCs do not make referrals based on cultural differences (A.6.e). Finally, rehabilitation counselors who use the CRCC *Code* (2023) will find themselves governed by similar standards associated with culturally competent treatment plans (A.1.b), counselor values in termination and referral (A.7.b), and inclusion and cultural sensitivity of assessment and diagnosis practices (H.1.b, H.3.b, and H.5.c). As you can see, all the ethical codes focus on equitable practices across populations within assessment, diagnosis, interventions, treatment planning, and referrals in some way. While we cannot get into the particulars of each specialization and setting, we hope to communicate ways you can practice in ethically and culturally relevant ways.

TABLE 18.1 Ethical Codes and Cross-Cultural Counseling Process

ACA (2014)	AMHCA (2020)	ASCA (2022a)	CRCC (2022)	NBCC (2023)
A.2.c. Developmental and Cultural Sensitivity Counselors communicate information in ways that are both developmentally and culturally appropriate. Counselors use clear and understandable language when discussing issues related to informed consent. When clients have difficulty understanding the language that counselors use, counselors provide necessary services (e.g., arranging for a qualified interpreter or translator) to ensure comprehension by clients. In collaboration with clients, counselors consider cultural implications of informed consent procedures and, where possible, counselors adjust their practices accordingly.	B.1.a Treatment Plans CMHCs and their clients work jointly to devise integrated, individual treatment plans that offer reasonable promise of success and are consistent with the abilities; ethnic, social, cultural, and values backgrounds; and circumstances of the clients.	A.1.d Supporting Student Development Provide culturally responsive instruction and appraisal and advisement to students.	A.1.b Rehabilitation Counseling Plans CRCs/CCRCs and clients collaborate to develop client-centered, integrated, individualized, mutually agreed-upon, written rehabilitation counseling plans. This agreed-upon plan is consistent with the abilities and circumstances of clients. CRCs/CCRCs and clients regularly review rehabilitation counseling plans to assess their continued viability and effectiveness and revise them as needed, while respecting the client's informed decision-making.	7. Professional Responsibilities Counselors shall demonstrate multicultural counseling competence in practice. Counselors will not use counseling techniques or engage in any professional activities that discriminate against or show hostility toward individuals or groups based on gender, ethnicity, race, national origin, sex, sexual orientation, disability, religion, or any other legally prohibited basis.

(Continued)

TABLE 18.1 *(Continued)*

ACA (2014)	AMHCA (2020)	ASCA (2022a)	CRCC (2022)	NBCC (2023)
A.11.b. Values Within Termination and Referral Counselors refrain from referring prospective and current clients based solely on the counselor's personally held values, attitudes, beliefs, and behaviors. Counselors respect the diversity of clients and seek training in areas in which they are at risk of imposing their values onto clients, especially when the counselor's values are inconsistent with the client's goals or are discriminatory in nature.	C.1.g Competence Recognize the important need to be competent with respect to cultural diversity; CMHCs are sensitive to the diversity of different populations and to changes in cultural expectations and values over time.	A.1.j Supporting Student Development Advocate for equitable, anti-oppressive and anti-bias policies and procedures, systems and practices, and provide effective, evidence-based and culturally sustaining interventions to address student needs.	A.7.b Values Within Termination And Referral CRCs/CCRCs refrain from referring prospective and current clients to another provider based solely on CRCs/CCRCs personally held values, attitudes, beliefs, and behaviors. CRCs/CCRCs respect the diversity of clients and seek training in areas in which they are at risk of imposing their values onto clients, especially when CRCs/CCRCs values are inconsistent with the client's goals or are discriminatory in nature.	61. Testing, Appraisal, and Research Counselors shall only use current, valid tests and assessments specifically necessary for the provision of quality services, and that have been carefully considered in terms of the instrument's validity, reliability, psychometric limitations, and appropriateness for use with regard to a particular population or client.

ACA (2014)	AMHCA (2020)	ASCA (2022a)	CRCC (2022)	NBCC (2023)
E.5.b. Cultural Sensitivity Counselors recognize that culture affects the manner in which clients' problems are defined and experienced. Clients' socioeconomic and cultural experiences are considered when diagnosing mental disorders.	D.1.a Assessment and Diagnosis CMHCs choose assessment methods that are reliable, valid, and appropriate based on their client's age, gender, race, ability status, etc. If tests must be used in the absence of information regarding the aforementioned factors, the limitations of generalizability should be duly noted.	A.6.e Appropriate Collaboration, Advocacy, and Referrals Refrain from referring students based solely on the school counselor's personal beliefs or values rooted in one's religion, culture, ethnicity or personal worldview. School counselors maintain the highest respect for student cultural identities and worldviews. School counselors pursue additional training and supervision when their values are discriminatory in nature (e.g., sexual orientation, gender identity, gender expression, reproductive rights, race, religion, ability status). School counselors do not impose their values on students and/or families when making referrals to outside resources for student and/or family support.	H.1.b Avoiding Bias in Assessment As part of the assessment process, CRCs/CCRCs address concerns about bias that may impact the evaluation of a client by (1) choosing unbiased methods, instruments, and procedures based on the individual evaluee; (2) recognizing and addressing issues of bias when interpreting assessment results; and (3) communicating those issues when sharing the results of assessment with other parties who are entitled to receive them.	

(*Continued*)

TABLE 18.1 *(Continued)*

ACA (2014)	AMHCA (2020)	ASCA (2022a)	CRCC (2022)	NBCC (2023)
E.5.c Historical and Social Prejudices in the Diagnosis of Pathology Counselors recognize historical and social prejudices in the misdiagnosis and pathologizing of certain individuals and groups and strive to become aware of and address such biases in themselves or others.	D.2.b Interpretation and Reporting CMHCs consider multicultural factors in test interpretation, diagnosis, and the formulation of prognosis and treatment recommendations.	A.14.a Evaluation, Assessment, and Interpretation Use only valid and reliable research-based tests and assessments that are culturally sensitive, in the student's preferred language and free of bias.	H.3.b Multicultural Sensitivity CRCs/CCRCs recognize that culture affects the manner in which a client's symptoms are defined and experienced. A client's socioeconomic and cultural experiences are considered when diagnosing mental disorders. CRCs/CCRCs carefully consider the specific validity, reliability, and appropriateness of tests when selecting them for use in a given situation or with a particular individual. CRCs/CCRCs are cognizant of cultural considerations and impact when evaluating and interpreting the test results or test performance of individuals with disabilities, marginalized groups, or other persons who are not represented in the standardized norm group of the instrument being used.	

ACA (2014)	AMHCA (2020)	ASCA (2022a)	CRCC (2022)	NBCC (2023)
E.8. Multicultural Issues/ Diversity in Assessment Counselors select and use with caution assessment techniques normed on populations other than that of the client. Counselors recognize the effects of age, color, culture, disability, ethnic group, gender, race, language preference, religion, spirituality, sexual orientation, and socioeconomic status on test administration and interpretation, and they place test results in proper perspective with other relevant factors.			H.5.c Appropriate Use With Multicultural Populations CRCs/CCRCs are responsible for the appropriate application, scoring, interpretation, and use of assessment instruments relevant to the needs of the client, whether they score and interpret such assessments themselves or use technology or other professional evaluator/ psychometric service providers. CRCs/ CCRCs consider the sample group normative data when reporting results.	

BOX 18.1 **PAUSE AND REFLECT: ETHICAL CODES AND YOUR PRACTICE**

Drawing on what you have learned from previous chapters, identify an ethical code from Table 18.1 that will apply to your future practice. Considering that ethical code, think of how you would apply it to a population or group that you have learned about through this text.

What might this ethical code look like in actual practice with the population you selected?

Cross-Cultural Best Practices in Intake

As you have learned, becoming a multiculturally oriented counselor involves understanding one's own biases, identifying implicit or explicit biases you hold, and understanding your privileged and marginalized identities, particularly in relation to the identities of each client you serve. This process applies to intake, assessment, and diagnosis just as it does to the rest of the counseling relationship! In this section, we discuss how counselors apply cultural awareness, knowledge, and skills as part of the initial counseling process.

BOX 18.2 **PAUSE AND REFLECT: BIAS IN RECOGNIZED PRACTICES? REALLY?**

Before you began reading this chapter, had you ever considered that intake, assessment, and diagnosis can be biased? Afterall, these are established practices that have been revised over and over again by many people across the allied mental health professions. Could they really be *biased*?

Consider your cultural identities. What might a counselor say or do during intake, assessment, or diagnosis that would invalidate one of your identities and your associated worldviews, values, or beliefs? What thoughts or feelings would arise for you? How would you react? Take your reactions into account as you read further and use them to stimulate perspective taking about how clients might respond.

Office Spaces and Intake Processes

The intake session is often the first major encounter between the client and the clinician beyond any phone or email request for services. Just as the website should be welcoming of diverse populations, so should the intake process and forms. The purpose of the intake is essentially twofold: collecting data and building rapport between client and clinician (Pashak & Heron, 2022). Generally, it entails identifying a client's presenting concerns, demographics, biopsychosocial background, strengths, support systems (e.g., family, friends, faith), broad symptomology and screening for mental health disorders, substance use, and risk of harm to self or others (Rivas-Vazquez et al., 2001). As the intake form is generally the first step in the treatment process and therefore the first documented interaction, it is imperative that it is structured appropriately. Research has shown that asking open-ended questions when possible, offering more options on multiple-choice items, and explaining why certain questions are asked can be helpful (Cook et al., 2020). Furthermore, as many clients who are members of marginalized groups often feel disempowered, using strength-based questions that can focus on resiliency can lead to reduced reporting of presenting concerns only, more hope, recognizing more solutions, and better outcomes long term (Liang & Shepherd, 2020). Additional forms, such as informed consent, should be explained not only in content but also include why they are needed. In addition to collecting the intake information and beginning to build the relationship in a culturally competent manner, there are additional strategies counselors can employ.

Prior to meeting with clients, ensure your office is as safe a space as possible. A *safer space* means your office is accessible, comfortable, inclusive, and welcoming for people from all backgrounds and experiences. Minimize physical obstacles, triggering odors, and bright lights. Displaying inclusion indicators, for example, a rainbow flag or literature, can help LGBTQIA+ clients feel welcome, or having literature in Spanish can demonstrate to Latine clients that you value their first language. Minimizing displays of personal photographs and mono-religious artifacts can assuage negative reactions from clients. It is critically important to consider accessibility for persons with different abilities, disabilities, and body sizes, as discussed in Chapters 12 and 17.

FIGURE 18.1 Examples of how to create affirming spaces

Ensure your office is accessible for a client who has a wheelchair, walker, crutches, service animal, or other mobility device. Consider seating options to be inclusive of all body sizes: Chairs with arms are not comfortable for all people, while sofas and chairs with wider seats are likely to work for more clients.

Additionally, be aware that every client has a multitude of aspects of their identity and affirming their intersectional identities is critical to gaining insight and trust. As you have learned, intersecting identities can be related to socioeconomic status, gender, sexuality, race, ethnicity, education, age, physical and cognitive ability (Sue et al., 2022). Understanding clients' multiple identities and how any personal biases (either on the part of the client or clinician) may interfere is critical to establishing trust and building rapport. The therapeutic alliance is the key factor in realizing successful outcomes, and it is critical that clients feel as comfortable as possible in their intake interview.

Counselors explore clients' identities during the intake and throughout the counseling process. Counselors never assume a client's identity (e.g., being a member of the LGBTQ+ community, having a disability) or that their identities are the reason for seeking treatment. Making assumptions can be damaging to the therapeutic alliance and impact treatment—if the client even returns to counseling. Listen to the client and let them tell their story, using reflections, summaries, and affirming body language to convey you are hearing them correctly.

BOX 18.3 **FOCUS ON CLIENT CARE**

A client of Iranian ethnicity named Neghar presents in Joe's counseling office and, during the intake session, broaches the subject of spirituality. As Joe's only experience with anyone of Iranian background has been Muslim, he assumes that she is also Muslim and mentions the local mosque. The client shares that she is actually Catholic.

This misstep can negatively impact rapport and the client's willingness to proceed with Joe. She may view him as having biases and making assumptions versus listening and maintaining curiosity toward her concerns.

If you were Joe, how would you proceed with this session? Remember to consider all that you've learned about identity through this text and the important need for cultural humility.

Broaching During Intake

Broaching culture with a client and having cultural humility can minimize assumptions and open cultural conversations (Day-Vines et al., 2021; see Box 18.4). Broaching is a component of cultural humility (see Chapter 3). Demonstrating an intent to be inclusive and open via broaching can "serve to increase provider-client rapport" (Bishop et al., 2021, p. 432) and improve not only the experience of your client in the intake session but also improve the quality of data you collect. Remaining open-minded and expressing the willingness to listen and learn will strengthen the bond and thereby lead to better treatment outcomes.

BOX 18.4 **TIPS FOR PROFESSIONAL PRACTICE: SAMPLE BROACHING QUESTIONS**

The University of Maryland Counseling Center (2016) has created the following list of broaching questions:

1. Where were you born? Tell me about that place.
2. Whom do you consider your family and why?
3. What languages do you speak? When do you use what language?
4. Who are your social support circles?
5. What religious or spiritual practices, if any, did you grow up with?
6. What activities do you enjoy?
7. How would you describe your cultural background?
8. What cultural traditions are most important to you?
9. Whom do you usually turn to for help when facing a problem?

Cross-Cultural Best Practices in Assessment

As you learned, the intake is a component of your overall assessment in the counseling relationship. Assessment occurs throughout the counseling process regardless of the setting or population served. Clinical counselors assess in each session, and school counselors have numerous opportunities to assess their students: in sessions, in classroom guidance, in groups, and in observations of the student throughout the school environment. It is critical to remember that assessment is happening whenever you are with the client or receiving information from relevant stakeholders (e.g., parents, teachers, case managers). Your values and biases can be a significant factor in how you assess. If you are unaware of your values, biases, and subsequent judgments, you risk collecting inaccurate data about the client or *missing* opportunities to collect data.

Similar to the intake, cultural knowledge and attunement are critical to accurate, relevant, and informative assessments. The goal of assessment is to gain insight into the client's presenting concerns, their support systems, and the overall impact of the situation and symptoms on their daily functioning. It is well-accepted that standard mental health assessment and professional practice in the United States were developed within Western cultural contexts (Sue, 2001). Few formal assessment instruments have been validated for cultural contexts outside those for which they were developed (Perry et al., 2019). Many psychometric assessments have been created and validated using White, middle-class, college student samples (because they are easily accessible to the researchers creating those assessments!). As such, clinicians need to use caution when administering and interpreting assessment results, especially with clients whose identities do not match the sample on which the assessment was normed. Inquiring beyond formal assessment results and understanding the client's perspective is the best means of establishing what is clinically significant.

One means of inclusive assessment is using the Cultural Formulation Interview (CFI) in the *Diagnostic and Statistical Manual of Mental Disorders Fifth Edition-Text Revision* (*DSM-5-TR*; APA, 2022). The CFI is a client-centered template for ascertaining the influence of cultural factors on the presenting concerns in psychiatric assessment (Strand & Bäärnhielm, 2021). The open-ended question format allows the client to share their perspective on topics like health, family relationships, treatment, spirituality, and other support mechanisms (Strand & Bäärnhielm, 2021). Learning this information can be critical to building the therapeutic alliance and discerning culturally appropriate case conceptualizations and treatment plans. There are supplemental modules to the CFI that target specific populations like older adults or refugees that can assist you with exploring further the impact of their culture on symptomatology.

Let's work through an example of how exploring culture with a client who has just experienced the death of a loved one can inform the counselor's assessment. Some cultures dictate that grieving is "an outward process that one is expected to engage in for years" (Boghosian, 2011, p. 58), while in other cultures, individuals are expected to *move on* after a few months. If your client is from a culture in which grief is expected to last for years, you may erroneously assess them as unable to process their grief and expressing abnormal depressive symptoms when in fact they are simply following their tradition (Boghosian, 2011). It is important that clinicians have the knowledge to differentiate between a culturally appropriate, culturally sanctioned practice and the need for formal diagnosis, such as prolonged grief disorder (APA, 2022).

Through culturally informed assessment, counselors collaborate effectively with the client to achieve the client's desired outcomes. As such, counselors select appropriate assessments that are most likely to provide informative results (see Box 18.5 for an example). Appropriate assessment can strengthen the bond between client and clinician, as well as deepen the client's understanding of their situation and symptoms. This process is repeated throughout treatment, as it allows for accurate diagnosis, treatment planning, and, thus, healing, the overall goal of counseling.

Culturally Informed Assessment in School Settings

Appraisal is used by school counselors to identify students' abilities, interests, and skills to support achievement (ASCA, 2019). It is essential for PSCs to understand various assessment instruments used in the school setting so they can interpret and analyze results in ways that support students and the development of individualized career, academic, and/or social-emotional plans. PSCs work conjointly with school psychologists, speech and language pathologists, school-based mental health counselors, teachers, and other educational professionals on multidisciplinary teams to assess the whole child and provide interventions accordingly. Importantly, PSCs, too, must ensure that assessment instruments are culturally appropriate for the student. Furthermore, PSCs play a critical role in multidisciplinary teams to ensure that students are being treated equitably and that their cultural identities are being accounted for and supported rather than pathologized.

Assessment in the school setting can be a challenge depending on what tools are available to them and, once accessed, how they are used to identify additional interventions or counseling support (Bardhoshi et al., 2019). Teacher observations, parent interviews, disciplinary reports, and medical documents are included in the assessment process at schools in addition to formal assessments (Bardhoshi et al., 2019). The use of universal screeners within the MTSS model is discussed later in the chapter.

Youth PTSD Assessment Examples

Adapted from Perry et al. (2019), the following assessments have been modified for diverse and marginalized children and teens.

1. Psychological Screening for Young Children (PSYCa 3–6)
   Originally validated in White Western populations, the new assessment is adjusted for educational levels and has been normed and validated in populations in Niger, Colombia, and Kenya.
2. UCLA Post-Traumatic Stress Disorder-Reaction Index (PTSD-RI)
   Transcultural validation is being achieved using criterion validity with key members and cultural informants in local cultures in Zambia.
3. The Post-Traumatic Cognitions Inventory (PTCI)
   Transcultural validation has been conducted in east Asian countries to account for cultural differences, such as cultural differences in individual relationships to self-blame.

Cross-Cultural Best Practices in Diagnosis

Diagnosis is a common event in clinical and rehabilitation counseling settings. School counselors typically do not diagnose but certainly will work with students who have mental health diagnoses. So, while not all counselors engage in diagnosing, all counselors must understand diagnoses and their potential impacts on clients. Diagnosis has positive and negative effects in counseling settings. Diagnosis can be positive, as it can help provide clinical language for client experiences, help clients learn about their own challenges, help them feel a sense of relief with a clinical explanation and name for their symptoms, and ultimately, can better help the profession understand different diagnoses via research, treatment interventions, and outcomes. Diagnosis is also necessary for third-party (insurance) reimbursement in most cases, which can help increase access to services for clients and ensure that counselors themselves are financially secure. Diagnosis also has negative components, which can include the prevalence of misdiagnosis, the lack of cultural inclusivity in diagnosis and diagnostic procedures, and possible stigmatization that accompanies some diagnoses. Diagnosis can be complicated when considering culture, and there is a great deal of debate regarding its efficacy and appropriateness with marginalized populations. However, diagnosis is common and used frequently across counseling settings following the assessment phase.

Once assessments are completed, clients in clinical settings are assigned one or more *DSM-5-TR* diagnoses (APA, 2022). Again, "culture must be viewed not as a distraction, but as a key factor in psychiatric diagnosis and central to the definition of mental and behavioral disorders" (Andary et al., 2003, p. 2). As the *DSM-5-TR* is based on the White Western medical model, it may not always be inclusive of cultural presentations or cultural differences. In many cultures, fear of bewitchment, avoiding eye contact, and extended grief (as discussed previously) are common. Not accounting for nondominant cultural norms and variances during diagnosis would be inaccurate and likely harmful to clients.

As an example, there is a common disorder in Nigeria known as *brain fag (fog) syndrome.* While the term *fag* is pejorative in the United States, it does not have the same definition in Nigeria as it does in the United States. Brain fag syndrome describes the mental and physical fogginess a person experiences and feels. Most clients present with fatigue, burning pain in the head or neck, difficulty focusing, sleep disturbances, and even blurred vision (Ayonrinde et al., 2015). While this disorder primarily affects students, it can affect others under stress as well. If a client who has recently immigrated from Nigeria presented with these symptoms and the counselor disregarded their cultural background, it would be easy for the counselor to assign an incorrect diagnosis of depression, anxiety, a neurological disorder, a somatic symptom disorder, or even schizophrenia. Misdiagnosis can result in more stress, and the client could become even more symptomatic! However, if they were given a diagnosis of brain fag in line with their cultural background, they may feel relief (Ayonrinde et al., 2015). Understanding culture-specific syndromes, ensuring client expressions of symptoms and clinician interpretations match, and awareness of cultural behaviors such as eye contact are all critical to accurate diagnosis (Perry et al., 2019). By reviewing a client's intersecting identities and incorporating follow-up questions into the intake interview, assessment, and diagnostic process, the counselor actively works to strengthen the therapeutic alliance through continued collaboration, increasing the likelihood of better client outcomes.

Case Conceptualization, Treatment Planning, and Interventions

A thorough assessment and thoughtful diagnosis sets the stage for the next phase: Case conceptualization. In this phase, counselors, with the client, create a full picture of the presenting problem that explains why the problem is a problem; this process lays the foundation for the treatment planning phase. While treatment plans are adapted as clients progress, the initial treatment plan lists goals and how clients will accomplish them through culturally responsive and appropriate interventions. As with case conceptualization, counselors work collaboratively with clients to create their treatment plan.

Case Conceptualization

Following intake, assessment, and diagnosis, counselors must seek to understand the presenting problem and the systems in place that help to maintain it. This is the core purpose of case conceptualization. Case conceptualization is not diagnosis but rather the *story* behind the stated problem; it requires the counselor to understand the client and their culture, including experiences with oppression, environment, strengths, and resources. Case conceptualization is where the art and science of counseling intersect. Culturally responsive counselors assess if and the extent to which external factors have contributed to the problem. The counselor investigates the key components listed below by asking key open questions and thoroughly listening carefully to the client's story.

Key Case Conceptualization Components

- Client identifying information
- Summary of what you know about the client
- Time line of events
- Lists of strengths and opportunities, noting how these inform diagnosis and treatment
- Diagnostic impression
- Prognosis statement
- Proposed course of treatment

The formal, written case conceptualization has several components that inform treatment planning. Counselors should explore things like who is the client? How did they come to be? What has been their journey? Case conceptualization is a process and tool, and like other tools, it has an identified purpose. When used correctly, it acknowledges and accounts for clients' lived experiences and leads to an effective treatment plan. When used incorrectly, it can interject bias, cause harm, and result in a treatment plan that is not appropriate for the client.

Treatment Planning and Interventions

Counselors create a map of how they will work with clients. This map is the treatment plan: an individualized, goal-focused plan that documents how counselors will work with clients to achieve their stated goals. Counselors collaborate with clients to cocreate this plan that includes structured, measurable goals, objectives, and interventions. A key aspect of treatment planning is understanding the importance of the client's culture. This requires that the counselor works to establish trust and connection with the client before diving into addressing the presenting concern—this means *not* problem-solving too quickly! Acknowledging that the counselor's culture is different from that of the client and leaving space to explore this is an important aspect of treatment planning (i.e., broaching). Before and while developing a plan for treatment, counselors must consider the impact of culture given cultures differ in their beliefs and attitudes about managing life challenges.

The treatment plan begins with a statement of the problem or a list of problems/symptomology, along with evidence for each. For example, if depression is listed as a problem/diagnosis, list assessment evidence (e.g., *BDI (Beck Depression Inventory) score of 52*) and the symptoms that are most troubling or pronounced based on client report (e.g., *Client reported loss of appetite all days for two weeks, sleeping 11 hours a day, missing work, frequent bouts of crying, feeling hopeless most of the day*).

After listing the problem(s), the counselor works with the client to develop SMART (Specific, Measurable, Achievable, Realistic and Time-limited) goals. The intention of goal-setting with clients is to set them up for success; SMART goals assist in this process. Below is an example of a SMART goal for a client who is seeking treatment for anxiety when delivering class presentations.

Example: Smart Goal Development

Goal Statement: During the fall semester, I will volunteer to present first in at least two courses to decrease anxiety related to giving oral presentations
Specific: Answer the 5Ws – who, what, when, where and why?

- Who: "I" client
- What: Volunteers to present first
- When: During the fall semester
- Where: In two courses
- Why: To reduce anxiety

***M*easurable:** Include a metric so clients know where they are currently and how far they have to go to achieve the goal.

- Metric: First to present in at least two courses; currently, always one of the last students to present.

***A*ttainable:** Can the client achieve this goal?

- Yes, it's doable: two out of four courses.

***R*ealistic:** Assess whether the goal can be accomplished reasonably by this specific client.

- Yes, the client has the skills and the opportunities to complete the goal.

***T*ime-bound**: Provide a timeline for when the goal will be completed.

- During the fall semester

Objectives and Interventions

Goals outline what the client will do, while objectives address how they will do it. Interventions are counselor-focused; they detail what actions the counselor will take to bring about change. Let's continue with the above example case. Consider how a counselor would help develop objectives and interventions for the following goal statement.

Goal Statement: During the fall semester, I will volunteer to present first in at least two courses to decrease anxiety related to giving oral presentations.

Example Objectives:
Objectives are active-focused and use action words to detail exactly what clients will do to move toward the stated goal.

- I will implement positive self-talk to reduce presentation-related anxiety.
- I will identify and verbalize worries and/or fears that contribute to anxiety.

Example Interventions:
Interventions are actions the counselor takes to support the client in achieving their goals. Typically, they are grounded in the counselor's theoretical orientation.

- The client will develop reality-based messages and use thought-stopping to increase confidence and reduce anxiety.
- The client will develop a robust list of coping strategies the client can use to manage anxiety.

Cultural sensitivity is important when developing treatment plans. Culturally sensitive counselors are open-minded and ask well-timed, appropriate questions without badgering or interrogating the client. They ensure that the goals and objectives listed in the treatment plan are culturally acceptable. For example, a counselor might consider how a minority client may respond to a standardized assessment like the BDI depending on that client's unique history or how the objectives and interventions align with the client's cultural values, beliefs, and ways of being.

Culturally Responsive Interventions

A key component of culturally responsive interventions is the ability to adapt interventions so they align with clients' values, beliefs, worldviews, and needs. Counselors incorporate cultural considerations when they recommend treatment, including culturally adapting EBPs. One example of such an adaptation is with CBT, a well-known EBP for a variety of mental health conditions. Interweaving cultural adaptations can make the treatment more culturally responsive and improve client outcomes. The question then becomes, how might a counselor identify cultural adaptation as an option, and how should they approach doing so? While this process does not follow a linear pathway, it can be helpful to think about this using a step-wise approach. Each step of this process is dependent on a foundation of trust that is strengthened when counselors are open to understanding clients' unique experiences and the role that culture plays in them. They must value diversity and have attitudes and core beliefs consistent with working effectively across cultures. This necessitates that counselors are aware of their own culture and how they are positioned within the larger sociocultural context. Then, they must have the knowledge to recognize when a cultural adaptation is indicated and understand the risk of implementing without adaptation. Next, counselors need the necessary skills to effectively adapt interventions while maintaining fidelity to the treatment.

CBT is an evidence-based practice when treatment is implemented with fidelity. When adapting treatment to enhance culture , it is important to be strategic and intentional with adaptations. Culturally adapted or Culturally-Focused CBT offers a systematic approach to adapting traditional CBT, which has its roots in Western culture, to promote better outcomes for clients from varying cultural backgrounds (Naeem et al., 2023). It is crucial that counselors understand when and how to adapt treatment and which specific pieces of the intervention are most amenable to adaptation. One such example is providing the option for clients to complete assignments in their preferred language. For some clients, including family members in the therapeutic process is a culturally responsive intervention that could enhance treatment effectiveness. For other clients, discerning *our* interventions (i.e., interventions that involve collaborative processes) rather than *I* interventions (i.e., individual actions) can be empowering. Other examples of culturally responsive interventions include language matching, having open discussions about culture-specific issues, attending to nonverbal behaviors, and the use of non-Eurocentric treatment modalities.

BOX 18.5 **FOCUS ON CLIENT CARE**

Consider:

- A Latiné client who is supported to complete counseling homework assignments in her first language (Spanish) rather than English. What positive effect might this have on the client and the therapeutic relationship?
- An Asian American client. Traditionally, psychotherapy is rooted in self-disclosure and emotional expression, which are antithetical to some Asian American cultural norms. When working with clients from this cultural group, counselors should consider more directive treatment like CBT or solution-focused therapy instead of relying on insight-focused interventions typical of psychodynamic therapies, depending on the client. What positive effect might this have on the client and the therapeutic relationship?

Culturally Informed Referrals and Recommendations

Referrals are common in counseling settings and occur for a variety of reasons. A counselor may make a referral for a client to receive additional mental health assessment, for health-care resources, for case management, or for additional self-care resources. Counselors make referrals when terminating the counseling relationship if their caseload is full, and in some cases, counselors may refer clients because the client's diagnosis is out of their scope of practice. Unfortunately, the parameters of the referral process are not always clearly described in the literature, which can leave counselors feeling directionless.

Referrals that are not made intentionally increase the likelihood a client may experience discrimination or cultural harm if the referral is not well vetted or if referrals are made unethically (see Table 18.1 earlier in this chapter). Beyond referrals to other counseling professionals, counselors sometimes make recommendations as part of the client's treatment plan (e.g., yoga for stress management and a dietician to support healthy eating goals). Next, we explore the common reasons for referrals with specific guidance related to cultural competence and inclusion.

Referral for Additional Mental Health Assessment

At some point, counselors of all specializations refer clients for additional mental health assessment. Additional mental health assessments are typically conducted by psychologists who specialize in testing and assessment for specific mental health disorders. For example, it is not uncommon for counselors to refer clients for additional assessment for neurodevelopmental disorders such as attention deficit hyperactivity disorder (ADHD) or ASD or for *DSM-5-TR* disorders classified in the schizophrenia spectrum and other psychotic disorders class.

BOX 18.6 **PAUSE AND REFLECT: BIAS IN AN ASSESSMENT REPORT**

Once, I (Dr. Clark) was reading an assessment report for a client I had been seeing at a nonprofit that served unhoused and formerly unhoused families. I had referred my client to a local psychology practice for an assessment; this client had Medicaid, and this was the only place she could go. My client had been unhoused, was experiencing poverty (acutely and generationally), and presented with severe and persistent mental illness. Upon receipt of the report, I read it thoroughly and discovered, to my dismay, really biased language. The assessor called my client "lazy," "uneducated," and "poor." While we can expect a mental status exam and client presentation to be included in reports such as these, I was shocked to see my client written about in such a biased way. It was clear to me that the assessor's bias about an unhoused woman of color was coming through, and it made me wonder about the veracity of the report. I processed the report with the client, including the language used and my client's experience during the assessment.

Consider this professional's choice of language: Why do you think words like *poor* and *uneducated* are problematic in this report and in how we would describe another person?

What might you do in this scenario? How would you process it with the client? What might you say to the assessor, if anything at all?

When making referrals for external mental health assessments, it is very important to understand the cultural competence of the provider to whom you are referring clients. Take, for example, ASD. We know that ASD presents differently in people assigned female at birth (AFAB) and People of Color. If you are sending an adolescent client who is Black a female for an ASD assessment, are you certain that the referral is competent to work with your client with intersecting identities?

Some questions you may want to ask providers about their competence *prior to* referring the client to them:

1. Tell me about the assessments you use. Are they inclusive of diverse and minoritized populations?
2. What type of language do you use to write about marginalized populations in your assessment reports?
3. How do you make your assessment process as inclusive as possible?

Referral for Health-Care Resources

In addition to referrals for mental health assessments, it is very common to make referrals to health-care providers for physical or mental health needs. For example, mental health referrals to psychiatrists and psychiatric nurse practitioners for psychotropic medications are common. Also, there are instances in which clients may not have health care at all and need support finding resources to access physical health care for chronic or acute conditions or a yearly physical.

In the United States, where health care is not accessible for all, it is important that your referral list includes physical health-care providers and/or organizations that can provide services to clients who do not have health insurance. Your referral list for health-care services should consider the cultural competence and inclusivity of the provider and the ability of clients across social classes to access those services. You will learn more about how to develop this list and screen other professionals later in this chapter.

BOX 18.7 **FOCUS ON CLIENT CARE**

Health care is extremely expensive in the United States, and without universal health care, many people are left without care. To help clients find qualified providers who provide services on a sliding scale, you can use this tool: https://findahealthcenter.hrsa.gov/.

Referral for Case Management

Counselors who work in outpatient mental health settings, especially in community mental health or the Veterans Administration, sometimes make referrals for case management. This referral is often made when clients have multiple intersecting challenges, such as challenges with severe and persistent mental illness (SPMI), housing, employment, health care, and/or legal issues. These barriers are considerable and represent clients' unique, diverse, and intersecting experiences! Case management can help with these challenges, and it often provides a more direct and hands-on, solution-focused approach that isn't achievable through counseling alone. Although the cultural competency of case managers is for another field and another text, it is important that you, as the client's counselor and advocate, ensure that your collaborative relationship (with appropriate releases, of course) with their case manager is positive and does not use biased language about your shared client. Counselors should continue to be social justice advocates and culturally adept helpers when working in the continuum of care.

BOX 18.8 **FOCUS ON CLIENT CARE**

It isn't uncommon that counselors are advocates for their clients and students within their employment settings with their coworkers, like teachers, administrators, case managers, and other allied health professionals. How might you address the below case?

You are a counselor working at a community agency. You share a client with a case manager named Lea. Lea expresses their frustration with you in a consultation meeting regarding the client's, Phyllis, progress. Lea says, "Phyllis just can't seem to get her life together. It's exhausting to have to teach her basic things and deal with her attitude. She just really doesn't care about making her life better."

To provide additional context, Phyllis is a Black single mother in her mid-50s pursuing SSDI (Social Security Disability Insurance) for an injury she sustained while working in her former factory job. Lea is a White woman in her 20s. You work with Phyllis weekly for issues associated with major depressive disorder (MDD) and trauma history.

1. How can you attend to Lea's frustrations without agreeing with her language regarding Phyllis?
2. How can you communicate your role as Phyllis's advocate without breaking confidentiality?

Referrals and Recommendations for Other Self-Care Resources

Counselors across settings make referrals to resources that are outside the traditional health-care system; this might include things like books (bibliotherapy), apps for symptom management and self-care, or even other self-care needs such as yoga, exercise, or time outdoors. While these resources can be incredibly useful for helping clients engage in their healing process inside and outside the counseling setting, there is little research about how counselors can do this effectively (e.g., Gamby et al., 2020) and with cultural considerations in mind.

When making referrals to these types of resources/services, it is important to assess what your client might be interested in or have room for in their life. For example, it might not make sense to refer a busy graduate student who is on a tight budget to an expensive yoga studio that conflicts with their courses or clinical placement. Another consideration is the welcoming and affirming positions of the resource. It would not be appropriate to refer a gender-expansive client of color to a group exercise course that doesn't actively welcome and include POC and gender-expansive people. We want to ensure that the referrals we give our clients are affirming to their identities and do not cause harm! Beyond affirmation of client identity and client safety, you must consider the accessibility of the referral. Is the referral accessible to the client financially? Is it accessible to their ability/disability? To their lifestyle? Their value system?

Referrals for Scope of Practice

Sometimes, counselors make referrals to other licensed mental health professionals (e.g., counselors, social workers, psychologists) because a client's presenting concern is outside their training or what we call the *scope of practice*. Sometimes, this can be a slippery slope (e.g., see *Ward v. Wilbanks* case in Chapter 15) if counselors refer for lack of comfort or having a bias toward a population—that is unethical and inappropriate, as we reviewed in the ethics table earlier in this chapter (Natwick, 2017). Referrals for scope of practice should occur when the client's presenting concern does not match the training a counselor has related to a diagnosis (e.g., disordered eating, substance use) or a specialization such as couples counseling or family counseling.

For example, a counselor could begin a relationship with a client in which the initial presenting concern was anxiety and a history of anxiety and compulsive behaviors. After a few sessions and continued assessment, the counselor realizes the primary concern is disordered eating, a complicated diagnosis to assess and treat, and requires very specialized care across a continuum of professionals. In this case, it would likely be most appropriate to refer this client to a disordered eating treatment facility or another mental health professional with very specific training in disordered eating to assess for the appropriate level of care.

Another example is the role of PSCs. While PSCs don't diagnose, they are frequently one of the first to assess children and adolescents for presenting mental health issues. While diagnosis is not in the scope of PSCs, PSCs must be prepared to make referrals to clinical counselors. For example, a student who presents with nonsuicidal self-injury (NSSI) via cutting themselves with sharp objects in school. In this instance, the PSC refers the student, in accordance with school regulations and local laws, to an appropriate mental health counselor with experience working with adolescents and NSSI and continues to be the liaison between this provider and the school setting (as long as appropriate releases are signed!).

Regardless of the reason for a scope of practice referral, it is the counselor's responsibility to ensure that referrals are culturally appropriate and a good fit for the client's presenting concern. This means that you must create a robust list of professionals in your area who have expertise in areas you do not. It can be helpful to network with them via a quick email or a call to assess their goodness of fit for your clients and their cultural competence.

Referrals for Termination or Full Caseload

At times, counselors must make referrals to other counselors not because of issues of expertise or scope of practice but because their caseload is full (e.g., unable to take on a client) or because of termination of services. Termination occurs for a variety of reasons. Perhaps the client is moving, or maybe the counselor is changing jobs or moving themselves. Ethical referral is critical in these instances. As per the ACA *Code of Ethics* (2014), the needs of clients are the priority, even if your caseload is full! The *Code* specifically outlines abandonment and neglect of clients as an ethical violation: "Counselors assist in making appropriate arrangements for the continuation of treatment, when necessary, during interruptions such as vacations, illness and following termination" (ACA, 2014, p. 6). This also includes the terminations of clients that often occur following the conclusion of a practicum and/or internship placement, so it is very relevant to counselors in training!

In cases where you have a caseload that is full (many counselors do!), or you need to terminate a client for another reason, as outlined above, you must be prepared with a robust list of appropriate referrals. To be culturally inclusive, you need to have a list of other counseling professionals who are not only culturally oriented themselves (you need to assess this before adding them to the list) but also practitioners with diverse identities. As explained earlier in this text, it is common for clients to want to work with a counselor who is culturally similar to them, so make sure you have diverse counselors on your list! If you are a counselor of color, you may find that your caseload fills quickly by clients seeking your services, and you'll need to be ready with a list of alternatives who can meet client needs.

As you create your list of counseling professionals, remember you must assess if they are culturally competent and if their scope of practice is what your clients need. This may seem like a daunting task, yet it can be accomplished through networking and simple conversations over time rather than in one fell swoop. Some questions you can ask other counselors about their cultural competence include the following:

1. What are your values about diversity and equity in your counseling relationships?
2. How do those values show up in your theoretical orientation and interventions?
3. What groups are you best suited to work with? Are there any groups that are challenging for you?
4. What are your specializations?
5. Do you accept insurance? Do you accept Medicaid? Do you have sliding-scale fees for uninsured clients?
6. Are you accepting new clients? Can I add you to my referral list?

If your caseload isn't full, you can position yourself as a culturally competent referral resource for other counselors. Be prepared to answer the above questions when asked or share this type of information without prompting to convey your commitment. Network at conferences and within community organizations. Ensure that how you advertise your services (e.g., online) indicates that you are an affirming and culturally competent practitioner. The need for culturally oriented practitioners is high!

BOX 18.9 **TIPS FOR PROFESSIONAL PRACTICE: CREATE A DIVERSE REFERRAL LIST**

Shortly before my daughter was born, I (Dr. Clark) was seeking a new counselor to help me adjust to being a parent. I sought out a specific counselor who was a woman and dealt with issues related to parenting and motherhood. Her caseload was full (sigh—of course!—a common struggle that many can relate to, I'm sure). She sent me her referral list, which only included three other counselors. Of the three, one was a former student of mine, another was a supervisor I had regular contact with as a practicum instructor, and the last was one of my former students whose dissertation I had chaired! This is a small example but highlights the need for a robust referral list (and how hard it can be to find your own counselor when you're a counselor and counselor educator!).

Considerations for School Counselors and School Settings

The school setting offers a unique process for counseling intervention, as the school counselor role is embedded within a comprehensive school counseling program that addresses the social-emotional, academic, and college and career domains for all students (ASCA, 2019). PSCs work collaboratively with other educational professionals and families to improve outcomes for student behaviors and learning (ASCA, 2023). The ASCA *Ethical Standards for School Counselors* (2022a) mandates that PSCs have cultural sensitivity and implement culturally sustaining school counseling policies and practices that actively advocate for equity across systems for fair outcomes for all students.

To support culturally sustaining school counseling ethics obligations, ASCA recommends a comprehensive school counseling program combined with the implementation of an MTSS (ASCA, 2021). MTSS is a prevention-based framework that uses data to inform instruction and intervention through direct and indirect services (ASCA, 2021; Belser et al., 2016; Betters-Bubon et al., 2022; Edwin et al., 2021). PSCs support MTSS implementation at the school level, as well as aligning programs with MTSS to demonstrate how school counseling is an essential component of K–12 education (Goodman-Scott et al., 2022). MTSS ensures more equitable access to school counseling support because it reaches 100% of students while also allowing opportunities for PSCs to respond to individual differences in culturally sensitive ways within a diverse school community (Edwin et al., 2021).

Despite the underlying equitable efforts of MTSS, there are still disproportionate outcomes impacting culturally and linguistically diverse students (Betters-Bubon et al., 2022). To improve these outcomes, schools should explicitly teach staff members culturally responsive lessons, including implicit bias, multicultural awareness, and antiracist models within MTSS training (Edwin et al., 2021). Better-Bubon et al. (2022) created a model for equitable support and outcomes for all students with four steps (1-Introspection of Self; 2-Interrogation of School, District, Community, and Environment; 3-Action; and 4-Evaluation) surrounding each of the three tiers (Tier 1-Universal, Tier 2-Targeted, Tier 3-Intensive) within MTSS (See Figure 18.2).

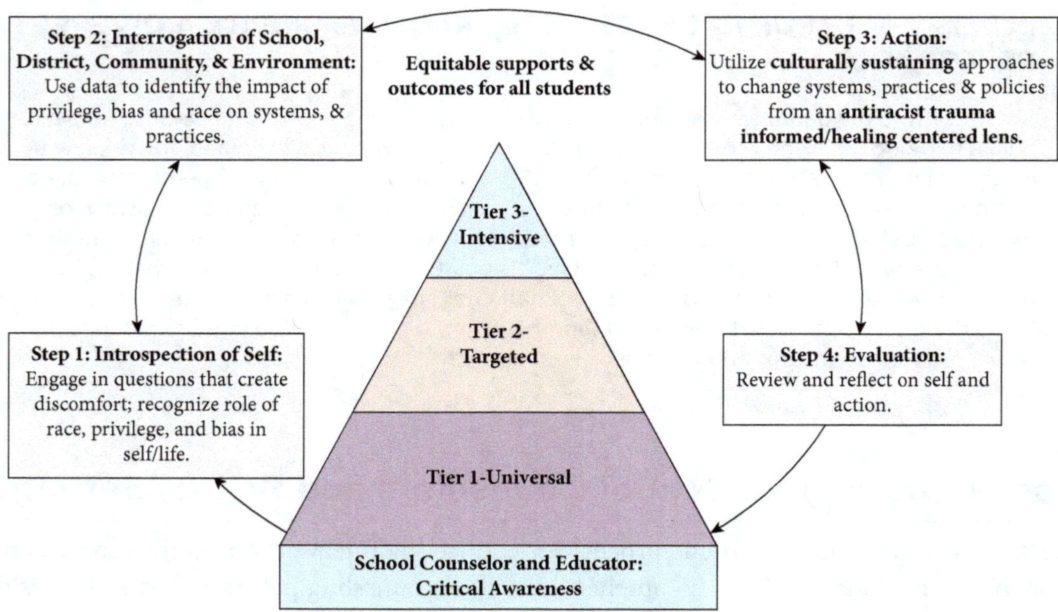

FIGURE 18.2 School Counselor and Education: Critical Awareness

Each school will have distinct student populations and each student will have several intersectional cultural variables that PSCs must be aware of and consider within each tiered level of support (Goodman-Scott et al., 2022). Universal screeners are instrumental in identifying students' academic, career, and social-emotional needs, which helps school counselors support students more equitably across the MTSS tiers (ASCA, 2023b). PSCs should also include student, family, and community member voices throughout the process by actively seeking input about different processes and policies (Goodman-Scott et al., 2022). Regardless of what the data identifies from universal screeners, PSCs and other school professionals should take the analysis to the next level by completing a data-equity walk to discuss outcomes and expose any gaps (Education Trust-West, 2021) throughout the initial identification and progress monitoring process of MTSS.

Tier 1-Universal is preventive in nature and includes whole school and classroom supports that impact the school climate and culture through proactive planning and instruction (ASCA, 2021). PSCs support the school through indirect services, such as identifying research-based strategies, consulting with parents and teachers, and collaborating with administrators and stakeholders regarding MTSS design and implementation (ASCA, 2021). Additionally, PSCs advocating for ASCA-recommended student-to-school counselor ratios are essential within Tier 1 of MTSS. The appropriate 250 students to each PSC ratio has been shown to improve outcomes for all students (Hilts et al., 2023). Without the proper delivery methods of Tier 1-Universal strategies, the direct services are less effective.

Direct services include incorporating an evidence-based curriculum that promotes a positive school climate into classroom counseling lessons. Various social-emotional learning (SEL) curricula that are research-based and/or evidence-based are available for universal instruction. Not all SEL curricula are equal: It is necessary for PSCs to analyze the research results of the selected curriculum to determine if the results match their student population to help predict potential outcomes. The Collaborative for Academic, Social, and Emotional Learning (CASEL) has a continuously updated program guide to help educational teams determine the best fit for an evidence-based SEL curriculum (CASEL, n.d.). Additionally, PSCs must include equity-elaborated SEL competencies to address the findings that SELs have been perceived as attempting to control Black students (Zyromski & Dimmitt, 2022). The universal Tier 1 directly informs the targeted interventions in Tier 2, which is an added layer to the counseling interventions.

Tier 2-Targeted includes small group interventions and responsive support for individuals. When students need additional support to meet the desired outcomes academically or behaviorally, PSCs are able to provide small-group counseling services that are goal specific. Additionally, if students are going through a personal or interpersonal issue and are assessed as requiring additional counseling support, PSCs are able to be responsive to specific situations. It is best practice for PSCs to use evidence-based counseling interventions for targeted counseling while enhancing the protective factors of students (Zyromski & Dimmitt, 2022). Therefore, Tier 2 evidence-based school counseling needs to include a deeper understanding of the mental health and learning needs of a diverse student population and how interventions can support all students at the systemic level (Zyromski & Dimmitt, 2022). Tier 2 indirect services also include consulting with educational professionals and outside agencies working with families and students (ASCA, 2021).

Tier 3-Intensive includes individual counseling and behavioral support for students, as well as referral practices with concerns beyond the scope of the PSC. Comprehensive school counseling programs use short-term counseling strategies for individual students (ASCA, 2019). Although individual counseling in schools is typically limited to 6–8 weeks for about 20–30 minutes per session, PSCs use cultural humility with all students on their caseloads to intervene appropriately. The assessment process, goal-setting process, treatment planning, and concluding and/or referring out for counseling require a PSC to be culturally sensitive and aware of systemic barriers for all students (Goodman-Scott et al., 2020).

Culturally Oriented Examples Across Counseling Settings

Counselors provide treatment in a variety of settings. The setting type depends largely on the type of treatment needed and symptom severity. Counselors provide services across multiple settings, including inpatient (e.g., hospitals), outpatient settings (such as community mental health or private practice settings), and schools (among others). While counselors can and do work anywhere, we summarize the above three common settings for professional counseling work below.

Inpatient Settings

Generally speaking, inpatient mental health care, meaning care involving an overnight stay in a hospital, is reserved for those diagnosed with SPMI, such as schizophrenia, psychosis, bipolar disorder, or MDD, among others (Maura & Weisman de Mamani, 2017). It may involve self-harm or aggressive behaviors (e.g., suicidality and homicidality). However, there is evidence of disparities in admissions and treatment strategies based on more than diagnosis. Research indicates that instead of using community outpatient resources, more racial/ethnic minorities seek care from emergency rooms and are more likely to be hospitalized when they do. Beyond that, more African Americans are involuntarily hospitalized than Whites. Perhaps even more concerning is the fact that race "was the strongest predictor of an admission diagnosis of schizophrenia" (Maura & Weisman de Mamani, 2017, p. 189). This information has troubling implications, improper diagnosis and overmedicating among them. And this is just one example.

While hospitalization/inpatient is warranted in some cases, it should not be pursued without considering the impact it may have on the client (e.g., trauma history) and the client's presenting concerns. Always make sure you are thoroughly assessing risk while considering the client's cultural presentation and needs. When hospitalization/inpatient care is warranted, the relationship with the counselor should still strive to maintain a strong therapeutic relationship with the client, and when possible, clients should be admitted to hospitals known to use cultural sensitivity.

TABLE 18.2 Mental Health Disparities and Reduction Strategies

Sociocultural Variable	Community Strategies	Provider Strategies	Patient Strategies
Stigma	Anti-stigma messages by cultural/religious community leaders Outreach efforts at community events Provision of non-traditional services (e.g., home visits) Bilingual/bicultural staff	Naturalistic, interpersonal contact between providers and patients (e.g., volunteer groups, community activities) Use of cultural brokers in program development	Engagement in peer support groups/community clubhouses Engagement in psychosocial interventions specific to stigma reduction
Trust/confidence in mental health systems	Increased diversity among providers	Collaborative care Empathetic communication Customization of content, approach, or delivery of intervention to consider culture	Patient involvement in treatment decisions (e.g., treatment preferences, treatment options, treatment planning)
Family involvement	Provision of family-focused treatment and psychoeducational programs in community settings Increased access to providers with family therapy training	Provider education in family stigma/burden, family stress and coping, and information exchange with family members Identification and inclusion of family support persons in treatment	Involvement of family members in treatment planning
Religious/spiritual values	Incorporation of religious/spiritual practices, beliefs, and community networks into treatment Provision of services in nonclinical settings (e.g., churches)	In-depth assessments of religiosity/spirituality Consideration of both patient and provider religious/spiritual values when conceptualizing cases and developing treatment plans	Involvement of significant religious/spiritual supports (e.g., religious mentors and/or healers) in treatment planning Engagement in religious/spiritually oriented treatment interventions
Culture	Involvement of family and community members, religious/spiritual supports, and indigenous providers in treatment development and delivery	Promoting cultural competence in service providers Inquiring about cultural history and identity Awareness of within-group diversity	Engagement in culturally adapted treatment interventions

Source: Maura and Wiseman de Mamani (2017)

Inpatient mental health patients are already subjected to "not uncommon coercive practices and experiences, including forced medication adherence, seclusion, restraint, verbal and physical aggression, and involuntary detention" (Wilson et al., 2017, p. 327). These activities can retraumatize those who have experienced previous trauma and actually traumatize those who have not. Obviously, some of these actions cannot be avoided.

BOX 18.10 **FOCUS ON CLIENT CARE**

Amelia is a 30-year-old female who emigrated to the United States from Sudan as a young child. She was witness to many acts of violence during the Sudanese war. She was raised practicing the animist religion of her tribe, which strongly believes in the power of the dead and the ability of ancestors to intervene in people's lives. While she has since converted to Christianity, Amelia still subscribes to this belief. Over the past few weeks, she has increasingly felt the presence of her grandmother and feels she is driving her to make decisions that her spouse finds reckless (impulse behavior, angry outbursts, impulsive spending), along with sleeping very few hours, if any, each night. Her husband reports that she is also highly distracted and "talking when no one is there." This has led to several arguments with her husband, and he has brought her to the emergency room as he feels she is experiencing psychosis. As her clinician, how might you proceed with Amelia?

Outpatient Settings

Among all clinical settings, the outpatient setting is often the most varied. Outpatient settings include private practice, group practice, and community mental health centers. Because of this variety, often limited oversight, and high potential for client harm, cultural competence is crucial for counselors working in these settings. A culturally competent counselor provides client-centered care that affirms the cultural traditions of individual clients. Counselors working in these settings must center clients as experts and as architects of their cultures, lives, and experiences. This centering requires that counselors focus more on *being* rather than doing. While interventions are necessary aspects of the counseling experience, the absence of humility and culturally relevant practice can diminish the quality of care provided (Guerrero and Andrews, 2011).

One method of enhancing cultural relevance and improving client outcomes is ethnic or cultural matching (Cabral and Smith, 2011), though this is not without controversy. Ethnic or cultural matching is the process of matching a client's ethnicity and culture to that of the counselor (Ibakair & Hall, 2014). While this likely happens naturally when some clients research counselors to contact, ethnic matching proposes a more intentional process. This matching can increase rapport between the counselor and client while also easing the discussion of ethnicity and culture within the counselor relationship (Ibakari & Hall, 2014). The limiting factor is that oftentimes, an ethnic or cultural match is not possible because of the predominance of White mental health counselors (88%; U.S. Bureau of Labor Statistics, 2019) and the limited availability of counselors of color. This means that all counselors must be prepared and competent to not only work with but also provide culturally responsive counseling to clients of all diverse and marginalized identities.

BOX 18.11 **FOCUS ON CLIENT CARE**

Consider the case of a 23-year-old biracial (Black/White) male who presented for counseling because of a self-reported history of anxiety and recently worsening depression. While discussing his presenting problem during the intake session, the client stated, "I'm really struggling with being a Black man in today's America." It would be easy to assume that the client's presenting problem is related to his identity and rush to dive into this. Instead, the multiculturally oriented counselor hears this and is aware of the history of racial oppression, acknowledges such, and then continues to listen intently, using minimal encouragers to help the client continue sharing his story.

Upon further assessment, the client shared that he was raised solely by his mom and currently lives with his mother and two younger siblings. He then (reluctantly) shares that his mother and other siblings are all White. Again, this sounds like a story about ethnicity and race, though the self-reported problems are anxiety and depression. The client felt misunderstood and therefore isolated both within his family and in society at large. While these contributed to the presenting problem, culturally competent counselors consider how culture and ethnicity play a significant role. Given the client's story and presentation, a diagnosis of MDD was suggested. The client's treatment included individual weekly therapy sessions with the goal of decreasing depression and anxiety. The client was also given a referral to psychiatry to explore medication options to assist with managing depression and anxiety. What other culturally responsive interventions would you use in this case?

Culturally informed treatment for men of color, particularly Black men, must focus on healing and restoration. It should be trauma-informed, strength-focused, holistic, and address the multiple intersecting identities of Black men. Counselors must develop comfort and competence in broaching; it is essential to address and discuss racism openly and directly while operating from a therapeutic stance. The history of mistrust of (mental health) systems can render traditional therapeutic techniques ineffective for Black men. Counselors should develop comfort embracing and engaging with community-based interventions that immerse clients into their culture while providing community support and therapeutic guidance. Identifying group therapy settings where clients can benefit from the collective stories of others who share their culture can be a transformative experience.

School-Based Settings

It is necessary for school counselors to be aware of the intersectionality of all students within their caseload in the school setting while also considering their own worldview and intersectionality within the specific school. Let's look at how school counselors can intervene appropriately in culturally responsive ways through the following case examples.

Example #1

During the Islamic holiday of Ramadan, several Muslim students at a predominately White suburban high school fast as part of their religious observations. There are 30 minutes built into each student's schedule for lunch in the cafeteria. A multiculturally oriented PSC who is aware of the student population has brought the students' potential discomfort of being in the cafeteria while peers were eating lunch to the attention of the administration well before the beginning of Ramadan. Together, the school counseling team and administration were able to designate an optional, separate location for students to go to during their lunch period for the month of Ramadan observation. Additionally, the PSC worked with community members to coordinate meaningful activities and speakers as a way to further support their students.

Example #2

The school counseling program has been given a $500 grant to purchase books for the school counseling office. At first, the books were specifically selected to meet the social, emotional, academic, and behavioral needs of the students. After analyzing the selected books, it was evident that many of the main characters and authors were White. A culturally aligned PSC intervened and sought books that were representative of all students, featuring characters of diverse backgrounds, abilities, family units, and cultures.

Conclusion

In this chapter, we have discussed the application of assessment, diagnosis, case conceptualization, treatment planning, therapeutic interventions, and referrals with diverse clients. We hope that this provides an introduction to these topics in a variety of counseling settings that help to build your confidence and connect your learning to your other courses in your chosen specialization. This chapter is not exhaustive, and there will always be more to learn regarding culturally competent and inclusive counseling applications. As discussed throughout this text, consider how your knowledge now can and should be continuously expanded, be culturally responsive and humble, and be cognizant of future learning opportunities to expand your own skills and knowledge as a professional counselor.

Questions for Reflection

Consider what you learned in this chapter as you respond to the questions and prompts below.

1. Considering the counseling setting you would like to work in, what information from this chapter has been the most useful to you?
2. How will you use assessment, diagnosis, and treatment planning in your own counseling work?
3. Identify how you can use formal and informal assessment to support culturally competent practice in your counseling setting of choice.

4. What are some culturally inclusive interventions that you can use in a treatment plan?
5. What are some skills that you need to expand to be an effective counselor for diverse populations?

Applying What You Have Learned

Complete each of the following activities, considering what you learned from this chapter.

Activity #1: Creating SMART Goals

Select one of the scenarios below. Using the text as a guide, create culturally inclusive SMART goals to support the client.

Client 1:
A sixth-grade junior high school student approaches her PSC, reporting that she is being teased about her stepfather being a trans man. His transition began when she was in first grade and was complete when she was in fourth grade. The peers at her elementary school were supportive, and she had limited social issues regarding her stepdad.

Client 2:
A multiracial 8-year-old boy who was recently adopted by White parents has been experiencing behavioral concerns in his new school setting. As part of the new student interview with parents, you learned that he has been in foster care since he was 4 years old. He was removed from the care of his mother when he was 18 months old and then lived with his grandmother until she died unexpectedly when he was 4. Over the past 4 years, he went to a Title 1 public school for pre–K through second grade in an urban city while living with the same foster family. He did not have a history of behavioral reports in his previous school setting, yet he was diagnosed by his pediatrician with oppositional defiant disorder and ADHD based on behavioral reports at home from his foster parents. He was also prescribed stimulant medication, as well as a sleep aid by the pediatrician, which the adopted parents are hoping to "wean him off of" over the next few months.

Credits

Fig. 18.1a: Copyright © 2019 Depositphotos/Technicsorn.
Fig. 18.1b: Copyright © 2019 Depositphotos/photographee.eu.
Fig. 18.1c: Copyright © 2018 Depositphotos/extracoin.
Fig. 18.1d: Copyright © 2024 Depositphotos/serezniy.

Appendix

In this appendix, you will find additional resources that can supplement and extend your learning organized by selected chapters.

Chapter 3: Cultural Humility

1. Developing Cultural Humility Assessment

Have you ever wondered how assessment scales are developed? Listen to this podcast on assessment talks from the Association of Assessment and Research in Counseling that focused on the work of Dr. Peitao Zhu, who developed a Cultural Humility Scale. *Cultural Humility with Dr. Peitao Zhu*: https://anchor.fm/association-for-assessment-and-research-in-counseling/episodes/Cultural-Humility-with-Dr--Peitao-Zhu-e185rru/a-a6kemi3

2. Improving Cultural Responsiveness

In this short video, Dr. Jesse Owens discusses ways to improve cultural responsiveness in psychotherapy. https://youtu.be/IqplgWGFCZc?si=ilBVx38qOT36WG9w. Watch this video and consider:

How can multicultural orientation help clinicians better account for the intersectionality of client's identities?

Consider this quote from the video, "When judgment comes up, that's when humility matters." What does this mean to you?

From 14:15 to 15:01, Dr. Owens discusses cultural comfort. Consider what you have read in this section of the chapter and the video. Reflect on the concept of "information avoidance" mentioned in the video.

From 16:24 to 18:37, Dr. Owens discusses ways to increase cultural comfort. Of those suggested, what could you implement in your life?

Chapter 4: Systems and Structural Oppression

1. Suggested Books, Movies, and TV Series

Books

Women, Race, and Class by Angela Y. Davis
Fading Scars: My Queer Disability History by Corbett Joan O'Toole

On Intersectionality by Kimberlé Crenshaw
Pedagogy of the Oppressed by Paulo Freire
Caste: The Origins of Our Discontents by Isabel Wilkerson

Movies

When They See Us
Believer
13th

TV Series

Mrs. America
Orange Is the New Black
The Handmaid's Tale

Podcasts

Hear to Slay with Roxane Gay and Tressie McMillan Cottom
Intersectionality Matters with Kimberlé Crenshaw
Undistracted with Brittany Packnett Cunningham

2. Research for Further Reading

Meyer, I. H. (2003). Prejudice, social stress, and mental health in lesbian, gay, and bisexual populations: Conceptual issues and research evidence. *Psychology Bulletin, 129*(5), 674–697. https://doi.org/10.1037/0033-2909.129.5.674

Johnson, K. F., & Brookover, D. L. (2021). School counselors' knowledge, actions, and recommendations for addressing social determinants of health with students, families, and in communities. *Professional School Counseling, 25*(1). https://doi.org /10.1177/2156759X20985847

Neal Keith, S., Coleman, M. L., Hicks Becton, L. Y., & Springfield, J. (2023). Assessing the social determinants of mental health in counseling practice. *Journal of Counseling & Development, 101*, 381–391. https://doi.org/10.1002/jcad.12470

3. More on the MSJCC

The multicultural and social justice counseling competencies (MSJCC) is a cornerstone of professional counseling competence, and we encourage you to become familiar with the model. To further immerse yourself in this important resource, we encourage the following:

1. Read the *Counseling Today* article "Multicultural and Social Justice Counseling Competencies: Practical Applications in Counseling" (2016) by Manivong J. Ratts, Anneliese A. Singh, S. Kent Butler, Sylvia Nassar-McMillan, and Julien Rafferty McCullough here: https://ct.counseling.org/2016/01/multicultural-and-social-justice-counseling-competencies-practical-applications-in-counseling/

2. Read the original MSJCC document adopted by the American Counseling Association (ACA) in 2015 by Ratts et al.: https://www.counseling.org/docs/default-source/competencies/multicultural-and-social-justice-counseling-competencies.pdf?sfvrsn=20
3. And finally, read the academic article written by Ratts et al., 2015, citation below: Ratts, M. J., Singh, A. A., Butler, S. K., Nassar Mc-Millan, S., & McCullough, J. R. (2016). Multicultural and social justice counseling competencies: Guidelines for the counseling profession. *Journal of Multicultural Counseling and Development, 44*. 28–48. https://doi.org/10.1002/jmcd.12035

Chapter 5: Social Justice, Advocacy, and Skills: Application in Counseling

American Counseling Association Vodcast

We would like to introduce a series of vodcasts that address important issues in the counseling community, including advocacy, racial justice, equity, cultural responsiveness, and mental health care. Each episode invites experts and mental health advocates with various perspectives and backgrounds.

> ***The Voice of Counseling (2021–present)***
>
> "The Voice of Counseling is a Vodcast series for the professional counseling community that showcases essential issues relevant to advocacy, racial justice, and how counselors help to competently create equity in the lives of our clients, students, and the world. Hosted by Dr. S. Kent Butler, the American Counseling Association's 70th president, each episode welcomes special guests to a conversation about all things counseling. We will have engaging dialogues about a counselors' professional work and identity, the business of counseling, and mental health care. Counseling students to seasoned practitioners with decades of experience will find something relevant to their work."

Chapter 7: Race, Racism, and Colorism

Media Examples of Anti-Blackness

The references below are examples of anti-Blackness in the media. They are not meant to represent the entirety of this concept. Rather, they are meant to showcase how it is represented.

K-Pop (https://www.theguardian.com/music/2020/jul/20/k-pop-black-fans-creatives-industry-accountable-race)

Swifty Blue (https://www.msn.com/en-us/music/news/mexican-rapper-swifty-blue-gets-dragged-for-saying-he-would-never-sign-with-a-black-owned-record-label/ar-AA10BDMk?item=flights%3Aprg-tipsubsc-v1a&ocid=windirect)

Wong and Lui (2022) (https://muse.jhu.edu/pub/1/article/869666/pdf)

Nury Martinez (https://www.latimes.com/politics/story/2022-10-17/nury-martinez-los-angeles-city-council-anti-blackness-latinos-racism)

Chapter 8: Ethnicity, National Identity, and Ethnocentrism

1. Movies

Rabbit-Proof Fence https://en.wikipedia.org/wiki/Rabbit-Proof_Fence

I Am Not Your Negro https://agoodmovietowatch.com/not-negro-2016/

Gather https://agoodmovietowatch.com/gather/

Winter on Fire: Ukraine's Fight for Freedom https://agoodmovietowatch.com/winter-on-fire-ukraines-fight-for-freedom-2015/

Bao https://en.wikipedia.org/wiki/Bao_(film)

The Half of It https://www.netflix.com/title/81005150

Avalon https://www.imdb.com/title/tt0099073/

2. Ted Talks

Your Culture Is Not Better Than Mine https://www.youtube.com/watch?v=qnNpFYVaXIc

Weird or Just Different? https://www.ted.com/talks/derek_sivers_weird_or_just_different

The Lies Our Culture Is Telling Us About What Matters https://www.ted.com/talks/david_brooks_the_lies_our_culture_tells_us_about_what_matters_and_a_better_way_to_live?language=en

How to Overcome Our Biases? https://www.ted.com/talks/verna_myers_how_to_overcome_our_biases_walk_boldly_toward_them?language=en

Want to Help Someone? Shut Up and Listen https://www.ted.com/talks/ernesto_sirolli_want_to_help_someone_shut_up_and_listen/transcript?language=en

Chapter 9: Immigrants, Refugees, Diasporas, and Xenomisia

Pop Culture Tools/Examples

Movies

Gardner, D., Kleiner, J., & Oh, Christina (Producers), & Chung, L. I. (Director). (2020). *Minari* [Motion picture]. A24.

Gurtubai, I., Lamont, A. (Producers), & Sharrock, B. (Director). (2020). *Limbo* [Motion picture]. United Kingdom: MUBI (United Kingdom and Ireland) and Universal Pictures (International).

Merino, Y., Spencer, C. (Producers), Bush, J., & Howard, B. (Directors). (2021). *Encanto* [Motion picture]. Walt Disney Pictures Studios Motion Picture.

Skalski, M. J., London, M. (Producers), & McCarthy, T. (Director). (2007). *the Visitor* [Motion picture]. Overture Films.

Weiwei, A., Yap, C-C., Cohen, A. (Producers), & Weiwei, A. (Director). (2017). *Human Flow* [Motion picture]. NFP Marketing & Distribution (Germany and Lionsgate International).

Podcasts

Hernandez, E. (Host). (2019–2020). *My immigrant life* [Audio podcast]. https://podcasts.apple.com/us/podcast/my-immigrant-life/id1463741510

Holton, J. (Host). (2017–present). *Refugees' stories* [Audio podcast]. https://www.refugeesstoriespodcast.org/refugees-stories-podcast-episodes

Khan, S. (Host). (2018–present). *Immigrantly: Cross-cultural conversations* [Audio podcast]. https://immigrantlypod.com/

Rani, A. (Host). (2023). *Forced to flee* [Audio podcast]. UNHCR. https://www.unhcr.org/forced-to-flee-podcast/

Chapter 10: Indigenous, Native, First Nations Groups, and Settler Colonialism

1. Watch and Listen

- *Colorado Experience: Sand Creek Massacre:* Documentary on the attack of the Cheyenne and Arapaho https://www.pbs.org/video/colorado-experience-sand-creek-massacre/
- *Mauna Kea Movie: The Conflict on Mauna Kea* https://youtu.be/4J3ZCzHMMPQ
- *The Hawaiian Language:* PBS documentary on the Hawaiian Language https://www.pbs.org/video/the-hawaiian-language-3pbtby/
- *Hawaii: The Stolen Paradise:* Documentary on the overthrow of the Hawaiian Kingdom https://documentaries.io/hawaii-the-stolen-paradise-full-documentary-tracks/
- Native Stories: Audio platform that provides access to stories of Native people, places, culture, and history: https://Nativestories.org
- Native Voices: Native and Indigenous interviews and stories as well as resources, lesson plans, and activities: https://www.nlm.nih.gov/Nativevoices/index.html
- Remembering Resilience: Podcasts on Native and Indigenous resilience https://rememberingresilience.home.blog
- *The Wellbriety Journey to Forgiveness*: A documentary on the abuses of Boarding Schools https://www.youtube.com/watch?v=vZwF9NnQbWM&t=3700s
- *We Shall Remain*: Docuseries on the plight of Native Americans https://www.pbs.org/wgbh/americanexperience/films/weshallremain/

2. Websites, Readings, and Resources

- *The 1491s Poetry*: A series of spoken word poems as well as comedy shorts relating to the Native experience. https://www.youtube.com/watch?v=3FUgDutdauQ&feature=youtu.be
- Indigenous Story Studio: Illustrations, posters, videos and comic books on health and social issues for Indigenous youth: https://istorystudio.com
- IWGIA: Organization that promotes recognition and respect of Indigenous persons and culture: https://www.iwgia.org/en/usa.html
- Native-land.ca: Enter an address to learn about Indigenous persons and language of an area.
- Pacific Northwest Indian Collection: Digital collection of images, documents, essays, and other resources for Pacific Northwest Indians: https://content.lib.washington.edu/aipnw/
- Pew Research Center: https://www.pewresearch.org/fact-tank/2015/06/11/american-indian-and-white-but-not-multiracial/
- Goo, S. K. (2015). After 200 years, Native Hawaiians make a comeback. https://www.pewresearch.org/fact-tank/2015/04/06/Native-hawaiian-population/
- Puʻuhonua o Puʻuhuluhulu: Established by the Kiaʻi to protect Mauna Kea and provide education of the movement: https://www.puuhuluhulu.com
- A Tribe Called Red (ATCR): A First Nations music group. Songs celebrate Native culture and provide a narrative of mistreatment of Indigenous peoples. http://atribecalledred.com
- Well for Culture: An "Indigenous wellness initiative" that seeks to reclaim and revitalize Indigenous health and wellness https://www.wellforculture.com/
- We R Native: A health resource for Native youth that provides content and stories on culture, mind, body, relationships, environment, and more https://www.wernative.org/
- White, R. K., Hanks, A., Branco, S., Meade, N., Burth, I. (2020). A collective voice: Indigenous resilience and a call for advocacy. *Counseling Today*. https://ct.counse
- ling.org/tag/Native-americans/

Chapter 11: Social Class and Classism

1. Suggested Books, Movies, and TV Series

Books

A People's History of Poverty in America (2011) by Stephen Pimpare
Capital in the Twenty-First Century (2013) by Thomas Piketty
Hand to Mouth: Living in Bootstrap America (2014) by Linda Tirado
The Oxford Handbook of Social Class in Counseling (2013) by William M. Liu
We Have Never Been Middle Class: How Social Mobility Misleads Us (2019) by Hadas Weiss
We Are Not Like Them (2021) by Christin Pride and Jo Piazza

Where We Stand: Class Matters (2000) by bell hooks
White Trash. The 400-Year Untold History of Class in the United States (2017) by Nancy Isenberg

Movies

The Breadwinner (2017)
The Color Purple (1985)
Dirty Dancing (1987)
The Florida Project (2017)
Good Will Hunting (1997)
Parasite (2019)
The Pursuit of Happyness (2006)
Snowpiercer (2013)

TV Series

Everybody Hates Chris (2005)
Ginny & Georgia (2021)
Good Times (1974)
Jane the Virgin (2014)
The Jeffersons (1975)
Roseanne (1988)
Shameless (2011)

2. Research for Further Reading

Clark, M., Ausloos, C., Delaney, C., Waters, L., Salpietro, L., & Tippett, H. (2020). Best practices for counseling clients experiencing poverty: A grounded theory. *Journal of Counseling and Development, 98*, 283–294. https://doi.org/10/1002/jcad.12323

Cook, J. M., & Lawson, G. (2016). Counselors' social class and socioeconomic status understanding and awareness. *Journal of Counseling and Development*, 94(4), 442–453. http://dx.doi.org/10.1002/jcad.12103

Long, S. M., Clark, M., Ausloos, C. D., Jacoby, R., & McGhee, C. (2019). The wellness and self-care experiences of single mothers in poverty: Strategies for mental health counselors. *Journal of Mental Health Counseling, 41*, 343–358.https://doi.org/10.17733/mehc.41.4.05

Chapter 14: Sex, Gender, Patriarchy, and Transmisia

1. House Bill (HB) 1557: Parental Rights in Education

HB 1557: Parental Rights in Education is an act that protects parents' rights to control their child's upbringing and information they are exposed to in public schools. The act requires school boards to notify parents at the start of each school year to inform them of healthcare services and specific content within the curriculum that will be shared with their children. Parents then have the option to withhold consent for services and education. One such designation in the act notes that "classroom instruction by school personnel or third parties on sexual orientation or gender identity may not occur in kindergarten through grade 3 or in a manner that is not age-appropriate or developmentally appropriate for students ..." (Laws of Florida, Ch. 2022-22). HB 1557 was first proposed to the Florida Governor in January of 2022, was approved in March of 2022, and took effect July of 2022. The state was required to update all policies and procedures around parent consent and educational materials by June of 2023.

HB 1557: Websites

https://www.flsenate.gov/Committees/BillSummaries/2022/html/2825
http://laws.flrulesEorg/2022/22

2. Pop Culture Examples

Podcasts

The Thoughtful Counselor Podcast, Episode 214: Creating Inclusive Spaces for Transgender and Gender Expansive Young People in K–12 Settings with Dr. Clark D. Ausloos;

Loud and Queerly Podcast, Society for Sexual, Affectional, Intersex, and Gender Expansive Identities (SAIGE)

Books

Redefining Realness (2014) by Janet Mock
Affirmative Counseling with LGBTQI+ People edited by Misty M. Ginicola, Cheri Smith, and Joel M. Filmore

Shows

Laverne Cox in *Orange Is the New Black*
Elliot Page in *The Umbrella Academy*
Mason Alexander Park in *The Sandman*

Movies

Disclosure (2020): Documentary on transgender depictions in Hollywood
The Trans List (2016): Interviews with gender-expansive people to learn about their lived experiences
Hidden Figures (2017): Explores civil rights, feminism, and STEM achievements of women. Stars Jenelle Monáe, a nonbinary actress
Everything, Everywhere, All at Once (2022): Michelle Yeoh is the first Asian woman to win the Academy Award for Best Actress
Moonlight (2016): Follows a young Black man into manhood, exploration of masculinity
The Mask You Live In (2015): Documentary on the impact of gender norms and masculinity on young boys

Music

"Unholy" by Sam Smith (nonbinary) and Kim Petras (transgender woman). Kim because the first openly transgender artist with a #1 hit on the Billboard Hot 100.

3. For Further Reading

Ausloos, C., Clark, M., Hansori, J., Dari, T., & Litam, S. D. A. (2022). A call for action: School counselor competence in working with trans students. *The Professional Counselor, 12*(1), 65–81. https://doi.org/10.15241/cda.12.1.65

Compton, E. & Morgan, G., (2022). The experiences of psychological therapy amongst people who identify as transgender or gender non-conforming: A systemic review of qualitative research. *Journal of Feminist Family Therapy, 34*(3–4), 225–248. https://doi.org/10.1080/08952833.2022.2068843

Di Bianca, M., & Mahalik, J. R. (2022). A relational-cultural framework for promoting healthy masculinities. *American Psychologist, 77*(3), 321–332. https://doi.org/10.1037/amp0000929

Salpietro, L., Ausloos, A., & Clark, M. (2019). Cisgender professional counselors' experiences with trans* clients. *Journal of LGBT Issues in Counseling, 13*(3), 198–215. https://doi.org/10.1080/15538605.2019.1627975

Chapter 15: Romantic and Affection Identity and Queer Oppression

1. RAI Resources/Organizations

Resource	Description	Web Address
Centers for Disease Control and Prevention (CDC)	Provides resources from the CDC, other government agencies, and community organizations for LGBT Youth, their friends, educators, parents, and family members to support positive environments.	https://www.cdc.gov/lgbthealth/youth-resources.htm
Child Welfare Information Gateway	Advocacy and support organizations for lesbian, gay, bisexual, transgender, and questioning (LGBTQ) communities	https://www.childwelfare.gov/
GLAAD	A media advocacy organization that increases media accountability and community engagement that ensures authentic LGBTQ stories are seen, heard, and actualized	https://www.glaad.org/resources
Human Rights Campaign (HRC)	Works to ensure that all LGBTQ+ people, and particularly those of us who are trans, People of Color, and HIV+, are treated as full and equal citizens within our movement, across our country and around the world	https://www.hrc.org/resources
National Alliance on Mental Illness (NAMI)	NAMI provides advocacy, education, support, and public awareness so that all individuals and families affected by mental illness can build better lives.	https://www.nami.org/Your-Journey/Identity-and-Cultural-Dimensions/LGBTQI

(*Continued*)

The National LGBTQIA+ Health Education Center	Provides educational programs, resources, consultation to health-care organizations with the goal of optimizing quality, cost-effective health care for LGBTQIA+ people	https://www.lgbtqiahealtheducation.org/
National Resource Center on LGBTQ+ Aging	A technical assistance resource center focused on improving the quality of services and supports offered to lesbian, gay, bisexual and/or transgender older adults, their families and caregivers.	https://www.lgbtagingcenter.org/
Society for Sexual, Affectional, Intersex, and Gender Expansive Identities	A division of the American Counseling Association that is a home for queer and trans counselors, ally counselors, and advocates to connect and grow, share research and resources.	https://saigecounseling.org/
Stonewall International (UK)	Campaigns as part of a global movement since 1989 and has helped create transformative change in the lives of LGBTQ+ people across communities in the United Kingdom.	https://www.stonewall.org.uk/our-work/international/international-resources
The Fenway Institute	The mission of the Fenway Institute is to optimize health and well-being for sexual and gender minorities and those affected by HIV.	https://fenwayhealth.org/the-fenway-institute/
The Trevor Project	Resources and mental health counseling support resources.	https://www.thetrevorproject.org/resources/
Two Spirit/Native LGBTQ Resources	Tribal justice personnel and others devoted to supporting and strengthening tribal justice systems through education, information sharing, and advocacy.	www.naicja.org

2. Diverse RAIs in Media and Pop Culture

Movies

Angels in America (2003)
The Boys in the Band (1970)
Call Me by Your Name (2017)
Hedwig and the Angry Inch (2001)
Moonlight (2016)
The Normal Heart (2014)
Portrait of a Lady on Fire (2019)
The Times of Harvey Milk (1984)

Documentaries

A Secret Love (2020)
All in My Family (2019)
The Death and Life of Marsha P. Johnson (2017)
Gayby Baby (2015)
How to Survive a Plague (2012)
Paris Is Burning (1990)
Pray Away (2021)

Podcasts

Lez Hang Out (2017–present)
The Flame: A Podcast Musical (2022)
Pants (2020–present)
QUEERY (2017–present)

Chapter 16: Spirituality, Religion, and Religious Persecution

ASERVIC Competencies (2023)

https://aservic.org/spiritual-and-religious-competencies/

Chapter 17: Emerging Areas

1. Fat-Positive Pop Culture Tools

Media	**Recommendation**	**Author(s)/Artists**
Podcast	*Maintenance Phase*	Aubrey Gordon and Michael Hobbes
Book	*What We Don't Talk About When We Talk About Fat*	Aubrey Gordon
Book	*"You Just Need to Lose Weight" and 19 Other Myths About Fat People*	Aubrey Gordon
Book	*Thickening Fat: Fat Bodies, Intersectionality, and Social Justice*	Edited By May Friedman, Carla Rice, Jen Rinaldi
Book	*Shrill*	Lindy West
TV Series (Hulu)	*Shrill*	Lindy West
Book	*Fearing the Black Body*	Sabrina Strings
Book	*The Body Is Not an Apology*	Sonya Renee Taylor

2. Professional Organizations for Addiction Treatment

International Association of Addictions and Offender Counseling (https://www.iaaoc.org/)
Association for Addiction Professionals (https://www.naadac.org/)
American Society of Addiction Medicine (https://www.asam.org/)

3. Resources for Further Reading

Divergent Mind: Thriving in a World That Wasn't Designed for You by Jenara Nerenberg (2020)
NeuroTribes: The Legacy of Autism and the Future of Neurodiversity by Steve Silberman et al. (2015)
Women and Girls with Autism Spectrum Disorder by Sarah Hendrix and Judith Gould (2021)
Odd Girl Out by Laura James and Lucinda Clare (2018)
Uniquely Human: The Podcast (2020)
ADDitude ADHD Experts Podcast **(2022)**
ADDitudeMag.com (1998–2022)
Autistic Self Advocacy Network (ASAN) (2022)
Nothing About Us Without Us: Increasing Neurodiversity and Social Justice Advocacy Groups (Hughes, 2022)
Special Interest Group for Neurodiversity. Stanford Neurodiversity Project. Stanford School of Medicine.
Are Prisons Obsolete? by Angela Y. Davis (2003)
Mass Incarceration in the Age of Colorblindness: The New Jim Crow by Michelle Alexander (2010)
Chained in Silence: Black Women and Convict Labor in the New South by Talitha L. LeFlouria (2015)
Writing My Wrongs: Death, Life and Redemption in an American Prison by Shaka Senghor (2017)
Crack in America: Demon Drugs and Social Justice? by Craig Reinarman (1997)
Judging Addictions; Drug Courts and Coercion in the Justice System by Rebecca Tiger (2012)
From the Ashes by Jesse Thistle (2019)
Dopesick by Beth Macy (2018)
U.S. Climate Resilience Toolkit https://toolkit.climate.gov/
Intersectional Environmentalist https://www.intersectionalenvironmentalist.com/
Ologies (Podcast) Meteorology EP296 (Weather & Climate) https://www.alieward.com/ologies/meteorology
How to Save a Planet (Podcast) https://gimletmedia.com/shows/howtosaveaplanet
The Uninhabitable Earth, Life After Warming by David Wallace-Wells (2019)
Learning to Build Resilience in the Face of "Climate Anxiety" (ACA, 2021)
A Terrible Thing To Waste: Environmental Racism and Its Assault on the American Mind by Harriet A. Washington (2019)
The Intergovernmental Panel on Climate Change *Activities* https://www.ipcc.ch/activities/

Glossary

Acquired Disability (see Chapter 13). A disability that develops during a person's lifetime rather than at birth. Antonym: *congenital disability.*

Adventitious Disability (see Chapter 13). A disability that occurs after birth. Antonym: *congenital disability.*

Advocacy (see Chapter 5). Proactively supporting and promoting the overall well-being of individuals and groups at individual, community, and national levels by minimizing systemic barriers that prevent them from achieving their optimal potential.

Ageism (see Chapter 14). Stereotypes, prejudice, and discrimination against someone of the nondominant age group.

Agender (see Chapter 14). A person who identifies without a gender.

Androgyny (see Chapter 14). A form of gender expression in which gendered appearance is ambiguous or not clearly identifiable as culturally defined as feminine or masculine.

Anti-Blackness (see Chapter 7). Systematic discrimination, marginalization, and devaluing of Black people and/or those perceived to be of African descent.

Apparent Disability (see Chapter 12). A disability that can be noticed by another person without being disclosed intentionally by the person with a disability. Also referred to as a *visible disability.*

Assessment (see Chapter 18). The process by which a counselor gathers information about a client to make decisions about their needs and to inform treatment planning.

Assigned Sex (see Chapter 14). The biological sex a person is given at the time of birth based on external anatomy. Also referred to as *sex assigned at birth* or *biological sex assigned at birth.*

Assimilation (see Chapter 9). The process by which individuals or groups conform to a new or different culture and customs.

Asylum Seeker (see Chapter 9). A person who has left their home country and is seeking protection in another but has not been legally recognized as a refugee.

Backhanded Compliments (see Chapter 17). Statements that may be made with good intent that have a harmful impact. Understood to be a microaggression.

Bias (see Chapter 1). To prefer one thing (e.g., idea, philosophy, identity, way of being) over another.

BIPOC (see Chapter 7). An acronym that stands for Black, Indigenous, and People of Color.

Case Conceptualization (see Chapter 18). The process by which counselors build a map of clients' experiences, needs, access to resources, barriers, privileges, oppressions, presenting concerns, and other variables that impact client cases.

Chronosystem (see Chapter 2). The fifth level of Bronfenbrenner's ecological systems theory. This system accounts for how things unfold over time—both what changes and what stays the same. It can include sociocultural and shared historical events (e.g., wars, shared tragedies, social movements, technological advancements), as well as significant individual life events, both normative (e.g., graduating from high school, establishing a career) and non-normative (e.g., death of a sibling in childhood, winning the lottery).

Cisgender (see Chapter 14). A person whose gender identity is congruent with the sex they were assigned at birth (e.g., a person whose assigned sex is female, and they identify as a woman).

Cisnormativity (see Chapter 14). The assumption that all people are cisgender or identify with the gender they were assigned at birth.

Cissexism (see Chapter 14). Behaviors that promote preferential treatment of cisgender people and discrimination and prejudice against those who are not cisgender.

Classism (see Chapter 11). An overarching term that includes bias, prejudice, discrimination, and/or oppression based on an individual's actual or perceived social class or SES group membership.

Collectivism (see Chapter 8). The belief and action of putting the group, family, or community needs first over individual needs. Antonym: *individualism.*

Colonization (see Chapter 10). The act of taking over an area or country by force and sending people from your own country to live in that area/country. Also includes imposing values, beliefs, traditions, etc., that override those who lived in an area/country originally.

Colorism (see Chapter 7). A form of discrimination perpetrated by those outside and within a racial or ethnic group whereby people with lighter skin are favored over those with darker skin.

Concern Trolling (see Chapter 17). The phenomenon of someone feigning sympathy for a perspective (e.g., obesity, those who are overweight) while actually seeking to change a person's behavior.

Coming Out (see Chapters 14 and 15). The process in which individuals choose to disclose their gender, sexual, affectual, and/or relational identities.

Community Cultural Wealth Model (see Chapter 8). A framework in which cultural wealth is defined by six forms of capital: aspirational, linguistic, familial, social, navigational, and resistance. All forms can be used throughout the lifecycle and be highlighted and explored within counseling to acknowledge strengths and resiliencies.

Congenital Disability (see Chapter 12). A disability that develops prenatally (within the womb) that may be detected before birth, at birth, or later in life. Antonym: *acquired disability.*

Contact Hypothesis (see Chapter 1). Having brief or limited experiences with groups/individuals with identities different from your own tends to result in strengthening stereotypes and prejudices rather than ameliorating them. Conversely, having extended, meaningful experiences and relationships with groups/individuals with identities different from your own often results in reducing stereotypes and prejudices.

Critical Thinking (see Chapter 2). Applying the full information at one's disposal to consider multiple perspectives, processes, causes, and outcomes using depth and nuance. Critical thinkers avoid one-dimensional thinking and do not use limited or one-sided information.

Cultural Appropriation (see Chapter 10). Inappropriate adaptation of the customs, practices, and ideas of another's culture.

Cultural Broaching (see Chapter 5). A counselor's deliberate and receptive approach to integrating sociocultural elements and individual cultural identities into the counseling relationship. Coined by Day-Vines et al. (2007).

Cultural Comfort (see Chapter 3). Feeling either stress or ease before, during, and after culturally relevant conversations with clients.

Cultural Genocide (see Chapter 10). Intentional destruction of a culture that may or may not involve killing or violence. This can include the eradication of cultural activities, artifacts, language, and traditions.

Cultural Humility (see Chapter 3). An accurate perception of your cultural values while maintaining an other-oriented perspective that involves respect, lack of superiority, and attunement regarding your own cultural beliefs and values.

Cultural Opportunities (see Chapter 3). Counselors look for occasions and natural transition points to invite clients to explore their beliefs, values, or other aspects of clients' cultural identities as they pertain to the presenting concern.

Cultural Racism (see Chapter 7). Societal beliefs and customs that endorse the assumption that White culture, language, and traditions are superior to those of other races.

Culturally-Bound Strengths (see Chapter 1). Skills, dispositions, and resiliencies developed as a result of one's membership in a specific cultural group.

Curiosity (see Chapter 2). Having interest and demonstrating engagement with ideas, people, concepts, philosophies, experiences, and more, with that which is familiar and unfamiliar. The genuine desire to want to learn more.

Diagnosis (see Chapter 18). The process by which a counselor uses the data gathered through assessment to determine a named mental health disorder using established diagnostic criteria.

Diaspora (see Chapter 9). Individuals whose heritage (e.g., ethnicity, culture) is historically rooted in certain geographical areas, nations, or territories but who now live in several different places around the world.

Discernment (see Chapter 2). Considering multiple perspectives, data sources, and evidence to make choices that reflect sound reasoning and thoughtful consideration.

Discrimination (see Chapters 1 and 4). When members of the dominant culture transform prejudices into actions in which they treat people with nondominant identities differently, inequitably, unjustly. Only those with sociocultural power (i.e., the dominant culture) can perpetrate discrimination.

Documented (see Chapter 9). Immigrants who reside in the United States with a valid visa and documentation.

Dominant Identities (see Chapter 1). Identities that hold sociocultural power and privilege.

Ecological Systems Theory (see Chapter 4). The perspective that individuals and groups interactions with different systems influences individual's beliefs and behaviors.

Emic (see Chapter 1). Having an inside or lived experience perspective on a cultural group's beliefs, traditions, ways of being, etc., because one is a member of that cultural group.

Emotional and Psychological Wounding (see Chapter 10). A series of events that cause emotional and psychological pain.

Ethical Practice (see Chapter 2). Applying the ethical codes of one's professional organization(s) to all professional responsibilities and actions.

Etic (see Chapter 1). Learning about a cultural group to which one does not belong, an outside perspective rather than a lived experience perspective.

Ethnic Identity (see Chapter 8). The ways in which individuals within a specific ethnic group shape and reshape their self-definition—influenced by external social, economic, and political processes.

Ethnicity (see Chapters 7 and 8). A term used to distinguish groups based on shared culture (e.g., country of origin, religion), characteristics, experiences, and background.

Ethnocentrism (see Chapter 8). The attitude that one's own ethnic group and/or nationality is superior to others.

Evidence-Based Practices (see Chapter 18). Interventions and/or programs that have established efficacy through research in a controlled setting.

Exosystem (see Chapter 2). The third level of Bronfenbrenner's ecological systems theory. Systems that affect the individual but with which the individual typically does not have direct contact nor the individual power to influence (e.g., local and national government, mass media, school boards, company owners, police, social services).

Fatmisia (see Chapter 17). Discrimination against fat people.

Feminism (see Chapter 14). Ideologies and movements aimed to identify and change social, political, and economic inequalities that are rooted in patriarchy.

Gender Affirming Medical Care (see Chapter 14). Surgical, hormonal, or other medical interventions or procedures used to change one's body to align with their gender identity or desired gender expression.

Gender Binary (see Chapter 14). A system in which woman and man are the two and only distinct categories of gender.

Gender Dysphoria (see Chapter 14). Classified in the *Diagnostic and Statistical Manual of Mental Disorders, Fifth edition, Text Revision* as incongruence between one's expressed gender and one's assigned gender.

Gender Expansive (see Chapter 14). A person whose gender identity and/or expression do not align with cultural and social expectations of masculinity and femininity.

Gender Expression (see Chapter 14). A person's external representation of gender identity through clothes, hairstyle, demeanor, body language, behaviors, and interests.

Gender Fluidity (see Chapter 14). The ability for gender identity and expression to Gender change across time and space.

Gender Identity (see Chapter 14). A person's internal concept and experience of gender.

Gender Roles (see Chapter 14). Culturally and socially created norms that dictate accepted behaviors associated with being a man or a woman.

Genocide (see Chapter 10). Violent attacks with the intent to destroy a national, ethnic, racial, or religious group.

Gerontology (see Chapter 13). The study of the aging process, ageism, and specific concerns of old age.

Historical Trauma/Traumatization (see Chapter 10). Collective experiences of a community or generation, such as genocide, economic depression, war, slavery, or colonization.

Hypodescent Phenomenon (see Chapter 10). Categorizing biracial individuals by their nondominant race (e.g., a biracial person who is Black and White will be categorized as Black predominantly).

Immigrant (see Chapter 9). Those who have moved from their country of origin to a new country permanently for work or for better living conditions.

Indigenous Historical Trauma (see Chapter 10). Cumulative emotional and psychological wounding over one's lifetime and from generation to generation following the loss of lives, land, and vital aspects of culture.

Indigenous Persons/Populations (see Chapter 10). Populations with historical claim and continuity with preinvasion and precolonial societies that developed on their territories. They have retained social, cultural, and political characteristics that are distinct from dominant societies.

Individual Discrimination (see Chapter 4). Oppressive acts enacted by dominant culture individuals toward persons based on their nondominant identities (e.g., race, gender, social class).

Individual Racism (see Chapter 7). An individual's attitudes, beliefs, and behaviors that represent White superiority and inferiority of nondominant racial groups.

Individualism (see Chapter 8). The belief and action of putting self needs over group or community needs in favor of self-reliance and independence. Antonym: *collectivism.*

Institutional Racism (see Chapter 7). Laws, social policies, and regulations that enable social and economic advantage of Whites over Black, Indigenous, and People of Color (BIPOC).

-isms (see Chapter 1). Structural oppression based on a specific, nondominant cultural identity (e.g., racism, classism, sexism).

Intersectionality (see Chapters 4, 11, and 13). The social, economic, and political ways in which identity-based systems of oppression and privilege connect, overlap, and influence one another.

Intersectionality Theory (see Chapter 14). The notion that people occupy several social-cultural positions simultaneously and have intersecting social and cultural identities that expose them to multiple, intersecting forms of oppression.

Intersex (see Chapter 14). A person who has more than one sex characteristics.

Low Social Class (see Chapter 11). The social class group with the lowest form of wealth. Includes individuals living in poverty.

Macrosystem (see Chapter 2). The fourth level of Bronfenbrenner's ecological systems theory. Cultural identities and the values, beliefs, customs, and ways of being that stem from cultural identities and cultural group membership. Cultural identities can include race, ethnicity, socioeconomic status, social class, ability status, religious/spiritual affiliation, gender, sex, sexual/affectual orientation, immigration status, language, and age. Marginalization, privilege, and power have a central role in individuals' experiences based on their identities.

Marginalization (see Chapter 1). The act of putting a person or a group at the *margins* or the edges of society based on their nondominant identity(ies).

Mesosystem (see Chapter 2). The second level of Bronfenbrenner's ecological systems theory. The relationships or interactions between groups within the microsystem that impact the individual (e.g., family's relationship with the individual's school, partner's relationship with the individual's friends) but with the individual does not have direct contact.

Microaggressions (see Chapters 1 and 15). Verbal, behavioral, or environmental slights that are hostile, derogatory, and/or negative attitudes toward people with nondominant or marginalized identities. Coined by Sue et al., 2007.

Microsystem (see Chapter 2). The first level of Bronfenbrenner's ecological systems theory. The individuals and groups with whom the individual has direct contact (e.g., family, friends, intimate relationships, colleagues, clubs, religious involvement). The individuals and groups that impact the individual will likely shift over time depending on where they are in the lifespan (e.g., child, adolescent, adult).

Middle Social Class (see Chapter 11). A social class group that falls between upper and lower social class. Considered the dominant social class cultural group in the United States because of the cultural value placed on middle-class values, beliefs, and ways of being.

Migrant (see Chapters 8 and 9). The movement of any person from their home/residence within and/or across countries, irrespective of their legal status, voluntary or involuntary, or length of stay, with the intent of improving their economic and social conditions.

Migration/Migrancy (see Chapter 9). Movement from one place to another in search of work, better living conditions, and opportunities.

Misgender (see Chapter 14). To refer to a person using pronouns or gendered language that do not align with the person's gender identity.

Misogynoir (see Chapter 14). The intersectional oppression of misogyny and racism.

Misogyny (see Chapter 14). Prejudice and discrimination against those who are women/female or perceived to be women/female.

-misias (see Chapter 1). Having an intense hatred toward a group based on their nondominant cultural identity (e.g., transmisia, homomisia, Islamomisia)

Multicultural Orientation (see Chapter 3). A way of being that demonstrates respect and openness toward clients' culture. Multicultural orientation is comprised of three concepts: cultural humility, cultural comfort, and cultural opportunities. Differs from *multicultural competence* because *competence* implies completion rather than an ongoing growth mindset.

Multicultural Orientation Model (see Chapter 3). A model in which the creators aimed to shift the conversation away from competencies to focusing on the bigger picture of the quality of the therapeutic relationship and how that relationship is impacted by the client and the counselor's cultural factors.

Multiculturalism (see Chapter 5). A paradigm that acknowledges and values diverse cultural backgrounds, identities, and life experiences of individuals.

Multitiered System of Supports (see Chapter 18). A prevention-based framework that uses data to inform instruction and intervention through direct and indirect services in educational settings.

National Identity (see Chapters 8 and 9). A component of ethnicity that refers to one's national origin (e.g., Canada, Columbia, Germany) and/or generational status (e.g., second-generation American).

Native Persons/Populations (see Chapter 10). Social and cultural groups that share ancestral ties to the lands where they lived, occupied, and from which have been displaced because of colonialism.

Nonbinary (see Chapter 14). The classification of gender into more than two distinct categories (i.e., man and woman) that are not separate and distinct.

Nondominant Identities (see Chapter 1). Identities that have been marginalized and oppressed because they deviate from the dominant culture's norm and are perceived to be *preferred*.

Nonjudgment (see Chapter 2). The ability to suspend critique while taking in information (e.g., listening, reading, experiencing events), making decisions, and interacting with others.

Open-mindedness (see Chapter 2). A mental state in which one suspends judgment by bracketing biases, preconceived notions, prior knowledge, and/or prior experiences to fully hear and be present for others.

Oppression (see Chapter 1). Acts by dominant culture individuals, groups, or systems in which they inflict unjust treatment, power, control, and/or limit or prohibit access to vital resources to people in nondominant cultural groups.

Passing (see Chapter 14). A term used to describe when a transgender person is assumed to be a cisgender person based on their external gender expression.

Pathologizing (see Chapter 11). To characterize and/or to treat someone differently based on their non-normative or nondominant behaviors or characteristics. Synonym: *abnormal.*

Patriarchy (see Chapter 14). Attitudes, beliefs, values, and actions that reinforce the notion that men are and should be in control of all things.

Perspective Taking (see Chapter 2). The ability to consider more multiple viewpoints, especially those that are not typical for one to take or those that seem counter to one's worldviews or values.

Poverty (see Chapter 11). A social class group and a federal designation for those who earn below the minimum income threshold. Living in poverty is an intersectional experience that interacts with other identities, all of which have distinct and interrelated effects on well-being.

Power (see Chapter 1). The direct influence or control over others on both individual and systemic levels based on sociocultural privilege—how individuals and systems use their privilege within society.

Privilege (see Chapter 1). Advantages people with dominant identities in all domains experience just for being who they are.

Pronouns (see Chapter 14). A term used to speak about a person (e.g., he, she, they) when not using a person's name.

Queer (see Chapters 14 and 15). An umbrella term for people who are not heterosexual or cisgender.

Race (see Chapters 7 and 8). A social and political human classification system based on physical characteristics that is not scientific or biologically based.

Racial Colorblindness (see Chapters 7 and 8). The belief that one's racial group should not be considered or even noticed as a strategy to manage discrimination.

Racism (see Chapters 7 and 8). An oppressive system based on race that advantages those whose race is dominant (i.e., White in the United States). Perpetrated by a racially dominant culture, individual, group, community, or institution against a racially nondominant person, group or community based on their actual or perceived race.

Referrals (see Chapter 18). The process by which counselors make recommendations to clients to access other health-care professionals, either to augment current counseling services or to begin treatment with another counseling provider.

Refugee (see Chapter 9). People who have fled their home country because of war or violence and who have crossed an international border seeking safety. Legally, it can indicate an individual whose situation has been assessed and has been awarded either temporary or permanent permission to stay in a host country.

Religion (see Chapter 16). An organized, structured belief system and worship of a God or gods.

Reservation (see Chapter 10). Federal land designated as *reserved* for a tribe or tribes who have been displaced via colonialism.

RESPECTFUL Model (see Chapter 4). A cultural identity acronym counselors use to attend to multiple areas of clients' culture. R: Religion/Spirituality E: Economic Class Background S: Sexual Identity P: Psychological Development E: Ethnic/Racial Identity C: Chronological/Lifespan Challenges T: Trauma F: Family Background U: Unique Physical Characteristics L: Location/Language.

Self-awareness (see Chapter 2). An individual's capacity to examine their thoughts, emotions, values, worldviews, and experiences from a nonjudgmental and curious perspective with the intent to learn and grow from what they learn about themselves.

Sexual Orientation (see Chapter 15). See *affectual orientation* (preferred term). Refers to who individuals are attracted to and want to have a relationship with.

Social Class (see Chapter 11). Groupings based on factors of wealth, income, education, occupation, and experiences and interactions with socioeconomic status or how they *do* their socioeconomic status. Social class includes socioeconomic status but is not socioeconomic status in and of itself.

Social Justice Counseling (see Chapter 5). A counseling approach that employs a range of strategies and interventions aimed at addressing oppressive systems of power and privilege that impact clients.

Socioeconomic Status (SES) (see Chapter 11). A combination of income, education, and occupation. Can be used to group individuals based on these factors.

Spatial Discrimination (see Chapter 17). The intentional exclusion of fat people from public spaces that were not designed for their bodies.

Spirituality (see Chapter 16). Recognition of a feeling, sense, or belief that there is something greater than oneself.

Structural Inequality (see Chapter 4). The inequitable distribution of resources that come from discriminatory practices of institutions such as legal, education, government, and health-care systems.

Structural Oppression (see Chapter 4). Institutional discrimination against individuals based on their nondominant identities (e.g., race, gender, social class) that hinders their opportunities and access to valued resources.

Systems Theory (see Chapter 4). An overarching approach used in couple, marriage, and family counseling that works with the *system* as the client. Also a broad term to denote the connections and relationships within and amongst societal structures.

Tolerance for Ambiguity (see Chapter 2). The capacity to hold multiple thoughts, ideas, facts, and feelings simultaneously, even if they conflict with one another, without needing to seek to resolve them immediately.

Transgender (see Chapter 14). A person whose gender identity does not match their assigned sex at birth.

Treatment Planning (see Chapter 18). Establishing, in collaboration with the client, what will occur in the counseling process based on the counselor's assessment, diagnosis, and case conceptualization to help the client reach their goals.

Two-Spirit (see Chapter 10). A person who identifies as having both masculine and feminine qualities or *spirit.* A term used by Indigenous Native Americans that describes sexual, gender, and spiritual identities.

Undocumented (see Chapter 9). Individuals born outside the United States who are living in the United States and do not possess a valid visa or other immigration documentation.

Upper Social Class (see Chapter 11). A social class group with the greatest wealth.

Visibility of Disability (see Chapter 12). A disability that can be noticed by another person without being disclosed intentionally by the person with a disability. Also referred to as an *apparent disability.*

Weight Stigma (see Chapter 17). Discrimination and oppression faced by people with large bodies (i.e., *fat people*) in U.S. society.

White Privilege (see Chapter 1). A set of unearned, social-cultural privileges that White people have due to their race.

Working Class (see Chapter 11). A social class group designated by performing manual labor or working in industrial settings.

Worldview (see Chapter 1). Each individual's personal collection of beliefs, attitudes, and values about the world.

Xenomisia (see Chapter 1). Hatred of people with actual or perceived nondominant ethnic identities or based on their country of origin.

Bibliography

Aboriginal Healing Foundation. (2004). Historic trauma and Aboriginal healing. Ottawa, Ontario. https://firstnationspedagogy.com/historic_trauma.pdf

ALGBTIC LGBQQIA Competencies Taskforce, Harper, A., Finnerty, P., Martinez, M., Brace, A., Crethar, H. C., Loos, B., Harper, B., Graham, S., Singh, A., Kocet, M., Travis, M., Lambert, S., Burnes, T., L Dickey, L. M & Hammer, T. R. (2013). Association for Lesbian, Gay, Bisexual, and Transgender Issues in Counseling Competencies for Counseling with Lesbian, Gay, Bisexual, Queer, Questioning, Intersex, and Ally Individuals, *Journal of LGBT Issues in Counseling, 7*(2), 2-43. http://dx.doi.org/10.1080/15538605.2013.755444

American Counseling Association. (2017). *Nondiscrimination Position Statement.*

American Counseling Association (1995). *1995 ACA code of ethics & standards of practice.*

American Mental Health Counselors Association (2021). *AMHCA standards from the practice of clinical mental health counseling.*

American Mental Health Counselors Association (2010). *AMHCA code of ethics.*

American Mental Health Counselors Association. (2015). *AMHCA code of ethics.*

American School Counselor Association (ASCA). (2019). *ASCA national model: A framework for school counseling programs* (4th ed.).

American School Counselor Association (ASCA). (2021). *The school counselor and multitiered systems of support. ASCA position statements.* https://www.schoolcounselor.org/Standards-Positions/Position-Statements/ASCA-Position-Statements/The-School-Counselor-and-Multitiered-System-of-Sup

American School Counselor Association (ASCA). (2022). *The school counselor and cultural diversity.*

Aaron, S. P., Gazaway, S. B., Harrell, E. R., & Elk, R. (2021). Disparities and racism experienced among older African Americans nearing end of life. *Current Geriatrics Reports, 10*(4), 157–166. https://doi.org/10.1007/s13670-021-00366-6

AARP. (2022). *Dignity 2022: The experience of LGBTQ older adults.* https://www.aarp.org/content/dam/aarp/research/surveys_statistics/life-leisure/2022/lgbtq-community-dignity-2022-report.doi.10.26419-2Fres.00549.001.pdf

AARP. (n.d). *Welcome to the network of age friendly states and communities.* Retrieved April 6, 2023, from https://www.aarp.org/livable-communities/network-age-friendly-communities/

Abrams, J. A., Maxwell, M., Pope, M., & Belgrave, F. Z. (2014). Carrying the world with the grace of a lady and the grit of a warrior: Deepening our understanding of the "strong black woman" schema. *Psychology of Women Quarterly, 38*(4), 503–518.

Administration on Aging. (2021). *2020 profile of older Americans.* Administration for Community Living, U.S. Department of Health and Human Services. https://acl.gov/sites/default/files/aging%20and%20Disability%20In%20America/2020Profileolderamericans.final_.pdf

Administration on Aging. (2022). *2021 profile of older Americans.* Administration on Community Living. https://acl.gov/sites/default/files/Profile%20of%20OA/2021%20Profile%20of%20OA/2021ProfileOlderAmericans_508.pdf

Adnan, A., Athar, F. B., Nazir, A., Mago, A., Ochani, S., & Siddiqui, A. (2023). Xenophobia amidst and post-COVID-19 pandemic. *Health Science Reports*, *6*(5), e1252. https://doi.org/10.1002/hsr2.1252

AIDS Coalition to Unleash Power. (n.d.). *ACT UP NY | End AIDS*! https://actupny.com/

Al-Azhari, S. (Ed.). (2023, June 21). *Five pillars of Islam*. Islamic Relief UK. https://www.islamic-relief.org.uk/resources/knowledge-base/five-pillars-of-islam/

Alexander, M. (2012). *The new Jim Crow: Mass incarceration in the age of colorblindness*. The New Press.

ALGBTIC LGBQQIA Competencies Taskforce, Harper, A, Finnerty, P., Martinez, M., Brace, A., Crethar, H. C., Loos, B., Harper, B., Graham, S., Singh, A., Kocet, M., Travis, L., Lambert, S., Burnes, T., Dickey, L. M., & Hammer, T. R. (2013). Association for Lesbian, Gay, Bisexual, and Transgender issues in counseling competencies for counseling with lesbian, gay, bisexual, queer, questioning, intersex, and ally individuals. *Journal of LGBT Issues in Counseling*, *7*(1), 2–43. https://doi.org/10.1080/15538605.2013.755444

Alhusen, J. L., Bower, K., Epstein, E., & Sharps, P. (2016). Racial discrimination and adverse birth outcomes: An integrative review. *Journal of Midwifery Women's Health*, *61*(6), 707–720. https://www.doi.org/10.1111/jmwh.12490.

Allen, B. J. (2023). *Difference matters: Communicating social identity* (3rd ed.). Waveland Press, Inc.

Allport, G. W. (1954). *The nature of prejudice*. Cambridge Press.

American Association for Marriage and Family Therapy. (2021). *Clinical Guidelines for LGBTQIA-affirming marriage and family therapy*. https://www.aamft.org/lgbtqiaguidelines

American Civil Liberties Union. (2023, March 17*). Mapping attacks on LGBTQ rights in U.S. State Legislatures*. https://www.aclu.org/legislation-affecting-lgbtq-rights-across-country

American Counseling Association. (ACA). (2014). *ACA code of ethics*. https://www.counseling.org/resources/aca-code-of-ethics.pdf

American Counselor Association. (ACA). (2017a). *Nondiscrimination position statement*.

American Counseling Association (ACA). (2017b). *Resolution on reparative therapy/conversion therapy/sexual orientation change efforts (SOCE) as a significant and serious violation of the ACA code of ethics*. Governing Council Motion. https://www.counseling.org/docs/default-source/resolutions/reparative-therapy-resoltution-letter—final.pdf?sfvrsn=d7ad512c_4

American Counseling Association. (2022). *We did it! Medicare reimbursement now law*. https://www.counseling.org/news/news-detail/2022/12/23/we-did-it!-medicare-reimbursement-now-law

American Medical Association (AMA). (2019, June 10). *AMA adopts new polices on first day of voting at 2019 annual meeting*. https://www.ama-assn.org/press-center/press-

American Mental Health Counselors Association. (AMHCA). (2020). *AMHCA code of ethics*. https://www.counseling.org/resources/aca-code-of-ethics.pdf

American Psychiatric Association (APA). (1968). *Diagnostic and statistical manual of mental disorders* (2nd ed.).

American Psychiatric Association (APA). (1973). *Homosexuality and sexuality orientation disturbance*: Proposed change in DSM-II (APA Document Reference No. 730008, 6th printing, p. 44).

American Psychiatric Association (APA). (1980). *Diagnostic and statistical manual of mental disorders* (3rd ed.).

American Psychiatric Association (APA). (2000). *Diagnostic and statistical manual of mental Disorders: DSM-IV-TR* (4th ed., text revision). https ://doi.org/10.1176/appi.books.9780890420249.dsm-iv-tr

American Psychiatric Association (APA). (2021). *New APA poll reveals that Americans are increasingly anxious about climate change's impact on planet, mental health.* https ://www.psychiatry.org/newsroom/news-releases/climate-poll-2020

American Psychiatric Association. (APA). (2022). *Diagnostic and statistical manual of mental disorders: DSM-5-TR* (5th ed., text revision).

American Psychological Association. (2017). *Multicultural guidelines: An ecological approach to context, identity, and intersectionality.* http://www.apa.org/about/policy/multicultural-guidelines.pdf

American Psychological Association (APA). (2020). *APA guidelines for psychological assessment and evaluation.* https://www.apa.org/about/policy/guidelines-psychological-assessment-evaluation.pdf

American Psychological Association (APA). (2023a). *APA dictionary of psychology.* https://dictionary.apa.org/

American Psychological Association (APA). (2023b). *APA dictionary of psychology: Intake interview.* https://dictionary.apa.org/intake-interview

American Psychological Association (APA). (n.d.). *APA style & grammar guidelines: Bias-free language.* https://apastyle.apa.org/style-grammar-guidelines/bias-free-language/gender

American Psychological Association, APA Task Force on Psychological Practice with Sexual Minority Persons. (2021). *Guidelines for psychological practice with sexual minority persons.* www.apa.org/about/policy/psychological-practice-sexual-minority-persons.pdf

American School Counselor Association (ASCA). (2019). *ASCA national model: A framework for school counseling programs* (4th ed.).

American School Counselor Association (ASCA). (2021). *The school counselor and multitiered systems of support. ASCA position statements.* https://www.schoolcounselor.org/Standards-Positions/Position-Statements/ASCA-Position-Statements/The-School-Counselor-and-Multitiered-System-of-Sup

American School Counselor Association (ASCA). (2022a). *ASCA ethical standards for school counselors.* https://www.schoolcounselor.org/About-School-Counseling/Ethical-Legal-Responsibilities/ASCA-Ethical-Standards-for-School-Counselors-(1)

American School Counselor Association (ASCA). (2022b). *The school counselor and cultural diversity.*

American School Counselor Association (ASCA). (2022c). *The school counselor and LGBTQ+ youth.* https://www.schoolcounselor.org/Standards-Positions/Position-Statements/ASCA-Position-Statements/The-School-Counselor-and-LGBTQ-Youth

American School Counselor Association. (2023a). *The school counselor and school counseling programs. ASCA position statements.* https://www.schoolcounselor.org/Standards-Positions/Position-Statements/ASCA-Position-Statements/The-School-Counselor-and-School-Counseling-Program

American School Counselor Association. (2023b). *The school counselor and universal screening. ASCA position statements.* https://www.schoolcounselor.org/Standards-Positions/Position-Statements/ASCA-Position-Statements/The-School-Counselor-and-Universal-Screening

American Society of Addiction Medicine. (2022). *Definition of addiction.* https://www.asam.org/quality-care/definition-of-addiction

Amlund, D. (2020). Everyone should be fat activists or fat-allies. *Conjunctions*, *7*(1) 1–14. https://doi.org/10.7146/tjcp.v7i1.119859

Anapol, D. (2010). *Polyamory in the 21st century: Love and intimacy with multiple partners.* Rowman & Littlefield.

Andary, L., Klimidis, S., & Stolk, Y. (2003). *Assessing mental health across cultures*. Australian Academic Press.

Anderson, R. E., Geier, T. J., & Cahill, S. P. (2016). Epidemiological associations between posttraumatic stress disorder and incarceration in the national survey of American life. *Criminal Behaviour & Mental Health, 26*(2), 110–123. https://doi.org/10.1002/cbm.1951

Andler, M. (2021). The sexual orientation/identity discussion. *Hypatia, 36*(2), 259–275. https://doi.org/10.1017/hyp.2021.13

Anti-Muslim Discrimination. (2022). *American Civil Liberties Union* (ACLU). https://www.aclu.org/issues/national-security/discriminatory-profiling/anti-muslim-discrimination

Appelbaum, K., Hickey, J. M., & Packer, I. (2001). The role of correctional officers in multidisciplinary mental health care in prisons. *Psychiatric Services, 52*, 1343–1347. https://doi.org/10.1176/appi.ps.52.10.1343

Arab American Institute. (2023). *National Arab American demographics*. https://www.aaiusa.org/demographics

Aragão, C. (2023, March 1). *Gender pay gap in U.S. hasn't changed much in two decades*. Pew Research Center. https://www.pewresearch.org/fact-.

Arends-Tóth, J., & Van de Vijver, F.J.R. (2004). Domains and dimensions in acculturation: Implicit theories of Turkish–Dutch. *International Journal of Intercultural Relations, 28*(1), 19–35. https://doi.org/10.1016/j.ijintrel.2003.09.001

Arnault, D. (2009). Cultural determinants of help seeking: A model for research and practice. *Research and Theory for Nursing Practice, 23*(4), 259–278. https://doi.org/10.1891/1541-6577.23.4.259

Arredondo, P., Gallardo-Cooper, M., Delgado-Romero, E. A., & Zapata, A. L. (2014). *Culturally responsive counseling with Latinas/os*. American Counseling Association.

Artiga, S., Hill, L., Ranji, U., & Gomez, I. (2022, July 15). *What are the implications of overturning Roe v. Wade for racial disparities*? Kaiser Family Foundation. https://www.kff.org/racial-equity-and-health-policy/issue-brief/what-are-the-implications-of-the-overturning-of-roe-v-wade-for-racial-disparities/

Aschauer, W., & Mayerl, J. (2019). The dynamics of ethnocentrism in Europe. A comparison of enduring and emerging determinants of solidarity towards immigrants. *European Societies, 21*(5), 672–703. https://doi.org/10.1080/14616696.2019.1616791

Associated Press. (2023). *Antisemitic incidents on rise across the US, report finds*. https://www.pbs.org/newshour/politics/antisemitic-incidents-on-rise-across-the-u-s-report-finds

Association for Lesbian, Gay, Bisexual, and Transgender Issues in Counseling LGBQQIA Competencies Taskforce. (2013). Association for lesbian, gay, bisexual, and transgender issues in counseling competencies for counseling with lesbian, gay, bisexual, queer, questioning, intersex, and ally individuals. *Journal of LGBT Issues in Counseling, 7*(1), 2–43. https://doi.org/10.1080/15538605.2013.755444

Association for Spiritual, Ethical, and Religious Values in Counseling (ASERVIC). (2009). *Competencies for addressing spiritual and religious issues in counseling.* http://www.aservic.org/wp-content/uploads/2017/02/ASERVIC-Spiritual-Competencies_FINAL.pdf.

Association for Spiritual, Ethical, and Religious Issues in Counseling (ASERVIC). (2021). *A white paper of the Association for Spiritual, Ethical, and Religious Values in Counseling.* https://aservic.org/aservic-white-paper/aservic-white-paper-2/

Astramovich, R. L., & Hoskins, W. J. (2013). Evaluating addictions counseling programs: Promoting best practices, accountability, and advocacy. *Journal of Addictions & Offender Counseling, 34*(2), 114–124. https://doi.org/10.1002/j.2161-1874.2013.00019.x

Ataga, J., Swank, J. M., McNeice, Z. P., Rabess, A., & Gay, J. L. (2021). Year of return: Black clinicians connecting across the West-African diaspora. *International Journal for the Advancement of Counselling, 43*(3), 302–319. https://doi.org/10.1007/s10447-021-09444-y

Atkinson, D. R., Morten, G., & Sue, D. W. (1998). Counseling American minorities: A cross-cultural perspective (5th ed.). Boston, MA: McGraw-Hill.

Ausloos, C. (2023a). Homonegativity. In S. Dermer & J. Abdullah (Eds.), *The SAGE encyclopedia of multicultural counseling, social justice, and advocacy.* SAGE Publications.

Ausloos, C. (2023b). LGBTQI+ affirmative counseling. In S. Dermer & J. Abdullah (Eds.), *The SAGE encyclopedia of multicultural counseling, social justice, and advocacy.* SAGE Publications.

Ausloos, C., & Salpietro, L. (2022). Culturally responsive counseling for transgender clients. In L. Summer & L. Nelson (Eds.), *Multicultural counseling: Responding with cultural humility, empathy and advocacy.* Springer.

Autistic Self Advocacy Network (ASAN). (2022). Identity-First Language. https://autisticadvocacy.org/about-asan/identity-first-language/

Avent, J. R., & Cashwell, C. S. (2015). The black church: Theology and implications for counseling African Americans. *The Professional Counselor, 5*, 81–90.

Ayonrinde, O. A., Obuaya, C., & Adeyemi, S. O. (2015). Brain fag syndrome: A culture-bound syndrome that may be approaching extinction. *BJPsych Bulletin, 39*(4), 156–161. https://doi.org/10.1192/pb.bp.114.049049

Baboolall, D., Greenberg, S., Obeid, M., & Zucker J. (2021, November 10). *Being transgender at work.* Mckinsey & Company. https://www.mckinsey.com/featured-insights/diversity-

Bacigalupo, A. M, (2007). *Shamans of the foye tree: Gender, power, and healing among Chilean Mapuche.* University of Texas Press.

Backer, R., & Chang, E. S. (2023). *Ageism as an invisible form of bigotry.* https://www.bu.edu/antiracism-center/files/2022/06/Ageism.pdf

Bacon, J. G., Scheltema, K. E., & Robinson, B. E. (2001). Fat Phobia Scale revisited: The short form. *International Journal of Obesity and Related Metabolic Disorders, 25*(11), 252–157. https://doj.org/10.1038/siijo.0801537

Bacon, L. (2010). *Health at every size: The surprising truth about your weight.* BenBella Books, Inc.

Baker, S. J., & Lucas, K. (2017). Is it safe to bring myself to work? Understanding LGBTQ experiences of workplace dignity. *Canadian Journal of Administrative Sciences, 34*, 133–148. https://doi.org/10.1002/cjas.1439

Ballard, J., Wieling, E., Solheim, C., & Lang, D. (n.d.). *Bioecological systems theory.* Iowa State University. https://iastate.pressbooks.pub/parentingfamilydiversity/chapter/bronfenbrenner/

Balsam, K. F., Huang, B., Fieland, K. C., Simoni, J. M., & Walters, K. L. (2004). Culture, trauma, and wellness: A comparison of heterosexual and lesbian, gay, bisexual, and two-spirit Native Americans. *Cultural Diversity and Ethnic Minority Psychology, 10*(3), 287–301. https://doi.org/10.1037/1099-9809.10.3.287

Balsam, K. F., Molina, Y., Beadnell, B., Simoni, J., & Walters, K. (2011). Measuring multiple minority stress: The LGBT people of color microaggressions scale. *Cultural Diversity Ethnic Minority Psychology, 17*(2), 163–174. https://doi.org/10.1037/a0023244

Bandura, A. (1986). *Social foundations of thought and action: A social cognitive theory.* Prentice Hall.

Bandura, A. (1997). *Self-efficacy: The exercise of control.* Macmillan.

Banerjee, R., & Dittmar, H. (2008). Individual Differences in Children's Materialism: The Role of Peer Relations. *Personality and Social Psychology Bulletin*, 34(1), 17-31. https://doi.org/10.1177/0146167207309196

Banks-VanAllen, C. (2023). Conceptualizing diagnosis through a social justice lens. *Counseling Today.* https://ct.counseling.org/2023/05/conceptualizing-diagnosis-through-a-social-justice-lens/

Bardhoshi, G., Cobb, N., & Erford, B. T. (2019). Determining evidence-based outcomes in school-aged youth: Free-access instruments for school counselor use. *Professional School Counseling, 22*(1b), 2156759X1983443. https://doi.org/10.1177/2156759x19834431

Barideaux Jr., K., Crossby, A., & Crosby, D. (2021). Colorism and criminality; The effects of skin tone and crime type on judgements of guilt. *Applied Psychology in Criminal Justice, 16*(2), 181–199.

Barker, D. (1992). Fetal and infant origins of adult disease. *British Medical Journal, 301*(6761), 1111.

Barker, M. (1981). *The new racism: Conservatives and the ideology of the tribe*. Aletheia Books.

Barnes, S. F. (2011). *Third age—The golden years of adulthood*. San Diego State University Interwork Institute. http://calbooming.sdsu.edu/documents/TheFourthAge.pdf

Bartels, S. J., Blow, F. C., Brockmann, L. M., & Van Citters, A. D. (2005). *Substance abuse and mental health among older Americans: The state of the knowledge and future directions*. Older Americans Substance Abuse and Mental Health Technical Assistance Center, Substance Abuse and Mental Health Services Administration.

Bartels, S. J., & Naslund, J. A. (2013). The underside of the silver tsunami—older adults and mental health care. *New England Journal of Medicine, 368*(6), 493–496. https://doi.org/10.1056/nejmx130007

Bathje, G. J., Pillersdorf, D., & Eddir, H. (2022). Multicultural competence as a common factor in the process and outcome of counseling. *Journal of Humanistic Psychology*. http://dx.doi.org/10.1177/00221678221099679

Baudon, P., & Jachens, L. (2021). A scoping review of interventions for the treatment of eco-anxiety. *International Journal of Environmental Research and Public Health, 18*(18), 9636. https://doi.org/10.3390/ijerph18189636

Baumann, A. A., Kuhlberg, J. A., & Zayas, L. H. (2010). Familism, mother-daughter mutuality, and suicide attempts of adolescent Latinas. *Journal of Family Psychology, 24*, 616–624. https://doi.org/10.1037/a0020584

Baumhofer, N. K., & Yamane, C. (2019). Multilevel racism and Native Hawaiian health. In C. Ford, D. M. Griffith, & M. A. Bruce (Eds.), *Racism: Science & tools for the public health professional* (Vol. 1). American Public Health Association. https://doi.org/10.2105/9780875533049ch19

Baylor, E. (2012). Ethnocentrism. *Oxford Bibliographies*. https://doi.org.10.1093/obo/9780199766567-0045

Beck, A. J. (2021, January). *Race and ethnicity of violent crime offenders and arrestees, 2018.* Bureau of Justice Statistics. https://bjs.ojp.gov/library/publications/race-and-ethnicity-violent-crime-offenders-and-arrestees-2018

Beeghley, L. (2000). *The structure of social stratification in the United States* (3rd ed.). Allyn & Bacon.

Beemyn, G. (2014). Transgender history in the United States. In L. Erickson-Schroth (Ed.), *Trans bodies, trans selves* (pp.). Oxford.

Bell, D. (1995). Who's afraid of critical race theory? *University of Illinois Law Review, 4*, 893–910.

Belser, C. T., Shillingford, M. A., & Joe, J. R. (2016). The ASCA model and a multi-tiered system of supports: A framework to support students of color with problem behavior. *The Professional Counselor, 6*(3), 251–262. https://doi.org/10.15241/cb.6.3.251

Beltran, A. (2017, February 21). Children and families fleeing gang violence in Central America. *Washington Office on Latin America*. https://www.wola.org/analysis/people-leaving-central-americas-northern-triangle/

Bem, L. S. (1981). Gender schema theory: A cognitive account of sex typing. *Psychological Review, 88*, 354–364.

Bemak, F., Talleyrand, R. M., Jones, H., & Daquin, J. (2011). Implementing multicultural social justice strategies in counselor education training programs. *Journal for Social Action in Counseling & Psychology, 3*(1), 29–43.

Benyshek, D. C. (2005). Type 2 diabetes and fetal origins: The promise of prevention programs focusing on prenatal health in high prevalence Native American communities. *Human Organization, 64*(2), 192–200. https://doi.org/10.17730/humo.64.2.kk7y77qhna0819bj

Berberian, A. G., Gonzalez, D. J. X., & Cushing, L. J. (2022). Racial disparities in climate change-related health effects in the United States. *Current Environmental Health Reports, 9*, 451–464. https://doi.org/10.1007/s40572-022-00360-w

Bergin, A. E. (1980). Psychotherapy and religious values. *Journal of Consulting and Clinical Psychology, 48*(1), 95–105.

Bernal, M. E., & Knight, G. P. (1993). *Ethnic Identity: Formation and transmission among Hispanics and other minorities. SUNY Series, United States Hispanic Studies.*

Berry, J. W. (1992), Acculturation and adaptation in a new society. *International Migration, 30*, 69–85. https://doi.org/10.1111/j.1468-2435.1992.tb00776.x

Berry, J. W. (1997). Immigration, acculturation and adaptation. *Applied Psychology, 46*(1), 5–34. http://dx.doi.org/10.1111/j.1464-0597.1997.tb01087.x

Berry, J. W. (2008). Globalization and acculturation. *International Journal of Intercultural Relations, 32*, 328–336. https://doi.org/10.1016/j.ijintrel.2008.04.001

Berry, J. W. (2015). Acculturation. In J. E. Grusec & P. D. Hastings (Eds.), *Handbook of socialization: Theory and research* (pp. 520–538). The Guilford Press.

Berry, J. W. (2019). Acculturation. In K. D. Keith (Eds.), *Cambridge elements: Elements in psychology and culture* (pp. 1–66). Cambridge University Press. http://dx.doi.org/10.1017/9781108589666

Bertosa, B. (2009). Sacrifice to Eros and homosexuality in the Spartan army. *War & Society, 28*(2), 1–19. https://doi.org/10.1179/072924709793054624

Betters-Bubon J., Brunner T., & Kansteiner A. (2016). Success for all? The role of the school counselor in creating and sustaining culturally responsive positive behavior interventions and supports programs. *The Professional Counselor, 6*(3), 263–277. https://doi.org/10.15241/jbb.6.3.263

Betters-Bubon, J., Pianta, R., Sweeney, D., & Goodman-Scott, E. (2022). Antiracism starts with us: School counselor critical reflection within an multitiered systems of support framework. *Professional School Counseling, 26*(1), 2156759X2210867. https://doi.org/10.1177/2156759x221086747

Bhati, K. S. (2014). Effect of client-therapist gender match on the therapeutic relationship: An exploratory analysis. *Psychological Reports: Relationships and Communications, 115*(2), 565–583. https://doi.org/10.2466/21.02.PR0.115c23z1

Biles, K., Mphande-Finn, J., & Stroud, D (2012). Social class and schools: Beyond Ruby Payne. In D. C. Sturm & D. M. Gibson (Eds.), *Social class and the helping professions* (pp. 151–166). Routledge.

Billingsley, A. (1968). *Black families in white America*. Prentice-Hall.

Bilodeau, B. L., & Renn, K. A. (2005). Analysis of LGBT identity development models and implications for practice. *New Directions for Student Services, 111*, 25–39.

Bioecological Systems Theory. (2022). LibreTexts: Social sciences. https://socialsci.libretexts.org/Bookshelves/Early_Childhood_Education/Child_Family_Community%3A_The_Socialization_of_Diverse_Children/01%3A_Introduction_to_Socialization_and_Theories/1.04%3A_Bronfenbrenner

Bishop, J., Crisp, D., & Scholz, B. (2021). The real and ideal experiences of what culturally competent counseling or psychotherapy service provision means to lesbian, gay and bisexual people. *Counseling and Psychotherapy Research, 22*(2), 429–438. https://doi.org/10.1002/capr.12469

Black Elk. (1989). *The sacred pipe: Black Elk's account of the Oglala Sioux*. University of Oklahoma Press. (Original work published 1953). https://search.library.wisc.edu/catalog/999666656002121

Blake, J. J., Keith, V. M., Luo, W., Le, H., & Salter, P. (2017). The role of colorism in explaining African American females' suspension risk. *School Psychology Quarterly, 32*(1), 118.

Blakemore, E. (2019, February 23). Race and ethnicity, explained. *National Geographic*. https://www.nationalgeographic.co.uk/history/2019/02/race-and-ethnicity-explained

Blanchflower, D. G., & Oswald, A. J. (2008). Is well-being U-shaped over the life cycle? *Soc Sci Med, 66*(8), 1733–1749. http://dx.doi.org/10.1016/j.socscimed.2008.01.030

Blau, F. D., & Mackie, C. (Eds.). (2017). *The economic and fiscal consequences of immigration*. National Academies Press.

Blay, Y. A. (2011). Skin bleaching and global white supremacy: By way of introduction. *The Journal of Pan African Studies, 4*(4), 4–46.

Blomley, N. (2019). The territorialization of property in land: Space, power and practice. *Territory, Politics, Governance, 7*(2), 233–249. https://doi.org/10.1080/21622671.2017.1359107

Blosnich, J. R., Henderson, E. R., Coulter, R. W. S., Goldbach, J. T., & Meyer, I. H. (2020). Sexual orientation change efforts, adverse childhood experiences, and suicide ideation and attempt among sexual minority adults, United States, 2016–2018. *American Journal of Public Health, 110*(7), 1024–1030. https://doi.org/10.2105/AJPH.2020.305637

Bockting, W., & Coleman, E. (2007). Developmental stages of the transgender coming out process: Toward an integrated identity. In R. Ettner, S. Monstrey, & E. Coleman (Eds.), *Principles of transgender medicine and surgery* (pp. 185–208). The Haworth Press.

Bockting, W., & Coleman, E. (2016). Developmental stages of the transgender coming-out process. In R. Ettner, S. Monstrey, & E. Coleman (Eds.), *Principles of transgender medicine and surgery* (2nd ed., pp.). Routledge.

Bockting, W., Robinson, B., Benner, A., & Scheltema, K. (2004). Patient satisfaction with transgender health services. *Journal of Sex & Marital Therapy, 30*(4), 277–294, https://doi.org/10.1080/00926230490422467

Bodner, E., Shrira, A., Bergman, Y. S., Cohen-Fridel, S., & Grossman, E. S. (2015). The interaction between aging and death anxieties predicts ageism. *Personality and Individual Differences, 86*, 15–19. https://doi.org/10.1016/j.paid.2015.05.022

Boghosian, S. (2011). *Counseling and psychotherapy with clients of Middle Eastern descent: A qualitative inquiry*. (Order No. 3453570) [Doctoral Dissertation, Utah State University]. https://login.libweb.lib.utsa.edu/login?url=https://www.proquest.com/dissertations-theses/counseling-psychotherapy-with-clients-middle/docview/867841069/se-2

Bosman, J. (2019, November 20). How the collapse of local news is causing a 'national crisis.' *New York Times*. https://www.nytimes.com/2019/11/20/us/local-news-disappear-pen-america.html

Bosomworth, N. J. (2012). The downside of weight loss: Realistic intervention in body-weight trajectory. *Canadian Family Physician Medecin de Famille Canadien, 58*(5), 517–523.

Bostock v. Clayton County, 590 U.S. (2020). https://www.supremecourt.gov/opinions/19pdf/17-1618_hfci.pdf

Bowen, D. (2011). An initial Christian counselor internship program for Ukraine. *Journal of Psychology and Theology, 39*(4), 356–363. http://www.thefreelibrary.com/An+initial+Christian+counselor+internship+program+for+Ukraine.-a0278526794

Bowman, P. J., Muhammad, R., & Ifatunji, M. (2004). Skin tone, class, and racial attitudes among African Americans. *Skin deep: How race and complexion matter in the "color-blind" era* (pp. 128–158). University of Illinois Press.

Brady, A. (2019, January 4). *Blind not broken* [Video]. Ted. https://www.ted.com/talks/annie_brady_blind_not_broken

Bram, J. T., Warwick-Clark, B., Obeysekare, E., & Mehta, K. (2015). Utilization and monetization of healthcare data in developing countries. *Big Data, 3*(2), 59–66.

Brave Heart, M. Y. H. (1999). Gender differences in the historical trauma response among the Lakota. *Journal of Health & Social Policy, 10*(4), 1–21. https://doi.org/10.1300/J045v10n04_01

Brave Heart, M. Y. H. (2003). The historical trauma response among natives and its relationship with substance abuse: A Lakota Illustration. *Journal of Psychoactive Drugs, 35*(1), *7–13. https://doi.org/10.1080/02791072.2003.10399988*

Brave Heart, M. Y. H., Chase, J., Elkins, J., & Altschul, D. (2011). Historical trauma among indigenous peoples of the Americas: Concepts, Research, and Clinical Considerations. *Journal of Psychoactive Drugs, 43*(4), 282–290. https://doi.org/10.1080/02791072.2011.628913

Brave Heart, M. Y. H., & DeBruyn, L. (1998). The American Indian holocaust: Healing historical unresolved grief. *American Indian/Alaskan Native Mental Health Research, 8*(2), 56–78.

Brinkman, A. H., Rea-Sandin, G., Lund, E. M., Fitzpatrick, O. M., Gusman, M. S., & Boness, C. L. (2023). Shifting the discourse on disability: Moving to an inclusive, intersectional focus. *American Journal of Orthopsychiatry, 93*(1), 50–62. https://doi-org.spot.lib.auburn.edu/10.1037/ort0000653.supp

Brochu, P. M. (2020). Testing the effectiveness of a weight bias educational intervention among clinical psychology trainees. *Journal of Applied Social Psychology*. https://doi.org/10.1111/jasp.12653

Bronfenbrenner, U. (1977). Toward an experimental ecology of human development. *American Psychologist*, 513–531.

Bronfenbrenner, U. (1979). *The ecology of human development: Experiments by nature and design*. Harvard University Press.

Bronfenbrenner, U. (1986). Ecology of the family as a context for human development: Research perspectives. *Developmental Psychology, 22*(6), 723–742. https://doi.org/10.1037/0012-1649.22.6.723

Bronfenbrenner, U. (1994). Ecological models of human development. In *International Encyclopedia of Education,* (Vol. 3, 2nd ed., pp. 37–43). Elsevier.

Bronfenbrenner, U. (2005). *Making human beings human: Bioecological perspectives on human development*. SAGE Publishing.

Bronfenbrenner, U., & Morris, P. A. (2006). The bioecological model of human development. In R. M. Lerner & W. Damon (Eds.), *Handbook of child psychology: Theoretical models of human development* (pp. 793–828). John Wiley & Sons Inc.

Brown, K. (2014). In the eye of the beholder: Definitions of beauty in popular black magazines. In *Soul Thieves: The Appropriation and Misrepresentation of African American Popular Culture* (pp. 77–90). Palgrave Macmillan US.

Brown, L. B. (1997). *Two spirit people.* Routledge.

Brown, L. S., Riepe, L. E., & Coffey, R. L. (2005). Beyond color and culture: Feminist contributions to paradigms of human difference. In M. Hill & M. Ballou (Eds.), *The foundation and future of feminist therapy* (pp. 63–92). The Hawthorn Press.

Brown, R. A., Dickerson, D. L., & D'Amico, E. J. (2016). Cultural Identity among Urban American Indian/Native Alaskan Youth: Implications for Alcohol and Drug Use. *Prevention Science: The Official Journal of the Society for Prevention Research, 17*(7), 852–861. https://doi.org/10.1007/s11121-016-0680-1

Brown, T. (2002). A proposed model of bisexual identity development that elaborates on experiential differences of women and men. *Journal of Bisexuality, 2*(4), 67–91. https://doi.org/10.1300/j159v02n04_05

Brulle, R. J., & Pellow, D. N. (2006). Environmental justice: Human health and environmental inequalities. *Annual Review of Public Health, 27*(3), 103–124. https://doi.org/10.1146/annurev.27.021405.102124

Buckland, R. (1986). *Buckland's complete book of witchcraft.* Llewellyn Publications.

Burkard, A. W., Edwards, L. M., & Adams, H. A. (2015). Racial color blindness in counseling, therapy, and supervision. *College of Education Faculty Research and Publications*, 383. https://epublications.marquette.edu/edu_fac/383

Burke, M., & Embrich, D. G. (2008). Colorism. *International encyclopedia of the social sciences, 2*, 17–18.

Burlingame, G. M., McClendon D. T., & Chongming Y. (2018). Cohesion in group therapy: A meta-analysis. *Psychotherapy, 55* (4), 384–398

Burnes, D., Sheppard, C., Henderson, C. R., Jr., Wassel, M., Cope, R., Barber, C., & Pillemer, K. (2019). Interventions to reduce ageism against older adults: A systematic review and meta-analysis. *American Journal of Public Health, 109*(8), e1–e9. https://doi.org/10.2105/AJPH.2019.305123

Bussey, K. (2011). Gender identity development. In S. J. Schwartz, K. Luyckx, & V. L. Vignoles (Eds.), *Handbook of identity theory and research* (pp. 603–628). Springer Science + Business Media. https://doi.org/10.1007/978-1-4419-7988-9_25

Bussey, K., & Bandura, A. (1999). Social cognitive theory of gender development and differentiation. *Psychological Review, 106*(4), 676–713. https://doi.org/10.1037/0033-295x.106.4.676.

Butler, K. (Host). (2021–present). *The voice of counseling* [Audio podcast]. American Counseling Association. https://www.youtube.com/playlist?list=PLpZf4HErnqmeYzy0dU22CPjuryhRVwAW1

Butler, R. N. (2002). *Why survive? Being old in America.* John Hopkins University Press.

Byers, L. E., & Williams, H. M. (2022). Hollywood's slim pickings for fat characters: A textual analysis of *Gilmore Girls, Sweet Magnolias, This Is Us, Shrill*, and *Dietland. Fat Studies*, 1–13.

Cabral, R. R., & Smith, T. B. (2011). Racial/ethnic matching of clients and therapists in mental health services: A meta-analytic review of preferences, perceptions, and outcomes. *Journal of Counseling Psychology, 58*(4), 537–554. https://doi.org/10.1037/a0025266

Calabrese, E. (2020, January 7). *5 ways to spot disinformation on your social media feeds.* ABC News. https://abcnews.go.com/US/ways-spot-disinformation-social-media-feeds/story?id=67784438

Caldwell, J. (2011). Disability identity of leaders in the self-advocacy movement. *Intellectual and Developmental Disabilities, 49,* 315–326. http://dx.doi.org/10.1352/1934-9556-49.5.315

Campbell, S. M. (2022). Expanding notions of equity: Body diversity and social justice. *Psychology in the Schools, 59*(12), 2387–2404.

Campion, A. (2021, November). *The language of social justice* [Video]. YouTube. https://youtu.be/FJkEDpWw45c?si=vQ_AvQBFIg5ah99M

Campos, P., Saguy, A., Ernsberger, P., Oliver, E., & Gaesser, G. (2006). The epidemiology of overweight and obesity: Public health crisis or moral panic?. *International journal of epidemiology, 35*(1), 55–60.

Carjuzaa, J. (2017). Revitalizing Indigenous languages, cultures, and histories in Montana, across the United States and around the globe. *Cogent Education, 4*(1), 1371822. https://doi.org/10.1080/2331186X.2017.1371822

Carrola, P. A., & Brown, C. H. (2018). Integrating the multicultural and social justice counseling competencies in correctional counseling. *Journal of Counselor Leadership & Advocacy, 5*(2), 109–121. https://doi.org/gf4b26

CASEL. (n.d.). *Collaborative for academic, social, and emotional learning program guide.* https://casel.s3.us-east-2.amazonaws.com/sites/4/PROGRAM-GUIDE-QUICK-START-DOWNLOAD.pdf

Cashwell, C. S. (2017). Putting the "E" in ASERVIC. *Counseling and Values, 62*(1), 8–10. https://doi.org/10.1002/cvj.12045

Cashwell, C. S., & Sweeney, T. J. (2016). Jane E. Myers: Legacy of a life well lived. *Journal of Counselor Leadership and Advocacy, 3*(1), 4–11.

Cashwell, C. S., & Young, J. S. (Eds.). (2011). *Integrating spirituality and religion into counseling: A guide to competent practice* (2nd ed.). American Counseling Association.

Cass, V. C. (1979). Homosexual identity formation: A theoretical model. *Journal of Homosexuality, 4*(3), 219–235. https://doi.org/10.1300/J082v04n03_01

Cassaniti, J. (2015). *Living Buddhism: Mind, self, and emotion in a Thai community.* Cornell University Press.

Castaño, Á., Bélanger, J. J., & Moyano, M. (2022). Cult conversion from the perspective of families: Implications for prevention and psychological intervention. *Psychology of Religion and Spirituality, 14*(1), 148–160. https://doi.org/10.1037/rel0000410

Caston, R. J. (1989). Dimensions of occupational inequality index and Duncan's socioeconomic index. *Sociological Forum, 4*(3), 329–348. http://dx.doi.org/10.1007/BF01115013

Castro, E. L., & Cortez, E. (2017) Exploring the Lived experiences and intersectionalities of Mexican community college transfer students: Qualitative insights toward expanding a transfer receptive culture. *Community College Journal of Research and Practice, 41*(2), 77-92. https://doi.org/10.1080/10668926.2016.1158672

Center on Positive Behavioral Interventions and Supports. (2021). *What is PBIS*? https://www.pbis.org/pbis/what-is-pbis

Centers for Disease Control and Prevention (CDC). (2020, September 16). *Prevalence of disability and disability type.* https://www.cdc.gov/ncbddd/disabilityandhealth/features/disability-prevalence-rural-urban.html

Centers for Disease Control and Prevention (CDC). (2022). *What is health equity*? https://www.cdc.gov/healthequity/whatis/index.html

Chacko, E. (2019). Fitting in and standing out: Identity and transnationalism among second-generation African immigrants in the United States. *African and Black Diaspora, 12*(2), 228–242. https://doi.org/10.1080/17528631.2018.1559789

Chan, C. D. (2021, January). The forces that could shape counseling's future. *Counseling Today, 63*(7), 22–57.

Chan, C. D., DeDiego, A. C., & Band, M. P. (2019). Moving counselor educator to influential roles as advocates: An ecological systems approach to student-focused advocacy. *Journal of Counselor Leadership and Advocacy, 6*(1), 30–41.

Chang, C. Y., & O'Hara, C. (2013). The initial interview with Asian American clients. *Journal of Contemporary Psychotherapy, 43*, 33-42.

Chang, C. Y., McDonald, C. P., & O'Hara, C. (2014). *Counseling for multiculturalism and social justice: integration, theory, and application*. Wiley.

Chang, D. F., & Berk, A. (2009). Making cross-racial therapy work: A phenomenological study of clients' experiences of cross-racial therapy. *Journal of Counseling Psychology, 56*(4), 521.

Chang, E. C. (2001). Cultural influences on optimism and pessimism: Differences in Western and Eastern conceptualizations of the self. In E. C. Chang (Ed.), *Optimism and pessimism: Theory, research, and practice* (pp. 257–280). American Psychological Association.

Chang, E. S., Monin, J. K., Zeterman, D., & Levy, B. R. (2021). Impact of structural ageism on greater violence against older persons: A cross-national study of 56 countries. *BMJ Open, 11*(5), e042580. https://doi.org/10/1136/bmjopen-2020-042580

Chang, S. C., Singh, A. A., & Dickey, l. M. (2018). *A clinician's guide to gender-affirming care: Working with transgender and gender nonconforming clients*. Context Press.

Chapin, M., McCarthy, H., Shaw, L., Bradham-Cousar, M., Chapman, R., Nosek, M., Peterson, S., Yilmaz, Z., & Ysasi, N. (2018). *Disability-related counseling competencies. American Rehabilitation Counseling Association (ARCA) Task Force on Competencies for Counseling for Persons with Disabilities*. https://www.counseling.org/docs/default-source/competencies/arca-disability-related-counseling-competencies-final-version-5-15-19

Chapman, R. (2021). Neurodiversity and the social ecology of mental functions. *Perspectives on Psychological Science, 16*(6), 1360–1372. https://doi.org/10.1177/1745691620959833

Chapman, R., & Botha, M. (2022). Neurodivergence-informed therapy. *Developmental Medicine & Child Neurology*, 1–8. http://doi.org/10.1111/dmcn.15384

Charmaz, K. (1994). Identity dilemmas of chronically ill men. *The Sociological Quarterly, 35*, 269–288. http://dx.doi.org/10.1111/j.1533-8525.1994.tb00410.x.

Charmaz, K. (1995). The body, identity, and self: Adapting to impairment. *The Sociological Quarterly, 36*, 657–680. http://dx.doi.org/10.1111/j.1533- 8525.1995.tb00459.x

Chen, H.-Y., & Jablonski, N. G. (2023). Stay out of the sun: Exploring African American college women's thoughts on the dynamics between colorism and sun-related behavior. *Journal of Black Psychology, 49*(4), 529–560. https://doi.org/10.1177/00957984221128374

Cherney, J. L. (2011). The rhetoric of ableism. *Disability Studies Quarterly, 31*(3), 7. https://doi.org/10.18061/dsq.v31i3.1665

Cherney, J. L. (2019). *Ableist rhetoric: How we know, value, and see disability.* The Pennsylvania State University Press.

Choi, G., Mallinckrodt, B., & Richardson, J. D. (2015). Effect of international student counselors' broaching statements about cultural and language differences on participants' perceptions of counselors. *Journal of Multicultural Counseling and Development, 43*, 25–37.

Chopik, W. J., O'Brien, E., & Konrath, S. H. (2017). Differences in empathic concern and perspective taking across 63 countries. *Journal of Cross-Cultural Psychology, 48*(1), 23–38. https://doi.org/10.1177/0022022116673910

Chopp, S. (2017). Communities of concentrated poverty. Retrieved from: https://www.pdx.edu/policy-consensus-center/policy-consensus-center/sites/policyconsensuscenter.web.wdt.pdx.edu/files/2020-06/1-Communities-of-Concentrated-Poverty.pdf

Chowdhury, D., Lund, E. M., Carey, C. D., & Li, Q. (2022). Intersection of discriminations: Experiences of women with disabilities with advanced degrees in professional sector in the United States. *Rehabilitation Psychology, 67*(1), 28–41. https://doi.org/10.1037/rep0000419

The Church of Jesus Christ of Latter-day Saints. (n.d.). Polygamy: What Latter-day Saints really believe. https://ph.churchofjesuschrist.org/polygamy-mormons-plural-marriage

Cima, M., Smeets T., & Jelicic, M. (2008). Self-reported trauma, cortisol levels, and aggression in psychopathic and non-psychopathic prison inmates. *Biological Psychology, 78*(1), 75–86. https://doi.org/10.1016/j.biopsycho.2007.12.001

Cislaghi, B. & Heise, L. (2019). Gender norms and social norms: differences, similarities and why they matter in prevention science. *Sociology of Health & Illness, 42*(2), 407–422. https://doi.org/10.1111/1467-9566.13008

Civil Rights Act of 1964 § 7, 42 U.S.C. § 2000e *et seq.* (1964). https://www.eeoc.gov/statutes/title-vii-civil-rights-act-1964

Clark, J. M., Brown, J. C., & Hochstein, L. M. (1990) Institutional religion and gay/lesbian oppression. In M. B. Sussman (Ed.) *Homosexuality and family relations* (pp. 265-284). Routledge.

Clark, M. (2016). The relationship between counselors' multicultural counseling competence and poverty beliefs. *Counselor Education and Supervision, 56*, 261–275. https://doi.org/10.1002/ ceas.12084

Clark, M. (2019). Experiences of intersections of privilege and oppression. In M. Pope, M. Gonzalez, E. Cameron, & J. S. Pangelinan (Eds.), *Experiential activities for teaching social justice and advocacy competence in counseling.* Routledge.

Clark, M., Ausloos, C., Delaney, C., Waters, L., Salpietro, L., & Tippett, H. (2020). Best practices for counseling clients experiencing poverty: A grounded theory. *Journal of Counseling and Development, 98*, 283–294. https://doi.org/10/1002/jcad.12323

Clark, M., Cook, J. M., Nair, D., & Wojcik, K. (2018). A content analysis of social class in ACA journals from 2000–2016. *Counseling Outcome Research and Evaluation, 9*(1), 1–12. http://dx.doi.org/10.1080/21501378.2017.1409599

Clark, M., Neukrug, E., & Long, S. M, (2018). Relational-cultural therapy (feminist therapy). In E. Neukrug (Ed.), *Counseling theory and practice* (2nd ed., pp. 519–552). Cognella.

Clinical implementation of the cultural formulation interview. (2015). *DSM-5® handbook on the cultural formulation interview.* https://doi.org/10.1176/appi.books.9781615373567.rlf04

Coffey, Y., Bhullar, N., Durkin, J., Islam, Md. S., & Usher, K. (2021). Understanding eco-anxiety: A systematic scoping review of current literature and identified knowledge gaps. *Journal of Climate Change and Health, 3,* 1–6. https://doi.org/10.1016/j.joclim.2021.100047

Cohen, I. G., Shachar, C., Silvers, A., & Stein, M. A. (2020). *Disability, health, law, and bioethics.* Cambridge University Press.

Cohen, J. A., Kassan, A., & Wada, K. (2022). Learning from the standpoints of minoritized students: An exploration of multicultural and social justice counselling training. *The Qualitative Report, 27*(2), 385–413.

Cohn, D. (2015, September 30). How U.S. immigration laws and rules have changes through history. *Pew Research Center.* https://www.pewresearch.org/fact-tank/2015/09/30/how-u-s-immigration-laws-and-rules-have-changed-through-history/

Coleman, E. (1982). Developmental stages of the coming out process. I. J. Gonsiorek (Ed.), *Homosexuality and psychotherapy: A practitioner's handbook of affirmative models* (31–44). Haworth Press.

Coleman, T. J., Hood, R. W., & Streib, H. (2018). An introduction to atheism, agnosticism, and nonreligious worldviews. *Psychology of Religion and Spirituality, 10*(3), 203–206. https://doi.org/10.1037/rel0000213

Collins Online Dictionary. (n.d). Diaspora. In *Collinsdictionary.com.* Retrieved October 24, 2022. https:// www. collinsdictionary.com/dictionary/english/diaspora

Collins, P. H. (2015). Intersectionality's definitional dilemmas. *Annual Review of Sociology, 41*(1), 1–20. https://doi.org/10.1146/annurev-soc-073014-112142

Coma, M. T., & Hunter, Q. (2018). Empathy, humanism, and mindfulness in multicultural counseling and social justice work. *The William & Mary Educational Review, 6*(1), 70–90.

Commission on Rehabilitation Counselor Certification (2017). *Code of professional ethics for certified rehabilitation counselors (CRC).*

Commission on Rehabilitation Counselor Certification (CRCC). (2023). *Code of professional ethics for certified rehabilitation counselors.* https://crccertification.com/wp-content/uploads/2023/01/2023-Code-of-Ethics-1.pdf

Compton, E. & Morgan, G., (2022). The experiences of psychological therapy amongst people who identify as transgender or gender non-conforming: A systemic review of qualitative research. *Journal of Feminist Family Therapy, 34*(3–4), 225–248. https://doi.org/10.1080/08952833.2022.2068843

Comstock, D. L., Hammer, T. R., Strentzsch, J., Cannon, K., Parsons, J., & II, G. S. (2008). Relational-cultural theory: A framework for bridging relational, multicultural, and social justice competencies. *Journal of Counseling & Development, 86*(3), 279–287.

Consolidated Appropriations Act of 2023, Pub. L. 117-328, 136 Stat. 4459 (2023).

Conyne, R. K., & Cook, E. P. (Eds.). (2004). *Ecological counseling: An innovative approach to conceptualizing person–environment interaction.* American Counseling Association.

Cook, E. P. (2012). *Understanding people in context: The ecological perspective in counseling.* American Counseling Association.

Cook, E. P., & Coaston, S. C. (2015). Behavior is changeable. In E. P. Cook (Ed.), *Understanding people in context: The ecological perspective in counseling* (pp.). John Wiley & Sons.

Cook, J. M. (2017). Social class bias: A phenomenological study. *Journal of Counselor Preparation and Supervision*, *9*(1). http://dx.doi.org/10.7729/91.1167

Cook, J. M. (2020). The advocacy action plan. In Pope, M., Gonzalez, M., Cameron, E., & Pangelinan, J. S. (Eds.), *Social justice and advocacy in counseling: Experiential activities for teaching* (pp. 74–80). Routledge

Cook, J. M., & Lawson, G. (2016). Counselors' social class and socioeconomic status understanding and awareness. *Journal of Counseling and Development*, *94*(4), 442–453. http://dx.doi.org/10.1002/jcad.12103

Cook, J. M., & O'Hara, C. (2019). An emerging theory of the persistence of social class microaggressions: An interpretative phenomenological study. *Counselling Psychology Quarterly*, *33*(4), 516–540 http://dx.doi.org/10.1080/09515070.2019.1596880

Cook, J. M., Ong, L., & Zavgorodnya, O. (2021). A mixed methods examination of counselors' social class and socioeconomic status perceptions. *Journal of Humanistic Counseling*, *60*(2), 117–136. https://doi.org/10.1002/johc.12160

Cook, J. M., Skaistis, S. M., Borden, S., & Nair, B. (2020). Inquiring about client cultural identities: A content analysis of intake paperwork. *Journal of Mental Health Counseling*, *42*(3), 220–233. https://doi.org/10.17744/mehc.42.3

Cook, R. M., Jones, C. T., & Welfare, L. E. (2020). Supervisor cultural humility predicts intentional nondisclosure by post-master's counselors. *Counselor Education and Supervision*, *59*(2), 160–167.

Córdova, D., & Cervantes, R. C. (2010). Intergroup and within-group perceived discrimination among U.S.-Born and foreign-Born Latino youth. *Hispanic Journal of Behavioral Sciences*, *32*(2), 259–274. https://doi.org/10.1177/0739986310362371

Corey, G. (n.d.). *Integrating spirituality in counseling practice*. American Counseling Association. https://www.counseling.org/docs/default-source/vistas/integrating-spirituality-in-counseling-practice.pdf?sfvrsn=7ddd7e2c_10

Council for Accreditation of Counseling and Related Educational Programs (CACREP). (2015). *2016 CACREP standards*. http://www.cacrep.org/wp

Council for Accreditation of Counseling and Related Educational Programs (CACREP). (2023). *CACREP vital statistics 2023: Results from a national survey of accredited programs*.

Counselors for Social Justice. (2001). The counselors for social justice (CSJ) code of ethics. *Journal for Social Action in Counseling & Psychology*, *3*(2), 1–21. https://doi.org/10.33043/JSACP.3.2.1-21

Counselors for Social Justice. (n.d.). *Definition of social justice*.

Covey, H. C. (1998). *Social perceptions of people with disabilities in history*. Charles C. Thomas.

Covey, S. R. (1989). *The 7 habits of highly effective people: Powerful lessons in personal change*. Franklin Covey Co.

Craig, S. L., McInroy, L., McCready, L. T., Alaggia, R. (2015). Media: A catalyst for resilience in lesbian, gay, bisexual, transgender, and queer youth. *Journal of LGBT Youth*, *12*(3), 254–275.

Crenshaw, K. W. (1988). Race, reform, and retrenchment: Transformation and legitimation in antidiscrimination law. *Harvard Law Review*, *101*(7), 1331–1387. https://doi.org/10.2307/1341398

Crenshaw, K. W. (1991). Mapping the margins: Intersectionality, identity politics, and violence against women of color. *Stanford Law Review*, *43*(6), 1241–1299. https://doi.org/10.2307/1229039

Cressey, J. (2019). Developing culturally responsive social, emotional, and behavioral supports. *Journal of Research in Innovative Teaching & Learning, 12*(1), 53–67. https://doi.org/10.1108/jrit-01-2019-0015

Croff, R., Hedmann M., & Barnes L. L. (2021). Whitest city in America: A smaller black community's experience of gentrification, displacement, and aging in place. *The Gerontologist, 61*(8), 1254–1265. https://doi.org/10.1093/geront/gnab041

Cross Jr., W. E. (1971). Negro-to-black conversion experience: Toward a psychology of black liberation. *Black World, 20*(9), 93–122.

Cross Jr., W. E. (1995). The psychology of nigrescence: Revising the Cross model. In J. G. Ponterotto, J. M. Casas, L. A. Suzuki, & C. M. Alexander (Eds.), Handbook of multicultural counseling (pp. 93–122). SAGE Publications.

Cross, W. E. Jr. (1971). A two-factor theory of Black identity: Implications for the study of identity development in minority children. In J. S. Phinney & M. J. Rotherman (Eds.), Children's ethnic socialization: Pluralism and development (pp. 117–133). SAGE Publications.

Crutchfield, J., Keyes, L., Williams, M., & Eugene, D. R. (2022). A scoping review of colorism in schools: Academic, social, and emotional experiences of students of color. *Social Sciences, 11*(1),15.

Cvitkovich, Y., & Wister, A. (2001). Bringing in the life course: A modification to Lawton's ecological model of aging. *Hallym International Journal of Aging, 4*(1), 15–29. https://doi.org/10.2190/l3lk-gd09-522r-7u22

Cyrus, K. (2017). Multiple minorities as multiply marginalized: Applying the minority stress theory to LGBTQ people of color. *Journal of Gay & Lesbian Mental Health, 21*(3), 194–202. https://doi.org/10.1080/19359705.2017.1320739

D.C. Law 21-95. LGBTQ Cultural Competency Continuing Education Amendment Act of 2016, 63 DCR 2203 (2016). https://code.dccouncil.us/us/dc/council/laws/21-95

D'Andrea, M., & Daniels, J. (1997, December). RESPECTFUL counseling: A new way of thinking about diversity counseling, *Counseling Today, 40*(6), 30–34.

da Silva Rebelo, M. J., Fernandez, M., & Achotegui, J. (2018). Mistrust, anger, and hostility in refugees, asylum seekers, and immigrants: A systematic review. *Canadian Psychology, 59*(3), 239–251. http://dx.doi.org/10.1037/cap0000131

Damiano, S. R., Paxton, S. J., Wertheim, E. H., McLean, S. A., & Gregg, K. J. (2015). Dietary restraint of 5-year-old girls: Associations with internalization of the thin ideal and maternal, media, and peer influences. *International Journal of Eating Disorders, 48*(8), 1166–1169.

Danieli, Y. (1998. Ed.). *International handbook of multigenerational legacies of trauma.* Plenum Press.

Data USA. (2023). *Counselors.* https://datausa.io/profile/soc/counselors#demographics

David, E. J. R., Okazaki, S., & Saw, A. (2009). Bicultural self-efficacy among college students: Initial scale development and mental health correlates. *Journal of Counseling Psychology, 56*(2), 211–226.

Davis, C. T., & Gates Jr, H. L. (Eds.). (1991). *The slave's narrative.* Oxford University Press.

Davis, D. E., & Hook, J. N. (2013). Measuring humility and its positive effects. *APS Observer, 26.*

Davis, D. E., DeBlaere, C., Brubaker, K., Owen, J., Jordan, T. A., Hook, J. N., & Van Tongeren, D. R. (2016). Microaggressions and perceptions of cultural humility in counseling. *Journal of Counseling & Development, 94*(4), 483–493.

Davis, D. E., DeBlaere, C., Owen, J., Hook, J. N., Rivera, D. P., Choe, E., Van Tongeren, D. R., Worthington Jr, E. L., & Placeres, V. (2018). The multicultural orientation framework: A narrative review. *Psychotherapy, 55*(1), 89.

Davis, D. E., Worthington Jr, E. L., & Hook, J. N. (2010). Humility: Review of measurement strategies and conceptualization as personality judgment. *The Journal of Positive Psychology, 5*(4), 243–252.

Davis, D. E., Worthington Jr, E. L., Hook, J. N., Emmons, R. A., Hill, P. C., Bollinger, R. A., & Van Tongeren, D. R. (2013). Humility and the development and repair of social bonds: Two longitudinal studies. *Self and Identity, 12*(1), 58–77.

Davis, D., DeBlaere, C., Hook, J. N., & Owen, J. (2020). *Mindfulness-based practices in therapy: A cultural humility approach.* American Psychological Association.

Day-Vines, Booker Ammah, B., Steen, S., & Arnold, K. M. (2018). Getting comfortable with discomfort: Preparing counselor trainees to broach racial, ethnic, and cultural factors with clients during counseling. *International Journal for the Advancement of Counselling, 40*(2), 89–104. https://doi.org/10.1007/s10447-017-9308-9

Day-Vines, N. L., Cluxton-Keller, F., Agorsor, C., & Gubara, S. (2021). Strategies for broaching the subjects of race, ethnicity, and culture. *Journal of Counseling and Development, 99*(3), 348–357 https://doi.org/10.1002/jcad.12380

Day-Vines, N. L., Cluxton-Keller, F., Agorsor, C., Gubara, S., & Otabil, N. A. A. (2020). The Multidimensional Model of Broaching Behavior. *Journal of Counseling & Development, 98*, 107–118. https://doi.org/10.1002/jcad.12304

Day-Vines, N. L., Wood, S. M., Grothaus, T., Craigen, L., Holman, A., Dotson-Blake, K., & Douglass, M. J. (2007). Broaching the subjects of race, ethnicity, and culture during the counseling process. *Journal of Counseling & Development, 85*(4), 401–409.

de Brey, C., Musu, L., McFarland, J., Wilkinson-Flicker, S., Diliberti, M., Zhang, A., Branstetter, C., & Wang, X. (2019). *Status and trends in the education of racial and ethnic groups 2018* (NCES 2019-038). U.S. Department of Education. National Center for Education Statistics. Retrieved March 12, 2023, from https://nces.ed.gov/ pubsearch/

de Coninck, H., Revi, A., Babiker, M., Bertoldi, P., Buckeridge, M., Cartwright, A., Dong, W., Ford, J., Fuss, S., Hourcade, J. C., Ley, D., Mechler, R., Newman, P., Revokatova, A., Schultz, S., Steg, L., Sugiyama, T., Araos, M., Bakker, S. … Singh, C. (2018). Strengthening and implementing the global response. In: *Global warming of 1.5°C. An IPCC special report on the impacts of global warming of 1.5°C above pre-industrial levels and related global greenhouse gas emission pathways, in the context of strengthening the global response to the threat of climate change, sustainable development, and efforts to eradicate poverty* (pp. 313–444). https://doi.org/10.1017/9781009157940.006.

Death Café. (n.d.). *Home page.* https://deathcafe.com/

DeBruyn, L., Chino, M., Serna, P., & Fullerton-Gleason, L. (2001). Child maltreatment in American Indian and Alaska Native Communities: Integrating culture, history, and public health for intervention and prevention. *Child Maltreatment, 6*(2), 89–102. https://doi.org/10.1177/1077559501006002002

DeCuir-Gunby, J. T. (2009). A review of the racial identity development of African American adolescents: The role of education. *Review of Educational Research, 79*(1), 103–124. https://doi.org/10.3102/0034654308325897

Defense of Marriage Act, 1 U.S.C. § 7. (1996). http://uscode.house.gov/view.xhtml?req=granuleid:USC-prelim-title1-section7&num=0&edition=prelim

Dempsey, C. (2020). *What are the earth system's four spheres*? https://www.geographyrealm.com/what-are-the-earths-systems/

den Houting, J. (2019). Neurodiversity: An insider's perspective. *Autism*, *23*(2), 271—273. https://doi.org/10.1177/1362361318820762

Department of Homeland Security (DHS). (n.d.). *Definition of terms*. https://www.dhs.gov/immigration-statistics/data-standards-and-definitions/definition-terms#18

Derani, S., & Reynish, J. (Trans.). (2020). *The Qur'an*. Prolance.

Deroche, M. D., Herlihy, B. J., & Lyons, M. L. (2020). Counselor trainee self-perceived disability competence: Implications for training. *Counselor Education and Supervision*, *59*(3), 187–199. https://doi.org/10.1002/ceas.12183

Deroche, M. D., Ong, L., & Cook, J. (2023). Ableist microaggressions, disability characteristics, and nondominant identities. *The Professional Counselor.*

Di Bianca, M. & Mahalik, J. R. (2022). A relational-cultural framework for promoting healthy masculinities. *American Psychologist*, *77*(3), 321–332. https://doi.org/10.1037/amp0000929

Dickinson, R., Haskins, M., & Saunders, J. A. (2021). The impact of the National Coalition Building Institute (NCBI): Cultivating cultural humility among social work students. *Social Work Education*, 1–20. https://doi.org/10.1080/02615479.2021.1928623

DiFranco, R. (2020). I wrote this paper for the Lulz: The ethics of internet trolling. *Ethical Theory & Moral Practice*, *23*(5), 931–945. https://doi-org.nec.gmilcs.org/10.1007/s10677-020-10115-x

Di Giovanni, M. (2009). *Council for standards in human service education legacy: Past, present and future.* Council for Standards in Human Service Education

Dirth, T. P., & Branscombe, N. R. (2017). Disability models affect disability policy support through awareness of structural discrimination. *Journal of Social Issues*, *73*(2), 413—442. https://doi.org/10.1111/josi.12224

Diversity Pride. (n.d.). *Let's call it like it is: It's hatred not fear.* https://diversitypride.org/misiapledge.html

Dixon, A. R., & Telles, E. E. (2017). Skin color and colorism: Global research, concepts, and measurement. *Annual Review of Sociology*, *43*, 405–424. https://doi.org/10.1146/annurev-soc-060116-053315

Dixon, K. M., Kivlighan, D. M., Jr., Hill, C. E., & Gelso, C. J. (2021). Cultural humility, working alliance, and outcome rating scale in psychodynamic psychotherapy: Between-therapist, within-therapist, and within-client effects. *Journal of Counseling Psychology.* http://dx.doi.org.ezproxy.proxy.library.oregonstate.edu/10.1037/cou0000590

Dobbs v. Jackson Women's Health Organization, 597 U.S. ___ (2022). https://www.supremecourt.gov/opinions/21pdf/19-1392_6j37.pdf

Dolcos, F., Hohl, K., Hu, Y., & Dolcos, S. (2021). *Religiosity and resilience: Cognitive reappraisal and coping self-efficacy mediate the link between religious coping and well-being.* National Library of Medicine. https://www.ncbi.nlm.nih.gov/pmc/articles/PMC7790337/#:~:text=In%20turn%2C%20habitual%20engagement%20of,and%20maintain%20emotional%20well%2Dbeing

Don't Ask, Don't Tell Repeal Act of 2010, 10 U.S.C. § 654. (2010). https://www.congress.gov/111/plaws/publ321/PLAW-111publ321.pdf

Donato, K. M., & Perez, S. L. (2017). Crossing the Mexico-U.S. border: Illegality and children's migration to the United States. *RSF: The Russell Sage Foundation Journal of the Social Sciences, 3*(4), 116–135. http://dx.doi.org/10.7758/rsf.2017.3.4.07

Donovan, R. A., & West, L. M. (2015). Stress and mental health: Moderating role of the strong Black woman stereotype. *Journal of Black Psychology, 41*(4), 384–396.

Doty, M. M., Horstman, C., Shah, A., Ayo-Vaughan, M., & Zephyrin, L. C. (2022). *How discrimination in health care affects older Americans, and what health systems and providers can do.* The Commonwealth Fund. https://www.commonwealthfund.org/publications/issue-briefs/2022/apr/how-discrimination-in-health-care-affects-older-americans

Douglas, P., Cetron, M., & Spiegel, P. (2019). Definitions matter: Migrants, immigrants, asylum seekers and refugees. *Journal of Travel Medicine, 26*(2), 1–3. http://dx.doi.org/10.1093/jtm/taz005

Dovchin, S. (2021). Translanguaging, emotionality, and English as a second language immigrants: Mongolian background women in Australia. *TESOL Quarterly,* 55(3), 839–865. https://doi.org/10.1002/tesq.3015

Downing, N. E., Roush, K. L. (1985) From passive acceptance to active commitment: A model of feminist identity development for women. *The Counseling Psychologist, 13,* 695–709.

Drake, S. C., & Cayton, H. R. (1970). *Black metropolis: A study of Negro life in a northern city* (Vol. 2).

Drapeau, C. W., & McIntosh, J. L. (2021). U.S.A. suicide: *2020 Official final data.* Suicide Awareness Voices of Education (SAVE). https://save.org/about-suicide/suicidestatistics

Drinane, J. M., Owen, J., & Tao, K. W. (2018). Cultural concealment and therapy outcomes. *Journal of Counseling Psychology, 65,* 239–246. https://doi.org/10.1037/cou0000246

Duffey, T. (2005). A musical chronology and the emerging life song. *Journal of Creativity in Mental Health, 1,* 141–147. http://dx.doi.org/10.1300/J456v01n01_09

Dumas, M. J. (2016). Against the dark: Antiblackness in education policy and discourse. *Theory Into Practice, 55*(1), 11–19.

Duncan, B. (2010). On becoming a better therapist. Washington, DC: American Psychological Association.

Duncombe, S. (2007). *Cultural resistance.* The Blackwell Encyclopedia of Sociology. https://doi.org/10.1002/9781405165518.wbeosc178

Dunn, A. B., & Dawes, S. J. (1999). Spirituality-focused genograms: Keys to uncovering spiritual resources in African American families. *Journal of Multicultural Counseling and Development, 27*(4), 240–254. https://doi.org/10.1002/j.2161-1912.1999.tb00338.x

Dunn, D. S., & Andrews, E. E. (2015). Person-first and identity-first language: Developing psychologists' cultural competence using disability language. *American Psychologist, 70*(3), 255.

Duponte, K., Martin, T., Mokuau, N., & Paglinawan, L. (2010). ʻIke Hawaiʻi – A training program for working with Native Hawaiians. *Journal of Indigenous Voices in Social Work, 1*(1), 1–24.

Duran, E. (2019). *Healing the soul wound: Trauma-informed counseling for indigenous communities* (2nd ed.). Teachers College Press.

Duriez, B., & Hutsebaut, D. (2000). The relation between religion and racism: The role of post-critical beliefs. *Mental Health, Religion & Culture, 3*(1), 85–102. https://doi.org/10.1080/13674670050002135

Dworin, J. E., & Bomer, R. (2008). What we all (supposedly) know about the poor: A critical discourse analysis of Ruby Payne's "framework." *English Education*, *40(*2), 101–121.

Dwyer, P. (2022). The neurodiversity approach(es): What are they and what do they mean for researchers? *Human Development*, 66, 73–92. https://doi.org/10.1159/000523723

Earley, P. C. (2002). Redefining interactions across cultures and organizations: Moving forward with cultural intelligence. *Research in organizational behavior, 24*, 271–299.

Early, P. C., & Mosakowski, E. (2004). Cultural intelligence. *Harward Business Review*. https://hbr.org/2004/10/cultural-intelligence

Eason, A. E., Pope, T., Becenti, K. M., & Fryberg, S. A. (2020). Sanitizing history: National identification, negative stereotypes, and support for eliminating Columbus Day and adopting Indigenous Peoples Day. *Cultural Diversity and Ethnic Minority Psychology*. https://doi.org/10.1037/cdp0000345

Edirmanasinghe, N. A., Goodman-Scott E., Smith-Durkin S., & Tarver, S. Z. (2022). Supporting all students: Multitiered systems of support from an antiracist lens. *Professional School Counseling, 26*(1), 3. https://doi.org/10.1177/2156759X221109154

Education Trust-West. (2021). *Data equity walk toolkit*. https://west.edtrust.org/data-equity-walk-toolkit/.

Edwards, B. H. (2014). Diaspora. In *Keywords for American cultural studies*. Retrieved October 24, 2022, from https://keywords.nyupress.org/american-cultural-studies/essay/diaspora/

Edwards, F. L., & Thompson, G. B. (2010). The legal creation of raced space: The subtle and ongoing discrimination created through Jim Crow laws. *Berkeley J. Afr.-Am. L. & Pol'y, 12*, 145.

Edwin, M., & Bahr, M. W. (2021). Development and exploratory factor analysis of the interventionist multitiered systems of support multicultural competence scale. *Professional School Counseling, 25*(1), 2156759X2110504. https://doi.org/10.1177/2156759x211050409

Ehrensaft, M., Cohen, P., Brown, J., Smailes, E., Chen, H., & Johnson, J. (2003). Intergenerational transmission of partner violence: A 20-year prospective study. *Journal of Consulting and Clinical Psychology, 71*(4), 741–753. https://doi.org/10.1037/0022-006X.71.4.741

Eisenberg, L. (2001). From molecules to mind. *EMHJ-Eastern Mediterranean Health Journal, 7* (3), 363–366. http://dx.doi.org/10.26719/2001.7.3.363

Ellis, A. (2005). *The myth of self-esteem: How rational emotive behavior therapy can change your life forever*. Prometheus Books.

Ellison, C. W. (1983). Spiritual well-being: Conceptualization and measurement. *Journal of Psychology and Theology*, 11, 330–340.

Emanuel, I., Filakti, H., Alberman, E., & Evans, S. (1992). Intergenerational studies of human birthweight from the 1958 birth cohort: Evidence for a multigenerational effect. *British Journal of Obstetrics and Gynaecology, 99*(1), 67–74.

Emmy's. (n.d.). *The Golden Girls awards & nomination. https://www.emmys.com/shows/golden-girls*

Episkenew, J. (2009). *Taking back our spirits: Indigenous literature, public policy, and healing*. University of Manitoba Press.

Erickson, E. H. (1958). *Young man Luther: A study in psychoanalysis and history*. Norton.

Erikson, E. H. (1963). *Childhood and society*. Norton.

Eriksson, M., Ghazinour, M., & Hammarström, A. (2018). Different uses of Bronfenbrenner's ecological theory in public mental health research: What is their value for guiding public mental health policy and practice? *Soc Theory Health, 16*, 414–433. https://doi.org/10.1057/s41285-018-0065-6

Estrada, D., Singh, A. A., & Harper, A. J. (2017). Becoming an ally: Personal, clinical, and school-based social justice interventions. In M. M. Ginicola, C. Smith, & J. M. Filmore (Eds.), *Affirmative counseling with LGBTQI+people* (pp. 343–358). American Counseling Association.

Evans, B., Bias, S., & Colls, R. (2021). The dys-appearing fat body: Bodily intensities and fatphobic sociomaterialities when flying while fat. *Annals of the American Association of Geographers, 111*(6), 1816–1832. http://dx.doi.org/10.1080/24694452.2020.1866485

Evans, W. N., & Fitzgerald, D. (2017). *The economic and social outcomes of refugees in the United States: Evidence from the ACS* (Working Paper 23498). National Bureau of Economic Research. https://www.nber.org/papers/w23498.pdf

FairyGodBoss. (2017). *Forget your resume: Sadly, how you look is more important in a job interview.* https://fairygodboss.com/career-topics/job-seeker-appearance

Faridi, N., Vakilian, K., & Yousefi, A. A. (2023). The effect of empowerment-based counseling on increasing the main indices of safe sex in women with substance use disorder. *International Journal of Healthcare Management, 16*(1), 70–78. https://doi.org/10.1080/20479700.2022.2071804

Farrell, I. C., & Barrio Minton, C. A. (2019). Advocacy among counseling leaders: The three-tiered legislative professional advocacy model. *Journal of Counselor Leadership and Advocacy, 6*(2), 144–159. https://doi.org/10.1080/2326716X.2019.1644254

Farvid, P., Vance, T. A., Klein, S. L., Nikiforova, Y., Rubin, L. R., & Lopez, F. G. (2021). The health and wellbeing of transgender and gender non-conforming people of colour in the United States: A systematic literature search and review. *Journal of Community & Applied Social Psychology, 31*(6), 703–731. https://doi.org/10.1002/casp.2555

Fassinger, R. & Morrow, S. L. (1995). Overcome: Repositioning lesbian sexualities. In L. Diamant & R McAnulty (Eds), *The psychology of sexual orientation, behavior and identity: A handbook* (pp. 197–219). Greenwood.

Fatima, S., Sharif, S., & Khalid, I. (2018). How does religiosity enhance psychological well-being? Roles of self-efficacy and perceived social support. *Psychology of Religion and Spirituality, 10*(2), 119–127. https://doi.org/10.1037/rel0000168

Fattoracci, E. S. M., Revels-Macalinao, M., & Huynh, Q.-L. (2021). Greater than the sum of racism and heterosexism: Intersectional microaggressions toward racial/ethnic and sexual minority group members. *Cultural Diversity and Ethnic Minority Psychology, 27*(2), 176–188. https://doi.org/10.1037/cdp0000329

Favario, M. (2022, January). Share of those 65 and older who are tech users has grown in the past decade. *Pew Research Center.* https://www.pewresearch.org/fact-tank/2022/01/13/share-of-those-65-and-older-who-are-tech-users-has-grown-in-the-past-decade/

Feagin, J. R. (2010). *Racist America: Roots, current realities, and future reparations* (2nd ed.). Routledge.

Feder, R. (2022). Psychotherapy for eco-anxiety: Shifting from catastrophizing to action. *American Psychiatric Association Psychiatric News.* https://doi.org/10.1176/appi.pn.2022.09.9.29

Federal Bureau of Investigation. (2022, December 13). *Facts and statistics: 2021 hate crime statistics.* United States Department of Justice. https://www.justice.gov/hatecrimes/hate-crime-statistics

Felitti, V. J., Anda, R. F., Nordenberg, D., Williamson, D. F., Spitz, A. M., Edwards, V., Koss, M. P., & Marks, J. S. (2019). Reprint of relationship of childhood abuse and household dysfunction to many of the leading causes of death in adults: the adverse childhood experiences (ace) study. *American Journal of Preventive Medicine, 56*(6), 774–786. https://doi-org.echo.louisville.edu/10.1016/j.amepre.2019.04.001

Felton, B. J., & Shinn, M. (1981). Ideology and practice of deinstitutionalization. *Journal of Social Issues, 37*(3), 158–172. https://doi.org/d5z5z8

Fenton, S. 2003, Ethnicity Polity Press, Cambridge.

Ferdman, B. M., & Gallegos, P. I. (2001). Racial identity development and Latinos in the United States. In W. C. L. Ed & J. B. W. I. Ed (Eds.), New perspectives on racial identity development: A theoretical and practical anthology (pp. 32–60). New York University Press.

Ferguson, H., Boivard, S., & Mueller, M. (2007). The impact of poverty on educational outcomes for children. *Paediatric Child Health, 12*(8), 701–706. https://doi.org/10.1093/pch/12.8.701

Feucht, T. E, & Gfroerer, J. (2011). *Mental and substance use disorders among adult men on probation or parole: Some success against a persistent challenge.* Substance Abuse and Mental Health Services Administration.

Finn, S. E., & Tonsager, M. E. (2002). How therapeutic assessment became humanistic. *The Humanistic Psychologist, 30*(1–2), 10–22. https://doi.org/10.1080/08873267.2002.9977019

Fisher, R., & Ury, W. (1991). *Getting to yes: Negotiating agreement without giving in* (2nd ed.). Penguin Books.

Fisher-Borne, M., Cain, J. M., & Martin, S. L. (2015). From mastery to accountability: Cultural humility as an alternative to cultural competence. *Social Work Education, 34*(2), 165–181.

Fleischer, D. Z., & Zames, F. (2001). *The disability rights movement: From charity to confrontation.* Temple University Press.

Flint, S. W., Čadek, M., Codreanu, S. C., Ivić, V., Zomer, C., & Gomoiu, A. (2016). Obesity discrimination in the recruitment process: "You're not hired!" *Frontiers in psychology, 7,* 647.

Flores, A. R., Meyer, I. H., Langton, L., & Herman, J. L. (2021). Gender identity disparities in criminal victimization: National crime victimization survey 2017–2018. *Am J Public Health, 111*(4), 726–729. https://www.doi.org/10.2105/AJPH.2020.306099

Florda Senate Education Committee. (2022). CS/CS/HB 1557—Parental Rights in Education. https://www.flsenate.gov/Committees/billsummaries/2022/html/2825

Forber-Pratt, A. J., Lyew, D. A., Mueller, C., & Samples, L. B. (2017). Disability identity development: A systematic review of the literature. *Rehabilitation Psychology, 62*(2), 198–207. https://doi.org/10.1037/rep0000134

Forber-Pratt, A. J., Mueller, C. O., & Andrews, E. E. (2019). Disability identity and disability allyship in rehabilitation psychology: Sit, stand, sign, and show up. *Rehabilitation Psychology, 64,* 119–129. https://doi.org/10.1037/rep0000256

Foronda, C., Baptiste, D.-L., Reinholdt, M. M., & Ousman, K. (2016). Cultural humility: A concept analysis. *Journal of Transcultural Nursing, 27*(3), 210–217. https://doi.org/10.1177/1043659615592677

Foss, L. L., Generali, M. M., & Kress, V. E. (2011). Counseling people living in poverty: The care model. *Journal of Humanistic Counseling,* 50, 161–171. https://doi.org/10.1002/j.2161-1939.2011.tb00115.x

Foss-Kelly, L. L., Generali, M. M., & Kress, V. (2017). Counseling strategies for empowering people living in poverty: The I-CARE model. *Journal of Multicultural Counseling and Development, 45*(3), 201–213. https:/doi.org/10.1002/jmcd.12074

Foster, R. D., & Holden, J. M. (2014). Human and spiritual development and transformation. In *Integrating spirituality and religion into counseling: A guide to competent practice* (2nd ed., pp. 83–97). Wiley.

Fouad, N. A., Gerstein, L. H., & Toporek, R. L. (2006). Social justice and counseling psychology in context. In R. L. Toporek, L. H. Gerstein, N. A. Fouad, G. Roysircar, & T. Israel (Eds.), *Handbook for social justice in counseling psychology: Leadership, vision, and action* (pp. 1–16). SAGE Publications. https://doi.org/10.4135/9781412976220.n1

Fowler, J. W. (1981). *Stages of faith: The psychology of human development.* Harper & Row.

Fox, R. S., Merz, E. L., Solórzano, M. T., & Roesch, S. C. (2013). Further examining berry's model. *Measurement and Evaluation in Counseling and Development*, (4), 270-2–88. https://doi.org/10.1177/0748175613497036

Frame, M. W. (2000). The spiritual genogram in family therapy. *Journal of Marital and Family Therapy, 26*(2), 211–216.

Frank, L. E., & Nagel, S. K. (2017). Addiction and moralization: The role of the underlying model of addiction. *Neuroethics, 10* (1), 129–139. https://doi.org/10.1007/s12152-017-9307-x

Frank, R. G. (2000). The creation of Medicare and Medicaid: The emergence of insurance and markets for mental health services. *Psychiatric Services, 51*(4), 465–468. https://doi.org/10.1176/appi.ps.51.4.465

Fredriksen-Goldsen, K. I., & Kim, H-J. (2017). The science of conducting research with LGBT older adults—An introduction to aging with pride: National Health, Aging, and Sexuality/Gender Study (NHAS). *The Gerontologist, 57*(1), 1–14. https://doi.org/10.1093/geront/gnw212

Freedman, V. (2021). *National health and aging trends study: Trends dashboard.* University of Michigan. https://micda.isr.umich.edu/research/nhats-trends-dashboards/

Freire, P. (2011). *Pedagogy of the oppressed.* Continuum International Publishing Group.

Frey, L. L. (2013). Relational-cultural therapy: Theory, research, and application to counseling competencies. *Professional Psychology: Research and Practice, 44*(3), 177–185. https://doi.org/10.1037/a0033121

Frideres, J. S., & Gadacz, R. R. (2011). *Aboriginal peoples in Canada* (9th ed.). Pearson Education Canada.

Friedlander, M.L., Escudero, V., Welmers-van de Poll, M.J., & Heatherington, L. (2018). Meta-analysis of the alliance-outcome relation in couple and family therapy. *Psychotherapy, 55*(4):356-371. doi: 10.1037/pst0000161.

Friend, T. (2017, November 13). Why ageism never gets old. *The New Yorker.* https://www.newyorker.com/magazine/2017/11/20/why-ageism-never-gets-old

Fryhofer, S. (2013). *Is obesity a disease?* The Council on Science and Public Health. https://www.ama-assn.org/sites/ama-assn.org/files/corp/media-browser/public/about-ama/councils/Council%20Reports/council-on-science-public-health/a13csaph3.pdf

Fullen, M. C. (2018). Ageism and the counseling profession: Causes, consequences, and methods for counteraction. *The Professional Counselor, 8*(2), 104–114. https://doi.org/10.15241/mcf.8.2.104

Fullen, M. C. (2019). Defining wellness in older adulthood: Toward a comprehensive framework. *Journal of Counseling & Development, 97*(1), 62–74. https://doi.org/10.1002/jcad.12236

Fullen, M. C., & Gorby, S. R. (2016). Reframing resilience: Pilot evaluation of a program to promote resilience in marginalized older adults. *Educational Gerontology, 42*(9), 660–671. https://doi.org/10.1080/03601277.2016.1205409

Fullen, M. C., Smith, J. L., Clarke, P. B., Westcott, J. B., McCoy, R., & Tomlin, C. C. (2023). Holistic wellness coaching for older adults: Preliminary evidence for a novel wellness intervention in senior living communities. *Journal of Applied Gerontology, 42*(3), 427–437. http://dx.doi.org/10.1177/07334648221135582

Fullen, M. C., Wiley, J. D., & Morgan, A. A. (2019). The Medicare mental health coverage gap: How licensed professional counselors navigate Medicare-ineligible provider status. *The Professional Counselor, 9*, 310–323. https://doi.org/10.15241/mcf.9.4.310

Fundamentalist Mormons. The Church of Jesus Christ of Latter-day Saints. (2002, February 6). *Fundamentalist Mormons.* https://newsroom.churchofjesuschrist.org/commentary/fundamentalist-mormons

Furer, P., & Walker, J. R. (2008). Death anxiety: A cognitive-behavioral approach. *Journal of Cognitive Psychotherapy, 22*(2), 167–182. https://doi.org/10.1891/0889-8391.22.2.167

Gallardo, M. E., & Gibson, J. (2005). Culturally diverse individuals with disabilities: Meeting therapeutic needs. Micro Training and Multicultural Development.

Gamby, K., Clark, M., O'Hara, C., Ausloos, C., Delaney, C., & Granello, P. (2020). Professional counselors' referral processes to complementary health practitioners. *Journal of Creativity in Mental Health, 16*, 1–16. http://dx.doi.org/10.1080/15401383.2020.1781723

Garcia, F., & Anderson, J. (2018). *Guide to Indigenous land and territorial acknowledgements for cultural institutions.* New York University.

García, J. (2020). *Testimonios of first-generation Chicana faculty in counselor education: A narrative inquiry* [Doctoral dissertation, the University of Texas at San Antonio].

Garrett, M. T., Portman, T.A.A., Choudhuri, D. D., & Santiago-Rivera, A. (2011). *Counseling and diversity: Counseling Native Americans.* Cengage.

Garrett-Walker, J. J., & Torres, V. M. (2017). Negative religious rhetoric in the lives of Black cisgender queer emerging adult men: A qualitative analysis. *Journal of Homosexuality*, 64(13), 1816–1831. https://doi.org/10.1080/00918369.2016.1267465

Gay, J. (1986). "Mummies and babies" and friends and lovers in Lesotho. *Journal of Homosexuality, 11*(3–4), 97–116. https://doi.org/10.1300/J082v11n03_07.

Gay, R. (2014). *Bad feminist: Essays.* Harper Perennial.

Gee, G., Akutsu, P., & Shih, M. (2010). Culture and mental health: Risk, prevention and treatment for Asian Americans. *AAPI Nexus: Policy, Practice and Community, 8*(2), v–xiv.

Geertsma, E. J., & Cummings, A. L. (2004). Midlife transition and women's spirituality. Groups: A preliminary investigation. *Counseling and Values, 49*(1), 27–36. https://doi-org.nsula.idm.oclc.org/10.1002/j.2161-007X.2004.tb00250.x

George, L. K. (2010). Still happy after all these years: Research frontiers on subjective well-being in later life. *The Journals of Gerontology: Series B, 65*, 331–339. http://dx.doi.org/10.1093/geronb/gbq006

Gerend, M. A., Patel, S., Ott, N., Wetzel, K., Sutin, A. R., Terracciano, A., & Maner, J. K. (2022). A qualitative analysis of people's experiences with weight-based discrimination. *Psychology & Health, 37*(9), 1093–1110.

Gerlach, L., Solway, E., Singer, D., Kullgren, J., Kirch, M., & Malani, P. (2021). *Mental health among older adults before and during the COVID-19 pandemic.* University of Michigan National Poll on Healthy Aging. http://dx.doi.org/10.7302/983

Gharehgozli, O., & Atal, V. (2020). Revisiting the gender wage gap in the United States. *Economic Analysis and Policy, 66*, 207–216. https://doi.org/10.1016/j.eap.2020.04.008

Gibson, D. M., Dollarhide, C. T., & Moss, J. M. (2010). Professional identity development: A grounded theory of transformational tasks of new counselors. Counselor Education and Supervision, 50(1), 21–38. https://doi.org/10.1002/j.1556-6978.2010.tb00106.x

Gibson, J. (2006). Disability and clinical competency: An introduction. *The California Psychologist, 39,* 6–10.

Gibson, M. (1988). *Sikh immigrants in an American high school.* Cornell University Press.

Gill, C. J. (1997). Four types of integration in disability-identity development. *Journal of Vocational Rehabilitation, 9,* 39–46. http://dx.doi.org/10.1016/S1052-2263(97)00020-2.

Gilligan, C. (1977). In a different voice: Women's conceptions of self and morality. *Harvard Educational Review, 47,* 481–517.

Ginicola, M. M. (2017). Counseling two-spirit clients. In M. M. Ginicola, C. Smith, & J. M. Filmore (Eds.), *Affirmative counseling with LGBTQI + people* (pp. 259–269). American Counseling Association.

Ginicola, M. M., Smith, C., & Filmore, J. M. (2017). *Affirmative counseling with LGBTQI+ People.* American Counseling Association.

GLAAD. (n.d.). Media reference guide: *LGBTQ Community Calendar, 11.*

Gladding, S. T., & Newsome, D. W. (2018). *Clinical mental health counseling in community and agency settings.* (5th ed.). Pearson Education.

Gloria, A. M., & Rodriguez, E. R. (2000). Counseling Latino university students: Psychosociocultural issues for consideration. *Journal of Counseling & Development, 78,* 145–154. https://doi.org/10.1002/j.1556-6676.2000.tb02572.x

Glosoff, H. L., & Kocet, M.M. (2006). Highlights of the 2005 ACA codes of ethics. In G.R. Walz, J. Bleuer, & R.K. Yep (Eds.), *VISTAS: Compelling perspectives on counseling, 2006* (pp. 5–9). American Counseling Association.

GLSEN, ASCA, ACSSW, & SSWAA. (2019). *Supporting safe and healthy schools for lesbian, gay, bisexual, transgender, and queer students: A national survey of school counselors, social workers, and psychologists.* https://www.glsen.org/sites/default/files/2019-11/Supporting_Safe_and_Healthy_Schools_%20Mental_Health_Professionals_2019.pdf

Gockel, A. (2011). Client perspectives on spirituality in the therapeutic relationship. *The Humanistic Psychologist, 39*(2), 154–168. https://doi.org/10.1080/08873267.2011.564959

Goebert, D., Alvarez, A., Andrade, N. N., Balberde-Kamalii, J., Carlton, B. S., Chock, S., Chung-Do, J. J., Eckert, M. D., Hooper, K., Kaninau-Santos, K., Kaulukukui, G., Kelly, C., Pike, M. J., Rehuher, D., & Sugimoto-Matsuda, J. (2018). Hope, help, and healing: Culturally embedded approaches to suicide prevention, intervention and postvention services with native Hawaiian youth. *Psychological Services, 15*(3), 332–339. https://doi.org/10.1037/ser0000227

Gone, J. P., & Trimble, J. E. (2012). American Indian and Alaska native mental health: Diverse perspectives on enduring disparities. *Annual Review of Clinical Psychology, 8*(1), 131–160. https://doi.org/10.1146/annurev-clinpsy-032511-14312

Gonyea, J. G., & Hudson, R. B. (2020). In an era of deepening partisan divide, what is the meaning of age or generational differences in political values? *Public Policy & Aging Report, 30*(2), 52–55. https://doi.org/10.1093/ppar/praa003

Gonzales, L., Davidoff, K. C., Natal, K. L., & Yanos, P. T. (2015). Microaggressions experienced by persons with mental illness: An exploratory study. *Psychiatric Rehabilitation Journal, 38*(3), 234–241. https://doi.org/10.1037/prj0000096

Gonzalez, E., Sperandio, K. R., Mullen, P. R., & Tuazon, V. E. (2021). Development and initial testing of the multidimensional cultural humility scale. Measurement and evaluation in counseling and development, 54(1), 56–70. https://doi.org/10.1080/07481756.2020.1745648

Gonzalez, J. M., & Connell, N. M. (2014). Mental health of prisoners: Identifying barriers to mental health treatment and medication continuity. *American Journal of Public Health, 104*(12), 2328–2333. https://doi.org/f6vc92

Goodman, L. A., Liang, B., Helms, J. E., Latta, R. E., Sparks, E., & Weintraub, S. R. (2004). Training counseling psychologists as social justice agents: Feminist and multicultural principles in action. *The Counseling Psychologist, 32*(6), 793– 836. https://doi.org/10.1177/0011000004268802

Goodman, L. A., Pugach, M., Skolnik, A., & Smith, L. (2012). Poverty and mental health practice: Within and beyond the 50-minute hour. *Journal of Clinical Psychology: In Session, 69*(2), 182–190. https://doi.org/10.1002/jclp.21957

Goodman, R. D., Vesely, C. K., Letiecq, B., & Cleaveland, C. L. (2017). Trauma and resilience among refugee and undocumented immigrant women. *Journal of Counseling and Development, 95*(3), 309–321. https://doi.org/10.1002/jcad.12145

Goodman-Scott, E. C., Edirmanasinghe, N. A., Moe, J., & Boulden, R. (2022). Assessing the influence of multitiered systems of support training on school counselors' perceptions of school counseling activities: Results of a national study. *Professional School Counseling, 26*(1), 2156759X2211382. https://doi.org/10.1177/2156759x221138232

Goodman-Scott, E., Donohue, P., & Betters-Bubon, J. (2023). A phenomenological investigation of universal mental health screening: Making meaning for school counseling. *Professional School Counseling, 27*(1), 2156759X2211500. https://doi.org/10.1177/2156759x221150008

Goodrich, K. M. & Brammer, M. K. (2021). Cass's homosexual identity formation: A critical analysis. *Journal of Multicultural Counseling & Development, 49*(4), 239–253. https://doi.org/10.1002/jmcd.12228

Goodrich, K. M., Luke, M., & Smith, A. J. (2016). Queer humanism: Toward an epistemology of socially just, culturally responsive change. *Journal of Humanistic Psychology, 56*(6), 612–623. https://doi.org/10.1177/0022167816652534

Gracia, J. J. (2015). Hispanic/Latino identity. *Debating Race, Ethnicity, and Latino Identity*, 147–180. https://doi.org/10.7312/columbia/9780231169448.003.0013

Graham, R. J. (1981). The role of perception of time in consumer research. *Journal of Consumer Research, 7*(4), 335–342. https://doi.org/10.1086/208823

Gramlich, J. (2017, September 29). *Hispanic dropout rate hits new low, college enrollment at new high.* Pew Research Center. https://www.pewresearch.org/short-reads/2017/09/29/hispanic-dropout-rate-hits-new-low-college-enrollment-at-new-high/

Gray, J. S., & Rose, W. J. (2012). Cultural adaptation for therapy with American Indians and Alaska Natives. *Journal of Multicultural Counseling and Development, 40*(2), 82–92. https://doi.org/10.1002/j.2161-1912.2012.00008.x

Greenberg, M. (2014). The moral impact theory of law. *The Yale Law Journal, 123*(5), 1288–1342. http://www.jstor.org/stable/23744443

Greenfield, E. (2012). Using ecological frameworks to advance a field of research, practice, and policy on aging-in-place initiatives. *The Gerontologist, 52*(1), 1–12. https://doi.org/10.1093/geront/gnr108

Greenleaf, R. K. (1977). *Servant leadership: A journey into the nature of legitimate power & greatness* (25th Anniversary Ed.). Paulist Press.

Greenleaf, R. K. (2002). *Servant leadership: A journey into the nature of legitimate power and greatness.* Paulist Press.

Groot, S. D. (2019). Two spirit. In Howard Chiang (Ed.), *Global encyclopedia of lesbian, gay, bisexual, transgender, and queer (LGBTQ) history* (1st ed.). Gale. https://search-credoreference-com.ezproxylr.med.und.edu/content/entry/galelesbian/two_spirit/0

Groven, K. S., Råheim, M., & Engelsrud, G. (2010). "My quality of life is worse compared to my earlier life" living with chronic problems after weight loss surgery. *International Journal of Qualitative Studies on Health and Well-Being, 5*(4), 5553.

Gu, M. (Michelle). (2015). A complex interplay between religion, gender and marginalization: Pakistani schoolgirls in Hong Kong. *Ethnic and Racial Studies*, 38(11), 1934–1951.

Guthrie, R. V. (2004). *Even the rat was white: A historical view of psychology* (2nd ed.). Pearson Education.

Gutierrez, D., Fox, J., Jones, K., & Fallon, E. (2018) The treatment planning of experienced counselors: A qualitative examination. *Journal of Counseling & Development, 96*(1), 86–96. https://doi.org/10.1002/jcad.12180

Haines, K. M., Boyer, C. R., Giovanazzi, C., & Galupo, M. P. (2017). "Not a real family": Microaggressions directed toward LGBTQ families. *Journal of Homosexuality, 65*(9), 1138–1151. https://doi.org/10.1080/00918369.2017.1406217

Hairston, T. R., Laux, J. M., O'Hara, C., Roseman, C. P., & Gore, S. (2018). Counselor education students' perceptions of wellness and mental health in African American men: The effects of colorism. *Journal of Multicultural Counseling and Development, 46*(3), 171–185.

Hall, C. (1980). *The ethnic identity of racially mixed people: A study of Black-Japanese* [Unpublished doctoral dissertation]. University of California, Los Angeles.

Hall, R. (1995). The bleaching syndrome: African Americans' response to cultural domination vis-à-vis skin color. *Journal of Black studies, 26*(2), 172–184.

Hall, R. E. (1994). The "bleaching syndrome": Implications of light skin for Hispanic American assimilation. *Hispanic Journal of Behavioral Sciences, 16*(3), 307–314.

Hall, R. E. (1997). Eurogamy among Asian-Americans: A note on Western assimilation. *The Social Science Journal, 34*(3), 403–408.

Handy, E. S. C., & Pukui, M. K. (1998). *The Polynesian family system in Ka'u*, Hawai'i. Mutual Publishing.

Hansen, I., Jackson, V., & Ryder, A. (2017). Religion and oppression: Cross-national and experimental investigations. *Religion, Brain & Behavior, 8*(4), 369–393. https://doi.org/10.1080/2153599x.2017.1358208

Hansson, A., Hilleras, P., & Forsell, Y. (2005). What kind of self-care strategies do people report using and is there an association with well-being? *Social Indicator Research, 73*, 133–139. https://doi.org/10/1007/s11205-00400995-3

Hardiman, R., & Jackson, B. W. (1992). Racial identity development: Understanding racial dynamics in college classrooms and on campus. *New Directions for Teaching and Learning*, 1992(52), 21–37. https://doi.org/10.1002/tl.37219925204

Hardy, K. V., & Laszloffy, T. A. (1995). The cultural genogram: Key to training culturally competent family therapists. *Journal of Marital and Family Therapy, 21*, 227–237. https://doi.org/10.1111/j.1752-0606.1995.tb00158.x

Harney, N. D., & Baldassar, L. (2007). Tracking transnationalism: Migrancy and its futures. *Journal of Ethnic and Migration Studies*, *32*(2), 189–198. http://dx.doi.org/10.1080/13691830601154088

Harper, A., Clayton, A., Bailey, M., Foss-Kelly, L., Sernyak, M. J., & Rowe, M. (2015). Financial health and mental health among clients of a community mental health center: Making the connections. *Psychiatric Services*, *66*(12), 1271–1276. https://doi.org/10.1176/appi.ps.201400438

Harper, G. W., Serrano, P.A., Bruce, D. & Bauermeister, J.A. (2016). The internet's multiple roles in facilitating the sexual orientation identity development of gay and bisexual male adolescents. *American Journal of Men's Health*, *10*(5), 359–376. https://doi.org/10.1177/1557988314566227

Harper, K. (2017, January 12). *5 Things to know about racial and ethnic disparities in special education.* Child Trends. https://www.childtrends.org/publications/5-things-to-know-about-racial-and-ethnic-disparities-in-special-education

Harrichand, J. J. S., Kirk, K. E., & Mwendwa, J. M. (2020). Deepa's discovery: An examination of intersectionality when multiple identities collide—Managing family roles, doctoral work, and clashing Eurocentric worldviews. In B. King, & T. Stewart (Eds.), *Cases on cross-cultural counseling strategies* (pp. 192–218). IGI Global. https://doi.org/10.4018/978-1-7998-0022-4.ch010

Harrichand, J. J. S., Su, Y-W., Hyun, J., & Anandavalli, S. (2022). School counselors and refugee students: Application of the refugee well-being project intervention to address the social determinants of health. *Professional School Counseling*, *26*(1b), 1–8. https://doi.org/10.1177/2156759X221106810

Harriger, J. A., Schaefer, L. M., Thompson, J. K., & Cao, L. (2019). You can buy a child a curvy Barbie doll, but you can't make her like it: Young girls' beliefs about Barbie dolls with diverse shapes and sizes. *Body Image*, *30*, 107–113.

Harro, B. (2000). The cycle of socialization. In Adams M. et al. (Eds.) *Readings for diversity and social justice* (2nd ed., pp. 45–52). Routledge.

Hartling, L. M., & Lindner, E. G. (2016). Healing humiliation: From reaction to creative action. *Journal of Counseling & Development*, *94*(4), 383-390.

Hartmann, W. E., & Gone, J. P. (2014). American Indian historical trauma: Community perspectives from Two Great Plains medicine men. *American Journal of Community Psychology*, *54*(3/4), 274–288. https://doi.org/10.1007/s10464-014-9671-1

Hartmann, W. E., Wendt, D. C., Burrage, R. L., Pomerville, A., & Gone, J. P. (2019). American Indian historical trauma: Anticolonial prescriptions for healing, resilience, and survivance. *The American Psychologist*, *74*(1), 6–19. https://doi-org.echo.louisville.edu/10.1037/amp0000326

Haugen, I., & Kunst, J. R. (2017). A two-way process? A qualitative and quantitative investigation of majority members' acculturation. *International Journal of Intercultural Relations*, *60*, 67–82. https://doi.org/10.1016/j.ijintrel.2017.07.004

Haynes, C. C., & Thomas, O. S. (2007). *Finding common ground: A First Amendment guide to religion and public schools.* First Amendment Center.

Haynes-Mendez, J., & Engelsmeier, J. (2020). Cultivating cultural humility in education. *Childhood Education*, *96*(3), 22–29. https://doi.org/10.1080/00094056.2020.1766656

Hays, P. A. (2001). *Addressing cultural complexities in practice: A framework for clinicians and counselors.* American Psychological Association. https://doi.org/10.1037/10411-000

Hays, P. A. (2008). *Addressing cultural complexities in practice: Assessment, diagnosis, and therapy.* American Psychological Association. https://doi.org/10.1037/11650-000

HB 1840/SB 1556, 109th General Assembly (Tn. 2016). https://wapp.capitol.tn.gov/apps/Billinfo/default.aspx?BillNumber=HB1840&ga=109 https://www.capitol.tn.gov/Bills/109/Fiscal/FM2060.pdf

Heck, N. C., Flentje, A., & Cochran, B. N. (2011). Offsetting risks: High school gay-straight alliances and lesbian, gay, bisexual, and transgender (LGBT) youth. *School Psychology Quarterly, 26*(2), 161–174.

Helms, J. E. (1993). *Black and white racial identity: Theory, research, and Practice*. Praeger.

Helms, J. E. (2020). *Race is a nice thing to have.* Cognella.

Henne, P. S., & Klocek, J. (2019). Taming the Gods: How religious conflict shapes state repression. *Journal of Conflict Resolution, 63*(1), 112–138. https://doi.org/10.1177/0022002717728104

Hersey, T. (2022). *Rest is resistance: A manifesto.* Hachette UK.

Hilgenkamp, K., & Pescaia, C. (2003). Traditional Hawaiian healing and western influence. *Californian Journal of Health Promotion, 1*(SI), 34–39. https://doi.org/10.32398/cjhp.v1iSI.556

Hill, L., Artiga, S., & Ranji, U. (2022, November 1). *Racial disparities in maternal and infant health: Current status and efforts to address them.* Kaiser Family Foundation. https://www.kff.org/racial-equity-and-health-policy/issue-brief/racial-disparities-in-maternal-and-infant-health-current-status-and-efforts-to-address-them/

Hilts, D., Liu, Y., & Guo, X. (2023). Student-To-School-Counselor Ratios, School-Level Factors, and Leadership Practices of School Counselors: A National Investigation. *Professional School Counseling, 27*(1). https://doi.org/10.1177/2156759X231182135

Hipolito-Delgado, C. P. (2010). Exploring the etiology of ethnic self-hatred: Internalized racism in Chicana/o and Latina/o college students. *Journal of College Student Development, 51*(3), 319-331.

Hipolito-Delgado, C. P., & Lee, C. C. (2007). Empowerment theory for the professional school counselor: A manifesto for what really matters. *Professional School Counseling, 10*(4), 327-332. https://doi.org/10.1177/2156759X0701000401.

Ho`omanawanui, K., Fujikane, C., & Kagawa-Viviani, A. K. (2019). Teaching for Maunakea: Kiaʻi Perspectives. *Amerasia Journal, 45*(2), 1–6.

Hobcraft, J., Menken, J., & Preston, S. (1982). Age, period, and cohort effects in demography: A review. *Population Index, 48*(1), 4–43. https://doi.org/10.2307/2736356

Hodge, D. R. (2000). Spiritual ecomaps: A new diagrammatic tool for assessing marital and family spirituality. *Journal of Marital and Family Therapy, 26*(2), 217–228.

Hodge, D., Limb, G., & Cross, T. (2009). Moving from Colonization toward balance and harmony: A Native American perspective on wellness. *Social Work, 54*(3), 211–219.

Hoffman, K. M., Trawalter, S., Axt, J. R., & Oliver, M. N. (2016). Racial bias in pain assessment and treatment recommendations, and false beliefs about biological differences between blacks and whites. *Proceedings of the National Academy of Sciences of the United States of America, 113*(16), 4296–4301. https://doi.org/10.1073/pnas.1516047113

Hoffman, R. J. (1980). Some cultural aspects of Greek male homosexuality. *Journal of Homosexuality, 5*(3), 217–226. https://doi.org/10.1300/J082v05n03_05

Hohenshil, T. H., Amundson, N. E., & Niles, S. G. (2015). *Counseling around the world: An international handbook.* American Counseling Association.

Holcomb-McCoy, C., & Bryan, J. (2010). Advocacy and empowerment in parent consultation: Implications for theory and practice. *Journal of Counseling & Development, 88*(3), 259–268. https://doi.org/10.1002/j.1556-6678.2010.tb00021.x

Holi, E. (2019). *Health concerns and moral distaste—'concern trolling' as a moralizing rhetoric.*

Holloway, R. A., Waldrip, A. M., & Ickes, W. (2009). Evidence that a simpático self-schema accounts for differences in the self-concepts and social behavior of Latinos versus Whites (and Blacks). *Journal of Personality and Social Psychology, 96*, 1012–1028. https://doi.org/10.1037/a0013883

Hook, J. N., Davis, D. E., Owen, J., Worthington, E. L., & Utsey, S. O. (2013). Cultural humility: Measuring openness to culturally diverse clients. *Journal of Counseling Psychology, 60*(3), 353–366. https://doi.org/10.1037/a0032595

Hook, J. N., Davis, D., Owen, J., & DeBlaere, C. (2017). *Cultural humility: Engaging diverse identities in therapy.* American Psychological Association. https://doi.org10.1037/0000037-000

Hook, J. N., Farrell, J. E., Davis, D. E., DeBlaere, C., Van Tongeren, D. R., & Utsey, S. O. (2016). Cultural humility and racial microaggressions in counseling. *Journal of Counseling Psychology, 63*(3), 269.

hooks, b. (2000). *Feminist theory: From margin to center.* Pluto Press.

Hope, D. A., Holt, N. R., Woodruff, N., Mocarski, R., Meyer, H. M., Puckett, J. A., Eyer, J., Craig, S., Feldman, J., Irwin, J., Pachankis, J., Rawson, K. J., Sevelius, J., & Butler, S. (2022). Bridging the gap between practice guidelines and the therapy room: Community-derived practice adaptations for psychological services with transgender and gender diverse adults in the central United States. *Professional Psychology: Research and Practice*, 53(4), 351–361. https://doi.org/10.1037/pro0000448

Hopkins, P. (2019). Social geography I: Intersectionality. *Progress in Human Geography, 43*(5), 937–947. https://doi.org/10.1177/0309132517743677

Horse, P. G. (2001). Reflections on American Indian identity. In C. Wijeyesinghe & B. Jackson (Eds.), *New perspectives on racial identity development: A theoretical and practical anthology* (pp. 91-107). New York: New York University Press.

Horse, P. G. (2005). Native American identity. *Special Issue: Serving Native American Students, 2005*(109), 61–68. https://doi.org/10.1002/ss.154

Horse, P. G. (2012). Reflections on American Indian identity. In *New perspectives on racial identity development: A theoretical and practical anthology* (pp. 91–107). NYU Press.

Hoyert D. L. (2022) *Maternal mortality rates in the United States, 2020.* National Center for Health Statistics. https://stacks.cdc.gov/view/cdc/113967

Hudson, K. D., & Romanelli, M. (2020). "We are powerful people": Health-promoting strengths of LGBTQ communities of color. *Qualitative Health Research, 30*(8), 1156–1170. https://doi.org/10.1177/104973231983757

Huey Jr., S. J., Tilley, J. L., Jones, E. O., & Smith, C. A. (2014). The contribution of cultural competence to evidence-based care for ethnically diverse populations. *Annual Review of Clinical Psychology, 10*, 305–338.

Huffaker, D. A., & Calvert, S. L. (2005). Gender, identity, and language use in teenage blogs. *Journal of Computer-Mediated Communication, 10*(2). https://doi.org/10.1111/j.1083-6101.2005.tb00238.x

Huffman, J. M., Warlick, C., Frey, B., & Kerr, B. (2020). Religiosity, spirituality, gender identity, and sexual orientation of sexual minorities. *Translational Issues in Psychological Science, 6*(4), 356–371. https://doi.org/10.1037/tps0000262

Hughes, J. (2020). Does the heterogeneity of autism undermine the neurodiversity paradigm? *Bioethics*, 1—14. https://doi.org/10.1111/bioe.12780

Hughes, J. M. F. (2013). *Increasing neurodiversity in disability and social justice advocacy groups.* Autism Advocacy Network. https://autisticadvocacy.org/wp-content/uploads/2016/06/whitepaper-Increasing-Neurodiversity-in-Disability-and-Social-Justice-Advocacy-Groups.pdf

Hughes, J. M. F. (2015). *Changing conversations about autism: A critical, action implicative discourse analysis of U.S. neurodiversity advocacy online* [Doctoral dissertation]. https://gradworks.umi.com/37/21/3721820.html

Human Rights Campaign (HRC), (2022a, December 5). *An epidemic of violence in 2022.* https://reports.hrc.org/an-epidemic-of-violence

Human Rights Campaign (HRC). (2022b). *State equality index* https://www.hrc.org/resources/state-equality-index

Human Rights Campaign (HRC). (n.d.) *Glossary of terms.* https://www.hrc.org/resources/glossary-of-terms

Human Rights Watch. (2021). *"I just try to make it home safe": Violence and the human rights of transgender people in the United States.* https://www.hrw.org/sites/default/files/media_2021/11/us_lgbt1121_web_0.pdf

Hunt, B., Matthews, C., Milsom, A., & Lammel, J. A. (2006). Lesbians with physical disabilities: A qualitative study of their experiences with counseling. *Journal of Counseling and Development, 84*(2), 163–173. https://doi.org/10.1002/j.1556-6678.2006.tb00392.x

Hunter, M. (2007). The persistent problem of colorism: Skin tone, status, and inequality. *Sociology Compass, 1*(1), 237–254.

Hurley D. A., Kostelecky, S. R., & Townsend, L. (2022). *Cultural humility.* ALA Editions.

Ibakari, A., & Hall, G. C. (2014). The components of cultural match in psychotherapy. *Journal of Social and Clinical Psychology, 33*(10), 936–953. https://doi.org/10.1521/jscp.2014.33.10.936

Immortal Technique (f. Chuck D., Killer Mike, & Brother Ali). (2011). Civil war. [Song]. Viper Records.

Institute of Medicine. (2012). *The mental health and substance use workforce for older adults: In whose hands*? The National Academies Press.

Intergovernmental Panel on Climate Change (IPCC). (2022). *Climate change 2022: Impacts, adaption, and vulnerability.* Contribution of Working Group II to the Sixth Assessment Report of the Intergovernmental Panel on Climate Change, 1–3068. https://doi.org/10.1017/9781009325844

Inton-Campbell, M. (2021). Transnational transness: Imagining the connections between Southeast Asian queer identities. In E.S.A. Gadong (Ed.), *ASEAN queer imaginings: Collection of writings by LGBTIQ thinkers* (pp. 27–36). ASEAN SOGIE Caucus.

Isajiw, W. W. (1993). Definition and dimensions of ethnicity: A theoretical framework. *Challenges of measuring an ethnic world: Science, politics and reality*, 407–427.

Ivey, A. E., D'Andrea, M. J., & Ivey, M. B. (2012). *Theories of counseling and psychotherapy: A multicultural perspective: A multicultural perspective* (7th ed.). SAGE Publications.

Ivey, A. E., Ivey, M. B., & Zalaquett, C. P. (2018). *Intentional interviewing and counseling: Facilitating client development in a multicultural society.* Cengage Learning, Inc.

Iwarsson, S., Wahl, H.W., Nygren, C., Oswald, F., Sixsmith, A., Sixsmith, J., Széman. Z., & Tomsone, S. (2007). Importance of the home environment for healthy aging: Conceptual and methodological background of the European ENABLE-AGE Project. *The Gerontologist, 47*(1), 78–84. https://doi.org/10.1093/geront/47.1.78

Jackson, S. D., Mohr, J. J., & Kindahl, A. M. (2021). Intersectional experiences: A mixed methods experience sampling approach to studying an elusive phenomenon. *Journal of Counseling Psychology, 68*(3), 299–315. https://doi.org/10.1037/cou0000537

Jacobs, B. (2019). Indigenous identity: Summary and future directions. *Statistical Journal of the IAOS, 35*(1), 147–157. https://doi.org/10.3233/sji-190496

James, S. E., Herman, J. L., Rankin, S., Keisling, M., Mottet, L., & Anafi, M. (2016). *The report of the 2015 U.S. transgender survey.* National Center for Transgender Equality. https://transequality.org/sites/default/files/docs/usts/USTS-Full-Report-Dec17.pdf

Jamtgaard, L., & Lewis, L. M. (2023). The monetization of emergency medicine. *Missouri Medicine, 120*(3), 172.

Jha, M. R. (2015). *The global beauty industry: Colorism, racism, and the national body.* Routledge.

Ji, Y., Huang, Q., Liu, H., & Phillips, C. (2021). Weight bias 2.0: The effect of perceived weight change on performance evaluation and the moderating role of anti-fat bias. *Frontiers in Psychology, 12*, 679802. https://doi.org/10.3389/fpsyg.2021.679802

Johnson, A. G. (2018). *Privilege, power, and difference* (3rd ed.). McGraw Hill.

Johnson, K. F., & Brookover, D. L. (2021). School counselors' knowledge, actions, and recommendations for addressing social determinants of health with students, families, and in communities. *Professional School Counseling, 25*(1). https://doi.org /10.1177/2156759X20985847

Johnson, S. B. (2012, April). Addressing the obesity epidemic: Why should psychologists care? *Monitor on Psychology, 43*(4). http://www.apa.org/monitor/2012/04/pc

Jones, C. T., & Branco, S. F. (2020). The interconnectedness between cultural humility and broaching in clinical supervision: Working from the multicultural orientation framework. *The Clinical Supervisor,* 39(2), 178–189. https://doi.org/10.1080/07325223.2020.1830327

Jones, J. (1982). "My mother was much of a woman": Black women, work, and the family under slavery. *Feminist Studies, 8*(2), 235–269.

Jones, L., & Castellanos, J. (2003). Preface. In J. Castellanos & L. Jones (Eds.), *The majority in the minority: Expanding the representation of Latina/o faculty, administrators and students in higher education* (pp. xiii–xxvi). Stylus Publishing.

Jones, M. K., & Pritchett-Johnson, B. (2018). "Invincible black women": Group therapy for black college women. *The Journal for Specialists in Group Work, 43*(4), 349–375.

Jongen, C., McCalman, J., & Bainbridge, R. (2018). Health workforce cultural competency interventions: A systematic scoping review. *BMC Health Services Research, 18*(1). https://doi.org/10.1186/s12913-018-3001-5

Jordan, J. V. (2001). A relational-cultural model: Healing through mutual empathy. *Bulletin of the Menninger Clinic, 65*(1: Special issue), 92-103.

Jordan, W. D., & Spickard, P. (2014). Historical origins of the one-drop racial rule in the United States. *Journal of Critical Mixed Race Studies, 1*(1), 98–132.

Joseph, B. (2018). *What does Indigenous knowledge mean? A Compilation of attributes.* Indigenous Corporate Training, Inc. https://www.ictinc.ca/blog/what-does-indigenous-knowledge-mean

Joshi, K. Y. (2020). *White Christian privilege*. New York University Press.

Josiah, N., Shoola, H., Rodney, T., Arscott, J., Ndzi, M., Bush, A. D., Wilson, P. R., Jacues, K., Baptiste, D-L, & Starks, S. (2023). Addressing systemic racism and intergenerational transmission of anxiety using Bowenian family therapy with African American populations: A discursive paper. *Journal of Advanced Nursing*, *79*(5), 1714–1723.

Justice in Aging. (2015). *LGBT older adults in long-term care facilities*. https://justiceinaging.org/wp-content/uploads/2015/06/Stories-from-the-Field.pdf

Justice in Aging. (2018). *Older women & poverty*. http://www.justiceinaging.org/wp-content/uploads/2018/12/Older-Women-and-Poverty.pdf

Justin, T. (2021). Fear, freaks, and fat phobia: an examination of how My 600 lbs life displays "fat" black women. *Feminist Media Studies*, 1–14.

Kaholokula, J. K., Hermosura, A., & Antonio, M. C. K. (2019). Physical wellbeing of Native Hawaiians, the Indigenous people of Hawai'i. In C. Fleming & M. Manning (Eds.), *Routledge handbook of Indigenous wellbeing* (1st ed., p. 388). Routledge.

Kaiser Family Foundation. (2019). *How much do Medicare beneficiaries spend out of pocket on health care?* https://www.kff.org/medicare/issue-brief/how-much-do-medicare-beneficiaries-spend-out-of-pocket-on-health-care/

Kaplan, D. (2006, June 2). A new focus on cultural sensitivity. *Counseling Today*. https://ct.counseling.org/2006/06/ct-online-ethics-update-7/

Kaplan, D. M., Tarvydas, V. M., & Gladding, S. T. (2014). 20/20: A vision for the future of counseling: The new consensus definition of counseling. *Journal of Counseling & Development*, *92*(3), 366–372. https://doi.org/10.1002/j.1556-6676.2014.00164.x

Karasawa, M., Curhan, K. B., Markus, H. R., Kitayama, S. S., Love, G. D., Radler, B. T., & Ryff, C. D. (2011). Cultural perspectives on aging and well-being: A comparison of Japan and the U.S. *The International Journal of Aging and Human Development*, *73*(1), 73–98. https://doi.org/10.2190/AG.73.1.d

Kaufman, J. D., & Hajat, A. (2021). Confronting environmental racism. *Environmental Health Perspectives*, *129*(5), 1—2. https://doi.org/10.1289/EHP9511

Keeton v. Anderson-Wiley, 664 F.3d 865 (U.S. Ct. App., 11th Cir. 2011).

Keeton v. Anderson-Wiley, 733 F. Supp. 2d 1368 (Dist. Ct., S.D. Ga. 2010).

Keller, R. M., & Galgay, C. E. (2010). Microaggressive experiences of people with disabilities. In D. Sue (Ed.), *Microaggressions and marginality: Manifestations, dynamics, and impact* (pp. 241–268). Wiley.

Kelley, D., Majbouri, M., & Randolph, A. (2021, May 11). Black women are more likely to start a business than white men. *Harvard Business Review*. https://hbr.org/2021/05/black-women-are-more-likely-to-start-a-business-than-white-men

Kemp, N. T., & Mallinckrodt, B. (1996). Impact of professional training on case conceptualization of clients with a disability. *Professional Psychology: Research and Practice*, *27*(4), 378–385. https://doi.org/10.1037/0735-7028.27.4.378

Kemperman, A., van den Berg, P., Weijs-Perrée, M., & Uijtdewillegen, K. (2019). Loneliness of older adults: Social network and the living environment. *International Journal of Environmental Research and Public Health*, *16*(3), 406. https://doi.org/10.3390/ijerph16030406

Kenneady, D. A. & Oswalt, S.B. (2014). Is Cas"s model of homosexual identity formation relevant to today's society? *American Journal of Sexuality Education, 9*(2), 229–246. https://doi.org/10.1080/15546128.2014.900465

Kerwin, M., Walker-Smith, K., & Kirby, K. (2006). Comparative analysis of state requirements for the training of substance abuse and mental health counselors. *Journal of Substance Abuse Treatment, 30*, 173–181. https://doi:10.1016/j.jsat.2005.11.004

Khannaa, N. (Ed.). (2020). *Whiter: Asian American women on skin color and colorism*. NYU Press. http://www.jstor.org/stable/j.ctv1jk0hxw

Killermann, S. (2017). *A guide to gender: The social justice advocate's handbook*. Impetus Books.

Killian, T., Peters, H. C., & Brottem, L. J. (2019). Religious and spiritual values conflicts in queer partnerships: Implications for couples and family counselors. *The Family Journal: Counseling and Therapy for Couples and Families, 27*(3), 250–256. https://doi.org/10.1177/1066480719853012

Kim, J. (1981). Processes of Asian American identity development: A study of Japanese American women's perceptions of their struggle to achieve positive identities as Americans of Asian ancestry, *Dissertations Abstracts International, 42*, 155, 1–49.

Kim, S., & Cardemil, E. (2012). Effective psychotherapy with low-income clients: The importance of attending to social class. *Journal of Contemporary Psychotherapy, 42*, 27–35. https://doi.org/10.1007/s10879-011-9194-0

King, K. M. (2021). "I want to, but how?" Defining counselor broaching in core tenets and debated components. *Journal of Multicultural Counseling and Development, 49*(2), 87–100. https://doi.org/10.1002/jmcd.12208

Kitano, H. H. L. (1982). Mental health in the Japanese American community. In E. E. Jones & S. J. Korchin (Eds.), *Minority mental health* (pp. 149–164). Praeger.

Kivlighan III, D. M., & Chapman, N. A. (2018). Extending the multicultural orientation (MCO) framework to group psychotherapy: A clinical illustration. *Psychotherapy, 55*(1), 39.

Klein, F. (2014). Are you sure you're heterosexual? Or homosexual? Or even bisexual? *Journal of Bisexuality, 14*(3–4), 341–346.

Klonoff, E. A., & Landrine, H. (2000). Is skin color a marker for racial discrimination? Explaining the skin color–hypertension relationship. *Journal of Behavioral Medicine, 23*(4), 329–338. https://doi.org/10.1023/A:1005580300128

Knight, B. G. (1996). *Psychotherapy with older adults*. SAGE Publications.

Knight, B. G. (2009). *Psychotherapy and older adults: Resource guide*. American Psychological Association. https://www.apa.org/pi/aging/resources/guides/psychotherapy

Kocet, M. M., & Herlihy, B. J. (2014). Addressing value-based conflicts within the counseling relationship: A decision-making model. *Journal of Counseling & Development, 92*(2), 180–186. https://doi.org/10.1002/j.1556-6676.2014.00146.x

Kochhar, R., (2023, March 1). *The enduring grip of the gender pay gap*. Pew Research Center. https://www.pewresearch.org/social-trends/2023/03/01/the-enduring-grip-of-the-gender-

Kofta, M., Soral, W., & Bilewicz, M. (2020). What breeds conspiracy antisemitism? The role of political uncontrollability and uncertainty in the belief in Jewish conspiracy. Journal of Personality and Social Psychology, 118(5), 900–918. https://doi.org/10.1037/pspa0000183

Kohlberg, L. (1963). Moral development and identification. In H. W. Stevenson (Ed.) & J. Kagan, C. Spiker (Collaborators) & N. B. Henry, H. G. Richey (Eds.), *Child psychology: The sixty-second yearbook of the National Society for the Study of Education, Part 1* (pp. 277–332). National Society for the Study of Education; University of Chicago Press. https://doi.org/10.1037/13101-008

Kohlberg, L. (1963). The development of children's orientations toward a moral order. *Human Development, 6*(1–2), 11–33. https://doi.org/10.1159/000269667

Kortsmit, K., Mandel, M. G., Reeves, J. A., Clark, E., Pagano, P., Nguyen, A., Petersen, E. E, & Whiteman, M. K. (2021). Abortion Surveillance—United States, 2019. *Surveillance Summaries, 70*(9), 1–29. http://dx.doi.org/10.15585/mmwr.ss7009a1

Koss, M. P., Yuan, N. P., Dightman, D., Prince, R. J., Polacca, M., Sanderson, B., & Goldman, D. (2003). Adverse childhood exposures and alcohol dependence among seven Native American tribes. *American Journal of Preventive Medicine, 25*(3), 238–244.

Kraus, M. W., Piff, P. K., Mendoza-Denton, R., Rheinschmidt, M. L., & Keltner, D. (2012). Social class, solipsism, and contextualism: How the rich are different from the poor. *Psychological Review, 119*, 546–572. https://doi.org/10.1037/a0028756

Kress, V. E., Seligman, L., & Reichenberg, L. W. (2021). *Theories of counseling and psychotherapy* (5th ed.). Pearson.

Krogstad, J. M., Alvarado, J., & Mohamed, B. (2023, April 13). *Among US Latinos, Catholicism continues to decline but is still the largest faith*. Pew Research Center. https://www.pewresearch.org/religion/2023/04/13/among-u-s-latinos-catholicism-continues-to-decline-but-is-still-the-largest-faith/#:~:text=U.S.%2Dborn%20Latinos%20are%20less,been%20relatively%20stable%20since%202010.

Kudrna, L., Furnham, A., & Swami, V. (2010). The influence of social class salience on self-assessed intelligence. *Social Behavior and Personality, 38*, 859–864. https://doi.org/10.2224/sbp.2010.38.6.859

Küng, H. (2001). *The Catholic Church: A short history.* Modern Library.

Kunst, J. R., & Sam, D. L. (2013). Expanding the margins of identity: A critique of marginalization in a globalized world. *International Perspectives in Psychology: Research, Practice, Consultation, 2*(4), 225–241. https://doi.org/10.1037/ipp0000008.

LaFromboise, T., Coleman, H. L. K., & Gerton, J. (1993). Psychological impact of biculturalism: Evidence and theory. *Psychological Bulletin, 114*(3), 395–412.

Lamb, R. H., & Weinberger, L. E. (2005). The shift of psychiatric inpatient care from hospitals to jails and prisons. *Journal of the American Academy of Psychiatry and the Law, 33*(4), 5290534. https://www.ncbi.nlm.nih.gov/pubmed/16394231

Lane, M. (2019). Understanding cultural humility through the lens of a military culture. *Reflections: Narratives of Professional Helping, 25*(1), 90–100.

Lardier, D. T., Pinto, S. A., Brammer, M. K., Garcia-Reid, P., & Reid, R. (2020). The relationship between queer identity, social connection, school bullying, and suicidal ideations among youth of color. *Journal of LGBT Issues in Counseling, 14*(2), 74–99. https://doi.org/10.1080/15538605.2020.1753623

Larson, E. H., Patterson, D. G., Garberson, L. A., & Andrilla, C.H.A. (2016). *Supply and distribution of the behavioral health workforce in rural America (Data Brief #160).* WWAMI Rural Health Center, University of Washington.

Lawrence v. Texas, 539 U.S. 558 (2003). https://tile.loc.gov/storage-services/service/ll/usrep/usrep539/usrep539558/usrep539558.pdf

Lawrence, S. E., Puhl, R. M., Schwartz, M. B., Watson, R. J., & Foster, G. D. (2022). "The most hurtful thing I've ever experienced": A qualitative examination of the nature of experiences of weight stigma by family members. *SSM-Qualitative Research in Health*, *2*, 100073.

Lawson, J. E., Cruz, R. A., & Knollman, G. A. (2017). Increasing positive attitudes toward individuals with disabilities through community service learning. *Research in Developmental Disabilities*, *69*, 1–7. https://doi.org/10.1016/j.ridd.2017.07.013

Lee, K. C. G., & Tang, J. L. K. (2023). Note, know, choose: A psychospiritual treatment model based on early Buddhist teachings. *Spirituality in Clinical Practice*, *10*(2), 150–167. https://doi.org/10.1037/scp0000220

Lee, S. B., Oh, J. H., Park, J. H., Choi, S. P., & Wee, J. H. (2018). Differences in youngest-old, middle-old, and oldest-old patients who visit emergency department. *Clinical Experiences in Emergency Medicine*, *5*(4), 249–255. https://doi.org/10.15441/ceem.17.261

Leigh-Osroosh, K., & Hutchison, B. (2019). Cultural identity silencing of Native Americans in education. *Race and Pedagogy Journal: Teaching and Learning for Justice*, *4*(1), Article 3. https://soundideas.pugetsound.edu/rpj/vol4/iss1/3

Lemanski, M. (2001). *A history of addiction and recovery in the United States*. Sharp Press.

Lenz, E. M. (2017). Influence of experienced and internalized weight stigma and coping on weight loss outcomes among adults [Doctoral dissertation, University of Connecticut].

Lenz, S. (2016). Relational-cultural theory: Fostering the growth of a paradigm through empirical research. *Journal of Counseling & Development*, *94*(4), 415–428. https://doi.org/10.1002/jcad.12100

Leppma, M., & Jones, K. D. (2013). Multiple assessment methods and sources in counseling: Ethical considerations. *VISTAS*, *1*(37), 1–12.

Lerner, G. (1986). *The creation of the patriarchy*. Oxford University Press.

Lev, A. I. (2004). *Transgender Emergence: Therapeutic Guidelines for Working with Gender-Variant People and their Families*. New York, NY: Haworth Clinical Practice Press

Levinthal, C.F. (2011). *Drugs, crime and criminal justice* (3rd ed.). Prentice Hall.

Levy, B. (2009). Stereotype embodiment. *Current Directions in Psychological Science*, *18*(6), 332–336. https://doi.org/10.1111/j.1467-8721.2009.01662.x

Levy, B. (2023). *Breaking the age code: How your beliefs about aging determine how long and well you live*. William Morrow.

Levy, B. R., Slade, M. D., Kunkel, S. R., & Kasl, S. V. (2002). Longevity increased by positive self-perceptions of aging. *Journal of Personality and Social Psychology*, *83*(2), 261–270. https://doi.org/10.1037/0022-3514.83.2.261

Lewis, J. A., Arnold, M. S., House, R., & Toporek, R. L. (2002). *ACA advocacy competencies*. https://counseling.org/resources/competencies/advocacy_competencies.pdf

LGBT Center, UNC-Chapel Hill. (2022). https://lgbtq.unc.edu/resources/exploring-identities/asexuality-attraction-and-romantic-orientation/

Li, W. W., Singh, S., & Keerthigha, C. (2021). A cross-cultural study of filial piety and palliative care knowledge: Moderating effect of culture and universality of filial piety. *Frontiers in Psychology, 12*. https://doi.org/10.3389/fpsyg.2021.787724

Liang, Y.-S., & Shepherd, M. A. (2020). A multicultural content analysis of mental health private practices' websites and intake forms. *Professional Psychology: Research and Practice, 51*(4), 325–334. https://doi.org/10.1037/pro0000305

Liao, K. Y. H., Wei, M., & Yin, M. (2020). The misunderstood schema of the strong Black woman: Exploring its mental health consequences and coping responses among African American women. *Psychology of Women Quarterly, 44*(1), 84–104.

Liboro, R. (2014). Community-level interventions for reconciling conflicting religious and sexual domains in identity incongruity. *Journal of Religion and Health, 54*(4), 1206–1220. https://doi.org/10.1007/s10943-014-9845-z

Limb, G. E., Hodge, D. R., & Panos, P. (2008). Social work with native people: Orienting child welfare workers to the beliefs, values, and practices of Native American families and children. *Journal of Public Child Welfare, 2*(3), 383–397. https://doi.org/10.1080/15548730802463595

Lindsey, R., & Dahlman, L. (2022). *Climate change: Global temperature.* https://www.climate.gov/news-features/understanding-climate/climate-change-global-temperature

Lingsome, S. (2008). Invisible impairments: Dilemmas of concealment and disclosure. Norwegian *Journal of Disability Research, 10*(1), 2–16. https://doi.org/10.1080/15017410701391567

Litam, S.D.A. (2020). "Take your Kung-Flu back to Wuhan": Counseling Asians, Asian Americans, and Pacific Islanders with race-based trauma related to COVID-19. *The Professional Counselor, 10*(2), 144–156. https://doi.org/10.15241/sdal.10.2.144

Liu, W. M. (2001, August 24-28). *Poverty and depression among men: The social class worldview model and counseling implications* [Paper presentation]. 109th Annual Meeting of the American Psychological Association, San Francisco, CA.

Liu, W. M. (2011). *Social class and Classism in the helping professions: Research, theory, and practice.* SAGE Publications.

Liu, W. M., & Pope-Davis, D. B. (2003). Understanding classism to effect personal change. In *Practicing multiculturalism: Affirming diversity in counseling and psychology* (pp. 294–310). Pearson.

Liu, W. M., (2004). Using social class in counseling psychology and research. *Journal of Counseling Psychology, 51*, 3–18. https://doi.org/10.1037/0022-0167.51.1.3

Liu, W. M., Alt, M. C., & Pittsinger, R. F. (2013). The role of the social class worldview model in the assessment, diagnosis, and treatment of mental and physical health. In *Handbook of multicultural mental health* (2nd ed., pp. 111–125). Elsevier Chapters.

Liu, W. M., Soleck, G., Hopps, J., Dunston, K., & Pickett, T., Jr. (2004). A new framework to understand social class in counseling: The social class worldview model and modern classism theory. *Journal of Multicultural Counseling and Development, 32*, 95–122. https://doi.org10.1002/j.2161-1912.2004.tb00364.x

Livingston, G. (2019). *Americans 60 and older are spending more time in front of their screens than a decade ago.* Pew Research Center. https://www.pewresearch.org/fact-tank/2019/06/18/americans-60-and-older-are-spending-more-time-in-front-of-their-screens-than-a-decade-ago/

Löckenhoff, C. E., De Fruyt, F., Terracciano, A., McCrae, R. R., De Bolle, M., Costa, P. T., Jr, Aguilar-Vafaie, M. E., Ahn, C. K., Ahn, H. N., Alcalay, L., Allik, J., Avdeyeva, T. V., Barbaranelli, C., Benet-Martinez, V., Blatný, M., Bratko, D., Cain, T. R., Crawford, J. T., Lima, M. P., Ficková, E., Gheorghiu, G., Halberstadt, J., Hřebíčková, M., Jussim, L., Klinkosz, W., Knežević, G., Leibovich de Figueroa, N., Martin, T. A.,

Marušić, I., Mastor, K. A., Miramontez, D. R., Nakazato, K., Nansubuga, F., Pramila, V. S., Purić, D., Realo, A., Reátegui, N., Rolland, J-P., Rossier, J., Schmidt, V., Sekowski, A., Shakespeare-Finch, J., Shimonaka, Y., Simonetti, F., Siuta, J., Smith, P. B., Szmigielska, B., Wang, L., & Yik, M. (2009). Perceptions of aging across 26 cultures and their culture-level associates. *Psychology and Aging, 24*(4), 941–954. https://doi.org/10.1037/a0016901

Long, S. M., Clark, M., Ausloos, C. D., Jacoby, R., & McGhee, C, (2019). The wellness and self-care experiences of single mothers in poverty: Strategies for mental health counselors. *Journal of Mental Health Counseling, 41*, 343–358. https://doi.org/10.17733/mehc.41.4.05

Long, S. M., Clark, M., Reed, L., & Raghavan, E. (2022). Wellness integration in professional counseling: A grounded theory. *Journal of Counseling & Development, 100*(4), 442–453.

Lovinger, R. J. (1984). *Working with religious issues in therapy.* Jason Aronson.

Lownsdale, S. (1997). Faith development across the life span: Fowler's integrative work. *Journal of Psychology and Theology, 25*(1), 49–63. https://doi.org/10.1177/009164719702500105

Lupien, S., King, S., Meaney, M,, & McEwen, B. (2000). Child's stress hormone levels correlated with mother's socioeconomic status and depressive state. *Biological Psychiatry, 48*(10), 976–980.

Lutz, J. S. (2009). *Makúk: A new history of aboriginal-white relations* (ills. ed.). UBC Press.

Lyons, R. D. (1973, December 16). Psychiatrists, in a shift, declare homosexuality no mental illness. *The New York Times.* https://www.nytimes.com/1973/12/16/archives/psychiatrists-in-a-shift-declare-homosexuality-no-mental-illness.html

Macintyre, S., McKay, L., & Ellaway, A. (2004). Are rich people or poor people more likely to be ill? Lay perceptions, by social class and neighborhood, of inequalities in health. *Social Science & Medicine, 60*(2), 313–317. https://doi.org/10.1016/j.socscimed.2004.08.001

MacKenzie, M. K., Serrano, S., & Kaulukukui, K. L. (2007). Environmental Justice for Indigenous Hawaiians: Reclaiming Land and Resources. NR&E.

Mackrael, K., & Cameron, D. (2020, April 21). Coronavirus sends one-fifth of workers to unemployment line in some states. *The Wall Street Journal.* https://www.wsj.com/articles/coronavirus-sends-one-fifth-of-workers-to-unemployment-line-in-some-states-11587461401

Madathil, J., & Benshoff, J. M. (2008). Importance of marital characteristics and marital satisfaction: A comparison of Asian Indians in arranged marriages and Americans in marriages of choice. *The Family Journal, 16*(3), 222–230. https://doi.org/10.1177/1066480708317504

Madden, E. F. (2019). Intervention stigma: How medication-assisted treatment marginalizes patients and providers. *Social Science & Medicine, 232*, 324–331. https://doi.org/10.1016/j.socscimed.2019.05.027

Magni, G. (2017). Indigenous knowledge and implications for the sustainable development agenda. *European Journal of Education, 52*(4), 437–447. https://doi.org/10.1111/ejed.12238

Malinowska, A. (2020). Waves of feminism. In K. Ross (Ed.). *The international encyclopedia of gender, media, and communication.* John Wiley & Sons, Inc. https://doi.org/10.1002/9781119429128.iegmc096

Manly, J. J., Jones, R. N., Langa, K. M., Ryan, L. H., Levine, D. A., McCammon, R., Heeringa, S. G., & Weir, D. (2022). Estimating the prevalence of dementia and mild cognitive impairment in the US: The 2016 health and retirement study harmonized cognitive assessment protocol project. *JAMA Neurology, 79*(12), 1242–1249. https://doi.org/10.1001/jamaneurol.2022.3543

Mann, T., Tomiyama, A. J., & Ward, A. (2015). Promoting public health in the context of the "obesity epidemic": False starts and promising new directions. *Perspectives on Psychological Science, 10*(6), 706–710. https://doi.org/10.1177/1745691615586401

Manson, S. M., Beals, J., Klein, S. A., & Croy, C. D. (2005). Social epidemiology of trauma among 2 American Indian reservation populations. *American Journal of Public Health, 95*(5), 851–859.

Marbley, A. F., Rouson, L., Burley, H., Ross, W., Bonner, F. A., Lértora, I., & Huang, S-H. (2017). 3-C models teaching tools to promote social justice. *Multicultural Education, 24*(2), 2–10. https://eric.ed.gov/?id=EJ1150937

Marín, G., & Marín, B. V. (1991). *Research with Hispanic populations: Applied social science research methods series volume 23.* SAGE Publications.

Marira, T. D., & Mitra, P. (2013). Colorism: Ubiquitous yet understudied. *Industrial and Organizational Psychology, 6*(1), 103–107.

Mark, J. J. (2020). *European colonization of the Americans.* World History. https://www.worldhistory.org/European_Colonization_of_the_Americas/

Markides, K. S. & Gerst-Emerson, K. (2014). Introduction: Minorities, aging, and health. In *Handbook of minority aging* (pp. 105–109). Springer.

Marks, L. D., Dollahite, D. C., & Young, K. P. (2019). Struggles experienced by religious minority families in the United States: Strangers in their own land. *Psychology of Religion and Spirituality,* 11, 247–256

Marshall, E. A., Butler, K., Roche, T., Cumming, J., & Taknint, J. T. (2016). Refugee youth: A review of mental health counselling issues and practices. *Educational Psychology and Leadership, 57*(4), 308–319. http://dx.doi.org.proxy.lib.odu.edu/10.1037/cap0000068

Marshall, W. L., Serran, G. A., Fernandez, Y. M., Mulloy, R., Mann, R. E., & Thornton, D. (2003). Therapist characteristics in the treatment of sexual offenders: Tentative data on their relationship with indices of behaviour change. *Journal of Sexual Aggression, 9*(1), 25–30. https://doi.org/10.1080/355260031000137940

Martens, A., Goldenberg, J. L., & Greenberg, J. (2005). A terror management perspective on ageism. *Journal of Social Issues, 61*(2), 223–239. https://doi.org/10.1111/j.1540-4560.2005.00403.x

Martin, L. C., Ruble, N. D., Szkrybalo, J. (2002). Cognitive theories of early gender development. *Psychological Bulletin, 128,* 903–933.

Martin, T. K., & Godinet, M. (2018). Using the Lōkahi wheel: A culturally sensitive approach to engage Native Hawaiians in Child Welfare Services. *Journal of Indigenous Social Development, 7*(2), Article 2. https://journalhosting.ucalgary.ca/index.php/jisd/article/view/58482

Martiny, S. E., & Rubin, M. (2016). Towards a clearer understanding of social identity theory's self-esteem hypothesis. In S. McKeown, R. Haji, & N. Ferguson (Eds.), *Understanding peace and conflict through social identity theory: Contemporary global perspectives* (pp. 19–32). Springer. https://doi.org/10.1007/978-3-319-29869-6_2

Maslow, A. H. (1968). *Toward a psychology of being.* Van Nostrand.

Maslow, A. H. (1970). *Motivation and personality* (2nd ed.). Harper & Row.

Masten, A. (2001). Ordinary magic: Resilience processes in development. *American Psychologist, 56*(3), 227–238. http://dx.doi.org/10.1037/0003-066X.56.3.227

Masters, C., Robinson, D., Faulkner, S., Patterson, E., McIlraith, T., & Ansari, A. (2019). Addressing biases in patient care with the 5Rs of cultural humility, a clinician coaching tool. *Journal of General Internal Medicine*, *34*, 627–630.

Masters, J. (2022). *The top 10 global weather and climate change events of 2021.* Yale Climate Connections. https://yaleclimateconnections.org/2022/01/the-top-10-global-weather-and-climate-change-events-of-2021/

Matsuno, E., & Israel, T. (2018). Psychological interventions promoting resilience among transgender individuals: Transgender resilience intervention model (TRIM). *The Counseling Psychologist*, *46*(5), 632–655. https://doi.org/10.1177/0011000018787261

Matthes, E. H. (2016). Cultural appropriation without cultural essentialism? *Social Theory & Practice*, *42*(2), 343–366. https://doi.org/10.5840/soctheorpract201642219

Matthew Shepard and James Byrd, Jr., Hate Crimes Prevention Act of 2009, 18 U.S.C. § 249 (2009). https://uscode.house.gov/statviewer.htm?volume=123&page=2835#

Mauer, M., & King, R. (2007). *A 25-year quagmire: The war on drugs and its impact on American society.* The Sentencing Project.

Maura, J., & Weisman de Mamani, A. (2017). Mental health disparities, treatment engagement, and attrition among racial/ethnic minorities with severe mental illness: A Review. *Journal of Clinical Psychology in Medical Settings*, *24*(3–4), 187–210. https://doi.org/10.1007/s10880-017-9510-2

McCarn, S. R., & Fassinger, R. E. (1996). Revisioning Sexual Minority Identity Formation: A New Model of Lesbian Identity and its Implications for Counseling and Research. *The Counseling Psychologist*, 24(3), 508-534. https://doi.org/10.1177/0011000096243011

McCarthy, H. (2003). The disability rights movement: Experiences and perspectives of selected leaders in the disability community. *Rehabilitation Counseling Bulletin*, *46*, 209–223. https://doi.org/10.1177/003435520304600402

McCarty, T. L., & Nicholas, S. E. (2014). Reclaiming Indigenous languages: A reconsideration of the roles and responsibilities of schools. *Review of Research in Education*, *38*(1), 106–136. https://doi.org/10.3102/0091732X13507894

McCaughey, M. (2008). *The caveman mystique: Pop-Darwinism and the debates over sex, violence, and science*. Routledge, Taylor and Francis Group.

McClellan, J. M., Susser, E., & King, M.-C. (2006). Maternal famine, de novo mutations, and schizophrenia. *JAMA*, *296*(5), 582–584. https://doi.org/10.1001/jama.296.5.582

McConnell, E. A., Birkett, M. A., & Mustanski, B. (2015). Typologies of social support and associations with mental health outcomes among LGBT youth. *LGBT Health*, *2*(1), 55–61.

McCubbin, L. D., & Marsella, A. (2009). Native Hawaiians and psychology: The cultural and historical context of Indigenous ways of knowing. *Cultural Diversity and Ethnic Minority Psychology*, *15*(4), 374–387. https://doi.org/10.1037/a0016774

McCubbin, L., McCubbin, H. I., Zhang, W., Kehl, L., & Strom, I. (2013). Relational well-being: An Indigenous perspective and measure. *Family Relations*, *62*(2), 354–365. https://doi.org/10.1111/fare.12007

Mcintosh, P. (2003). White privilege: Unpacking the invisible knapsack. In S. Plous (Ed.), *Understanding prejudice and discrimination* (pp. 19--196). McGraw Hill.

McLaughlin, J. S., & Neumark, D. (2022). *Gendered ageism and disablism and employment of older workers*. National Bureau of Economic Research, Working Paper 30355. *https://doi.org/10.3386/w30355*

McLeod, A. M. (2015). Prison abolition and grounded justice. *UCLA Law Review, 62*(5), 1156–1239.

Mcleod, S. (2023, February 13). *Social identity theory: Definition, history, examples, & facts*. Simply Psychology. https://simplypsychology.org/social-identity-theory.html

McLeroy, K. R., Bibeau, D., Steckler, A., & Glanz, K. (1988). An ecological perspective on health promotion programs. *Health Education & Behavior, 15*(4), 351–377. https://doi.org/10.1177/109019818801500401

McMahon, H. G., Mason, E. C. M., Daluga-Guenther, N., & Ruiz, A. (2014). An ecological model of professional school counseling. *Journal of Counseling & Development, 92*(4), 459–471. https://doi.org/10.1002/j.1556-6676.2014.00172.x

McMahon, H. G., Paisley, P. O., & Skudrzyk, B. (2018). Individuals and families of European descent. In D. G. Hays & B. T. Erford (Eds.), *Developing multicultural counseling competence: A systems approach* (3rd ed., pp. 431–470). Pearson.

McMichael, A. (1999). Prisoners of the proximate: Loosening the constraints on epidemiology in an age of change. *American Journal of Epidemiology, 149*(10), 887–897.

MediaSmarts. (n.d.). *Representation of diversity in media—overview.* Retrieved April 6, 2023, from https://mediasmarts.ca/digital-media-literacy/media-issues/diversity-media/representation-diversity-media-%E2%80%93-overview

Mejia, M., Hyman, S. M., Behbahani, S., & Farrell-Turner, K. (2018). Death anxiety and ageist attitudes are related to trainees' interest in working with older adults. *Gerontology & Geriatrics Education, 39*(3), 341-356. http://dx.doi.org/10.1080/02701960.2016.1247063

Melnyck, B. M., Fineout-Overholt, E., Stillwell, S. B., & Williamson, K. M. (2010). Evidence-based practice step by step: The seven steps of evidence-based practice. *American Journal of Nursing, 110*(1), 51–52. https://doi.org/10/1097/01. NAJ.0000366056.06605.d2

Mental Health of America (MHA). (2023). *Black and African American communities and mental health*. https://www.mhanational.org/issues/black-and-african-american-communities-and-mental-health#:~:text=Sixteen%20percent%20(4.8%20million)%20of,people%20between%202008%20and%202018.

Mercado, V. (2003). *Effects of language brokering on children of Latino immigrants.* Pace University.

Mesa-Miles, S. (2018). Two spirit: The trials and tribulations of gender identity in the 21st century. *Indian Country Today.* https://indiancountrytoday.com/archive/two-spirit-the-trials-and-tribulations-of-gender-identity-in-the-21st-century

Meyer, I. H. (2003). Prejudice, social stress, and mental health in lesbian, gay, and bisexual populations: Conceptual issues and research evidence. *Psychol Bull, 129*(5), 674–697. https://doi.org/10.1037/0033-2909.129.5.674

Meyer, S. & Schwitzer, A. (2008). Stages of identity development among college students with minority sexual orientations. *Journal of College Student Psychotherapy, 13*(4), 41n65. https://doi.org/10.1300/J035v13n04_05

Meyer, Z. (2021, July 7). *Millennials face yet another workplace challenge—ageism.* Fast Company. https://www.fastcompany.com/90651334/millennials-face-yet-another-workplace-challenge-ageism

Meyerowitz, J. (2002). *How sex changed: A history of transsexuality in the United States.* Harvard University Press.

Meyerowitz, J. (2008). A history of "gender." *The American Historical Review, 113*(5), 1346–1356. https://www.jstor.org/stable/30223445

Meyers, L. (2014). A living document of ethical guidance. *Counseling Today*, 56(12), 32-40. https://ctarchive.counseling.org/2014/05/a-living-document-of-ethical-guidance/

Meyers, L. (2016). Immigration's growing impact on counseling. *Counseling Today, 58*(8), 22–31. https://ct.counseling.org/2016/01/immigrations-growing-impact-on-counseling/

Meyers, L. (2020). Climate in crisis: Counselors needed. *Counseling Today*, 20–27. https://www.counseling.org/docs/default-source/default-document-library/ct_sept_2020lr.pdf?sfvrsn=cc37232c_2

Middleton, T. J., Arjune, B., Peebles, E., Hughes, D., & Dollarhide, C. T. (2022). Optimal Theory and educational realities for African Americans: Suggestions for humanistic counselors working K–16. *The Journal of Humanistic Counseling, 62*, 15–24.

Miller, C. F. (2016). Gender development, theories of. In A. Wong, M. Wickramasinghe, r. hoogland and N.A. Naples (Eds.), *The Wiley Blackwell encyclopedia of gender and sexuality studies* (pp.). https://doi.org/10.1002/9781118663219.wbegss590

Mink, Gwendolyn & Alice O'Conner (eds.). *Poverty in the United States: An Encyclopedia of History, Politics and Policy* . Santa Barbara, CA, ABC-CLIO, 2004. ASU REF HC110.P6 P598 2004 v1 and 2.

Miranda, A. R., Perez-Brumer, A., & Charlton, B. M. (2023). Latino? Latinx? Latine? A call for inclusive categories in epidemiologic research. *American Journal of Epidemiology, 192*(12), 1929–1932.

Miranda, L. (2010, December 1). *Get the facts on the dream act.* The White House President Obama. https://obamawhitehouse.archives.gov/blog/2010/12/01/get-facts-dream-act

Miserandino, C. (n.d.). *The spoon theory.* But You Don't Look Sick. https://butyoudontlooksick.com/articles/written-by-christine/the-spoon-theory/

Mitchell, U. A., Nishida, A., Fletcher, F. E., & Molina, Y. (2021). The long arm of oppression: How structural stigma against marginalized communities perpetuates within-group health disparities. *Health Education & Behavior, 48*(3), 342–351. https://doi.org/10.1177/10901981211011927

Mitran, C. L. (2022). Experiences of licensed counselors and other licensed mental health providers working with neurodiverse adults: An instrumental case study. *The Family Journal*, 1–10.

Mizock, L., & Lundquist, C. (2016). Missteps in psychotherapy with transgender clients: Promoting gender sensitivity in counseling and psychological practice. *Psychology of Sexual Orientation and Gender Diversity, 3*(2), 148–155.

Mohajan, H. K. (2022). Four waves of feminism: A blessing for global humanity. *Studies in Social Science and Humanities, 1*(2), 1–8. https://doi.org/10.56397/SSSH.2022.09.01

Mohammed, Y. N., Ferri-Guerra, J., Salguero, D., Baskaran, D., Aparicio-Ugarriza, R., Mintzer, M. J., & Ruiz, J. G. (2019). The association of ageist attitudes with all-cause hospitalizations and mortality. *Gerontology and Geriatric Medicine, 5*, 233372141989268. https://doi.org/10.1177/2333721419892687

Mohatt, N. V., Fok, C. C. T., Burket, R., Henry, D., & Allen, J. (2011). Assessment of awareness of connectedness as a culturally-based protective factor for Alaska native youth. *Cultural Diversity and Ethnic Minority Psychology, 17*(4), 444–455. https://doi.org/10.1037/a0025456

Moon, S. H., & Sandage, S. J. (2019). Cultural humility for people of color: Critique of current theory and practice. *Journal of Psychology and Theology, 47*(2), 76–86. https://doi.org/10.1177/0091647119842407

Moore, L. A., Aarons, G. A., Davis, J. H., & Novins, D. K. (2015). How do providers serving American Indians and Alaska Natives with substance abuse problems define evidence-based treatment? *Psychological Services, 12*(2), 92.

Moorhead, H. J., Duncan, K., & Fernandez, M. S. (2023). The critical need for professional advocacy: A call to the counseling profession to value professional counselor identity. *Journal of Counselor Leadership and Advocacy, 10*(1), 3-17. https://doi.org/10.1080/2326716X.2023.2178985

Moorehead, V. D., Gone, J. P., & December, D. (2015). A gathering of Native American healers: Exploring the interface of indigenous tradition and professional practice. *American Journal of Community Psychology, 56*(3/4), 383–394. https://doi-org.ezp.waldenulibrary.org/10.1007/s10464-015-9747-6

Mora, L. (2022, October 7). *Hispanic enrollment reaches new high at four-year colleges in the US, but affordability remains an obstacle.* Pew Research Center. https://www.pewresearch.org/short-reads/2022/10/07/hispanic-enrollment-reaches-new-high-at-four-year-colleges-in-the-u-s-but-affordability-remains-an-obstacle/

Moradi, B., & Grzanka, P. R. (2017). Using intersectionality responsibly: Toward critical epistemology, structural analysis, and social justice activism. *Journal of Counseling Psychology, 64*(5), 500–513. https://doi.org/10.1037/cou0000203

Moradi, B., Subich, L. M., & Phillips, J. C. (2002). Revisiting feminist identity development theory, research, and practice. *The Counseling Psychologist, 30*(1), 6–43. https://doi.org/10.1177/0011000002301002

Moran, J., & Bussey, M. (2007). Results of an alcohol prevention program with urban American Indian youth. *Child and Adolescent Social Work Journal, 24*(1), 1–21. https://doi.org/10.1007/s10560-006-0049-6

Moreland, C., & Leach, M. M. (2001). The relationship between black racial identity and moral development. *Journal of Black Psychology, 27*(3), 255–271.

Morrison, M., & Brown, S. F. (1991). *Judaism.* Oxford University Press.

Morrison, S., Steele, J. M., & Henry, L. (2015). Recommendations for counselors working with Jamaican immigrant families and children. *Ideas and Research You Can Use: VISTAS Online*, 1–12. https://www.counseling.org/docs/default-source/vistas/recommendations-for-counselors-working-with-jamaican-immigrant-families-and-children.pdf?sfvrsn=8

Morse, B. W. (1985). *Aboriginal peoples and the law: Indian, Metis, and Inuit rights in Canada.* Carleton University Press.

Mosher, D. K., Hook, J. N., Captari, L. E., Davis, D. E., DeBlaere, C., & Owen, J. (2017). Cultural humility: A therapeutic framework for engaging diverse clients. *Practice Innovations, 2*(4), 221–233. https://doi.org/10.1037/pri0000055

Mosley, D. V., Hargons, C. N., Meiller, C., Angyal, B., Wheeler, P., Davis, C. & Stevens-Watkins, D. (2021). Critical consciousness of anti-black racism: A practical model to prevent and resist racial trauma. *Journal of Counseling Psychology, 68*(1), 1–16. http://dx.doi.org/10.1037/cou0000430

Moslimani, M., Tamir. C., Budiman, A., Noe-Bustamante, L., & Mora, L. (2023, March 2). *Facts about the US Black population.* Pew Research Center. https://www.pewresearch.org/social-trends/fact-sheet/facts-about-the-us-black-population/

Moullin, J. C., Moore, L. A., Novins, D. K., & Aarons, G. A. (2019). Attitudes towards evidence-based practice in substance use treatment programs serving American Indian Native communities. *Journal of Behavioral Health Services & Research, 46*(3), 509–520. https://doi-org.ezp.waldenulibrary.org/10.1007/s11414-018-9643-6

Movement Advancement Project (MAP) (2023). *Equality maps: Employment nondiscrimination laws.* https://www.lgbtmap.org/equality_maps/employment_non_discrimination_laws.

Movement Advancement Project (MAP) and National LGBTQ Workers Center [NLGBTQWC]. (2018). *LGBT people in the workplace: Demographics, experiences and pathways to equity.* https://www.lgbtmap.org/lgbt-workers-brief

Movement Advancement Project (MAP). (n.d.). *Identity document laws and policies.* Retrieved March 31, 2023, from https://www.lgbtmap.org/equalitymaps/identity_ document laws#:~:text= Additionally%2C%20states%20may%20allow%20individuals, female%2C%20nonbinary)%20are%20available

Moyano, M., & Trujillo, H. M. (2014). Intention of activism and radicalism among Muslim and Christian youth in a marginal neighbourhood in a Spanish city. *Revista de Psicología Social, 29*(1), 90–120. https://doi.org/10.1080/02134748.2013.878571

Mulligan, C. J. (2021). Systemic racism can get under our skin and into our genes. *American Journal of Physical Anthropology, 175*(2), 399–405.

Murray, K. E., Davidson, G. R., & Schweitzer, R. D. (2010). Review of refugee mental health interventions following resettlement: Best practices and recommendations. *American Journal of Orthopsychiatry, 80*(4), 576–585. https://doi.org/10.1111/j.1939-0025.2010.01062.x

Myers, J. E., & Schweibert, V. L. (1996). *Competencies for gerontological counseling.* American Counseling Association.

Myers, J., & Sweeney, T. (2008). Wellness counseling: The evidence base for practice. *Journal of Counseling and Development, 86*, 482–492. https://doi.org10.1002/j.1556-6678.2008.tb00536

Myers, L. J., Speight, S. L., Highlen, P. S., Cox, C. I., Reynolds, A. L., Adams, E. M., & Hanley, C. P. (1991). Identity development and worldview: Toward an optimal conceptualization. *Journal of counseling & development, 70*(1), 54–63.

Nadal, K. L., Issa, M.-A., Leon, J., Meterko, V., Wideman, M., & Wong, Y. (2011). Sexual orientation microaggressions: "Death by a thousand cuts" for lesbian, gay, and bisexual youth. *Journal of LGBT Youth, 8*(3), 234–259.

Nadal, K. L., Skolnik, A., & Wong, Y. (2012). Interpersonal and systemic microaggressions toward transgender people: Implications for counseling. *Journal of LGBT Issues in Counseling, 6*(1), 55–82. https://doi.org/10.1080/15538605.2012.648583

Naeem, F., Sajid, S., Naz, S., & Phiri, P. (2023). Culturally adapted CBT—the evolution of psychotherapy adaptation frameworks and evidence. *The Cognitive Behaviour Therapist, 16*, e10. https://doi.org/10.1017/S1754470X2300003X

Nagel, J. (1994). Constructing ethnicity: Creating and recreating ethnic identity and culture. *Social Problems, 41*(1), 152–176.

Nario-Redmon, M. R., Kemerling, A. A., & Silverman, A. (2019). Hostile, benevolent, and ambivalent ableism: Contemporary manifestations. *Journal of Social Issues, 75*(3), 726–756. https://doi.org/10.1111/josi.12337

NASA Global Climate Change. (n.d.). *What's the difference between climate change and global warming?* https://climate.nasa.gov/faq/12/whats-the-difference-between-climate-change-and-global-warming/

National Archives. (n.d.). *Milestone documents: Medicare and Medicaid Acts* (1965). Retrieved February 8, 2022, from https://www.archives.gov/milestone-documents/medicare-and-medicaid-act

National Association to Advance Fat Acceptance, Inc. https://static1.squarespace.com/static/5e7be2c55ceb-261b71eadde2/t/5e7fb20e554fd6780a9d60f1/1585426959255/Constitution-VER09.pdf

National Association to Advance Fat Acceptance. (2011). *Constitution for the*

National Board for Certified Counselors (2005). *Code of ethics.*

National Board for Certified Counselors (NBCC). (2016). *National Board for Certified Counselors (NBCC) code of ethics.*

National Board for Certified Counselors (NBCC). (2023). NBCC *code of ethics.* https://www.nbcc.org/assets/Ethics/NBCCCodeofEthics.pdf

National Center for Education Statistics (NCES). (n.d.). *Fast facts: Students with disabilities.* Retrieved August 22, 2022, from https://nces.ed.gov/fastfacts/display.asp?id=64

National Center for Health Statistics. (2017). *Health, United States, 2016: With chartbook on long-term trends in health.* National Center for Health Statistics. http://www.ncbi.nlm.nih.gov/books/NBK453378/

National Immigration Forum. (2018, June 14). *Immigrants as economic contributors: Refugees are a fiscal success story for America.* https://immigrationforum.org/article/immigrants-as-economic-contributors-refugees-are-a-fiscal-success-story-for-america/

National Institute on Aging. (n.d.). *Understanding the dynamics of the aging process.* National Institutes of Health. https://www.nia.nih.gov/about/aging-strategic-directions-research/understanding-dynamics-aging

National Library of Medicine (n.d.). Medicine ways: Traditional healers and healing. https://www.nlm.nih.gov/nativevoices/exhibition/healing-ways/medicine-ways/medicine-wheel.html

National Oceanic and Atmospheric Administration [NOAA] (n.d.). *What's the difference between climate and weather*? https://www.climate.gov/maps-data/climate-data-primer/whats-difference-between-climate-and-weather

National Park Service. (2022, August 13). *Stonewall national monument.* https://www.nps.gov/ston/index.htm

Native Governance Center. (2019). *A guide to Indigenous land acknowledgment.* https://Nativegov.org/a-guide-to-Indigenous-land-acknowledgment/

Natwick, J. (2017). On the ethics of ending: Terminations and referrals. *Counseling Today.* https://www.counseling.org/docs/default-source/ethics/

Navarro, M. (2002). Against *Marianismo.* In R. Montoya, L. J. Frazier, J. Hurtig (Eds.), *Gender's place.* Palgrave Macmillan. https://doi.org/10.1007/978-1-137-12227-8_13

Neihardt, J. G., Deloria, P., & DeMallie, R. (2014). *Black Elk speaks: The complete edition.* University of Nebraska Press, Bison Books.

Nelson, C. M. (2021). *The predictors of counselor moral and ethical reflection: Spiritual intelligence, meditation, clinical experience, and ethical climate* (Order No. 28415485) [Doctoral Dissertation, University of North Carolina]. ProQuest One Academic (2528579087). https://login.libweb.lib.utsa.edu/login?url=https://www.proquest.com/dissertations-theses/predictors-counselor-moral-ethical-reflection/docview/2528579087/se-2

Nelson, T. D. (2005). Ageism: Prejudice against our feared future self. *Journal of Social Issues, 61*(2), 207–221. https://doi.org/10.1111/j.1540-4560.2005.00402.x

Neuman, G. L. (1993). The lost century of American immigration law (1776-1875). *Columbia Law Review, 93*(8), 1833–1901. https://doi.org/10.2307/1123006

Newcomb, H. (2022). *The weight of living: An analysis of anti-fat bias and fatphobia in women's working relationships* [Doctoral dissertation, Middle Tennessee State University].

Newcomb, M. E., & Mustanski, B. (2010). Internalized homophobia and internalizing mental health problems: a meta-analytic review. *Clinical Psychology Review, 30*(8), 1019-29. doi:10.1016/j.cpr.2010.07

Newman, B. M. (2020). Ecological theories. In P. R. Newman (Ed.), *Theories of adolescent development* (pp. 313–335). Academic Press.

Ngo, B., & Lee, S. J. (2007). Complicating the image of model minority success: A review of Southeast Asian American education. *Review of Educational Research, 77*(4), 415–453.

Nikalje, A., & Çiftçi, A. (2023). Colonial mentality, racism, and depressive symptoms: Asian Indians in the United States. *Asian American Journal of Psychology, 14*(1), 73–85. https://doi.org/10.1037/aap0000262

Norcross, J. C., & Lambert, M. J. (2018). Psychotherapy relationships that work III. *Psychotherapy, 55*(4), 303–315. https://doi.org/10.1037/pst0000193

Norcross, J. C., & Wampold, B. E. (2011). Evidence-based therapy relationships: research conclusions and clinical practices. *Psychotherapy, 48*(1), 98.

NPR. (2021, August 21). *More than 9,000 anti-Asian incidents have been reported since the pandemic began.* NPR. https://www.npr.org/2021/08/12/1027236499/anti-asian-hate-crimes-assaults-pandemic-incidents-aapi

Nutton, J., & Fast, E. (2015). Historical trauma, substance use, and indigenous peoples: Seven generations of harm from a "big event." *Substance Use & Misuse, 50*(7), 839–847. https://doi.org/10.3109/10826084.2015.1018755

O'Hara, C., Dispenza, F., Brack, G., & Blood, R.A.C. (2013). The preparedness of counselors in training to work with transgender clients: A mixed methods investigation. *Journal of LGBT Issues in Counseling, 7*(3), 236–256. https://doi.org/10.1080/15538605.2013.812929

Obergefell v. Hodges, 576 U.S. ___ (2015). https://www.supremecourt.gov/opinions/14pdf/14-556_3204.pdf

Oberlander, J. (2003). *The political life of Medicare.* University of Chicago Press.

Ocampo, A. C., & Soodjinda, D. (2016). Invisible Asian Americans: The intersection of sexuality, race, and education among gay Asian Americans. *Race Ethnicity and Education, 19*(3), 480–499.

Office of Immigration Statistics. (2019). *Legal immigration and adjustment of statistics report FY2019, Quarter 4.* https://www.dhs.gov/immigration-statistics/special-reports/legal-immigration

Office of Management and Budget. (2023). *Initial proposals for updating OMB's race and ethnicity statistical standards.* https://www.federalregister.gov/documents/2023/01/27/2023-01635/initial-proposals-for-updating-ombs-race-and-ethnicity-statistical-standards

Office of Minority Health. (2023). Hispanic/Latino Health. U.S. Department of Health and Human Services, National Institutes of Health. https://minorityhealth.hhs.gov/hispaniclatino-health

Ogunbode, C. A., Doran, R., Hanss, D., Ojala, M., Salmela-Aro, K., van den Broek, K. L., Bhullar, N., Aquino, S. D., Marot, T., Schermer, J. A., Wlodarczyk., Lu, S., Jiang, F. Maran, D. A., Yadav, R., Ardi, R., Chegeni, R., Ghanbarian, E., Zand, S., Najafi, R., Park, J. … & Karasu, M. (2022). Climate anxiety, well-being and pro-environmental action: Correlates of negative emotional responses to climate change in 32 countries. *Journal of Environmental Psychology, 84*, 1–14. https://doi.org/10.1016/j.jenvp.2022.101887

Oh, H., Lincoln, K., & Waldman, K. (2021). Perceived colorism and lifetime psychiatric disorders among Black American adults: Findings from the national survey of american life. *Soc Psychiatry Epidemiol*, 56, 1509–1512. https://doi.org/10.1007/s00127-021-02102-z

O'Hara, C., & Cook, J. M. (2018). Doctoral level counseling students' experiences of social class microaggressions. *Counselor Education and Supervision, 57*(4), 255-270. http://dx.doi.org/10.1002/ceas.12115

Okoro, C. A., Hollid, N. D., Cyrus, A. C., & Griffin-Blake, S. (2018). Prevalence of disabilities and health care access by disability status and type among adults—United States, 2016. *Morbidity and Mortality Weekly Report, 67*(32), 882–887. http://dx.doi.org/10.15585/mmwr.mm6732a3

Oliphant, J. B., & Cerda, A. (2022, September 8). *Republicans and democrats have different top priorities for U.S. immigration policy.* Pew Research Center. https://www.pewresearch.org/fact-tank/2022/09/08/republicans-and-democrats-have-different-top-priorities-for-u-s-immigration-policy/

Olkin, R. (1999). *What psychotherapists should know about disability.* Guilford Press.

Olkin, R. (2022, March 29). *Conceptualizing disability: Three models of disability.* https://www.apa.org/ed/precollege/psychology-teacher-network/introductory-psychology/disability-models

O'Neill, B., Gidengil, E., Côté, C., & Young, L. (2015). Freedom of religion, women's agency and banning the face veil: The role of feminist beliefs in shaping women's opinion. *Ethnic and Racial Studies*, 38(11), 1886–1901. https://doi.org/10.1080/01419870.2014.887744

Orenstein, G. A. & Lewis, L. (2022). *Erikson's stages of psychosocial development.* StatPearls. https://pubmed.ncbi.nlm.nih.gov/32310556/

Organista, K. C. (2007). *Solving Latino psychosocial and health problems: Theory, practice, and populations.* John Wiley & Sons.

Ortman, J. M., Velkoff, V. A., & Hogan, H. (2014). An aging nation: The older population in the United States. *Current Population Reports, P25-1140.* U.S. Census Bureau. https://www.census.gov/library/publications/2014/demo/p25-1140.html

Osterman, M.J.K., Hamilton, B. E., Martin, J. A., Driscoll, A. K., & Valenzuela, C. P. (2022, February 7). Births: Final data for 2020. *National Vital Statistics Reports, 70*(17). U.S. Department of Health and Human Services. https://www.cdc.gov/nchs/data/nvsr/nvsr70/nvsr70-17.pdf

Owen, J. (2013). Early career perspectives on psychotherapy research and practice: Psychotherapist effects, multicultural orientation, and couple interventions. *Psychotherapy, 50*(4), 496.

Owen, J. J., Tao, K., Leach, M., & Rodolfa, E. (2011). Clients' perceptions of their psychotherapists' multicultural orientation. *Psychotherapy, 48*, 274 –282. http://dx.doi.org/10.1037/a0022065

Owen, J., Drinane, J., Tao, K. W., Adelson, J. L., Hook, J. N., Davis, D., & Fookune, N. (2017). Racial/ethnic disparities in client unilateral termination: The role of therapists' cultural comfort. *Psychotherapy Research, 27*(1), 102–111. https://doi.org/10.1080/10503307.2015.1078517

Owen, J., Jordan, T. A., Turner, D., Davis, D. E., Hook, J. N., & Leach, M. M. (2014). Therapists' multicultural orientation: Client perceptions of cultural humility, spiritual/religious commitment, and therapy outcomes. *Journal of Psychology and Theology, 42*(1), 91–98.

Owen, J., Tao, K. W., Drinane, J. M., Hook, J., Davis, D. E., & Kune, N. F. (2016). Client perceptions of therapists' multicultural orientation: Cultural (missed) opportunities and cultural humility. *Professional Psychology: Research and Practice, 47*(1), 30.

Page, R. L., Chilton, J., Montalvo-Liendo, N., Matthews, D., & Nava, A. (2017). Empowerment in Latina immigrant women recovering from interpersonal violence: A concept analysis. *Journal of Transcultural Nursing, 28*(6), 531–539. http://dx.doi.org/10.1177/1043659617707014

Paglinawan, L. K., Paglinawan, R. L., Kauahi, D., & Kanuha, V. K. (2020). *Nāna Nāna I Ke Kumu Helu 'Ekoulu* (Vol. III). Lili'uokalani Trust.

Paine, T. (2012). *Rights of man: Being an answer to Mr. Burke's attack on the French revolution.* Cambridge University Press. (Original work published 1791).

Palmer, C. A. (2018). Defining and studying the modern African diaspora. *Journal of Pan African Studies, 11*(2), 214–221.

Parker M. (2004). Memory, narrative, and myth in the construction of national identity: A rhetorical analysis of the senate debate over reparations for Japanese Americans. In G. A. Hauser & A. Grim (Eds.), *Rhetorical democracy: Discursive practices of civil engagement* (pp. 277–284). Lawrence Erlbaum Associates Publishers.

Parks, C. A., Hughes, T. L., & Matthews, A. K. (2004). Race/ethnicity and sexual orientation: Intersecting identities. *Cultural Diversity and Ethnic Minority Psychology, 10*(3), 241–254. https://doi.org/10.1037/1099-9809.10.3.241

Pashak, T. J., & Heron, M. R. (2022). Build rapport and collect data: A teaching resource on the clinical interviewing intake. *Discovery Psychology, 2*(20). https://doi.org/10.1007/s44202-022-00019-5

Passel, J. S., & Cohn, D. (2018). *U.S. unauthorized immigrant total dips to lowest level in a decade.* Pew Research Center. https://www.pewresearch.org/hispanic/2018/11/27/u-s-unauthorized-immigrant-total-dips-to-lowest-level-in-a-decade/

Patil, V. (2013). From patriarchy to intersectionality: A transnational feminist assessment of how far we've really come. *Signs: Journal of Women in Culture and Society, 38*(4), 847–867. https://doi.org/10.1086/669560

Payne, J. S. (2022). *Out of the fire: Healing black trauma caused by systemic racism using acceptance and commitment therapy.* New Harbinger Publications.

Payne, R. K. (2005). *A framework for understanding poverty* (4th ed.) aha! Process, Inc.

Pear, V. A., Ponicki, W. R., Gaidus, A., Keyes, K. M., Martins, S. S., Fink, D. S., Rivera-Aguirre, A., Gruenewald, P. J., & Cerdá, M. (2019). Urban-rural variation in the socioeconomic determinants of opioid overdose. *Drug & Alcohol Dependence, 195*, 66–73. https://doi.org/10.1016/j.drugalcdep.2018.11.024

Peck, M.S. (1998). *The road less traveled and beyond: Spiritual growth in an age of anxiety.* Touchstone.

Percy, W. A. (1996). *Pederasty and pedagogy in archaic Greece.* University of Illinois Press.

Perez, W., Espinoza, R., Ramos, K., Coronado, H. M., & Cortes, R. (2009). Academic Resilience Among Undocumented Latino Students. *Hispanic Journal of Behavioral Sciences*, 31(2), 149-181. https://doi.org/10.1177/0739986309333020

Pérez-Rojas, A. E., Bartholomew, T. T., Lockard, A. J., & Gonzalez, J. M. (2019). Development and initial validation of the therapist cultural comfort scale. *Journal of Counseling Psychology, 66*(5), 534–549. http://dx.doi.org/10.1037/cou0000344

Perreira, K. M., & Ornelas, I. (2013). Painful passages: Traumatic experiences and post-traumatic stress among U.S. immigrant Latino adolescents and their primary caregivers. *The International Migration Review, 47*(4), 976–1005. http://dx.doi.org/10.1111/imre.12050

Perry, J. M., Modesti, C., Talamo, A., & Nicolais, G. (2019). Culturally sensitive PTSD screening in non-Western youth: Reflections and indications for mental health practitioners. *Journal of Refugee Studies, 32*(Special_Issue_1), 151–161. https://doi.org/10.1093/jrs/fez053

Perry, P. (2001). White means never having to say you're ethnic: White youth and the construction of "cultureless" identities. *Journal of Contemporary Ethnography, 30*(1), 56–91. https://doi.org/10.1177/089124101030001002

Peters, R. H., Kremling, J., Bekman, N. M., & Caudy, M. S. (2012). Co-occurring disorders in treatment-based courts: Results of a national survey. *Behavioral Sciences & the Law, 30*, 800–820. https://doi.org/f4gp24

Petersen, E. E., Davis, N. L., Goodman, D., Cox, S., Syverson, C., Seed, K., Shapiro-Mendoza, C., Callaghan, W. M., & Barfield, W. (2019). Racial/ethnic disparities in pregnancy-related deaths — United States, 2007–2016. MMWR. *Morbidity and Mortality Weekly Report, 68*(35), 762–765.

Pettitt, P. (2010). *The palaeolithic origins of human burial*. https://doi.org/10.4324/9780203813300

PettyJohn, M. E., Tseng, C. F., & Blow, A. J. (2020). Therapeutic utility of discussing therapist/client intersectionality in treatment: When and how?. *Family Process, 59*(2), 313–327. https://doi.org/10.1111/famp.12471

Pew Charitable Trusts. (2013). *Moving on up*. http://www.pewtrusts.org/en/research-and-analysis/reports/0001/01/01/moving-on-up

Pew Research Center (PRC). (2014). *Religious landscape study*. https://www.pewforum.org/religious-landscape-study/

Pew Research Center (PRC). (2018, March). *Trends in party affiliation among demographic groups*. https://www.pewresearch.org/politics/2018/03/20/1-trends-in-party-affiliation-among-demographic-groups/

Pew Research Center (PRC). (2019, December). *In a politically polarized era, sharp divides in both partisan coalitions*. https://www.people-press.org/2019/12/17/in-a-politically-polarized-era-sharp-divides-in-both-partisan-coalitions/

Pew Research Center (PRC). (2022, December 21). *Religious composition by country, 2010–2050*. Pew Research Center's Religion & Public Life Project. https://www.pewresearch.org/religion/interactives/religious-composition-by-country-2010-2050/

Pew Research Center. (2023, March). *The enduring grip of the gender pay gap*. https://www.pewresearch.org/social-trends/2023/03/01/the-enduring-grip-of-the-gender-pay-gap

Phillips, G., Felt, D, Perez-Bill, E., Ruprecht, M. M. & Glenn, E. E. (2022). Principles of LGBTQ+ evaluation. *New Directions for Evaluation*. https://doi.org/10.1002/ev.20519

Phinney, J. S. (1989). Stages of ethnic identity development in minority group adolescents. *Journal of Early Adolescence, 9*, 34–49.

Piaget, J. (1932). *The moral development of the child*. Routledge & Kegan Paul.

Piaget, J. (1954). *The Construction of Reality in the Child*. Cook, M., Trans., KBasic Books. https://doi.org/10.1037/11168-000

Pierce, C. (1970). *Offensive mechanisms in black seventies*. Porter Sargent.

Pimpare, S. (2008). *A people's history of poverty in America*. The New Press.

Pinto, S. A. & Blueford, J. M. (2022). Culturally affirming school counseling for LGBTGEQIAP+ youth. In S. Brant-Rajahn, E. Gibson, & M. Cook Sandifer (Eds.), *Developing, delivering, and sustaining school counseling practices through a culturally affirming lens* (pp. 97–127). IGI Global. https://doi.org/10.4018/978-1-7998-9514-5.ch006

Pitts, C., & Kawahara, D. M. (2017). Radical visionaries—feminist psychotherapists: 1970–1975, *Women & Therapy, 40*(3–4), 256–259. https://doi.org/10.1080/02703149.2017.1241558

Plummer, R. S., Alter, Z., Lee, R. M., Gordon, A. R., Cory, H., Brion-Meisels, G., … & Kenney, E. L. (2022). “It’s not the stereotypical 80s movie bullying”: A qualitative study on the high school environment, body image, and weight stigma. *Journal of School Health, 92*(12), 1165–1176.

Pomerville, A., Burrage, R. L., & Gone, J. P. (2016). Empirical findings from psychotherapy research with Indigenous populations: A systematic review. *Journal of Consulting and Clinical Psychology, 84*(12), 1023–1038. https://doi.org/10.1037/ccp0000150

Poston, W. S. (1990). The biracial identity development model: A needed addition. *Journal of Counseling and Development, 69*, 152–155.

Poupart, L. M. (2003). The familiar face of genocide: Internalized oppression among American Indians. *Hypatia, 18*, 86–100.

Prilleltensky, I. (1994). *The morals and politics of psychology: Psychological discourse and the status quo.* State University of New York Press.

Primeau, A., Bowers, T. G., Harrison, M. A., & XuXu. (2013). Deinstitutionalization of the mentally ill: Evidence for transinstitutionalization from psychiatric hospitals to penal institutions. *Comprehensive Psychology, 2*, 16-02. https://doi.org/10.2466/16.02.13.CP.2.2

Proujansky, R. A. & Panchankis, J. E. (2014). Toward formulating evidence-based principles of LGB-affirmative psychotherapy. *Pragmatic Case Studies in Psychotherapy, 10*(2), 117–131. https://doi.org/10.14713/pcsp.v10i2.1854

Proulx, G., & Crane, N. J. (2020). “To see things in an objective light”: The Dakota Access Pipeline and the ongoing construction of settler colonial landscapes. *Journal of Cultural Geography, 37*(1), 46–66. https://doi.org/10.1080/08873631.2019.1665856

Puhl, R. M., & Heuer, C. A. (2010). Obesity stigma: important considerations for public health. *American Journal of Public Health, 100*(6), 1019–1028.

Puhl, R. M., Moss-Racusin, C. A., Schwartz, M. B., & Brownell, K. D. (2008). Weight stigmatization and bias reduction: Perspectives of overweight and obese adults. *Health Education Research, 23*(2), 347–358.

Puhl, R. M., Peterson, J. L., DePierre, J. A., & Luedicke, J. (2013). Headless, hungry, and unhealthy: A video content analysis of obese persons portrayed in online news. *Journal of Health Communication, 18*(6), 686–702.

Pukui, M. K., & Elbert, S. H. (1986). *Hawaiian dictionary: Hawaiian-English English-Hawaiian revised and enlarged edition.* University of Hawaii Press.

Quffa, W. A. (2016). A review of the history of gender equality in the United States of America. *Social Sciences and Education Research Review, 3*(2), 143–149.

Quillian, L., Lee, J. J., & Honoré, B. (2020). Racial discrimination in the US housing and mortgage lending markets: a quantitative review of trends, 1976–2016. *Race and Social Problems, 12*, 13–28.

Rahman, F. (1993). Islam. In *Encarta encyclopedia.* Microsoft.

Rata, A., Liu, J. H., & Hutchings, J. (2014). Creation narratives as metaphors for indigenous identity development: The P whiri identity negotiation framework. *Psychology & Developing Societies, 26*(2), 291–319. https://doi.org/10.1177/0971333614549144

Ratts, M. J. (2009). Social justice counseling: Toward the development of a fifth force among counseling paradigms. *The Journal of Humanistic Counseling, Education and Development*, *48*(2), 160–172. https://doi.org/10.1002/j.2161-1939.2009.tb00076.x

Ratts, M. J., & Greenleaf, A. T. (2018). Counselor–advocate–scholar model: Changing the dominant discourse in counseling. *Journal of Multicultural Counseling and Development*, *46*(2), 78–96. https://doi.org/10.1002/jmcd.12094

Ratts, M. J., & Pedersen, P. B. (2014). *Counseling for multiculturalism and social justice: Integration, theory, and application*. John Wiley & Sons.

Ratts, M. J., Singh, A. A., Nassar-McMillan, S., Butler, S. K., & McCullough, J. R. (2015). *Multicultural and social justice counseling competencies*. Association for Multicultural Counseling and Development. https://www.counseling.org/docs/default-source/competencies/multicultural-and-social-justice-counseling-competencies.pdf?sfvrsn=8573422c_24

Ratts, M. J., Singh, A. A., Nassar-McMillan, S., Butler, S. K., & McCullough, J. R. (2016). Multicultural and social justice counseling competencies: Guidelines for the counseling profession. *Journal of Multicultural Counseling and Development*, *44*(1), 28–48.

Ratts, M., D'Andrea, M., & Arredondo, P. (2004). Social justice counseling: "Fifth force" in field. *Counseling Today*, *47*(1), 28–30.

Ravelli, G, Stein, Z, & Susser, M. (1976). Obesity in young men after famine exposure in-utero and early infancy. *New England Journal of Medicine*, *295*(7), 349–353.

Ray, R. & DeLoatch, N. (2018, November 13). *Race*. Oxford Bibliographies. https://www.oxfordbibliographies.com/display/document/obo-9780199756384/obo-9780199756384-0173.xml

Redfield, R., Linton, R., & Herskovits, M. J. (1936). Memorandum for the study of acculturation. *American Anthropologist*, *38*(1), 149–152. http://dx.doi.org/10.1525/aa.1936.38.1.02a00330

Redmond, L., & Gittlesohn, J. (2019). Chronic disease among Native North Americans. In C. Fleming & M. Manning (Eds.), *Routledge handbook of Indigenous wellbeing* (1st ed., pp. 22–34). Routledge.

Reece, R. L. (2020). Whitewashing slavery: Legacy of slavery and white social outcomes. *Social Problems*, *67*(2), 304–323.

Reed, E. (2018). The heterogeneity of family: Responses to representational invisibility by LGBTQ parents. *Journal of Family Issues*, *39*(18), 4204–4225. https://doi.org/10.1177/0192513X18810952

Reese, R. F., & Lewis, T. F. (2019). Greening counseling: Examining multivariate relationships between ecowellness and holistic wellness. *Journal of Humanistic Counseling*, *58*, 53–67. https://doi.org/10/1002/johc.12089

Reese, R. F., Myers, J. E. (2012). Ecowellness: The missing factor in holistic wellness models. *Journal of Counseling & Development*, *90*, 400—408. https://doi.org/10.1002/j.1556-6676.2012.00050.x

Reiheld, A. (2020). Microaggressions as a disciplinary technique for fat and potentially fat bodies. In *Microaggressions and philosophy* (pp. 205–225). Routledge.

Respect for Marriage Act, H.R. 8404, 117th Cong. (2022). https://www.congress.gov/117/bills/hr8404/BILLS-117hr8404pcs.pdf

Rezentes III, W. C. (1996). *Ka lama kukui Hawaiian psychology: An introduction*. A'ali'i Books.

Rhodes, M., & Baron, A. (2019). The development of social categorization. *Annual Review of Developmental Psychology*, *1*, 359–386. https://doi.org/10.1146/annurev-devpsych-121318-084824

Riabchuk, M. (2015). 'Two Ukraines' reconsidered: The end of Ukrainian ambivalence? *Academy of Science of Ukraine, 15*(1), 138–156. https://doi.org/10.1111/sena.12120

Richards, P. S., & Bergin, A. E. (1997). *A spiritual strategy for counseling and psychotherapy.* American Psychological Association. https://doi.org/10.1037/10241-000

Richmond, L. J., & Guindon, M. H. (2013). Culturally alert counseling with European Americans. In G. J. McAuliffe (Ed.), *Culturally alert counseling: A comprehensive introduction* (pp. 231–262). SAGE Publications.

Rinaldi, J., Rice, C., Kotow, C., & Lind, E. (2020). Mapping the circulation of fat hatred. *Fat Studies, 9*(1), 37–50.

Rio, J. L., Laux, J. M., Clark, M., Walker, T., Goodlin, F. W., Heckman, L., & DelRe, J. (2022). A model for professional counselors to integrate multiculturalism and social justice into correctional settings. *Journal of Addictions & Offender Counseling, 43*(1), 62–75. https://doi.org/10.1002/jaoc.12104

Rios, J. (2011). *7 men from FLDS sect adjust to life behind bars.* Corrections1. https://www.corrections1.com/arrests-and-sentencing/articles/7-men-from-flds-sect-adjust-to-life-behind-bars-r3r5YpTbSC9yfC-qK/#:~:text=Dutson%20and%20six%20other%20FLDS,FLDSowned%20ranch%20in%20Schleicher%20County.

Rivas, M., & Hill, N. R. (2018). Counselor trainees' experiences counseling disability: A phenomenological study. *Counselor Education and Supervision, 57*(2), 116–131. https://doi.org/10.1002/ceas.12097

Rivas-Vazquez, R. A., Blais, M. A., Rey, G. J., & Rivas-Vazquez, A. A. (2001). A brief reminder about documenting the psychological consultation. *Professional Psychology: Research and Practice, 32*(2), 194–199. https://doi.org/10.1037/0735-7028.32.2.194

Robinson, M. (2020). Two-Spirit identity in a time of gender fluidity. *Journal of Homosexuality, 67*(12), 1675–1690. https://doi.org/10.1080/00918369.2019.1613853

Roe v. Wade, 410 U.S. 113 (1973).

Rogers, C. R. (1951). *Client-centered therapy, its current practice, implications, and theory.* Houghton Mifflin.

Rogers, C. R. (1957). The necessary and sufficient conditions of therapeutic personality change. *Journal of Consulting Psychology, 21*(2), 95–103. https://doi.org/10.1037/h0045357

Rogers, C. R. (1961). *On becoming a person: A therapist's view of psychotherapy.* Constable.

Rogers-Sirin, L., Melendez, F., Refano, C., & Zegarra, Y. (2015). Immigrant perceptions of therapists' cultural competence: A qualitative investigation. *Professional Psychology: Research and Practice, 46*(4), 258–269. https://doi.org/10.1037/pro0000033

Root, M. P. P. (1990). Resolving "other" status: Identity development of biracial individuals. In L. S. Brown & M. P. P. Root (Eds.), *Diversity and complexity in feminist theory* (pp. 185–205). Haworth.

Rosario, R. J., Minor, I., & Rogers, L. O. (2021). "Oh, you're pretty for a dark-skinned girl": Black adolescent girls' identities and resistance to colorism. *Journal of Adolescent Research, 36*(5), 501–534.

Rosenberg, C. (1995). *The care of strangers: The rise of America's hospital system.* John Hopkins University Press.

Rosenkrantz, D. E., Black, W. W., Abreu, R. L., Aleshire, M. E., & Fallin-Bennett, K. (2017). Health and health care of rural sexual and gender minorities: A systematic review. *Stigma and Health, 2*(3), 229. https://doi.org/10.1037/sah0000055

Ross, T. (2015, September 8). *30 years later, 'The Golden Girls' is still the most progressive show on television.* Medium. https://medium.com/@traceylross/30-years-later-the-golden-girls-is-still-the-most-progressive-show-on-television-b63aadd2edec

Rovitto, T. L. (2020a). (Cultural) humility in practice: Engaging first-generation college students. *Journal of College Student Psychotherapy, 36*(6), 1–16. https://doi.org/10.1080/87568225.2020.1819924

Rovitto, T. L. (2020b). (Cultural) humility in practice: Engaging first-generation college students. *Journal of College Student Psychotherapy, 36*(3), 294–309.

Royal Commission on Aboriginal Peoples. (2016). *Report of the Royal Commission on Aboriginal Peoples.* Government of Canada. https://www.bac-lac.gc.ca/eng/discover/aboriginal-heritage/royal-commission-aboriginal-peoples/Pages/final-report.aspx

Rubin, M., & Stuart, R. (2017). Kill or cure? Different types of social class identification amplify and buffer the relation between social class and mental health. *Journal of Social Psychology, 158*, 236 – 251. https://doi.org10.3102/0013189X14528373

Ruiz, N. G., Horowitz, J., & Tamir, C. (2020, July 1). *Many Black and Asian Americans say they have experienced discrimination amid the COVID-19 outbreak.* Pew Research Center. https://www.pewresearch.org/social-trends/2020/07/01/many-black-and-asian-americans-say-they-have-experienced-discrimination-amid-the-covid-19-outbreak/

Runnels, R. C., & Thompkins, A. (2020). Using Fowler's stages of faith to understand the development of aspiring social workers. *Social Work & Christianity, 47*(4), 19–29. https://doi.org/10.34043/swc.v47i3.80

Rybak, C., & Decker-Fitts, A. (2009). Understanding Native American healing practices. *Counselling Psychology Quarterly, 22*(3), 333–342. https://doi.org/10.1080/09515070903270900

tripart -Ouriaghli, I., Godfrey, E., Bridge, L., Meade, L., & Brown, J.S.L. (2019). Improving mental health service utilization among men: A systematic review and synthesis of behavior change techniques within interventions targeting help-seeking. *American Journal of Men's Health, 13*(3). https://doi.org/10.1177/1557988319857009

Salmon, L. (2017). The four questions: A framework for integrating an understanding of oppression dynamics in clinical work and supervision. In R. Allan & S. S. Poulsen (Eds.), *Creating cultural safety in couple and family therapy* (pp. 11–22). AFTA Springer Briefs in Family Therapy. https://doi.org/10.1007/978-3-319-64617-6

Samers, M., & Collyer, M. (2017). *Migration* (2nd ed.). Routledge. http://dx.doi.org/10.4324/9781315684307

Savage, T. A., Harley, D. A., & Nowak, T. M. (2005). Applying social empowerment strategies as tools for self-advocacy in counseling and lesbian and gay male clients. *Journal of Counseling & Development, 83*(2), 131–137. https://doi.org/10.1002/j.1556-6678.2005.tb00589.x

Schafer, M. H., & Shippee, T. P. (2010). Age identity in context: Stress and the subjective side of aging. *Social Psychology Quarterly, 73*(3), 245–264. https://doi.org/10.1177/0190272510379751

Scharron-del Rio, M. R. (2017). Teaching at the intersections: Liberatory and anti-oppressive pedagogical praxis in the multicultural counseling classroom as a queer Puerto Rican educator. *Feminist Teacher, 27*(2–3), 90–105.

Scheim, A. I., Perez-Brumer, A. G., & Bauer, G. R. (2020). Gender-concordant identity documents and mental health among transgender adults in the USA: A cross-sectional study. *The Lancet: Public Health, 5*(4), E196–E203. https://doi.org/10.1016/S2468-2667(20)30032-3

Scherrer, K. S. (2008). Coming to an asexual identity: Negotiating Identity, negotiating desire. Sexualities, *11*(5), 621–641. https://doi.org/10.1177/1363460708094269

Schlosser, L. Z. (2003). Christian privilege: Breaking a sacred taboo. Journal of Multicultural Counseling and Development, 31(1), 44–51. https://doi.org/10.1002/j.2161-1912.2003.tb00530.x

Schmalbach, I., Albani, C., Perowski, K., & Brähler, E. (2022). Client-therapist dyads and therapy outcome: Does sex matching matters? A cross-sectional study. *BMC Psychology*, *52*(10), 1–13. https://doi.org/10.1186/s40359-022-00761-4

Schmalz, H. (2021). *Fatphobia as marginalization: The impacts on women in the public sphere.*

Schmitz, R. M., & Tyler, K. A. (2019). 'Life has actually become more clear': An examination of resilience among LGBTQ young adults. *Sexualities*, *22*(4), 710–733. https://doi.org/10.1177/1363460718770451

Schvey, N. A., Puhl, R. M., & Brownell, K. D. (2014). The stress of stigma: Exploring the effect of weight stigma on cortisol reactivity. *Psychosomatic Medicine*, *76*(2), 156–162.

Schwartz, R. C., & Blankenship, D. M. (2014). Racial disparities in psychotic disorder diagnosis: A review of empirical literature. *World Journal of Psychiatry*, *4*(4), 133.

Schwartz, S. J., Unger, J. B., Zamboanga, B. L., & Szapocznik, J. (2010). Rethinking the concept of acculturation: Implications for theory and research. American Psychologist, 65, 237–251. https://doi.org/10.1037/a0019330

Scuro, J., Reynolds, J. M., Havis, D. N., & Brown, L. X. Z. (2018). *Addressing ableism: philosophical questions via disability studies*. Lexington Books.

Sears, B. & Mallory, C. (2011). Documented evidence of employment discrimination & it's effects on LGBT people. *The University of California School of Law*. https://escholarship.org/content/qt03m1g5sg/qt03m1g5sg.pdf?t=mccaje

Seaton, E. K., Gee, G. C., Neblett, E., & Spanierman, L. (2018). New directions for racial discrimination research as inspired by the integrative model. *American Psychologist*, *73*(6), 768–780. https://doi.org/10.1037/amp0000315

Seifert, T. (2007). Understanding Christian privilege: Managing the tensions of spiritual plurality. *About Campus*, *12*(2), 10–17. https://doi.org/10.1002/abc.206

Shafranske, E. P. (1996). Religious beliefs, affiliations, and practices of clinical psychologists. In E. P. Shafranske (Ed.), *Religion and the clinical practice of psychology* (pp. 149–162). American Psychological Association. https://doi.org/10.1037/10199-005

Shakespeare, T. (2018). *Disability: The basics*. Routledge.

Shakespeare, T., Watson, N., & Alghaib, O. A. (2017). Blaming the victim, all over again: Waddell and Aylward's biopsychosocial (BPS) model of disability. *Critical Social Policy*, *37*(1), 22–41. https://doi.org/10.1177/0261018316649120

Shangani, S., Gamarel, K. E., Ogunbajo, A., Cai, J., & Operario, D. (2020). Intersectional minority stress disparities among sexual minority adults in the USA: The role of race/ethnicity and socioeconomic status. *Culture, Health & Sexuality*, *22*(4), 398–412. https://doi.org/10.1080/13691058.2019.1604994

Sheperis, C. J., Cuff, P., & Sheperis, D. (2023). Educating professional counselors about the social determinants of mental health. *Journal of Counseling & Development*, *101*, 429–439. https://doi.org/10.1002/jcad.12486

Shewan, A. (2021). *Intersections or roots: Understanding anti-fat bias through the lens of anti-black racism and the applicability to counselling practice.*

Shore, J. H., Richardson Jr, W. J., Bair, B., & Manson, S. (2015). Traditional healing concepts and psychiatry: Collaboration and integration in psychiatric practice. *Psychiatric Times, 32*(6), 1–5.

Sigelman, C. K., & Rider, E. A. (2022). *Lifespan: Human development* (10th ed.). Cengage.

Silva, N. K. (2000). Kanawai e ho'opau i na hula kuolo Hawai'i: The political economy of banning the hula. *Hawaii Journal of History, 34*, 29–48. http://evols.library.manoa.hawaii.edu/handle/10524/347

Simmons University Library. (2019). *Anti-oppression: Anti-transmisia*. https://simmons.libguides.com/anti-oppression/anti-transmisia

Simmons University Library. (2022, December 21). *Anti-oppression: Anti-fatmisia*. https://simmons.libguides.com/anti-oppression/anti-fatmisia

Simons, J., Grant, L., & Rodas, J. M. (2020). Transgender people of color: Coping and support during the school-age years. https://doi.org/10.31235/osf.io/epdsx

Simons, J., Grant, L., & Rodas, J. (2021) Transgender people of color: Experiences and coping during the school-age years. *Journal of LGBTQ Issues in Counseling, 15*(1), 16–37. https://doi.org/10.1080/15538605.2021.1868380

Singer, B. & Deschamps, D. (2017). *LGBTQ stats: Lesbian, gay, bisexual, transgender, and queer people by the numbers*. The New Press.

Singer, J. (1998). *Odd people in: The birth of community amongst people on the autistic spectrum. A personal exploration based on neurological diversity* [Honors thesis, University of Technology, Sydney], 1–56. https://www.academia.edu/27033194/Odd_People_In_The_Birth_of_Community_amongst_people_on_the_Autistic_Spectrum_A_personal_exploration_based_on_neurological_diversity

Singer, J. (n.d.). What is neurodiversity? *Reflections on Neurodiversity*. https://neurodiversity2.blogspot.com/p/what.html

Singh, A.A., Appling, B., & Trepal, H. (2020), Using the multicultural and social justice counseling competencies to decolonize counseling practice: The important roles of theory, power, and action. *Journal of Counseling & Development, 98*, 261–271. https://doi.org/10.1002/jcad.12321

Singh A. A., Hwhang S. J., Chang, S. C., & White, B. (2017). Affirmative counseling with trans/gender-variant people of color. In A. A. Singh & L. M. Dickey (Eds.). *Trans-affirmative counseling and psychological practice*. American Psychological Association.

Singh, A. A., Nassar-McMillan, S., Butler, S. K., & McCullough, J. R. (2016). Multicultural and social justice counseling competencies: Guidelines for the counseling profession. *Journal of Multicultural Counseling and Development, 44*(1), 28–48. https://doi.org/10.1002/jmcd.12035

Sink, C. A., & Ockerman, M. S. (2016). Introduction to the special issue—school counselors and a multitiered system of supports: Cultivating systemic change and equitable outcomes. *The Professional Counselor, 6*(3), v–ix. https://doi.org/10.15241/csmo.6.3.v

Skaistis, S., Cook, J. M., Nair, D., & Borden, S. (2018). A content analysis of intake paperwork: An exploration of how clinicians ask about gender, sex, and sexual/affectual orientation. *Journal of LGBT Issues in Counseling, 12*(2), 87–100. http://dx.doi.org/10.1080/15538605.2018.1455555

Skerrett, K., Spira, M., & Chandy, J. (2022). Emerging elderhood: Transitions from midlife. *Clinical Social Work Journal, 50*(4), 377–386. https://doi.org/10.1007/s10615-021-00791-2

Smart, J. (2019). *Disability across the developmental lifespan*. (2nd ed.). Springer.

Smart, J. F. (2009). The power of models of disability. *Journal of Rehabilitation*, *75*(2), 3–11. http://www.nationalrehab.org/website/pubs/index.html

Smart, J. F. & Smart, D. W. (2006). Models of disability: Implications for the counseling profession. *Journal of Counseling and Development*, *84*(1), 29–40. http://doi.org/10.1002/j.1556-6678.2006

Smedley, A., & Smedley, B. D. (2005). Race as biology is fiction, racism as a social problem is real: Anthropological and historical perspectives on the social construction of race. *American Psychologist*, *60*(1), 16–26. https://doi.org/10.1037/0003-066X.60.1.16

Smith, E. J., (2006). The strengths-based counseling model. *The Counseling Psychologist*, *34*(1), 13–79. http://doi.org/10.1177/0011000005277018

Smith, E. R., Perrin, P. B., & Sutter, M. E. (2020). Factor analysis of the heterosexist harassment, rejection, and discrimination scale in lesbian, gay, bisexual, transgender, and queer people of colour. *International Journal of Psychology*, *55*(3), 405–412.

Smith, L. (2005). Psychotherapy, classism, and the poor: Conspicuous by their absence. *American Psychologist*, *60*(7), 687–696. http://dx.doi.org/10.1037/0003-066X.60.7.687

Smith, L., Li, V., Dykema, S., Hamlet, D., & Shellman, A. (2013). "Honoring somebody that society doesn't honor": Therapists working in the context of poverty. *Journal of Clinical Psychology*, *69*(2), 138–151. http://dx.doi.org/10.1002/jclp.21953

Smith, S. D., Reynolds, C. A, & Rovnak, A (2009). A critical analysis of the social advocacy movement in counseling. *Journal of Counseling & Development*, *87*, 483–491. https://doi.org/10.1002/j.1556-6678.2009.tb00133.x

Smith, S. L., Pieder, K., & Choueiti, M. (2017). Seniors on the small screen: Aging in popular television content. *Media, Diversity, & Social Change Initiative*. USC Annenberg. http://assets.uscannenberg.org/docs/Seniors_on_the_Small_Screen-Dr_Stacy_L_Smith_9-12-17.pdf

Smith, T. B., & Trimble, J. E. (2016). Matching clients with therapists on the basis of race or ethnicity: A meta-analysis of clients' level of participation in treatment. In *Foundations of Multicultural Psychology: Research to Inform Effective Practice* (pp. 115–128). American Psychological Association. http://www.jstor.org/stable/j.ctv1chs8nz.9

Smuts, B. (1985). The evolutionary origins of patriarchy. *Human Nature*, *6*(1), 1–32.

Snow, J. (2019, May 14). Portraits of gender and sexual identities in the Hawaiian community. *Honolulu Magazine*. https://www.honolulumagazine.com/portraits-of-gender-and-sexual-identities-in-the-hawaiian-community/

Snow, K. C., Harrichand, J. J. S., & Mwendwa, J. M. (2021). Advocacy and social justice approaches with immigrants and refugees in counsellor education. *Canadian Journal of Counselling and Psychotherapy*, *55*(1), 7–27. https://doi.org/10.47634/cjcp.v55i1.68482

Snow, K. C., Mwendwa, J. M., & Harrichand, J. J. S. (2020). Getting personal with immigrants and refugees: Advocacy and social justice counseling concerns. In M. Pope, M. Gonzalez, E. Cameron, & J. S. Pangelinan (Eds.), *Social justice and advocacy in counseling: Experiential activities for teaching* (1st ed., pp. 132–137). Routledge. http://dx.doi.org/10.4324/9781315180687-34

Social Security Administration. (2023). *Fact sheet Social Security*. https://www.ssa.gov/news/press/factsheets/basicfact-alt.pdf

Sommers-Flanagan, J. (2015). Evidence-based relationship practice: Enhancing counselor competence. *Journal of Mental Health Counseling, 37*(2), 95–108. http://dx.doi.org/10.17744/mehc.37.2.g13472044600588r

Song, S. J. (2021). Mental health of unaccompanied children: Effects of U.S. immigration policies. *BJPsych Open, 7*(6). https://doi.org/10.1192/bjo.2021.1016

Sotero, M. (2006). A conceptual model of historical trauma: Implications for public health practice and research. *Journal of Health Disparities Research and Practice, 1*(1), 93–108.

Sperry, J., & Sperry, L. (2020). Case conceptualization: Key to highly effective counseling. *Counseling Today.* https://ct.counseling.org/2020/12/case-conceptualization-key-to-highly-effective-counseling/

Spreckley, M., Seidell, J., & Halberstadt, J. (2021). Perspectives into the experience of successful, substantial long-term weight-loss maintenance: A systematic review. *International Journal of Qualitative Studies on Health and Well-Being, 16*(1), 1862481.

Stanton, A. G., Jerald, M. C., Ward, L. M., & Avery, L. R. (2017). Social media contributions to strong Black woman ideal endorsement and Black women's mental health. *Psychology of Women Quarterly, 41*(4), 465–478.

Stapleton, D. C., O'Day, B. L., Livermore, G. A., & Imparato, A. J. (2006). Dismantling the poverty trap: Disability policy for the twenty-first century. *Milbank Quarterly, 84*(4), 701–732. https://doi.org/10.1111/j.1468-0009.2006.00465.x

Stephan, R. (2021, April 30). *The story of Arab Americans' beginning in America—and the quest for fair representation.* US Department of State. https://www.state.gov/dipnote-u-s-department-of-state-official-blog/the-story-of-arab-americans-beginning-in-america-and-the-quest-for-fair-representation/

Stevens, G., & Featherman, D. L. (1981). A revised socioeconomic index of occupational status. *Social Science Research, 10*(4), 364–395. https://doi.org/10.1016/0049-089X(81)90011-9

Stewart, H., Jameson, J. P., & Curtin, L. (2015). The relationship between stigma and self-reported willingness to use mental health services among rural and urban older adults. *Psychological Services, 12*(2), 141–148. https://doi.org/10.1037/a0038651

Stewart, J. L. & Wiener, K. K. K. (2021). Does supervisor gender moderate the mediation of job embeddedness between LMX and job satisfaction? *Gender in Management, 36*(4), 536–552. https://doi.org/10.1108/GM-07-2019-0137

Stonequist, E. V. (1937). *The marginal man: a study in personality and culture conflict.* Scribner/Simon & Schuster.

Strand, M., & Bäärnhielm, S. (2021). Could the DSM-5 cultural formulation interview hold therapeutic potential? Suggestions for further exploration and adaptation within a framework of therapeutic assessment. *Culture, Medicine, and Psychiatry, 46*(4), 846–863. https://doi.org/10.1007/s11013-021-09761-2

Strings, S. (2019). *Fearing the black body.* New York University Press.

Strum, D. C., Daniels, J., Metz, A. L., Stauffer, M., Reese, R., Milner, R., & Torres-Rivera, E. (2020). *Empower clients to address the mental health impacts of climate change, 1—14.* Counseling.org. https://www.counseling.org/docs/default-source/resources-for-counselors/climate-change-fact-sheet-revised.pdf?sfvrsn=3004292c_4

Su, L., Monga, A. S., & Jiang, Y. (2021). How life-role transitions shape consumer responses to brand extensions. *Journal of Marketing Research, 58*(3), 579–594. https://doi.org/10.1177/0022243720986546

Substance Abuse and Mental Health Services Administration (SAMHSA). (2014). *SAMHSA's concept of trauma and guidance for a trauma-informed approach.* HHS Publication No. (SMA)-14-4884.

Substance Abuse and Mental Health Services Administration (SAMHSA). (2015). *Screening and assessment of co-occurring disorders in the justice system.* HHS Publication No. (SMA)-15-4930.

Substance Abuse and Mental Health Services Administration (SAMHSA). (2017). *Racial/Ethnic Differences in Substance Use, Substance Use Disorders, and Substance Use Treatment Utilization among People Aged 12 or Older (2015–2019).* https://www.samhsa.gov/data/sites/default/files/reports/rpt35326/2021NSDUHSUChartbook102221B.pdf

Substance Abuse and Mental Health Services Administration (SAMHSA). (2022). *Key substance use and mental health indicators in the United States: Results from the 2021 National Survey on Drug Use and Health* (HHS Publication No. PEP22-07-01-005, NSDUH Series H-57). Center for Behavioral Health Statistics and Quality, Substance Abuse and Mental Health Services Administration. https://www.samhsa.gov/data/report/2021-nsduh-annual-national-report

Sue, S., & Sue, D. W. (1971). Chinese American personality and mental health. *Amerasian Journal*, 1, 36–49.

Sue, D. W. (2001). Multidimensional facets of cultural competence. *The Counseling Psychologist, 29*(6), 790–821. https://doi.org/10.1177/0011000001296002

Sue, D. W. (2021). Microaggressions: Death by a thousand cuts. *Scientific American*, 48–50.

Sue, D. W., Bernier, J. E., Durran, A., Feinberg, L., Pedersen, P., Smith, E. J., & Vasquez-Nuttall, E. (1982). Position paper: Cross-cultural counseling competencies. *The Counseling Psychologist, 10*(2), 45–52. https://doi.org/10.1177/0011000082102008

Sue, D. W., Capodilupo, C. M., Torino, G. C., Bucceri, J. M., Holder, A., Nadal, K. L., & Esquilin, M. (2007). Racial microaggressions in everyday life: Implications for clinical practice. *American Psychologist, 62*(4), 271.

Sue, D. W., & Sue, D. (1999). Racial and cultural identity development: Therapeutic implications. In D. W. Sue & D. Sue (Eds), *World views in multicultural counselling and therapy* (pp. 121–142). John Wiley & Sons.

Sue, D. W., Sue, D., Neville, H. A., & Smith, L. (2013). Asian American identity models. In *Counseling the culturally diverse: Theory and practice* (pp. 293–295). Wiley.

Sue, D. W., Sue, D., Neville, H. A., & Smith, L. (2022). *Counseling the culturally diverse: Theory and practice.* John Wiley & Sons.

Sue, D. W., Arredondo, P., & McDavis, R. J. (1992). Multicultural counseling competencies and standards: A call to the profession. *Journal of Counseling & Development, 70*(4), 477–486. https://doi.org/10.1002/j.1556-6676.1992.tb01642.x

Sue, S. (2003). In defense of cultural competency in psychotherapy and treatment. *American Psychologist, 58*(11), 964.

Suprina, J. S., Matthew, C. H., Kakkar, S., Harrell, D., Brace, A., Sadler-Gerhardt, C., Kocet, M. M. & Association for Lesbian, Gay, Bisexual, and Transgender Issues in Counseling (ALGBTIC). (2019). Best practices in cross-cultural counseling: The intersection of spiritual/religious identity and affectional/sexual identity. *Journal of LGBT Issues in Counseling, 13*(4), 293–325. https://doi.org/10.1080/15538605.2019.1662360

Tajfel, H. (1979). Individuals and groups in social psychology. *British Journal of Social and Clinical Psychology, 18*(2), 183–190. https://doi.org/10.1111/j.2044-8260.1979.tb00324.x

Tatum, B. D. (2001). *Defining racism:"Can we talk?"*

Taylor, Y., & Becker, M. J. (1999). *I was born a slave. An anthology of classic slave narratives, two volumes.* Lawrence Hill Books.

Tello, A. M. (2015). *The psychosocial experiences of Latina first-generation college graduates who received financial and cultural capital support: A constructivist grounded theory* [Doctoral dissertation].

Tello, A. M. (2020). Lucia's journey of bridging two worlds: Counseling Latinx first-generation college students. In B. C. King & T. A Steward (Eds.), *Cases on cross-cultural counseling strategies.* IGI Global.

Tello, A. M., & Lonn, M. R. (2017). The role of high school and college counselors in supporting the psychosocial and emotional needs of Latinx first-generation college students. *The Professional Counselor, 7*(4), 349–359. https://doi.org/10.5241/amt.7.4.349

Terlizzi, E. P. & Schiller, J. S. (2022). *Mental health treatment among adults aged 18–44: United States (2019–2021).* NCHS Data Brief, no 444. National Center for Health Statistics. https://dx.doi.org/10.15620/cdc:120293.

Terry, R. W. (1981). The negative impact on white values. In B. P. Bowser & R. G. Hunt (Eds.), *Impacts of racism on white Americans* (pp. 119–151). Sage Publications.

Tervalon, M., & Murray-García, J. (1998). Cultural humility versus cultural competence: A critical distinction in defining physician training outcomes in multicultural education. *Journal of Health Care for the Poor and Underserved*, 9(2), 117–125. https://doi.org/10.1353/hpu.2010.0233

Thacker, N., & Barrio Minton, C. A. (2021). Minoritized professionals' experiences in counselor education: A review of research. *Counselor Education and Supervision, 60*(1), 35–50. https://doi.org/10.1002/ceas.12195

The Church of Jesus Christ of Latter-day Saint in the Philippines. (n.d.). *Polygamy: What Latter-Day Saints really believe.* https://ph.churchofjesuschrist.org/polygamy-mormons-plural-marriage

The Sentencing Project. (2018). *Report of the Sentencing Project to the United Nations Special Rapporteur on contemporary forms of racism, racial discrimination, xenophobia, and related intolerance: Regarding racial disparities in the United States criminal justice system.* The Sentencing Project. https://www.sentencingproject.org/publications/un-report-on-racial-disparities/

Theoretical Framework. (n.d.). Santa Clara University. https://www.scu.edu/oml/about-us/theoretical-framework/

The White House. (2021). *A proclamation on Indigenous Peoples' Day, 2021.* The White House. https://www.whitehouse.gov/briefing-room/presidential-actions/2021/10/08/a-proclamation-indigenous-peoples-day-2021/

Thomas, M. E., Moye, R., Henderson, L., & Horton, H. D. (2018). Separate and unequal: The impact of socioeconomic status, segregation, and the great recession on racial disparities in housing values. *Sociology of Race and Ethnicity, 4*(2), 229–244.

Thomas, S. L., Hyde, J., Karunaratne, A., Herbert, D., & Komesaroff, P. A. (2008). Being 'fat' in today's world: A qualitative study of the lived experiences of people with obesity in Australia. *Health Expectations, 11*(4), 321–330.

Thomason, T. C. (2011). Best practice in counseling Native Americans. *Journal of Indigenous Research, 1*(1), Article 3.

Thompson, J., & Lowry, D. (2016). The girls and the "others": Analyzing villainy in the first season of *The Powerpuff Girls. Unconventional Wisdom: University of Montevallo TRIO McNair Scholars Program*

2016 Research Journal, 4, 242–283. https://www.montevallo.edu/wp-content/uploads/2018/09/journal-2016-complete.pdf

Tobin-Tyler, E. T., & Brockmann, B. (2017). Returning home: Incarceration, reentry, stigma and the perpetuation of racial and socioeconomic health inequity. *Journal of Law, Medicine & Ethics, 45*(4), 545–557. https://doi.org/10.1177/1073110517750595

Todres, J., & Villamizar Fink, D. (2020). The Trauma of Trump's family separation and child detention actions: A children's rights perspective. *Wash. L. Rev., 95*, 377.

Tokar, D. M., & Swanson, J. L. (1991). An investigation of the validity of Helms's (1984) model of white racial identity development. *Journal of Counseling Psychology, 38*(3), 296–301. https://doi.org/10.1037/0022-0167.38.3.296

Tomiyama, A. J., Epel, E. S., McClatchey, T. M., Poelke, G., Kemeny, M. E., McCoy, S. K., & Daubenmier, J. (2014). Associations of weight stigma with cortisol and oxidative stress independent of adiposity. *Health Psychology, 33*(8), 862.

Toomey, & Carlson, R. G. (2022). Leaning into student discomfort with LGBTQ issues in the counselor education classroom. *Journal of LGBTQ Issues in Counseling, 16*(1), 86–103. https://doi.org/10.1080/15538605.2021.1972895

Toporek, R. L. (2013). Social class, classism, and social justice. In W.M. Liu (Ed.). *The Oxford handbook of social class in counseling* (pp. 3–20). Oxford University Press.

Toporek, R. L., & Daniels, J. (2018). *American counseling association advocacy competencies: Updated.* American Counselling Association.

Tran, T. S., & Rubel, D. J., 2022. *Two interpretative phenomenological analysis studies: How American midwestern white school counselors experience developing cultural humility and experience cultural humility while working with students of color.* [Doctoral Thesis, Oregon State University]. Oregon State University Scholars Archive. https://ir.library.oregonstate.edu/concern/graduate_thesis_or_dissertations/j098zj83g

Trepal, H., Tello, A. M., Haiyasoso, M., Castellon, N., Garcia, J., & Martinez-Smith, C. (2019). Supervision strategies used to support Spanish-speaking bilingual counselors. *Teaching and Supervision in Counseling, 1*(1), 19–32. https://doi.org/10.7290/tsc010103

Trevino, R. R. (2006*). The church in the barrio: Mexican American ethno-Catholicism in Houston.* The University of North Carolina Press.

The Trevor Project. (2022). Homelessness and Housing Instability Among LGBTQ Youth https://www.thetrevorproject.org/wp-content/uploads/2022/02/Trevor-Project-Homelessness-Report.pdf

Trippany, R. L., Kress, V. E. W., & Wilcoxon, S. A. (2004). Preventing vicarious trauma: What counselors should know when working with trauma survivors. *Journal of Counseling & Development, 82*(1), 31–37.

Trombley, J., & Chalupka, S. (2017). Climate change and mental health. *American Journal of Nursing, 117*(4), 44–52. https://doi.org/10.1097/01.NAJ.0000515232.51795.fa

Trott, A., & Reeves, A. (2018). Social class and the therapeutic relationship: The perspective of therapists as clients. A qualitative study using a questionnaire survey. *Counseling and Psychotherapy Research, 18*(2), 166–177. https://doi.org/10.1002/capr.12163

Tskhay, K. O., & Rule, N. O. (2015). Sexual orientation across culture and time. In S. Safdar, & N. Kosakowska-Berezecka (Eds.), *Psychology of gender through the lens of culture: Theories and applications* (pp. 55–73). Springer.

Tuck, E. (2009). Suspending damage: A letter to communities. *Harvard Educational Review, 79*, 409–427. https://doi.org/10.17763/haer.79.3.n0016675661t3n15

Tulchinsky, T., & Varavikova, E. (2000). *The new public health: An introduction for the 21st century* (1st ed.). Academic Press.

Tulshyan, R. (2022). We need to retire the term "microaggressions." *Harvard Business Review.* https://hbr.org/2022/03/we-need-to-retire-the-term-microaggressions

US Citizenship and Immigration Services. (2020 July 30). *Early American immigration policies.* https://www.uscis.gov/about-us/our-history/overview-of-ins-history/early-american-immigration-policies#:~:-text=The%20general%20Immigration%20Act%20of,for%20new%20federal%20enforcement%20authorities.

U. S. Constitution, Amendment 1.

U.S. Bureau of Labor Statistics, (2019). *Employed persons by detailed occupation, sex, race, and Hispanic or Latino ethnicity.* U.S. Bureau of Labor Statistics (bls.gov)

U.S. Bureau of Labor Statistics. (n.d.). *Standard occupational classification.* https://www.bls.gov/soc/2018/#classification

U.S. Census Bureau. (2019). *American community survey.* https://www.census.gov/programs-surveys/acs

U.S. Census Bureau. (2022). *Quick facts.* https://www.census.gov/quickfacts/fact/table/US/RHI225222

U.S. Census Bureau. (2023a). *Annual estimates of the resident population by sex, race, and hispanic origin for the United States: April 1, 2020 to July 1, 2022.* https://www.census.gov/newsroom/facts-for-features/2023/hispanic-heritage-month.html#:~:text=63.7%20million,19.1%25%20of%20the%20total%20population.

U.S. Census Bureau. (2023b). *Multiracial heritage week; June 7–14, 2023.* https://www.census.gov/newsroom/stories/multiracial-heritage-week.html

U.S. Citizenship and Immigration Services (USCIS). (2020a). *Early American immigration policies.* https://www.uscis.gov/about-us/our-history/history-office-and-library/our-history/overview-of-ins-history/early-american-immigration-policies

U.S. Citizenship and Immigration Services (USCIS). (2020b). *Refugee timeline.* https://www.uscis.gov/about-us/our-history/history-office-and-library/featured-stories-from-the-uscis-history-office-and-library/refugee-timeline

U.S. Customs and Border Patrol (USCBP). (2023, July 24). *Border wall system.* https://www.cbp.gov/border-security/along-us-borders/border-wall-system

U.S. Department of Justice (DOJ). (n.d.). *Introduction to the Americans with Disabilities Act.* https://www.ada.gov/topics/intro-to-ada/

U.S. Department of State. (2022, March 31). *X gender marker available on U.S. passports starting April 11* [Press release]. https://www.state.gov/x-gender-marker-available-on-u-s-passports-starting-april-11/

U.S. Environmental Protections Agency (EPA). (2022a). *Climate change indicators: Weather and climate.* https://www.epa.gov/climate-indicators/weather-climate

U.S. Environmental Protections Agency (EPA). (2022b). *Frequently asked questions about climate change.* https://www.epa.gov/climatechange-science/frequently-asked-questions-about-climate-change#climate-change

U.S. Environmental Protections Agency (EPA). (2022c). *Basics of climate change.* https://www.epa.gov/climatechange-science/basics-climate-change

U.S. Environmental Protections Agency (EPA). (2022d). *Inventory of U.S. greenhouse gas emissions and sinks*: 1990–2020. 1–841. https://www.epa.gov/system/files/documents/2022-04/us-ghg-inventory-2022-main-text.pdf

U.S. Environmental Protections Agency (EPA). (2022e). *Impacts of climate change.* https://www.epa.gov/climatechange-science/impacts-climate-change

U.S. Environmental Protections Agency (EPA) (2022f). *View the indicators.* https://www.epa.gov/climate-indicators/view-indicators

U.S. Environmental Protection Agency (EPA). (2022g). *Understanding the connection between climate change and human health.* https://www.epa.gov/climate-indicators/understanding-connections-between-climate-change-and-human-health

U.S. Environmental Protection Agency (EPA). (2022h). *Learn about environmental justice.* https://www.epa.gov/environmentaljustice/learn-about-environmental-justice

U.S. Holocaust Memorial Museum. (n.d.). What is anti-Semitism? https://www.ushmm.org/antisemitism/what-is-antisemitism

Udo, T., Purcell, K., & Grilo, C. M. (2016). Perceived weight discrimination and chronic medical conditions in adults with overweight and obesity. *International Journal of Clinical Practice, 70*(12), 1003–1011. https://doi.org/10.1111/ijcp.12902

Ungar, M., Ghazinour, M., & Richter, J. (2013). Annual research review: What is resilience within the social ecology of human development? *Journal of Child Psychology and Psychiatry, 54*(4), 348–366. http://dx.doi.org/10.1111/jcpp.12025

United Nations Department of Economic and Social Affairs. (2017). *Population facts.* https://www.un.org/en/development/desa/population/migration/publications/populationfacts/docs/MigrationPopFacts20175.pdf

United Nations Department of Economic and Social Affairs. (n.d.). *Convention on the rights of persons with disabilities* (CRPD). https://www.un.org/development/desa/disabilities/convention-on-the-rights-of-persons-with-disabilities.html

United Nations Educational, Scientific, and Cultural Organization (UNESCO). (2020). *Poverty.* http://www.unesco.org/new/en/social-and-human-sciences/themes/international-migration/glossary/poverty/

United Nations High Commissioner for Refugees. (UNHCR; 2022). *Climate change and disaster displacement.* https://www.unhcr.org/en-us/climate-change-and-disasters.html

United Nations. (n.d.). *Shifting demographics.* https://www.un.org/en/un75/shifting-demographics

United Negro College Fund (UNCF). (2023). *K–12 disparity facts and statistics.* https://uncf.org/pages/k-12-disparity-facts-and-stats

University of Maryland Counseling Center (2016). *New peer assisted learning coordinators training manual* (Unpublished training manual). University of Maryland.

University of Nebraska-Lincoln. (2023). *LGBTQA+ center awareness days.* https://lgbtqa.unl.edu/awareness-days

University of North Carolina at Chapel Hill. (n.d.). *LGBTQ Resources: Asexuality, attraction, and romantic orientation.* https://lgbtq.unc.edu/resources/exploring-identities/asexuality-attraction-and-romantic-orientation/

USA.gov. (n.d.). *Federally recognized Indian tribes and resources for Native Americans*. https://www.usa.gov/indian-tribes-alaska-native

Van Breda, A. D. (2018). A critical review of resilience theory and its relevance for social work. *Social Work, 54*(1), 1–18.

Van Lith, T., Bullock, L., Horbal, I., & Lvov, A. (2017). A Brief evaluation to identify level of satisfaction of srt therapy with undergraduate Ukrainian students. *International Journal for the Advancement of Counselling 39*, 282–294. https://doi.org/10.1007/s10447-017-9297-8

Van Vleck, M. (2021, October 26). *"Kids these days": Why youth-directed ageism is an issue for everyone*. Institute for Public Health. https://publichealth.wustl.edu/kids-these-days-why-youth-directed-ageism-is-an-issue-for-everyone/

Vauclair, C-M., Hanke, K., Huang, L-L., & Abrams, D. (2017). Are Asian cultures really less ageist than Western ones? It depends on the questions. *International Journal of Psychology, 52*(2), 136–144. https://doi.org/10.1002/ijop.12292

Vejar, C. M., & Quach, A. S. (2013). Sex slavery in Thailand. https://www.semanticscholar.org/paper/Sex-Slavery-in-Thailand-Vejar-Quach/af286e13fc88636ed6be1d3f2179835a0693663c

Vélez, V. N. (2016). Organizing for change: Latinx im/migrant parents, school decision-making, and the racial politics of parent leadership in social reform. *Association of Mexican American Educators Journal, 10*(3), 108–125. https://eric.ed.gov/?id=EJ1124412

Vera, E. M., & Speight, S. L. (2003). Multicultural competence, social justice, and counseling psychology: Expanding our roles. *The Counseling Psychologist, 31*(3), 253–272. https://doi.org/10.1177/0011000003031003001

Vespa, J., Medina, L., and Armstrong, D. M., (2022). *Demographic turning points for the United States: Population projections for 2020 to 2060.* Current Population Reports, P25-1144, U.S. Census Bureau. https://www.census.gov/content/dam/Census/library/publications/2020/demo/p25-1144.pdf

Villalba, J. A. (2009). Addressing immigrant and refugee issues in multicultural counselor education. *Journal of Professional Counseling, Practice, Theory, & Research, 37*(1), 1–12. https://doi.org/110.1080/15566382.2009.12033851

Vontress, C. E. (2011). Social class influences on counseling. *Counseling and Human Development, 44*, 1–12.

Vrtis, C. (2022). Defending the Patriarchy: The monstrous (queer) other and the anti-carnivalesque. In Chemers, M., & Santana, A. (Eds.), *Monsters in performance: Essays on the aesthetics of disqualification* (1st ed., pp. 99–110). Routledge. https://doi.org/10.4324/9781003137337

Walker, A. (1983). *In search of our mothers' gardens: Womanist prose.* Houghton Mifflin Harcourt.

Walker, N. (2014). *Neurodiversity: Some basic terms and definitions* [Web log post]. http://neurocosmopolitanism.com/neurodiversity-some-basic-terms-definitions/

Walker, N. (2021). *Neuroqueer heresies: Notes on the neurodiversity paradigm, autistic empowerment, and postmornal.* Autonomous Press. https://autonomous-press.myshopify.com/products/neuroqueer-heresies

Walker, T. L., & Bruns, K. L. (2022). Cross-racial interactions in the counselor education classroom: The impact of racial perception. *Journal of Multicultural Counseling and Development, 50*(2), 94–105.

Walton, Q. L., Campbell, R. D., & Blakey, J. M. (2021). Black women and COVID-19: The need for targeted mental health research and practice. *Qualitative Social Work, 20*(1–2), 247–255.

Wampold, B. E. (2015). How important are the common factors in psychotherapy? An update. *World Psychiatry, 14*, 270–277. https://doi:10.1002/wps.20238

Wang, D., & Chonody, J. (2013). Social workers' attitudes toward older adults: A review of the literature. *Journal of Social Work Education, 49*(1), 150–172. https://doi.org/10.1080/10437797.2013.755104

Wang, D. S., Chonody, J. M., & Krase, K. (2013). Social work faculty's knowledge of aging: Results from a national sample. *Educational Gerontology, 39*(6), 428–440. https://doi.org/10.1080/03601277.2012.7011288 Wang, M. and Dovchin, S. (2022). *"Why should I not speak my own language (Chinese) in public in America?": Linguistic racism, symbolic violence, and resistance.* TESOL J. https://doi.org/10.1002/tesq.3179

Ward v. Polite, 667 F.3d. 727 (U.S. Ct. App., 6th Cir. 2012).

Ward v. Wilbanks, 700 F. Supp. 2d. 803 (Dist. Ct., S.D. Mich. 2010).

Wardecker, B. M., & Matsick, J. L. (2020). Families of choice and community connectedness: A brief guide to the social strengths of LGBTQ older adults. *Journal of Gerontological Nursing, 46*(2). https://doi.org/10.3928/00989134-20200113-01

Warhol, L. (2011). *Native American language policy in the United States.* Center for Applied Linguistics. Heritage Language in America.

Warner, W. L., Meeker, M., & Eells, K. (1960). *Social class in America.* Harper & Row.

Warschauer, M., Donaghy, K., & Kuamoyo, H. (1997). Leoki: A powerful voice of Hawaiian language revitalization. *Computer Assisted Language Learning, 10*(4), 349–361.

Watkins, C. E., Hook, J. N., Mosher, D. K., & Callahan, J. L. (2019). Humility in clinical supervision: Fundamental, foundational, and transformational. *The Clinical Supervisor, 38*(1), 58–78.

Webb, L. M., & Chen, C. Y. (2022). The COVID-19 pandemic's impact on older adults' mental health: Contributing factors, coping strategies, and opportunities for improvement. *International Journal of Geriatric Psychiatry, 37*(1), 10.1002/gps.5647. https://doi.org/10.1002/gps.5647

Weeber, J. E. (2004). Disability community leaders' disability-identity development: A journey of integration and expansion [Unpublished doctoral dissertation]. Department of Educational Research, Leadership, and Counselor Education, North Carolina State University, Raleigh, NC.

Weikert, D. (2010). Person-centered therapy, masculinity, and violence. *The Person-Centered Journal, 17*(1–2), 100–107.

Weinberg, M. S., Williams, C. J., & Pryor, D. W. (1994). *Dual attraction: Understanding bisexuality.* Oxford University Press.

Weissman, J., Pratt, L.A., Miller, E.A., & Parker, J.D. (2015). *Serious psychological distress among adults: United States, 2009–2013.* (National Center for Health Statistics Data Brief no. 203). National Center for Health Statistics.

Wendt, D. C., & Gone, J. P. (2016). Integrating professional and indigenous therapies: An urban American Indian narrative clinical case study. *The Counseling Psychologist, 44*(5), 695–729.

West, A. (2015). A brief review of cognitive theories in gender development. *Behavioral Sciences Undergraduate Journal, 2*(1), 59–66. https://doi.org/10.29173/bsuj288

Westermann, S., Rief, W., Euteneuer, F., & Kohlmann, S. (2015). Social exclusion and shame in obesity. *Eating behaviors, 17*, 74–76. https://doi.org/10.1016/j.eatbeh.2015.01.001

Westman J. C. (1991). Juvenile ageism: unrecognized prejudice and discrimination against the young. *Child psychiatry and human development, 21*(4), 237–256. https://doi.org/10.1007/BF00705929

Whaley, B. A., & Williamson, P. (2023). The Americans with Disabilities Act, addiction, and recovery. *Journal of Vocational Rehabilitation, 58*(3), 299–305. https://doi.org/10.3233/JVR-230018

White, K. (2016). *Strains of skin tone bias: Implications for adolescent delinquency and residential segregation for blacks.* [Doctoral dissertation].

White, W. (1998). *Slaying the dragon: The history of addiction treatment and recovery in America.* Chesnut Health Systems.

Whitmarsh, L., Player, L., Jiongco, A., James, M., Williams, M., Marks, E., & Kennedy-Willams, P. (2022). Climate anxiety: What predicts it and how is it related to climate action. *Journal of Environmental Psychology, 83,* 1–10. https://doi.org/10.1016/j.jenvp.2022.101866

Wiggins-Frame, M. (2003). Integrating religion and spirituality into counseling: A comprehensive approach. Brooks/Cole-Thomson Learning.

Wiieyesinghe, C. L. (2012). The intersectional model of multiracial identity. *New Perspectives on Racial Identity Development: Integrating Emerging Frameworks*, 81.

Wilcox, C., & Lida, R. (2011). Evangelicals, the Christian right, and gay and lesbian rights in the United States: Simple and complex stories. In D. Rayside, & C. Wilcox (Eds.), *Faith, politics, and sexual diversity in Canada and the United States* (pp. 101–120). UBC Press.

Wilcox, W. B., Wang, W. R., & Mincy, R. B. (2018, July 3). *Black men are succeeding in America.* CNN. https://www.cnn.com/2018/07/03/opinions/good-news-for-black-men-in-america-opinion-wilcox-wang-mincy/index.html

Wilderson, F. B. (2010). *Red, white, and black: Cinema and the Structure of U.S. Antagonisms.* Duke University Press.

Willging, C. E., Salvador, M., & Kano, M. (2006). Brief reports: Unequal treatment: Mental health care for sexual and gender minority groups in a rural state. *Psychiatric Services, 57*(6), 867–870. https://doi.org/10.1176/ps.2006.57.6.867

Williams, D. R., Neighbors, H. W., & Jackson, J. S. (2003). Racial/ethnic discrimination and health: Community studies. *American Journal of Public Health, 93*(2), 200–208. https://doi.org/10.2105/AJPH.93.2.200

Wilson, A., Hutchinson, M., & Hurley, J. (2017). Literature review of trauma-informed care: Implications for mental health nurses working in acute inpatient settings in Australia. *International Journal of Mental Health Nursing, 26*(4), 326–343. https://doi.org/10.1111/inm.12344

Wilson, B. D. M., Choi, S. K., Harper, G. W., Lightfoot, M., Russell, S., & Meyer, I. H. (2020). Homelessness among LGBT adults in the US. *The Williams Institute.* https://williamsinstitute.law.ucla.edu/wp-content/uploads/LGBT-Homelessness-May-2020.pdf

Wilson, M. (2001). Black women and mental health: Working towards inclusive mental health services. *Feminist Review, 68*(1), 34–51.

Winant, H. (2006). Race and racism: Towards a global future. *Ethnic and Racial studies, 29*(5), 986–1003. https://hbr.org/2021/05/black-women-are-more-likely-to-start-a-business-than-white-men

Wingfield, A. H. (2007). The modern mammy and the angry Black man: African American professionals' experiences with gendered racism in the workplace. *Race, Gender & Class*, 196–212.

Winkeljohn Black, S., Gold, A. P., Hook, J. N., & Davis, D. E. (2019). Trainees' cultural humility and implicit associations about clients and religious, areligious, and spiritual identities: A mixed-method investigation. *Journal of Psychology and Theology, 47*(3), 202–216. https://doi.org/10.1177/0091647119837019

Winsor, M. (2019). Over 380,000 gallons of oil spill from Keystone pipeline in North Dakota. *ABC News*. https://abcnews.go.com/US/380000-gallons-oil-spill-keystone-pipeline-north-dakota/story?id=66683075

Wintersmith, S. (2022, March 9). *Arab Americans say the census and other forms don't consider their roots*. NPR. https://www.npr.org/2022/03/09/1085355634/arab-americans-say-the-census-and-other-forms-dont-consider-their-roots

Witherspoon, R., & Theodore, P. (2021). Exploring minority stress and resilience in a polyamorous sample. *Archives of Sexual Behavior, 50*, 1367–1388. https://doi.org/10.1007/s10508-021-01995-w

Wong, C. F., Schrager, S. M., Holloway, I. W., Meyer, I. H., Kipke, M. D. (2014). Minority stress experiences and psychological well-being: The impact of support from and connection to social networks within the Los Angeles house and ball communities. *Prevention Science, 15*, 44–55.

Woo, J. (2020). The myth of filial piety as a pillar for care of older adults among Chinese populations. *Advances in Geriatric Medicine and Research, 2*(2). https://doi.org/10.20900/agmr20200012

Wooldridge, S. (2023). Writing respectfully: *Person-first and identity-first language*. National Institutes of Health. https://www.nih.gov/about-nih/what-we-do/science-health-public-trust/perspectives/writing-respectfully-person-first-identity-first-language

World Health Organization (WHO). (n.d.). *Ageism*. World Health Organization. Retrieved April 9, 2023, from https://www.who.int/health-topics/ageism#tab=tab_1

World Health Organization. (2021, November 25). *Abortion*. https://www.who.int/news-room/fact-sheets/detail/abortion

World Population Review. (2023). *Religion by country 2023*. https://worldpopulationreview.com/country-rankings/religion-by-country

World Professional Association for Transgender Health (WPATH). (2022). Standards of care for the health and care of transgender and gender diverse people, Version 8. *International Journal of Transgender Health, 23*(S1), S1–S258. https://doi.org/10.1080/26895269.2022.2100644

Worthington, E. L., Jr., & Sandage, S. J. (2002). Religion and spirituality. In J. C. Norcross (Ed.), *Psychotherapy relationships that work: Therapist contributions and responsiveness to patients* (pp. 383–399). Oxford University Press.

Worthington, R. L., Soth-McNett, A. M., & Moreno, M. V. (2007). Multicultural counseling competencies research: A 20-year content analysis. *Journal of Counseling Psychology, 54*, 351–361.

Woulfe, J. M., & Goodman, L. A. (2020). Weaponized oppression: Identity abuse and mental health in the lesbian, gay, bisexual, transgender, and queer community. *Psychology of Violence, 10*(1), 100–109. https://doi.org/10.1037/vio0000251

Wray, M. (2006). *Not quite white: White trash and the boundaries of whiteness*. Duke University Press.

Wright State University. (2023). Division of inclusive excellence: International LGBTQA dates to know. https://www.wright.edu/inclusive-excellence/culture-and-identity-centers/lgbtqa-center/international-lgbtqa-dates-to-know

Yakushko, O., Mack, T., Iwamoto, D. (2010). Minority identity development model. In C. S. Clauss-Ehlers (Eds.), *Encyclopedia of cross-cultural school psychology*. Springer. https://doi.org/10.1007/978-0-387-71799-9_257

Yale Sustainability. (2020, November). How to support environmental justice everyday. *The Yale Sustainability Blog.* https://sustainability.yale.edu/blog/how-support-environmental-justice-everyday

Yalom, I. D. (2008). *Staring at the sun: Overcoming the terror of death.* Jossey-Bass.

Yang, M. (2020). An intimate dialogue between race and gender at women's suffrage centennial. *Humanities & Social Sciences Communications, 65*(7), 1–13. https://doi.org/10.1057/s41599-020-00554-3

Yankovsky, S. (2011). Neoliberal transitions in Ukraine: The view from psychiatry. *Anthropology of East Europe Review, 29*(1), 35–49. https://scholarworks.iu.edu/journals/index.php/aeer/article/view/1057/1146

Yearby, R. (2018). Racial disparities in health status and access to healthcare: The continuation of inequality in the United States due to structural racism. *American Journal of Economics and Sociology, 77*(3–4), 1113–1152.

Yosso, T. J. (2005). Whose culture has capital? A critical race theory discussion of community cultural wealth. *Race Ethnicity and Education, 8*(1), 69–91.

Yosso, T. J., Smith, W. A., Ceja, M., & Solórzano, D. G. (2009). Critical race theory, racial microaggressions, and campus racial climate for Latina/o undergraduates. *Harvard Educational Review, 79,* 659–690.

Young, D. M., Sanchez, D. T., Pauker, K., & Gaither, S. E. (2021). A meta-analytic review of hypodescent patterns in categorizing multiracial and racially ambiguous targets. *Personality & Social Psychology Bulletin, 47*(5), 705–727. https://doi-org.echo.louisville.edu/10.1177/0146167220941321

Young, J. S., Wiggins-Frame, M., & Cashwell, C. S. (2007). Spirituality and counselor competence: A national survey of American Counseling Association members. *Journal of Counseling & Development,* 85, 47–52.

Young, M. E. (2021). *Learning the art of helping: Building blocks and techniques.* Pearson.

Young, S. (2014, June 24). *I'm not your inspiration, thank you very much* [Video]. Ted Conferences. https://www.ted.com/talks/stella_young_i_m_not_your_inspiration_thank_you_very_much/transcript?language=en

Zayid, M. (2013, December). *I've got 99 problems … palsy is just one* [Video]. Ted Conferences.https://www.ted.com/talks/maysoon_zayid_i_got_99_problems_palsy_is_just_one

Zhang, H., Watkins Jr., C. E., Hook, J. N., Hodge, A. S., Davis, C. W., Norton, J., Wilcox, M. M., Davis, D. E., DeBlaere, C. and Owen, J. (2022). Cultural humility in psychotherapy and clinical supervision: A research review. *Counselling and Psychotherapy Research, 22*(3), 548–557.

Zhong, W., Cristofori, I., Bulbulia, J., Krueger, F., & Grafman, J. (2017). Biological and cognitive underpinnings of religious fundamentalism. *Neuropsychologia,100,* 18-25. https://doi.org/10.1016/j.neuropsychologia.2017.04.009.

Zhu, P., Isawi, D. T., & Luke, M. M. (2022b). A discourse analysis of cultural humility within counseling dyads. *Journal of Counseling & Development, 101*(2), 167–179. http://dx.doi.org/10.1002/jcad.12457

Zhu, P., Liu, Y., Luke, M. M., & Wang, Q. (2022a). The development and initial validation of the cultural humility and enactment scale in counseling. *Measurement and Evaluation in Counseling and Development, 55*(2), 98–115.

Zhu, P., Luke, M., & Bellini, J. (2021). A grounded theory analysis of cultural humility in counseling and counselor education. *Counselor Education and Supervision, 60*(1), 73–89.

Zilcha-Mano, S., Muran, J.C., Hungr, C., Eubanks, C. F., Safran, J. D., & Winston, A. (2016). The relationship between alliance and outcome: Analysis of a two-person perspective on alliance and session outcome. *Journal of Consulting and Clinical Psychology, 84*(6), 484–496. https://doi.org/10.1037/ccp0000058

Zong, J. (2022). *A mosaic, not a monolith; A profile of the US Latino population, 2000–2020.* UCLA Latino Policy & Politics Institute. https://latino.ucla.edu/research/latino-population-2000-2020/

Zyromski, B., & Dimmitt, C. (2022). Evidence-based school counseling: Embracing challenges/changes to the existing paradigm. *Professional School Counseling, 26*(1), 2156759X2210867. https://doi.org/10.1177/2156759x221086729

Index

Symbols

3-C model, 117

A

AANHPI. *See* Asian American, Native Hawaiian, and Pacific Islander
ableism, 292, 300–301. *See also* disability
ableist microaggressions, 300–301
ACA. *See* American Counseling Association (ACA)
ACA Advocacy Competencies, 108, 109
accent discrimination, 188
acceptance, 135, 140, 155
  identity, 149
  of identity society, 140
  passive, 135, 145
accessibility, 316
acculturation models, 133, 142, 199–200, 214–215
acquired disability, 155, 297, 332
active commitment, 145
active learner, 21
ADA. *See* American Disabilities Act (ADA); Americans with Disabilities Act (ADA)
adaptable and functional strengths. *See* resiliencies
ADDRESSING model, 116, 125
ADHD. *See* attention deficit hyperactivity disorder (ADHD)
adolescent lesbian and gay identity development model, 149–150
advanced directive, 342
adventitious disability, 302
advocacy, 74, 108, 286–287, 317, 379, 411–412, 465–466
  and allyship, 317
  and social justice, 104–128
  applications of, 118–121
  at macrolevel, 287
  at microlevel, 119–120, 287
  circle of influence, 118–119, 120–121
  codes, 110–112
  defined, 107–108
  ecological system and, 119
  in counseling, 117–118, 123–127
  interventions, 286–287
advocacy interventions
  and counseling, 345–346, 439–443
  music chronology, 442–443
  neurodivergence, 461
  religion and spirituality, 443
  spiritual ecomaps, 441
  spiritual genograms, 441, 442
AFAB. *See* assigned female at birth (AFAB)
affectional identity, defined, 389
affectional orientation, 385
affirmative counseling, 397
affirmative therapy, 385
age/aging/ageism, 323–350
  across the lifespan, 335–336
  age-period-cohort model, 332–334
  and environment, 332
  combating, 336–337
  counseling, 334, 339
  cultural diversity in, 326–329
  defined, 325
  developmental theories, 325–326
  discrimination, 330, 335
  historical context of, 338
  in counseling practice, 347
  intersectionality and, 336
  overview, 323
  role of ageism, 334–335
  within ecological framework, 329–332
agender, 143, 353
agents of change, 99, 127, 317
age-period-cohort model, 333
alien, 212
alloromantic, 385
allosexual, 386
Allport's scale of prejudice, 95, 96
allyship, 317
AMA. *See* American Medical Association (AMA)
AMCD. *See* Association for Multicultural Counseling and Development (AMCD)
American Counseling Association (ACA), 26, 34–36, 61, 110, 182, 226, 316, 338, 378, 396, 407, 443, 484, 517
American Disabilities Act (ADA), 468
American Indian identity development model, 136–137
American Medical Association (AMA), 368, 452
American Mental Health Counselors Association (AMHCA), 26, 36–37, 61, 111, 182, 227, 316, 346, 409, 411, 484, 485–489
American Personnel and Guidance Association (APGA). *See* American Counseling Association (ACA)
American Rehabilitation Counseling Association (ARCA), 69, 309
American School Counseling Association (ASCA), 42, 46, 51, 111, 182, 378, 379–380, 381
American School Counselor Association (ASCA), 26, 37–38, 182, 226, 316
American Society of Addiction Medicine (ASAM), 467
Americans with Disabilities Act (ADA), 294, 306
AMHCA. *See* American Mental Health Counselors Association (AMHCA)
androgyny, 353
anti-Blackness
  and racism, 453
  defined, 168
anti-semitism, 435
anti-slavery movement, 93
apparent disability, 297–298
applying the label, 150
The Arab American Institution, 174
aromantic, 386
The Art of Counseling (May), 422
ASAM. *See* American Society of Addiction Medicine (ASAM)
ASAN. *See* Autistic Self Advocacy Network (ASAN)
ASCA. *See* American School Counseling Association (ASCA)
Aschauer, W., 188
ASD. *See* Autism spectrum disorder (ASD)
ASERVIC. *See* Association for Spiritual, Ethical, and Religious Values in Counseling (ASERVIC)
asexual, 386

Asian American identity development model, 137
Asian American, Native Hawaiian, and Pacific Islander (AANHPI), 169–171
as model minorities, 170
colorism in, 169–170
counselors relationship with, 176
familial structure of, 171
history of, 169
Asian Americans from other countries and Pacific Islanders (AAPI), 137
aspirational capital, 204
assessment, 284, 482
assigned female at birth (AFAB), 428, 501
assigned sex. *See* sex
assimilation, 142
Association for Multicultural Counseling and Development (AMCD), 413, 436, 446
Association for Spiritual, Ethical, and Religious Values in Counseling (ASERVIC), 423, 436, 437, 439, 446
asylum seekers, 210, 213, 225
Atkinson, D. R., 134
attention deficit hyperactivity disorder (ADHD), 458, 459, 501, 513
Autism spectrum disorder (ASD), 297, 458, 501
Autistic Self Advocacy Network (ASAN), 457, 526
autonomy, 346, 347, 365, 402, 427, 453, 461
autonomy schema, 140
Avent, J. R., 200
awareness, 150
Awareness of Cultural Connectedness Scale (ACS), 260

B

backhanded compliments, 452
Bacon, Frances, 302
Bandura, A., 145
Barrio Minton, C. A., 118
Baumhofer, Kauʻi, 258
BCE. *See* before the common era (BCE)
Becker, Ernest, 335
before the common era (BCE), 80, 214, 423
Bell, Derrick, 9
Benjamin, Harry, 359
Benson, 422
Berry, J. W., 142, 215
Betters-Bubon, J., 506
bias, 12–13
individual, 94–95
unconscious, 22
biculturalism, 142, 192
Biden, Joe, 169, 174, 241
Big Brother, 170
Billingsley, A., 167
bi/multiracial identity development model, 133, 140–141
BIPOC. *See* Black, Indigenous, and People of Color (BIPOC)
biromantic, 386
bisexual, 386
bisexual identity development, 150–151
Black American identity development model, 137–138
Black feminism, 93–94
Black, Indigenous, and People of Color (BIPOC), 65, 133, 168, 187, 242, 472
Black Lives Matter, 164
Black people, 163–164, 165–168
and African American, 163, 165
anti-Blackness, 168
colorism in, 166–168
families of, 165–166
identity development, 137–138
racism in, 163–165, 166–168
religion and spirituality, 166
slavery of, 164, 167
Blay, Y. A., 174
bleaching syndrome, 170
Bockting, W., 144, 146
Bodner, E., 337
body mass index (BMI), 452, 453
braille, 305
brain fag syndrome, 496
Braun, Erik, 417, 427–428
Brave Heart, M.Y.H., 239
Brinkman, A. H., 308
Bronfenbrenner, U., 44, 80, 109, 119, 200, 208, 220–222, 272, 307, 329, 334, 399, 402, 430, 431
model, 325
Brown, Margaret, 83
Brown, R. A., 253
Brown-Smythe, Claudette, 230
Brown v. Board of Education, 9
Bruns, Kristin, 179
Buckland's Complete Book of Witchcraft (Buckland), 428
Buck vs.Bell, 302
Buddhism, 425–426
Burke, Tarana, 361
Burnes, D., 337
Bush, George H. W., 306
Bussey, K., 145
Butler, Robert, 334

C

Campion, A., 121
CARE model, 280
CAS. *See* counselor advocate scholar model (CAS)
case conceptualization, 482, 496–497
CASEL. *See* Collaborative for Academic, Social, and Emotional Learning (CASEL)
Cashwell, C. S, 200
Cass, V. C., 149
Caucasian, 6–7
CBT. *See* cognitive behavioral therapy (CBT)
CCMSCM. *See* contextual cohort-based, maturity, specific challenge model (CCMSCM)
CCW. *See* community cultural wealth (CCW)
CDC. *See* Centers for Disease Control and Prevention (CDC)
Centers for Disease Control and Prevention (CDC), 97, 293, 330
certified rehabilitation counselors (CRC), 11, 39, 255, 443
CFI. *See* Cultural Formulation Interview (CFI)
Chan, C. D., 116, 119
Charmaz, K., 155
chattel enslavement, 95, 162, 164
chattel slavery, 83
Chinese Exclusion Act, 169
Chisholm, Shirley, 93
Christianity, 423–424
chronic/generational poverty, 275, 276
chronic health conditions, 342, 462
chronic illness, 298–299. *See also* disability
chronosystem, 46–49, 81, 195–196, 221, 329, 365, 405
Ciftci, A., 425
circle of influence, 118–119, 120–121, 129–130
cisgender, 274, 353
cisnormativity, 353
cissexism, 353
Civil Rights Act, 306, 359, 394
Clark, M., 8, 77, 102, 265, 375, 383, 480
classism, 268–269, 272–277. *See also* social class
and counseling, 276–277
defined, 268–269
impact on poverty, 274–275
in ecological contexts, 272–273
clients empowerment, 126–127
client welfare, 346, 347, 412
client worldview, 345, 437–438

climate anxiety. *See* eco-anxiety
climate crisis
  and well-being, 470–475
  counseling in, 473–474
  ecological advocacy and, 475
  environmental justice, 472–473
  overview, 470
climate, defined, 470–471
clinical mental health counselors (CMHC), 26, 36, 234, 484
Clotida, 83
CMHC. *See* clinical mental health counselors (CMHC)
Coco, 172
COD. *See* co-occurring disorders (COD)
Coelho, Paolo, 2
cognitive behavioral therapy (CBT), 254, 337, 397, 499, 500
cognitive disabilities, 296, 297, 302
cognitive dissonance, 9
cohort, 333
Coleman, E., 144, 146, 149
Collaborative for Academic, Social, and Emotional Learning (CASEL), 507
collectivism, 19–20, 192–193
colonization, 238–239, 251, 253–254
color-based discrimination. *See* colorism
color-blindness, 139
colorism, 160, 162, 166–170. *See also* race/racism
  defined, 166
  history of, 167–168
  in AANHPI, 169–170
  in black communities, 166–168
  overview, 160
Columbus, Christopher, 240
Columbus day. *See* Indigenous People's Day
combat ageism, 336–337
coming out concept, 146, 149, 354, 386, 389
Commission on Rehabilitation Counselor Certification (CRCC), 26, 38–40, 111–112, 182, 226, 316, 409, 484, 485–489
commitment, 71–74, 136, 138, 145, 150
  active, 145
  deepening and, 150
  internalization and, 136, 138
  multicultural orientation model, 74
  personal, 20–21
  strengths and growing edges, 72
  to personal cultural development, 73
community cultural wealth (CCW), 203–205
Competency Continuing Education Amendment Act, 413
Compton, E., 372
concern trolling, 452
conformity, 134
Confucius, 57, 417
confusion, 149, 150
congenital disability, 154–155, 297, 302
congruence, 17, 18
conjunctive faith, 152
consensual nonmonogamy, 386
consultation, 412
contact hypothesis, 13–14
contact schema, 140
contextual cohort-based, maturity, specific challenge model (CCMSCM), 341
contextual, referes to, 341
continuing education, 345, 378, 380, 410, 412–413
Contreras, Jacqueline, 205
Convention on the Rights of Persons with Disabilities, 307
co-occurring disorders (COD), 463, 464, 466
Cook, J. M., 8, 276
Cottom, Tressie McMillan, 93
Council for Accreditation of Counseling and Related Educational Programs (CACREP), 41, 257
counseling/counseling practice, 346, 347. *See also* autonomy
  accessibility in, 316
  acculturation models, 133, 142, 199–200, 214–215
  advocacy in, 106–108, 109, 117–118, 286–287, 345–346, 437, 439–443
  affirmative, 397
  applications to, 334, 454–455, 463–464
  challenges, and barriers related to, 225
  clients with poverty, 280–281
  client worldview, 345
  cognitive behavioral therapy, 254, 337, 397
  communication for, 199
  cultural approaches, 257, 261
  cultural broaching in, 124, 125–126, 372
  deficit-based *vs.* resilience focused, 253–254
  ethical codes in, 25–54, 182–183, 206–207, 226–227, 277, 377, 378, 381
  ethical considerations, 346–347
  fostering wellness, 408–409
  generational considerations, 259
  historical context, 338
  humanistic strategies, 281–283, 407
  I-CARE model, 229–232, 233, 280
  implication for Volodymyr, 232–233, 234
  importance of intersectionality in, 92
  liberatory, 397
  MSJCC, 177, 201–202, 227–229, 251–252, 277–278, 344, 373–374, 407–408, 436–437
  multicultural approaches in, 255
  multicultural orientation model, 74
  neurodiversity, 459–460
  person-centered, 16–19, 37, 197, 255, 281–283, 369–370
  queer oppression in, 395–396
  recommendations, 178
  relationship, 176–177, 345–346, 371–372, 405–406, 454
  religion and spirituality (R/S) in, 436–437
  resiliencies, 19–20, 180–182, 203–205, 232, 233, 315, 408–409
  school-based settings, 511–512
  SOCE, 407
  social class, 280, 284
  social justice in, 106–108, 109, 114–117
  spiritual and religious support, 200–201
  standards, 397–398
  strengths, 180–182, 203–205, 232–233, 254, 315, 408–409, 443
  systems theory in, 79
  therapeutic rapport, 255–256
  traditional healing, 261–262
  trauma-informed approach in, 233
  use of assessments in, 315
  wellness in, 180–182, 203–205, 232, 315, 332, 374, 408–409
counseling relationship, 345–346, 371–372, 405–406, 438–439, 454. *See also* social justice and advocacy
  clients empowerment, 126–127
  cultural broaching, 124–126
  cultural humility, 123–124
counseling settings, 508–512
  inpatient, 508–510
  outpatient, 510–511
  quadrants model of, 92
  school-based settings, 511–512
counseling standards, 397–398
counselor, 2–22. *See also* ethical code
  ACA Advocacy Competencies, 108, 109
  CAS model, 117–118
  client worldview, 437–438
  core conditions for, 16–19

culturally relevant practice, 5, 27–28, 29, 314
ethical practice, 26–27
guidelines for, 313
inclusive language, 445
MSJCC, 436–437
overview, 2–3
personal commitment, 21–22
professional responsibility of, 29
recommendations for, 436–438
responses to oppression and discrimination, 189–190
responsibilities of, 99–101
role of, 112, 117–118, 127
scope of practice, 445
self-awareness of, 228, 309–310, 344, 370, 397, 408, 437
training process of, 4–5
working with clients, 444–445
counselor advocate scholar model (CAS), 117, 118
Covey, Stephen, 118
COVID-19 Hate Crimes Act, 169
COVID-19 pandemic, 48, 49, 165, 169, 196, 308, 329, 332, 333, 339, 346
CRC. *See* Certified Rehabilitation Counselors (CRC)
CRCC. *See* Commission on Rehabilitation Counselor Certification (CRCC)
creative and expressive arts personal growth (CAPG), 217
Crenshaw, Kimberle, 9, 92
critical race theory (CRT), 8–9, 24, 203
critical thinking, 30, 32
cross-cultural best practices
cultural broaching, 492
in assessment, 493–494
in diagnosis, 495–496
in intake, 490–492
Cross, W. E. Jr, 137, 141
Crow, Jim, 164, 172, 187
cults, features, 426–427
cultural appropriation, 261
cultural broaching, 124–126, 314–315, 343, 345. *See also* cultural humility
cultural capital, 156
cultural comfort, 59, 65–66, 67–70
cultural concealment, 406
cultural connectedness, 260
cultural diversity, 326–329
Cultural Formulation Interview (CFI), 494
cultural genocide, 238, 240, 254
cultural humility, 57–75, 123–124, 515
and enactment scale, 72–73
attributes of, 62–63
commitment, 71–74
cultural broaching, 124
cultural comfort, 65–66, 67–70
cultural opportunities, 70–71
defined, 58–59
empirical support, 64–65
historical context of, 63–64
multicultural orientation model, 58–70
overview, 57
cultural identity
and connectedness, 260
categories, 9–11
disability as, 296
racial and, 134–135
cultural identity development models, 131–158. *See also* identity development models (IDMs)
defined, 132
overview, 132–133
cultural intelligence (CQ), 198
culturally adapted health interventions, 247
culturally bound strengths, 19
culturally competent skills, 480–512
case conceptualization, 496–497
cross-cultural best practices, 490–496
culturally responsive interventions, 499–500
ethical considerations, 484–490
overview, 480
referrals and recommendations, 500–505
terms and models, 482–483
treatment planning and interventions, 497–499
culturally relevant practice, 5, 27–28, 29, 314
cultural opportunities, 59, 70–71
cultural racism, 134
cultural relativism (CR), 198
cultural relevance, 5, 25, 27–28, 29, 42, 314
ethical code interpretation, perspectives, 41–54
ethical practice and, 26–28
multiculturalism in ethical codes, 33–41
overview, 25
professional responsibility, 29–33
cultural resiliencies, 24
cultural resistance, 200
cultural strengths and weaknesses, 23
Cunningham, Brittany Packnett, 93
curiosity, 30

D

Dakota Access Pipeline (DAPL), 243–245
Darwin, Charles, 302
David, E.J.R., 192
Davis, Angela, 93, 160
Davis, D. E., 61
Day-Vines, N. L., 201
D/deaf, 302
death anxiety, 335, 337
death, dying, and loss, 342
Defense of Marriage Act (DOMA), 393
DEI. *See* diversity, equity, and inclusion (DEI)
Delgado, Richard, 9
demiromantic person, 386
demisexual, 386
Dennis-Morgan, Ciara, 179
Department of Health and Human Services, 275
Deroche, M. D., 301
Descendant, 83
developmental theories, 325–326
Bronfenbrenner's bioecological model, 325
Erikson's theory, 325
Freud's psychoanalytic stages of development, 325
Kohlberg's stages of moral development, 325
Piaget's periods of cognitive development, 325
diagnosis, 482
Diagnostic and Statistical Manual of Mental Disorders Fifth Edition-Text Revision (DSM-5-TR), 14, 257, 354, 458, 494
diasporas, concept of, 214
Di Bianca, M., 376–377
disability, 292–319. *See also* counseling/counseling practice
additional practice for, 317–318
biopsychosocial model of, 296
categories of, 296
classification and visibility of, 296–298
defined, 294
functional and environmental models of, 295
historical context of, 301–303
intersectional perspective of, 307–309
medical model of, 295
minority group model of, 295–296
models of, 294–296
moral model of, 294
onset and course of, 296, 297
overview, 292

disability identity development model, 154–155
disability rights movement, 295, 303–307
discernment, 30
Discoverers' Day, 241
discrimination, 12, 14, 94–95, 188–190, 334. *See also* prejudice
disintegration schema, 140
dispositions, 29–32
dissonance, 134
diversity, 448–476
  climate crisis and mental health, 470–475
  fatmisia, 450–456
  incarcerated populations, 462–466
  neurodiversity/neurodivergence, 457
  overview, 448
  Substance use disorders (SUD), 463, 466–475
diversity, equity, and inclusion (DEI), 5–6
Dobbs v. Jackson Women's Health Organization, 360, 361, 365
documented immigrants, 212, 213
Dolcos, F., 440
DOMA. *See* Defense of Marriage Act (DOMA)
dominant identities, 9–11
double-jeopardy hypothesis, 336
Dovchin, S., 188–189
Downing, N. E., 144, 145
Dream Act, 172
DSM-5-TR. *See Diagnostic and Statistical Manual of Mental Disorders Fifth Edition-Text Revision* (DSM-5-TR)
Duffey, T., 442, 443
Duncan Socioeconomic Index, 267
Duncombe, S., 200

E

EBP. *See* Evidence-Based Practices (EBP)
eco-anxiety, 471, 472, 473, 475
ecological contexts
  chronosystem, 365, 405
  exosystem, 363, 404
  homonegativity, 401
  macrosystem, 364, 404
  mesosystem, 362, 402–404
  microsystem, 361–362, 402–404
  RAIs, homelessness, and youth, 401–402
ecological framework, aging, 329–332
ecological systems theory (EST), 44–45, 79–82, 109, 195, 220–221, 307
  chronosystem, 46–49, 81, 195–196, 221
  exosystem, 46, 81, 330, 363
  macrosystem, 46–49, 81, 195, 221, 364
  microsystem, 45–46, 49, 80–81, 220, 329, 361
economic cultures (EC), 156
Education for All Handicapped Children Act. *See* Individuals with Disabilities Education Act
Elk, Black, 250, 261
Ellis, A., 421
emanation, 145
embeddedness, 145
emerging life song, steps for, 442–443
emic perspective, 19
emotional and psychological wounding, 239
empathy, 17, 18, 31
empirical support, 60–61, 64
Encanto, 172
encounter, 136, 138
Equal Pay Act, 359, 363
Erickson, E. H., 141, 144, 147
Erikson, E., 339, 348
Erikson's theory, 325
ESP. *See* evidence-supported practices (ESP)
essential models, 246–250. *See also* indigenous and native people
  indigenous ways of knowing, 246
  medicine wheel, 250
  native models of wellness, 246–247
  pathways to wellness, 247–249
EST. *See* ecological systems theory (EST)
ethical behaviors, 21
ethical codes, 25–54, 182–183, 206–207
  ACA, 26, 34–36, 182, 226, 316, 378
  advocacy in, 50–54, 110–112, 411–412
  AMHCA, 26, 36–37, 182, 227, 316
  and cross-cultural counseling process, 485–489
  application of, 182–183, 377–381, 409–413, 443–444
  ASCA, 26, 37–38, 182, 226, 316, 378
  cases in point, 410–411
  comparision of, 377
  conflicts, 37
  consultation, 412
  continuing education, 412–413
  counselor scope of practice, 455
  counselors working with clients, 444–445
  CRCC, 26, 38–40, 182, 226, 316
  culture in, 49–50
  defined, 346
  development of, 42–44
  HB 1557: Parental Rights in Education, 377
  history of, 33–41
  inclusive language, 445
  interpretation perspectives, 41–54
  multicultural integration in, 33–41
  NBCC, 26, 40–41, 182, 227, 255, 316
  perspectives, 41–54
  professional responsibility in, 29
  social justice in, 50–54, 110–112
ethical considerations, 226–227, 346–347, 409, 443, 480, 484
ethical practice, 26–29
ethical responsibility, 277
Ethical Standards for School Counselors, 255
ethnic awareness, 137
ethnicity/ethnic identities, 160, 163, 185–208, 518. *See also* counseling/counseling practice
  achievement, 141
  biculturalism, 192
  diversity within diversity, 190–191
  ecological and sociopolitical contexts, 195–196
  ethnocentric definitions of, 186–187
  historical context of, 186–188
  identity formation, 141
  influenced by, 185
  nondominant ethnic groups, 190–195
  overview, 185
  racial and, 61, 133, 135, 142, 173, 189, 231, 301, 468
  refers to, 185, 186
  search/moratorium, 141
  spectrum of collectivism and individualism, 193–194
  spiritual and religious beliefs, 191
  unexamined, 141
ethnocentrism, 160, 187–188, 189, 195–196, 199
etic perspective, 19
evidence-based practices (EBP), 17, 257, 482–483, 490, 499
evidence-supported practices (ESP), 483
evidence-supported treatments (EST). *See* evidence-supported practices (ESP)
EWB. *See* existential well-being (EWB)
existential well-being (EWB), 420

exosystem, 46, 81, 330, 363, 404, 430, 431
exploration, 146, 150

F

faith, 152
familial capital, 204
Farrell, I. C., 118
Fassinger, R. E., 150
Fast, E., 254
fatmisia, 450–456
in media, 453
microaggressions, 451–452
overview, 450
power of language, 450–451
weight stigma, 451
Fattoracci, E. S. M., 190
Federal Poverty Level (FPL), 275–276
feminism, 355
feminist identity development model, 145
feminist movement, 92
Ferdman, B. M., 138
first-generation college student (FGCS), 205–206
Fisher, R., 120
Fleming, Melissa W., 318
Forber-Pratt, A. J., 317
Forristal, Kaitlyn M., 448, 450
Fort Laramie, 244
Foss-Kelly, L. L., 229, 231
fostering wellness, 180, 203, 232, 408, 455
Fouad, N. A., 115
Fowler, J. W., 152–153
Fowler's model, 152–153
Frankl, Viktor, 421–423
fraysexual/ignotasexual, 386
Freire, P., 114
Freud, S., 234, 339, 421
Freud's psychoanalytic stages, 325
fundamentalist, 427

G

Galgay, C. E., 300
Gallegos, P. I., 138
Game of Thrones, 333
Gay, 386
Gay, Roxane, 77, 91
gender, 351–382, 521–523
binary, 354
concepts of, 356–357
defined, 353, 356
dysphoria, 354
ecological and sociopolitical contexts, 361–365
equality, 358–361, 360–363
ethical code application, 377–381
expression, 354
fluidity, 354
historical context of, 357–361
identity, 354
nondominant group identities, 365–369
oppression, 93
overview, 351
pay gap, 363
professional counseling practice applications, 369–377
role of, 355, 358
socialization, 358, 376
terminology, 353–356
gender-affirming medical care, 354
gender-expansive, 354
gender identity development models, 143–147
extending, 147
feminist identity development, 145
overview of, 144
psychosocial development, 144
social cognitive theory of, 144–145
TPOC, 146–147
transgender identity, 146
generation, concept of, 332–333
generational differences, 332–334
genocide, 238
genogram, 142, 284
genuineness, 17–18
gerontology, 338
Gibson, M., 200
Gilligan, C., 141, 155
The Golden Girls, 330
Goodrich, K. M., 389, 407
Gray Asexual (Graysexual; Gray-A), 386
Gray, J. S., 257
Greenleaf, A. T., 116, 117
growth mindset, 20–21

H

Hairston, T. R., 167
Hall, R. E., 170
Harbor, Pearl, 169
Hardiman-Jackson identity development model, 135
Harper, A., 231
Harrichand, J.J.S., 222
Harris, Cheryl, 9
Harris, Kamala, 361
The Harrison Act, 468
Hate Crimes and Prevention Act, 393
Hawaiian renaissance, 240. *See also* indigenous and native people
Hays, P. A., 125
HB 1557: Parental Rights in Education, 377, 521–522
Hegemonic masculinity, 370, 376–377
Helms, J. E., 139
The Help, 194
Hersey, Tricia, 181
Hester, Rita, 360
heterosexism
concepts of, 345, 364
defined, 387
heterosexual, 387
Heumann, Judith E., 305
hidden disability. *See* nonapparent disability
hidden rules of social class (Payne), 268
Hinduism, concept in, 425
Hipolito-Delgado, C. P., 115
Hippocrates, 480
historical trauma, 238–239
HIV/AIDS epidemic, 345, 394, 409
homomisia, 434
homonegativity, 387, 399, 401
homophobia/misia, 14, 387
homosexual, 387
homosexual identity formation model, 149
Hook, J. N., 60, 65, 71
hooks, bell, 265, 448
Hopkins, P., 252
House Bill 1557, 377–381
House Bill 1840, 37
HRC. *See* Human Rights Campaign (HRC)
humanistic, 407
and person-centered perspectives, 407–409
application of, 407
Human Rights Campaign (HRC), 368, 523
Human Rights Watch, 368
Hurston, Zora Neale, 93
H. W. Bush, George, 306, 393
hypodescent phenomenon, 242

I

I-CARE Model, 229–232, 233, 280
acknowledge realities, 231
cultivating relationship, 230
expand on strengths, 231–232
internally reflect, 229
remove barriers, 231
IDEA. *See* Individuals with Disabilities Education Act
identities/identification
acceptance, 149
as new racial group, 141
comparison, 149

confusion, 149
integration, 146
intersectionality, 11
nondominant group, 162–174
pride, 149
synthesis, 149
tolerance, 149
with both racial groups, 141
with single racial group, 141
identity development models (IDMs), 131–157
acculturation, 142
American Indian, 136–137
areas without, 156
Asian American, 137
bi/multiracial, 140–141
Black American, 137–138
categories, 133
defined, 132
disability, 154–155
ethics and, 157
ethnic, 141
for clients, 158
gender, 143–147
Hardiman-Jackson, 135
Latinx, 138–139
minority, 135–136
overview of, 131, 133
racial/cultural, 134–135
racial/ethnic, 133–134, 142
religious and spiritual, 152
romantic and affectual, 148–151
White and nonracist white, 139, 140
identity-first language, 357
immersion, 135
immersion/emersion, 136, 138, 140
immigrants and refugees, 210–234, 518–519. *See also* counseling/counseling practice
asylum seekers, 121
ecological and sociopolitical perspectives, 220–222
environment impact on, 220
historical context of, 218–220
immigration laws, 218–220
nondominant group identities, 216
overview, 210
terminology of, 211–212
traumas of, 221
immigration, 172, 212–213, 218–220, 222
Immigration Act, 172
Immigration and Nationality Act (INA), 212
incarcerated populations, 462–466
counseling applications, 463–464
historical context of, 463
MSJCC application, 464–466
overview, 462
inclusive language, 148, 377, 405, 445
income, 267
incorporation, 137
Indigenous and native people, 236–264, 519–520. *See also* counseling/counseling practice
and experiences, 238
cases of, 240–245
colonization impact on, 238, 240
components of, 248
deficit-based narrative of, 253–254
environmental consequences on, 243
essential models for, 246–250
gender and sexuality of, 253
healing practices for, 246, 251, 261–262
historical context of, 238–239
historical trauma, 238–239
language preservation of, 241
overview, 236–237
refer to, 238
renaissance of, 240
resilience of, 240
resurgence of, 240–243
spaces and lands of, 243
wellness of, 247–250
Indigenous historical trauma (IHT), 238–239
Indigenous knowledge, 246
Indigenous knowledge systems, 246
Indigenous People's Day, 240–241
individual bias, 94–95
individual discrimination *vs.* structural oppression, 84–96
individualism, 19, 192–193
individual racism, 133
Individuals with Disabilities Education Act, 293, 306
individuative reflective faith, 152
in-groups, 10
In Search of Our Mothers' Gardens (Walker), 166
Institute for Human-Centered Design, 316
institutional juvenile ageism, 335
institutional racism, 133
intake, 483
integration, 142, 146, 150
integrative awareness, 135
Intergovernmental Panel on Climate Change (IPCC), 471, 472
internalization, 135, 136, 138, 150
internalized fatmisia, defined, 451
internalized homophobia/ homonegativity, 387, 390
interpersonal, 69
intersectional identity, 93, 94, 102–103, 453
intersectionality, 252–253, 390
and ageism, 336
defined, 92
theory, 92, 328
intersectionality theory, 92, 328
intersex, 355
interventions
as agents of change, 99–101
culturally responsive, 499–500
treatment planning and, 497–499
intimacy, 146
intracounseling broaching dimension, 372
intrapersonal, 67
introspection, 135
intuitive projective faith, 152
IPCC. *See* Intergovernmental Panel on Climate Change (IPCC)
Islam, 424–425
Islamomisia, 435–436
-isms, defined, 14
Israel, T., 374
iterative process, 19
Ivey, A. E., 126

J

James Byrd, Jr., 393
Jones, J., 133
Jorgensen, Christine, 359
Judaism, 424
Judeo-Christian practices, 392, 420, 423
Jung, Carl, 421

K

Keeton, Jennifer, 396
Keller, R. M., 300
Keystone Pipeline, 243, 245
Kim, J., 137
Klipper, 422
Knight, Bob, 341
Kohlberg, L., 152, 153
Kohlberg's stages, 325

L

LaFromboise, T., 192
Landrine, H., 168
language brokering, 199
language preservation, 241
Latina/o/x, 138–139, 171–173
and hispanic communities, 171–173
biracial and multiracial individuals, 172–173

characteristics of, 172
history of, 171–172
identity development model, 138–139
refers to, 171
White culture in, 139
Latinx as "other,", 139
Latinx-identified, 139
Latinx identity development model, 138–139
Latinx-integrated, 138
Latter-day Saints (LDS), 427, 432
LDS. *See* Latter-day Saints (LDS)
League of the Physically Handicapped, 304
Ledbetter Equal Pay Act, 363
Lee, C. C., 115
lesbian, 387
Levy's, 335
LGBQIA+, 412–413
LGBTGEQIAP+, 143, 151, 387
LGBT groups, 120, 357, 359, 408, 428–429, 434
LGBQIA+, 412–413
LGBTGEQIAP+, 143, 387, 408
LGBTQ+, 48, 120, 216
liberatory counseling, 396, 397, 406
life review and reminiscence therapy, 337
life role transitions, 342
linguistic capital, 204
linguistic racism, 189
Litam, S.D.A., 169
Liu, W. M., 156
longevity, 334, 335
Long, S. M., 182, 265, 448, 457, 470
Lonn, M. R., 193
Lorde, Audre, 93, 181
low social class, 270, 272, 276, 277, 281, 286, 287
Luger, Brynn, 236, 254
Lyons, Mary, 243

M

macrosystem, 46–49, 81, 195, 221, 364
Magni, G., 246
Mahalik, J. R., 376–377
Man's Search for Meaning (Frankl), 422
MAP. *See* Movement Advancement Project (MAP)
marginalization, 11, 12, 142
Marks, L. D., 432, 435
Martin, Trayvon, 49
Maslow, A. H., 231
Masten, A., 315
MAT. *See* medication-assisted treatment (MAT)
Matsuno, E., 374
Matthew Shepard, 393
Mauna Kea, 245
Mayerl, J., 188
May, Rollo, 422
MCC. *See* multicultural counseling competencies (MCC)
McCarn, S. R., 150
McCarty, T. L., 241
McCubbin, L. D., 242
Mcintosh, Peggy, 310
McLeroy, K. R., 109
Meaher, Timothy, 83
MEAs. *See* Middle Eastern Americans (MEAs)
Mecca, defined, 425
Medicare and Medicaid Act. *See* Social Security Amendments of 1965
medicare program, 327, 338
medication-assisted treatment (MAT), 468–469
mesosystem, 329–330, 362, 402
MeToo Movement, 361
Meyers, L., 225
microaggressions, 14–16, 276, 300, 355, 402–403, 426, 431, 451–452, 459
microsystem, 45–46, 49, 80–81, 220, 329–330, 361–362, 402
Middle Eastern Americans (MEAs), 174–175
middle social class, 270, 272–273, 276, 281
migrant, defined, 211
migration, 211–212, 225
Milk, Harvey, 383, 414, 524
minority identity model, 135–136
minority stress, 390
Miserandino, Christine, 298
misgender, 355, 410
-misias, defined, 14
misogynoir, 328
misogyny, 328, 455
M. Long, Susan, 265, 448, 457, 470
MMBB. *See* multidimensional model of broaching behavior (MMBB)
MMSM. *See* multiple minority stress model (MMSM)
model minority, 170, 216
"mongoloid,", 7
Moonves, Julie Chen, 170
Moore, L. A., 257
Moorhead, H. J., 118, 257
moral and medical models, 467
Morgan, G., 372
Morris, P. A., 329
Moullin, J. C., 257
Movement Advancement Project (MAP), 403
MSJCC. *See* multicultural and social justice counseling competencies (MSJCC)
MTSS. *See* Multi-Tiered System of Supports (MTSS)
multicultural and social justice counseling competencies (MSJCC), 344–345, 373, 407–409, 456, 460, 465, 469
application, 177, 373–374, 407–408, 456, 464–465, 469
domains of, 227
in counseling, 177, 201, 210, 227, 251–252, 277–278, 309
marginalization, 251, 277
power and privilege, 116
structural oppression, 91–92
multicultural competence, 5
multicultural counseling competencies (MCC), 100, 109, 201, 323, 397
multiculturalism, defined, 107
multicultural orientation model, 5, 58–70, 74
advocacy, 74
components of, 58–60, 70
cultural humility, 61–70
diversity, equity, and inclusion (DEI) in, 5–6
empirical support, 60–61
multidimensional model of broaching behavior (MMBB), 125
multiple minority stress model (MMSM), 94
Multi-Tiered System of Supports (MTSS), 483
Murray-Garcia, J., 58, 63, 123
Murray, K. E., 233
music chronology, 442–443. *See also* emerging life song
mythic literal faith, 152
The Myth of Self-Esteem (Ellis), 421

N

National Academies of Sciences, Engineering, and Medicine, 222
National Board for Certified Counselors (NBCC), 26, 40–41, 112, 182, 227, 255, 316, 409, 412, 484, 485–489
National Health Statistics Report, 165
national identity, 186–187
Native American Languages Act, 241
navigational capital, 204
NBCC. *See* National Board for Certified Counselors (NBCC)
Negro, 7, 172

"negroid,", 7
Nelson, T. D., 336
Neuman, G. L., 218
neurocognitive disorders, 340
neurodivergence-informed therapy, 460–461
neurodivergent, 458, 461
neurodiversity movement, 458–459
neurodiversity/neurodivergence, 457–461
  concept of, 457
  counseling applications, 459–460
  forms of, 458
  historical context of, 459
  models of disability, 458–459
  neurodivergent, 458
  neurodiversity paradigm, 458–459
  neurotypical (NT), 458, 459
  overview, 457
neurodiversity paradigm, 458–459
neurotypical (NT), 309, 458, 459
Nicholas, S. E., 241
Nikalje, A., 425
Nixon, Richard, 304, 468
nonapparent disability, 298
nonbinary, 355
nondominant identities, 9–11, 162–174, 190–193, 365–369, 399–400
  AANHPI, 169–171
  African American and Black Communities, 163–164, 165–168
  Arab and Middle Eastern Americans, 174–175
  cisgender women, 367–368
  concept of, 190
  dominant and, 9–11
  ethnic, 190–193
  intersectionality in, 190
  Latina/o/x and Hispanic Communities, 171–173
  nonbinary people, 369
  related to religion and spirituality, 428–430
  religiosity/spirituality, 400
  transgender people, 368
nonracist White identity, 140
nonsuicidal self-injury (NSSI), 504
nontokenization, 21
NSSI. *See* nonsuicidal self-injury (NSSI)
Nutton, J., 254

O

obesity epidemic, 453
occupation, 267
O'Hara, C., 276, 278
older adults, 326, 328
Oluo, Ijeoma, 104
one-drop rule, 167, 172
open-mindedness, 30
opioid use disorder (OUD), 468–469
oppressed *vs.* oppressor, 89–90
oppression, 11, 12, 188, 189, 328–329
  forms of, 434–436
  gender based, 93–94
  structural, 82–83
  white christian privilege, 432–433
  within sociopolitical contexts, 432–436
oppressor *vs.* oppressed, 89–90
optimal theory, 178
OUD. *See* opioid use disorder (OUD)
out-groups, 10
overculture, defined, 94
Owen, J., 57, 60, 61, 69

P

Paine, T., 272
Palmer, C. A., 163
panromantic, 387
pansexual, 387
parentification, 199
Park, Christine, 236
passing, 355
passive acceptance, 135, 145
passive awareness, 154
patriarchy, defined, 355
Payne, R. K., 268
PCT. *See* person-centered therapy (PCT)
Pear, V. A., 468
Pedersen, P. B., 115
People of Color, 160, 270
people with disabilities (PWD), 292–319
  accessible environment for, 316
  advocacy for, 304
  forced sterilization of, 302
  historical context of, 301–303
  media depictions of, 303
  nondominant identities of, 308
  perceptions and actions, 307–308
  policy and language of, 307
period, 333
Perry, J. M., 495
personal cultural development, 73
personal values, 55–56
person-centered approaches/perspectives, 340, 369, 407, 454, 463, 465, 469. *See also* humanistic
person-centered skills, 21
person-centered therapy (PCT), 16–19, 369, 370, 422
  techniques, 370
person-first language, 357
perspective taking, defined, 30, 32, 42
PettyJohn, M. E., 202
Pew Research Center (PRC), 213, 329, 363, 423
Phinney, J. S., 141
physical disabilities, 296, 297
Piaget, J., 152, 153
Piaget's periods of cognitive development, 325
Pierce, C., 451
POC. *See* People of Color
polyamory, 387, 399
polyromantic, 387
polysexual, 388
Portlock, Katie, 259
Post-Traumatic Cognitions Inventory (PTCI), 495
Post-Traumatic Stress Disorder-Reaction Index (PTSD-RI), 495
poverty, 274–276, 280–281
  barriers to, 274, 276
  defined, 274
  five-point model for, 280
  practice for clients with, 280–281
  resource-based, 275
power, 8–9, 10, 11, 12, 81, 107, 114–115
PRC. *See* Pew Research Center (PRC)
prejudice, 12, 13, 95, 107, 109, 112, 168, 214, 300, 334
Pridhidko, Alena, 185, 194
primal faith, 152
privilege, 8–9, 10, 11, 12, 81, 107, 114–115
professional counseling, 69–70
professional responsibility, 29–33
  dispositions, 29–33
  skills, 29–33
professional school counselors (PSC), 37–38, 99, 484
professional values, 55–56
pronouns, 355
protective factors, 247
PSC. *See* professional school counselors (PSC)
pseudo-independent schema, 140
PSYCa, 3–6. *See* Psychological Screening for Young Children (PSYCa 3-6)
psychiatric disabilities, 296, 297
Psychological Screening for Young Children (PSYCa 3-6), 495
psychosocial development, 144
PTCI. *See* Post-Traumatic Cognitions Inventory (PTCI)
PTSD-RI. *See* Post-Traumatic Stress Disorder-Reaction Index (PTSD-RI)
Purge, 121

Q

QPOC. *See* Queer People of Color (QPOC)
queer, 388
queer oppression, 385, 393–396, 402, 406, 409, 410, 412
Queer People of Color (QPOC), 390, 399

R

race/racism, 160–183, 517–518. *See also* counseling/counseling practice
  abandonment of, 140
  and anti-blackness, 453
  cultural, 134
  ecological and sociopolitical contexts of, 174–175
  ethical code application, 182–183
  historical overview, 160, 162
  identity development, 133–134, 135
  in AANHPI, 169–171
  in black communities, 163–165, 166–168
  in counseling practice, 160, 176–182
  individual and systemic, 134
  in Hispanic/Latinx community, 171–173
  institutional, 133
  linguistic, 189
  nondominant group identities, 162–174
  to express White identity, 137
  types of, 133–134
racial/cultural identity development model, 134–135
racial, ethnic, and cultural (REC), 125
racial groups, 140–141
racial identity development, 133–134
racial slavery, 167
racial socialization, 167, 179
RAIs, homelessness, and youth, 401–402
Ratts, M. J., 115, 116, 117, 201, 397
Raymond, Janice, 360
RCT. *See* relational-cultural theory (RCT)
Reagan, Ronald, 392
realization, 154
REC. *See* racial, ethnic,and cultural (REC)
redefinition, 135
redirection, 137
referrals
  and recommendations, 500–505
  defined, 483
  for additional mental health assessment, 500–501
  for case management, 502
  for health-care resources, 501–502
  for other self-care resources, 503
  for scope of practice, 503–504
  for termination or full caseload, 504–505
refugees, 212, 213, 225
Rehabilitation Act, 304
reintegration schema, 140
relational-cultural therapy (RCT), 84, 100, 175, 178, 369, 375, 376–377, 483
relationship, 150, 176–177, 197–198, 230, 346
  counseling, 345–346
  enhancer, 405–406, 416
relative poverty, 274–275
Relaxation Response (Benson and Klipper), 422
religion, 152
religion and spirituality, 417–446, 525–526
  as a form of resilience, 443
  belief systems, 423–426
  defined, 417
  ecological context, 430–432
  historical context of, 421–423
  morals and values, 420–421
  overview, 417
  spiritual ecomaps, 441
  spiritual genograms, 441, 442
religiously unaffiliated, 426
religious/spiritual identity development models, 152–153, 417–446. *See also* Fowler's model
  Fowler's model, 152–153
  well-being, 420
religious trauma
  cults, 426–427
  nondominant group identities, 428–430
religious well-being (RWB), 420
reservation, 238
resilience, 233, 254, 315, 332, 343–344, 374, 408–409, 443
resiliencies, 20
resiliency-focused approach, 19–20
resistance, 135
resistant capital, 204
RESPECTFUL models, 125–126
Rest Is Resistance (Hersey), 181
revelation, 145
reverse racism, 196
Rhyne, Diana Yum, 311
Rights of Man (Paine), 272
Rio, Jennifer, 448, 462, 466, 618
rite of purification, 261
Roberts, E., 304
Rogers, C., 16–17, 422, 438
romantic and affectional identity (RAI) development models, 148–151, 151, 383–415
  adolescent lesbian and gay identity, 149–150
  application, 406
  bisexual identity, 150–151
  gaps, 151
  historical context of, 392–398
  homosexual identity formation model, 149
  impact of colonization on, 392–393
  lesbian identity development, 150
  overview, 383
  religiosity/spirituality and, 400
  terminology of, 385–389
romantic identity/orientation, 388
Root, M. P. P., 140
Rorie, Tanesha, 160
Rosario, R. J., 167
Rose, W. J., 257
Roush, K. L., 144, 145
RWB. *See* religious well-being (RWB)

S

schizophrenia, 471, 496, 501, 508
school-based settings, 511–512
school counselors, 505–508
  and education, 506
  and school settings, 505–508
Schwitzer, Albert, 25
SCWM. *See* social class worldview model (SCWM)
SCWM-Revised (SCWM-R), 155–156
SDOH. *See* social determinants of health (SDOH)
section, 304–307, 504
SEL. *See* social-emotional learning (SEL)
self-assessment, 129
self-awareness, 30, 32
self-disclosure, 176, 192, 255, 370
self-esteem, 137, 167
self-identification, 145
semisexual, 388
separation, 142
SES. *See* socioeconomic status (SES)
settling into identity, 151
severe and persistent mental illness (SPMI), 290, 502, 508
sex, 521–523
  concepts of, 356–357
  ecological and sociopolitical contexts, 361–365
  ethical code application, 377–381
  historical context of, 357–361
  nondominant group identities, 365–369

professional counseling practice applications, 369–377
sexism, 434–435
sexual identity, 388–389
sexuality, 388
sexually-fluid, 388
sexual orientation, 388, 395
Sexual Orientation Change Measures (SOCE), 388, 395, 396, 405, 407, 416
sexual prejudice, 388
Shakespeare, T., 296
Shire, Warsan, 210
Shore, J. H., 251
Simons, J., 146
Singer, J., 457
Singh, A.A., 189
Sirleaf, Ellen Johnson, 185
Skerrett, K., 342
skills in, 313–315
skin tone bias. *See* colorism
skoliosexual, 389
Smart, D. W., 295
Smart, J. F., 295
Smith, L., 276
smudging, 261
Snow, Kevin C., 210
SOCE. *See* Sexual Orientation Change Measures (SOCE)
social capital, defined, 156, 204
social class/classism, 265–288, 520–521. *See also* counseling/counseling practice
  and related topics, 271–272
  assessment, 284
  bias, 268, 272, 281
  CARE and I-CARE model, 278
  classism in, 273
  genogram, 284
  historical context of, 271–272
  microaggressions, 276
  poverty as, 274–275
  socioeconomic status and, 267–268
  stratification, 269–271
  systemic and ecological contexts, 272–273
  terminology of, 267–271
social class groups, 269–271
social class worldview model (SCWM), 155–156
social cognitive theory (SCT), 144–145
social determinants of health (SDOH), 96–99, 239
social-emotional learning (SEL), 507
social identity theory, 336
social justice
  3-C model, 117
  and advocacy, 104–128
  Black feminism, importance, 93–94
  counseling, 114–117
  counselors, 115–116
  defined, 107, 115
  historical knowledge of, 114–115
  self-aware, 115–116
  skills, 116–117
social justice and advocacy, 50–54, 104–128, 517
  clients empowerment, 126–127
  communicating about, 107–108
  cultural broaching, 124–125
  cultural humility, 123–124
  ethical codes related to, 110–112
  historical context of, 109–110
  in counseling relationship, 123–127
  overview, 104
  role of, 106–107
social media, 49, 81, 120, 317, 404
social-political consciousness, 137
Social Security Amendments of 1965, 338
social support strategies, 286
socioecological model, 109, 251
socioeconomic status (SES), 266, 267–268
sociopolitical contexts, 174–175, 195–197, 361–365. *See also* ecological contexts
Sommers-Flanagan, J., 17
Sosin, Lisa, 217
Sotero, M., 239
spatial discrimination, 451–452
spiritual genograms, 441, 442
spirituality, 152, 200. *See also* religion and spirituality
SPMI. *See* severe and persistent mental illness (SPMI)
spoon theory, 298–299
stagnancy, 145
Stalin, Joseph, 234
STAR. *See* Street Transvestite Action Revolutionaries (STAR)
Stark, Susan, 38
stereotype embodiment theory, 334–335, 336, 337
stereotypes, 12, 13
story of Kau'i, 258
story of Volodymyr, 232–234
straight people, 388
Street Transvestite Action Revolutionaries (STAR), 359
strength-based approaches, 19–20
strengths, 19–20, 233, 254, 315, 332, 374, 408–409, 443
structural inequality, 83
structural oppression, 82–101, 515–517
  Black feminism, 93–94
  dismantling, 103
  examples of, 85–88,
  historical context of, 83–84
  intersectionality, 92
  MSJCC, 91–92
  oppressed *vs.*oppressor, 89–90
  outcomes of, 96–99
  social determinants of health, 96–99
  systemic oppression *vs.* individual bias and discrimination, 94–95
  vs. individual discrimination, 84–96
subgroup-identified, 139
substance use disorders (SUD), 463, 466–475
  and disability, 468–469
  counseling applications, 469–470
  criminalization of, 468
  disparities in, 468
  historical context of, 467–469
  overview, 466
SUD. *See* Substance use disorders (SUD)
Sue, D. W., 15
sun dance, 262
Sunim, Haemin, 417
Suprina, J. S., 400
symbolic violence, 188–189
synthesis, 145, 150
synthetic conventional faith, 152
systemic oppression *vs.* individual bias and discrimination, 94–95
systems-level impacts, 21
systems theory, 78–79
  ecological, 80–82
  in counseling, 79

T

Tagaq, Tanya, 236–262
Tello, A. M., 185, 193
temperance movement, 467
terror management theory, 335, 337
Tervalon, M., 58, 63, 123
theoretical orientations, 100–101
Thirty Meter Telescope (TMT), 245
Thomason, T. C., 255, 257
time line of gender equality, 358–361
tolerance for ambiguity, 30
traditional healing practices, 261–262. *See also* indigenous and native people
  examples of, 261
  rite of purification, 261
  sun dance, 262
transgender, 356
transgender people of color (TPOC), 146–147

transgender resilience intervention model (TRIM), 374
transinstitutionalization, 338
transition, 356
transmisia, 356, 361–362, 363, 364, 373
transsexual, 356
The Transsexual Empire: The Making of the She- Male (Raymond), 360
transsexualism. *See* under gender
The Transsexual Phenomenon (Benjamin), 359
traumatic brain injury (TBI), 297
treatment planning, 483, 497–499
Treaty of Fort Laramie, 244
Tremaine and Julianne, case, 410–411
trephining, 303
Trevino, R. R., 191
TRIM. *See* transgender resilience intervention model (TRIM)
Truth, Sojourner, 93, 359
two-spirit, 253
Tyrell, Olenna, 334
Tyson, Cicely, 323

U

uncertainty/identity maintenance, 151
Unconditional Positive Regard (UPR), 17, 18–19
unconscious bias, 22
undifferentiated, 139
undocumented immigrants, 212–213
unexamined ethnic identity, 141
Ungar, M., 308
universalizing faith, 152
University of California, 304
The University of Hawaii Institute for Astronomy, 245
upper social class, 166, 266, 270
Ury, W., 120
U.S. Citizenship and Immigration Services, 218
U.S. Department of Homeland Security, 212

V

Van Lith, T., 234
Vauclair, C-M., 327
Vietnam War, 332
visibility of disability. *See* apparent disability

W

Walker, Alice, 166
Wang, M., 188
Ward, Julea, 396
warmth, 17, 18
Web Content Accessibility Guidelines (WCAG), 316
weight stigma, 451
Weinberg, M. S., 150
wellness, 315, 332, 374, 408–409
Wells, Ida B., 93
Westman J. C., 335
White Christian Privilege, 432–433
White gaze, 190
White identification, 137
White identity development model, 139–140
White people, 6–9
White Privilege: Unpacking the Invisible Knapsack (Mcintosh), 310
White supremacy, 7, 84–85, 90, 93, 94, 164, 166, 174, 175, 181
WHO. *See* World Health Organization (WHO)
Wilderson, F. B., 168
Willis, Raquel, 93
Wolpe, Joseph, 422
World Health Organization (WHO), 334
World Population Review, 417
The World Professional Association for Transgender Health (WPATH), 360, 373
World War II, 187, 218, 393, 421
WPATH. *See* The World Professional Association for Transgender Health (WPATH)
Wray, M., 270

X

xenomisia, defined, 214
xenophobia, 14

Y

Yosso, T. J., 203
Young, Stella, 292

Z

Zhong, W., 432
Zhu, P., 61
Zimmerman, George, 49
zsexual, 389

About the Editors

Jennifer (Jenn) M. Cook, PhD, LPC, NCC, ACS ***(she/her)*** is an associate professor of counselor education at the University of Texas at San Antonio. She resides and works on the traditional lands of the Jumanos, Coahuiltecan, Ndé Kónitsąąíí Gokíyaa (Lipan Apache), and Tonkawa peoples. Jenn earned her PhD in counselor education from Virginia Tech, her M.A. in counseling psychology and counselor education with a couples and family specialization from the University of Colorado at Denver, and a M.Div. from Iliff School of Theology. Her research focuses on counselor cultural development and culturally relevant client care with specific emphasis on social class and identity intersectionality, as well as addiction prevention and harm reduction. She has published extensively, completed over 40 national and international peer-reviewed presentations, and served several counseling organizations. Jenn is an avid reader, loves walking and being outdoors in every season, and is a *hodophile* (in addition to being a self-proclaimed word nut), yet loves coming home to her two cats.

Madeline (Maddie) Clark, PhD, LCPC (NV), LPC (VA), NCC, CCMHC, ACS ***(she/they)*** is an associate professor of counselor education at the University of Nevada, Las Vegas. She resides and completes her work on the traditional lands of the Nuwu and Southern Paiute peoples. Maddie earned her PhD in counselor education and supervision from Old Dominion University (ODU) in Norfolk, Virginia and a M.S.Ed. in clinical mental health counseling, also from ODU. She focuses her research broadly on diversity, equity, and inclusion in counseling and counselor education with a specific focus on poverty and counseling outcomes for clients experiencing poverty. She has published over 40 peer-reviewed publications and presented locally, regionally, and nationally. She is a former president of the Association for Research and Assessment in Counseling (AARC) and has won numerous awards, including the American Counseling Association's Research Best Practices Award. She is a descendant of European American settlers from the farming Midwest and mining Appalachian regions, a first generation academic, and is neurodivergent. When not working, you can find her doing CrossFit and olympic weightlifting, enjoying time with her partner Viktor and daughter Maxine, or spending time outdoors with her two rescued pit bulls, Moses and Jude, or inside with her two cats, George and Babadook.

About the Contributors

Charmayne R. Adams, PhD, LIMHP. (she/her). Assistant Dean of Student Health, Counseling, and Wellness, Gonzaga University. Dr. Charmayne Adams is an independently Licensed Counselor in the state of Nebraska and a supervisor for provisionally licensed counselors. Dr. Adams's specialty areas are crisis, trauma, and stress response, especially as they pertain to counseling students and clients who hold marginalized identities. Clinically and academically, Dr. Adams focuses on social justice counseling and empowering clients to examine barriers and use their strengths to overcome life's challenges.

Clark D. Ausloos, PhD, LPCC, LPSC, NCC. (he/him). Clinical Assistant Professor, University of Denver. Dr. Ausloos earned a BFA in musical theater and dance, an MA in counseling (with both school and clinical foci), and a PhD in counselor education. Dr. Ausloos has worked in elementary, intermediate, and junior high school settings, as well as in private practice and in higher education. Dr. Ausloos has worked with learners at the College of William and Mary, as well as Palo Alto University, and now serves as Clinical Assistant Professor in the SchoolCounseling@Denver program. Dr. Ausloos continues to work toward making classrooms safe and accessible for students, especially marginalized populations like queer and trans youth. Dr. Ausloos has authored several published peer-reviewed manuscripts, book chapters and encyclopedia terms in press and is highly active in research around the world. Through intentional research, Dr. Ausloos aims to empower and promote ethical, affirming training and professional practices within counselor education programs, and within clinical and school settings.

Jillian M. Blueford, PhD, LPC, NCC, FT. (she/her). Clinical Assistant Professor, University of Denver. Dr. Jillian Blueford is a Clinical Assistant Professor for the school counseling program at the University of Denver, a Licensed Professional Counselor in the state of Colorado, and a Fellow in Thanatology: Death, Dying, and Bereavement. Over the years, Dr. Blueford has provided grief counseling to individuals of all backgrounds in various settings, including schools, outpatient facilities, and currently in private practice in the Denver area. Further, Dr. Blueford is a grief and loss scholar who has conducted research and scholarship via her dissertation, peer-reviewed publications, webinars, podcast features, and several regional, national, and international presentations. Seeking that all counseling professionals are equipped and competent in grief counseling, Dr. Blueford also works with other educators and clinicians as Co-chair of the Grief Counseling Competencies Task Force to develop key competencies for the training programs.

Lisa M. Boyd, PhD. (she/her). Graduate Student, Virginia Tech. Dr. Lisa Boyd is a graduate student in counselor education at Virginia Tech. Dr. Boyd earned her doctorate in Sociology and Demography from Pennsylvania State University and completed a National Institute of Mental Health T32 postdoctoral fellowship in women's health and community health interventions at the Yale School of Public Health. Upon completing her postdoc, she worked as a social determinants of health researcher in academic and industry settings until returning to graduate school in 2022 to study clinical mental health counseling.

Erik Braun, PhD, NCC. (he/him). Associate Professor, Bradley University. Dr. Braun was born and raised in Riverside, Illinois, a suburb of Chicago. Dr. Braun's professional background includes community mental health and substance abuse counseling from an existential and rational-emotive behavioral therapy perspective. His interests also include spirituality, multiculturalism, and mindfulness. Dr. Braun has experience in community agency, university, and residential settings. Dr. Braun teaches mental health counseling courses, including pre-practicum, group counseling, and ethics, among other topics. Dr. Braun's research interests include multicultural issues, especially gender identity and spirituality. His work has been published in several journals and has included the topics of gender identity, multicultural issues in supervision, and counselor education. Dr. Braun is a member of the American Counseling Association and the Association for Counselor Education and Supervision. Currently, Dr. Braun also serves as a coach for Bradley's Grappling and Jiu-Jitsu Club.

Janice Byrd, PhD. (she/her). Assistant Professor, Pennsylvania State University. Dr. Janice A. Byrd is an Assistant Professor in the Counselor Education Program at Pennsylvania State University. She earned her PhD in counselor education and supervision from the University of Iowa and an MEd in counselor education (K–12 school counseling) from South Carolina State University. She has previous experience as a school counselor, career counselor, teaching in secondary settings, and serving as a university-wide diversity, equity and inclusion (DEI) affiliate. As a community-engaged critical qualitative researcher, Dr. Byrd's areas of expertise include policies and practices that influence the development and mental health of Black girls/women in educational settings; college and career readiness (at the intersections of identities); and research and teaching in counselor education and supervision. She has been nationally recognized for her scholarship, teaching, and service, and her work appears in various peer-reviewed journals.

Tabitha Cude, PhD. (she/her). Assistant Professor, University of Tennessee at Martin. Dr. Tabitha Cude is an Assistant Professor of Counseling in the Department of Educational Studies at the University of Tennessee at Martin. Her teaching primarily focuses on school counseling, but she teaches both school counseling and clinical counseling students. She is also the School Counseling Practicum and Internship Coordinator. She has received a PhD in Professional Counseling from Amridge University. Her professional and scholarly pursuits are centered around mental health care in schools and in rural communities and school counseling–related topics.

Nicolette Castagna, LMHC, MPH, CDP. (she/her). Licensed Mental Health Counselor, Florida State University College of Medicine Department of Geriatrics. Nicolette Castagna is a Licensed Mental Health Counselor and a Certified Dementia Practitioner with a background in public health and aging. She earned a master's degree in clinical mental health counseling from Wake Forest University and a master's in public health from Florida State University. She is part of the Florida State University College of Medicine Department of Geriatrics Health Resources and Services Administration H-funded Geriatrics Workforce Enhancement Partnership leadership team since its inception in 2015 and works as a counselor at the Tallahassee Senior Center supporting older adults experiencing loneliness, social isolation, and depression. Her work centers around age-friendly health care and communities, dementia sensitivity trainings, family caregiver support, and strengthening collaborations between aging network sectors to promote system improvements and synergies.

Monica L. Coleman MS, NCC, CRC. (she/her). Doctoral Candidate, University of Mississippi and Program Officer, Robert Wood Johnson Foundation. Monica is a recognized leader and advocate for community-powered research and evaluation. She leverages her expertise in counselor education, journalism, community organizing, and public policy advocacy to instigate and engage in grantmaking that bridges the gap between communities, scholars, and policymakers. Her research and evaluation work centers the leadership, voice, and power of those most impacted by structural oppression in efforts to foster a more just society.

Melissa D. Deroche, PhD, LPC-S, ACS, NCC. (she/her). Assistant Professor, Tarleton State University. Dr. Melissa D. Deroche earned her PhD in counselor education, master's degree in mental health counseling, and bachelor's degree in psychology—all from the University of New Orleans. Dr. Deroche holds licenses as a Licensed Professional Counselor and Supervisor (LPC-S) and certifications as an Approved Clinical Supervisor (ACS) and National Certified Counselor (NCC). For approximately 15 years, she worked as a professional counselor in a variety of settings with individuals who were diagnosed with mental health, cognitive, and physical disabilities. Dr. Deroche's scholarly interests include multicultural and diversity education, training, and competence specific to people with disabilities, as well as the ableist microaggression experiences and social justice concerns of this diverse community, and she has conducted over 20 peer-reviewed presentations on these topics.

Tabitha Fabin, BA. (she/her). Masters Student, Bradley University. Tabitha Fabin was born and raised in a suburb of Chicago. Tabitha's educational background includes obtaining a bachelor's degree in psychology from Saint Mary's University of Minnesota. During her undergraduate years, she also triple minored in global diversity and social justice, leadership, and criminal justice. She graduated with departmental distinction in psychology and the social sciences, and became a member of the International Honors Society of Psychology (Psi Chi). Tabitha is currently enrolled in a master's program at Bradley University, where she will graduate with a degree in clinical mental health counseling. Her interests in the field include working with children and eventually obtaining her PhD. Tabitha also has experience with research, including topics such as spirituality, body image, and self-esteem. Currently, Tabitha also works at the Bradley University Writing Center as a graduate assistant writing consultant.

Kaitlyn M. Forristal, PhD, LPCC-S, NCC, ACS. (she/her). Visiting Assistant Professor, John Carroll University. Dr. Kate Forristal (she/her) has earned a PhD in counselor education and supervision, an MA in clinical mental health counseling, and a BA in psychology from The University of Toledo in Toledo. She has been teaching since 2015 and currently serves as a Visiting Assistant Professor in the Counseling Department at John Carroll University after 5 years as an Assistant Professor and Program Director of Clinical Mental Health Counseling at

New England College. Kate is an LPCC-S in Ohio, where she was born and raised on unceded Erie land, and holds NCC and ACS credentials. Dr. Forristal's research interests are equity in counseling for marginalized communities with a primary focus on anti-fat bias, fatmisia, and counseling relationships and counselor training. She has published and presented on this topic at many state, regional, and national conferences. In her spare time, Dr. Forristal enjoys cooking, baking, swimming, and spending time with her cats.

Matthew Fullen, PhD, MDiv, LPCC. (he/him). Associate Professor, Virginia Tech. Dr. Matthew Fullen is an Associate Professor at Virginia Tech, where he teaches counselor education. His research, teaching, and advocacy focus on the mental health needs of older adults, with an emphasis on addressing gaps in Medicare mental health policy and developing programs to enhance resilience and wellness and prevent suicide among older adults. Dr. Fullen is the counseling profession's most active scholar on aging and mental health, and he has received research grant funding from both public and private entities, including the U.S. Department of Health and Human Services, as well as the Mather Institute, to develop programs that support older adults' mental health. In recognition of his research and professional leadership related to Medicare mental health advocacy, he has received three national awards from the American Counseling Association: the Counselor Educator Advocacy Award (2023), the ACA Research Award (2021), and the Carl D. Perkins Government Relations Award (2020).

John J. S. Harrichand, PhD, LPC-S, LMHC, NCC, CCMHC, ACS, CCTP. (he/him). Assistant Professor, University of Texas at San Antonio. Dr. John Harrichand Harrichand is a Canadian of Chinese and East Indian ancestry, an immigrant to Canada who was born and raised in Guyana, South America. He is a proud International Faculty, serving as an Assistant Professor in the Department of Counseling at the University of Texas at San Antonio. Dr. Harrichand's scholarship centers on counselor education leadership, development, and burnout; cross-cultural counseling and minority populations (i.e., LGBTQ+, immigrants, refugees, international students, sex-trafficked survivors); clinical supervision and gatekeeping; and ethical, professional, and social justice advocacy using qualitative and quantitative methodologies. Dr. Harrichand is passionate about creating access to affordable mental health services while advocating for minoritized and systemically excluded communities. He was recognized with the AMCD Young Emerging Leader Award, the SACES Outstanding Pre-tenure Counselor Educator Award, and the ACES Leadership Award.

Alexandria Hepburn, LPC. (she/her). Doctoral Candidate, The University of Toledo. Alexandria Hepburn, LPC (Ohio) is a practicing clinician (Ohio) with experience working in community mental health, private practice and school-based programs. She holds classroom experience teaching counseling-based courses over the Council for Accreditation of Counseling and Related Educational Programs (CACREP) standards, including Counseling Theories, Fundamentals of Mental Health, Cultural Competencies, Skills and Group. Alexandria committed her research, practice and pedagogical energy to working with and advocating for underserved and marginalized communities. Service and mentorship have served as a priority, as seen through her efforts in the development of DEI-based initiatives.

Gwendolyn (Gwen) Hooks, MA, LPC. (she/her). Doctoral Candidate, The University of Toledo. Gwendolyn Hooks is a second-year counselor education doctoral student at The University of Toledo in Toledo, Ohio. She earned a master's degree in counseling psychology from Bowie State University in 2010 and currently holds active independent licensure as a professional counselor in the state of Michigan. She has had a variety of clinical experiences, including two years working in intellectual disabilities, several more in community mental health and severe and persistent mental illness, and most recently in the private practice setting. She is now focused on serving the Veteran population. She is passionate about evidenced-informed treatment with research interests that include promoting the use of evidence-based practices, understanding barriers to their use, and how these intersect with health equity and culturally responsive practices.

Jeongwoon Jeong, PhD, LMHC, NCC. (he/him). Assistant Professor, University of New Mexico. Dr. Jeongwoon Jeong is an Assistant Professor of Counselor Education in the Department of Individual, Family, and Community Education at the University of New Mexico. He received a PhD in counselor education and supervision and MA in educational measurement and statistics from the University of Iowa. His scholarly work mainly focuses on mental health and addiction issues of marginalized populations, multicultural counseling, multicultural counselor education, and counseling self-efficacy of counselors and counselors in training. He is serving as an editorial board member of the *International Journal for the Advancement of Counseling* and the peer-review board of the *Journal of International Students.*

ZeVida A. Jones, EdD, LPSC, LPC, NCC. (she/her). Assistant Professor, University of Tennessee at Martin. ZeVida A. Jones is an Assistant Professor of Counselor Education in the Department of Educational Studies at the University of Tennessee at Martin. She received an EdD in counselor education and supervision, EdS in school counseling, and an MA in liberal studies from the University of Memphis. She served as the Secondary Counselor and Interim Deputy Principal of Xiamen International School in Xiamen, China, as well as the Graduation Coach and High School Counselor for the Shelby County Schools District and Gestalt Community Schools. Dr. Jones is the author of *So You Call Yourself a Counselor?: High School Counselors' Impact on First-Generation African American College Students' Post-Secondary Aspirations* and is the owner of Empowering Books Publishing House. Her research interests include the experiences of first-generation African American college students, low-income and minority students, and the counselor-student relationship.

Krista E. Kirk, PhD, LMHC, NCC, ACS, BC-TMH. (she/her). Associate Professor, Southeastern University. Dr. Krista Kirk is an Associate Professor of counseling at Messiah University in Mechanicsburg, PA. In addition to being a professor, Dr. Kirk runs a private counseling practice in the New York City metropolitan area, where she seeks to meet the needs of underserved populations. After earning her doctorate in counselor education and supervision, Dr. Kirk became a professor and taught in the graduate Clinical Mental Health Counseling Program at Liberty University, and eventually transitioned to also teach in their doctoral counselor education and supervision program. Dr. Kirk actively engages in professional development, publishing her work in the areas of gatekeeping and psychological safety in counselor education, mental illness stigma in religious communities, and multicultural competence in the counseling profession.

Kathleen Klein, MA, MEd, LPC. (she/her). Doctoral Student, The University of Toledo. Kathleen Klein is a second-year counselor education doctoral student at The University of Toledo in Toledo, Ohio. She earned a master's degree in education from The University of Toledo in 1999 and a master's degree in counseling from Northwestern University in 2022. She currently holds active licensure as a professional counselor in the state of Ohio. She is trained in Dialectical Behavior Therapy and Collaborative Assessment and Management of Suicidality. She is currently in private practice, where she treats a diversified client base for a wide variety of disorders. Her interests include addressing the unique concerns of those with acquired disability and chronic illness. Prior to becoming a counselor, she worked in human resource development and program management within both the service and manufacturing realms.

Donghun Lee, PhD. (he/him). Assistant Professor, University of Texas at San Antonio. Dr. Donghun Lee currently serves as an Assistant Professor in the Department of Counseling at the University of Texas at San Antonio and has obtained his doctoral degree in Counselor Education and Supervision at the University of Arkansas. His primary research interests lie in the areas of professional identity and development, counselor burnout and wellness, multicultural counseling and social justice, and dispositional assessment. He is an active member of diverse counseling associations and is currently serving as an editorial board member of the *Journal of Asia Pacific Counseling* and the *International Journal for the Advancement of Counselling.*

Susan M. Long, PhD, LPCC-S. Assistant Professor, The University of Toledo. Susan M. Long, PhD, LPCC-S, is an Assistant Professor at The University of Toledo. Dr. Long's scholarship is focused on the integration of holistic wellness and neuroeducation in professional counseling. In addition to teaching and research, Dr. Long is engaged in provision of clinical supervision and counseling in the community.

Brynn Luger, PhD, LPCC, NCC. (she/her). Assistant Professor, University of North Dakota School of Medicine and Health Sciences. Dr. Brynn Luger is from the Standing Rock Sioux Tribe in North Dakota. She has 15 years of experience in clinical counseling, counselor education, and supervision. Dr. Luger specializes in treating depression, anxiety, childhood and adult trauma, and the emotional and social issues surrounding substance abuse. Her research areas are Indigenous mental health and healing practices and secondary trauma among Native American counselors.

Rachel Mattingly, LPCA. (she/her). Doctoral Candidate, The University of Toledo. Rachel Mattingly received her master of arts in education through Western Kentucky University's Clinical Mental Health Counseling Program and is a doctoral student at The University of Toledo studying counselor education and supervision. Rachel has several years of experience working in residential and outpatient substance abuse treatment centers and community mental health agencies. Rachel seeks to empower individuals, couples, and families through mental health advocacy, substance use education, and healthy conflict skills. Rachel uses a person-centered approach along with strengths-based cognitive-behavioral therapy and often uses tenets of the

Gottman method with groups and individuals. Rachel values utilizing psychoeducation and mental health counseling to evoke systemic change within families and communities.

Elizabeth K. Mautz, PhD, MPA, CRC, LPC. (she/her). Adjunct Professor, Troy University. Dr. Elizabeth Kelley Mautz holds a PhD in counselor education and supervision from Auburn University and master's degrees in rehabilitation counseling from Georgia State University and public administration from the University of Georgia. She is a Certified Program Evaluator, Certified Rehabilitation Counselor, and Licensed Professional Counselor in the state of Alabama. Dr. Mautz is an Adjunct Professor at Troy University in Montgomery, Alabama, and serves as the Deputy Commissioner of the Alabama Department of Corrections (ADOC), where she oversees operations for three statewide facilities serving the female incarcerated population and the coordination of ADOC services and programming for females housed at the Alabama Therapeutic and Educational Facility. Prior to working for ADOC, Dr. Mautz worked with persons with brain and spinal cord injuries and at-risk youth, and coordinated services serving low socioeconomic status families.

Laurie "Lali" McCubbin, PhD, LP. (she/her). Professor and Chair, University of Kentucky. Dr. Laurie "Lali" McCubbin is a Professor and Chair at the University of Kentucky in the Department of Educational, School and Counseling Psychology and an Indigenous/multiracial scholar (Native Hawaiian Kanaka ʻŌiwi Japanese/White). She received her master's degree from Boston College and her PhD from the University of Wisconsin-Madison. Her research interests and expertise include resilience, recovery, and well-being among Black, Indigenous, and People of Color folx, cultural identity development, decolonization in psychology training programs, and stress and cultural factors related to trauma, recovery, and resistance at the individual, family, and community levels. She is currently the Executive Director of the Resilience, Adaptation and Well-Being Project (www.mccubbinresilience.org). She has served as past Chair of the Children, Youth, and Families Committee for the American Psychological Association and past President of the Council of Counseling Psychology Training Programs. She currently serves as an Associate Editor for the *Training and Education in Professional Psychology Journal* and editorial member for the *Journal of Counseling Psychology, Asian American Journal of Psychology*, and *The Counseling Psychologist.*

Mary Chase Mize, PhD, LPC, ACS, NCC. (she/her). Assistant Professor, Agnes Scott College. Dr. Mary Chase Mize is an Assistant Professor of Clinical Mental Health Counseling at Agnes Scott College in Decatur, Georgia. She earned her PhD in counselor education and practice, a master's degree in clinical mental health counseling, and a master's degree in gerontology with an emphasis in aging program administration from Georgia State University. Dr. Mize is a Licensed Professional Counselor, and since 2018, she has worked with clients at Jewish Family and Career Services of Atlanta, where she specializes in working with older adults and their families, individuals experiencing thoughts of suicide, and individuals and groups experiencing grief, bereavement, and major life transitions. Dr. Mize's research agenda is focused on community-based suicide prevention and intervention efforts with older adults, equipping faith-based communities to respond to suicide, and preparing counselors to work with older adults.

Chase Morgan-Swaney, PhD, LPCC-S, NCC, CCMHC, ACS. (he/him). Senior Lecturer, The University of Akron. Chase Morgan-Swaney is a Licensed Professional Clinical Counselor in Ohio, as well as an NCC and Certified Clinical Mental Health Counselor through the National Board for Certified Counselors. Chase is a Senior Lecturer in the CACREP-accredited Counselor Education and Supervision PhD program within the School of Counseling at the University of Akron, where he is also a part-time faculty member. Additionally, Chase is a private practitioner at Arbor Sana Counseling and Wellness, Inc. in Cleveland, Ohio, where he predominantly serves adolescent and adult LGBTGEQIAP+ clients. Chase is a past President of the Society for Sexual, Affectional, Intersex, and Gender Expansive Identities of Ohio. In addition to being a published scholar, Chase has over 50 international, national, state, and invited presentations. His presentations have covered a range of topics, though mostly focused on LGBTGEQIAP+ issues in counseling, supervision, social justice, and advocacy.

Joy M. Mwendwa PhD, LPC-S (VA), NCC, ACS. (she/her). Associate Professor, Liberty University. Joy Maweu Mwendwa is an Associate Professor in the Department of Counselor Education and Family Studies at Liberty University. She holds a PhD in counselor education and supervision from Old Dominion University. With over 15 years in the counseling profession, her work settings have included a college counseling center, community mental health, churches, and internationally in Kenya, Tanzania, and Malawi. As an LPC and LPC-S (Virginia), she mostly works with women of color, immigrants, international students, and international professionals. Her research interests are focused on qualitative and Indigenous research methodologies, the development of the profession of counseling internationally, the supervisory relationship, and multicultural competence.

Sojeong Nam, PhD, LMHC, NCC. (she/her). Assistant Professor, University of New Mexico. Dr. Sojeong Nam is an Assistant Professor of Counselor Education in the Department of Individual, Family, and Community Education at the University of New Mexico. She has received a PhD in counselor education and supervision from the University of Iowa. Her professional and scholarly pursuits are centered on comprehending and reducing mental health disparities. Currently, her research efforts concentrate on investigating and deconstructing implicit biases in counseling students, addressing the issues of mental health literacy and stigma within underserved populations, and developing culturally responsive interventions for suicide survivors.

Christie Nelson PhD, LCMHC-S, BCMHP. (she/her). Assistant Professor, Bradley University. Dr. Nelson earned her PhD in counselor education and supervision from the University of North Carolina at Charlotte and her MA and EdS in mental health counseling from Gardner-Webb University. Her clinical experience includes providing counseling, supervision, and case management in the areas of mental health, addictions, and developmental disabilities in hospital, outpatient, residential, and community settings. Dr. Nelson's research interests include contemplative practices, meditation, spirituality, and spiritual intelligence.

Christine Park, PhD, LMHC, REAT, NCC. (she/her). Assistant Professor, Adler Graduate School. Dr. Christine Park lives in Hawaiʻi and was born and raised on Hawaiʻi Island (kamaʻāina). She is a Licensed Mental Health Counselor and has degrees in special education, counseling psychology, and counselor education and supervision. Her work experiences include counseling in school, community, and private practice settings. She is also a graduate-level professor in counselor education and works in her community to assist dislocated and disadvantaged adults' transition to college or employment. She provides advocacy and service at the state and national levels, and her passion lies in advocating for mental health and wellness, normalizing access to mental health care, and supporting disadvantaged populations and Native and Indigenous communities.

Jacob Perez, MS, RMHCI. (he/him). Doctoral Student, Florida State University. Jacob is a PhD student in counseling and school psychology at Florida State University. He graduated from the University of North Florida's Clinical Mental Health Counseling Master's Program. He is a dedicated advocate for developing the concrete practice of multicultural competence within the mental health professions and for inclusive, comprehensive sexual health education.

Stacy Pinto, PhD, NCC, LPCC. (she/her, they/them). Clinical Assistant Professor, University of Denver. Dr. Stacy Pinto is a Clinical Assistant Professor in the Department of Counseling Psychology and the Program Director for the School Counseling program at the University of Denver. She earned her PhD in counselor education from Montclair State University and holds credentials as a certified school counselor (New Jersey), Licensed Professional Counselor candidate (Colorado), and NCC. Dr. Pinto's experience spans a variety of counseling and educational settings, including K–12, post-secondary, in-home, and community-based environments. She has served the counseling profession through roles such as President (2024–2025) of the Society for Sexual, Affectional, Intersex, and Gender Expansive Identities (SAIGE), President (2022–2023) of Colorado SAIGE, and as a member of the Editorial Board for the *Journal of LGBTQ Issues in Counseling*. Dr. Pinto's scholarly interests include intersectionality, sexual identity labeling and language, and the development and maintenance of affirming, sustaining counseling environments.

Alena Prikhidko, PhD, LMFT. (she/her). Associate professor, Clinical Coordinator, Counseling Program, Florida International University. Dr. Alena Prikhidko is an Assistant Professor in the Counselor Education program. Previously, she worked as an Assistant Professor of Social Psychology at the Russian State University for the Humanities, specializing in social psychology of emotions and group counseling. She obtained her PhD in counselor education at the University of Florida. Dr. Prikhidko had worked as a Mental Health and Marriage and Family counselor in Russia and in the United States. Her research interests include emotion regulation, emotion socialization, ethics in counseling and counselors' development. Dr. Prikhidko currently has more than 30 publications in peer-reviewed journals, several book chapters and actively presents at state, regional, national, and international levels.

Diana Yum Rhyne MBA, MS, LPC-IT, CRC, NCC, CTP. (she/her). Mental Health Counselor, Department of Veterans Affairs. Diana earned her first master's degree in business administration from the University of Wisconsin-Parkside. As a recipient of the Rehabilitation Services Administration Scholarship, Diana earned her second master's degree in clinical mental health counseling, specializing in rehabilitation counseling at Marquette University in Milwaukee, WI. Diana has years of experience working within the criminal justice system in pretrial risk assessment, prison reentry, and as a court-appointed mediator before making a career change in mental health. Following her internship at a short-term residential facility for psychiatric stabilization, working with clients with severe persistent mental illness in psychiatric crises, she worked as a vocational rehabilitation counselor fellow in the Psychosocial Recovery and Rehabilitation Center at the VA before being hired as a permanent staff position as a therapist, the first LPC to do so in the Milwaukee VA. She is a certified trauma professional, group facilitator for Social Skills Training for Schizophrenia, and is currently in the consultation phase of training for integrative behavioral couple therapy.

Jennifer Rio, PhD, LPC, CAADC. (she/her). Assistant Professor, Hazelden Betty Ford Graduate School of Addiction Studies. Dr. Jennifer Rio is an Assistant Professor at Hazelden Betty Ford Graduate School of Addiction Studies. She has a PhD in Counselor Education and Supervision with research interests in co-occurring mental health and substance use disorders, persons who have offended, and multicultural and social justice competencies in counseling. Her clinical experiences include counseling in a residential prison setting, community mental health, and private practice. She is a Licensed Professional Counselor and a Certified Advanced Drug and Alcohol Counselor in Michigan.

Tanesha Rorie, PhD. (she/her). Assistant Professor, Xavier University. Dr. Tanesha L. Rorie is an Assistant Professor at Xavier University, specializing in clinical mental health counseling. She has taught in counseling programs since 2015 and has served in various capacities in professional organizations, currently serving as the past President of the Ohio Association for Counselor Education and Supervision and the Chair of the Advocacy Interest Network of the Association for Counselor Education and Supervision. Dr. Rorie's research passions fall in the areas of cross-cultural counseling and supervision, social justice and advocacy, and Black mental health experience. She has publications in peer-reviewed journals, including the *Journal of Counseling and Development* and the *Journal of Multicultural Counseling and Development.* Dr. Rorie is passionate about the training and guidance of future counselors as a way to service marginalized populations in surrounding communities. She currently has a private practice in which she specializes in interpersonal therapeutic practices through a cultural feminist framework.

Lena Salpietro, PhD, LPCC, NCC. (she/her). Assistant Professor, Kent State University. Dr. Lena Salpietro is an Assistant Professor in the Clinical Mental Health Counseling Program at Kent State University. She has experience providing clinical services in college counseling, community, and private practice settings. She currently works as a telehealth counselor with expertise in counseling survivors of sexual assault, individuals who identify as gender expansive or sexually/affectionally expansive, and individuals who live with chronic illness/pain or medical trauma. Her scholarly work focuses on gatekeeping and remediation in counselor education, the mental wellness and counseling experiences of LGBTGEQIAP+ people, and counselors who have lost a client to suicide.

Derrick Shepard, PhD. (he/him). Assistant Professor, University of Tennessee at Martin. Dr. Derrick Shepard is an Assistant Professor at the University of Tennessee, Martin. He received his bachelor's degree from the University of Tennessee, Chattanooga, master's degree from Tennessee Tech. University, and doctorate of counselor education from the University of Tennessee, Knoxville.

He regularly presents at state, regional, and national conferences such as the Tennessee Counseling Association, Southern Association for Counselor Education and Supervision, and the American Counseling Association. He has published in refereed journals and authored a book chapter. His research interests include multiculturalism in counseling, social class awareness and skills related to counselor preparation, and pedagogical practices in counselor education and supervision.

Kevin C. Snow, PhD, NCC, ACS. (he/him). Assistant Professor of Human Services, Old Dominion University. Dr. Kevin C. Snow is an Assistant Professor of Human Services at Old Dominion University. Previously, he was an Associate Professor, Clinical Mental Health Program Director, and Chair of the Department of Psychology and Counseling at Marywood University. He has extensive clinical experience in diverse community mental health settings. His research interests include spirituality/competence/inclusion, qualitative research, advocacy in social justice, diversity issues, and international counseling. He has served on the editorial review boards of *Counselor Education and Supervision*, the *Journal of Counselor Leadership and Advocacy*, and the *Canadian Journal of Counselling and Psychotherapy*, and was co-editor of the *Journal of Human Services*. He is the author of many articles, book chapters, and reports, and is co-author of *The Dictionary of Counseling and Human Services*. He is active in professional associations, including NOHS, ACA, ACES, CSI, and IAC, and is past President of the Northeast Pennsylvania Counseling Association.

Renee Stack, MS, LPSC. (she/her). doctoral candidate, The University of Toledo. Renee Stack is a counselor education and supervision doctoral student at The University of Toledo in Toledo, Ohio. She earned her master's degree in applied educational psychology from Northeastern University in Boston, Massachusetts, and her bachelor's degree in psychology from Capital University in Columbus, Ohio. She has worked in the public school setting as a school counselor for over 12 years in Title 1 schools with a diverse population of students. Renee is interested in promoting the professional identity of school counselors to proactively address the mental health, social-emotional, and academic needs of students through a comprehensive program that is preventive, responsive, and equitable.

Angelica M. Tello, PhD, LPC-S, NCC. (she/her). Associate Professor, University of Houston–Clear Lake. Angelica M. Tello is an Associate Professor in the Counseling Program at the University of Houston–Clear Lake. She received her doctoral degree in counselor education and supervision from the University of Texas at San Antonio (UTSA). Dr. Tello also holds a master's degree in Community Counseling from UTSA and is a Licensed Professor Counselor-Supervisor (LPC-S) in the state of Texas. In 2015, Dr. Tello received the American Counseling Association's Courtland C. Lee Multicultural Excellence Award for her commitment to providing counseling services to underserved clients. She also has been recognized as a 2013 NBCC Minority Fellow and a 2013 ACES Presidential Fellow. Moreover, she has presented at counseling conferences on the state, regional, national, and international levels. Her presentations focus on topics related to multicultural counseling, diversity, and social justice. Dr. Tello's counseling and research publications include working with first-generation college students, bilingual counselor supervision, and Latinx counseling experiences.

Kassie Terrell, PhD, LMHC, NCC, CCIS-II. (she/her). Associate Professor, University of North Florida. Dr. Kassie Terrell is an Associate Professor in the Clinical Mental Health Counseling Program at the University of North Florida. She has a personal and professional commitment to social justice, advocacy, and honoring diversity, equity, and inclusion. Her clinical practice and research involve exploring and understanding competencies in working with LGBTQIA+ clients; exploring dynamics of same-sex relationships; understanding how sex, gender, sexuality, and minority stress affect mental health; crisis counseling and safety planning when working with victims of domestic violence; relationship counseling; exploring the impact social media has on young women; sizeism and fat phobia; slut shaming; pedagogy for increasing tolerance among master's students when working with diverse populations; enhancing infusion of cultural diversity training into counseling courses; and ethical and legal dilemmas in teaching tolerance.

Thang S. Tran, PhD. (he/him). Counselor Educator, University of Nebraska Omaha. Dr. Tran has over 20 years of experience in education, serving students and families as a middle school science teacher and counselor in Illinois and Nebraska. He is a licensed professional school counselor in Nebraska and currently serves as an assistant professor at the University of Nebraska Omaha, teaching multiple courses in school and clinical mental health counseling. He recently completed his PhD at Oregon State University in counselor education and supervision, with a dissertation on cultural humility in school counseling. His research interests include school and mental health counseling collaboration, digital media and adolescent development, and integrating artificial intelligence in counselor education and school counseling. He continues to be grateful for the small but important role he plays in educating and impacting the next generation of counselors and educators, as his students teach him as much (if not more) as he teaches them.

Shreya Vaishnav, PhD. (she/her). Assistant Professor Palo Alto University. Dr. Shreya Vaishnav is an Assistant Professor in the Department of Counseling at Palo Alto University. She has held leadership and has been a member of diverse counseling organizations. In addition to her leadership experiences, Dr. Vaishnav has led several research projects on the impact of microaggressions on students from marginalized identities and facilitated workshops on navigating and responding to microaggressions in academia. Her research has also focused on effective mentoring practices for students and faculty, strengths-based approaches in working with students from marginalized backgrounds, and social justice advocacy. Clinically, Dr. Vaishnav's expertise is in working with immigrant populations on cross-cultural issues, especially South Asian immigrants and first-generation Asian Americans.

Jordan B. Westcott, PhD, NCC. (she/her). Assistant Professor, University of Tennessee Knoxville. Dr. Jordan Wescott is an Assistant Professor of Counselor Education at the University of Tennessee Knoxville. She graduated with her PhD in counselor education from Virginia Tech and received her master of science in clinical mental health counseling from Northeastern State University. Her research focuses on health equity for sexual and gender minority populations using a developmental perspective, especially in later life. In her past clinical experience, she worked with clients across the lifespan in community and hospital settings. She is a strong advocate for mental health policy at both the state and federal levels, alongside advocating for LGBTQIA+-inclusive policies.

Julianna Williams, MAEd. (she/her). Doctoral Candidate, University of Tennessee Knoxville. Julie Williams is a doctoral candidate in counselor education at the University of Tennessee, Knoxville. She holds an MAEd in clinical mental health counseling from Virginia Tech and currently practices as a counselor at the UTK Counselor Training Clinic and the Student Counseling Center. Julie also has experience in an employee assistance program and middle and high school counseling programs. Her research agenda includes the impacts of mass incarceration, sexuality in education and counseling, and mental health parity. She is particularly interested in social justice and legislative advocacy and has participated in advocacy for issues such as Medicare reimbursement and LGBTQ+ equity.

Ryan Wisniewski, M.Ed., LPC, NCC. (he/him). Doctoral Candidate, The University of Toledo. Ryan Wisniewski is a doctoral candidate and adjunct professor at The University of Toledo. He is also a Licensed Professional Counselor (Ohio) with experience in community mental health and university settings. With an emphasis on his passion and advocacy through research, Ryan has presented on men's mental health and other research-related topics at state, regional, and national conferences. Ryan's research experience involves factors influencing men who are counselor education students' use of personal counseling, use of artificial intelligence in pedagogical practices, and information processing within counseling and counselor education. Ryan is committed to the de-stigmatization of mental health and the advancement of clinical approaches in counselor education.

Discussion

BVQ

1 - Ch 1-3 Dispositions + skills for you
Cultural humility - Jesus
p. 30-35 - MCC Text

2 Ch 4-6 - MCC Text - Enculturation vs Acculturation
How - McFee's 150% person
Black Lives Matter
Cultural Identity Analysis
Identity model

3 Ch 7+8 Identify privileges you have + how you might use it to advocate for clients of color
None

4 Ch 9 + 10 What are Challenges + barriers refugees face (-Olena)
None

5 Ch 11, 12, 13 What does growing older mean to you?
None

6 Ch 14 + 15 Do I Know nondominant RAI peple in my personal/prof life? How do I perceive/engage w/ them?
Immersion Experience

7 Ch 16 + 17 + 18 No Discussion oh yea!
Group Advocacy

8 Final Exam!

www.ingramcontent.com/pod-product-compliance
Lightning Source LLC
LaVergne TN
LVHW082332230126
830529LV00045B/1121